CONFLICT OF LAWS IN THE PEOPLE'S REPUBLIC OF CHINA

ELGAR ASIAN COMMERCIAL LAW AND PRACTICE

Series Editors: Douglas Arner, Xian Chu Zhang and Chin Leng Lim, *University of Hong Kong*

The Elgar Asian Commercial Law and Practice series is a library of works by leading practitioners and scholars covering discrete areas of law in the field of Asian Commercial Law. Each title is analytical in approach, highlighting and unpicking the legal issues that are most critical and relevant to practice. Designed to be detailed, focused reference works, the books in this series aim to offer an authoritative statement on the law and practice in key topics within the field, including corporate, dispute resolution, taxation, and cross-border transactions.

CONFLICT OF LAWS IN THE PEOPLE'S REPUBLIC OF CHINA

ZHENG SOPHIA TANG

Professor, Newcastle University and Barrister (Middle Temple), UK

YONGPING XIAO

Cheung Kong Scholars Distinguished Professor, Wuhan University, China

ZHENGXIN HUO

Professor, China University of Political Science and Law, China

ELGAR ASIAN COMMERCIAL LAW AND PRACTICE

Edward Elgar
PUBLISHING

Cheltenham, UK • Northampton, MA, USA

Published by
Edward Elgar Publishing Limited
The Lypiatts
15 Lansdown Road
Cheltenham
Glos GL50 2JA
UK

Edward Elgar Publishing, Inc.
William Pratt House
9 Dewey Court
Northampton
Massachusetts 01060
USA

A catalogue record for this book
is available from the British Library

Library of Congress Control Number: 2016935779

This book is available electronically in the **Elgar**online
Law subject collection
DOI 10.4337/9781849808590

MIX
Paper from
responsible sources
FSC® C013056

ISBN 978 1 84980 858 3 (cased)
ISBN 978 1 84980 859 0 (eBook)

Printed and bound in Great Britain by TJ International Ltd, Padstow, Cornwall

Typeset by Columns Design XML Ltd, Reading

CONTENTS

EXTENDED TABLE OF CONTENTS

PART II JURISDICTION, PROCEDURE, FOREIGN JUDGMENTS AND AWARDS

5. SELECTED PROCEDURAL ISSUES IN FOREIGN-RELATED LITIGATION IN CHINA

6. RECOGNITION AND ENFORCEMENT OF FOREIGN JUDGMENTS IN CHINESE COURTS

11. CHOICE OF LAW IN PROPERTY

12. CHOICE OF LAW IN INTELLECTUAL PROPERTY

PART IV INTERREGIONAL CONFLICTS AND COOPERATION

13. INTERREGIONAL CONFLICTS AND COOPERATION BETWEEN MAINLAND, HONG KONG, MACAU AND TAIWAN

PART V FINAL REMARKS

14. CHINESE CONFLICT OF LAWS: PAST, PRESENT AND FUTURE

PREFACE

Conflict of laws in China has gone through a fundamental development in the past three decades. Since China adopted a new policy of reform and of opening up to the world after 1978, it has been the world's fastest-growing major economy. Economic development and international trade and globalization have led to transformations in almost every area of Chinese law, including private international law. The development of international cooperation in trade and commerce increases the number and complexity of foreign-related disputes brought to the Chinese courts. The early conflicts system was fully established in the 1990s. For a long time afterwards, there was limited improvement in the legislation although the system was enriched and improved in a piecemeal manner by judicial interpretations and judicial directions of the Supreme People's Court. Only after China's accession to the WTO in 2001 did the greater proliferation of international trade relations and commercial disputes bring about the need to modernize the Chinese conflicts system. The handover of Hong Kong and Macau has also generated new interregional conflicts problems. Against this background, the Chinese conflicts system experienced a second important leap, marked by the enactment of the Conflicts Act in 2010, the reform of Civil Procedure Law in 2012, and the Supreme People's Court's new jurisdiction interpretation on the Conflicts Act in 2012 and the Civil Procedure Law in 2015. It is fair to argue that China has established a comprehensive and up-to-date conflicts system since the 2010s, and the Chinese conflicts system now enters into the modernization stage.

Compared to the remarkable development of the Chinese conflicts system, it is disappointing that there is no proliferation of comprehensive and quality literature on Chinese conflict of laws. Although numerous journal articles are published in this field in international journals, a wide-ranging, updated, analytical and critical monograph on this subject is lacking in the current market. This monograph aims to fill this gap. However, it is not only a book providing rule-by-rule analysis of current Chinese conflict of laws. It combines historic, theoretic, political and economic backgrounds, and recognizes the scholarly contribution made by Chinese scholars to this field. It compares rules of Chinese characteristics and international practices to assess the current Chinese conflicts system and proposes a modernization strategy for the future. Given the ambitious goal, multiple research methods are adopted. The monograph primarily implements doctrinal research, focusing on analyzing the current conflicts rules. Judicial decisions provide recommendatory and directive value to interpret Chinese law and provide invaluable evidence to demonstrate how the conflicts rules are implemented in practice. This monograph therefore also provides sophisticated analysis of representative case laws. It also includes empirical data to show how the law is enforced in reality. The historic, theoretical and comparative analysis is adopted in various sections. It concludes with a proposal for the future modernization of the Chinese conflicts system.

Since the conflict of laws covers almost every civil and commercial perspective, it is impossible to provide in-depth analysis of all conflicts matters in this book, thus it excludes family-related matters and only focuses on other civil and commercial matters. It does not mean family matters are not important in China. On the contrary, more and more foreign-related marriages, divorces, adoptions and matrimonial property matters are brought to Chinese courts. Chinese conflicts rules in family matters have also been reformed and modernized, and in certain issues are quicker in pace than other civil and commercial matters. For example, although recognition and enforcement of foreign civil judgments is still subject to a rigid principle of reciprocity, a more liberal approach is adopted to recognizing and enforcing foreign divorce decrees. Since family conflict of laws can be a stand-alone subject, it is not included in this book given its volume and will be included in a follow-up book project.

It is necessary to note that a large amount of Chinese material is used in this book, including legislation, judicial interpretation, cases, government papers, books, journal articles, speeches and newspaper articles. The citation and translation of Chinese materials was a daunting task in this project. In order to avoid extremely long and redundant references, the book only provides Pingyin and English translation of Chinese materials in the text and references. Since many resources have no uniform translation, the provision of 'Pingyin' aims to help readers, who do not read original Chinese to know the pronunciation of the Chinese materials, which helps to identify relevant resources. The Table of Legislation, Table of Cases and Bibliography provide a full list of all Chinese materials used, including the English translation, original Chinese characteristics and Pingyin. As to the secondary resources included in the Bibliography, the author's name will be cited as it is in the original resources. If the secondary resource is in Chinese, the English translation will follows the original order of the author's name in the Chinese resource with the surname capitalized.

This is a collaborative project between three professors based in the UK and in China. Professor Zheng Sophia Tang is responsible for writing Chapters 3, 4, 5, 8, 10, 12, and 14, and contributes to Chapters 6 (IV.1), 7 (IV.5), 9 (III.2.iv, v, vi; IV and V), 11 (I.2, and III.5), and 13 (II and III), Professor Zhengxin Huo is responsible for Chapters 1, 2, 9, and 11, and Professor Yongping Xiao Chapters 6, 7 and 13.

ACKNOWLEDGEMENTS

This book could not have been completed without the help and support of our colleagues, families and close friends. In particular, this project is supported by the 中国社科基金中华学术外译项目（项目编号：11WFX001) [Guojia Shehui Kexue Jijin Zhonghua Xueshu Waiyi Xiangmu] [Academic Translation Project of National Social Science Foundation of China] (Project Number: 11WFX001). We want to thank the National Social Science Foundation of China for its financial support and the editors of Edward Elgar Publishing for their assistance and hard work.

Professor Tang wants to thank Professor Paul Beaumont at the University of Aberdeen and Professor Jonathan Harris at King's College London, who have provided her with invaluable guidance and support throughout her academic career. She is also grateful to Ms Lu Xu, who read a chapter of the book and provided useful comments. Professor Yongping Xiao wishes to thank Dr Wenwen Liang at the international Law Institution of Wuahn University, who assisted in collecting materials and proofreading, and two PhD candidates at the Wuhan University, Hantao Ding and Saixiao Tang, who contributed in collecting materials used in this probject.

ZS Tang, YP Xiao and ZX Huo
15 October 2015

ABBREVIATIONS

BPC	Basic People's Court
CADMFA	Consular Affair Department of the Ministry of Foreign Affairs
CPL	Civil Procedure Law
FJR	Foreign Judgment Recognition
GPCL	General Principles of Civil Law
HKSAR	Hong Kong Special Administrative Regime
HPC	High People's Court
ICC	International Chamber of Commerce
IPC	Intermediate People's Court
IPR	Intellectual property right
JRE	Judgment recognition and enforcement
MASAR	Macau Special Administrative Regime
NPC	National People's Congress
NYC	New York Convention
PRC	People's Republic of China
SAR	Special administrative region
SCNPC	Standard Committee of the National People's Congress
SPC	Supreme People's Court
SPP	Supreme People's Procuratorate

TABLE OF CASES

CHINA

PRC Supreme People's Court Cases

PRC Local Courts Cases

NATIONAL AND EUROPEAN UNION CASES

Australia

Belgium

European Union

Germany

Hong Kong

Japan

Switzerland

UK

USA

TABLE OF LEGISLATION

CHINA

Statute

National People's Congress's Decision

Administrative Regulations

PRC Supreme People's Court Judicial Interpretation

PRC Supreme People's Court – Other Judicial Guidance

PRC High People's Court – Judicial Guidance

Other Documents

INTERNATIONAL CONVENTIONS AND EU LEGISLATION

NATIONAL LEGISLATION

Croatia

France

Gabon

Germany

Italy

Japan

Hong Kong

Macau

Russia

Switzerland

United Kingdom

United States of America

Part I

CONFLICT OF LAWS IN CHINA—HISTORY AND CONCEPT

1

CONFLICT OF LAWS IN CHINA—A HISTORICAL PERSPECTIVE

I. INTRODUCTION

China is a country that boasts both a splendid ancient civilization and a long history whose legal origin may date back thousands of years. During its history great achievements have been made in various aspects, including law. Chinese law has been widely recognized as one of the world's major law families, which significantly influenced the East Asian countries, such as Japan, Korea and Vietnam.[1] However, Chinese social and legal development lagged far behind the western world since the nineteenth century. Since the twentieth century, however, Chinese law has been strongly influenced by the western law; consequently, law in China today has become a complex blend of traditional Chinese approaches and western influences. **1.01**

In ancient China, the legal system had been largely based on the Confucian philosophy of social control through moral education, as well as the 'Legalist' emphasis on codified law and criminal sanction.[2] Following the Chinese Revolution of 1911, the Republic of China, the first republic in Asia, adopted a largely western-style legal code following the civil law tradition (specifically influenced by Germany). In 1949, the People's Republic of China (PRC) was **1.02**

1 Since the Chinese civilization and Chinese Empires persisted in unbroken continuity to modern times, they have dominated East Asia in a way that no western country had dominated the West. Consequently the political and legal diversity that has characterized the West since the fall of Rome did not develop in East Asia. See L.S. Stavrianos, *A Global History: From Prehistory to the 21st Century* (Prentice Hall 1999) 223; K. Zweigert and H. Kötz, *Introduction to Comparative Law* (3rd ed., Clarendon Press 1998) 286–94.

2 A.H. Chen, *An Introduction to the Legal System of the People's Republic of China* (LexisNexis 2004) 10–15.

established. The first step of the PRC Government was the abolition of the existing legal system, which was regarded as having supported feudal and colonial rules. Nonetheless, because of the extreme left-wing ideology, there was not very much effort to create a new legal system from the 1950s to the 1970s. Instead, the legal sector was one of the targets of deliberate attacks during the Cultural Revolution (1966–76). The first three decades after the founding of the PRC resulted in little legislative progress.

1.03 In the late 1970s, China adopted a new policy of reform and began opening up to the world. Since then, it has been the world's fastest-growing major economy. By the year of 2011, it had become the world's second largest economy. During the past three decades, the law and legal system in the PRC have been undergoing fundamental reform, as many elements inside and outside China emphasize the need to strengthen the rule of law in fostering economic development. International trade and globalization spur transformations in almost every area of Chinese law, including private international law. Chinese law in almost every aspect has been developing by leaps and bounds, and the differences between Chinese law (including private international law) and western law have become less and less noticeable with the acceleration of globalization.

II. PRIVATE INTERNATIONAL LAW IN ANCIENT CHINA

1.04 Private international law occurs as a combined consequence of four basic conditions:[3] (i) differences in laws and the legal systems of different countries; (ii) indispensable civil relations and business transactions among the countries; (iii) granting of civil status to foreigners by the forum country; and (iv) recognition of the extraterritorial effects of foreign laws in civil and commercial matters.[4]

1.05 Some Chinese scholars believe that such conditions existed as early as the seventh century, when the Tang Dynasty came into its prime and international trade was active in East Asia, especially in Chang'an, the capital of the

3 In Chinese textbooks, the classic definition of private international law is the 'branch of law that regulates international civil and commercial relations', or 'the branch of law that deals with civil and commercial relations that involve foreign elements'. HAN Depei, *Guoji Sifa [Private International Law]* (Gaodeng Jiaoyu Chubanshe [China Higher Education Press], 2000) 1; HUANG Jin, *Guoji Sifa [Private International Law]* (2nd ed., Falv Chubanshe [China Law Press] 2005) 1.

4 See HUANG Jin, *supra* n 3,12–15.

Chinese Empire.[5] The Tang Dynasty furnished the earliest choice-of-law rule ever discovered in China.

The Tang Code was enacted in 624 A.D., revised in 627 A.D. and 637 A.D. respectively, and enhanced with a commentary.[6] It is the oldest legal code in the history of Chinese law and represents the greatest achievement of ancient Chinese law. It consists of 12 sections and contains 502 articles, forming the basis of the later codes of the Song, Yuan, Ming and Qing dynasties. **1.06**

The first title of the Tang Code is 'Mingli' which provided the fundamentals of the Code where a typical conflicts rule was incorporated. Article 6 of this title may be translated as follows: 'If both parties of infringement belong to the same foreign ethnic group, the customary law of their own shall apply; if the parties belong to different ethnic groups, law of the Tang Empire shall apply.'[7] With scholastic acumen, Chinese scholars conclude that this is the earliest conflicts rule that China had enacted.[8] They specify that the article is a combination of *lex partriae* and *lex loci actus* insofar as the first part embodies *lex partriae* whereas the second part *lex loci actus*. Chinese scholars feel proud of the article in the sense that it reflected a cosmopolitan approach to solving conflicts problems, a manifestation of both confidence and strength of the Tang Dynasty in the seventh century.[9] It should be noted that, in Chinese history, a code, if any, applied to both civil and criminal cases; and in this respect, the argument that the above provision reflects the earliest conflicts rule in China is highly arguable. **1.07**

Between 1271 and 1368, China was occupied by the Mongols, a period of time in history that the Chinese call the Yuan Dynasty. The Mongolian tribes that destroyed the Song Dynasty, Tang's successor, introduced their own laws, but did not eradicate Chinese law. Consequently, once the invaders had formally settled in Chinese territories, they lived together with people whose legal relations were governed by different rules. The Mongols established a four-level class system: the Mongols were the highest and ruling class at the top of the system; the ethnic groups from west and central Asia, including Uyghurs, immigrants from the west and some clans of Central Asia, belonged to the second class;[10] the third class was occupied by the northern Chinese, **1.08**

5 See HAN Depei, *supra* n 3, 1.

6 The Chinese name for the Tang Code is Tanglvshuyi (唐律疏议). Legal historians disagree over the actual date of the Tang Code, some suggesting it was only published in 652.

7 The original Chinese text is: 诸化外人，同类自相犯者，各依本俗法;异类相犯者，以法律论.

8 HUANG Jin, *supra* n 3, 119.

9 Ibid.

10 These ethnic groups were called 'semu ren', literally meaning 'persons with coloured eyes'.

Kitans, Jurchens and Koreans, from the north of the empire; and they were followed by the lowest level constituted of southern Chinese of the conquered Song dynasty. If persons from different classes were involved in one legal dispute, they would be subject to different rules. In this respect, the legal environment of Yuan Dynasty in China was quite similar to the Personal Law Period of the Middle Ages in west Europe.[11]

1.09 The Ming Dynasty and the Qing Dynasty, for most of the time, adopted a closed-door policy, enacted strict bans on private maritime activities, and tried to remain separate, or isolated, from the rest of the world. For example, the law of the Ming Dynasty prohibited overseas business, and refused to recognize the effect of foreign law which provided that 'any violation committed by the foreign ethnic people shall be governed by law of the Ming Empire'.[12] This provision suggested that the Ming Dynasty followed an approach of absolute territorialism, refusing to recognize the effect of any foreign law. The rationale behind this approach is that 'these foreign ethnic people, although not the subjects of the Ming Dynasty originally, are regarded as so once they submit themselves to the authority of the Ming Dynasty. … Hence law of the Ming Dynasty shall apply'.[13] Essentially, the deep-rooted sense of superiority of the Chinese empire over all other nations was a major reason, inter alia, for disregarding the status of foreign people and the effect of foreign law. Another issue worthy of note is that the wording of the above provision indicates definitely that it was a criminal rule in nature, inapplicable to civil disputes, as opposed to the rule contained in the Tang Code which applied to both civil and criminal disputes.

1.10 The isolation of China from the outside world and the blind arrogance, together with the tradition of Chinese law, i.e., emphasizing criminal penalty while disregarding civil remedy,[14] suffocated the systematic development of private international law in China until the nineteenth century. Under the influence of Chinese culture and law, most East Asia countries also did not provide a spawning ground for private international law during this time.

---

11 See F.K. Juenger, *Choice of Law and Multistate Justice* (Transnational Publishers 2000) 10.

12 The original Chinese text is 凡化外人犯罪者，并依律拟断.

13 The original Chinese text is 原虽非我族者，归附即是王民，… … 并依常法律拟段.

14 Chen, *supra* n 2, 15.

III. CHINA'S EFFORTS TO CODIFY PRIVATE INTERNATIONAL LAW AT THE TURN OF THE TWENTIETH CENTURY

As noted above, China had isolated itself from the outside world since the Ming Dynasty, whose social, economic and legal system stagnated for centuries. However, after the mid-nineteenth century, the political and legal situation dramatically changed when China had to enter into many unequal treaties with western powers including the United Kingdom, France, Germany, Russia, the United States and Japan. These powers opened up Chinese ports and trading centres, granted extraterritoriality and a degree of separate jurisdiction to foreign nationals which was called 'foreign consular jurisdiction', and involved the cession or 'lease' of territories on the edge of the Chinese Empire. Under the 'consular jurisdiction', nationals of these western countries, who resided in the territory of China, were not subject to the jurisdiction of Chinese courts. If they committed crimes or became defendants in civil litigation, they could be tried only in the consular courts of their respective countries. These consular courts were located in the 'leased' territory in China, where Chinese authority could not intervene. In this manner, the judicial sovereignty of China was seriously undermined.[15] **1.11**

In 1899, the great powers, apparently in preparation for a grand annexation of the whole of China, entered into a treaty, which divided up the territory among them into 'spheres of interest'.[16] As a matter of fact, the crisis that China faced at that time fundamentally changed the course of the historic development of Chinese society thoroughly wiping out the arrogance and the sense of superiority that the nation had treasured for thousands of years. As LI Hongzhang, the then Prime Minister of the Qing Dynasty lamented: '[T]he great changes that China is witnessing have never happened during the last three thousand years, and the formidable enemies that China is fighting against have never emerged during the last three thousand years.'[17] **1.12**

It was only under these circumstances that the rulers of the late Qing Dynasty came to realize that fundamental internal reforms were needed if China wanted to withstand competition from the European powers. In the ensuing legal reform, the late Qing Dynasty attempted to establish a legal system based on European models. Because Japan acted as the bridge for the Qing Dynasty **1.13**

15 Ibid., at 22. For more on the consular jurisdiction, see Z. Mao, '"Friendship" or Aggression?', in MAO Tse-Tung, *Selected Work of Mao Tse-Tung*, Vol. IV (1st ed., People's Publishing House, Peking 1961) (in English) 450, note 1.

16 Zweigert and Kötz, *supra* n 1 291.

17 GUO Tinyi, *Jianmin Zhongguo Xiandaishi [A Brief of Modern Chinese History]* (Shanghai People's Press 2009) 121.

to understand the western political and legal system, the Chinese law reform was assisted by learning from Japanese law that developed during the Meiji period. The Japanese law and legal terminology largely benefited from translations of European laws (especially German law). Also because Germany had won the Franco-Prussian war, the enacted new codes were modelled after that of Germany. During this period, modern private international law was introduced into China for the first time in history.[18]

1.14 In the early 1900s, the Qing Dynasty began to enact various codes successively, following the Japanese and German law. It should be noted that in 1906, a draft of Civil and Criminal Procedure was submitted to the Emperor, which contained five chapters and 256 articles. Chapter V of the draft was entitled 'cases between Chinese and foreign parties',[19] which provided some articles involving foreign civil litigation. The inclusion of such articles in the draft suggested that the need for private international law was gradually being recognized by the rulers, although a comprehensive code of private international law was not listed in the legislative reform.

1.15 It is perhaps needless to say that the reforms aimed at saving the Qing Dynasty from collapse came too late. The crumbling Empire was powerless abroad; and internally there were riots against foreigners, there were power struggles between reformists and conservatives, and the foreign debt was skyrocketing. All these led to the complete collapse of the Qing Dynasty in 1911, whereupon the Republic of China, the first republic country in Asia, was established.

1.16 The republican government during the following years was admittedly only a weak government, which never established control over the whole of China because of the dual factors of domestic strife between the Kuomintang (Nationalist Party) and the Chinese Communists and of military aggression on the part of Japan. Nonetheless, a large number of laws were codified during this period.

1.17 On 5 August 1918, 'Act on the Application of Law' was promulgated which heralded that China had its code of private international law for the first time in history. The Act, principally based on the Japanese *Hōrei* of 1898,[20]

---

18 See SHEN Juan, *Guoji Sifa [Private International Law]* (China Social Sciences Press 2006) 43. Jin Huang, Zhengxin Huo, 'A Commentary on Private International Law in East Asia', in Wen-Yeu Wang (ed.), *Codification in East Asia: Selected Papers from the 2nd IACL Thematic Conference* (Springer 2014) 215, 221.

19 See LI Guilian, *Shen Jiaben Zhuan [Biography of Shen Jiaben]* (China Law Press 2000) 107.

20 Japan introduced Chinese characters to express Japanese in writing around the First and Fourth century B.C. Even today, a large number off Chinese characters are still used in modern Japanese language. The

contained seven chapters and 27 articles, which provided both general principles and various specific conflicts rules for personal status, succession, property and formal validity of conduct.[21] A close examination of the Act finds that it was not only similar in content to the *Hōrei*, but also incorporated a number of legal terms from Japanese *Hōrei* which did not exist in Chinese legal language at that time.[22]

Objectively speaking, this Act was well drafted and incorporated the most advanced doctrines of private international law at that time; it was regarded as one of the most detailed and comprehensive codes available in those days.[23] Regrettably, under the general legal and political background during the early twentieth century the Act was never put into operation. The unequal treaties with foreign countries, and 'foreign consular jurisdiction', in particular, made the Act almost unenforceable.[24] **1.18**

When the PRC was founded in 1949, it abolished all the laws of the Republic of China. The Act on the Applicable Law, therefore, ceased to take effect in mainland China after 1949, although it was still effective in Taiwan until 1953 when it was replaced by a new act entitled 'the Act on the Application of Law in Civil Matters involving Foreign Elements'.[25] **1.19**

IV. DEVELOPMENT AFTER THE FOUNDING OF THE PEOPLE'S REPUBLIC OF CHINA

IV.1 Introduction

At the end of the Chinese civil war, the losing Kuomintang-headed central government moved to the island of Taiwan in 1949, followed by a large number of mainlanders who eventually accounted for about 13 per cent of Taiwan's entire population. From then, mainland China and Taiwan have had different laws and legal systems.[26] **1.20**

Chinese characters of '*Hōrei*' are '法例'. The term '*Hōrei*' was used in ancient China in the Jin Dynasty (265–420) as the name of the general rules for its statutes; however, it had been forgotten in China and not used since the fall of the Dynasty.

21 See LU Jun, *Guojisifa zhi Lilun Yu Shijian [Theory and Practice of Private International Law]* (China University of Political Science and Law Press 1998) 331–4.

22 SHEN Juan, *supra* n 18, 48.

23 Ibid., 49.

24 See HUANG Jin, *supra* n 3, 119.

25 XIAO Yongping, *Zhongguo Chongtufa Lifa Wenti Yanjiu [A Study on the Legislative Issues of China's Conflicts Law]* (Wuhan University Press 1996) 3.

26 For more discussion on Mainland-Taiwan conflict of laws, see Ch 13.

1.21 In the mainland, once the PRC was established, the Communists abolished all Kuomintang laws including the Act on the Application of Law of 1918, and judicial organs. The newly established regime claimed it would build a brand new legal system of New China as soon as possible. Nevertheless, 61 years had passed when its first Conflicts Act was enacted by the Standing Committee of the National's People's Congress in October 2010. Indeed, looking back at these 61 years of legislative and judiciary development, mainland Chinese scholars hold the common view that 'while significant achievements have been made, painfully mistakes have also been committed at some stages; the journey has not been an easy and straightforward one'.[27]

1.22 In general, the legislative development of private international law in the PRC has been full of setbacks.[28] It should be noted that private international law has only been regarded as an independent discipline after 1978, when mainland China adopted a new policy of reform and opened up to the outside world. Before that, private international law was regarded by scholars in mainland China as a forbidden, even perilous, academic pursuit. The anti-foreign sentiments that dominated mainland China from the 1950s to the 1970s were so pervasive that it was difficult to associate with any Western ideas or influence, even in academic study. The same attitude was also manifested by the legislature and the judiciary, in their reluctance to recognize the effect of foreign law in civil cases involving foreign elements.[29]

1.23 However, this attitude has become untenable for the PRC due to the reform and the open-door policy. With the development of external economic cooperation and trade, increasing numbers of disputes involving foreign factors have arisen, and have been brought to the Chinese people's courts. Moreover, China's accession to the WTO in 2001 has resulted in a greater proliferation of international civil and commercial disputes of ever increasing complexity. Meanwhile, with a huge number of Chinese civilians overseas, China began to realize conflicts rules were needed to coordinate the interaction between the legal systems involved in order to deal with the rights and obligations of Chinese nationals. Under such a circumstance, private international law was introduced in China in the late 1970s to assist in the resolution of these disputes.

---

27 A.H Chen, *supra* n 2, 25.

28 Compared with mainland China, the development of private international law in Taiwan has been smoother basically due to two reasons. First, while all laws of the Republic of China were abolished in mainland China in 1949, they, including the 'Act on the Application of Law' of 1918, continue to be effective in Taiwan; second, Taiwan's economy is more foreign-oriented and its economic take-off happened around two decades earlier than the economic reform in mainland China.

29 T.P. Chen, 'Private International Law of the People's Republic of China: An Overview', (1987) 35 *Am J Comp L* 445.

IV.2 Jurisdiction and judicial cooperation

In the past three decades, private international law in mainland China has made significant progress. Since 1982, the Civil Procedure Law (for Trial Implementation) has provided special procedural rules for civil litigation involving foreigners, non-nationalists, foreign enterprises and organizations.[30] It regulates the basic procedural issues, including the right to sue, language and translation, legal representation, service of judicial documents, limitation period, security and provisional measures, arbitration and judicial assistance. The special rules, however, only apply if one party is a non-Chinese national. In other words, the special rules apply very narrowly and would be irrelevant if a party is a Chinese national habitually residing abroad, or the subject matter or the legal relationship is located abroad. Furthermore, it does not provide international jurisdiction rules. Instead, the special procedural rules apply to all litigation involving non-Chinese nationals in Chinese courts. It implies that Chinese courts would take jurisdiction in any circumstances. This extreme attitude to assert jurisdiction over all disputes is clearly incompatible with the needs of international trade and exchanges. **1.24**

The 1982 Act was replaced in 1991 by the Civil Procedure Law (CPL), which provided more detailed rules on service of judicial documents abroad, enforcement of foreign judgments and arbitral awards, and arbitration in general, applying to all foreign-related proceedings, although no interpretation was provided as to the meaning of 'foreign-related'. The 1991 CPL also provided special jurisdiction rules for a Chinese court to assert jurisdiction in foreign-related disputes.[31] Chinese courts no longer take all disputes that are brought to them but have to decide whether they are competent according to the established standard. Jurisdiction may be based on the exclusive sovereign control, defendant's submission, parties' agreement, defendant's domicile and multiple objective connecting factors. Although the jurisdiction rules may be criticized for simplicity, ambiguity and too sovereign-oriented,[32] they are comprehensive and generally appropriate and practical at that time. The 1991 CPL also improved and enriched the rules on procedural matters.[33] **1.25**

30 Ch 5.
31 Arts 243–246.
32 See Ch 3 below.
33 Ch 5 below.

1.26 The 1991 CPL was later supplemented by the Supreme People's Court's (SPC) judicial interpretation, mainly the 1992 Opinion[34] and a number of judicial directions. These interpretations provide more detailed rules to implement the CPL rules in practice. The CPL was later amended in 2007 and 2012, without significant changes in international jurisdiction and procedural rules, except limited updates and re-arrangement of provisions.[35] Nevertheless, the SPC published a new judicial interpretation in 2015,[36] which has made significant improvements compared to the 1992 Opinion. In particular, it officially permits the Chinese courts to exercise discretion not to take jurisdiction, which is the so-called Chinese-style *forum non conveniens*.[37] It also provides more detailed guidance for enforcement of foreign judgments.[38] All these demonstrate that China has taken one step further to opening its judicial system to the rest of the world, to better integrate into the international community and to internationalize its conflicts rules.

1.27 Despite these developments, Chinese law on jurisdiction, foreign-related procedure and international judicial cooperation still needs modernization. From the perspective of legislative skills, spreading relevant rules in multiple legal resources would be increasingly difficulty in practice;[39] the effectiveness of the derogation power of a foreign jurisdiction clause has never been officially clarified;[40] the maintenance of the principle of reciprocity in enforcement of foreign judgments in most civil and commercial cases other than divorce continuously produce difficulties for the parties;[41] and the relevant restricted way of allowing foreign judicial documents to be served in China making China-related disputes a huge challenge to foreign parties.[42]

---

34 SPC, 'Zuigao Renmin Fayuan Guanyu Guanyu Shiyong "Zhonghua Renmin Gongheguo Minshi Susongfa" Ruogan Wenti de Yijian' (Shixiao) ['Opinion on several Questions in the Implementation of the PRC Civil Procedure Act' (Abolished)] ('1992 Opinion'), Fa Fa [1992] 22

35 For example, the 2012 CPL no longer includes a separate prorogation jurisdiction for foreign-related proceedings, but provides the same choice of court agreement rule for both domestic and international cases. It updates the methods to serve judicial documents by permitting service by electronic means to reflect the current development of telecommunication.

36 SPC, 'Zuigao Renmin Fayuan Guanyu Shiyong "Zhonghua Renmin Gongheguo Minshi Susongfa" de Jieshi' ['Interpretation of the SPC on the Application of the PRC Civil Procedure Law' ('2015 Opinion')], Fa Shi [2015] No 5.

37 Art 532, 2015 Opinion. See Ch 4 below.

38 In particular, exception to the reciprocity principle is given to foreign divorce judgments by Art 544. This book, however, does not cover family and matrimonial matters.

39 See Ch 2 below for the necessity to rely on judicial interpretation to supplement legislation.

40 See Ch 4 below.

41 See Ch 6 below.

42 See Ch 6 below.

IV.3 Choice of law

Objectively speaking, prior to the promulgation of the Conflicts Act, Chinese legislation on private international law remained unsophisticated, compared with the United States, major European countries and its East Asian neighbours, such as South Korea and Japan. Before the new Conflicts Act of 2010, Chapter Eight of the General Principles of Civil Law (GPCL) was the most important source of private international law in mainland China.[43] However, like the rest of the GPCL, Chapter Eight did not purport to be a comprehensive codification. Instead, it contained nine articles that deal with contractual obligations, torts, and succession, and was often hard to follow, particularly in complicated cases. Although other relevant laws, such as the Maritime Law,[44] Civil Aviation Law[45] and Contract Act,[46] have been enacted consequently, and contain certain conflicts rules that fall within their scope of regulation respectively, legislation on Chinese Choice of Law during this period remained fragmentary, incomplete, and less influential than in other areas of private law. **1.28**

Chinese scholars argued that choice of law legislation in mainland China before the enactment of the Conflicts Act had five major defects: (1) the conflicts rules contained in various Chinese statutes and regulations were incomplete; (2) some statutory conflicts rules were insufficient or even out of date; (3) some conflicts rules contradicted each other; (4) some conflicts rules included in the judicial interpretations of the SPC were in disharmony with statutory conflicts rules; and (5) the existing Chinese choice of law legislation lacked a consistent legislative technique.[47] In light of this, Chinese scholars argued that Chinese choice of law legislation was in need of fundamental reform, and a code of private international law should be enacted as soon as possible.[48] **1.29**

---

43 Zhonghua Renmin Gongheguo Minfa Tongze [General Principles of Civil Law](GPCL hereafter) Chapter 8 (1986) (PRC). The GPCL was adopted at the Fourth Session of the Sixth National People's Congress on 12 April 1986, coming into force on 1 January 1987, and is still effective at present, assuming a prominent role in the area of civil law in China. Structurally, the GPCL has devoted an entire chapter to regulating the conflict of laws (i.e., Chapter Eight, Application of Laws to Civil Matters Involving Foreign Element), where nine articles can be found.

44 Zhonghua Renmin Gongheguo Haishangfa [Maritime Law] (1992) (PRC).

45 Zhonghua Renmin Gongheguo Minyong Hangkongfa [Civil Aviation Law] (1996) (PRC).

46 Zhonghua Renmin Gongheguo Hetongfa [Contract Law] (1999) (PRC).

47 For detailed discussion see Weizuo Chen, 'The Necessity of Codification of China's Private International Law and Arguments for a Statute on the Application of Laws as the Legislative Model' <http://www.tsinghua.edu.cn/docsn/fxy/tclr/issue/…/CHEN%20Weizuo.pdf>.; ZHAO Xianglin (ed), *Guojisifa [Private International Law]* (Press of China University of Political Science and Law, 2011) 56.

48 See HAN Depei, *supra* n 3, 17; Chinese Society of Private International Law, 'Model Law of Private International Law of the People's Republic of China', in Petar Sarcevic and Paul Volken (eds.), *Yearbook of Private International Law* (Kluwer Law Int'l) 349–90.

1.30 The restructuring of private international law first appeared on the agenda of the National People's Congress (NPC) in 2001. The Standing Committee of the Ninth NPC formulated an ambitious plan to draft the Civil Code of the PRC,[49] which would include not only substantive private law, such as contract law, property law, tort law, but also conflicts law.[50] After one year of preparation the Draft Civil Code had been drawn up, and was presented to the Standing Committee of the Ninth NPC for its first reading on 23 December 2002.[51] The Draft Civil Code consisted of nine books, and the ninth book,[52] entitled *The Law on the Application of Law over Foreign-related Civil Relationship*, was specifically concerned with choice-of-law problems. Chinese scholars were so optimistic about the legislative project that they predicted that the first Civil Code of the PRC would soon be adopted.

1.31 However, to their disappointment, the plan of drafting a comprehensive Civil Code was abandoned when the Tenth NPC and its Standing Committee were elected in March 2003.[53] Given the extensive coverage of the Civil Code, the newly-constituted legislature maintained that it would be unrealistic, and even risky, to enact the Civil Code in one stroke; therefore, it decided that the Civil Code would not be adopted as a whole but book by book. Within such a setting, the Property Law and the Tort Liability Law were adopted on 16 March 2007 and 26 December 2009 respectively.[54] No sooner had those two acts been enacted than the legislative process of the Conflicts Act was resumed. The drafting of the Conflicts Act was accelerated. Entrusted by the Legislative Affairs Committee of NPC's Standing Committee, the Chinese Society of Private International Law, an academic organization, established a

---

49 The National People's Congress (NPC) is elected for a term of five years. The NPC is in session once a year for not more than two weeks. It establishes a Standing Committee to exercise its authority when it is not in session. See Feng Lin, *Constitutional Law in China* (Sweet & Maxwell 2000) 63–4; Zhengxin Huo, 'A Tiger without Teeth: The Antitrust Law of the People's Republic of China' (2008) 10 *Asian Pac Law Pol J* 36.

50 See Weidong Zhu, 'China's Codification of the Conflict of Laws' (2008) 3 *Journal of Private International Law* 283, 306.

51 Under the Legislation Law of the PRC, a bill which has been put on the agenda of the Standing Committee session shall in general be deliberated three times in the current session of the Standing Committee before being voted on, and it needs a simple majority of the members of the Standing Committee for its adoption as a national law. After its adoption by the NPC Standing Committee, it will be signed and promulgated by the President of state. See Zhonghua Renmin Gongheguo Li Fafa [PRC Law on Legislation] (promulgated by the Standing Comm Nat'l People's Cong., 15 March 2000, effective 1 July 2000) Arts 40, 41 (PRC).

52 They are the GPCL, Property Law, Contract Law, the Law of Personality Rights, Marriage Law, Adoption Law, Succession Law, the Law of Tort and the Law on the Application of Law of Foreign-related Civil Relationship respectively in numerical order, among which Book One, Book Two, Book Four, Book Eight and Book Nine are new complements, and the third, fifth, sixth and the seventh books are just four ready-made laws inserted in the Draft, without any amendments. Weidong Zhu, n 50, 306.

53 See <www.npc.gov.cn/huiyi/cwh/1116/2010-08/28/content_1593162.htm>.

54 Zhonghua Renmin Gongheguo Wuquanfa [PRC Property Act] (2007) (PRC); Zhonghua Renmin Gongheguo Qinquanzerenfa [PRC Tort Liability Law] (2009) (PRC).

drafting group. After a year's discussion and preparation, the Society submitted a draft entitled *The Act on Application of Laws over Foreign-related Civil Relationships* ('Suggested Draft') at the end of March 2010, which was expected to serve as a blueprint for the NPC's Standing Committee to enact the conflicts code.[55] Based on the Suggested Draft, the task force, established by the Legislative Affairs Committee of the NPC's Standing Committee, created a draft bill of the Conflicts Act and submitted it to the Standing Committee of the Eleventh NPC for deliberation on 23 August 2010. The full text of the draft bill was soon published on the website of the NPC for public comment from 28 August to 20 September 2010.[56] After receiving the comments and suggestions, the Legislative Affairs Committee proceeded to prepare a final draft of the Conflicts Act in October 2010. The bill was submitted to the Seventeenth Session of the Standing Committee of the Eleventh NPC on 16 October 2010. Among the 158 members of the Standing Committee that attended the Session, all voted in favour of adopting the Conflicts Act.[57] Passed by the Chinese Legislature, the Conflicts Act was promulgated by President Jintao HU as 'Order of the President of the PRC No. 36 of 2010', and came into force on 1 April 2011.[58]

Entitled 'Act on the Application of Laws over Foreign-related Civil Relation- **1.32** ships', the new Chinese Conflicts Act contains eight chapters and 52 articles, with headings that are indicative of their respective scope: Chapter One, 'General Provisions' (Arts 1–10); Chapter Two, 'Civil Subjects' (Arts 11–20); Chapter Three, 'Marriage and Family' (Arts 21–30); Chapter Four, 'Succession' (Arts 31–35); Chapter Five, 'Property' (Arts 36–40); Chapter Six, 'Obligations' (Arts 41–47); Chapter Seven, 'Intellectual Property' (Arts 48–50); and Chapter Eight, 'Supplementary Provisions' (Arts 51–52).[59]

From the title and the structure of the Conflicts Act, the following two points **1.33** can be observed as the main style features of the Act. First, it is not a comprehensive private international law code. It contains choice-of-law issues on civil relationships, and excludes not only jurisdictional rules, rules of recognition and enforcement of foreign judgments and awards, but also

55 Detailed discussion on the draft, see Zhengxin Huo, 'China's Codification of Conflicts Law: Latest Efforts' (2010) 51 *Seoul Law Journal* 279–322.

56 See <http://www.npc.gov.cn/huiyi/cwh/1116/2010-08/28/content_1593162.htm>.

57 For the legislative rules and process, see n 51 above, and Law on Legislation, Arts 40, 41(2000)(PRC).

58 See Quanguo Renda Changweihui Gonggao [Bulletin of Standing Comm. Nat'l People's Cong, 30 August 2007] (PRC), <http://www.npc.gov.cn/wxzl/gongbao/2007-10/09/content_5374672.htm>.

59 For detailed discussion of the Conflicts Act, *see* Zhengxin Huo, 'An Imperfect Improvement: The New Conflict of Laws Act of the People's Republic of China', (2011) 60 ICLQ 1065.

choice-of-law issues on commercial relationships.[60] As various Chinese civil and commercial statutes have already included some conflicts rules, for the areas that are not covered by the new Act, such as Maritime Law,[61] Civil Aviation Law[62] and Negotiable Instrument Law,[63] the conflicts rules in the related statutes still apply. Such a model does not accord with the original expectation of most Chinese conflicts scholars, who had been espousing enacting a comprehensive code of private international law following the legislative model of Switzerland's Federal Code on Private International Law of 1987.[64]

1.34 Despite the scholars' calls, Chinese legislators have not showed enthusiasm for enacting a comprehensive conflicts code; on the contrary, they maintain that the first Conflicts Act should contain choice-of-law rules over civil relationships only. They hold to such a position, partly because of their conservative ideology,[65] and partly because of their concern that enacting a comprehensive code would require enormous amendments to many existing laws, such as the Civil Procedure Law, the Arbitration Law, the Contract Law, the Succession Law, and the Maritime Law, which would be a long and arduous work.[66]

1.35 Second, the Conflicts Act is not a simple recompilation of the existing conflicts rules that are scattered throughout different laws, regulations and judicial interpretations. Instead it establishes a relatively systematic regime in which general provisions are introduced and many new specific conflicts rules covering various areas are enacted. Strongly influenced and much inspired by modern foreign and international legislation, the Conflicts Act incorporates many of the most advanced developments discussed in private international

60 Under the Chinese scholarship, civil law has both broad and narrow definitions. In its broad sense, civil law is a body of law that governs proprietary and personal relationships between the parties that have equal status. In this respect, commercial law is a part of civil law. However, in its narrow sense, civil law refers to the section of private law excluding the area regulated by commercial law; and commercial law in this context is defined as the branch law of that governs company, insurance, bankruptcy, negotiable instruments, and admiralty. As civil law in its broad sense includes such an extensive coverage, law professors in China now usually embrace the narrow scope of civil law. Thus a typical Chinese textbook on civil law would include contract law, family law, tort law, and property law only. This view has also been endorsed by the Chinese legislators, which is reflected by the structure of the General Principle of Civil Law of the PRC. See Law Institute of the Chinese Academy of Social Science (ed), *Faxue Cidian* [*Law Dictionary*] 425, 646 (2004).

61 Maritime Law, Arts 270, 271, 272.

62 Civil Aviation Law, Arts 185, 186, 187.

63 Zhonghua Renmin Gongheguo Piaojufa [Negotiable Instrument Contract Law] arts 96, 97, 98, 99, 100, 101 (1999, revised in 2004) (PRC).

64 See HAN Depei, *supra* n 3, 18.

65 Even today, some of Chinese legislators are still of the opinion that the application of foreign law is an offence of China's sovereignty. See Weidong Zhu, supra n 50, 306.

66 See ibid 284; <http://www.npc.gov.cn/huiyi/cwh/1116/2010–08/28/content_1593162.htm>.

law.[67] For instance, the principle of the closest connection has been stipulated as a subsidiary principle of application of laws; party autonomy has been confirmed and expanded, to torts and real rights in movables; the Conflicts Act reflects the notion of the protection of weaker parties; and most impressively, abandoning the Chinese tradition, the Conflicts Act adopts habitual residence, rather than nationality, as the principal connecting factor to determine *lex personalis*. This represents a significant improvement in building a modern system of private international law.[68]

Basically, the promulgation of the Conflicts Act shows that China has **1.36** succeeded in achieving the goal of codifying substantial parts of its choice of law the significance of which cannot be overestimated. Nonetheless, the progress represented by the enactment of the Conflicts Act is but 'an imperfect improvement'.[69] The Act is not comprehensive and some rules are too simple, ambiguous, or not fully thought-through.

It is not surprising that no sooner had the Conflicts Act been implemented **1.37** than the SPC initiated the work of enacting the judicial interpretation.[70] Entrusted by the Judicial Committee of the SPC,[71] a drafting group was established that included experienced judges from the Fourth Civil Division of the SPC in January 2012.[72] Given that the Act had been implemented for only a short period and that the actual effect of its various articles in judicial practice had still to be observed, the Group considered adopting a single interpretation on the Act at one stroke too risky. Consequently, it decided to take two successive steps: it would first adopt the interpretation on Chapter One (General Provisions) of Act; and later, when the time was right, it would then adopt the interpretation on the remaining parts of the Act.[73]

---

67 According to the legislators, during the process of drafting, the conflicts statutes of some foreign countries, principally Germany, Switzerland and Japan, and the conventions of the Hague Conference of Private International Law and some Europe Union's regulations have been referred to. <http://www.npc.gov.cn/huiyi/cwh/1116/2010–08/28/content_1593162.htm>.

68 Zhengxin Huo, *supra* n 59,1065–93

69 Ibid.,, 1069–70.

70 ZHANG Xianming, 'Zhengquen Shenli Shewai Minshi Anjian, Qieshi Weihu Shehui Gonggong Liyi [Trying the Foreign-related Civil Cases in an Appropriate Way to Safeguard the Social Public Interests, Answer of the Fourth Civil Division of the SPC to the Press]', *People's Court Daily*, Jan. 7, 2013, 6.

71 According to the Organic Law of People's Courts, Chinese courts at all levels set up a Judicial Committee. The president of a People's Court presides over meetings of the judicial committee within that court. The tasks of a judicial committee include the summing up of judicial experience and the discussion of important or difficult cases and other issues relating to its judicial work. Zhonghua Renmin Gongheguo Renmin Fayuan Zuzhifa,[Organic Law of People's Courts] art 11 (1979, revised in 1983)(P.R.C.).

72 The People's Courts decide cases according to their nature, so that cases can be tried by specialist judges. The Fourth Civil Division of the SPC is the professional court that tries foreign-related civil cases and maritime cases falling under the jurisdiction of the SPC. See Feng Lin, *supra* n 49, 218.

73 The Private International Law Act, see para 1.32 above. See also Huo, *supra* n 59, 1069.

1.38 In this light, after preparation, discussion and investigation, the Group submitted a draft bill entitled 'Interpretation (I) on the Implementation of the Act on the Application of Laws over Foreign-related Civil Relationships' (hereinafter Conflicts Act Interpretation I) to the Judicial Committee of the SPC in December 2012. On January 6, 2013, the bill of Conflicts Act Interpretation I was passed at the 1563th Conference of the Judicial Committee of the SPC, which came into force on 7 January 2013.[74] The promulgation of the Conflicts Act Interpretation I can be regarded as an important effort made by China's judiciary to build a modern private international law system with Chinese characteristics, which cannot only solve the problems of the Conflicts Act to a considerable degree but also pave the way for the substantive amendment of the Act by the legislature in the future.[75]

74 SPC, 'Conflicts Act Interpretation I'.

75 Some materials in this chapter are reproduced from Zhengxin Huo, *supra* n 59, 1065; Zhengxin Huo, *supra* n 77.

2

CONCEPTS AND PRELIMINARY QUESTIONS

I. THE NATURE OF CONFLICT OF LAWS

There are three groups of thought on the nature of conflict of laws: universalism, particularism and dualism. Universalism insists on the uniform, universal and obligatory norms that private international law imposes to all states in the world. Friedrich Carl von Savigny and Pasquale Stanislao Mancini are the leading advocates. Particularism is represented by Albert Venn Dicey and Martin Wolff, holding each state creates its own private international law norms pursuing its own policy, making private international law domestic law instead of international law.[1] Duralists include Ernest Zitelmann and Rudolf Bystricky, who believe that private international law regulates both domestic and international legal relations whose sources include not only domestic law **2.01**

1 As Wolff puts it: 'Today undoubtedly private international law is national law. There exists an English private international law as distinct from a French, a German, an Italian private international law. The rules on the conflict of laws in the various countries differ nearly as much from each other as do those on internal (municipal) law.' Martin Wolff, *Private International Law* (2nd ed., Clarendon Press 1950) 11.

but also international conventions and custom; therefore, private international law is both internal and international in nature.[2]

2.02 Chinese scholars approach this issue from the perspective of historical materialism believing in an evolutionary process, by virtue of which private international law has been progressing from internal law to international law. In the earlier period private international law comprised conflicts rules only in domestic legislation; in other words, private international law undoubtedly originated from internal law in nature. Only after the nineteenth century, when international conventions and custom gradually became the sources of private international law, did scholars have disagreements on the nature of the discipline. Based on the historic background, the discipline depends on the specific stage where private international law is situated now in its evolutionary process.

2.03 Private international law in the early twenty-first century is thus a blend of internal and international law. The evolution of private international law suggests that the discipline is striding towards the realm of international law, notwithstanding the fact that its current sources are primarily domestic legislation and case law.[3]

II. JUSTIFICATION FOR CONFLICT OF LAWS

2.04 The premise of modern conflict of laws is that domestic law and foreign law are equal in multi-state civil and commercial disputes, and that judges may choose one from the relevant competing rules, domestic or foreign, which should apply. In theory there is a similar, if not an equal, opportunity for a foreign law to be applied by domestic courts.

2.05 Why should foreign law be applied in a domestic court? The parties have come before a domestic court, and the local lawyers and judges know domestic law much better than they know foreign laws. Moreover, it may be difficult for a domestic court to discover accurately what the relevant rule of foreign law is. Furthermore, one may wonder if the use of a foreign law means the surrender of the sovereignty to a foreign country. These concerns existed in Chinese history. However, the past three decades have witnessed a substantial change in China's attitude in the application of foreign law. China has gradually but

2 HUANG Jin, *Guoji Sifa [Private International Law]* (2nd ed., China Law Press 2005) 28.
3 SHEN Juan (ed.), *Guoji Sifa [Private International Law]* (China Social Sciences Press 2006) 674.

steadily moved from sovereignty-sensitive exclusion to foreign law to reform-served openness to apply foreign law.[4] This positive change has stimulated Chinese private international law scholarship. With regard to the reason or justification for the application of foreign law, many western theories, such as 'comity' and 'vested right', are now well received in China. Nevertheless, Chinese scholars are not satisfied with the introduction and discussion of foreign theories; instead they have been exploring new doctrines to justify the application of foreign law.[5] Chinese legal research has developed from a complete blank of private international law scholarship to the existence of various doctrines boasting 'Chinese characteristics'. However, at present, Chinese doctrines, in spite of their preferable ideology, still need to be further refined and improved before they can gain international recognition.

II.1 The theory of mutual benefits in international relations

The most dominant theory in China is that of mutual benefits in international **2.06** relations.[6] According to this doctrine, the application of foreign law in transnational civil and commercial disputes is an inevitable consequence of the development of human society.[7] With the rapid development of international trade and the acceleration of globalization, the civil and commercial disputes that involve the interests of more than one country have become unprecedentedly common and the interest of different countries have become interrelated and interacted with each other. The pursuit of absolute self-interest is no longer tenable, and it becomes necessary for a court to apply foreign law in transnational civil cases, subject to certain conditions. Otherwise, the interest of the forum state and the benefit of the international community as a whole will, in the long run, be undermined.[8] Although the theory of mutual benefits focuses on the benefit of the international community as a whole, the fundamental purpose is to protect the national interest. It emphasizes the fact that national interest cannot be fully protected in the age of globalization without recognizing and respecting the interest of other countries, including applying foreign law in the domestic court.

---

4 Mo Zhang, 'Choice of Law in Contracts: A Chinese Approach' (2006) 26 *Northwestern Journal of International Law & Business* 299, 304; Zhengxin Huo, 'Choice of Law in Tort', (2009) 4 *Journal of Cambridge Studies* 82, 83.

5 See ibid.

6 See YU Xianyu (ed.), *Chongtufa [Conflict of Laws]* (China Law Press, Beijing 1989) 89; XIAO Yongping, *Guojisifa Yuanli [The Principle of Private International Law]* (Law Press, Beijing 2003) 47; YU Fei, *Zhongguo Guoji Sifa Lilun yu Lifa [Theory and Legislation of Chinese Private International Law]* (China Law Press 2004) 154–5.

7 HUANG Jin, *supra* n 2, 166.

8 Ibid.

2.07 For example, in order to judge whether a foreign corporation investing in China is a qualified corporate body, the law of this foreign country, not Chinese law, shall apply.[9] The civil capacity of foreigners as well as foreign corporations should be determined by the *lex personalis*. If Chinese courts were to insist on applying Chinese law instead of *lex personalis*, capacity of foreign companies, incorporated under the law of the place of incorporation, would be subject to two different laws, which could cause extra difficulty for potential international investors and would eventually harm the Chinese economy.

2.08 Furthermore, China should safeguard the stability of legal relations established under foreign laws in order to facilitate international trade. For example, if a Chinese company enters into a trade relationship with its foreign partner, the transaction is conducted abroad and the parties agree that their legal relationship should be subject to the foreign law, insisting on applying Chinese law may hamper the parties' intention and jeopardize commercial certainty. This approach would prejudice all Chinese parties in international transactions, hamper stable development of international civil and economic relations, and harm Chinese national interest as a whole.[10]

2.09 It is necessary to note here that the theory of mutual benefits differs from reciprocity. The purpose of applying foreign law is to achieve national interests through benefiting another country. It does not require the foreign country to apply Chinese law reciprocally. However, reciprocity may be a pleasant result of the theory of mutual benefits. If all countries recognize the importance of mutual benefits, which are indispensable to national interests, all countries would be willing to apply foreign law in certain circumstances. Chinese law would naturally be given effect out of jurisdiction. The mutual application of each other's law would largely promote mutual benefits to all countries, and the protection of community interest would in return benefit each individual country.

II.2 The theory of benefit promotion

2.10 The theory of mutual benefits, however, is logically challenged. In order to receive 'mutual benefits', the application of foreign law should mutually benefit more than one party with equal footing and also bring benefits to more than one relevant country. If the application of foreign law only benefits the Chinese party or promotes Chinese interest, the foreign law should not be applied. As has been stated above, the fundamental purpose of the theory of

9 Ibid.
10 Zhang, *supra* n 4, 304.

mutual benefits is to protect national interests through promoting mutual benefits in the international community. However, national interest and the interest of the international community are not always consistent. Where conflicts exist between benefiting the home state and benefiting the international community, most countries will decide to protect national interest, which challenges the viability of the theory of mutual benefits in practice. It is reasonable to argue that 'mutual benefits' is only the means, not the aim, to achieve national interest. The fundamental reason to apply foreign law is to promote national interest, which leads to the theory of benefit promotion. This theory abandons the internationalization or cosmopolitan approach and returns to the position of national interest. A national court will apply foreign law not because it wants to promote mutual benefits but because applying foreign law is beneficial to this country and its citizens.[11]

The theory of benefit promotion is more realistic than the theory of mutual benefits and may be more easily accepted by most countries in the world. However, it is hard to know whether applying foreign law would be more beneficial to the local country and its citizens. For example, does it depend on the substance of the law, the parties' intention and expectation, the stability of economic development or the interest and policy in legislation? If the legislative policy is taken into account, the theory of benefit promotion is close to the government interest analysis theory, proposed by Currie.[12] **2.11**

From the practical perspective, the theory of benefit promotion may result in a case-by-case analysis of choice of law. Since the reason behind applying foreign law is to promote national interest, the court must exercise its discretion to decide whether, in a particular case, the foreign law is more beneficial to national interest than the forum law. This approach, however, is incompatible with Chinese judicial tradition under which judges have very limited discretion and should apply the pre-designed choice of law rules according to legislation or judicial interpretation. **2.12**

---

11 YU Fei, *supra* n 5, 155–6.

12 L. Brilmayer, 'Governmental Interest Analysis', (1985) 46 *Ohio State Law Journal* 459; H.H. Kay, 'Currie's Interest Analysis in the 21st Century', (2001) 37 *Willamette Law Review* 123.

III. SOURCES OF CONFLICT OF LAWS

III.1 Statutes

2.13 Sources of law are the materials and processes out of which the legal rules and principles regulating the human community develop. Chinese scholars usually define the term as something (such as a constitution, treaty, statute or custom) providing manifestation of the law and its creation.[13] In civil law countries, statutes adopted by legislature are the primary source of law; whereas in common law countries, case law is traditionally regarded as the major source of law. Nevertheless, with the convergence of two law families, the traditional differences on the sources of law are no longer as distinct as they used to be. China has a civil law tradition and statutes are the most important source of law, including private international law.

2.14 China had no specific choice of law statute until October 2010. Before that, choice of law rules were scattered among various statutes and regulations, the dominant and most important of which is the General Principles of Civil Law (GPCL) 1986.[14] The GPCL has devoted an entire chapter to regulating the conflict of laws (i.e., Chapter Eight, Application of Laws to Civil Matters Involving Foreign Element), where nine conflicts rules can be found. On 28 October 2010, the Standing Committee of the Eleventh National People's Congress (NPC) adopted the first statute of the P.R. China on Conflicts Law – Law on the Application of Laws over Foreign-related Civil Relationships' (Conflicts Act).[15] This is considered a milestone in demonstrating that conflict of laws has eventually been modernized in China. More importantly, the passage of this long-expected Act marks that 'the socialist legal system with Chinese characteristics' has been successfully established as scheduled, which implies that China, the largest developing country, can now claim to

---

13 However, as Holland pointed out, the phrase of 'source of law' is ambiguous. It is commonly used in four senses, i.e., to refer to: (1) the place from which we obtain our knowledge of the law, e.g., whether from the statute-book, the reports, or treaties (literary source); (2) the ultimate authority that backs up the law (formal source); (3) the causes that have, seemingly automatically, brought into existence rules that have subsequently acquired legal force, such as custom, religion, and scientific discussion (historical or material source); or (4) the organs through which the state either grant legal recognition to rules previously unauthoritative, or itself creates new law, such as legislation and adjudication (legal source). See HAN Depei, *Guoji Sifa* [*Private International Law*] (China Higher Education Press 2001) 20.

14 Zhonghua Renmin Gongheguo Minfa Tongze [PRC General Principle of Civil Law] (GPCL) (1986).

15 Zhonghua Renmin Gongheheguo Shewai Minshi Falvguanxi Shiyongfa [Act on the Application of Laws over Foreign-related Civil Relationships] ('Conflicts Act') (2010). Detailed discussion, see Zhengxin Huo, 'An Imperfect Improvement: The New Conflict of Laws Act of the People's Republic of China' (2011) 60 *International and Comparative Law Quarterly* 1065, 1070.

have a systematic legal system.[16] Hence, after its implementation on 1 April 2011, the Conflicts Act becomes the major source of Chinese Choice of Law.[17]

The major piece of legislation governing international civil litigation is Civil Procedure Law of the People's Republic of China (hereinafter referred to as the CPL).[18] Promulgated on 4 April 1991, revised on 28 October 2007, and 31 August 2012 respectively, the CPL is the major law for the People's Court to follow in the process of the adjudication of civil cases. Among the provisions of the CPL, the most relevant ones are contained in Part Four, entitled 'Special Provisions of Civil Procedures for Cases Involving Foreign Elements'. **2.15**

In addition, some other national laws, such as Contract Law,[19] Maritime Law,[20] and Civil Aviation Law,[21] also contain certain conflicts rules that fall within their scope of regulation respectively. **2.16**

III.2 Judicial interpretation

Besides national laws, the judicial interpretations promulgated by the SPC enjoy the de facto status of an important source of Chinese law, including private international law. It should be noted that the meaning of the term 'judicial interpretation' may be different in China than in other countries. According to the Organic Law of the People's Courts, the SPC is the only court that has the authority to provide judicial interpretation. Under Article 32 of the Law, when a new statute or decree is enacted, the SPC is entitled to give a general interpretation about how the legislation should be implemented in adjudication.[22] Although this article has raised the issue of constitutionality,[23] most Chinese scholars argue that this practice is desirable for China's circumstances. First, judicial interpretation can supplement the inappropriateness of **2.17**

16 At the 15th National Congress of the Communist Party of China, the rule of law principle was established as a fundamental principle for the administration of the country, and in order to implement the principle the Party put forward a legislative plan pursuant to which the socialist legal system with Chinese characteristics would be shaped by the year 2010. To ensure the accomplishment of the legislative plan, the National People's Congress, China's supreme legislature, has obviously accelerated legislation after 2005. See Collection of Documents of the 15th National Congress of the Communist Party of China, 5–6 (1997). Zhonghua Renmin Gongheguo Wuquanfa [PRC Property Law] (2007); Zhonghua Renmin Gongheguo Qinquanzerenfa [PRC Tort Liability Law] (2009); see also Zhengxin Huo, 'China's Codification of Conflicts Law: Latest Efforts', (2010) 51 *Seoul L J* 283.

17 For more discussion, see Ch 1, IV.3.

18 Zhonghua Renmin Gongheguo Minshi Susongfa [PRC Civil Procedure Law] (1991, revised 2007 and 2012).

19 Zhonghua Renmin Gongheguo Hetongfa [PRC Contract Law] (1999).

20 Zhonghua Renmin Gongheguo Haishangfa [PRC Maritime Law] (1993).

21 Zhonghua Renmin Gongheguo Minyong Hangkongfa [PRC Civil Aviation Law] (1996).

22 Feng Lin, *Constitutional Law in China* (Sweet & Maxwell 2000) 222.

legislation, such as inconsistencies between different legislation, gaps left by legislation, etc. Secondly, it can provide sound experience and conditions for the future legislation or the amendment of the existing legislation. As legislation in China is far from perfect at the current stage, such judicial interpretation is both beneficial and necessary.[24]

2.18 Judicial interpretation has played an increasingly prominent role within the Chinese legal system since the 1980s. It is a paradox that the SPC, a relatively weak supreme court in a communist country, enjoys such wide authority to interpret law that can hardly be imagined by the supreme courts of any other country.[25] Although some commentators argue that many judicial interpretations issued by the SPC have exceeded the authorization by law, most of them acknowledge the merits and the necessity of this development under the current Chinese legal and political background.[26]

2.19 The major reason for the growing role played by judicial interpretation is the intrinsic defect of the Chinese legislative system. As the NPC is in session for about two weeks each year, it has little time to adopt more sophisticated statutes or to review problems associated with the application of existing statutes.[27] Although the Standing Committee of the National People's Congress (SCNPC) enjoys legislative authority when the NPC is not in session, it is not capable of performing such a duty, as it is basically composed of retired senior officials and not legal professionals.[28] Consequently, many Chinese statutes have suffered from being either inapplicable due to their ambiguous language or outdated by rapid social changes.[29]

2.20 Under these circumstances, the SPC, which has been composed largely of legal professionals, stepped into the vacuum left by the Chinese legislatures, providing much needed help. Hence it is not surprising that the NPC and its Standing Committee are not only aware of the SPC *ultra vires* interpretations,

---

23 Some authors believe that the exercise of such judicial interpretation by the SPC is a usurpation of the legislative authority of the national legislature. *See* Li Wei, 'Judicial Interpretation in China' (1997) 5 *Willamette Journal of International Law & Dispute Resolution* 87, 104.

24 *See* Lin, *supra* n 22, 222.

25 YUAN Mingsheng, 'Sifa Jieshi Lifahua Xianxiang Tanwei [A Commentary on the Legitimacy of Judicial Interpretation of the SPC]' (2003) 2 Fashang Yanjiu [Studies in Law & Business] 3.

26 CHEN Chenglong, 'Zhongguo Sifajieshi de Diwei yu Gongneng [The Status and Function of Judicial Interpretation in China]' (2003) 1 Zhongguo Faxue [China Legal Science)] 24.

27 Zhengxin Huo, 'Two Steps Forward, One Step Back: A Commentary on the Judicial Interpretation on the Private International Law Act of China' (2013) 43 *Hong Kong Law Journal* 710.

28 See HU Angang, 'Reforming the Standing Committee of the NPC, Optimizing the Composition of its Members' 21 Jan. (2003) Global News of the 21st Century 15. Available at http://news.sina.com.cn/c/2003-01-21/1509882585.shtml (visited 20 April 2013).

29 Huo, *supra* n 27, 710.

but also have apparently enjoyed the benefit of the SPC's judicial interpretations that effectively relieved them from the burden of reviewing and amending statutes.[30]

2.21 In this light, it is understandable why the Conflicts Act and the CPL, like many other statutes, are fraught with problems such as their simplistic framework and ambiguous language, and why the legislators decided to leave various complex issues to the SPC when they enacted the Act. For the same reason, the importance of the judicial interpretations issued by the SPC is comparable to the national statutes. Indeed, as judicial interpretations usually contain more detailed provisions and provide solutions to certain complex issues, they are indispensable not only for Chinese judges in court trials, but also for lawyers inside and outside China.[31]

2.22 So far, major judicial interpretations concerning private international law include, inter alia, 'Interpretation of the SPC on the Application of the PRC Civil Procedure Law' (2015),[32] 'Interpretation (I) on the Implementation of the Act on the Application of Laws over Foreign-related Civil Relationships of the People's Republic of China' (2012),[33] and 'Opinions of the SPC on Implementing the General Principles of Civil Law of the People's Republic of China' (1988).[34]

III.3 International treaties

2.23 Another important source of Chinese private international law is international treaties to which China is a party. Since the 1980s, China has participated actively in the codification and unification movement of private international law and has cooperated fruitfully with international communities in order to settle foreign-related disputes more efficiently. It has acceded to dozens of multinational treaties on private international law matters and has signed 78

30 HU Tugui, 'Quanguo Renda Ying Chongfen Xingshihao Lifaquan [The NPC Should Fully Exercise Its Legislative Power]' (1995) 2 Faxue [Legal Science] 8, 9.

31 Huo, *supra* n 27, 711.

32 SPC, 'Zuigao Renmin Fayuan Guanyu Shiyong 'Zhonghua Renmin Gongheguo Minshi Susongfa' de Jieshi [Interpretation of the SPC on the Application of the PRC Civil Procedure Law' (2015 Opinion)]', Fa Shi [2015] No 5.

33 SPC, 'Zuigao Renmin Fayuan Guanyu Shiyong 'Zhonghua Renmin Gongheguo Shewai Minshi Guanxi Falv Shiyong Fa' Ruogan Wenti de Jieshi (Yi)' ['Interpretations of the SPC on Several Issues Concerning Application of the Law of the People's Republic of China on Choice of Law for Foreign-Related Civil Relationships (I)' ('Conflicts Act Interpretation I')], Fa Shi [2012] No 24.

34 SPC, 'Zuigao Renmin Fayuan Guanyu Guanche Zhixing "Zhonghua Renmin Gongheguo Minfa Tongze" Ruogan Wenti de Yijian (Shixing)(Shixiao) [Opinion of the SPC about Several Issues on the Implementation of the "General Principle of Civil Law" (For the Trial Purpose)]' ('Opinion on GPCL'), Fa (Ban) Fa [1988] No 6 (abolished).

bilateral agreements on judicial assistance with other countries up to 2 July 2006.[35] It should be emphasized that in the aspect of civil law, international treaty stipulations prevail over domestic Chinese law when in conflict, Article 142(2) of the GPCL provides as follows:

> If any international treaty concluded or acceded to by the People's Republic of China contains provisions differing from those in the civil laws of the People's Republic of China, the provisions of the international treaty shall apply, unless the provisions are ones on which the People's Republic of China has announced reservations.

III.4 International customs and common practice

2.24 In addition to treaties, a further source of private international law is international practice, Article 142(3) of the GPCL provides that international practice may be applied to matters for which neither the law of the PRC nor any international treaty concluded or acceded to by the PRC has any provisions.

2.25 This provision shows that international practice is a source of private international law in China. However, its status is lower than both international treaties and Chinese domestic civil laws. What is more, under this provision, the application of international practice is in any case a matter of discretion, rather than being mandatory.

III.5 Court decisions and academic opinions

2.26 Finally, decisions and rulings of Chinese courts and the opinions of Chinese academics are also potential sources of private international law. Even though civil law countries normally do not recognize the doctrine of *stare decisis* as such, there is no doubt that in China, where the system of private international law remains substantially incomplete, judicial opinions and the decisions are often resorted to in resolving conflicts problems where no other authorities are available.[36]

IV. CHARACTERIZATION

2.27 Chinese conflicts system is rule-based, which means pre-designated rules are provided to direct the court to apply the law of a particular country. Due to the

35 See HUANG Jin, *supra* n 2, 56.
36 Han, *supra* n 13, 25.

large variety of disputes of different nature, it is impossible to provide one simple choice of law rules for all foreign-related disputes. Specifically designed conflicts rules are provided for different types of claim. But before the court can identify the correct conflicts rule to apply, it needs to characterize the matter into a particular judicial category. In other words, the court must initially, whether consciously or not, go through the process of determining the nature of the problem. The process is called 'characterization'.

IV.1 Practice before the Conflicts Act

Although characterization is one of the most interesting issues in private international law theory, the Chinese legislation and judicial interpretations were silent on this matter before the enactment of the Conflicts Act. No guidance has been provided for general characterization problems except limitation.[37] Before the implementation of the Conflicts Act, Chinese courts usually applied the *lex fori* for characterization. Nevertheless, the courts had sometimes been inconsistent in characterizations in adjudicating foreign-related disputes. For example, releasing goods without presentation of the original bill of lading was held as breach of contract in some cases,[38] but tort in others.[39] In *Wanbao Group Company Guangzhou Feida Electronic Factory v. America President Liners*,[40] while the People's Court of first instance and of second instance held the disputes as tort, the SPC characterized the claims as breach of contract and reversed the classification. In another example, *TMT Trading Ltd. v. Guangdong Light Industrial Products Import-Export (Group) Co*,[41] disputes arose out of the agreement under which the claimant provided the defendant with the exclusive rights to use the claimant's trademark to produce products and to become the sole distributor of the products. The High People's Court of Guangdong Province characterized the dispute as contract of agency, while the SPC as legal relation of trust. The SPC made 2.28

37 Article 195 of the Judicial Interpretation of the SPC: 'Time limitation for action shall be determined according to the applicable law governing the civil legal relation that is determined pursuant to the rule of conflict of laws.' In view of this, time limitations for actions are characterized as substantive issues. SPC, 'Opinion on GPCL', n 26, Art 195.

38 *Yuehai Electronic Co. Ltd. v. China Merchants Warehouse & Transportation Co. Ltd*, (1997) 1 Zhonghua Renmin Gongheguo Zuigao Renmin Fayuan Gongbao [PRC SPC Gazette] No 14; discussed in Zhenjia Jin, *Zhongguo Dianxing Haishi Anli Pingxi [An Analysis of Typical Chinese Maritime Cases]* (China Law Press 1998) 312–22. This is a decision made by the SPC in 1994.

39 Qingjiang Kong and Mingfei Hu, 'The Chinese Practice of Private International Law', (2002) 3 *Melbourne Journal of International Law* 202.

40 [2001] Min Er Zhong Zi No 166.

41 [1998] Zhi Zhong Zi No 8.

such a characterization at the time when trust was not a recognized legal relationship under Chinese law.[42]

IV.2 Conflicts Act

2.29 In order to provide a clear guideline for Chinese judges to follow when they characterize foreign-related disputes, the Conflicts Act of 2010 incorporates a choice-of-law rule for characterization in Article 8, which provides that '[T]he classification of foreign-related relationships shall be governed by the law of forum.'[43]

2.30 Characterization is effected on the basis of the law of the forum. This is the accepted position under the common law and in most civilian systems. However, it is also widely accepted that the *lex fori* in this context should be interpreted in a liberal manner, not insisting that all its technical requirements in the domestic substantive law are complied with. Moreover, the court should not be deterred by the fact that the particular foreign claim was not recognized under the *lex fori*. Under that circumstance, it should characterize it in accordance with what it considered to be the closest equivalent under the *lex fori*. This method of characterization could be referred to as the 'liberal' or 'enlightened' *lex fori*.[44] It is suggested that the SPC should interpret Article 8 as soon as possible; otherwise, if a foreign legal institution or a rule of foreign law is unknown to Chinese law, the Chinese court seized will be in an awkward position.[45]

V. *RENVOI*

2.31 In private international law, *renvoi* arises whenever a court of the forum (Country A), by applying its own choice-of-law rule, is directed to the 'law' of a foreign country (Country B), while the choice-of-law rules of Country B designate the 'law' of Country A as the applicable law (remission), or refers to the law of a third country (Country C) (transmission).[46]

---

42 Discussed in Vai Io Lo and Xiaowen Tian, *Law and Investment in China: The Legal and Business Environment after China's WTO Accession* (Routledge 2005) 188.

43 Conflicts Act, Art 8 (2010).

44 George Panagopoulous, *Restitution in Private International Law* (Oxford 2000), 33.

45 Zhengxin Huo, *supra* n 15, 1075.

46 See William M. Richman, and Milliam L. Reynolds, *Understanding Conflict of Laws* (LexisNexis 2003) 167–8.

According to the position of the SPC of China, *renvoi* has no place in Chinese judicial practice. Paragraph 2 of Article 178 of the 'Opinion on GPCL' provides that: '[U]pon handling the cases involving foreign elements, the People's Court shall determine the applicable substantive law according to the regulations of Chapter VIII of the GPCL.'[47] This provision indicates that when Chinese courts determine that the law of a certain state applies, they apply its 'substantive law' directly, thus excluding the conflicts rules of the designated state. **2.32**

It should be noted that there is one reported case in China in which the doctrine of *renvoi* was allegedly to apply, i.e., *Chancery plc (United Kingdom) v. Sukissed Marine Co Ltd. (Greece)* decided by Guangzhou Maritime Court.[48] In this case, the parties agreed that their dispute should be governed by Chinese law. However, Guangzhou Maritime Court referred to the conflicts rule of Chinese law instead of Chinese substantive law based on the parties' choice. The court referred to Article 271 of the PRC Maritime Law which provides that 'mortgage of a ship shall be determined by the law of the flag State of the ship'.[49] The court, then, referred to the substantive law of Cyprus as the applicable law according to the above conflicts rule. **2.33**

This decision was alleged to be based on the doctrine of *renvoi*. Nevertheless, it is submitted that Guangzhou Maritime Court made a mistake in applying the doctrine in such a manner. First, according to its definition, *renvoi* occurs when a forum court applies a foreign choice-of-law rule that selects law different from that chosen by the forum's conflicts rule. In the present case, after the parties had explicitly chosen Chinese law as the applicable law, Guangzhou Maritime Court applied the choice-of-law rule of China, which directs to Cyprus. The application of the substantive law of Cyprus, therefore, was the result of the repeated resort to the choice-of-law rules of the forum. **2.34**

Secondly, as mentioned above, under the 'Opinion on GPCL', *renvoi* is categorically excluded. It was unjustified that the Guangzhou Maritime Court should refer to the conflicts rule rather than substantive rules even if presuming that the repeated application of the choice-of-law rules of the forum suited the definition of the doctrine of *renvoi*. As a matter of fact, since the GPCL upholds party autonomy in contracts involving foreign elements and its judicial interpretation excludes *renvoi*, the Chinese law chosen by the parties in this case should have been Chinese substantive law. Referring to another **2.35**

47 SPC, 'Opinions on GPCL', *supra* n 37.

48 *Chancery plc (United Kingdom) v. Sukissed Marine Co Ltd (Greece)*, Guangzhou Maritime Court, 29 February 1996; Jin, *supra* n 38, 17–18.

49 Maritime Law, Art 271.

Chinese choice-of-law rule, which pointed to the law of another country, was not only contrary to the expectation of the parties but also violated law. The alleged application of *renvoi* by Guangzhou Maritime Court misused the concept of *renvoi*, deviated from the provisions of the GPCL as well as its judicial interpretation, and frustrated the parties' expectation.

2.36 While Chinese legislation long contained no *renvoi* provision, the majority of Chinese scholars advocate adopting partial *renvoi* in certain cases, basically, in matters concerning personal or family status. This point of view is fully reflected in the Model Law of Private International Law of People's Republic of China, Article 8 of which provides:[50]

> The applicable law provided under this law means the current, effective civil and commercial substantive law and does not include conflicts rules unless otherwise provided by this law. In matters concerning personal or family status, a reference back (*Renvoi*) to the PRC law by foreign conflicts rules shall be accepted.

2.37 Based on the Model Law, Chinese conflicts scholars have been advocating that the Conflicts Act of 2010 should permit *renvoi* in certain fields, such as the matters concerning personal or family status, which, on the one hand, may expand the application of the *lex fori*, and promote international decisional harmony on the other.

2.38 Nevertheless, the legislators did not accept such suggestions and decided to reject *renvoi* entirely, as Article 9 of the Conflicts Act of 2010 stipulates that: 'The foreign law applicable to a foreign-related civil relationship does not include the conflicts law of that foreign country.'

2.39 The most important reason for the complete rejection of *renvoi* is that the Chinese legislators worry that permitting it, even partially, may further complicate the judicial task of Chinese judges. That consideration may be comprehensible at present; however, given the quality of Chinese judges has been, and will be, continuously improving, this worry seems, in the long run, to be unnecessary.[51]

---

50 In August 2000, the Chinese Society of Private International Law, an academic organization located in China, drew up the 'Model Law of Private International Law of the People's Republic of China', which embodies the latest and highest level of research in China in the field of private international law. Chinese Society of Private International Law, Model Law of Private International Law of the People's Republic of China (2000); English version, 3 *Yearbook of Private International Law* (Petar Sarczvic and Paul Volken eds.) (Kluwer Law International 2001) 349–90.

51 Huo, *supra* n 15, 1070.

VI. PROOF OF FOREIGN LAW

Establishing the contents of foreign law is an essential part of any litigation that involves transnational parties or transactions. The proof of foreign law largely depends on the classification of foreign law, i.e., whether a foreign law is classified as a matter of fact or law? In many foreign states, this is a fundamental question that has a direct bearing on the specific methods and procedures for the proof of foreign law. However, Chinese law fails to provide a clear answer. Some Chinese scholars even argue that it is meaningless to address this question in light of Chinese legislation, insofar as CPL provides that '[I]n trying civil cases, the People's Courts must base themselves on facts and take the law as the criterion.'[52] These scholars note that under the wording of this provision, there is no difference between fact and law in Chinese civil procedure at all. No matter whether a foreign law is classified as a fact or law, the judge has the duty to ascertain it. Therefore, the classification of foreign law as fact or as law is pointless in judicial practice.[53] **2.40**

Unlike common law jurisdictions, Chinese courts do not depend on pleadings and proof by the parties concerned, because the Chinese civil procedure adopts an inquisitorial system rather than adversarial system, in which the judge is not just the passive adjudicator of the parties but a 'truth-seeker' whose duty is to actively take the initiative and select appropriate means to ascertain the objective truth underlying a legal dispute. Therefore, it is an established principle that where a People's Court applies foreign law as the applicable law, it has to identify the law *ex officio*.[54] However, although it is the court's duty to ascertain the content of foreign law, in China, as well as in many other civil law states, the judge may require the parties to assist in proving its content.[55] **2.41**

VI.1 Practice before the Conflicts Act

According to the 'Opinion on GPCL', the applicable foreign laws may be found in the following ways: (1) provided by the litigant; (2) provided by the central organization of the country having entered into the judicial assistance treaty with this country; (3) provided by the consulate of that country in China; (4) provided by the embassy of that country in China; or (5) provided by the legal experts at home and abroad.[56] **2.42**

---

52 Civil Procedure Law, Art 7 (2012).

53 Huang, *supra* n 2, 205.

54 Kong and Hu, *supra* n 39, 204.

55 Zhengxin Huo, *supra* n 4, 91.

56 SPC, 'Opinions on GPCL', *supra* n 37, Art 193(1).

2.43 In the event that the foreign law cannot be ascertained, rather than applying the most closely ascertainable law, Chinese courts will, out of pragmatic considerations and as a result of the 'homeward trend', apply Chinese law instead. Article 193(2) of the Guidelines of the SPC on Implementing the GPCL provides unambiguously that: '[I]f the applicable foreign laws are unable to be ascertained with the above-said ways, the case shall be applicable for the law of the People's Republic of China.' This provision, greatly simplifies the task of Chinese judges, but encourages the 'homeward trend'. In practice, it is often the case that Chinese courts are too ready to conclude that the applicable foreign laws are unable to be ascertained and apply Chinese law.[57] For example, in *MV Trade Quicker v. MV Yanan*,[58] although Panamanian law should have applied as both colliding ships were registered in Panama, the difficulty in ascertaining Panamanian law by both the parties and the court left the Tianjin Maritime Court no choice but to apply Chinese law as an alternative.[59]

2.44 On 23 July 2007, SPC promulgated 'Provisions on Several Issues Concerning the Application of Laws in Hearing the Cases Involving Foreign-related Civil or Commercial Contractual Disputes' (herein after referred to as 'Provisions of 2007'), which provides more detailed stipulations on the proof of foreign law in contract disputes. The relevant articles are as follows:[60]

> Article 9
>
> Where the parties concerned choose or alter the choice of the law applicable to contractual disputes to be a foreign law, the parties concerned shall provide or prove the relevant content of such foreign law.
>
> When the People's Court determines a foreign law as the law applicable to contractual disputes based on the principle of closest connection, it may ascertain such foreign law in accordance with its power, or may request the parties concerned to provide or prove the content of such foreign law.
>
> Where neither the parties concerned nor the People's Court can ascertain the content of the foreign law by appropriate means, the People's Court may apply the law of the People's Republic of China.

---

57 See Shen, *Private International Law, supra* n 3, 128; Huo, *supra* n 4, 91–2.

58 *Trade Quicker Inc v. Golden Light Overseas Management SA*, SPC, *Selected Cases of People's Courts* (1996) 1896–1902 (Tianjin Maritime Court, 1992).

59 In the case of the collision between the ships Huayu and Coral Island, the Maritime Court concerned failed to ascertain the foreign law chosen by the parties; therefore, it applied Chinese law instead.

60 See SPC, 'Zuigao Renmin Fayuan Guanyu Guanyu Shenli Shewai Minshi huo Shangshi Hetong Jiufen Anjian Falv Shiyong Ruogan Wenti de Guiding [Provisions of the SPC on the Relevant Issues concerning the Application of Law in Hearing Foreign-Related Contractual Dispute Cases in Civil and Commercial Matters]' ('2007 Provisions on applicable law'), Fa Shi [2007] 14 (abolished), Arts 9, 10.

Article 10

If the parties concerned raise no objection to the ascertained content of the foreign law after cross-examination, the People's Court shall confirm it. If the parties concerned raise any objection, the People's Court shall examine and determine it.

From the above provisions, some interesting changes are noted compared with Article 193(1) of the Opinion on GPCL.

First, re-affirming that both the judges and the parties have the duty to prove foreign law, the new provisions go on to make a more detailed classification. Where the parties select a foreign law as the governing law, the parties shall bear the burden of proof in ascertaining the content of the foreign law. This is because the choice of the foreign law implies that the parties are familiar with the law in question and so should possess the material to ascertain its content in order to make such a choice.[61] Where the People's Court decides to apply a foreign law in the absence of choice, the judge and the parties share the burden of proof. Since the law is determined by the court *ex officio*, requesting the parties and the judges to share the duty of proof is more beneficial to the accomplishment of the task. **2.45**

Secondly, given the development of modern science and technology and the close relation between the countries, the new provisions do not list the specific channels to ascertain foreign law, thus providing more flexible solutions. **2.46**

Thirdly, the new provisions make it clear that where the parties reach agreement on the content of the foreign law after cross-examination, the People's Court will confirm the argument. If the parties raise any objection, the People's Court shall examine and determine the content of the foreign law. This provision is in conformity with the laws of most countries. **2.47**

Last, but not least, the Provisions of 2007 reflects some changes in the consequence of the failure to prove foreign law, insofar as Article 9(3) provides that '[W]here neither the parties concerned nor the People's Court can ascertain the content of the foreign law by appropriate means, the People's Court *may* apply the law of the People's Republic of China (emphasis added).' The wording of 'may', instead of 'shall' implies that the application of the law of forum now becomes a matter of discretion, which is obviously different from Article 193 of the Opinion on GPCL. This change is believed to discourage the 'homeward trend', which has been a striking tendency in **2.48**

61 Huo, *supra* n 15, 1076.

Chinese judicial practice. However, it does not provide what alternative means are available in such circumstances other than applying domestic law.

VI.2 Conflicts Act and its judicial interpretation

2.49 The specific means to prove the content of foreign law has been provided by the judicial interpretations issued by the SPC, but provisions contained in different judicial interpretations remained fragmented, with some articles being outdated or contradictory. Hence, the Conflicts Act of 2010 provides a more systematic solution, as stipulated in Article 10:

> The foreign law applicable to a foreign-related relationship shall be ascertained by the relevant People's Court, arbitration institution, or administrative agency; where the parties choose to apply a foreign law, the parties concerned shall ascertain such foreign law; in case the foreign law cannot be ascertained or there is no pertinent rule of law after ascertainment, the law of the PRC shall apply.

2.50 A careful reading of the above article indicates that it is not a mere recompilation of the existing rules; instead, it attempts to provide a systematic solution. First of all, the article follows the tradition of civil law. It establishes that, as a general principle, courts or other quasi-judicial institutions shall prove the content of foreign law *ex officio*. Secondly, based on Article 9 of the Provisions of 2007, the Act makes it clear that where the parties choose a foreign law as the applicable law, the parties shall ascertain the content of the chosen law. Thirdly, this article states clearly that failure to prove the content of foreign law or the lack of pertinent rules of law after proof would lead to the consequence that Chinese law will be applied. It should be noted that Article 10 of the Conflicts Act of 2010 apparently ignores both the improvement made by Article 9(3) of the Provisions of 2007 and the suggestions put forward by many Chinese scholars who worry that the automatic application of the *lex fori* in this case would encourage the 'homeward trend'.

2.51 Moreover, having acknowledged that proof of foreign law is one of the major obstacles for the People's Courts improving judicial efficiency in foreign-related cases, the SPC considers it necessary to provide more detailed provisions.[62] Article 17 of the Conflicts Act Interpretation I states that:

---

62 Zhang Xianming, 'Zhengque Shenli Shewai Minshi Anjian Qieshi Weihu Shehui Gonggong Liyi [Trying the Foreign-related Civil Cases in an Appropriate Way to Safeguard the Social Public Interests, Answer of the Fourth Civil Division of the SPC to the Press]' 7 Jan 2013, Renmin Fayuanbao [People's Court Daily], 6.

> If a foreign law cannot be which China is a party, by the parties' submission, by expert witness, or other appropriate methods, the People's Court may hold that the foreign law cannot be proved.
>
> Where the parties bear the burden of proving a foreign law chosen by them, the People's Court may hold that the foreign law cannot be proved if they fail to fulfill this duty within the reasonable period designated by the Court.

It merits particularly strong emphasis that judges are left with much more discretion under the above article compared with the judicial interpretation issued by the SPC previously, which is reflected in the following two aspects. First, when the People's Court ascertain the content of foreign law *ex officio*, it shall fulfil its duty pursuant to Article 17 of the Conflicts Act Interpretation I, with no need to exhaust the five methods enumerated by Article 193(1) of the Opinion on GPCL.[63] Second, when the parties bear the burden of proving the foreign law, they shall fulfil the duty within a reasonable period specified by the People's Court; otherwise, they have to face the consequence that the law chosen by them is unable to be ascertained.[64] **2.52**

Obviously, the SPC attempts to improve judicial efficiency by vesting judges with such wide discretion. Nevertheless, given that failure to prove the foreign law would lead to the application of the *lex fori*, it is submitted that Article 17 of the Conflicts Act Interpretation I would encourage the application of Chinese law. Indeed, as many Chinese judges are still reluctant to recognize the effect of foreign law in foreign-related civil litigation,[65] it is highly possible that this article would be manipulated by Chinese judges to expand the application of *lex fori*, and if this is the case, the fundamental principle of the Conflicts Act would be undermined.[66] **2.53**

Furthermore, since Chinese judges are generally unfamiliar with foreign law, especially with case law in Anglo-American jurisdictions, Article 18 of the Conflicts Act Interpretation I provides that the People's Court should listen to the parties' statement on the content of foreign law, should they reach **2.54**

---

63 Zhengxin Huo, *supra* n 30, 709.

64 Conflicts Act Interpretation I, Art 17; *See* Zhang, *supra* n 64, 6.

65 Although the number of foreign civil cases has grown by leaps and bounds over the years, the precedents of the application of the conflicts rules by the People's Courts have been quite limited. According to the statistics, among all the foreign civil and commercial cases that have been trialed by the People's Courts, only less than 10 per cent applied the conflicts rules, and the overwhelming majority of these cases applied domestic Chinese law without any explanations. For many Chinese judges, applying foreign law is both costly and difficult; therefore, they are reluctant to recognize the effect of foreign law in civil cases involving foreign elements; and whenever possible, they are inclined to apply domestic Chinese law directly or by misusing some escaping devices, such as characterization, *ordre public* reservation and failure to prove foreign law.

66 Conflicts Act Interpretation I, Art 1. Huo, *supra* n 19, 1076.

consensus, the court may confirm it; should they fail to do so, the court shall examine and determine it. In other words, if the parties reach agreement on the content of a foreign law, the court may confirm it directly, even where the court shall prove foreign law *ex officio.*[67] The purpose of such an arrangement, needless to say, is to lighten the burden of Chinese judges, thus enhancing judicial efficiency in foreign-related cases.[68]

2.55 It is necessary to note that in China legal opinion submitted by lawyers of the relevant foreign country are usually inadequate to prove foreign law. In *Standard Chartered (Asia) Ltd v. Guangxi Zhuang Autonomous Region Huajian Co*,[69] for example, the People's Court refused to accept the legal opinion of a Hong Kong lawyer as adequate evidence to prove the content of Hong Kong law, which was chosen by the parties, because the party submitting the evidence failed to prove that the content of the legal opinion was true and accurate. It is unclear what additional evidence may be admitted to prove the accuracy of the legal opinion. Furthermore, it is also uncertain whether a certified legal opinion could be admitted as evidence to prove the content of foreign law.

2.56 In some common law systems, foreign law is considered as a 'fact' to be proven, and not as 'law'. In these jurisdictions, where access to appellate review is restricted to mistakes of law, mistakes in the application of foreign law are not adequate grounds for review. In contrast, all court decisions in China are appealable to a higher court, whether the mistake alleged is one of the fact or of the law, as Article 168 of the Civil Procedure Law provides: '[W]ith respect to an appealed case, the People's Court of second instance shall review the relevant facts and the application of the law.'[70] Therefore, mistakes in the application of the foreign law by the lower court, as well as mistakes in the application of the conflicts rules of the forum, can be appealed to a higher court in China.

VII. EVASION OF LAW

2.57 A person who by compulsory legal rules is prevented from achieving his aims often tries to evade them by establishing in an abnormal way a set of facts to which the legal rules do not apply. Such *fraus legi facta* may occur either within

67 Zhang, *supra* n 64, 6.

68 Conflicts Act Interpretation I, Art 17.

69 SPC, Selected Cases of People's Courts (1996) 1135–41 (Higher People's Court of Guangxi Zhuang Autonomous Region, 1993). Kong and Hu, *supra* n 39, 206.

70 Civil Procedure Law, Art 7.

or outside the boundaries of the internal law. If it is the latter case, an evasion of law in private international law may occur. As a matter of fact, in the area of private international law, such evasions are frequent. The parties, who wish to produce a certain legal effect forbidden by the law of country A, establish in an artificial and unusual connection with country B where the law is favourable for their purpose. The following are some illustrations:

(1) A company which intends to carry on business solely in mainland China is incorporated in Hong Kong SAR where the rules are less stringent or income tax is lower than in the mainland.
(2) In making a contract, the parties subject it to a legal system which considers as valid certain clauses that under the normally applicable law would be void.
(3) A Frenchman residing at *Evian-les-Bains* on the French shore of the lake of Geneva wishes to promise a gift. As French law requires a deed attested by a notary public, and Swiss law declares a written document to be sufficient, he crosses the lake and makes his promise in Switzerland in order to save the notary fee.

All the above examples constitute the evasion of law in private international law, the common thread being that when a party breaks off the existing connection between a fact in issue and the governing jurisdiction, and creates a new connecting factor (e.g., by changing domicile or nationality) leading to a different governing law or jurisdiction.[71] The purpose of changing the connecting factor is to avoid the law that would otherwise have been applicable. **2.58**

The position on evasion of law is very different between civil law and common law systems. Typically civil law usually assumes a hostile attitude towards evasions of law whereby the court can reject a connection established for the purpose of evading the laws of a particular jurisdiction. For example, French law has developed an all-embracing doctrine to reject evasion of law by the fraudulent change of connection on the basis of an old adage '*fraus omina corrumpit*'. Any 'fraudulent' exclusion of a legal rule by establishing a foreign connection is regarded in France as invalid, and therefore the excluded rule applies as if it had not been excluded.[72] An act is considered as fraudulent if it suffers from a '*défaut de sincérité*' – a rather vague formula. The same view has **2.59**

71 Tung-Pi Chen, 'Private International Law of the People's Republic of China: An Overview' (1987) 35 *Am J Comp L* 445, 449.
72 Wolff, *supra* n 1, 143.

been taken by Italian courts.[73] The common law, however, does not attach significance under its conflicts analysis to fraudulent evasions.[74]

2.60 The Conflict of Laws Act of 2010 does not contain an article on evasion of the law.[75] The SPC provides in Article 11 of the Conflicts Act Interpretation I that the People's Court shall not recognize the effect of an otherwise applicable foreign law where a party to a foreign-related relationship evades the mandatory rules contained in law or administrative regulations of the PRC by deliberately establishing a connecting factor.[76] Under this provision, if a new connecting factor is created for the sole purpose of evading the application of a mandatory rule contained in Chinese law, then a civil relationship, which may otherwise be valid under the normal Chinese conflicts rule, will be deemed void.[77]

2.61 Although mandatory rules and evasion of law are two different concepts in private international law, they do occasionally overlap.[78] If this case arises, neither the Act nor the Conflicts Act Interpretation I provides a solution. Chinese scholars argue that judges, in such a situation, should place priority on mandatory rules, as the application of this notion is objective, neutral and simple, without the need to check the parties' intentions and consequences of a potential evasion.[79]

VIII. THE PRELIMINARY QUESTION

2.62 The preliminary question, or the incidental question, in the context of private international law presumes the existence of three facts:[80] (i) the main issue should, under the private international rules of the forum, be governed by a foreign law; (ii) there should be a subsidiary question involving a foreign element which could have arisen separately and which has its own independent choice of law rule; and (iii) this choice of law rule should lead to a conclusion different from that which would have been reached had the law governing the main question been applied. Consequently, it seldom occurs in

---

73 Ibid.

74 E. Rabel, *The Conflict of Laws, A Comparative Study* (University of Michigan 1968) 250.

75 *Cf.* Opinion on the GPCL, *supra* n 26, Art 194.

76 Conflicts Act Interpretation I, Art 11.

77 Huo, *supra* n 27, 705

78 See Michal Wojewoda, 'Mandatory Rules in Private International Law' 7 (2000) *Maastricht J Eur & Comp L* 183, 1209.

79 Yongping Xiao and Weidi Long, 'Mandatory Rules in China's Private International Law' (2012) 10 *Social Sciences in China* 107, 122.

80 J.J. Fawcett and J. Carruthers, *Cheshire and North's Private International Law* (14th ed., OUP 2008) 47.

judicial practice. For this reason, the Conflict of Laws Act of 2010 does not contain a provision on it. Nonetheless, for the purpose of improving the Chinese private international law regime, the SPC considers it necessary to close the legal loophole. Thus, the Conflicts Act Interpretation I makes the following provision for the preliminary question in Article 12: 'In case the resolution of a foreign-related dispute depends on the resolution of a preliminary issue, the Peoples' Court shall determine the applicable law to the preliminary issue by its nature.'[81]

The preliminary question, ever since the scholars discovered it, has been acknowledged as a technical problem of considerable difficulty.[82] Some jurists support the law governing the main issue, and others the choice of law rules of the forum.[83] As the solution compels a choice between two evils, either choice is equally unpalatable.[84] Recently, more and more scholars have suggested that a priori reasoning should be avoided and a flexible approach adopted, taking the nature of the individual case and the policy of the forum thereto into account.[85] It is perfectly understandable that Article 12 of the Conflicts Act Interpretation I provides that the determination of the preliminary question will depend on its nature, which affords judges considerable leeway when they deal with this issue.[86] **2.63**

IX. MANDATORY RULES

The concept of 'mandatory rules' ('*lois d' application immédiate*') has only recently been introduced into Chinese law. Under Chinese scholarship and legislation, mandatory rules only refer to international mandatory rules that cannot be derogated from even if the law of a foreign country applies.[87] This concept does not cover mandatory rules of the domestic sense, which cannot be derogated from by contracts if the legal system to which the law belongs governs the disputes, but may be derogated from if the governing law is the **2.64**

81 Conflicts Act Interpretation I, Art 12.

82 The discovery of the problem is often attributed to the German jurists Melchior and Wengler in 1932–34. See Collins (et al) eds, *Dicey, Morris and Collins on the Conflict of Laws* (Lawrence Collins ed., 15th ed., Sweet & Maxwell 2012) 55.

83 Fawcett and Carruthers, *supra* n 80, 47

84 See Friedrich K. Juenger, *Choice of Law and Multistate Justice* (Transnational 2000), 75.

85 *Dicey, Morris and Collins*, *supra* n 82, 62.

86 Huo, *supra* n 27, 709.

87 Huo, *supra* n 15, 1073; HUANG Jin (ed), *Zhonghua Renmin Gongheguo Shewai Minshi Falvguanxi Shiyongfa: Shiyi yu Fenxi [Understanding Act on the Application of Laws on Foreign-related Civil Relationships]* (China Law Press, 2011) 20.

law of another country.[88] The concept of domestic mandatory rules is generally unknown in Chinese legal writing. Chinese conflict of laws thus does not include any rules granting domestic mandatory rules any overriding effect in exceptional circumstances where the disputes have closer connections with China and applying domestic mandatory rules may be more appropriate to satisfy Chinese interest.[89]

2.65 Article 4 of the Conflicts Act of 2010 provides: '[T]he laws of the People's Republic of China which are mandatorily applicable to foreign-related civil relationships shall be applied directly.' This provision only requires the Chinese Court to apply the mandatory rules of the forum. In other words, no effect should be provided to differently expressed mandatory rules of a foreign country. However, effect should also be given to mandatory rules contained in an international convention provided that China is a contracting party to that convention.[90] As a result, mandatory rules in China are classified as mandatory rules of the forum, mandatory rules of the *lex causae*, mandatory rules of the third country, and mandatory rules of international convention.[91] All may be given effect in China, except mandatory rules of the third country.

2.66 The SPC observes that the incorporation of mandatory rules into the Conflicts Act represents a significant legislative development.[92] Nevertheless, as Chinese judges are generally unfamiliar with the notion of mandatory rules, Article 10 of the Conflicts Act Interpretation I provides a definition which consists of a general description and a specific enumeration. According to this

---

88 For the concept of domestic mandatory rules and international mandatory rules, see P. Rogerson, *Collier's Conflict of Laws* (4th ed., CUP 2013) 434.

89 For example, the law may provide that in certain circumstances, the domestic mandatory rules of the habitual residence of the consumer, insured or employee may apply irrespective of the governing law. See, e.g., Regulation (EC) No 593/2008 on the law applicable to contractual obligations (Rome I) [2009] OJ L 177/6, Arts 6, 7 and 8.

90 The GPCL has confirmed the principle of the superiority of international convention. Art 142(2) of the GPCL provides as follows:

> If any international treaty concluded or acceded to by the People's Republic of China contains provisions differing from those in the civil laws of the People's Republic of China, the provisions of the international treaty shall apply, unless the provisions are ones on which the People's Republic of China has announced reservations.

GPCL, Art 142(2); Huo, *supra* n 15, 1073.

91 It is commonly believed that international mandatory rules are classified into three categories: international mandatory rules belonging to the *lex cause*, international mandatory rules of the forum, and international mandatory rules of third countries. Kwang Hyun Suk, 'The New Conflict of Laws Act of the Republic of Korea', in P. Sarczvic and P. Volken eds., *Yearbook of Private International Law* (Kluwer Law International 2003)110; *See* also Wojewoda, *supra* n 78, 190–91.

92 Zhang Xianming, *supra* n 62. 6.

article, mandatory rules, for the purpose of the Conflicts Act, means the provisions in laws or administrative regulations directly applicable to foreign-related civil relations which concern the socio-public interests of the PRC and which cannot be derogated from by agreement. They may include rules as follows: (i) the provisions that bear on the protection of labourers' rights; (ii) the provisions that bear on the safety of food or public sanitation; (iii) the provisions that bear on environmental safety; (iv) the provisions that bear on financial safety, e.g., administration of foreign exchange; (v) the provisions that bear on antitrust and antidumping; and (vi) other rules that should be regarded as mandatory rules.

Obviously, under Article 4 of the Conflicts Act and Article 10 of the Conflicts Act Interpretation I, Chinese judges are left with considerable discretion in deciding whether to invoke mandatory rules in any particular case. However, judges should be very scrupulous when exercising such power. It would be very unfortunate if the notion of mandatory rules were to be employed to thwart the application of all foreign laws which would otherwise apply.[93] **2.67**

X. *ORDRE PUBLIC*

X.1 Introduction

Ordre public (public order) is one of the most ancient doctrines in the conflict of laws. In accordance with this doctrine, a foreign law that is otherwise applicable is disregarded if its application would violate the fundamental interest, basic policy, general principle of justice, or prevailing concept of good morals in the forum. This notion surfaced during the late Middle Ages in the works of the great Bartolus (1314–57) who distinguished the 'favourable' from 'odious' statutes.[94] Later, many scholars such as Huber (1636–94), Story (1802–55), Savigny (1779–1861) and Mancini (1817–88) built upon such a distinction with variations of their own, ushering in a new doctrine of considerable importance. It bears mentioning that in general, the civil law doctrine of *ordre public* has assumed more prominence than its corresponding doctrine of public policy in the laws of the Anglo-American family, since the former is broader in scope than the latter.[95] **2.68**

---

93 Huo, *supra* n 27, 710.

94 *See* Juenger, *supra* n 84, 15.

95 *See* J.G. Collier, Conflict of Laws (3rd ed., CUP 2001) 361. It is generally believed that common law judges used public policy in a purely defensive manner to bar the application of foreign rules, whereas civil law jurisdictions also seize upon this reservation to justify the application of forum law.

2.69 Serving as a corrective measure of last resort, the doctrine of *ordre public* is essential in guarding against the injurious effect of offensive foreign rules, in maintaining the stability of local legal systems, and in protecting the public welfare of the forum. As a result, this doctrine has been vividly compared to a 'safety valve'.[96] However, it is worth emphasizing that the doctrine suffers from vagueness, amorphousness, and uncertainty in application, so that no attempt to define the doctrine precisely has ever succeeded. Legal scholars have acknowledged that: 'The danger of a doctrine so vague as this is that it may be interpreted to embrace such a multitude of domestic rules as to provide a fatally easy excuse for the application of the law of the forum and thus to defeat the underlying purpose of private international law.'[97]

2.70 Furthermore, the application of the doctrine is of an inconstant and evolving nature, changing as society and general notions of justice change.[98] Whether a foreign rule is repugnant to the *ordre public* is an issue to be determined by the criteria of the law of the forum; therefore, there is no uniform measure of *ordre public* for all times and for all countries.

2.71 Nonetheless, the doctrine has edged its way into the modern legal theory and plays an active and important role in private international law. As one scholar points out, it is hard to find a legal doctrine such as *ordre public*, which has endured such extensive criticism and nonetheless survived.[99]

X.2 From GPCL to Conflicts Act

2.72 China has consistently adopted an affirmative attitude towards the application of the doctrine of *ordre public*. Since the founding of the People's Republic of China in 1949, the doctrine has been reflected in the relevant legislation and is invoked occasionally in civil litigation involving foreign elements.[100]

2.73 The *ordre public* reservation rule prescribed by the GPCL is the first elaborate expression of the doctrine of *ordre public* within China's private international law. Article 150 provides that:

---

96 *See* Juenger, *supra* n 84, 157.

97 Fawcett and Carruthers, *supra* n 80, 106.

98 Michael Mousa Karayanni, 'The Public policy Exception to the Enforcement of Forum Selection Clause' (1996) 34 *Duq L Rev* 1009.

99 Ibid.

100 Yongping Xiao and Zhengxin Huo, '*Ordre Public* in China's Private International Law' (2005) 53 *Am J Comp L* 653, 675.

> The application of foreign laws or international custom and usage in accordance with the provisions of this Chapter shall in no way violate the socio-public interests of the People's Republic of China.

Additionally, the Maritime Act of the People's Republic of China, effective as of 1 July 1993, and the Civil Aviation Act, effective as of 1 March 1996, contained verbatim the very provision noted above. **2.74**

The adoption of the doctrine manifests itself in two different ways, i.e., directly and indirectly. The adoption of *ordre public* in a direct way means that the conflicts rules explicitly indicate that the application of foreign law cannot violate the *ordre public* of the forum; while adoption in an indirect way means that the conflicts rules provide that some domestic laws are mandatory, thus necessarily excluding the application of foreign law, without express reference to the doctrine of *ordre public*. Between these two, the former, needless to say, assumes greater flexibility. Secondly, a distinction has been drawn between the foreign rule itself, on the one hand, and the outcome of its application, on the other. That is to say, a foreign law that would normally be applicable in a particular situation is not necessarily invalid, per se, but should be excluded only under circumstances in which the effect of its application is contrary to China's *ordre public*. Thirdly, and most strikingly, *ordre public* in China targets not only foreign laws but also international custom and usage, which is a phenomenon without parallel in the laws of any other countries thus far. **2.75**

Article 15 of the Conflicts Act contains an article incorporating *ordre public* which provides that: 'The application of a foreign law shall be excluded if such application is offensive to the socio-public interests of the PRC, and the law of the PRC shall apply.' **2.76**

A close reading of the above article manifests that the doctrine reflected in the new Conflicts Act has made some modifications. International custom and usage are no longer the targets of the doctrine. The above article also makes it clear that Chinese law shall apply after the relevant foreign law has been excluded.[101] **2.77**

101 Part of this chapter is reproduced with permission from Zhengxin Huo, *supra* n 15, 'An Imperfect Improvement', (2011) 60 International and Comparative Law Quarterly 1065; Yongping Xiao, Zhengxin Huo, *supra* n 100.

Part II

JURISDICTION, PROCEDURE, FOREIGN JUDGMENTS AND AWARDS

3

JURISDICTION IN CHINESE COURTS

I. INTRODUCTION

Jurisdiction in this book only refers to adjudication jurisdiction,[1] which is a court's competence to hear a dispute. In international civil and commercial matters, a dispute usually involves elements that are located in more than one country. In most cases, the connections with more than one country may lead to a conflict of jurisdiction between the different countries. Although the international community has conducted extensive work to establish judicial cooperation and harmonize jurisdiction rules, it has made some but rather limited progress.[2] Harmonized jurisdiction rules exist either regionally,[3] or in a **3.01**

1 American scholars classify jurisdiction into legislative jurisdiction, adjudication jurisdiction and enforcement jurisdiction. This book adopts the traditional English and European definition and focuses only on the adjudication jurisdiction.

2 The Hague Conference on Private International Law started the project to harmonize jurisdiction rules in civil and commercial matters which resulted in a partial harmonization of jurisdiction in choice of court agreements in the Hague Choice of Court Convention of 2005. This convention entered into force from 1 Oct 2015 between EU Member States and Mexico. However, US and Singapore have only signed but not ratified this Convention and China has not signed it. The Hague Choice of Court Convention only covers exclusive jurisdiction clauses in certain civil and commercial matters and is thus not comprehensive.

number of treaties concerning special matters in a piecemeal manner.[4] China is not within any jurisdiction treaties. Jurisdiction in Chinese courts, thus, is largely decided by Chinese domestic law, which primarily demonstrates the national interest and international policy, instead of judicial cooperation with other countries in the world. Many Chinese jurisdiction rules, as a result, are remarked as exorbitant and excessive. However, after a 40-year 'open door' policy and intensive connections with foreign countries, Chinese jurisdiction rules have gone through gradual development and modernization.

3.02 As in many other countries in the world, Chinese jurisdiction rules can be generally classified as 'positive jurisdiction rules' and 'negative jurisdiction rules'. The positive jurisdiction rules refer to rules based on which the courts are empowered to assert jurisdiction. The negative jurisdiction rules provide the otherwise competent courts with the discretion to decline exercising jurisdiction. Both rules are present in Chinese law. In history, Chinese law was much more developed in positive jurisdiction rules and did not include authorized measures to decline jurisdiction. This has been changed during judicial practice. This chapter focuses on positive jurisdiction rules; the negative jurisdiction rules are discussed in Chapter 4.

I.1 Legal sources

3.03 Chinese jurisdiction rules on foreign-related disputes are mainly covered in Part Four of the PRC Civil Procedure Law (CPL). CPL was adopted and promulgated on 9 April 1991,[5] amended by the Decision of the Standing Committee in 2007,[6] and in 2012.[7] Part Four of CPL is entitled 'Special Provisions for Civil Proceedings of Cases Involving Foreign Elements'. 'Cases involving foreign elements' are defined as: cases where either or both parties are foreign citizens, stateless persons, foreign corporates or organizations;

---

3 Such as the EU harmonization of jurisdiction and mutual recognition and enforcement of judgments. See the Regulation (EU) No 1215/2012 on jurisdiction and the recognition and enforcement of judgments in civil and commercial matters (Recast) [2012] OJ L 351/1. China is not a party to any regional jurisdiction treaties.

4 For example, the Convention for the Unification of Certain Rules for International Carriage by Air of 1999 (Montreal Convention) includes uniform jurisdiction rules for disputes arising out of international carriage by air contracts and this convention has been ratified by China. Since the international treaty ratified by China takes priority over Chinese domestic law, the Montreal jurisdiction rules thus will apply to international carriage by air disputes in China.

5 Zhonghua Renmin Gongheguo Minshi Susong Fa [Civil Procedure Law of the People's Republic of China], 1991.

6 The Decision of the Standing Committee of the National People's Congress on Amending the 'Civil Procedure Law of the People's Republic of China', 2007, came into effect from 1 April 2008.

7 The Decision of the Standing Committee of the National People's Congress on Amending the 'Civil Procedure Law of the People's Republic of China', 2012, went into effect from 1 January 2013.

either or both parties have their habitual residence outside China; the subject matter of the dispute is located abroad; the elements concerning establishment, variation and termination of the relationship between the parties are located abroad; and other cases that could be deemed to involve foreign elements.[8] The non-exhaustive list may cause uncertainty and the court is allowed to exercise discretion in 'other cases'. Besides the CPL, special legislation dealing with specific issues may also provide special jurisdiction rules. For example, jurisdiction rules in maritime disputes are not covered by the CPL, but by the Special Maritime Procedure Law of 1999.[9]

The CPL provisions are simple and succinct, but cause uncertainty and ambiguity in practice. More rules on jurisdiction can be found in the SPC judicial interpretation. In 1992, the SPC published the 'Opinion on several Questions in the Implementation of the PRC Civil Procedure Law' ('1992 Opinion'),[10] which had remained the most important source of law for over 20 years, irrespective of several amendments to the CPL. Although the SPC has published other supplementary judicial interpretations during this period, they are less important in both comprehensiveness and impact. After major amendments to the CPL in 2012, the 1992 Opinion was obviously outdated and could no longer satisfy the requirements of judicial practice. Based on the 2012 CPL amendment, the 1992 Opinion, and other SPC documents, the SPC published the new 'SPC Opinion on Interpretation about the Application of the CPL' ('2015 Opinion') in 2015,[11] which repealed the 1992 Opinion and is the most important CPL judicial interpretation in China. The 2015 Opinion constitutes 23 Chapters and 552 articles. It is the longest judicial interpretation with the largest number of articles in Chinese history. It not only modifies the 1992 Opinion by addressing the amendments but also provides more comprehensive and modern rules covering jurisdiction, adducing evidence, service of process, class action, mediation and enforcement. **3.04**

As well as SPC judicial interpretation, SPC judicial directions serve as an important source to understanding PRC law and practice. The difference between judicial interpretation and judicial direction is that the latter responds **3.05**

---

8 SPC, 'Zuigao Renmin Fayuan Guanyu Shiyong "Zhonghua Renmin Gongheguo Minshi Susongfa" de Jieshi [Interpretation of the SPC on the Application of the PRC Civil Procedure Law]' ('2015 Opinion'), Fa Shi [2015] No 5, Art 522.

9 Zhonghua Renmin Gongheguo Haishi Susong Tebie Chengxu Fa [Special Maritime Procedure Law of the People's Republic of China], 1999.

10 SPC, 'Zuigao Renmin Fayuan Guanyu Guanyu Shiyong "Zhonghua Renmin Gongheguo Minshi Susongfa" Ruogan Wenti de Yijian (Shixiao) [Opinion on several Questions in the Implementation of the PRC Civil Procedure Act]'('1992 Opinion') (Abolished), Fa Fa [1992] 22.

11 2015 Opinion, *supra* n 8. This Interpretation entered into force from 4 Feb 2015. The previous judicial interpretation, '1992 Opinion', *supra* n 10, was repealed.

to the inquiry of a local court concerning specific issues arising out of an individual case. SPC judicial directions, as a result, only bind the individual case and have no general binding effects. However, judicial directions may form convincing evidence of the SPC opinion on the authorized interpretation of the law. They are usually consistent with each other and provide valuable guidance for future practice. The principle adopted in the judicial direction may be included in the later judicial interpretation.

3.06 It is also important to note that cases and judicial decisions provide recommendatory and directive value to interpret Chinese law, although case precedent is not a source of law binding on the other courts. The SPC published the 'Notice of the SPC on Issuing the Third Five-Year Reform Outline for the People's Courts' in 2005, which first raised the needs to establish the Guiding Case System.[12] In 2010, the SPC published the 'Notice of the SPC on Issuing the Provisions on Case Guidance', which explicitly provides the People's Court with a duty to refer to the SPC guiding cases when making decisions.[13] A more detailed guidance was provided 2015, which further requires all people's courts to decide a case by referring to the guiding cases of the SPC.[14] The guidance also provides that the guiding cases cannot be referred to as the source of law but the ratio for the decision.[15]

I.2 Domestic hierarchical jurisdiction in foreign-related disputes

3.07 China has a relatively complex domestic court system. The Chinese judiciary is a hierarchical structure of courts at four levels. The highest judicial authority is the Supreme People's Court (SPC), followed by the High People's Court (HPC), the Intermediate People's Court (IPC) and the Basic People's Court (BPC). Hierarchical jurisdiction determines the competence between courts at different levels. Most domestic cases are heard by the BPCs at the first instance. The hierarchical jurisdiction, however, is fundamentally different in foreign-related disputes. The CPL provides that the IPC usually has jurisdiction to act as the court of the first instance for important foreign-related

---

12 SPC, 'Renmin Fayuan Di Er Ge Wunian Gaige Gangyao (2004–2008) [Notice of the SPC on Issuing the Second Five-Year Reform Outline for the People's Courts]', Fa Fa [2005] 18. Xingliang Chen, 'China's Guiding Case System: A Study on the Mechanisms of Rule Formation', (2014) 1 *Peking University Law Journal* 215.

13 SPC, 'Guanyu Anli Zhidao Gongzuo de Guiding [Notice of the SPC on Issuing the Provisions on Case Guidance]', Fa Fa [2010] 51, Art 7.

14 SPC, 'Zuigao Renmen Fayuan Yinfa '"Guanyu Anli Zhidao Gongzuo de Guiding" Shishi Xize' de Tongzhi [Detailed Rules on the Implementation of the "Notice of the SPC on Issuing the Provisions on Case Guidance"]' ('Detailed Rules on Guiding Cases'), Fa [2015] 130, Art 9.

15 'Detailed Rules on Guiding Cases', ibid., Art 10.

cases,[16] which include cases concerning a large sum of money; complicated facts and law; or multi-party disputes with significant impact.[17] It nevertheless implies that some BPCs may also be competent to hear transnational disputes classified as 'unimportant' taking into account the value of the subject matter, complexity and impact. The HPC is the competent first-instance court to hear foreign-related disputes that have significant impact in the territory of its jurisdiction,[18] and the SPC disputes which have significant impact over the country or which it considers appropriate to be tried in the SPC.[19] It is not known what is meant by 'important', and 'significant impact' in the region or country. Furthermore, the HPC and SPC could, in theory, have discretion to hear the foreign-related dispute even if the case, in normal circumstances, fell within the regime of the IPC.[20] Simply relying on the CPL to determine the hierarchical jurisdiction between different courts in foreign-related cases is perplexing and uncertain.

More guidance can be found in SPC judicial interpretations. In 2002, the SPC **3.08** published 'Provisions of the SPC on Some Issues Concerning the Jurisdiction of Civil and Commercial Cases Involving Foreign Elements' ('Jurisdiction Provisions'),[21] which provides that the court that has the first instance jurisdiction over a foreign-related civil and commercial dispute includes the BPCs in the economic and technological development zones approved by the State Council, IPCs in the capital cities of provinces, autonomous regions and central-direct-governed municipalities, IPCs in special economic regions and special-designated cities, other IPCs designated by the SPC, and HPCs.[22] The Jurisdiction Provisions apply to foreign-related contractual and tort disputes; disputes arising out of letters of credit; application to vacate, recognize or enforce international arbitral awards; application to review validity of foreign-related arbitration clauses; and application to recognize and enforce foreign judgments in civil and commercial cases.[23] It is noticeable that only limited IPCs and BPCs satisfying certain conditions may be competent to hear foreign-related disputes. The main purpose is to centralize first instance jurisdiction over foreign-related civil and commercial matters. These

16 CPL, Art 18(1).

17 2015 Opinion, Art 1(1).

18 CPL, Art 19.

19 CPL, Art 20.

20 For more on the transferred jurisdiction, see Yuwen Li, *The Judicial System and Reform in Post-Mao China* (Ashgate Publishing 2014) 15.

21 SPC, 'Zuigao Renmin Fayuan Guanyu Shewai Minshangshi Susong Guanxia Ruogan Wenti de Guiding [Provisions of the SPC on Some Issues Concerning the Jurisdiction of Civil and Commercial Cases Involving Foreign Elements]', Fa Shi [2002] No 5.

22 Article 1. See translation of the Provisions and Introduction in Yuwen Li, *supra* n 20, 19–20.

23 Article 3.

competent courts should establish special chambers specializing in foreign-related civil disputes and to provide special training to improve the competence of judges.[24]

3.09 The centralizing approach was necessary at the early stage as most Chinese judges lacked experience and specialized knowledge in handling foreign-related disputes. However, following the rapid development of international trade and transactions, the number of foreign-related disputes increased greatly and affected the efficiency of the centralization of the first instance jurisdiction. The workload of the competent court of the first instance increased, which caused delay and affected the quality of the judgments. In 2004, the SPC published another judicial interpretation, increasing the number of the competent courts in regions with advanced economy and foreign-related trade.[25] It provides that the HPC of Guangdong Province and other central-direct-governed municipalities could designate local BPCs as the first instance courts over foreign-related and Hong Kong, Macau or Taiwan-related commercial cases.[26] The designation should be reported to and recorded by the SPC.[27]

3.10 Although the 2004 Jurisdiction Notice expands the scope of competent courts of the first instance, the centralization of foreign-related jurisdiction provides competence to the HPCs in most regions except a few special regions with developed economic, technological and international relations. In most territories of China, the BPCs and IPCs have no jurisdiction to hear foreign-related disputes regardless of the express provisions of the CPL.[28] After 2004 the SPC no longer published general judicial interpretations to expand the competent first instance courts. Instead, the SPC gradually authorized more local IPCs and BPCs to hear foreign-related disputes upon the report and application of local HPCs. From 2005 to 2011, the SPCs approved first instance jurisdiction of over 167 IPCs and 71 BPCs. This proliferation in competent courts causes confusion on jurisdiction between BPCs, IPCs and HPCs. Furthermore, some BPCs and IPCs have a tendency to reserve

24 SPC, 'Zuigao Renmin Fayuan Guanyu Renzhen Xuexi Guanche "Guanyu Shewai Minshangshi Anjian Susong Guanxia Ruogan Wenti de Guiding" de Tongzhi [Notice of the SPC on Carefully Study and Implement the "Provisions on Some Issues Concerning the Jurisdiction of Civil and Commercial Cases Involving Foreign Elements"]', Fa [2002] No 22, Arts 2 and 3.

25 SPC, 'Zuigao Renmin Fayuan Guanyu Jiaqiang Shewai Shangshi Anjian Susong Guanxia Gongzuo de Tongzhi [Notice of the SPC about Strengthening the Jurisdiction of Foreign-Related Commercial Cases]' ('2004 Jurisdiction Notice'), Fa [2004] No 265.

26 2004 Jurisdiction Notice, ibid., Art 2.

27 Ibid.

28 Yuwen Li, *supra* n 20, 20–21.

jurisdiction to protect local interests, even if the dispute is more significant than those it would normally handle.[29]

I.3 Domestic territorial jurisdiction

Domestic territorial jurisdiction allocates cases between courts located in different judicial districts. In general, the rules determining internal territorial allocation of jurisdiction between different cities and provinces are similar to those applying to international cases. The courts in the district where real property is located has exclusive jurisdiction; in the absence of which, the defendant's domicile, the court chosen by the parties, and the district that has the closest connection with the case has jurisdiction; and furthermore, the defendant can also submit to the court selected by the claimant.[30] **3.11**

I.4 Outline of international jurisdiction

Chinese private international law generally constitutes five types of jurisdiction rules: exclusive jurisdiction; jurisdiction by submission; prorogation jurisdiction; general jurisdiction; and special jurisdiction. Exclusive jurisdiction stands at the top of the hierarchic structure, which grants the Chinese court jurisdiction for all disputes falling in its scope and cannot be derogated from by other jurisdiction grounds or international judicial collaboration. It is primarily based on the exclusive control and sovereign power over a subject matter, such as property disputes over land.[31] **3.12**

If the defendant submits to the Chinese court or enters appearance to raise a substantive defence, the Chinese court should have jurisdiction. This is mainly because the defendant is apparently not contesting the claimant's selection of court; the defendant's cooperation is, therefore, deemed acquiescent. Traditionally, Chinese scholarship treats jurisdiction by submission as an implied choice of the Chinese court by the parties, therefore, an implied choice of court agreement.[32] This construction is wrong. Although the defendant's submission has the same effect of a choice of court agreement, the parties have not had the required meeting of minds or agreement in any form. Jurisdiction by submission does not usually raise a lot of practical difficulties and it will not, therefore, be examined in details in the following sections.[33] **3.13**

29 Ibid., 21.

30 Chapter 2 of the CPL.

31 See section II below.

32 DU Xinli, *Guoji Sifa Shiwu Zhongde Falv Wenti [Legal Problems in Private International Law Practice]* (CITIC Publishing House 2005) 61.

33 Article 127 of the CPL. This jurisdiction ground will not be discussed in detail in this book.

3.14 Prorogation jurisdiction means that the parties, by agreement, submit to the jurisdiction of the Chinese court. If the parties have chosen a Chinese court, this court usually will take jurisdiction and will ignore the fact that other courts may also be competent. Prorogation jurisdiction, however, may generate complicated questions as to the content and scope, the validity and the exclusive/derogation effect of the choice. The current Chinese law does not provide clear rules and the practice is inconsistent in this area and causes uncertainty and criticism.[34]

3.15 General jurisdiction grants jurisdiction to the defendant's domicile, i.e., the Chinese court is competent to hear a dispute against the Chinese defendant. Special jurisdiction is based on objective connections between the dispute and China. These objective nexus establishes a link that makes taking jurisdiction reasonable and sometimes convenient for the trial purpose.[35] These two types of jurisdiction are alternatives in the hierarchic structure.

II. EXCLUSIVE JURISDICTION

3.16 Exclusive jurisdiction allows a court to assert jurisdiction to the exclusion of all other courts. Every country, no matter how deeply committed to international judicial cooperation, has reserved exclusive jurisdiction over crucial areas. Exclusive jurisdiction is established in order to protect the fundamental economic and social interest of a country, to reserve state sovereignty and to protect national interest.[36]

II.1 Exclusive jurisdiction of Chinese courts

3.17 Exclusive jurisdiction differs from country to country. The different grounds and scopes of exclusive jurisdiction depend on how a country defines its fundamental policy and national interest. Part Four of CPL only includes one

---

34 See section III below.

35 See section IV below.

36 Daniel J. Cloherty, 'Exclusive Jurisdiction and the Eleventh Amendment: Recognizing the Assumption of the State Court Availability in the Clear Statement Compromise' (1994) 82 *California Law Review* 1287; W.J. Wagner, 'The Original and Exclusive Jurisdiction of the United States SPC' (1952) 2 *Louisiana University Law J* 111; R.W. Pogue, 'Exclusive Jurisdiction' (1973) 43 *Antitrust* 313; ZENG Jianpin, 'Budongchan Jiufen Zhuanshu Guanxia Tanxi [Study of exclusive jurisdiction on immovable property]' (2008) 2 Xinan Nongye Daxue Xuebao (Shehui Kexue Ban) [South West Agriculture University Journal (Social Science)] 22; LI Hao, 'Minshi Susong Zhuanshu Guanxia Zhidu Yanjiu [Study of Exclusive Jurisdiction in Civil Procedure]' (2009) 26 Fashang Yanjiu [Study in Law and Business] 94–101; LIU Li, 'Shewai Jicheng Anjian Zhuanshu Guanxia Kao [Study on Exclusive Jurisdiction in Cross-Border Succession]' (2009) 2 Xiandai Faxue [Modern Law Science] 138.

article which provides that Chinese courts have exclusive jurisdiction over disputes arising out of performance of China-foreign equity joint ventures, China-foreign contractual joint ventures or China-foreign cooperation and development of natural resources.[37] It is doubtful whether this is the only ground for exclusive jurisdiction. If so, this ground is too narrow and Chinese courts do not reserve exclusive jurisdiction over immovable property located in China, which is traditionally subject to exclusive state control as an international common practice. Permitting any other country to hear disputes on the title of land located in China is impractical, contrary to Chinese public policy and certainly not the intention of the legislators. It is thus suggested that the exclusive jurisdiction provided in Article 33, which allocates jurisdiction in domestic cases, should also be applied to cross-border disputes.[38] Article 33 provides, as a general rule, that particular People's Courts shall have exclusive jurisdiction in disputes arising out of immovable property;[39] harbour operations;[40] and succession.[41]

The People's Court at the location of the immovable property has exclusive jurisdiction over disputes relating to that immovable property.[42] Exclusive jurisdiction over immovable property located within its territory is usually undisputable. The question is what are 'disputes relating to immovables'; and may include disputes on the proprietary right of immovable property. **3.18**

The People's Court at the location of the harbour has exclusive jurisdiction over harbour operations.[43] Harbour is defined as: 'an area composed of a certain scope of water area and land area, which has the functions for vessels to enter and exit, to berth, to anchor, for passengers to embark and disembark, and for goods to be loaded and unloaded, lightered, stored, etc., and which has the corresponding wharf facilities'.[44] Harbour operations refer to loading and unloading, lighterage and storage of goods and other work that is conducted in the area of the harbour, such as investigations, exploration, surveys, rescue, salvage, towing, dredging, demolition, etc.[45] The very nature of harbour **3.19**

37 Article 266.

38 See also Art 305 of the Opinion 1992.

39 CPL, Article 33(1).

40 Article 33(2).

41 Article 33(3)

42 Article 33(1).

43 Article 33(2).

44 Zhonghua Renmin Gongheguo Gangkou Fa [Port Law of the People's Republic of China], adopted at the Third Meeting of the Standing Committee of the Tenth National People's Congress on 28 June 2003 and promulgated by Order No 5 of the President of the People's Republic of China on 28 June 2003.

45 *Yueyang Tongda Cooling Air Condition v. Sino Trans Group,* see SPC, 'Zuigao Renmin Fayuan Guanyu Yueyang Tongda Zhileng Kongtiao Youxian Gongsi deng Sijia Gongsi Zhijian de Weituo Hetong yu Gangkou Zhuangxie Zuoye Jiufen Anjian Guanxiaquan Zhengyi de Chuli Yijia [Opinion on the Resolution

operations means that there is a high risk of damage to property and/or personal injury. Usually, the maritime court of the place where the harbour is located has exclusive jurisdiction. If there is no maritime court, the local court of the place has exclusive jurisdiction. It is believed that for disputes over harbour operations, the events occur in China, the evidence is located in China and the operation is regulated according to Chinese rules and code of practice.

3.20 However, it is questionable whether 'convenience' is a strong enough reason to justify exclusive jurisdiction. Exclusive jurisdiction, by its nature, should be used only in areas concerning the fundamental interest of a country. The consideration of the closest connection or convenience should be factors considered in special jurisdiction or exorbitant jurisdiction. The consideration of 'convenience' cannot exclude the possibility and necessity of international judicial cooperation, jurisdictional interest of other competent countries, and the parties from agreeing to choose an inconvenient forum by agreement.

3.21 Chinese courts have exclusive jurisdiction on a dispute over succession if China is the place where the decedent had his domicile upon death or where the principal part of his estate is located.[46] Exclusive jurisdiction over succession is controversial. Firstly, it grants the people's court exclusive jurisdiction on alternative grounds. This type of exclusive jurisdiction is very rare and has unduly expanded the exclusive control of Chinese courts. Secondly, it is hard to justify exclusive jurisdiction based on the domicile of the decedent. It has been mentioned above that exclusive jurisdiction is based either on the control of the court or state interest. Where the decedent had his domicile in China upon his death, but the principal part of his estate is located abroad, exercising exclusive jurisdiction based on the decedent's domicile is hardly appropriate. The exercise of jurisdiction does not have substantive connections with the country's sovereignty and it cannot be justified in terms of control or the convenience of the trial, if the principal part of the estate or the real estate is located abroad. Asserting exclusive jurisdiction on that ground may cause difficulty for the recognition and enforcement of judgments abroad.[47] It is doubtful whether including cross-border succession in exclusive jurisdiction was the original intention of Chinese legislators, noting that Article 33 is included in the part concerning domestic disputes and is interpreted to have extraterritorial effect by Chinese jurists. Although the extended effect works

of Dispute on Jurisdiction over Contract and Unloading in the Harbour between Four Companies including Yueyang Tongda Cooling Air Condition Ltd]', Fa Jing (1994) 158.

46 Article 33(3).

47 DU Huanfang, 'Zhongguo Fayuan Shewai Guanxiaquan Shizheng Yanjiu [Empirical Study of Extraterritorial Jurisdiction of Chinese Courts]' (2007) 2 Faxuejia [Jurist] 152, 155; LIU Li, *supra* n 36.

for immovable property,[48] it is incompatible with the original purpose to establish exclusive jurisdiction over succession.[49] A reform to adopt a more flexible approach over succession is required.

Contracts for Chinese-foreign equity joint ventures, Chinese-foreign contractual joint ventures and Chinese-foreign cooperative exploration and development of nature resources are all important contracts concerning international investment.[50] The subject matter relates to national sovereignty and concerns the fundamental economic, public and social order of a country.[51] Furthermore, if these contracts are performed within the territory of China, the performance concerns natural resources located in China. Asserting exclusive jurisdiction demonstrates sovereign control over immovable property. In addition, it is believed that exclusive jurisdiction is the best approach to protect the Chinese parties. **3.22**

This ground for exclusive jurisdiction, however, is criticized by commentators as being parochial and inconsistent with the policy to encourage international investment.[52] Chinese-foreign cooperative exploration and development of natural resources located in China can be justified in terms of public policy, national interest, state sovereignty and control of immovable property. It is, however, difficult to claim that all contracts of Chinese-foreign equity joint ventures and Chinese-foreign contractual joint ventures concern national interest and public policy. The importance of these contracts and their national or social impact depend on the content of the contracts and the subject matter. The only reason that Chinese legislators reserve exclusive jurisdiction over all Chinese-foreign joint ventures is to protect Chinese parties of such contracts. The purpose can hardly be justified in modern private international law, where judicial cooperation between different countries is the main trend. **3.23**

It is true that the three contracts, described above, if performed in China, have the closest connection with China. Permitting the Chinese courts to take jurisdiction could simplify the procedure, bring convenience to the parties, and **3.24**

48 Article 33(1).

49 DING Wei, 'Woguo Shewai Minshangshi Susong Guangxia Zhidu de Wanshan [On the Perfection in the Legal System of China's Jurisdiction over Foreign Civil and Commercial Disputes]' (2006) 24 Zhengfa Luntan [Journal of China University of Political Science and Law] 152, 161.

50 Article 266 of the Civil Procedure Law. Chinese-Foreign equity joint ventures: *Pearl Time Investments v. Tianjin Metal Instruments*, SPC, [2002] Min Si Zhong Zi 3; *Taiwan Fanmao v. Guangxi Medical University*, Guangxi Zhuang Autonomous Region HPC, (2006) Gui Min San Zhong Zi 16; Chinese-Foreign contract joint ventures: *Guangzhou Baiyun Foreign investment Services v. Xianggang Wancheng*, Guangdong Province Guangzhou Municipality IPC, (2006) Sui Zhong Fa Min Si Chu Zi 47.

51 DU Huanfang, *supra* n 47, 156.

52 DING Wei, *supra* n 49, 162.

help the recognition and enforcement of judgments. However, the most convenient and appropriate forum does not mean this forum should take exclusive jurisdiction to the exclusion of other courts. With the enhanced cooperation between Chinese and foreign companies, more and more Chinese-foreign joint ventures are established. Chinese legislation starts to provide the same substantive law governing Chinese companies and Chinese-foreign joint ventures. There is no sufficient reason to justify treating these two types of companies differently in terms of jurisdiction.[53]

3.25 The CPL and the 2015 Opinion do not include incorporation, legal capacity and dissolution of companies and the content and validity of IP rights in the exclusive jurisdiction. However, the judicial practice and other specific legislation in company and IP law suggest Chinese courts have taken de facto exclusive jurisdiction over these matters. It is clear that these matters all involve the activity of administrative organs. Pursuant to the ordinary jurisdiction principle, administrative matters should not be subject to international civil jurisdiction but should be reserved exclusively by the forum where the administrative organs are located. It is hard to imagine that China would be happy for a foreign court to decide the effect and validity of the administrative decision of Chinese Government.

II.2 Effects of exclusive jurisdiction

3.26 In China, exclusive jurisdiction cannot be derogated from by jurisdiction agreements but can be excluded by arbitration agreements. The second indent of Article 531 of the 2015 Opinion provides that the parties cannot choose the court of any other country for disputes subject to exclusive jurisdiction, except arbitration agreements. Both the Law of the PRC on Chinese-Foreign Contractual Joint Ventures[54] and the Law of the PRC on Chinese-Foreign Equity Joint Ventures[55] provide that although Chinese courts have exclusive jurisdiction on the disputes and the parties are not allowed to choose another competent court, they are permitted to designate an arbitral tribunal to resolve the dispute. Article 25 of the Act on Chinese-Foreign Contractual Joint Ventures provides that for '(a)ny dispute between the Chinese and foreign parties arising from the execution of the contract or the articles of association for a contractual joint venture' the Chinese and foreign parties may submit it to 'a Chinese arbitration agency or any other arbitration agency for arbitration'.

---

53 Ibid.

54 Zhonghua Renmin Gongheguo Zhongwai Hezuo Jingying Qiye Fa [Law of the PRC on Chinese-Foreign Contractual Joint Ventures], adopted in 1979, amended in 1990, and amended for the second time in 2001.

55 Zhonghua Renmin Gongheguo Zhongwai Hezi Jingying Qiye Fa [Law of PRC on Chinese-Foreign Equity Joint Ventures], adopted in 1988 and amended in 2000.

Article 15 of the Act on Chinese-Foreign Equity Joint Ventures provides that: 'Disputes arising between the parties to an equity joint venture which the board of directors has failed to settle through consultation may be settled through conciliation or arbitration by an arbitration agency of China or through arbitration by another arbitration agency agreed upon by the parties.' All these sources confirm one principle, if the parties have chosen an arbitral tribunal, either seated in China or abroad, the Chinese courts will not hear the disputes, even if they are subject to exclusive jurisdiction. In *Zhangjiagang Xingang v Brose International CmbH,*[56] a Chinese company and a German company entered into a contract for Chinese-Foreign equity joint ventures. The contract contained an arbitration agreement designating the arbitral tribunal seated in Switzerland. Although Chinese courts had exclusive jurisdiction over the subject matter, the SPC confirmed that the exclusive jurisdiction could be excluded by a valid arbitration agreement, designating a tribunal located either in China or in another country. The SPC thus ordered the local court to decline jurisdiction in favour of the Swiss arbitration.

It is hard to explain why the law permits the parties to use arbitration agreements to avoid exclusive jurisdiction.[57] If exclusive jurisdiction covers the area that represents strong public interest and sovereign concern, which is not freely disposable by the parties, the matter subject to exclusive jurisdiction would not be proper for the adjudication of either a foreign court or a private body.[58] In order words, exclusive jurisdiction usually would imply non-arbitrability.[59] **3.27**

II.3 Chinese exclusive jurisdiction – general remarks

Exclusive jurisdiction shows sovereign reservation of a country over cross-border disputes on civil and commercial matters. Although the current tendency in the world is the gradual relaxation of jurisdictional control in civil **3.28**

56 Jiangsu Province HPC, (2005) Su Min San Li Zhong Zi No 39, reversed by the SPC, *Re the Request for Instruction about the Arbitration Clause Validity between Zhangjiagang Electro and Best-Better Worldwide Ltd*, [2006] Min Si Ta Zi No 1.

57 See criticism in DING Wei, *supra* n 49, 162.

58 For example, in Croatian law, an arbitrable dispute must be the one not subject to exclusive jurisdiction of the Croatian courts. See M. Dika, 'Boundaries of Arbitrability—Reflections on Draft Croatian Law on Arbitration: Arbitrability and Exclusive Jurisdiction of Courts of Law' (1999) 6 *Croatian Arbitration Yearbook* 27, 29, 40; A. Uzelac, 'Arbitrability and Exclusive Jurisdiction' in S. Kroll, L.A. Mistelis, P. Perales Viscasillas and V. Rogers (eds), *International Arbitration and International Commercial Law: Synergy, Convergence and Evolution* (Kluwer Law International 2011) 451–66; for German practice, see L.A. Mistelis and S.L. Brekoulakis, *Arbitrability: International and Comparative Perspectives* (Kluwer Law International 2009) 105ff.

59 P. Sanders, *Het Nederlandse arbitragerecht – nationaal en internationaal,* (4th ed., Deventer: Kluwer 2001) 36–8. Cf. V. Lazic, 'Arbitration Law Reform in the Netherlands' (2007) 11 *Electronic Journal of Comparative Law* 17.

matters and the improvement of international judicial cooperation, every country reserves exclusive jurisdiction to protect the fundamental public interest of a country. From an international perspective, common grounds for exclusive jurisdiction include rights *in rem* in immovable property, the constitution, nullity or dissolution of companies or other legal persons, and registration or validity of patents or other intellectual property rights.[60] Exclusive jurisdiction in China, however, is inconsistent with the common practice.

3.29 Chinese courts reserve exclusive jurisdiction in succession, harbour operations and Chinese-foreign joint ventures and cooperation performed in China. There is no doubt that exclusive jurisdiction can be justified if the above-mentioned issues concern immovable property located in China or concern the fundamental interest and public order of the country. However, based on the above analysis, exclusive jurisdiction in most cases in these areas is established in order to facilitate a convenient and efficient trial, to improve recognition and enforcement of judgments, and to protect Chinese citizens/companies as a party. These reasons can no longer be justified in the modern world marked by cooperation and comity. A few reasons can be contributed to the unsatisfactory legislation: one is the poor legislative technique, which causes practical difficulty in reality; the second is the misunderstanding over exclusive jurisdiction and the confusion between fundamental public interest and the closest connection; the third is the traditional attitude to equalizing jurisdiction and sovereignty; and the fourth is the sceptical view towards international judicial cooperation.

3.30 On the other hand, China does not assert exclusive jurisdiction in registration of companies, intellectual property rights, and other issues that require the administration and governance of a public authority.[61] Disputes relating to the constitution or dissolution of a company registered in China, for example, cannot be properly heard in a country other than the place of registration. It is also improper for the courts located in another country to review the administrative work of a public authority. Although the Chinese courts could take jurisdiction in these matters according to other jurisdictional grounds, it is more appropriate to cover these sovereign-sensitive issues in exclusive jurisdiction and prevent any other countries from taking jurisdiction.

3.31 In conclusion, Chinese exclusive jurisdiction is outdated and improper. It covers issues that should not be exclusively controlled by a country, but leaves out issues where the intervention of another country should be excluded.

---

60 E.g., see Art 22 of the Brussels I Regulation.

61 DING Wei, *supra* n 49, 161.

III. PROROGATION JURISDICTION

Chinese law has recognized party autonomy in cross-border civil and commercial procedure ever since 1991 upon the enactment of the Civil Procedure Law 1991.[62] The original purpose to accept prorogation jurisdiction in Chinese law was to tackle the competing jurisdiction between different Chinese courts instead of addressing conflicts of jurisdiction between China and a foreign state.[63] However, prorogation jurisdiction is provided for both domestic and cross-border disputes. In both the 1991 version and the 2007 amendment, the CPL maintains two prorogation jurisdiction provisions, one concerning domestic disputes[64] and the other cross-border disputes.[65] In the 2012 amendment, the legislators deleted the provision concerning prorogation jurisdiction in foreign-related cases in Part Four. The only provision remaining is Article 34, which is traditionally interpreted as the jurisdiction rules applying to domestic cases. There are two possible explanations. The first is that the legislators wanted to remove the difference previously existing between domestic and international prorogation jurisdiction and decided to use one set of rules to govern all choice of court agreements, both domestically and internationally.[66] Before the amendment, commentators had criticized the separate treatment to jurisdiction agreements in domestic and international cases and recommended a uniform provision for both.[67] Another possibility is that the legislators considered the potential future international judicial cooperation in choice of court agreements. The deletion of the prorogation 3.32

62 Articles 25 and 244, adopted at the Fourth Session of the Seventh National People's Congress and promulgated by Order No 44 of the President of the PRC on 9 April 1991.

63 Minshi Susong Fa (Shixing) 1982 [The Civil Procedure Law (for Trial Implementation) 1982] did not recognize the parties' right to choose a competent court. This caused competing jurisdiction between Chinese domestic courts. WANG HanBin, 'Guanyu "Zhonghua Renmin Gongheguo Minshi Susongfa (Shixing)" (Xiugai Cao'an) de Shuoming [Explanation on the Civil Procedure Law of the People's Republic of China (for Trial Implementation)(Amendment Draft)]', the 4th Meeting of the Seventh NPC, 2 April 1991, section 2, the Chinese version is available at http://cpc.people.com.cn/GB/64184/64186/66684/4494177.html (accessed on 10 Oct 2013).

64 Article 35 of CPL 2007.

65 Article 342 of CPL 2007.

66 CHEN Yong Can, 'Jiedu Minshi Susongfa Xin Xiuding [Interpretation of the Amendment of the Civil Procedure Law]', published on 18.09.2012, available at http://www.wjnco.com/cn/articles_show.asp?Articles_id=248 (accessed on 04 June 2013); XU Yan, 'Interpretation of the 2012 New Civil Procedure Law Part II', published on the website of the Yun Xi District Court on 25.02.2013, available at http://yxqfy.chinacourt.org/public/detail.php?id=290 (accessed on 02 June 2013); WANG Fuhua, 'Xieyi Guanxia Zhidu de Jinbu yu Juxian [Development and Limits on Prorogation Jurisdiction]' (2012) 30 Falv Kexue: Xibei Zhengfa Xueyuan Xuebao [Law Science: Northwest University of Political Science and Law Journal] 163.

67 LIAO Zhonghong, 'Xieyi Guanxia: Wenti, Yuanyin Jiqi Gaige Shexiang [Agreement Jurisdiction: the Problems, Reasons and Reformation Plan]' (2008) 10 Xinan Zhengfa Daxue Xuebao [Journal of Southwest University of Political Science and Law] 110; WANG Qi, LU Jianhua, 'Woguo Guonei Xieyi Guanxia Zhidu de Wanshan [Improving Chinese Domestic Prorogation Jurisdiction]' (2009) *Hai Nan University Journal (Art and Social Science)* 167; WANG Fuhua, ibid.

jurisdiction from Part Four clears the way to implement the Hague Choice of Court Convention in the future.

3.33 No matter which interpretation is true, Article 34 is used to decide prorogation jurisdiction of a people's court in both domestic and international litigation for now. Article 34 provides:

> Parties to a dispute over a contract or other proprietary rights and interests may, through written agreement, choose the court of the place which has practical connections with the dispute to exercise jurisdiction. Such a choice shall not violate the provisions of this Law on jurisdiction by forum level and on exclusive jurisdiction.

3.34 This provision has recognized the basic doctrine of party autonomy. However, compared to legislation and legal practices in other countries, it fails to provide rules to determine exclusivity of a jurisdiction clause, establishes restrictive requirements as to the validity of a jurisdiction clause, and does not explicitly provide the effectiveness of a jurisdiction clause.

III.1 Exclusivity of a jurisdiction clause

3.35 Exclusivity of a jurisdiction clause is crucial in that it determines whether the agreement simply grants jurisdiction to a court or whether it also derogates jurisdiction to other competent courts. The Chinese law does not provide how to decide the exclusivity of a jurisdiction clause. If the parties clarify in their agreement that a jurisdiction clause is 'exclusive' or 'non-exclusive', the parties' intention will be respected.[68] Without expression, the parties' intention can also be inferred by construing contract terms and referring to other circumstances of the case. If no intention is expressed or can be inferred, there is no general presumption helping the Chinese courts to decide the exclusivity of a jurisdiction clause.[69] Some courts believe that unless the parties expressly state otherwise, a jurisdiction clause should be exclusive.[70] This interpretation is consistent with the legislative purpose. Prorogation jurisdiction was introduced with the purpose of preventing undue competition of jurisdiction

68 E.g., *Zhong An Housing Ltd v. Merchants Bank*, SPC (2001) Min Si Zhong Zi No 1.

69 Presumptions, however, exist in many other countries. For example, in Art 23(1) of the Brussels I Regulation, a jurisdiction clause is presumed to be exclusive unless the parties express otherwise. In the USA and Australia, a jurisdiction clause is presumed to be non-exclusive unless the parties express otherwise.

70 E.g., *Yacheng Automobile Fittings v. HSBC Holdings plc*, Jiangsu Province Wuxi Municipality IPC, (2006) No 23. See also DU Huanfang, 'Ruhe Queding yu Xingshi Shewai Minshangshi Guanxiaquan [How to determine jurisdiction in cross-border civil and commercial matters]', Renmin Fayuan [People's Court], published on 31.10.2006, available at http://www.zwmscp.com/a/susongchengxu/susongchengxu/2010/0709/6826.html (accessed on 10 Oct 2012).

between the competent courts.[71] A choice of court agreement could only prevent a competent court from competing for jurisdiction if it has the effect of derogation. The correct construction of a jurisdiction clause in the Chinese court should be that the parties' choice of court agreement is exclusive, unless the parties agree otherwise. However, other courts also attempt to interpret a neutral jurisdiction clause as non-exclusive, especially where a foreign court is chosen. In *Compania Sud Ameicana De Vapore S.A v. Hin-proInternational Logistics Ltd*,[72] the Zhejiang HPC held the jurisdiction clause stating 'disputes should be submitted to London High Court' was non-exclusive,[73] because the parties failed to explicitly provide exclusivity to the chosen court. This approach may be readily adopted by Chinese local courts as a legitimate means to assert jurisdiction irrespective of parties' agreement otherwise. This practice reflects the 'homeward trend' and local protectionism of some Chinese courts. The SPC or the legislators should provide judicial guidance to harmonize interpretation of exclusivity, and it is suggested the 'exclusive'-presumption should be adopted.

It is necessary to note that classification between exclusive and non-exclusive jurisdiction clauses only has importance where the law grants clear derogation effects to exclusive jurisdiction clauses. If the law does not recognize the parties the power to derogate from the jurisdiction of the competent local court by any means, the distinction between exclusive and non-exclusive jurisdiction clauses might be meaningless.[74] This is another difficulty in current Chinese law and practice and is discussed in details in subsection III.4 below. **3.36**

III.2 Validity of a jurisdiction clause

A jurisdiction clause cannot be enforced if it is invalid as to form or substance.[75] Validity of a contract term is a question of law and choice of law **3.37**

71 WANG HanBin, *supra* n 63.

72 Zhejiang HPC, (2013) Zhe Xia Zhong Zi No 145.

73 It is incorrect to hold the jurisdiction clause as non-exclusive, though the final decision is correct in Chinese law. England had no practical connection with this dispute and the choice was therefore invalid in Chinese law. See III.2 below.

74 Under the current Chinese law, a Chinese court may be able to take jurisdiction even if the parties' jurisdiction clause is intended to be 'exclusive'. See SPC, 'Zuigao Renmin Fayuan, "Di Er Ci Quanguo Shewai Shangshi Haishi Shenpan Gongzuo Huiyi Jiyao" [Summary of the Second National Conference on the Adjudication of Commercial and Maritime Cases with Foreign Elements]' ('2005 Summary') Fa Fa [2005] No 26, Art 12.

75 *Min Ye (HK) v. Liaoning Property*, SPC, 'The Reply of the SPC on jurisdiction of disputes on loan agreements between Min Ye Ltd (HK), Liaoning Property Group Ying Kou Trading Department, and Gai Zhou City Hong Da Property Co', Fa Han [1996] No 158; *ZHENG LiQiang v. Weifu Transport*, Guangzhou Maritime Court, (2005) No 267 (two exclusive jurisdiction clauses choosing US courts and

issues are relevant in an international context. Article 34 does not specify choice of law deciding the validity of a jurisdiction clause. The judicial practice of the Chinese courts demonstrates great diversity. Most courts use the *lex fori* to decide the validity of a jurisdiction clause and directly apply Article 34 requirements without considering choice of law issues at all.[76] Some courts have considered the choice of law questions but classified choice of court agreements as something relating to procedure subject to the *lex fori*.[77] An exceptional case is *Sumitomo Bank Ltd v Xinhua Estate*, where the SPC applied the *lex causae* to decide the validity of the parties' choice of court agreement.[78] Since the parties had chosen the applicable law governing the contract, the chosen law had been applied to interpret the meaning and to decide the validity of the choice of court agreement contained in the main contract.[79] There was, unfortunately, no attempt to harmonize the approaches. In practice, the third approach is used very rarely and most courts, following either the approach one or two, would apply Chinese law in determining validity of a jurisdiction clause.

3.38 It is fair to recognize that the Chinese substantive law on validity of a jurisdiction clause is improving slowly but steadily. Comparing the 2015 Opinion with previous practice, three important improvements are noticeable. The first is to recognize the choice of more than one court.[80] The 1992 Opinion invalidated a jurisdiction clause choosing more than one court,[81] based on the reason that such a choice is ambiguous and could not prevent competition of jurisdiction.[82] This justification is unconvincing. First, the choice of more than one court is not ambiguous as long as both courts are

English courts respectively are invalid because these two places have no connections to the dispute); *SBF (Korea) v. Teng (Beijing)*, Beijing Municipality HPC, (2005) Gao Min Zhong Zi No 98 (parties choose two alternative *fora*).

76 *Shandong Jufeng v. Korea MGame*, SPC, (2009) Min San Zhong Zi No 4; SPC, 'Zuigao Renmin Fayuan Guanyu Yinfa Zuigao Fayuan Zhishi Chanquan Niandu Baogao (2009) de Tongzhi [Annual Report of Intellectual Property Cases in the SPC (2009)]', [2010] Fa No 173, case 44.

77 *Shandong Jufeng v. MGame*, ibid. SPC, 'Zuigao Renmin Fayuan Guanyu Shenli She Gangao Jingji Jiufen Anjian Ruogan Wenti de Jieda [Answers to economic disputes relating to Hong Kong or Macau]', Fa (Jing) Fa [1987] No 28, Art 3(1) and (2); Guangdong HPC, 'Guanyu Queding Guangzhoushi deng Wuge Zhongji Renmin Fayuan dui Shewai Shegang'aotai Minshangshi Anjian de Quyu Guanxia Fanwei ji Shewai Shegang'aotai Minshangshi Anjian Jibie Guanxia deng Youguan Shixiang de Tongzhi [Notice on Issues about Deciding the Five IPCs of Guangzhou Municipality on the Territorial Jurisdiction and Jurisdiction by Forum Level on Civil and Commercial Matters Relating to Hong Kong and Macau]', Yue Gao Fa [2002] No 191, Art 13; *China Point Finance Ltd v. Zhuhai City Commercial Bank*, Guangdong Province HPC, (2004) No 263.

78 SPC, (1999) No 194.

79 Ibid.

80 Article 30 of the 2015 Opinion, 2nd indent.

81 '1992 Opinion', Art 24.

82 *SBF (Korea)*; *Zhongshan Shishen v. Auli*, Guangdong Province HPC, (2004) Yue Gao Fa Min Si Zhong Zi No 239.

clearly named and easily identifiable. The parties may express their intention in a clear manner that the claimant should have the right to choose. The competent court is thus affirmed at the point when the claimant makes the choice. Secondly, only an exclusive jurisdiction clause may exclude competition between courts, but no one would suggest that all non-exclusive jurisdiction clauses should be invalid. After over a decade, the SPC eventually decided to retreat. Article 30 of the 2015 Opinion expressly permits the choice of more than one court. Furthermore, choice by reference is also allowed. The parties do not need to identify the exact jurisdiction or the name of the court, but can simply decide that the court of the domicile of one party has jurisdiction.[83] If the named party has changed domicile afterwards, the chosen court is deemed to be the court of the place where this party had his domicile at the time of contracting. The third important development is that the SPC has finally paid attention to the necessity of protecting the weaker party in contracts. Article 31 of the 2015 Opinion provides that if the business and the consumer enter into the choice of court agreement in a standard-form contract, the choice of court agreement will not bind the consumer if the business does not provide him with reasonable notice. The Chinese SPC does not prima facie invalidate jurisdiction clauses in consumer contracts, but it regulates asymmetric information. The rationale is that once the consumer notices the jurisdiction clause and still decides to conclude the contract, genuine consent should be deemed to exist. This may not be convincing. First, it is hard to assess what amounts to 'reasonable notice'. Does it require the jurisdiction clause to be interpreted to the consumer in person? Does it require the jurisdiction clause to be highlighted or singled out? Or does it only require that the clause is properly referred to and not buried in lengthy contract terms? Secondly, even if reasonable notice is provided, it could not properly balance the inequality of bargaining power. Consumers are still in a take-it-or-leave-it position and there is no opportunity to bargain. Despite this, although the level of protection is low and inadequate, the recognition of the necessity to protect consumers in choice of court agreements is an important development in Chinese jurisdiction rules per se.

Noting the improvement, it is also necessary to recognize that Chinese law still provides rather restrictive requirements to the validity of a jurisdiction clause. Even if the chosen court is a foreign court, which has more flexible prerequisites, the resisting party may relatively easily escape the jurisdiction agreement by bringing actions in China. Article 34 of CPL includes at least three restrictions that are inconsistent with international commercial practice. 3.39

83 Article 32, 2015 Interpretaion.

First, a jurisdiction clause should be concluded in writing.[84] According to the PRC Contract Law,[85] the 'written form' is defined to include: 'any form which renders the information contained in a contract capable of being reproduced in tangible form such as a written agreement, a letter, or electronic text (including telegram, telex, facsimile, electronic data interchange and e-mail'.[86] Although the written form is extended to cover clauses concluded through most modern communication technology, it is uncertain whether an oral agreement that is recorded in writing or that can be proved is valid in form. So far there is no case law that has invalidated a jurisdiction clause because it is orally agreed and evidenced in writing.

3.40 Furthermore, Chinese law does not specify the format of 'writing'. In principle, a jurisdiction clause can be written in different formats, including being clearly written in the contract; contained in the standard terms of the general contract which is explicitly accepted by the parties; or contained in the small print on the back of the contract. If a contract is unilaterally drafted or is a standard form contract of one party, once the jurisdiction clause is properly notified to the other party, it is valid. The requirement of 'proper notice' demonstrates that some courts are ready to consider the format of writing to decide the authentic consent of the parties.[87] The proper notice requirement also applies to the valid incorporation of a jurisdiction clause contained in another contract. In a few disputes relating to the bill of lading, the Chinese courts have held that a dispute resolution clause contained in the charter could not be successfully incorporated in the bill of lading if the language of incorporation only refers to 'all the terms whatsoever of the Charter', instead of specifying the dispute resolution agreement,[88] or the dispute resolution clause is only referred at the back of the bill of lading.[89] It is necessary to provide more guidance to clarify the format requirements and harmonize the practice.

3.41 Secondly, Chinese law also restricts the nature of disputes where party autonomy could apply. Choice of court agreements are expressly allowed in

84 The 'written' requirement is later confirmed in the 2015 Opinion, Art 29.

85 Zhonghua Renmin Gongheguo Hetong Fa [PRC Contract Law], adopted at the Second Session of the Ninth National People's Congress on 15 March 1999 and promulgated by Order No 15 of the President of the PRC on 15 March 1999.

86 Article 11.

87 *Wenzhou Foreign Trade Co of Light Industry Arts and Crafts v. Compagniemaritimed Affretement (France)*, Fujian HPC, 1999, available at www.chinalawinfo.com, reference no CLI.C.21767 (the choice of court agreement was printed on the face of the bill of lading in red while all other provisions were in blue). The case number and citation is not available.

88 *SF Chemistry v. DB Seafreight*, Qingdao Maritime Court, (2009) Qing Hai Fa Shang Chu Zi No 277.

89 *China PingAn Insurance Dalian Branch v. Cosco Shipping Co and Guangzhou Ocean Shipping*, (2006) Min Si Ta Zi No 49.

disputes concerning contracts or proprietary rights.[90] It may imply that in non-contractual, non-proprietary obligations, the parties are not allowed to choose the competent forum. The law fails to interpret what 'proprietary' means. If it refers to obligations relating to property or property rights, all tort obligations may be excluded. However, in practice, if the parties in tort claims agree to subject their disputes to the Chinese court, there is no reason to invalidate this choice. Realizing the difficulty, the Chinese court usually adopts an extended interpretation if possible to apply prorogation jurisdiction to non-contractual, non-proprietary claims. This usually occurs if such claims arise out of a contract. In *Lai v. ABN AMRO Bank*,[91] the parties entered into a jurisdiction clause in an investment contract but the claimant sued the defendant in a non-chosen court on fraud, arguing that this type of claim was not subject to the jurisdiction agreement. The court ruled that since the dispute arose out of a contract, the jurisdiction clauses should be enforceable and the claimant could not manipulate the system by formulating its claim.[92]

Thirdly, the parties can only choose the court of the place with 'practical connections' with the dispute.[93] The parties could choose the court located in the domicile of the defendant, the place where the contract is performed, the place where the contract is concluded, the domicile of the claimant, the place where the object of the dispute is located, the place where tort occurs and other places which have practical connections with the dispute.[94] There is no consensus as to what 'other places' with practical connections with the dispute should be.[95] In *Shandong Jufeng*,[96] the SPC mentioned that the chosen court had no other practical connections with the dispute because none of the listed connections were located in the chosen court, and the law of another country was chosen by the parties as the governing law. It implies that the choice of law agreement or applicable law may also form a 'practical connection'. **3.42**

This interpretation is controversial. First, the parties' choice of law agreement is subjective. Allowing parties to create a subjective 'practical connection' may depart from the legislative purpose to only allow the submission to an objectively related court. Secondly, applicable law in the absence of choice, on **3.43**

---

90 CPL, Art 34; 2015 Opinion, Art 531.

91 Shanghai Municipality HPC, (2010) Hu Gao Min Wu (Shang) Zhong Zi No 49.

92 See also *Watanabe v. Culture & Art Press*, Shanghai Municipality No 1 IPC, (2008) Hu Yi Zhong Min Wu (Zhi) Chu Zi No 210.

93 Article 34 of CPL; Art 531, 2015 Opinion.

94 Article 531, 2015 Opinion.

95 *Shandong Jufeng*, *supra* n 76, see the next paragraph. However, some courts only permit the parties to choose from the five specified places and will not consider other connections. See e.g., XU *YAN Conghua v. Meihong and LIU Yueping*, Fujian Province HPC, (2010) Min Min Zhong Zi No 78.

96 *Shandong Jufeng*, *supra* n 76.

the other hand, may be an objective practical connection. However, it is not as straightforward and easy to determine as other connections listed in the provision. It is time-consuming and inefficient to decide the complicated choice of law issue at the jurisdiction stage.

3.44 The SPC interpretation in *Shandong Jufeng* suggests that the SPC might have noticed the undue restriction of 'practical connections' and have tried to relax the requirement by introducing subjective connections. A strict interpretation of practical connection requirement technically invalidates jurisdiction agreements choosing a neutral forum, which is a common practice in international trade. In *Zheng v. Wider Logistics Ltd*,[97] the bill of lading provided that all disputes arising out of the US Carriage of Goods by Sea Act 1936 should be heard exclusively in the New York court; for other disputes, the English courts had jurisdiction. The Chinese court instead took jurisdiction by holding that both New York and England were neutral fora and the jurisdiction clause was invalid. This approach is over-rigid and inappropriate in international commerce. The flexible interpretation in *Shandong Jufeng*, on the other hand, generates uncertainty in practice. It is suggested that the best approach is to completely remove the 'practical connection' requirement from the prorogation jurisdiction.

III.3 Third parties

3.45 A choice of court agreement usually only binds its parties and should not affect the rights of a third party, even where the third party is a party in a related contract and has known or ought to have known of the existence of this jurisdiction clause. In *China Agricultural Finance Co v Guangdong Samsung (Group)*,[98] the SPC held that the jurisdiction clause entered into between the debtor and the creditor did not bind the guarantor of the debtor.

3.46 Two exemptions, however, exist. First, a choice of court agreement binds the assignee as the new party to the agreement, unless the assignee does not know of the existence of the choice of court agreement at the time of assignment, or the assignment agreement provides otherwise, which has been agreed by the original debtor.[99] Before the 2015 Opinion, an assignee was automatically bound by the jurisdiction clause of the original contract, unless the assignee

97 Zheng v. Wider Logistics Ltd, Guangzhou Maritime Court, (2005) Guang Hai Fa Shu Zi No 267.
98 SPC, [2004] Min Si Zhong Zi No 23.
99 2015 Opinion, Art 33.

expressly objected to its application at the time of assignment, or the assignment agreement included a different choice of court agreement.[100] It presumed that in the absence of objection or different agreements, the assignee impliedly took over all the rights and obligations of the assignor in the original contract, including the jurisdiction clause.[101] The 2015 Opinion provides necessary protection for the assignee, who may not be aware of the existence of such a jurisdiction clause, negotiate a new jurisdiction clause or raise any objection. The practical difficulty is how to decide whether an assignee has knowledge of the original jurisdiction clause. The actual knowledge is hard to prove. Only constructive knowledge is required. Constructive knowledge exists if the sufficient notice is given, for example, by highlighting the jurisdiction clause in the assignment agreement, by obtaining the assignee's signature to the contract where the jurisdiction clause is contained, or by providing a clear reference to the contract where the jurisdiction clause is included. The assignee's experience, profession, and business relationship with either the assignor or the original debtor may also be taken into consideration.

Secondly, some Chinese courts and jurists hold that a jurisdiction clause in the bill of lading concluded between a carrier and a consignor binds the consignee.[102] It is believed that the commercial practice in carriage by sea requires the rights and obligations between the carrier, consignor and consignee to be determined by the bill of lading.[103] Binding the consignee meets the purpose of commercial convenience and reduces the business risk of the carrier. However, other Chinese courts still hold the view that a consignee does not demonstrate his consent to be bound by the jurisdiction agreement and should **3.47**

100 SPC, 'Zuigao Renmin Fayuan Guanyu Shenli Sheji Jinrong Zichan Guanli Gongsi Shougou, Guanli, Chuzhi Guoyou Yinhang Buliang Daikuan Xingcheng de Zichan de Anjian Shiyong Falv Ruogan Wenti de Guiding [Several Issues Concerning the Law Applicable to the Trial of Cases of Financial Asset Management Companies' Purchase, Management and Disposal of Assets formed by Bad Loans of State-Owned Banks]', Fa Shi [2001] No 12, Art 3(2); SPC, 'Zuigao Renmin Fayuan Guanyu Jinrong Zichan Guanli Gongsi Shougou, Chuzhi Yinhang Buliang Zichan Youguan Wenti de Buchong Tongzhi [Supplementary Notice about the Purchase and Disposal of Non-Performing Assets by Financial Asset Management Companies]', [2005] No 62, Art 1. *China Enterprise International Investment Co, Ltd v. China Haohua Chemical (Group) Co,* SPC, [2006] Min Er Zhong Zi No 186.

101 *China Enterprise International Investment Co*, ibid.

102 *Baron Motorcycles v. Awell Logistics Group,* Ningbo Maritime Court, (2008) Yong Hai Fa Shang Chu Zi No 277; *P & O Nedlloyd v. Wah Hing Seafreight (China),* Guangzhou Maritime Court, (2000) Guang Hai Fa Shi Zi No 037; ZHENG Zhi-Hua, 'Tidan Beimian Guanxia Tiaokuan Xingzhi Ruogan Wenti Tanxi [Analysis of Several Issues concerning Jurisdiction Clauses in the Back of the Bill of Lading]' (2004) 32 Haishi Sifa Luntan [Maritime Judicial Forum] 59; ZHAO Cheng-Tao, 'Yiqi Tidan Guanxiaquan Tiaokuan Jiufen'an zhi Wojian [A Dispute on the Jurisdiction Clause in the Bill of Lading]', (1999) Zhongguo Haishangfa Niankan [Yearbook of Chinese Maritime Law] 402, 404.

103 See also the Zhonghua Renmin Gongheguo Haishang Fa [PRC Maritime Law] 1992, Art 78(1).

be treated as an innocent third party.[104] Consistent interpretation needs to be provided by the SPC on this question.

III.4 Effect of a valid jurisdiction clause

3.48 If the parties have chosen the Chinese court in a valid jurisdiction agreement, the chosen court must take jurisdiction. According to the 2015 Opinion, a Chinese court is not allowed to decline jurisdiction if there is an agreement between the parties choosing the Chinese court, even if the foreign court may be more appropriate and convenient to hear the dispute.[105] The language is inclusive and does not distinguish between exclusive and non-exclusive jurisdiction clauses. In other words, if the parties have chosen the Chinese court in a non-exclusive jurisdiction clause and there is a foreign court that is more appropriate in which to hear the dispute, the Chinese court, by law, still cannot decline jurisdiction.[106] A non-exclusive jurisdiction is treated as an exclusive one as far as the Chinese court is chosen. It demonstrates the tendency of the SPC to favour local jurisdiction. However, if the parties have chosen the foreign court in an exclusive jurisdiction clause, the derogation effect against the Chinese court is much more uncertain in Chinese law. In the absence of compulsory requirements by law, some courts may nevertheless take jurisdiction under other jurisdiction grounds irrespective of a valid exclusive jurisdiction clause choosing a foreign court. This issue concerns declining jurisdiction by the Chinese courts and is discussed in detail in Chapter 4.[107]

III.5 Transferred jurisdiction

3.49 It has been stated that China has a complex domestic judicial system. Even if the parties agree to submit disputes to China as a competent forum in general, there are complicated issues concerning hierarchical jurisdiction and internal territorial jurisdiction.[108] The parties may conclude an ambiguous choice of court agreement, which states 'any disputes should be heard by the courts of PRC', or the parties clearly state that 'the IPC of Jinhua, Zhejiang should have jurisdiction'. In the first scenario, when disputes have arisen, the claimant is responsible for figuring out the competent domestic court by hierarchy and territory. In the second scenario, what if the parties have, by agreement, made a

---

104 E.g., *Xiamen PICCP &C v. Chipolbrok*, SPC, [2004] Min Si Ta Zi No 43; *Beijing Alison Import and Export v. Songa Shipholding (Singapore) and Solar Shipping Angtrading (Japan),* Hubei Province HPC, E' Gao Fa [2007] No 197, aff'd, SPC, [2007] Min Si Ta Zi No 14.

105 Article 532(2). See also SPC, '2005 Summary', *supra* n 74, Art 11.

106 For more discussion, see Ch 4, IV below.

107 See ibid.

108 See I.3 above.

choice incompatible with the Chinese law on hierarchical and domestic territorial jurisdiction?

One may argue that such a choice may be invalid as contrary to law. However, such an interpretation requires the parties to fully understand the complicated internal jurisdiction in China to identify the right court. This is an extra burden and the cost of learning would be inappropriate and proves inefficient in cross-border transactions. Many jurisdiction clauses in international transactions are part of standard-term contracts and it is commercially unviable to require a more specific designation of domestic courts. Furthermore, since the hierarchical jurisdiction is determined by considering the value of the dispute and the type and significance of cases, it cannot be accurately predicated before disputes have arisen. As a result, the choice of a Chinese court that is incompatible with the regulation on hierarchical jurisdiction should be valid. The claimant could have two options in this circumstance. First, the claimant could bring the dispute to the chosen court. CPL provides rules for the internal transfer of jurisdiction. If the competent court is the court at the higher hierarchy, the chosen court should report this issue to the higher court.[109] If the competent court is the lower court, the higher court could assume jurisdiction, but could also report to its supervisory court to approve transferring the case to the lower court.[110] Furthermore, if the competent court is at the same level as the chosen court, the chosen court could transfer the case to the competent court.[111] The second option, or the more convenient option, however, is to permit the claimant to bring the action in the correct competent court according to domestic law. The court should nevertheless take jurisdiction and treat the jurisdiction clause as a valid clause designating Chinese forum in general. 3.50

IV. GENERAL JURISDICTION

General jurisdiction is based on the defendant's domicile.[112] A Chinese court has general jurisdiction over a dispute if the defendant has his domicile in China. Domicile is a question of law and the definition differs in country to country.[113] The legislation and judicial practice in China have adopted the *lex* 3.51

109 CPL, Art 38.
110 Ibid.
111 CPL, Art 36.
112 Article 265.
113 For the concept of domicile, see R.J. Weintraub, 'An Inquiry into the Utility of "Domicile" as a Concept in Conflicts Analysis', (1965) 63 *Michigan Law Review* 961; Michael Mann, 'The Seventh Report of the

fori to apply the Chinese substantive law to decide whether a person has his domicile in China.[114]

3.52 What is domicile in Chinese law? Chinese legislation and the judicial guidance of the SPC all provide that the domicile of a legal person is its principal place of business.[115] If the principle place of business cannot be determined, the legal person has its domicile in the place of registration.[116] Domicile of a natural person, however, is more controversial. China is a country with a long history of controlling and monitoring citizen's residence and migration. Natural persons should register their permanent residence as a family member. This is also called family registry system (HuKou).[117] The concept of domicile in China has great connections with the family registry system. Article 3 of the 2015 Opinion provides that the domicile of a natural person should be the place of his registered residence.[118]

3.53 Treating the family registry as domicile is unique and is incompatible with the needs of the modern commercial world, where people may move more frequently and freely. It also makes it difficult to sue a foreign citizen in China under the general jurisdiction as they would not be registered in the family registry system. Habitual residence is thus introduced as a supplementary connecting factor to relax the rigidity of domicile. Article 15 of GPCL provides that if the habitual residence is different from the registered residence, the habitual residence is the domicile.[119] This provision relaxes the requirement for domicile and may allow a foreign citizen to be sued in China under the general jurisdiction, if the foreign citizen has habitual residence in China. Habitual residence is defined by the SPC as a place where a natural

---

Private International Law Committee on Domicile', (1963) 12 ICLQ 1326; P.B. Carter, 'Domicil: The Case for Radical Reform in the United Kingdom' (1987) 36 ICLQ 713.

114 Beside the *lex fori*, there are other approaches to decide domicile. One is to apply the substantive law of the relevant country in which the person is claimed to have his domicile, another is to use choice of law rules by designing special connection factors to decide domicile. See LI Wang, 'Guoji Sifa Zhongguoji he Zhusuo de Queding –Jianlun "Shewai Minshiguanxi de Falvshiyong fa (Cao'an)" di 6 Tiao he di 18 Tiao de Xianghu Guanxi [Determining the Chinese Nationality and Domicile in Private International Law]', (2010) 31 Faxue Zaizhi [Law Science Magazine] 62; WANG XiaoYan, Guoji Sifa zhong de Ziranren Zhusuo Zhidu Yanjiu [Study on Domicile of Natural Person in Private International Law], PhD Dissertation, Southwest University of Political Science and Law (2009), 62–93.

115 2015 Opinion, Art 3; GPCL, Art 39; Company Law of the People's Republic of China, Art 10.

116 2015 Opinion, Art 3.

117 Hukou [Family Registration] '户口'. SHEN Tirui, 'The People's Republic of China Domicile Administrative Work', The Ministry of Public Security of P.R China, East and South Asian Workshop on Strategies for Accelerating the Improvement of Civil Registration and Vital Statistics Systems, 29 Nov–3 Dec, 1993, Beijing, China, available at http://unstats.un.org/unsd/demographic/meetings/wshops/1993_China_CRVS/docs/1993_Doc.29_PRChina.pdf (accessed on 08 Oct 2012).

118 See also Art 15 of the CPR General Principle of Civil Law (GPCL) of 1986, in force from 1 Jan 1987, Art 15.

119 GPCL, Art 15.

person has resided for at least one consecutive year after he left his registered residence, unless this purpose of residing is medication.[120]

3.54 Chinese law requires a person, in terms of private international law, to have one, and at least one, domicile. If a citizen has changed his registered residence and has no habitual residence while the change is taking place, the previous registered residence is his domicile.[121] If the domicile of a person cannot be decided, the habitual residence can be treated as the domicile in such circumstances. What if the person has more than one habitual residence? It may lead to more than one domicile in law. According to the Opinion on GPCL, if a person has more than one domicile, he is deemed to have domicile in the place that has the closest connection with the dispute.[122] What if a person has no habitual residence? Under the current family registry system, it is possible that a person may fail to register; this person may not have habitual residence to replace domicile either. In such a case determining domicile will be a problem and no answer is officially given to the question. Two approaches may be the options: first, domicile of this person should be deemed to be the current place where the person resides;[123] or two, domicile of this person should be the place that has the closest connection with the person.[124]

3.55 The concept of domicile of a natural person is undeveloped in China. The law that links domicile with the family registry and Chinese nationality is no longer compatible with the development of cross-border transactions and other civil relationships. Furthermore, the current Chinese law fails to provide a practical relationship between domicile and habitual residence. Although it provides that habitual residence may be used to be the deemed domicile in certain circumstances, it is sometimes more difficult and uncertain to decide a person's habitual residence. It is also possible that a person may have more than

120 2015 Opinion, Art 4.

121 SPC, 'Zuigao Renmin Fayuan Guanyu Guanche Zhixing "Zhonghua Renmin Gongheguo Minfa Tongze" Ruogan Wenti de Yijian (Shixing)(Shixiao) [Opinion of the SPC about Several Issues on the Implementation of the "General Principle of Civil Law" (For the Trial Purpose)]' ('Opinion on GPCL'), Fa (Ban) Fa [1988] No 6 (abolished), Art 9.

122 Opinion on GPCL, Art 183.

123 Zhonghua Renmin Gongheguo Shewai Minshi Guanxi Falv Shiyong Fa [Law of the People's Republic of China on the Laws Applicable to Foreign-Related Civil Relations], adopted at the 17th session of the Standing Committee of the 11th National People's Congress, 28 October 2010, Art 20 provides that in terms of applicable law, if the habitual residence cannot be decided, the law of the present residence should apply.

124 YAN Lin, 'Guoji Sifa shang Ziranren Zhusuo Zhidu jiqi Jiejian Yiyi [Domicile of a Natural Person in Private International Law]' ((2007) 16 Journal of Huai Yin Gong Xue Yuan 31.

one habitual residence or no habitual residence.[125] The determination of the personal connecting factor in general jurisdiction needs systematic review and updating.

V. INTERNATIONAL TERRITORIAL JURISDICTION

3.56 A general characteristic of Chinese law concerning jurisdiction in cross-border civil and commercial matters is that China has a tendency to expand the scope of its jurisdiction.[126] This is clearly shown in the extended grounds of special jurisdiction. According to Article 265 of CPL, Chinese courts have jurisdiction in a contract dispute or other disputes over proprietary interests, if the contract is signed in China, if the contract is performed in China, if the object of the action is located in China, if the defendant has distrainable property in China, if the defendant has its representative office in China, or if the tort occurred in China.[127]

V.1 Exorbitant jurisdiction in contract

3.57 Chinese law does not distinguish contractual claims from non-contractual ones to provide different jurisdiction grounds for different types of claims. Instead, Article 265 of CPL provides six jurisdiction grounds covering all contract disputes and 'other disputes over proprietary rights and interests'. It is clear that some of the grounds are closely relevant to cross-border contracts, such as the place where the contract is signed; the place where the contract is performed; and the place where the subject matter of the contract is located. Other grounds aim to facilitate the enforcement of judgments, i.e., the defendant has distrainable property in China; or based on the extended personal connections with the defendant, i.e., the defendant has its representative office in China. These grounds can be applied to all types of cases, including contracts. However, one of the jurisdictional grounds provides that Chinese courts have jurisdiction if the tort occurred in China. This ground is traditionally used in the cases of tort and barely used in contracts. The only possibility for it to be used in contract is where there is concurrent action of contract and tort and the claimant brings the action in contract.

125 For more on domicile in Chinese law, see YU Fei, *Zhongguo Guoji Sifa Lilun yu Lifa [Theory and Legislation of Chinese Private International Law]* (China Law Press, 2004) 262ff.

126 ZHANG Yan, Lun Woguo Fayuan Shewai Anjian zhong Jujue Guanxia de Jichu, The Bases for the Chinese Court to Decline Jurisdiction, MPhil thesis submitted to Shanghai Jiao Tong University in 2008.

127 Article 265 of the CPL.

A very clear characteristic of exorbitant jurisdiction in contract is that the law unduly expands jurisdiction of Chinese courts over cross-border contracts. In other words, any connections between a contractual dispute and China could generate special jurisdiction of Chinese courts. Some of these connections are weak, such as the place where the contract is signed or the place where the subject matter of the contract, if not immovable, is located. In the modern commercial world, a lot of contracts are concluded at a distance and the place where the contract is signed can be located in more than one country. Modern technology also makes it possible to negotiate contracts at a distance, and the place where a contract is signed may be fortuitous and have no substantive connections to the negotiation or the formation of the contract at all. Furthermore, jurisdiction may be taken if the subject of the contract is located in China. If a movable is the subject and it should not be located in China pursuant to the contract and the parties' intention, one party could manipulate the jurisdiction ground easily by relocating the property to China. In *Zhejiang Dongyang Plastic v. David-Standard*,[128] for example, the parties had disputes on the quality of goods subject to a sale of goods contract. The defendant was a company domiciled in the US, and the contract was signed and performed in the US. The contract did not have close connections with China, however, the Chinese court took jurisdiction based on the fact that the subject matter of the contract was located in China. **3.58**

Some of these connections may be strong, such as the place of performance. However, it can be a problem deciding the place where the contract is to be performed. First, if the parties have made an agreement, the agreed place will be the place of performance.[129] It is, however, unclear whether the parties could agree on a place which has no connections with the factual place of performance. In practice, it is very likely that the parties may nevertheless agree on such a place in order to avoid the 'practical connection' restriction for choice of court agreements.[130] For example, if the parties agree China as the place of performance, even though China has no connection with the actual performance of the contract, China may have exorbitant jurisdiction over the contractual disputes instead. The SPC has the intention to avoid this result. It clearly provides that if the contract is not factually performed and none of the parties have their domicile in the agreed place of performance, the agreed place may not have jurisdiction and the dispute should be heard in the domicile of the defendant.[131] Although it does not explicitly state what may happen if the contract was performed in a place different from the agreement, the provision **3.59**

128 SPC, (1997) Jing Zhong Zi 318.
129 2015 Opinion, Art 18, first paragraph.
130 See section III.4 above.
131 2015 Opinion, Art 18, third indent.

suggests that the SPC will refuse to permit the parties to 'create' a factitious and artificial connecting factor by agreement.

3.60 In the absence of the designated place by consent, determining the place of performance is problematic in bilateral contracts where both parties have different obligations to perform. The contract is thus performed in different places depending on which party's obligation is taken into consideration. For example, the contract provides A delivers goods to B and B pays the price. When A sues B for non-payment, should the court consider the place where A delivers goods or B pays money to be the place of performance? The characteristic obligation approach requires the court to consider that the performance, which is more important and complex and carries more risk, could demonstrate the characteristic of the contract and could distinguish this contract from other types of contracts. This approach has the advantage of providing uniform results in all cases and jurisdiction does not depend on which party brings the action. The disadvantage is that the court, in all cases, only considers the characteristic obligation and not the other obligation, even if the dispute is about the other obligation. It may grant jurisdiction to a court in the absence of substantive connections to the dispute in question.[132] The 2015 Opinion, as a result, opts for the 'obligation in question' approach. If the dispute is about the payment of money, the court will consider where the money is or should be paid; if the dispute is about other obligations, the court will consider where these obligations subject to dispute have been performed.[133]

3.61 Furthermore, even if the court uses one obligation to determine the place of performance, this place may not be easy to identify. First, the place of performance of some obligations may be a question of law, which is determined by the governing law of this matter. A typical example is the place of payment. Under Chinese law, payment takes place in the domicile of the creditor.[134] Under German law, the place of payment is the debtor's domicile.[135] Chinese law does not provide any choice of law provisions for this issue. There is no judicial precedent to apply any foreign law to determine the place of performance. In practice, Chinese law will be applied systematically to this question, as confirmed by the SPC.[136] Secondly, some obligations may be complicated and require continuous performance in more than one country. One example is international carriage of goods. The performance includes

132 For more on characteristic performance, see Ch 8, III.2 below.

133 2015 Opinion, Art 18, second indent.

134 Ibid.

135 J. Hill and A. Chong, *International Commercial Disputes* (4th ed., Hart: Oxford 2014) 156.

136 2015 Opinion, Art 18, second indent.

selecting and training the crew, uploading the goods, and managing the seaworthy vessel, all performed in the place of departure; delivering the goods, which occurs in the place of destination; and carrying and transporting the goods from the place of departure to the destination, which occurs in more than one country or on the high sea. All the tasks are important and indispensable for the complete performance of the obligation. It is difficult to determine one country of performance. Different approaches may be suggested. The first one looks at the task in dispute. For example, if the claimant sues for a failure to provide seaworthy vessels, the place of performance is the place of departure; if the defendant is sued for deviation during transport, the country where deviation occurs is the place of performance; or if the claim is about the damage during delivery, the country of destination is the place of performance. This approach, however, cannot avoid the difficulty where the place of breach cannot be determined, for example, the goods are damaged during transit and the exact place is unknown; or the place of breach is not within the territory of any country, for example, deviation occurs on the high sea. In order to avoid this difficulty, the 2015 Opinion provides that, as a general rule, the place of performance is the place where the performer of the obligation in question has its domicile.[137]

Exceptions, however, are provided for a number of contracts. First, for a contract for the transfer of immovable property, the court of the situs of the property has jurisdiction.[138] This is consistent with international practice and exclusive jurisdiction in Chinese law. The contractual dispute on the transfer of immovable property usually can hardly be distinguished from the proprietary dispute. The latter is exclusively governed in the situs of the property and so should the former. Secondly, for a contract that is performed immediately on the spot, as both parties perform their obligations fully, instantly and in the same place, the place of performance is easy to determine and should prevail in the domicile of the performer. Thirdly, lease contracts are performed in the place where the property subject to lease is located.[139] Fourthly, in e-contracts without the parties' choice of place of performance, where the performance constitutes the supply of intangible products online, it is performed in the place of the buyer. For offline performance, the place where the goods are delivered should be the place of performance.[140] There is no reason to treat the performance of e-contracts differently from traditional contracts. It is true that determining the place of supply of e-products is difficult, but the place of performance in traditional contracts is not determined as a question of fact but **3.62**

137 2015 Opinion, Art 18, second indent.

138 Ibid.

139 2015 Opinion, Art 19.

140 Ibid., Art 20.

a question of law. Legal rules are provided to presume that the contract is performed in the place of the creditor or the place of the supplier. The same rules are unchallenged by e-commerce. Furthermore, the offline performance of e-contracts has no substantive difference from performance of traditional contracts. The SPC provides two sets of rules to determine the place of performance in e-contracts and traditional contracts, which is unnecessary and may cause complexity in practice. Sixthly, different rules are provided for insurance contracts. For indemnity insurance contracts, the court of the place where the vehicle is registered, the destination of transport, or the place where the accident occurs has jurisdiction. For life insurance contracts, the court of the place where the insured has his domicile has jurisdiction.[141]

V.2 Exorbitant jurisdiction in tort

3.63 The legislation is problematic in terms of special jurisdiction in tort. Article 265 of CPL does not state it applies to tort. The jurisdiction rules therein explicitly apply to 'an action concerning a contract dispute or other disputes over proprietary rights and interests'.[142] If a tort concerns property rights and interests, such as infringement of an IP right or damage to property caused by tort, Article 265 is applicable. In *Sichuan Nanjian v. BMW*,[143] the court took jurisdiction based on the place of the wrong over a claim on monetary damages caused by deficient products. The place where the tort occurs should have jurisdiction. The place of tort could refer to both the place where the wrong is committed and the place where the damage is suffered.[144]

3.64 However, there are also torts which have nothing to do with proprietary rights and interests, such as personal injury, libel and defamation, infringement of a citizen's or a legal person's right of name and portrait.[145] A literal interpretation of Article 265 suggests that jurisdiction grounds therein are irrelevant to decide extraterritorial jurisdiction on these types of claims. If this is the correct interpretation, Chinese courts only have jurisdiction over a cross-border non-proprietary tort if the defendant has domicile within the territory of China.[146] This, of course, is inconsistent with international commercial practice in the rest of world or the legislative intention. It is thus suggested that

141 2015 Opinion, Art 21.

142 CPL, Art 241.

143 *Sichuan Nanjian v. BMW*, Sichuan Province Luzhou Municipality IPC, 28.11.2000, the citation is not available.

144 2015 Opinion, Art 24.

145 GPCL, Art 120.

146 *International Hoteliers v. Shenzhen Xindu Hotel*, Guangdong Province Shenzhen Municipality IPC, (2003) Shen Zhong Fa Min Si Chu Zi No 15.

irrespective of the literal drafting of Article 265, a Chinese court has special jurisdiction over any tort claims if tort occurs in China.[147]

As contracts, all listed jurisdiction grounds may be applied to tort. Although some grounds, such as the place where tort occurs may be more relevant and specific to tort disputes. In *Xu v. Kraus & Naimer Gesellschaft*,[148] the defendant was sued on infringement of a domain name. The Chinese court took jurisdiction based on the location of the domain name. The court held that although the domain name was intangible, it was controlled by the administrative entity that was responsible for registering and managing domain names. A domain name, thus, was deemed to be located in the place where the administrative entity was located. Allowing the court of the place where the administrative entity was located to hear disputes over domain names also helped achieve a convenient and efficient trial. Jurisdiction is not taken based on the place of tort, but on the factor in relation to 'things', i.e., the place where the subject matter is located. This is another example showing the result of providing multiple jurisdiction connecting factors to unclassified disputes. It enables the Chinese court to take jurisdiction as far as any grounds are met, even if the ground is not usually used for this type of claim. **3.65**

i. Jurisdiction on online tort

The internet challenges traditional jurisdiction rules and makes it more difficult to designate an appropriate forum for online tort. Tort committed online usually has the following characteristics. First, damage usually occurs at a distance from where the delictual activities have taken place. Secondly, damage can easily occur in multiple jurisdictions. Thirdly, the nature of the internet may spread the damage to an extent more than the wrongdoer could predict. Fourthly, the involvement of the server may cause fortuitous connections. A typical example is online defamation. A wrongdoer domiciled in Country A may publish a defamatory article online. The website is registered in Country B, hosted on a server in Country C. The article damages the reputation of the victim who has his domicile in Country D. The article is accessible and downloaded in all countries with the internet connection. Special guidance is required to determine the place of wrong and the place of damage. It is important to avoid providing jurisdiction to the country that does not have substantive connections with the dispute, to designate countries that the wrongdoer could predict and to appropriately protect the victim. **3.66**

147 *Zhejiang Dongyang Plastic, supra* n 128.

148 Fujian Province Xiamen IPC, (2006) Xia Min Shu Zi No 193.

3.67 Article 25 of the 2015 Opinion provides a succinct interpretation. It provides that the place of wrong for online tort 'includes' the place where the computer or other information equipment are located that are used to facilitate the delictual activity. The place of damage 'includes' the place where the victim has his domicile. In an earlier SPC judicial interpretation 'Provisions of the SPC on Several Issues concerning the Application of Law in Hearing Civil Dispute Cases Involving Infringement of the Right of Dissemination on Information Networks',[149] the SPC provides a similar interpretation and includes the server or computer used by the defendant to commit the tort as the place of wrong. It further provides that if the place of the wrongful action and the domicile of the defendant are hard to determine or are located abroad, the equipment where the tort content is located can be deemed as the place of wrongful action.[150] This interpretation aims to extend the court's jurisdiction and provide protection for the claimant. Reading these interpretations together, it is concluded that for online tort, the dispute can be brought in the People's Court if it is either the place of wrong or the place of damage. The place of wrong includes the place where the computer or equipment which the defendant used to commit the tort, or where the computer or equipment that hosted the tort content is located. The place of damage includes the place where the victim has its domicile.

3.68 This interpretation is incomprehensive and unrealistic. It is incomprehensive because it uses the word 'include' to provide examples of places that may be relevant. In other words, other places may still be treated as the place of tort and have jurisdiction. It is unrealistic in that it focuses on the location of the 'equipment' instead of the location of the person. The wrongdoer may choose to locate the equipment in an irrelevant country, either accidentally or on purpose to conduct forum shopping.

ii. Special jurisdiction on online infringement of IPRs

3.69 The SPC has also provided judicial interpretation to determine jurisdiction on online infringement of copyright.[151] The SPC decides that both the place where the infringing act is committed and where the defendant has his domicile have jurisdiction. The SPC further provides that the place where the tort is committed shall include places where the equipment used to carry out the accused infringing acts, such as network servers or computer terminals,

149 SPC, 'Zuigao Renmin Fayuan Guanyu Shenli Qinhai Xinxi Wangluo Chuanboquan Minshi Jiufen Anjian Shiyong Falv Ruogan Wenti de Guiding [Provisions of the SPC on Several Issues concerning the Application of Law in Hearing Civil Dispute Cases Involving Infringement of the Right of Dissemination on Information Networks]' ('2012 Regulations') Fa Shi [2012] No 20.

150 SPC, '2012 Regulations', *supra* n 149, Art 15.

151 Ibid.

etc., is located.[152] Where the place in which an infringing act is committed or in which the defendant has its domicile, is difficult to determine or is located abroad, the place of the equipment, such as a computer terminal, in which the plaintiff has found the contents of infringement may be deemed as the place where the infringing act is committed.[153]

Article 15 of the 2012 Regulations is an amended version of Article 1 of the SPC's 2006 Interpretation on Copyright Disputes over Computer Network (abolished).[154] Both give priority to the place where the defendant has its domicile, or the place where the infringement act is committed, which, in most cases, coincides with the defendant's domicile.[155] The difference is that the 2006 Interpretation only allows the claimant to sue in the place of destination if the defendant's domicile or the place where tort is committed is hard to determine. In practice, a claimant must be able to certify the identity of the defendant in order to bring an action in court. The defendant's domicile, as a result, could be determined in most cases, even if the place where the infringement act occurs cannot easily be identified. The ground that enables a claimant to sue in its own domicile, thus, applies to exceptional, if any, cases.[156] In *Edko Film v. China Telecom Changde*,[157] a non-Chinese domiciliary committed the infringement act abroad. Since the defendant's domicile was identifiable, a Chinese claimant would not be able to bring the action in a Chinese court regardless of the fact that the claimant found the existence of the infringement in China and also suffered financial damages in there. In the 2012 Regulations, the knowledge of the defendant's domicile is no longer a bar to preventing a Chinese claimant from suing in the place of destination if the defendant is domiciled abroad. The 2012 amendment is designed to include cross-border disputes in its scope. It clearly adopts the approach of protecting the claimant in cross-border online infringement of IP rights. It creates an **3.70**

152 Ibid. It is consistent with Art 25 of the 2015 Opinion, which provides that for all online torts, the place where tort is committed includes the place where the equipment used is located.

153 Ibid.

154 SPC, 'Zuigao Renmin Fayuan Guanyu Shenli Sheji Jisua ji Wangluo Zhuzuoquan Jiufen Anjian Shiyong Falv Ruogan Wenti de Jieshi [Interpretation of the SPC on Several Issues Concerning the Applicable Law in the Trial of Cases Involving Copyright Disputes over Computer Network]', Fa Shi [2006] No 11. This interpretation is abolished since this 2012 Regulations entered into force from 1 Jan 2013. See 2012 Regulations, Art 16.

155 2012 Regulations, Art 15; 2006 Interpretations, Art 1. *Beijing Sohu v. HU Kai Chang*, Zhejiang HPC, (2008) Zhe Min Gao Zhong Zi No 100.

156 In majority of cases, the courts declined jurisdiction and transferred the cases to the defendant's domicile. E.g., *Beijing Wanbo Network Information Technology v. Shenzhen Hairun Advertisement*, Beijing Municipality No 1 IPC, (2003) Yi Zhong Min Chu Zi No 9020; *Yang v. Xinhua*, Shanghai No 2 IPC, (2002) Hu Er Zhong Min Wu (Zhi) Chu Zi No 166; *Bangbang v. Chinese Online Culture Development*, Beijing No 1 IPC, (2006) Yi Zhong Min Zhong Zi No 13999; *Tianhang Yuanjing v. Chinese Online Culture Development*, Beijing No 1 IPC, (2006) Yi Min Zhong Zi No 13998.

157 *Edko Film v. China Telecom Changde*, Zhejiang Province HPC, (2008) Zhe Min Gao Zhong Zi No 169.

additional jurisdictional ground and allows the Chinese claimant to choose. It is obviously more convenient for the Chinese claimant to sue in the place of destination, which usually will be in China. Chinese courts take exorbitant jurisdiction over online infringement of IP rights.

3.71 The country of destination approach on online tort aims to prevent a foreign domiciliary from infringing IP rights acquired by a Chinese domiciliary. If the infringement is found in China, Chinese courts would take jurisdiction irrespective of the place where the infringing act is committed. Defendants may claim that this approach causes uncertainty for foreign defendants because they cannot control the reach of a website. This argument, however, is not accepted in Chinese courts. Defendants could use technology to ring-fence the area where a website can be accessed. If defendants have taken no steps to control the reach of a website and the infringement is found in China, the defendant is deemed to subject itself to any places where the website can be accessed.

3.72 One potential problem with this interpretation is that granting jurisdiction to the place where the infringement is found may be different from the place where the damage occurs, though they may be the same in most cases.[158] The two places have significant differences in that the former may be fortuitous while the latter has substantive connections to the dispute. If the claimant has habitual residence abroad and has no substantive commercial interest in China, if he is travelling in China temporarily and happens to find the infringement while personally located there, taking jurisdiction by Chinese courts is arbitrary and improper. It is suggested that the 2012 Regulation may need to be amended to reconcile it with the wording in the 2015 Opinion.

3.73 If a claimant wants to sue the defendant in the place of origin, he could choose the place of the defendant's domicile, or the place where the infringing act is committed. How could the claimant prove the location of the server of a computer terminal where the infringement act is conducted? In *Shanghai Youdu Broadband v. Beijing Wangshang Culture*,[159] the claimant used www.168ip.com, which provided IP identification services, to check the infringement website's IP address. The claimant received the information that the infringement website was located in Zhejiang province, Hangzhou city, and brought an action there. The court, however, refused to admit the evidence, claiming the www.168ip.com was not an authorized official website

158 M.A. Zhang-Kai, 'Wangluo Zhuzuoquan Anjian "Sifa Jieshi" Pingjie [Comments on Network Copyright Disputes and the "Judicial Interpretation"]', http://www.china-review.com/laf.asp?id=13321, accessed on 20.11.2011.

159 Zhejiang Province Hangzhou Municipality IPC, (2010) Zhe Hang Zhi Chu Zi No 471–1.

run by government authorities, and the website included a declaration that 'All data provided are for reference purposes. The website is not liable for the accuracy of the IP address.' Furthermore, although the website showed the contact information, which included the local telephone code of Hangzhou, the court refused to find the telephone information decisive. The evidence can be admitted if the IP address is identified through an authority, such as the Ministry of Industry and Information Technology.[160] However, if the IP address and the location of the server is notarized, the authentic instrument can be accepted by the court as the valid evidence.[161]

iii. Product liability

Product liability is a special tort which is usually complicated by the internationalization of production and distribution, and concerns conflicts between the protection of business and innovation and the protection of personal safety. Industrialization and internationalization make the production of one product include the work of various parties located in various countries, which increases the difficulty in jurisdiction. Article 26 of the 2015 Opinion provides that product liability cases can be heard in the People's Court located in the place of manufacture, the place of distribution, the place where the services are provided, the place where tort is committed, and the place where the defendant has its domicile. **3.74**

Article 26 decides internal territorial jurisdiction of Chinese courts. Should it also apply to international disputes? Although the 2015 Opinion does not state explicitly, it is suggested that Article 26 could be used as convincing evidence to interpret foreign-related product liability jurisdiction rules. In particular, it helps to interpret the place of the tort. It expands the jurisdiction of Chinese courts, and allows Chinese courts to take jurisdiction as far as any relevant place is located in China. It is an important economic strategy for Chinese courts to assume jurisdiction over cross-border product liability disputes, in order to enforce Chinese economic policy to protect Chinese industry and companies. China may have a particular interest in avoiding strict product liability rules of some countries and especially to prevent punitive damages against Chinese companies on product liability. **3.75**

160 *Guangdong Zhongkai v. China Unicom,* Beijing HPC, (2008) Gao Min Zhong Zi No 1154.

161 *Chongqing Vip v. Chinese Journals of Practical Medicine,* Beijing No 1 IPC, (2008) Yi Zhong Min Zhong Zi No 7387.

V.3 Exorbitant jurisdiction in restitution

3.76 Chinese jurisdiction rules do not classify different claims. As a result, the six grounds are equally applicable to non-contractual obligations other than tort, such as unjust enrichment. In *Liang v. Forward Machinery Industrial Co*,[162] the claimant brought an action to claim the return of money paid to the defendant under a contract that was alleged to have been formed in China but did not exist in law. The defendant was a company registered in Hong Kong and had no representative in the mainland. The claimant passed the cheque to the defendant in China. The cheque was issued in Hong Kong and paid into the defendant's account in Hong Kong. However, these facts could not persuade the Chinese court to take jurisdiction. It was held that since there was no contract, the place where the contract was signed or performed was irrelevant. However, since the defendant had distrainable property in China, the Chinese court took jurisdiction based on this ground. It shows that some Chinese courts have taken a rigid interpretation of the provision and only assert jurisdiction of restitution claims if China is the place where the defendant, the representative of the defendant or the defendant's distrainable property is located.[163] In fact, a literal interpretation of Article 265 may suggest any grounds may be relied on to grant Chinese courts jurisdiction over such claims.[164]

V.4 Jurisdiction based on the enforcement of judgments

3.77 Most connecting factors provided by Article 265 of CPL are commonly used internationally. However, the connecting factor based on the defendant's distrainable property is unusual. The distrainable property may have no connections to the dispute in question and it is hard to justify why a court has interest to hear a dispute simply because the defendant has distrainable property in this country. The only justification is to facilitate recognition and enforcement of judgments. Although this ground is unusual, it has practical value. Since many foreign judgments may not be enforced in China,[165] if the defendant's assets are only located in China, the foreign judgment creditor

---

162 *Liang v. Forward Machinery Industrial Co*, Guangdong Province Foshan IPC, (2005) Fo Zhong Fa Min Si Chu Zi No 181.

163 In *Guizhou Wengfu v. Sino Transpac Co & Universal Chartering*, Guangdong Province HPC, (2004) Yue Gao Fa Min Si Zhong Zi No 53, the court also took jurisdiction based on the location of the distrainable property of the defendant after the court classified the dispute as unjust enrichment.

164 As a result, some non-contractual obligations arise out of matters relating to contracts, and some arise out of matters relating to tort, an ordinary understanding may suggest the Chinese court could take jurisdiction based on the place relating to contract or tort.

165 See Ch 6 for more discussion on enforcement of foreign judgments in China. In general, in the absence of treaty obligations, China will only enforce foreign judgments based on *de facto* reciprocity.

may have to bring a fresh action in China anyway to enforce its rights. Chinese courts will take jurisdiction at the enforcement stage, and the jurisdiction is indirectly based on the place of the defendant's disposable assets. Granting this extra jurisdictional ground would help prevent concurrent proceedings and save costs. This jurisdiction ground is thus important in China, given the relatively restrictive law in enforcing foreign judgments.[166]

VI. CONCLUSION

It should be recognized that Chinese jurisdiction rules have been gradually improved over the past few decades. However, there is still room for further improvement. The current positive jurisdiction rules show the following characteristics, to which the legislators need to pay more attention. **3.78**

First, there is a general trend towards expanding the jurisdiction of Chinese courts over international civil and commercial cases. This is evidenced by the broad scope of exclusive jurisdiction, the unclear way of determining the exclusivity of jurisdiction clauses, the compulsory nature of any jurisdiction clauses choosing a Chinese court, the uncertain derogation effect provided to the foreign jurisdiction clause, the broad multiple jurisdiction grounds for Chinese courts to assert exorbitant jurisdiction and the unusual connecting factors based on the defendant's disposable assets. Extending jurisdiction shows China's intention to protect its jurisdictional sovereignty. Chinese courts, thus, may more frequently face a positive conflict of jurisdiction, and compete for jurisdiction with foreign courts. It may also unduly increase the workload of Chinese courts and cost extra public resources. Given the relatively undeveloped rules on declining jurisdiction,[167] the extended grounds to assert jurisdiction are inappropriate. **3.79**

Secondly, legislative techniques need improvement. The CPL still fails to clarify the relationship between domestic jurisdiction rules and international ones. It is hard to decide whether a jurisdiction rule listed for domestic cases should be used in foreign-related cases. Special jurisdiction rules specifically provided for international cases are nevertheless too simple and incomprehensive. There are multiple legal sources, which may confuse practitioners and commercial participants, especially when they provide inconsistent rules. Article 265 on exorbitant jurisdiction is problematic in particular. Multiple territorial jurisdiction grounds are provided for all types of claims in the **3.80**

166 See Ch 6 below.
167 See Ch 4 below.

absence of classification. It is hard to judge if all grounds are applicable to all claims no matter how far-reaching the application may be.[168]

3.81 Thirdly, the rules on jurisdiction agreements need modernization. The restrictive validity requirements should be relaxed. In particular, the legislators should consider whether it is necessary, in the modern commercial world, to require 'practical connections' with the chosen court. It is also necessary to clarify how to decide the exclusivity of a jurisdiction clause and which law should be applied to decide the existence and validity of a jurisdiction clause. The most important issue that needs to be addressed is the clarification of the derogation effect of a foreign jurisdiction clause, which will be discussed in more detail in the next chapter.

3.82 It is, however, necessary to note that jurisdiction rules may not be improved alone. Reform and modernization cannot be done without considering the general legal background and the overall international litigation and enforcement system. Some of the above-mentioned weaknesses are affected by the rules in enforcement of foreign judgments. Since most foreign judgments cannot be easily recognized or enforced in China, keeping some weak aspects of jurisdiction rules may be inevitable. For example, due to the difficulty in enforcing foreign judgments, China adopts the exorbitant jurisdiction based on the defendant's assets;[169] since it is hard to enforce foreign judgment in China even if the parties may have chosen the foreign court, Chinese law may not be able to give compulsory derogation effects to a foreign exclusive jurisdiction clauses.[170] Modernizing jurisdiction rules depends on modernizing the whole conflicts system.

---

168 Such as applying the place of tort for contract claims, or the *situs* jurisdiction to tort disputes.

169 See V.4 above.

170 For more details, see Ch 4 below.

4

DECLINING JURISDICTION IN CHINESE COURTS

I. INTRODUCTION

The rules of positive jurisdiction grant jurisdiction to a particular country, designed to define and exercise national judicial sovereignty; to express national interest to adjudicate cross-border disputes; to enforce the extra-territorial policy of a country; and to protect the right of its citizens. Negative jurisdiction requires a court not to take jurisdiction, even if it is competent, which reflects other policies, including procedural efficiency, the ends of justice and international comity. **4.01**

Negative jurisdiction in Chinese law is undeveloped. This is mainly because Chinese authorities, for historic reasons,[1] place more emphasis on protecting judicial sovereignty. Judicial sovereignty takes priority over trial efficiency and international comity and the Civil Procedure Law (CPL) uses affirmative terms to make jurisdiction of Chinese courts compulsory. Article 123 of CPL **4.02**

1 See Ch 1 in general.

provides that: 'The people's court *must* entertain the lawsuits filed in conformity with the provisions of Article 119 of this Law …' Article 119 provides four conditions for a court to assert jurisdiction, namely a competent plaintiff, a definite defendant, a specific claim and the existence of jurisdiction.[2] These two articles suggest that once the four elements are satisfied, the court must hear the case unless the law explicitly provides otherwise.

4.03 However, it does not mean a Chinese court would never decline the jurisdiction granted to it by the positive jurisdiction rules. Jurisdiction may be declined in certain circumstances, including: the existence of a valid arbitration agreement; the existence of a valid foreign jurisdiction clause; the existence of other treaty obligations; and where the Chinese-style *forum non conveniens* comes into play.

II. PARALLEL PROCEEDINGS

4.04 Parallel proceedings means that the same actions between the same parties are heard in more than one forum. Parallel proceedings waste public funds, duplicate litigation costs, encourage abuse of process, and may result in irreconcilable judgments. From the perspective of individual interests, parallel proceedings should be avoided in order to improve efficiency and finality of cross-border litigation. From the perspective of the international community, parallel proceedings should be prevented in order to improve international cooperation and comity.

4.05 Parallel proceedings are handled through three measures. The first one is the *lis pendens* rule, which provides that in a case of parallel proceedings the second seized court should stay jurisdiction in favour of the first seized court. It is strictly based on a 'first-come-first-served' basis.[3] However, individual countries may be reluctant to adopt this rule in the absence of any judicial cooperation or mutual agreement with other countries. If a country adopts the *lis pendens* rule unilaterally and other countries do not adopt the similar rule, it may provide priority to the jurisdictional power of other countries and indirectly encourage avoidance of domestic jurisdiction by suing earlier in

2 Article 119 of the CPL provides:

> (1) the plaintiff must be a citizen, legal person or any other organization that has a direct interest in the case; (2) there must be a definite defendant; (3) there must be specific claim or claims, facts, and cause or causes for the suit; and (4) the suit must be within the scope of acceptance for civil actions by the people's courts and under the jurisdiction of the people's court where the suit is entertained.

3 E.g., Art 29 of the Brussels I Recast.

other fora. As a result, the *lis pendens* rule is usually only effectively implemented between countries with judicial cooperation and mutual respects, such as Member States of the European Union.

The second measure is to consider whether parallel proceedings may cause injustice in individual proceedings and whether staying jurisdiction in such cases may help to achieve the ends of justice. The existence of parallel proceedings is not decisive but just one factor in exercising discretion. Parallel proceedings may increase litigation costs but this does not necessarily suggest that the local court, instead of the foreign court, should stay jurisdiction. Justice may be done if the local court continues jurisdiction in cases where the foreign court is inappropriate and inconvenient. This approach is adopted in some common law countries as part of the doctrine of *forum non conveniens*.[4] Because the implementation of this approach depends on the competence of judges in exercising discretion and it may lead to uncertainty, it is not a measure adopted universally. **4.06**

The third measure is not to take any particular action to deal with parallel proceedings. Although parallel proceedings are problematic, no individual states should give up their jurisdictional power in favour of another sovereign state in the absence of treaty obligations. The difficulty caused by irreconcilable judgments can be handled at the enforcement stage. **4.07**

The third approach is adopted in China. The existence of parallel proceedings is not one of the major concerns within Chinese jurisdiction rules. Where both Chinese and foreign courts have jurisdiction and one party sues in the foreign court and another in China, the Chinese court could hear the case. If the Chinese court decides to take jurisdiction, the Chinese court will not recognize or enforce the foreign judgment, unless an international treaty to which both countries are parties provides differently.[5] This interpretation was first given in the 1992 Opinion, repeatedly confirmed by the SPC, and applied in a number of cases.[6] **4.08**

---

4 P. Rogerson, *Collier's Conflict of Laws* (4th ed., CUP 2013) 164–86.

5 2015 Opinion, Art 533, SPC, 'Zuigao Renmin Fayuan Guanyu Shiyong "Zhonghua Renmin Gongheguo Minshi Susongfa" de Jieshi [Interpretation of the SPC on the Application of the PRC Civil Procedure Law]' ('2015 Opinion'), Fa Shi [2015] No 5. The same interpretation was adopted in the SPC, 1992 Opinion, Art 306 and was followed in the Guangdong Province HPC, 'Guiding Opinions on Some Issues on Foreign-Related Commercial Trial', Yue Gao Fa Fa [2004] No 32, s1.10.

6 SPC, 'Zuigao Renmin Fayuan Guanyu Guanyu Shiyong "Zhonghua Renmin Gongheguo Minshi Susongfa" Ruogan Wenti de Yijian (Shixiao) [Opinion on several Questions in the Implementation of the PRC Civil Procedure Act (Abolished)]' ('1992 Opinion'), Fa Fa [1992] 22, Art 306. *Shanghai Saifeng International Trade Co Ltd v. Changzhou Branch of China Industrial and Commercial Bank*, Jiangsu Province Changzhou Municipality IPC, (2006) Su Min San Li Zhong Zi No 26; *Jiangmen Xinhua Paper Mill v. HK Tak Lee*

4.09 Chinese courts, thus, could take jurisdiction irrespective of the existence of concurrent proceedings. In *Shanghai Saifeng International Trade Co Ltd v. Changzhou Branch of China Industrial and Commercial Bank,*[7] a dispute arising between the claimant, a Chinese company, and the co-defendants, a Chinese bank and an Indian bank. The claimant provided the equipment to an Indian importer and required the first defendant Changzhou CICB to act as its agent to collect the payment and present the documents to the buyer in exchange. The first defendant forwarded the documents to the second defendant, the Indian bank, and instructed the latter to collect the debt. The Indian importer paid part of the price but the banks presented all the documents. The Chinese company sued two banks for loss and damage in China. The Indian bank challenged jurisdiction claiming that the dispute between the Indian importer, the claimant, and the two defendants has already been brought to the Indian court and the Chinese court should decline jurisdiction on the parallel proceedings. The trial court, however, took jurisdiction, recognizing that no *lis pendens* rule exits in Chinese law.[8] Chinese courts take jurisdiction over not only the same matter pending in the other forum, but also cases that have received final judgments in other countries, unless the foreign judgments have already been recognized in China. In *Jiangmen Xinhua Paper Mill v. Tak Lee Metal & Paper Co,*[9] the claimant sued the defendants for recovery of debts. Before the case was brought to the Jiangmen Municipality IPC, the claimant had brought the action in Hong Kong HPC, and received the judgment ordering the defendant to pay HKD two million. When the defendant failed to enforce the order, the claimant brought a fresh action in Jiangmen IPC. The Chinese court decided to hear the case and decided that it was not bound by the judgment of the foreign court. The court then moved to make a judgment different from the judgment of the Hong Kong court.

Metals & Paper, Guangdong HPC, (1999) Yue Fa Jing Er Zhong Zi No 322. SPC, 'Dierci Quanuo Shewai Shangshi Haishi Shenpan gongzuo Huiyi Jiyao [Summary of the Second National Conference on the Adjudication of Commercial and Maritime Cases with Foreign Elements]' ('2005 Summary'), Fa Fa [2005] No 26, Art 10.

7 *Shanghai Saifeng International Trade,* ibid.

8 Ibid.

9 Guangdong Province HPC, (1999) Yue Fa Jing Er Zhong Zi No 322.

III. EXISTENCE OF ARBITRATION AGREEMENTS

Although the language of CPL suggests that it is compulsory for a Chinese court to take jurisdiction, limited exceptions to avoid the compulsory nature of jurisdiction are laid down by Article 124 of CPL.[10] Article 124(2) of CPL expressly provides exception to the compulsory jurisdiction rules, which provides: **4.10**

> If, according to the law, both parties have on a voluntary basis reached a written agreement to submit their contract dispute to an arbitral organ for arbitration, they may not institute legal proceedings in a people's court. The people's court shall advise the plaintiff to apply to the arbitral institution for arbitration.

Furthermore, Article 271 of CPL provides that: **4.11**

> In the case of a dispute arising from the foreign economic, trade, transport or maritime activities, if the parties have had an arbitration clause in the contract concerned or have subsequently reached a written arbitration agreement stipulating the submission of the dispute for arbitration to an arbitral institution in the People's Republic of China handling cases involving foreign element, or to any other arbitral body, they may not bring an action in a people's court.
>
> If the parties have not had an arbitration clause in the contract concerned or have not subsequently reached a written arbitration agreement, they may bring an action in a people's court.

Article 215 of the 2015 Opinion of the SPC also provides that: **4.12**

> [W]ere the parties concluded an arbitration clause in the written contract, or entered into an arbitration agreement in writing after the dispute had arisen, if one party brings the dispute to the people's court, the court should advise the claimant to bring the dispute to the arbitral tribunal. If the claimant insists in suing in the court, the court should rule to decline jurisdiction, unless the arbitration clause or agreement is invalid, ineffective, or ambiguous and impossible to operate.

10 Exceptions include a lawsuit within the scope of administrative actions; both parties have on a voluntary basis reached a written agreement to submit their contract dispute for arbitration; disputes shall be dealt with by other organs; cases that are not under jurisdiction of the trial court in breach of internal allocation of jurisdiction; cases in which a judgment or order has already taken legal effect; an action that may not be filed within a specified period according to the law; a divorce case in which a judgment has been made disallowing the divorce, or in which both parties have become reconciled after conciliation, or in a case concerning adoptive relationship in which a judgment has been made or conciliation has been successfully conducted to maintain the adoptive relationship; and the plaintiff files a suit again within six months in the absence of any new developments or new reasons. CPL, Art 124.

4.13 In addition, Article 5 of the Arbitration Law provides:[11]

> If the parties have concluded an arbitration agreement and one party institutes an action in a people's court, the people's court shall not accept the case, unless the arbitration agreement is null and void.

4.14 Chinese legislation and judicial interpretation consistently protect the enforceability and effectiveness of an arbitration agreement. China accepts that the contractual parties, by entering into an arbitration agreement, could effectively exclude jurisdiction of a competent Chinese court. If one of the parties brings the action to the Chinese court, the court must, as a question of law, decline jurisdiction,[12] unless: (1) the arbitration clause does not exist or is invalid; or (2) the other party submits to the Chinese court.

III.1 The arbitration clause is invalid

4.15 The meaning of 'validity' is very broad and includes the formal and material requirement; existence; incorporation; clarity and interpretation of an agreement; the arbitrability of the subject matter; and the capacity of the parties to conclude the agreement.

4.16 The first issue that needs to be decided is whether a Chinese court has jurisdiction to decide the validity of an arbitration clause or if the preliminary matter relating to an arbitration clause should be decided exclusively by the arbitral tribunal chosen by the parties. In China, both the arbitral tribunal and the court have jurisdiction to decide the validity of an arbitration agreement.[13] It is thus completely up to the applicant to decide whether or not to bring the challenge in the court or arbitration commission. If raising the challenge in the court the applicant does not need to bring an independent action on the validity of the arbitration agreement. What the applicant could do is to bring the dispute subject to arbitration directly to the court for judgment. The court should then, by its own motion, decide whether the arbitration agreement is valid.

---

11 Zhonghua Renmin Gongheguo Zhongcai Fa [PRC Arbitration Law 1994].

12 SPC, 'Zuigao Renmin Fayuan Guanyu Dingyou Zhongcai Tiaokuan de Hetong Yifang Dangshiren Bu Chuting Yingsu Ying Ruhe Chuli de Fuhan [Re how to deal with cases where one party of a contract including an arbitration clause does not enter an appearance or make a defence]', [2008] Min Si Ta Zi No 3; *Action Construction Equipment v. Pheaton Shipping*, Shanghai Maritime Court, (2009) Hu Hai Fa Shang Chu Zi No 979; *Coast to Coast Building Supply LLC v. Jiangsu International Economic-Technology Cooperation,* Jiangsu Province HPC, (2008) Ning Min Wu Chu Zi No 93.

13 Arbitration Law, Art 20.

What if one party requests the arbitration commission to make a decision while another applies to the court for a ruling? Where concurrent proceedings on the validity of an arbitration clause are brought to the tribunal and the court respectively, Chinese Arbitration Law requires priority to be given to the court.[14] The court's decision on the validity of an arbitration agreement is final and can only be repealed on appeal, while an arbitral tribunal's decision is not final and can be repealed by courts when the party applies to revoke the award, or not to enforce the award. However, this approach could encourage a party to hamper the arbitration procedure by bringing the dispute to the court. In these circumstances, the arbitration procedure must be stayed until the court makes a decision. Even if the court eventually refers the parties to arbitration, there will be delays. **4.17**

A Chinese court does not have jurisdiction to decide the validity of an arbitral agreement at any time. The challenge of an arbitration clause must be raised prior to the first hearing of an arbitral tribunal.[15] If the party did not submit the challenge in time and applied to the Chinese court later, the court should refuse to hear the case.[16] The time restriction is justified by the following considerations. First, if the opposing party fails to challenge the validity of an arbitration agreement before the first hearing, the party is deemed to have impliedly accepted the validity of the agreement and is estoppled from challenging it at a later stage.[17] Secondly, it prevents a party from abusing procedure by challenging the validity of an arbitration clause after realizing, during the arbitration proceedings, that it may not get an award in its favour. Thirdly, it protects the efficiency of arbitration and prevents unnecessary costs and delays.[18] **4.18**

Furthermore, the power of a Chinese court to review the validity of an arbitration agreement at the trial stage is if the decision on the same issue has **4.19**

14 Ibid.

15 Ibid. This applies to the review of the validity of an arbitration agreement in both courts and tribunals. SPC, '*Re Request for Instruction on Revoking CIETAC Award* [2008] Zhongguo Maozhong Jing Cai Zi No 0044', 18.03.2009, Document number is not available; *Re Request for Instruction on Revoking Arbitral Award on Korea Taisei G-3 Changchun Yuanda*, [2008] Min Si Ta Zi No 28 (the applicant challenged the arbitration agreement during the first hearing).

16 SPC, 'Zuigao Renmin Fayuan Guanyu Shiyong "Zhonghua Renmin Gongheguo Zhongcaifa" Ruogan Wenti de Jieshi [Interpretation of the SPC concerning Some Issues on Application of the Arbitration Law of the People's Republic of China]' ('2006 Arbitration Law Interpretation'), Fa Shi [2006] No 7, Art 13.

17 *JIN Chongyang v. WANG Leyi*, Henan Province Jiaozhou Municipality IPC, (2010) Jiao Min Yi Chu Zi No 6.

18 LIU Jia-Liang, 'Shixian Minshi Susongfa Quanmian Xiugai de Lingyizhong Shijiao—"Zhongcaifa Jieshi" Pingjia [Complete Revision of Civil Procedure Law—Assessment of the Interpretation of Arbitration Law]', (2008) *Journal of Shandong Police College* 29.

already been made by the arbitral institution.[19] It prevents the applicant from bringing the same matter repeatedly to the arbitration commission and the court. If the applicant fails in his application to invalidate the arbitration agreement in a tribunal, he may take a second chance to sue in court, which causes delay, extra costs, procedural inefficiency and is unfair to the other party. However, this rule does not have much value in practice. Even if the applicant is barred from bringing the same challenge to the court at the trial stage, the applicant can do so after the tribunal gives the award by applying to the court to revoke the award or refusing the recognition and enforcement of such an award. The court nevertheless will take jurisdiction to decide the validity of the arbitration agreement regardless of the pre-existing tribunal ruling.

III.2 Internal report and review procedure

4.20 In order to prevent Chinese local courts from competing with arbitration institutions in taking jurisdiction and unreasonably expending that jurisdiction, the SPC establishes the internal report and review procedure in cross-border cases.[20] If an IPC decides to take jurisdiction of any cross-border disputes subject to an arbitration clause based on the reason that the clause is invalid or unenforceable, the court must stay the proceedings and refer the decision to the HPC for a review. If the HPC affirms the decision, the HPC should then refer the case for the final approval of the SPC. Only after the SPC approves that jurisdiction has been properly taken can the court continue the proceedings.[21] A local court cannot take jurisdiction in cases with an arbitration clause, without seeking the approval of the SPC.[22]

4.21 The internal report and review procedure was established against the background of many Chinese local courts not respecting party autonomy and tending to take excessive jurisdiction over disputes that should have been

19 SPC, 2006 Arbitration Law Interpretation, Art 13.

20 SPC, 'Zuigao Renmin Fayuan Guanyu Renmin Fayuan Chuli yu Shewai hongcai ji Waiguo Zhongcai Shixiang Youguan Wenti de Tongzhi [Notice Regarding Several Issues Relating to the People's Courts' Handling of Foreign-related and Foreign Arbitration Matters]', Fa Fa [1995] 18 *Re Dalian Branch of Pin An of China, the Plaintiff, and Zhong Yuan Shipping, Guangzhou Ocean Shipping, the defendants*, [2006] Min Si Ta Zi No 49, 9.

21 Ibid. Art 1. This is restated by Shanghai Municipality HPC Trial Committee, "Guanyu Zhixing 'Zhonghua Renmin Gongheguo Zhongcaifa" Ruogan Wenti de Chuli Yijian [Opinions on Several Issues Relating to the Execution of "Arbitration Law of the People's Republic of China"]', published on 03.01.2001, Art 8(2).

22 *Liberia Power Shipping v. China Chongqing Xinfu Food*, [2006] Min Si Ta Zi No 26; *Re the Validity of an Arbitration Agreement in CECT and Korea Mobile, Shanghai Ausheng Investment Dispute on Jurisdiction in Joint Venture Contract*, [2006] Min Si Ta Zi No 19.

submitted to arbitration.[23] In practice, the SPC has refused approval of local courts' invalidating arbitration clauses in a number of cases, including the wrongful application of Chinese law without considering choice of law rules,[24] failure to prove the foreign law,[25] confusion over the applicable law to the main contract and over that of the arbitration clause,[26] and where wrongful decisions were made by misinterpretation of applicable law, especially foreign law, in deciding the validity of an arbitration agreement.[27]

Although the purpose of the internal report and review procedure is to ensure the local courts will not take excessive jurisdiction or unreasonably compete with arbitration institutions on jurisdiction, the practical effect of the procedure is doubtful. First, the review can only be generated by the local court. If the local court does not refer the case, the HPC and the SPC will not voluntarily scrutinize the local court's jurisdiction. Some local courts do not follow the procedure. After they have made an order that the arbitration clause is invalid they immediately accept jurisdiction. The only remedy for the resisting party is to appeal the order to the higher court.[28] For example, in *Martin Yale International GmbH v. Shanghai Zengma*,[29] the Shanghai Municipality No 1 IPC ruled that the arbitration clause was invalid and directly made an order to accept jurisdiction without starting the report procedure. The losing party thus had to appeal to the HPC to have the order revoked.[30] The HPC approved the appeal by ruling the arbitration agreement valid and referring the parties to the arbitration tribunal as agreed in their contracts. Had the IPC followed the report procedure by referring the case to the HPC, the HPC would have recommended that the IPC decline jurisdiction. The same result can be reached by both appeal and the report and review procedure. However, generally speaking, the internal report and review procedure should be easier and cheaper for the parties.[31] On the other hand, if the HPC dismisses the appeal, since there is only one chance for appeal against an order on jurisdiction, the resisting party loses its chance for remedy and has to be subject to the court's jurisdiction. The report-and-review procedure, however, provides a maximum of two review chances by HPC and SPC respectively. **4.22**

---

23 DU Huanfang, 'Zhongguo Fayuan Shewai Guanxiaquan Shizheng Yanjiu [Empirical Study of Extra-territorial Jurisdiction of Chinese Courts]' (2007) 2 Faxuejia [Jurist] 152, 159.

24 *CECT and Korea Mobile*, *supra* n 23.

25 Ibid.

26 *Re the Request for Instruction about the Arbitration Clause Validity between Zhangjiagang Electro and Best-Better Worldwide Ltd*, [2006] Min Si Ta Zi No 1.

27 *Chengdu Qicai v. Chuangshi Fashion*, SPC, [2007] Min Si Ta Zi No 16.

28 CPL, Art 175.

29 (2005) Hu Yi Zhong Min Wu (Shang) Chu Zi No 151.

30 Shanghai Municipality HPC, (2005) Hu Gao Min Si (Shang) Zhong Zi No 65. See also *Ningxia Hebin Minzhu Electric Power v. HK Qilong Industrial*, Ningxia HPC, (2004) Ning Min Zhong Zhi Zi No 4.

31 DU Huanfang, *supra* n 24, 159.

4.23 Secondly, the special procedure applies only where a court of first instance accepts jurisdiction by ruling the arbitration clause invalid. It does not apply where the applicant only seeks a negative declaration. In *P & O Nedlloyd v. Wah Hing Seafreight*,[32] the applicant applied to the court to decide the validity of an arbitration clause and the court ordered negatively. This court did not report the order to the higher court for review, because the court had only made a negative declaration order instead of taking jurisdiction based on the ruling. If the court that makes the declaration does not take jurisdiction itself, it would effectively prevent the other party from bringing the dispute to the arbitration tribunal, which would usually take the court order into consideration. Furthermore, even if the tribunal takes jurisdiction regardless of the order, the existence of the order will serve as a shield to prevent the arbitral award from being recognized and enforced in courts.[33] Finally, usually more than one court has jurisdiction to hear a dispute. The claimant may seek declaratory relief in one court while suing the defendant in another court. The court seized to take jurisdiction to hear the dispute may apply the ruling of the other court and directly take jurisdiction. It is uncertain under current practice whether the report and review procedure applies to this situation but a strict literal interpretation probably means it does not. Since the application of the report and review procedure is narrow, this procedure is easily evaded by manipulating the civil procedure system.

4.24 Thirdly, the internal report and review procedure increases the case load of the HPCs and SPC and causes delay in judicial proceedings. Sometimes, the local IPC has made the right decision, but the proceedings cannot continue until the decision is approved by the HPC and SPC, which can take months. For example, in *Pacific Insurance v. Sunglide Maritime*, the Wuhan Maritime Court held the arbitration clause invalid and reported the case to the Hubei HPC on 1 July 2008; the Hubei HPC affirmed the decision and reported it to the SPC on 10 September 2008;[34] and the SPC finally approved jurisdiction on 24 February 2009.[35] The total procedure took around eight months simply to confirm the right ruling. Research on other cases where jurisdiction is approved by the SPC shows that the length between the report from the local

32 Guangzhou Maritime Court, (2000) Guang Hai Fa Shi Zi No 037.

33 Chinese judges can declare an arbitration clause invalid under the law agreed by the parties to the arbitration clause, failing any choice, the law of the place where the arbitration award is made or, without which the *lex fori*. The first two applicable law options are identical with the New York Convention, Art V.1(a) of which permits a court to refuse to recognize or enforce an arbitral award if the agreement is valid under the applicable law.

34 Hubei HPC, E Gao Fa [2008] No 393.

35 *Shanghai Branch of China Pacific Property Insurance Co Ltd (Plaintiff) v. Sunglide Maritime Ltd., Ocean Freighters Ltd. and the United Kingdom Mutual Steam Ship Assurance Association (Bermuda) Limited (Defendants)*, [2008] Min Si Ta Zi No 50.

HPC to the SPC and the final decision made by the SPC usually takes three to six months,[36] but in exceptional cases, the delay could be as long as a year. For example, in *Re the Request for Instruction about the Arbitration Clause Validity between Zhangjiagang Electro and Best-Better Worldwide Ltd*,[37] the SPC rejected Jiangsu HPC's decision and refused the local IPC its jurisdiction. It, however, took the SPC 15 months to reach the decision.[38] Comparatively, appeal might take less time, because under the civil procedure law, the losing party is only entitled to one appeal against the court order on jurisdiction. In *Tipco Asphalt v. Islamic Republic of Iran Shipping*,[39] the appeal on the order to take jurisdiction and the invalidity of an arbitration clause took only about one month. Of course, if the application of foreign law is involved, the procedure is likely to take much longer. For example, the appeal in *Samsung v. Shanghai Jinguang* took 17 months, because the applicable law to the arbitration agreement was the law of Singapore.[40] Ironically, the court of first instance that has made the right decision on the validity of an arbitration clause usually is more willing to follow the report and review procedure by referring the case to the higher court and to stay jurisdiction voluntarily during the review procedure. Those courts that have a hostile attitude towards arbitration and intend to compete with arbitration for jurisdiction usually do not commence the internal report and review procedure.

III.3 The other party submits to the Chinese court

Where a party brings an action in the Chinese court in breach of an arbitration agreement and the other party enters an appearance to make a defence on a substantive issue, the Chinese court has jurisdiction. In such a case, there is no necessity for the court to consider the validity of the arbitration clause. The defendant who submits to the court is deemed to agree to the abandonment of **4.25**

---

36 *Re Arbitration Clause Validity in the Dispute over Transfer Contract for Land-Use Rights in the Case of Hong Kong Ace Medical Packaging Co., Ltd. v. Dongguan Metal Product Factory Ltd. and Virgin Islands New Guanyu Industrial Co Ltd,* [2007] Min Si Ta Zi No 45 (Guangdong HPC reported on 19.11.2007; SPC responded on 5.4.2008); *RENT CORPORATION v. Complant Ningbo Imp. & Exp. Co., Ltd. and Dongguan Jianhua Construction Machinery Co., Ltd.*, [2008] Min Si Ta Zi No 4 (Guangdong HPC reported on 4.12.2007; SPC responded on 18.3.2008); *Re Arbitration Clause Validity in the Dispute Over Application for Company Dissolution in the Case of Tianjin Municipality Heping District Economic & Trade Commission v. Tianjin Goubuli Steamed Bun Frozen Foods Co Ltd and Hong Kong Haoping Development Co Ltd,* [2007] Min Si Ta Zi No 37 (three months); *China Beijing Ailisheng Export and Import Ltd v. Japan Sunglide Trading Ltd,* [2007] Min Si Ta Zi No 14 (Hubei HPC reported on 17.5.2007; SPC responded on 29.9.2007); *Re Arbitration Clause Validity in the Distribution Contract between Shenzhen Huahan Trade and Development Ltd and Xiongpai Far East Chemical Corporation,* [2005] Min Si Ta Zi No 41 (Guangdong HPC reported on 8.7.2005; SPC responded on 13.9.2005).

37 [2006] Min Si Ta Zi No 1.

38 One reason for the excessive delay was probably the application of foreign law to the arbitration clause.

39 Shanghai Municipality HPC, (2003) Hu Gao Min Si (Hai) Zhong No 133.

40 Shanghai HPC, (2001) Hu Gao Min Zhong Zi No 245.

their arbitration clause. Once the arbitration clause has been abandoned impliedly by the party's submission, neither party can rely on it to commence arbitration proceedings. In the SPC's Judicial Direction in *Tianyu Passenger and Freight Transport v. Xiamen Wanlishi*,[41] the consignor brought the court action in breach of a valid arbitration agreement concluded in the parties' carriage contract and the carrier entered an appearance in court to make a substantive defence. The court accepted jurisdiction based on the defendant's submission. However, when the court later rejected the suit, based on the fact that the plaintiff was an unqualified subject, the plaintiff lost the opportunity to bring the dispute in arbitration.

4.26 Could the other party submit to the court impliedly? For example, if the party, after being properly served failed to respond to the action or make his defence. Some defendants believe that the court should not take jurisdiction because of the existence of an arbitration agreement and, therefore, do not intend to enter an appearance. This is most likely to happen to a defendant not domiciled in China. It is suggested by the SPC that only an active submission has the legal effect of abolishing arbitration agreements. If the defendant does not appear to the court to challenge jurisdiction the court cannot presume the defendant accepts the court's jurisdiction; the court should decline jurisdiction unless it finds the arbitration clause invalid.[42]

III.4 Changing decision on jurisdiction

4.27 In many cases, the claimant brings the dispute subject to an arbitration clause directly to the court without disclosing the existence of such a clause. The court thus will accept jurisdiction. However, if the other party subsequently challenges jurisdiction by submitting the arbitration clause prior to the first hearing, the court shall decline jurisdiction unless the arbitration clause is null and void.[43]

4.28 However, a strict time requirement for bringing the challenge is placed on the defendant. If the defendant does not raise an objection prior to the first hearing, he is deemed to have renounced the arbitration clause and the court will continue to try the case.[44] The reason for this requirement is to encourage

41 *Re Arbitration Clause Validity between Tianyu Passenger and Freight Transport and Xiamen Wanlishi*, [2006] Min Si Ta Zi No 40.

42 SPC, 'Guanyu Dingyou Zhongcai Tiaokuan de Hetong Yifang Dangshiren Buchuting Yingsu Yinggai Ruhe Chuli de Fuhan [Re how to deal with cases where one party of a contract including an arbitration clause does not enter an appearance or make a defence]', [2008] Min Si Ta Zi No 3.

43 Arbitration Law, Art 26.

44 Ibid.

the party who intends to challenge jurisdiction to act promptly. If the party raises objection after a few hearings and after the submission of essential evidence and presence of witnesses, it causes delays, extra cost, and is a waste of resources.

IV. EXISTENCE OF A FOREIGN JURISDICTION CLAUSE

IV.1 Status quo

Chinese legislation and judicial interpretation have not provided clear guidance demanding that a Chinese court decline jurisdiction in favour of a valid exclusive jurisdiction clause choosing a foreign court. In its 'Summary of the Second National Conference on the Adjudication of Commercial and Maritime Cases with Foreign Elements' ('2005 Summary'), the SPC says an exclusive choice of court agreement choosing a foreign court could not exclude an otherwise competent Chinese court its jurisdiction.[45] A Chinese court is not obliged to decline jurisdiction even when faced with a valid exclusive jurisdiction clause choosing a foreign court. The practice in Chinese courts has demonstrated uncertainty and diversity.[46] In practice, many Chinese courts recognize the importance of party autonomy and voluntarily decline jurisdiction to give effect to the parties' intentions.[47] Some courts, however, still have valid concerns which make them reluctant to stay jurisdiction in favour of the chosen foreign court. Some courts do not provide any reasons or justification but others justify their decision by considering the difficulties of enforcing foreign judgments in China.[48] As a result, the effect of a foreign jurisdiction clause in China is uncertain. The existence of a valid jurisdiction clause **4.29**

45 SPC, 'Zuigao Renmin Fayuan, "Di Er Ci Quanguo Shewai Shangshi Haishi Shenpan Gongzuo Huiyi Jiyao" [Summary of the Second National Conference on the Adjudication of Commercial and Maritime Cases with Foreign Elements]', Fa Fa [2005] No 26, Art 12.

46 Chinese courts refused to decline jurisdiction in favour of a foreign choice of court agreement in *Kwok & Yih Law Firm v. Xiamen Huayang Color Printing Co*, Xiamen Municipality IPC, 2003.08.13, the case number is not available, but the judgment is accessible from http://www.lawinfochina.com/display.aspx?lib=case&id=284, or http://www.coolaw.com.cn/info/3f0427deba31a4aa2ad3b291333562ec (accessed on 10 Oct 2013); *NKK (Japan) v. Beijing Zhuangsheng*, Beijing Municipality HPC, (2008) Gao Min Zhong Zi No 919. In other cases, Chinese courts have enforced choice of court agreements by declining jurisdiction in *Lai v. ABN AMRO Bank*, Shanghai Municipality HPC, (2010) Hu Gao Min Wu (Shang) Zhong Zi No 49' *Yacheng Automobile Parts v. Huifeng*, Jiangsu Province Wuxi Municipality IPC, (2006) Xi Min San Chu Zi No 23; *Sojitz v. Xiao*, Shanghai Municipality HPC, (2004) Hu Gao Min San (Zhi) Zhong Zi No 72; *Wenzhou Foreign Trade Co of Light Article Industry v. CMA (France)* Fujian HPC, available at www.chinalawinfo.com, reference no CLI.C.21767; *Junichirou Watanabe v. Culture & Art Press*, Shanghai Municipality No 1 IPC, (2008) No 210.

47 *Lai v. ABN AMRO Bank*; *Yacheng Automobile Parts v. Huifeng*; *Sojitz v. Xiao*; *Wenzhou Foreign Trade Co of Light Article Industry v. CMA (France)*; *Junichirou Watanabe v. Culture & Art Press*, all ibid.

48 *Kwok & Yih Law Firm supra* n 47; *NKK (Japan) v. Beijing supra* n 47.

choosing a foreign court, at the moment, is not a compulsory reason for a Chinese court to decline jurisdiction.[49]

IV.2 Enforcing foreign judgments and choice of court clauses

4.30 Chinese courts may take jurisdiction irrespective of a foreign exclusive jurisdiction clause because the foreign judgment made pursuant to a valid jurisdiction clause may not be recognized and enforced in China. China has very narrow grounds for recognizing and enforcing foreign judgments, which is pursuant either to multilateral or bilateral treaties or to the principle of reciprocity.[50] Even if both prerequisites are met, judgments may not be recognized and enforced if they infringe the Chinese basic principle of law, state sovereignty, national security, social interest or pubic policy.[51] China has only entered into around 35 bilateral agreements with foreign countries or regions to recognize and enforce each other's judgments,[52] not including some major trade partners of China, such as Japan, the USA, Germany and the UK. The principle of reciprocity also applies restrictively. The SPC suggests that only de facto reciprocity is recognized, which means that the foreign country must have recognized and enforced the Chinese judgment in the past.[53] If the parties have chosen a forum that has no treaty agreement or reciprocity with China, the judgment cannot be enforced in the Chinese court.[54] The judgment creditor will have to bring a fresh action in China for the second time, with resulting extra costs and uncertainty.

---

49 See *supra* Ch 3.III.D. For discussion *see* Z.S. Tang, 'Effectiveness of Exclusive Jurisdiction Clauses in the Chinese Courts—A Pragmatic Study', (2012) 61 ICLQ 459.

50 CPL, Art 282.

51 Ibid.

52 See Ch 6, III.1 below. China entered into 36 bilateral treaties in general civil and commercial judicial corporation, but treaties with Singapore and Korea do not include reciprocal enforcement of judgments. China has also entered into a judicial cooperation treaty in investment matters with Australia including agreements on mutual enforcement of judgments.

53 SPC, 'Guanyu Woguo Renmin Fayuan Yingfou Chengren he Zhixing Ribenguo Fayuan Juyou Zhaiquan Zhaiwu Neirong Caipan de Fuhan [Re whether the People's Courts should recognize and enforce the Judgment given by the Japanese Court in Payment of Debts]', [1995] Min Ta Zi No 17; *NKK (Japan) v. Beijing Zhuangsheng, RNO v. Beijing International Music Festival Society,* Beijing No 2 IPC (2004) Er Zhong Min Te Zi No 928.

54 SPC, '1992 Opinion', Art 318:

> If the party applied to the competent intermediate court of the People's Republic of China for recognition and enforcement of foreign judgments or rulings, if the country where the foreign court is located and the People's Republic of China have not concluded or acceded to international treaties, or formed the relation of reciprocity, the applicant could sue in the People's Court for the competent People's Court to make judgment for enforcement.

For more discussion on recognition and enforcement of foreign judgments in China, see Ch 6 below.

This consideration is clearly demonstrated in *NKK (Japan) v. Beijing Zhuangsheng.*[55] In this case, a Japanese company and a Chinese company entered into a contract including an exclusive choice of court agreement choosing Hong Kong courts. The defendant, Beijing Zhuang Sheng, had assets located exclusively in China. The Hong Kong judgment could not be recognized and enforced in China and the claimant brought the same action in China. The Chinese court asserted jurisdiction. In *Kwok & Yih Law Firm v. Xiamen Huayang Color Printing Co*,[56] the Xiamen IPC refused to decline jurisdiction in favour of the Hong Kong court chosen in a non-exclusive jurisdiction clause. The court did not place too much emphasis on the non-exclusive nature of the jurisdiction clause, but focused on the importance of enforcing the judgment, i.e., all of the defendant's property was located in China and there was no reciprocal arrangement between Hong Kong and the mainland at the time when the judgment was made.[57] **4.31**

However, if a Chinese court enforces a foreign exclusive jurisdiction agreement without considering the potential consequence of judgment enforcement, it may cause an unreasonable result for the claimant and may also deny the ends of justice. In *Junichirou Watanabe v. Culture & Art Press*,[58] the Japanese party and the Chinese company had concluded a jurisdiction clause granting exclusive jurisdiction to the Japanese courts. The Japanese claimant later brought an action for the infringement of copyright, but, because the defendant had all its assets located in China and with the concomitant difficulty of enforcement, the action was raised in China, in breach of the jurisdiction clause. Unfortunately, the Chinese court insisted that the parties must be bound by the exclusive jurisdiction agreement and declined jurisdiction. The result was that, if even the claimant succeeded in the action in Japan, he would have to bring the same action in China again in order to have the judgment enforced.[59] **4.32**

This does not suggest that denying the derogation effect of an exclusive jurisdiction clause is justifiable. Where the parties enter into a genuine agreement to submit their disposable disputes to a particular forum, that intention should be respected. The difficulty in enforcing foreign judgments creates a dilemma for the Chinese court and also greatly hampers party **4.33**

---

55 *NKK (Japan) v. Beijing Zhuangsheng*, Beijing Municipality HPC, (2008) Gao Min Zhong Zi No 919.

56 *Kwok & Yih Law Firm supra* n 47.

57 It is necessary to note that judgment can now be enforced between the mainland and Hong Kong, pursuant to the Arrangement on Reciprocal Recognition and Enforcement of Judgments in Civil and Commercial Matters by the Courts of the Mainland and of the Hong Kong SAR Pursuant to Choice of Court Agreements between Parties Concerned 2006. See Ch 13, VI below.

58 *Junichirou Watanabe; Yacheng Automobile Parts; Sojitz v. Xiao; Wenzhou v. CMA (France)* all *supra* n 47.

59 For more discussion, see Z.S. Tang, *supra* n 50, 459.

autonomy and its advantages in international commerce. In order to improve the situation, the Chinese legislators should not only consider inserting an affirmative statement granting full effectiveness to a valid jurisdiction clause, but also reform the whole system on recognition and enforcement of foreign judgments.[60] The latter, obviously, is a more challenging task.[61]

IV.3 Reciprocity

4.34 It is questionable whether China will enforce foreign jurisdiction clauses based on reciprocity, i.e. a jurisdiction clause designating the foreign court may be enforced in China only if the foreign court enforces a jurisdiction clause choosing a Chinese court. This has been observed by commentators as the early practice of Chinese maritime courts.[62]

4.35 Since the principle of reciprocity is widely adopted in Chinese law and jurisprudence in dealing with foreign relations, implying this principle in the enforcement of foreign jurisdiction clauses is not unreasonable pursuant to Chinese legislative intention and policy. This is, however, not fully confirmed by recent judicial practice. First, the existence of reciprocity can be hard to prove. The court must be satisfied that the foreign court has declined jurisdiction where the parties have chosen the Chinese court in their agreement. It requires the court of the given foreign country to have decided a case where a choice of Chinese courts clause exists. Since China is not a popular forum in international litigation, such cases would be rare. Secondly, China does not have a formal and systematic case-report system and many decisions, especially those made by local courts, are unreported. None of the accessible decisions have explicitly relied on reciprocity to decline jurisdiction. As a result, it is hard to state with certainty that the principle of reciprocity is still a valid basis for enforcing foreign jurisdiction clauses in China.

IV.4 Hague Choice of Court Convention

4.36 Although the CPL does not include many provisions allowing Chinese courts to decline jurisdiction, Article 260 provides that an international treaty concluded or acceded to by China should supersede CPL. In other words, if

60 LIU En-yuan, 'Zhongguo Chengren yu Zhixing Waiguo Panjue de Jichu Tiaojian [Basic Conditions for China to Recognize and Enforce Foreign Judgments]', (2008) 23 Fazhi [*Journal of Shanghai University of Political Science and Law*] 63.

61 See Tang, *supra* n 50, 459; and Ch 6 below.

62 Zhang Jinxian, *China's Maritime Courts and Justice*, I.C.C. International Maritime Bureau (Witherby Publishers, London 1997) 48.

China has treaty obligations to decline jurisdiction, the People's Courts must decline jurisdiction.

China is a member of the New York Convention on recognition and enforcement of arbitral awards. Chinese courts, thus, decline jurisdiction in favour of a valid arbitration agreement not only pursuant to Chinese law but also to treaty obligations.[63] This explains the additional work conducted by the SPC to protect the enforcement of international arbitration agreements subject to the New York Convention and to prevent local courts from unduly competing with arbitral tribunals in jurisdiction. Although imperfect, the judicial practice in enforcing arbitration agreements is laudable and more advanced than in other fields. All demonstrate the SPC and legislators' decision to fulfil treaty obligations. **4.37**

China has not entered into an international judicial cooperation treaty in choice of court agreements. The Hague Convention on Choice of Court Agreement 2005 provides jurisdiction cooperation between contracting states to mutually enforce exclusive jurisdiction agreements. The Hague Choice of Court Convention has been signed by the US, the EU and Singapore, and ratified by Mexico and the EU. It has entered into force between EU Member States and Mexico from 1 October 2015.[64] If China ratifies the Hague Choice of Court Convention, China will have treaty obligations to decline jurisdiction in favour of the chosen court of the other contracting state. Since mutual enforcement of judgments pursuant to a valid exclusive jurisdiction clause is also ensured by the Hague Convention, concerns over the difficulty of enforcing foreign judgments will also be removed. **4.38**

Although China has not yet signed the Hague Choice of Court Convention, the Arrangement on Reciprocal Recognition and Enforcement of Judgments between China and Hong Kong has been in force since 2008 to handle judicial cooperation between China and Hong Kong.[65] The Arrangement provides that any monetary judgment made by a Hong Kong court pursuant to an exclusive jurisdiction clause may be recognized and enforced in China and vice versa.[66] It, however, does not compulsorily require a Chinese court to decline **4.39**

---

63 See section III above.

64 Mexico deposited the instrument of ratification, acceptance, approval or accession on 26 Sept 2007 and the EU on 11 June 2015. The Convention enters into force on the first day of the month after the expiration of three months of the second deposit. See Art 31. The status can be found at http://www.hcch.net/index_en.php?act=conventions.status&cid=98, accessed on 19 June 2015.

65 Interpretation No 9 [2008] of the Supreme People's Court on 3 July 2008; Mainland Judgments (Reciprocal Enforcement) Ordinance and its (Commencement) Notice, Ord No 9 of 2008, L.S. No 2 to Gazette No 27/2008. See Ch 13, V.1 below.

66 Art 1.

jurisdiction in favour of a valid exclusive jurisdiction clause choosing the Hong Kong court, although the mutual recognition and enforcement of judgments eliminates practical difficulties for declining jurisdiction. The existence of a jurisdiction agreement is one of the conditions to prove the ruling court has jurisdiction and thus the judgment, made by 35 countries which have signed bilateral treaties with China, may be enforceable pursuant to such an agreement in China.[67] Again, none require the court of either contracting state to decline jurisdiction facing a valid clause granting another court exclusive jurisdiction. Compared to the existing treaties and arrangements, the Hague Convention provides a fundamentally different requirement to Chinese courts and may raise a few diplomatic and political concerns.

4.40 It is hard to predict whether China will sign and ratify the Hague Convention in the short term. Most countries do not sign the Hague Convention and the practical benefit of the Hague Convention is uncertain. So is its potential risk. In the absence of an effective and operational international judicial collaboration scheme covering most of the countries in the world, a refusal to enforce a foreign jurisdiction clause may not bring too much harm to China, especially when enforcement of judgments is equally uncertain and difficult in many other countries. It may even allow Chinese courts to take jurisdiction over many cases involving a Chinese party and to protect Chinese interest. The difficulty in enforcing foreign judgments in China may also lead to a foreign party voluntarily giving up the jurisdiction clause but suing the Chinese defendant in China for the enforcement purpose.

4.41 However, it is very likely that China will eventually take part in the Convention, if the Convention is accepted by most countries internationally. Once the Convention enters into force and applies in a large number of countries, being out of the international judicial cooperation scheme would leave Chinese parties at a disadvantage. If a Chinese party is involved in a transaction, it may increase the risk of breaching the jurisdiction clause, the potential litigation cost and the difficulty of enforcing judgments. Trading with Chinese parties may be classified as risky and uncertain which would hamper competitiveness of Chinese companies in the international market.

---

67 Eg, Sino-Italy, Art 22(1)(3); Sino-Spain, Art 21(1)(2); Sino-Tunis, Art 23(1)(3); Sino-UAE, Art 19(3); Sino-Kuwait, Art 19(1)(3); Sino-Peru, Art 25(3); Sino-Egypt, Art 23(1)(3); Sino-Cyprus, Art 26(1)(3); Sino-Vietnam, Art 18(1)(3); Sino-Laos, Art 22(1)(3).

V. DECLINING DISCRETIONARY JURISDICTION

Declining discretionary jurisdiction permits a court to exercise its discretion when it is appropriate to do so. In common law countries this is called *forum non conveniens*. This discretionary doctrine has been adopted in China. However, due to the special characteristics of the Chinese judicial system and judicial practice, implementing this doctrine in Chinese courts is very different from that in common law countries. More restrictive guidance is provided and relatively limited power is granted to exercise discretion.[68] **4.42**

V.1 Brief history of *forum non conveniens* in China

No Chinese legislation has expressly or impliedly provided a court with the power to decline jurisdiction granted by law. Development in this area is contributed to by judicial practice. *Disputes in Property of ZHAO Biyan* is the first case where a Chinese court declined jurisdiction in favour of Japan based on the 'convenience' of the trial.[69] The plaintiff claimed ownership of property located in Japan. Although the plaintiff had her domicile and habitual residence in China, and some important evidence and witnesses were located in China, Japan was the more appropriate and convenient forum because it was the place where the property in dispute and other respondents were located. Since the early 1990s, the SPC started to use *forum non conveniens* to decline jurisdiction in exceptional cases where both parties were not Chinese citizens or Chinese companies and the dispute had no connection with China.[70] For example, in 1993, SPC instructed the Shenzhen IPC to refuse jurisdiction on a cross-border letter-of-credit dispute, because none of the parties were mainland companies and the dispute had no substantive connection with China.[71] In 1995, the SPC applied the concept of *forum non conveniens* again in *Sumitomo Bank v. Xinhua*,[72] because neither parties had **4.43**

---

68 For more discussion on *forum non conveniens* in China, see Z.S. Tang, 'Declining Jurisdiction by *Forum Non Conveniens* in Chinese Courts', (2015) 45 *Hong Kong Law Journal* 351.

69 See XUE Hui, *Zhongmei Pingxing Susong Wenti zhi Bijiao Yanjiu [Comparative Study of Parallel Proceedings between China and USA]*, MS Dissertation, Dalian Haishi University, submitted in 2007, 46–9; WU Yi-Min, 'Liangda Faxi zhong de Bufangbian Fayuan Yuanze ji zai Zhongguo de Heli Jiejian [Forum non conveniens in Two Legal Systems and its Adoption in China]', (2008) 1 Xinan Zhengfa Daxue Xuebao [Journal of SWUPL] 2; GUO SuLi, 'Guoji Minshangshi Guanxiaquan Chongtu Jiqi Jiuji—dui Zhongguo Shijian de Kaocha [Conflict of Civil and Commercial Jurisdiction and Remedies—A Study of Chinese Practice]' (2000) 7 Faxue [Legal Science] 12; ZHANG Yan, *Lun Woguo Fayuan Shewai Anjian zhong Jujue Guanxiaquan de Jichu [The Bases for the Chinese Court to Decline Jurisdiction]*, MPhil thesis submitted to Shanghai Jiao Tong University in 2008, 5.

70 ZHANG Yan, ibid., 6.

71 *Dongpeng Trade v. HK Bank of East Asia,* Guangdong Province HPC, (1995) Yue Fa Jing Er Jian Zi No 3.

72 SPC, (1999) Jing Zhong Zi No 194.

domicile in China, the contract was performed in Hong Kong, Hong Kong law was chosen, and there was a non-exclusion clause choosing Hong Kong courts.[73]

4.44 The early recognition of *forum non conveniens*, therefore, existed in Chinese judicial practice. Such practice is later recorded in more generic guidance during the 2000s. In 2004, the SPC published 'Answers to Questions Arising out of Trial Practice of Commercial and Maritime Cases with Foreign Elements' ('2004 Answers'),[74] according to which *forum non conveniens* can be used if both parties are foreigners; the main fact has no connection to China; the court finds it significantly difficult to determine the facts and to apply the governing law; and the judgment needs recognition and enforcement in another country. A more detailed guidance was provided in 2005 in the 'Summary of the Second National Conference on the Adjudication of Commercial and Maritime Cases with Foreign Elements' ('2005 Summary'),[75] and is echoed in the SPC 2015 Opinion to the Civil Procedure Law. Article 532 of the 2015 Opinion provides that the People's Court could decline jurisdiction and direct the claimant to the more convenient foreign court under the circumstances as follows: (1) the defendant pleads *forum non conveniens*, or the defendant challenges jurisdiction; (2) there is no agreement between the parties choosing Chinese courts; (3) the case is not one falling within the exclusive jurisdiction of China; (4) the case does not affect the interest of the state, citizens, legal persons or other organizations of China; (5) the main fact that gives rise to the dispute occurred outside China and the Chinese law is not applicable, causing the People's Court significant difficulty in deciding the facts or law; and (6) there is a foreign court that has jurisdiction and it is more convenient to try the case in that court. All theses conditions must be satisfied before the court can exercise discretion to decline jurisdiction under *forum non conveniens*.

V.2 Applying *forum non conveniens* in judicial practice

i. Defendant must challenge jurisdiction

4.45 First, Article 532(1) clearly provides that the defendant should plead *forum non conveniens*, or challenge jurisdiction. It means that *forum non conveniens*

73 Ibid.

74 SPC, 'Shewai Shangshi Haishi Shenpan Shiwu Wenti Jieda [Answers to Questions Arising out of Trial Practice of Commercial and Maritime Cases with Foreign Elements]', a Chinese version is available at http://www.lawtime.cn/info/maoyi/myzc/20081217111.html, answer 7, accessed on 20 May 2011.

75 SPC, '2005 Summary', Art 11. Du Huanfang, *supra* n 25, 157.

could be pled in the defendant's application,[76] or be considered by the court by its own motion as far as the defendant has challenged jurisdiction.[77]

Some commentators argue *forum non conveniens* should only be pleaded by the defendant, because if the defendant does not plead *forum non conveniens,* he is deemed to have accepted that the forum is convenient if competent. The court should not step in to help the defendant.[78] Furthermore, the main purpose of *forum non conveniens* is to balance the litigation power between the parties. Facilitating an efficient and convenient trial is the second consideration.[79] **4.46**

Other commentators see *forum non conveniens* as an instrument to prevent the excessive and inappropriate exercise of jurisdiction of a court,[80] not only as a mechanism to protect the defendant. Judicial practices in most countries have ranked sound administration of justice a more weighty reason to justify *forum non conveniens* than the defendant's interest, which can, in many cases, be counter-balanced by the claimant's right to sue.[81] Furthermore, some factors that are taken into consideration when deciding *forum non conveniens* are beyond the defendant's convenience, including the accessibility of evidence and witnesses and the enforceability of judgments. These factors will fundamentally jeopardize an efficient trial and waste time and public funds.[82] In such cases, a court should have the discretion to decide not to hear a case for the purpose of protecting public interest, either with or without the defendant's application.[83] **4.47**

The SPC does not wholly take the view that the Chinese court has the power to exercise its discretion voluntarily to maintain sound administration of justice. However, it recognizes that sometimes the defendant challenges jurisdiction but fails to rely on the ground of *forum non conveniens* because he lacks relevant knowledge. In order to keep a balance between different interests, the SPC allows a Chinese court to consider *forum non conveniens* only if jurisdiction is challenged by the defendant, either with or without the **4.48**

76 '2005 Summary', Art 11; *Dongpeng Trade supra* n 71; *Kwok & Yih Law Firm supra* n 47; *Cai v. Wang*, Fujian Province Quanzhou Municipality IPC, (1997) Quan Min Gao Zi No 27.

77 *Kwok & Yih Law Firm*; *Sumitomo Bank v. Xinhua.*

78 ZHANG Shu-Dian, 'Lun Woguo Bufangbian Fayuan Yuanze Shiyong de Ruogan Zhenyi Wenti [Study on Problems on forum non convenience in court]', (2009) 30 Xingzheng yu Fa [*Public Administration and Law*] 96, 97.

79 Ibid., 97.

80 Ibid.

81 HUANG Qiu-feng, 'Zhonngguo Ying Queli Bufangbian Fayuan Zhidu [Set up the Doctrine of Forum Non Conveniens in China]', (2010) 28 Hebei Faxue [*Hebei Law Science*] 70, 73.

82 For the public-private balance in *forum non convenines*, see E.J. Derr, 'Striking a Better Public-Private Balance in *Forum Non Conveniens*', (2008) 93 *Cornell Law Review* 819.

83 HUANG Qiu-feng, *supra* n 81, 73.

plea of *forum non conveniens*. Where the defendant does not challenge jurisdiction, the defendant is deemed to submit to the jurisdiction and the court should take jurisdiction without considering a convenient and efficient trial.

4.49 A related question is the burden of proof. There is no clear guidance as to the burden of proof in *forum non conveniens*. Usually, the defendant carries most of the burden. In most cases, it is not enough for the defendant simply to question the convenience and appropriateness of Chinese courts without comparing the alternative forum. The claimant is not normally required to prove issues relating to *forum non conveniens*, but only carries the burden of demonstrating the preliminary requirement that the seized court has jurisdiction.[84] However, in some cases, the claimant also provides evidence to dispute the defendant's *forum non conveniens* application, proving the seized court was more convenient than the alternative forum proposed by the defendant.[85] Of course, if the court voluntarily considers *forum non conveniens* without the defendant's application, the court does not require any party to discharge the burden of proof.[86]

ii. Parties' intention

4.50 The existence of a jurisdiction agreement has mixed effect in applying Chinese *forum non conveniens*. If the parties enter into a jurisdiction agreement choosing a Chinese court, the chosen court cannot decline jurisdiction based on *forum non conveniens*.[87] In practice, many Chinese courts have confirmed the absence of Chinese jurisdiction clauses before moving to consider *forum non conveniens*.[88] The language of the 2015 Opinion suggests that it makes no difference if the Chinese court is chosen in a non-exclusive jurisdiction agreement. Even if the parties do not use agreements to derogate other competent courts from their jurisdiction, the choice of Chinese courts implies that the parties accept Chinese courts.

4.51 To the contrary, the attitude given to the foreign jurisdiction clause is different. The choice of a foreign court is not a listed factor supporting *forum non conveniens* in Article 532 of the 2015 Opinion. In practice, even if a

84 *Cai v. Wang supra* n 76; ZHANG Shu-dian, *supra* n 78, 97.
85 *Kwok & Yih Law Firm supra* n 47; ZHANG Shu-dian, *supra* n 78, 97
86 *Sumitomo Bank v. Xinhua supra* n 72.
87 2015 Opinion, Art 532(2); 2005 Summary, Art 11(3).
88 *Baron Motorcycles Inc v. Awell Logistics Group Inc*, Ningbo Maritime Court, (2008) Yong Hai Fa Shang Chu Zi No 277 (the court referred to the lack of a jurisdiction clause choosing China as one of the factors supporting the use of *forum non conveniens* to decline jurisdiction); *Jaten Electronic v. Smartech Electronic*, Shanghai Municipality No 1 IPC, (2009) Hu Yi Zhong Min Wu (Shang) Chu Zi No 51.

foreign jurisdiction clause is chosen in an exclusive jurisdiction clause, it may not be a weighty factor in *forum non conveniens.* Before the promulgation of the 2015 Opinion, a few Chinese courts had already used *forum non conveniens* in practice, but none of them granted *forum non conveniens* based on the foreign jurisdiction clause. Some courts directly held the seized Chinese court not competent if the parties had concluded an exclusive jurisdiction agreement choosing a foreign court, which barred the use of *forum non conveniens.* Some other courts simply refused to recognize the derogation effect of a foreign jurisdiction clause and took jurisdiction irrespective of the parties' choice.

iii. Exclusive jurisdiction

Forum non conveniens cannot be applied if the dispute falls within the exclusive jurisdiction of the Chinese courts. Exclusive jurisdiction is there to reserve disputes exclusively to the court to protect state sovereignty and such jurisdiction cannot be derogated from by any means. The only criticism probably is that this ground is unnecessary. The legislation establishes exclusive jurisdiction based on a strong national and public interest. Disputes falling within the scope of exclusive jurisdiction will usually have close proximity with, and impact on, the local forum. Even without this condition, a court will not apply *forum non conveniens* in disputes subject to exclusive jurisdiction. **4.52**

iv. Impact in China

Chinese courts cannot decline jurisdiction if the dispute has an impact in China.[89] 'Impact' is defined as an effect on the interests of the state, citizens, legal persons or other organizations of China. If a dispute concerns the national or public interest, Chinese courts would have interest to take jurisdiction and it may be contrary to Chinese public policy to decline jurisdiction in this case. Impact should be the direct impact of the judgment and should not include indirect impact. In *Jaten Electronic v. Smartech Electronic,*[90] two Hong Kong companies (A and B) entered into a contract for the sale of electronic products (contract 1). The contract was concluded in Hong Kong and goods were delivered and stored in Hong Kong. The buyer B would resell the goods to the final purchaser (C), who was domiciled in China. Although the final purchaser was not a party to the current contract, this purchaser and its requirement to the goods was known to both parties.[91] When the dispute arose between A and B concerning the performance of **4.53**

89 '2005 Summary', Art 11(3).

90 *Jaten supra* n 88.

91 The defendant had a representative branch in Shanghai and the contract offer was faxed from the Shanghai branch. According to Art 241 of the Civil Procedure Law, Shanghai courts had jurisdiction. The issue was whether Shanghai courts should decline jurisdiction in favour of Hong Kong.

contract 1, the question faced by the trial court was whether the court should decline jurisdiction under *forum non conveniens* in favour of Hong Kong. It is clear that Hong Kong may have had close connections to the dispute and both parties were Hong Kong residents. The question was whether the dispute had impact in China, as the performance of the contract 1 would eventually affect the interests of C, a Chinese resident. The court decided that C was not a contract party and would not be directly affected by the judgment. The potential indirect impact of the judgment was insufficient to prove the existence of impact in China.

4.54 It is argued that the focus on 'direct' impact to the contract parties may not be appropriate. The purpose of this factor is to allow Chinese courts to keep jurisdiction once the Chinese general public may be affected by the case or the decision. The general public should not be the direct parties of the dispute. However, it is also wrong to claim that whenever a third party that may be affected by the judgment is Chinese, *forum non conveniens* cannot be applied. Attention should be paid to the significance of the impact. In *Jaten Electronic v. Smartech Electronic* mentioned above, the impact on C was private and hardly a significant impact in the general public. *Forum non convenines,* thus, should be allowed.

v. Proximity

4.55 *Forum non conveniens* will be applied if the main facts under dispute occurred outside China and Chinese law is not the applicable law, which makes it difficult for the People's Court to decide the fact and the law.

4.56 Before the 2015 Opinion, when declining jurisdiction based on the lack of proximity, great consideration was given to the parties' domicile. If both parties had common domicile in a foreign country and the fact giving rise to the claim occurred in the same country, the courts would be more willing to hold that the dispute had closer connections with the foreign country and decline jurisdiction.[92] Other facts, such as the location of the subject matter of the dispute; the place where the contract is concluded; and the application of a foreign law; were treated as inconclusive factors and could not work alone to support *forum non conveniens.*[93]

---

92 *Baron Motorcycles Inc supra* n 88; *Jaten Electronic supra* n 88.

93 *Baron Motorcycles* (US law was the possible applicable law); *Jaten Electronic* (Hong Kong law would apply under Chinese choice of law rules, continuing jurisdiction could cause difficulties); *Sumitomo Bank v. Xinhua supra* n 72 (parties chose Hong Kong law to govern the loan agreement). See comments in XI Xiao-Ming, 'Bufangbian Fayuan Zhidu de Jidian Sikao [Several Thoughts on Forum Non Conveniens]' (2002) 24 *Legal Study* 81, 90.

The 2015 Opinion clarifies two issues. First, when deciding proximity, both the factual connections and the applicable law should be taken into account. If the disputes have close nexuses with a foreign country but Chinese law applies, jurisdiction cannot be declined, and vice versa. The inconvenience should exist in determining both the fact and the law. Secondly, proximity in Chinese *forum non conveniens* does not mean Chinese courts will decline jurisdiction in favour of the natural forum or the centre of gravity. Jurisdiction will only be declined if the lack of proximity causes difficulty or inconvenience in the trial. If the fact giving rise to the claim occurs abroad, but all evidence is easily accessible in China, *forum non conveniens* will not be granted. If the foreign law applies, is not hard to prove and the content of which is not significantly different from Chinese law, *forum non conveniens* will not be applied. **4.57**

vi. Convenience of trial

The last requirement to rule *forum non conveniens* is that the foreign court should have jurisdiction and that it is more convenient for this foreign court to hear the dispute. First, it is necessary to prove there is a competent foreign court available. Otherwise, declining jurisdiction may be unfair to the claimant, who would be deprived of the right to access to court. Secondly, it should be comparatively more convenient for the foreign court to hear the dispute. The court should take discretion to determine the comparative convenience of the trial. Consideration should be given to the access to the evidence, to the application of law, to the availability of experts and witnesses, and the entry of appearance of both parties. **4.58**

It is necessary to note that one factor, which is not specifically mentioned in the 2015 Opinion, but should be taken into consideration and given much weight, is the enforcement of the judgment. In China, the enforcement of foreign judgments is subject to very restrictive conditions and will usually be refused in the absence of treaty obligations or reciprocity.[94] Given that difficulty, Chinese legislators have extended Chinese jurisdictional grounds to include disputes which might seek enforcement in China based on the location of the disposable assets in China. In *Kwok & Yih Law Firm v. Xiamen Huayang Color Printing Co*, the claimant proved that although Hong Kong was a more convenient forum to hear the dispute, the judgment could not be enforced in China.[95] The defendant's *forum non conveniens* application was refused.[96] It is suggested that the location of the defendant's assets and the **4.59**

94 2015 Opinion, Art 544. See Ch 6 below.

95 This case was decided in 1999 when there was no arrangement for mutual enforcement of court judgments between China and Hong Kong.

96 *Kwok & Yih supra* n 47.

possibility of enforcing the foreign judgment should be taken into account as one important factor in the comparative convenience of trial.

4.60 Furthermore, the word 'convenience' is not defined, and it is uncertain whether it could be given a broad meaning to cover not only procedural efficiency but also the quality of trial and the ends of justice. If the foreign court is the natural forum and the trial is significantly inconvenient in China, but requiring the claimant to sue in the foreign court may be vexatious or oppressive, for example, the foreign judicial system is not independent, the foreign country is in a war zone or under civil riot, the foreign court is seriously incompetent, or the claimant may suffer prejudice in that country for race, gender, or religious reasons, could this be considered a reason justifying that the foreign court is not a 'more convenient' one to hear the case? A literal meaning of the word 'convenience' in Chinese suggests that only procedural efficiency is relevant.[97] The past judicial practice or judicial guidance also did not suggest the Chinese courts have ever considered the ends of justice in *forum non conveniens* rulings. From the perspective of politics, China has the tradition of respecting other countries' sovereignty and non-interference in other country's internal affairs.[98] Based on this foreign policy, Chinese courts would be very reluctant to question the quality, competence and fairness of the judicial system of the other country. Chinese *forum non conveniens,* thus, primarily focuses on procedural efficiency.[99]

V.3 Conclusion

4.61 China, during over 20 years of judicial practice, has established a special Chinese style of *forum non conveniens.* This doctrine was created by Chinese judgments in judicial practice and later confirmed and recognized by the SPC. There is no statutory recognition of this doctrine though. However, it is undeniable that *forum non conveniens* exists in China and has worked well in some cases to improve more efficient and just trials.

4.62 However, the Chinese *forum non conveniens* is a premature version. The starting point of Chinese courts is that jurisdiction should only be declined in exceptional circumstances. The guidance provided in the 2015 Opinion focuses more on the control and restriction of *forum non conveniens.* Very

97 Convenience is called 'Fang Bian' (方便) in Chinese.

98 Both 'mutual respect of sovereignty' and 'non-interference of internal affairs' are included in the Five Principles for Peaceful Coexistence. See Lijiang Zhu, Chengyuan Ma, 'Chinese Practice in Public International Law', (2013) 12 *Chinese Journal of International Law* 363.

99 See in general, Tang, *supra* n 68, 351.

restrictive conditions are imposed and the court has limited room to exercise its discretion.

Some commentators oppose the adoption of *forum non conveniens* in China because they concern the qualification and competence of Chinese judges.[100] *Forum non conveniens* is based on discretion, even if the Chinese *forum non conveniens* largely limits the court's discretionary power. Most Chinese judges have not received proper training in exercising discretion.[101] Many judges wish to reduce the rate of successful appeals of their judgments to the higher courts in order to receive promotion.[102] They would not want to take the 'risk' by applying such a new doctrine in China and believe strictly applying CPL to be a safer approach. Finally, discretion means flexibility and that the judges are granted more power than in other cases. A discretionary approach may not work well if judges' professional ethics are in doubt and the judicial system is not free from concern of corruption.[103] **4.63**

All these concerns are valid. However, the quality of judges and judicial system should not be a reason against adopting any discretionary method in China, especially if this method could provide efficiency and justice to Chinese courts. Other commentators have noticed an improvement in judges' competence and professional skills in the past decades.[104] Further, Chinese *forum non conveniens* is developed gradually by judges. Many courts have demonstrated, in general, a satisfactory professional standard and legal analysis. The quality of judgments in applying *forum non conveniens* is also improving. Compared to earlier judgments, many judgments made after 2000 include detailed analysis and justification.[105] **4.64**

Forum non conveniens, if adopted in China, will inevitably have strong civil law characteristics in that more regulations will be imposed to limit the court's discretion. It is reasonable to predict that Chinese *forum non conveniens* will **4.65**

---

100 XU Gong-Wei, 'Woguo Buyi Caiyong Bufangbian Fayuan Yuanze [*Forum Non Conveniens* is Inappropriate for China]' (2006) 24 *Legal Forum* 146, 150; XU Gong-wei, 'Bufangbian Fayuan Yuanze zai Zhongguo de Yunyong [The Application of the Principle of *Forum Non Convenience* in China]', (2003) 21 *Tribune of Political Science and Law* 161, 166; HUANG Qiu-feng, *supra* n 81, 71.

101 XU Gong-wei, ibid., (2006) 24 *Legal Forum* 146, 150; HUANG Qiu-feng, *supra* n 81, 71.

102 LI Li-Min, 'Brief Study of the Quantitative Assessment of Judges', published on http://www.hicourt.gov.cn/theory/artilce_list.asp?id=1943&l_class=6 (accessed on 10 Oct 2013); Note, 'Man-made 'Judicial Justice' (in Chinese), http://view.163.com/special/reviews/falsejustice1120.html (accessed on 10 Oct 2013).

103 XU Gong-wei, *supra* n 101, 150; HUANG Qiu-feng, supra n 81, 71.

104 XU Qian-fei, 'Zhongguo Faguan Suzhi Pingxi [Evaluation of the Quality of Chinese Judges]', (2001) 9 People's Judicature 8; XU Qian-fei, 'Zailun Zhongguo Faguan de Suzhi [Re-Evaluation of Quality of Chinese Judges]', (2002) *People's Judicature* 33.

105 *Jiangdu Shipyard v. CICB Yangzhou Branch and China Bank HK*; *Kwok & Yih Law Firm v. Xiamen Huayang Color Printing Company*; *Jaten Electronic v. Smartech Electronic.*

not be developed into the same level of *forum non conveniens* in common law countries, such as the UK, the USA and Australia. However, it is a laudable practice to improve administration of international justice. The overall trend by adopting *forum non conveniens* in China is a positive sign of China's intention to modernize its jurisdiction system.

VI. CONCLUSION

4.66 Chinese law in declining jurisdiction shows clear improvement in the past decades. The protection to arbitration agreements and the development of the Chinese style *forum non conveniens* deserve recommendation. However, the system is still premature. There are three major problems. First, an exclusive jurisdiction clause is not given its full effectiveness and the derogation effect is frequently ignored by the Chinese courts. Secondly, no consideration is given to *lis pendens* and the Chinese courts takes no steps to prevent concurrent proceedings. Thirdly, *forum non conveniens* is used in a very restrictive manner, focuses only on procedural efficiency and pays little attention to the ends of justice.

4.67 The current law requires continuous modernization. It is necessary to recognize that many of these fallacies cannot be addressed independently because they are the result of, or have connections with, other problems in the whole legal system. First, the law cannot simply demand that all courts to decline jurisdiction in favour of a foreign court chosen in an exclusive jurisdiction clause without ensuring that the judgment, made pursuant to a valid jurisdiction clause, is enforceable in China. If the foreign judgment cannot be recognized and enforced in the Chinese court, the Chinese court will take jurisdiction to hear the dispute anyway if the judgment creditor chooses to bring a fresh claim in China. This part of law can only be improved with the fundamental reform of the recognition and enforcement of foreign judgments.[106] Secondly, unilateral *lis pendens* is inappropriate between countries in the absence of judicial cooperation and it may also encourage the parties to rush to the court. In order to reduce concurrent proceedings and to improve procedural efficiency, it is suggested that *lis pendens* should be one factor taken into consideration in the *forum non conveniens.* Thirdly, the restrictive rule on *forum non conveniens* is due to the civil law tradition and the lack of proper training in judges' exercise of discretion. A too broad discretion may leave uncertainty and cause inappropriate judgments. More discretion may only be granted gradually to the courts after a period of exercise and training.

106 For more discussion, see Ch 6 below. Also see Ch 3, VII.

Furthermore, the lack of consideration for the ends of justice in *forum non conveniens* is largely caused by the Chinese foreign policy of not judging the quality of justice of the judicial system of the other state. Lack of the ends of justice consideration may lead to unreasonable results for the parties, especially where the claimant has significant barriers preventing it from accessing to the most convenient forum. Declining jurisdiction may infringe the claimant's right to access to justice. This point, however, may hardly be addressed until there is an improvement in the Chinese concept and understanding of international comity.

5

SELECTED PROCEDURAL ISSUES IN FOREIGN-RELATED LITIGATION IN CHINA

I. INTRODUCTION

5.01 Although this book focuses on private international law questions, it cannot avoid some important procedural issues in foreign-related actions. These issues are closely connected to foreign-related actions and the implementation of private international law. Even if a Chinese court has jurisdiction and is willing to exert jurisdiction to hear a dispute, the proceedings cannot be commenced, nor can the purpose of the proceedings be achieved, if the defendant cannot be served, if the court cannot take evidence abroad, if the foreign claimant is required to provide security for cost and cannot pay, if one of the parties needs judicial aid but cannot acquire it, if the defendant continues the alleged wrong or infringement, or if the defendant hides or removes assets out of the jurisdiction. This chapter discusses these important procedural matters in foreign-related litigation in the Chinese courts.

II. SERVICE OF PROCESS ON FOREIGN DEFENDANTS

After the claimant commences legal proceedings in China, the Chinese court should serve process on the defendant. Service of process is an exercise of judicial sovereignty.[1] As a result, Chinese law provides restrictive rules on extraterritorial service, focusing on the protection of national and judicial sovereignty instead of pragmatic convenience and efficiency. **5.02**

If the defendant has no domicile in China, the court could serve the claim form through any means approved in Article 267 of the CPL. Article 267 provides eight authorized ways to serve judicial documents on defendants with no domicile in China.[2] **5.03**

II.1 Service out of jurisdiction

i. Treaty obligation

Where multilateral or bilateral international treaties have been concluded or acceded to by China and the relevant foreign country, the treaty regulations take priority over the domestic CPL rules. China has acceded to the Hague Convention on the Service Abroad of Judicial and Extrajudicial Documents in Civil and Commercial Matters 1965 ('Hague Service Convention'), which has been effective in China since 1 January 1992. **5.04**

The objective of the Hague Service Convention is to create an appropriate means for serving judicial documents abroad; to ensure adequate notice to the recipient; to improve mutual judicial assistance; and to simplify and expedite the process of extraterritorial service.[3] It applies to service of documents between contracting states. The main channel of the Convention is to serve process through the Central Authority of the relevant contracting state. Every contracting state should designate a Central Authority to receive and proceed the letter of request from the other contract state.[4] When China ratified the Hague Service Convention, the PRC Ministry of Justice was designated as the only Central Authority that could accept documents served through diplomatic channels. Although the Hague Service Convention permits any competent authority or judicial officer to forward the letter of request to the Central Authority of the country of destination, in the past China required **5.05**

1 LI Shuangyuan, *Guoji Sifa [Private International Law]* (2nd ed., Peking University Publishing 2007) 538.

2 CPL, Art 267. This chapter focuses only on how Chinese courts can serve the claim on a defendant domiciled abroad. It does not examine how foreign courts can serve on a defendant in the territory of China, this is examined in Ch 6, IV.2.

3 Hague Service Convention, Prelim.

4 Ibid., Art 2.

that all local courts should transmit the judicial documents to the SPC to be forwarded to the PRC Ministry of Justice, and only the Ministry of Justice could transmit the documents and the letter of request to the foreign Central Authority. This very restrictive and centralized regulation caused delays and inefficiencies. In 2003, in order to improve efficiency, the SPC decided to authorize the HPCs of Beijing and Shanghai Municipalities, and Guangdong, Zhejiang and Jiangsu Provinces to directly forward the judicial documents and the letter of request to the Central Authority of the country of destination.[5]

5.06 The second Conventional means to serve documents abroad is through consular and diplomatic channels. China has declared its opposition to such service within the territory of China unless the documents are served on a national of the state of origin.[6] However, China may serve judicial documents out of jurisdiction in the territory of other contracting states upon any recipients through consular and diplomatic channels, unless those states have made the same reservation.[7] Furthermore, there is nothing to prevent the other contracting state from adopting the principle of reciprocity with the effect of not permitting the Chinese service through consular or diplomatic channels upon a non-Chinese citizen within its territory. If service through diplomatic channels is adopted, the competent Chinese court should transmit all the relevant documents to the SPC. The SPC can then forward the documents directly or through the PRC Ministry of Justice to the Chinese consulate or embassy in the country of destination.[8]

5.07 The Convention also permits service by post, or through judicial officers, officials or other competent persons of the requested state.[9] China has made reservations to service through all these methods in China. China, however, could rely on these methods to serve documents in the territory of another contracting state, which does not object, unless the other contracting state

5 SPC, 'Guanyu Zhiding Beijingshi, Shanghaishi, Guangdongsheng, Zhejiangsheng, Jiangsusheng Gaoji Renmin Fayuan Yiju Haiya Songda Gongyue he Haiya Quzheng Gongyue Zhijie xiang Guowai Zhongyang Jiguan Tichu he Chuandi Sifa Xiezhu Qingqiu he Xiangguan Cailiao de Tongzhi [Notice of the SPC on Assigning the HPCs of Beijing Municipality, Shanghai Municipality, Guangdong, Zhejiang, and Jiansu Provinces to Directly Put Forward and Transfer Judicial Assistance Requests and Relevant Documents]', Fa Ban [2003] No 297.

6 Hague Service Convention, Art 8, 2nd paragraph.

7 Ibid., Art 8, 1st paragraph.

8 Service Convention Implementation Notice, Art. 9. SPC, Ministry of Foreign Affairs, Ministry of Justice, 'Guanyu Zhixing "Guanyu Xiang Guowai Songda Minshi huo Shangshi Sifa Wenshu he Sifa Wai Wenshu Gongyue" youguan Chengxu de Tongzhi [Notice on Relevant Procedure about Implementation of "Hague Convention on the Service Abroad of Judicial and Extra Judicial Documents in Civil and Commercial Matters"]', Wai Fa [1992] No 8, Art 5.

9 Hague Service Convention, Art 10.

applies the principle of reciprocity to refuse recognizing service by post or through competent persons from China.

ii. Diplomatic service

Service through diplomatic channels has been one of the major means of serving legal documents out of jurisdiction throughout Chinese history. It requires the Chinese court to issue a formal request to the court where the defendant has its domicile. This formal request cannot be transmitted directly between two courts. It requires the assistance of the Central Authorities of both countries. The court of origin should initially transmit the documents to the Central Authority of its home country, which forwards the documents to the Central Authority of the country of destination for the latter to forward to the local court of the destination. The local court will finally serve the documents on the defendant. **5.08**

Service through diplomatic channels has strict procedural and formal requirements. The legal documents provided by the local court should be investigated and approved by the supervisory HPC and forwarded to the Consular Affair Department of the Ministry of Foreign Affairs (CADMFA); the issuing HPC should also provide the name, gender, age, nationality and address of the defendant and the basic facts of the case; and the HPC should provide a letter of request and legal documents in the official language of the court of the destination.[10] The major weakness of service by diplomatic channels is its inefficiency. This form of service usually takes time, sometimes one or two years, and has a low success rate, around 30 per cent.[11] **5.09**

iii. Consular and embassy service

Chinese consular and embassy operating in the foreign country could serve legal documents on Chinese nationals domiciled in that country. The IPC or special court that takes jurisdiction to hear the dispute should transmit the judicial documents to its supervisory HPC for the latter to transmit to the SPC. The SPC then transmit the documents to the CADMFA to be forwarded **5.10**

---

10 SPC, Ministry of Foreign Affairs, Ministry of Justice, 'Guanyu Zhixing "Guanyu Xiang Guowai Songda Minshi huo Shangshi Sifawenshu he Sifawai Wenshu Gongyue" Youguan Chengxu de Tongzhi [Notice on several issues about service of legal documents through diplomatic channels between Chinese courts and foreign courts]', Wai Fa [1986] No 47.

11 The figures are provided by the then SPC Vice-President WAN E'Xiang in his speech in the Conference of National Foreign-Related Civil and Commercial Trial Work, included in *Zhongguo Shewai Shangshi Haishi Shenpan Zhidao yu Yanjiu [Guidance and Study of China Foreign-Related Civil and Commercial Trial]* (2002, Vol 1) 54.

and to the Chinese embassy or consulate in the relevant foreign country. The Chinese embassy or consulate then serves the documents on the defendant.[12]

iv. Service by post

5.11 Compared to the service through diplomatic channels or through consulates and embassies, service by post is usually quicker, more convenient and more efficient. However, it has two important drawbacks. First, it is sometimes difficult to prove whether the service has been successful. Both a receipt of service and a receipt of mail should be included in the post and the recipient is required to sign and return one of these to prove the service has been successful.[13] The SPC recommend that extraterritorial service should be conducted by the Express Mail Service (EMS);[14] it is unclear whether other post services may be deemed legally effective. For example, the mail may be delivered by recorded delivery instead of EMS. It is suggested that a functional equivalent approach should be adopted. As long as the mail can only be delivered when the recipient or its representative signs for it and the service is as effective as EMS in terms of security and evidence of proof, then, irrespective of the slower speed it should also be a valid service.

5.12 Special delivery (EMS) or recorded delivery usually requires the recipient's signature upon receiving mail which could prove the service has been successful. However, in exceptional circumstances, if no receipt is returned within three months of post, the service is deemed ineffective,[15] except where there is enough evidence proving otherwise. What evidence may be admitted by courts? If the recipient refuses to return either receipt, but mentions the content of the legal documents when it challenges the service, or performs according to the content of the legal documents, this should be enough evidence to prove the service is successful.[16] In such cases, the service is deemed effective on the first day three months after the posting date. However, if the defendant does nothing, the pro-defendant principle may suggest that the service is unsuccessful, which inevitably delays the proceedings.

---

12 SPC, 'Fayuan Guanyu Xiang Juzhu zai Waiguo de Woguo Gongmin Songda Sifa Wenshu Wenti de Fuhan [Reply of the SPC to Questions about Serving Judicial Documents to Chinese Citizens Residing Abroad]', published and effective on 19 Nov 1993, Art 1.

13 CPL, Art 267(6); 2015 Opinion, Art 536.

14 SPC, 'Guanyu yi Fayuan Zhuandi Fangshi Youji Songda Minshi Susong Wenshu de Ruogan Guiding [Several Provisions of the SPC on the Service of Civil Process by Post in the Manner of Special Delivery]', Fa Shi [2004] No 13.

15 2015 Opinion, Art 536.

16 SPC, 'Fayuan Guanyu Shewai Minshi Huo Shangshi Sifa Wenshu Songda Wenti Ruogan Guiding [Several Provisions of the SPC on the Service of Judicial Documents of Foreign-Related Civil or Commercial Cases]' ('Service of Judicial Documents Provisions'), Fa Shi [2006] No 5.

Furthermore, service by post is only permitted if it is a legitimate service method recognized in the country of destination. China has made reservation to the service by post in the Hague Service Convention. China does not allow foreign countries to serve documents on Chinese residents by post; and, following the principle of reciprocity, foreign countries may prevent service by post from China. This may seriously reduce the practical implementation of this method. China, on the other hand, is reluctant to abandon this reservation. There is a concern that allowing service in China by post may greatly increase the amount of litigation against Chinese residents.[17] It is predicted that China will not readily lift this reservation in the short term. **5.13**

v. Electronic service

Electronic service is the innovation introduced by the CPL in 2012. Electronic service includes service by fax, e-mail, electronic data exchange (EDI), telegram, or mobile short message service (SMS).[18] It is efficient, fast and inexpensive. However, some concerns need to be addressed before this service method can be widely and successfully adopted in practice. **5.14**

First, e-service imposes fundamentally different formal and substantive requirements from traditional service by post, and requires clear legal guidance on its formality and material validity. The law, however, is ambiguous and lacks detailed regulation on the process, formal requirement, effective date, security and the protection of recipients of electronic service.[19] **5.15**

Secondly, service by post requires the document to be posted to the country where the recipient has its domicile. The postal address and the domicile of the recipient are usually consistent and located in the same country. The e-mail address may be analogized with the physical address of the recipient. The document is thus served to the e-mail address, which may be registered in another country, remote from the domicile of the recipient. In theory, the documents are served in the territory of the country where the server is located.[20] There is a considerable chance that the location of the server is not the domicile or residence of the defendant or has any substantive connections with the defendant. **5.16**

17 HE Qisheng, 'Woguo Yuwai Songda Jizhi de Kunjing yu Xuanze [Difficulties and Reform for Service out of China]', (2005) 27 Faxue Yanjiu [*Cass Journal of Law*] 126, 137.

18 JIA Chenhao and LIU Yantao, 'Sifa Wenshu Dianzi Songda [Electronic Service of Legal Documents]', (2014) 240 Lilun Xuekan [*Theory Journal*] 107.

19 Ibid., 108.

20 JU Haiting, 'Dianzi Fangshi Songda Falv Wenshu Wenti Yanjiu [Study of Problems in Electronic Service of Legal Documents]', (2006) 6 Renmin Sifa [*People's Judicature*] 67, 68.

5.17 Thirdly, e-service may suffer challenges to its authority. Traditional legal documents are authorized by a stamp or a seal, e-documents rarely have similar means to ascertain their authority. Certification usually relies on an e-signature based on cryptographic technology.

5.18 Fourthly, there is a problem ensuring the defendant has been successfully served, i.e., the legal documents have reached the defendant and the defendant is aware of the service?[21] When service is by post, service can only be successful if the defendant or its representative has been required to sign the receipt of service or post. In e-commerce, the e-mail may be delivered to the defendant's e-mail address, which may not be frequently checked by the defendant. The e-mail may also be classified as unsolicited spam or other commercial mail and transferred automatically to the 'junk' folder. The CPL explicitly provides that legitimate electronic service must ascertain that the defendant has received the legal documents. 'Receive' means the legal documents have reached the control of the defendant in a way that the defendant knows or ought to have known their delivery. Mechanisms should be adopted to prove it. For example, the e-mail may require the defendant to send a receipt that the e-mail has been read. Once the receipt is sent, the defendant is successfully served. However, some defendants may refuse to send the delivery report as requested. In these circumstances proving service successful is difficult.

5.19 Fifthly, e-service imposes technical requirements to both the court administration and the recipient. Data may be lost, varied, damaged or stolen during transmission.[22] Adopting high technological security devices inevitably imposing the same technical requirements to the recipient, who needs relevant software or hardware and must have good computer literacy to decrypt the e-documents. The court needs to be sure that the recipient is well equipped to receive e-service before it could legally use this method.

5.20 Although accepting electronic service is a laudable development, the factual implementation requires more substantive work. Electronic service may suffer conceptual problems, practical difficulties and objections in the country of destination. Electronic service is still in the early stages of its development and it is a sensitive area that may easily generate a defence of procedural irregularity when judgments seek enforcement in the foreign country.

---

21 JIA and LIU, *supra* n 18, 108.
22 JU Haiting, *supra* n 20, 67.

vi. Public notice

If all the above methods fail, the foreign defendant may be served by public notice. The notice should be publicized for three months and the defendant is deemed served at the end of the period.[23] 5.21

In general, service on the defendant may only be effective if the method used provides the 'adequate notice' to the defendant in order to protect the defendant's right to be heard. Service by public notice, however, focuses more on the procedural efficiency and protection of the claimant's right to sue. The service is 'deemed' effective after a few conditions are fulfilled, even if the defendant has not actually read the notice. Therefore, it is necessary to provide additional conditions and requirements to protect the defendant's procedural rights. 5.22

Although not provided by the CPL, the 2015 Opinion provides that for domestic service, the public notice should include the reason why the service is by public notice; the claim form; the main issues in the case; the time limit for the defendant to respond; the time and venue of trial; and the consequences for not entering into appearance.[24] There is nothing to prevent the same requirements for extraterritorial public notice. The SPC in an earlier judicial interpretation also provided that to serve out of jurisdiction, the public notice must be published in the newspaper in both China and the country of destination.[25] It is questionable whether the public notice in a Chinese newspaper could serve the purpose of alerting a foreign defendant, especially if the defendant cannot read Chinese. It is also unclear what type of foreign newspaper should be chosen – national, regional, local, tabloid, or broadsheet? Public funding is spent to translate the document and to publish the notice abroad. The appropriateness, effectiveness and efficiency of the extraterritorial public notice are also subject to scepticism. 5.23

Another innovative issue about service by public notice in the digital era is whether the notice can be published on the website. This method has been adopted by some courts as a supplement to traditional public notices in domestic service. For example, the SPC official newspaper, *People's Court News*, publishes the public notice of all local courts on its website.[26] The parties could search and download the judicial documents. It is unclear whether the online notice alone could be a legally effective means to serve on 5.24

---

23 CPL, Art 367(8).

24 2015 Opinion, Art 139.

25 Service of Judicial Documents Provisions, *supra* n 16, Art 9.

26 www.rmfygg.com, accessed on 12 June 2015.

the defendant.[27] Since this method has only been used as a supplementary means to support traditional service, no clear answer has been provided. In general, the online notice may enjoy the characteristic of convenience, low-cost, and widespread broadcasting. However, it may not be able to provide adequate notice to the defendant; and the defendant has to be computer literate and have access to the website and also needs to visit the website that publishes the notice. Courts usually publish the notice on their own websites, frequent visitors to which are usually legal practitioners and not the general public. Furthermore, visiting a website differs from reading a newspaper. When reading a newspaper, the reader usually briefly browses each paper and selects the most interesting content to read. While browsing the newspaper, the reader may take a glance at some words printed on it and this would include the judiciary notice. Psychologically, the reader would be more sensitive to his name than to other information, which increases the chance of the notice being seen. The website is different; the homepage provides categories of the main sections and each main section may include subsections. The visitor will only browse the sections in which they are interested and, for most readers, this will not include the court notices. Unless the website automatically delivers the court notice in a pop-up window, the content will not be brought to the attention of the visitor. Furthermore, Chinese courts currently only publish the online notice on the website of the court system in Chinese. It is unreasonable to expect foreign defendants to visit the website or understand the notice. The only effective online notice may need judicial cooperation by publishing the notice on the website of the court of the destination and in the foreign language. But no such cooperation or arrangement exists.

II.2 Service within jurisdiction – service on the agent

5.25 Only Chinese lawyers may legally represent foreign clients in Chinese proceedings,[28] a foreign lawyer may represent a client as a non-lawyer.[29] Many foreign parties choose to appoint Chinese lawyers as their legal representatives partly because of their familiarity with the Chinese language, culture, law and procedure, and partly because of the unproved concern that Chinese lawyers may receive more favourable treatment over foreign lawyers in Chinese courts. If the foreign defendant has long-term business in China, it may recruit a Chinese lawyer who is fully authorized to handle all relevant legal affairs,

27 HUANG Liangyou and WEN Tingting, 'Wangshang Gonggao Songda Zhidu Yanjiu [Study of Service by Online Public Notice]', (2013) 34 Jishou Daxue Xuebao Shehui Kexueban [*Journal of Jishou University* (*Social Science Edition*)] 114, 115.

28 CPL, Art 263.

29 2015 Opinion, Art 528.

including receiving legal documents. In these circumstances, the legal document can be safely served on the representative within China instead of serving extraterritorially in the defendant's domicile.

The Chinese office or branch of the foreign defendant may also acquire the authority and act as its agent to receive legal documents. However, some foreign companies choose to establish subsidies in China, instead of a representative office or branch. These subsidies have separate legal personality and may refuse to receive service as the agent of the foreign company. For example, in 2000, Chinese consumers commenced a product liability action against Mercedes-Benz Germany. The Beijing Chaoyang District People's Court delivered the judicial documents to the defendant's Beijing office, but the latter refused to receive the documents arguing it was an independent entity not the authorized agent of the defendant. The refusal seriously delayed the action.[30] In *Qualcomm Shanghai v. Qualcomm US*, on the infringement of a trademark, the Chinese office of Qualcomm US claimed it had no authority to receive judicial documents on behalf of Qualcomm US. It took 12 months to serve the documents on the defendant out of jurisdiction through diplomatic channels.[31] **5.26**

In order to prevent an authorized agent from refusing to receive legal documents on behalf of the principal, the SPC provides that the service should be effective by leaving the legal documents in the premises of this agent.[32] However, this does not substantively resolve the difficulty. The preliminary request for leaving the legal documents in the premises of the agent is that this entity is indeed the authorized legal agent. In practice, however, foreign companies may establish agents or representative offices in China without authorizing them to receive legal documents in order to evade service on the agent within China. This alternative means to serve the process aims to provide efficiency and to protect the Chinese claimant's right to sue, but it is easily avoidable, which hampers the purpose of the legislation. It is necessary to consider whether the process can be served on much broader entities that have substantive connections with the foreign defendant, including representative offices, branches, subsidiaries and other establishments. Secondly, **5.27**

30 News, 'Chinese Consumer Sue Benz: An Endless Tough Road?', http://en.people.cn/200202/01/eng20020201_89758.shtml, accessed on 12 June 2015.

31 News, 'Qualcomm Shanghai v Qualcomm US', 18 Mar 2015. http://finance.takungpao.com/hkstock/qqgs/2015-03/2948554_print.html, accessed on 13 Aug 2015.

32 SPC, 'Guanyu Xiang Waiguo Gongsi Songda Sufa Wenshu Nengfou Xiangqi Zhuhua Daibiao Jigou Songda Bing Shiyong Liuzhi Songda Wenti de Pifu [Official Reply on Whether Judicial Documents to be Served on Foreign Companies can be Served on their Representative Agencies in China and on the Application of Service by Leaving the Said Documents]', Fa Shi [2002] No 15; SPC, 'Service of Judicial Documents Provisions', *supra* n 16, Art 12; 2015 Opinion, Art 130.

'authorization' may be interpreted to include both explicit authorization and implied authorization. If a Chinese entity has substantive connections with the foreign defendant and has acted as a *de facto* agent, service on this entity should be deemed successful. This interpretation, however, may cause other disadvantages, by unduly extending the judicial power of the Chinese court. Service in this matter may also generate difficulties in enforcement of judgments abroad and the defendant may bring a defence based on procedural irregularity.

II.3 Assessment of extraterritorial service in Chinese law

5.28 Extraterritorial service is a recognized problem in China. Although the CPL has provided multiple service methods, the most widely adopted ones are through diplomatic channels and by public notice.[33] The former is very slow and with a low success rate. The latter is questionable in terms of efficiency and adequate protection for the defendant. The legislators have recognized the necessity of updating the Chinese law. The new provisions in the CPL and the 2015 Opinion indeed have taken into account the more flexible approaches and the latest development in other countries. For example, service by post and electronic service are accepted. However, the law and guidance are not detailed enough to address all the practical issues and some conceptual concerns are not properly dealt with either. Adopting the new measures too quickly without being fully prepared or equipped with the necessary technology, skill and experience may lead to unexpectedly negative results. For example, some Chinese courts may exercise the service power over foreign defendants unduly and driven by local protectionism. The practice may not only cause diplomatic concerns and infringe international comity, it may also lead to the difficulty of enforcing judgments abroad in the future.

III. PROVISIONAL MEASURES

5.29 Provisional measures are important in assisting the effective trial, the enforcement of final judgments, and the factual outcome of the litigation. They are available in every jurisdiction to prevent the party from conducting any activities that may hamper the purpose of the trial, such as hiding or disposal of assets, destroying evidence, or continuing allegedly wrongful activities.

33 According to the research on the performance of Xiamen Intermediate People's Courts, between 2002 and 2006, about one-fifth of extraterritorial service is done by public notice. CAO Fagui, 'Xiamenshi Zhongji Renminfayuan Shewai Minshangshi Anjian de Shenli he Yanjiu [Adjudication of Foreign-Related Civil and Commercial Cases by the Xiamen Intermediate People's Court]', (2007) 3 Renmin Sifa [*People Judicature*] 46, 47.

III.1 Initiating provisional measures

Chinese law does not distinguish between domestic and international provisional measures; the same procedural rules apply to both. In China, three provisional measures are explicitly permitted, i.e., asset preservation, interim injunction and interim enforcement.[34] Provisional measures can be issued either upon the party's application or by the court's own motion when the court finds it 'necessary'.[35] The 'necessity' standard is ambiguous and may unreasonably expand the court's power to intervene in the parties' rights and obligations at an early stage, this may question the impartiality of the court and may also put pressure on the party against whom the interim measures are imposed forcing it to settle. **5.30**

III.2 Ancillary jurisdiction in provisional measures

Chinese law fails to provide exclusive jurisdiction rules on foreign-related provisional measures; it provides the same jurisdiction rules for both ancillary jurisdiction and substantive jurisdiction. In principle, any competent court should have ancillary jurisdiction to issue provisional measures over a substantive claim.[36] In practice, two scenarios exist. First, where the substantive dispute has already been commenced in a court, this court would wish to take ancillary jurisdiction to issue provisional measures to protect the progress of its action. The applicant may also feel it is more convenient to bring the petition to the same court, without realizing the potential difficulty of enforcement if the order should be executed overseas. Secondly, where the substantive dispute has not yet been brought to the court, and in an emergency case, the applicant may apply for the provisional measures before the commencement of litigation in the court of the place where the assets are located, where the applicant or the defendant has its domicile, or in any other competent court.[37] After the court issues the interim measures, there is a greater chance that the claimant may wish to bring the substantive action in the same court. **5.31**

Chinese law that mixes ancillary jurisdiction for provisional measures and substantive jurisdiction is improper. The court that hears the substantive dispute may not be the most appropriate one to order provisional measures. For example, the court may take substantive jurisdiction based on the defendant's domicile, while the defendant's seizable assets are located elsewhere. Or **5.32**

34 CPL, Art 100.
35 Ibid.
36 See Ch 3 for jurisdiction rules.
37 CPL, Art 101.

the court taking substantive jurisdiction is located in the place where the defamation victim has his domicile, while the interim injunction is sought to prevent the continuing publication of the alleged libel materials in another country.[38] In both cases, assistance from another court is required to enforce those provisional measures. In an international scenario, the enforcement of provisional measures depends on the judicial cooperation and assistance of the other country. In the absence of an international treaty between China and the foreign country concerned, the extraterritorial effect of the provisional measures order is questionable. Because of the difficulty of cross-border enforcement of provisional measures, some Chinese courts avoid issuing an order that involves extraterritorial enforcement. If the defendant has assets located in China, even if these assets have no connections with the dispute in question, the Chinese court may issue an assets preservation order against these assets instead of assets located in foreign countries which are the subject matter of the disputes. For example, in *China National Technical Import and Export Co v. Swiss Industrial Resource Inc*,[39] the assets subject to the dispute were located in Switzerland. The Chinese court, considering the convenience of enforcement, froze the defendant's assets located in China although they were irrelevant to the dispute.

5.33 What if the substantive disputes are brought abroad and the competent foreign court issues a provisional measure that needs to be enforced in China? The status quo is not promising. Foreign provisional measures are rarely enforced in China. The CPL and SPC interpretation do not include any provisions concerning the enforcement of foreign provisional measures. There is no international treaty available to facilitate international cooperation in this area. China has entered into a number of bilateral judicial cooperation treaties with foreign countries, but those treaties do not clearly define the term 'judgments' or 'rulings' to include rulings on provisional measures. Some treaties even expressly exclude mutual enforcement of provisional measures from the scope of judicial cooperation.[40] Furthermore, since interim measures are different from final judgments, it is unclear whether the Chinese law on enforcement of foreign judgments can be equally applied, i.e., whether foreign interim measures may be enforced by reciprocity.[41]

---

38 CPL, Art 265.

39 (1989) 1 SPC Gazette 26–28.

40 Such as the Sino-Kuwait and Sino-UAE Civil and Commercial Judicial Assistance Treaties.

41 For more discussion on Chinese law on enforcement of foreign judgments, see Ch 6 below.

The hostile attitude of Chinese courts against the enforcement of foreign interim measures is demonstrated in *Wahaha v. KPMG*,[42] where the substantive actions against the Chinese defendant were brought by the claimant Danone in the British Virgin Islands and Samoa respectively. Both courts issued interim freezing orders against the defendant's assets located in China. The claimant appointed KPMG, an accountancy firm, to enforce the order by taking over the assets in China. Chinese courts held KPMG liable in tort for enforcing foreign orders not authorized for enforcement by China. The courts also declared that the practice of KPMG infringed the China's sovereignty. **5.34**

III.3 Ancillary jurisdiction in maritime cases

A special jurisdiction rule is provided for jurisdiction over provisional measures in maritime claims. A Chinese court can issue compulsory preservation measures, maritime injunctions and maritime evidence preservation over vessels or goods within it territory. Jurisdiction is wholly based on the territorial location of the subject matter and the exclusive control of a court over property within its territory. Such ancillary jurisdiction is not subject to the limitation of exclusive jurisdiction or party autonomy. Ancillary jurisdiction in maritime claims is different from jurisdiction on the substance of the dispute. The applicant could bring the application before or during the litigation on merit in another court. If the litigation is not brought in another competent country and the applicant applies to the court that has taken the interim measure to take jurisdiction on the substance, the court can accept substantive jurisdiction.[43] Such practice is not unusual in maritime litigation. Since the 'convenience flag' is used widely in maritime practice, the flag of the vessel, in many cases, has no connection with the owner. When it is difficult to identify the real defendant, arresting the ship or issuing other compulsory interim measures may force the defendant to identify itself.[44] Furthermore, allowing the court that has taken process and control of the subject matter can also help enforcement after the court has given judgments on the merit of the dispute. Extending jurisdiction over maritime preservation and interim measures to the substance of the dispute is also recognized in the International Convention on the Arrest of Ships.[45] **5.35**

---

42 Jiangsu Province High People's Court, (2009) Su Min Er Zhong Zi 43.

43 Zhonghua Remin Gongheguo Haishi Susong Tebie Chengxu Fa (1999) [Special Maritime Procedure Law of the People's Republic of China (1999)], Arts 19, 61, 72.

44 DU Huanfang, 'Zhongguo Fayuan Shewai Guanxiaquan Shizheng Yanjiu [Empirical Study of Extraterritorial Jurisdiction of Chinese Courts]' (2007) 2 Faxuejia [Jurist] 152, 167.

45 Geneva, 12 March 1999.

IV. TAKING EVIDENCE ABROAD

5.36 Article 276 of the CPL provides that Chinese and foreign courts can each request the other to provide judicial assistance in taking evidence located in the territory of the other country pursuant to treaty obligations and the principle of reciprocity. Chinese courts can take evidence abroad through two channels.[46] First, evidence that is located abroad can be acquired according to treaty provisions. China has acceded to the Hague Convention 1970 on the Taking of Evidence Abroad in Civil or Commercial Matters ('Hague Evidence Convention') since 3 July 1997.[47] China and 42 countries can provide reciprocal assistance for evidence-taking pursuant to this Convention. The Convention provides two channels for taking evidence, i.e., through Central Authorities and through diplomatic officers, consular agents and commissioners. A contracting state should designate a Central Authority to receive letters of request from another contracting state and to transmit them to the competent national authority for execution.[48] China has made a reservation to the second channel, except that a Chinese diplomatic officer or consular agent may take the evidence from Chinese nationals in the territory of another contracting state.[49] The diplomatic officer or consular agent, however, cannot coercively acquire evidence from Chinese nationals. According to the principle of reciprocity, the diplomatic officer of the other contracting state may only take evidence from its citizens in China by the same means. The Hague Convention does not define the scope of evidence-taking activity, but it may include examining witnesses and inspecting documents or other property.[50]

5.37 As well as the Hague Evidence Convention, China has entered into bilateral judicial assistance treaties with more than 30 countries, such as France, Poland, Belgium, Russia, Mongolia, Cyprus, etc. The procedure described is similar in all the treaties. The competent court should provide the letter of request and relevant documents pursuant to the treaties, transmitting them to the SPC through the Higher People's Court of its district. The SPC will inspect the documents and translate them into the official language of the country of destination. The Chinese letter of request and documents together with the foreign language translation are then transmitted to the Ministry of Justice to be forwarded to the competent authority of the foreign country. Some

46 CPL, Art 277.

47 NPC, 'Quanguo Renmin Daibiao Dahui Changwu Weiyuanhui Guanyu Woguo Jiaru "Guanyu Cong Guowai Diaoqu Minshi huo Shangshi Zhengjude Gongyue" de Jueding [Decision of the Standing Committee of the NPC about China Acceded to "Convention on the Taking of Evidence Abroad in Civil or Commercial Matters"]' ('Decision to Accede to Evidence Convention'), 3 July 1997.

48 Hague Evidence Convention, Art 2,; Decision to Accede to Evidence Convention, ibid., Art 3.

49 Hague Evidence Convention, Art 15.

50 Ibid., Art 3.

countries enter into bilateral treaties with China and are also contracting states of the Hague Evidence Convention. The bilateral treaty should usually take priority over the Hague Evidence Convention in cases of conflict.

In the absence of treaties, overseas evidence can only be taken through diplomatic channels based on the principle of reciprocity.[51] The competent court should transmit the letter of request and relevant materials to the SPC for inspection. The SPC then transmits the documents to the Consular Affair Department of the Ministry of Foreign Affairs (CADMFA). CADMFA forwards the documents to the authority of the country of destination pursuant to its domestic law. **5.38**

V. COSTS, SECURITY FOR COSTS AND JUDICIAL AID

V.1 Costs and security for costs

The CPL and 2015 Opinion do not provide rules on court fees. The current regulation is primarily provided by the 'Notice of the SPC on the Application of the Measures for Paying Litigation Costs' ('Costs Notice')[52] and the State Council 'Measures on the Payment of Litigation Costs' ('Costs Order').[53] The Costs Notice and the Costs Order provide detailed guidance on the charge of litigation fees by the Chinese court. The same standard applies to both Chinese and foreign parties. However, if the court in which the foreign party has its citizenship treats the Chinese party differently from its own citizens, the Chinese court will apply the principle of reciprocity.[54] **5.39**

The ordinary rule that the loser pays the winner's costs is followed.[55] However, if the claimant is not a Chinese citizen, the court may order security for costs against the claimant. This rule was first provided by the SPC in 1984.[56] It does not suggest that the defendant should make an application or that the order can only be made under certain conditions. In other words, it seems that the 1984 Notice grants the court the power to order security for costs against all **5.40**

51 CPL, Art 277.

52 SPC, 'Guanyu Shiyong "Susong Feiyong Jiaona Banfa" de Tongzhi [Notice of the SPC on the Application of the Measures for Paying Litigation Costs]' 'Costs Notice', Fa Fa [2007] No 16.

53 State Council, 'Susong Feiyong Jiaona Banfa [Measures on the Payment of Litigation Costs]', Order of the State Council [2006] No 461.

54 Costs Notice, *supra* n 52, Art 5.

55 Ibid., Art 29.

56 SPC, 'Guanyu Yinfa "Minshi Susong Shoufei Banfa (Shixing)" de Tongzhi [Notice of the SPC on the Application of the Measures for Paying Litigation Costs (for the Trial Purpose)]' (abolished), Fa Ban Zi [1984] No 117, Art 14.

non-Chinese claimants in all cases by its own motion. This rule is designed to reduce the amount of litigation brought by foreign claimants in China, usually against Chinese defendants, and it clearly reflects local protectionism. The 1984 Notice was repealed by the 1989 Notice, which deleted the provision on security for costs. Following that, foreign claimants may have to provide security for costs only if the foreign country where they have their domicile or citizenship provides the same requirement for Chinese claimants. In other words, security for costs will only be ordered against foreign claimants based on the principle of reciprocity.[57]

5.41 Systematically ordering security for costs against foreign claimants is a parochial approach that is contrary to internationalization and international comity. However, the principle of reciprocity leaves the Chinese court in a passive position. When making an order, the Chinese court will not consider whether security for costs would be appropriate in an individual case, where, for example, the foreign claimant is suffering financial difficulties and the prospect of success is not high. The Chinese court will also apply the same procedural standards as used in the foreign court to make the order, for example, if the foreign court allows the court to exercise discretion, the Chinese court will exercise discretion in the same way, even if it may have no experience or insufficient knowledge of how discretion should be exercised.

5.42 It is thus suggested that simply relying on the principle of reciprocity is inappropriate and that more detailed guidance should be provided for Chinese courts to decide whether security for costs should be ordered. The order should not be initiated by the court by its own motion but based on the defendant's application. The defendant should also provide evidence to prove why it is considered necessary and reasonable to order security for costs. The court should then consider all relevant factors, including the claimant's link with China, its financial condition, the nature of the claim, the apparent prospects of success, any steps taken to relocate assets, and other factors that may prove that the claimant may evade the consequence of the action. In particular, the court should balance the interests between protecting foreign claimants' rights to bring a genuine action and preventing irresponsible and abusive litigation. It should be taken as the basic principle that the court should not unreasonably hinder a genuine claim. Therefore, security for costs may be ordered only in exceptional circumstances. The guidance should also provide the period when application may be made, and what securities may be accepted.

---

57 Costs Notice, *supra* n 52, Art 5.

V.2 Judicial aid

The judicial costs may be reduced, waived or deferred in exceptional circumstances.[58] This is called 'judicial aid' in China.[59] Judicial aid may be provided to a natural person who has proved that paying the judicial costs would cause financial difficulty.[60] The SPC further provides detailed guidance on when the financial difficulty is deemed to exist.[61] Although it does not explicitly apply to foreign parties, foreign parties may in principle receive the same standard of treatment.[62] In practice, however, judicial aid is difficult for foreign parties to access. **5.43**

First, many of the approved circumstances for judicial aid can only apply to Chinese citizens. For example, judicial aid may be granted to those receiving the rural minimum social security: 'five guarantees' in rural areas;[63] the social aid for serious poverty or job allowance;[64] social welfare institutes;[65] the claimant in the recourse of social insurance;[66] and migrant works from the rural area.[67] The standard is determined according to the national and local social welfare and allowance, which is not applicable to foreign parties. **5.44**

Secondly, some circumstances that entitle the victim to claim for judicial aid may exist in cross-border actions. For example, judicial aid may be granted to the party suing for payment of wages; for damages arising out of a traffic accident, a medical accident, injury in the workplace, product liability and other personal injury; for damages arising out of any action to protect the public interest of the society; or suffering financial difficulty caused by any natural disaster.[68] However, it does not mean that judicial aid should be granted whenever these circumstances exist. The court must be satisfied that the applicant does suffer financial difficulty. The question is whether the court **5.45**

---

58 CPL, Art 118.

59 Judicial aid is called 'Sifa Jiuzhu' in Chinese (司法救助). See Costs Notice, *supra* n 52, Ch 6. M. Palmer and C. Xi, 'The People's Republic of China', in C. Hodges, S. Vogenauer, M. Tulibacka (eds), *The Costs and Funding of Civil Litigation* (Bloomsbury, 2010) 261, 263.

60 Costs Notice, *supra* n 52, Art 44.

61 Ibid., Arts 44–47; SPC, 'Zuigao Renmin Fayuan Guanyu Dui Jingji Queyou Kunnan de Dangshiren Tigong Sifa Jiuzhu de Guiding [Provisions of the SPC on Providing Legal Assistance for Litigants with Confirmed Financial Difficulties]', Fa Fa [2005] No 6.

62 CPL, Art 5.

63 Costs Notice, *supra* n 52, Art 45(3). 'Five Guarantees' [wu bao](五保) is a social welfare system in China ensuring the low-income families the five basic guarantees for living, including food, clothing, medical care, housing and burial expenses. Judicial Aid Provisions, *supra* n 61, Art 3(2).

64 Costs Notice, *supra* n 52, Art 45(3); Judicial Aid Provisions, *supra* n 61, Art 3(9).

65 Costs Notice, *supra* n 52, Art 46(3).

66 Costs Notice, *supra* n 52, Art 47(1); Judicial Aid Provisions, *supra* n 61, Art 3(5).

67 Judicial Aid Provisions, *supra* n 61, Art 3(8).

68 Costs Notices, *supra* n 52, Art 45–47; Judicial Aid Provisions, *supra* n 61, Art 3.

should assess the financial status of the applicant according to the living standard and the local allowance of the applicant's domicile or the standard in the place where the court is located. Applying the local standard of the applicant's domicile may cause difficulty of proof. Where the applicant is domiciled in an economically advanced country, providing judicial aid may be prejudicial to Chinese citizens and waste Chinese public funds. Applying the local standard of the court would be more appropriate.

5.46 Thirdly, the judicial cost of cross-border litigation is usually higher than domestic actions, due to the additional requirements for translation, notarization, collecting evidence, extraterritorial service and proving foreign law. The foreign party also must bear the cost of travel, accommodation, interpretation, etc, when conducting proceedings in China. The extra cost probably would cause financial difficulty to the party, even if this party is not considered financially disadvantaged according to the local standard of the Chinese court. The cost of litigation, however, is not a relevant factor in the application for judicial aids, which may make the relevant rule unreasonable for foreign-related proceedings.

5.47 Fourthly, the court also needs to prevent the foreign claimant from abusive litigation. Providing judicial aid functions contrary to the security for costs. Where a foreign claimant in financial difficulty seizes the Chinese court to bring an action, the court may want to order security for cost to prevent this party from bringing unfounded claims, while the judicial aid system permits the court to reduce, waive or defer payment of the judicial cost. These two systems appear contradictory. China has largely abandoned the scheme for ordering security for cost from the foreign claimants. However, when granting judicial aid to foreign claimants, special caution is required. It is suggested that the court should first look at the expressed circumstances in the SPC guidance. Only those that fall in one of the circumstances may be considered for judicial aid. Secondly, the court should consider whether the claim is well-founded, genuine and has reasonable perspective to succeed. If yes, the legal aid may be granted.

VI. IDENTIFICATION OF THE FOREIGN PARTY

5.48 Where a foreign party participates in a legal action in China, it must submit authentic documents to the court to prove its identity. Natural persons should provide their passport.[69] More complicated requirements are imposed on

69 2015 Opinion, Art 523, para 1.

foreign companies or other entities. Foreign companies or entities should submit identification documents notarized in the relevant country and certified by the Chinese embassy or consulate in that country, or other certified documents pursuant to the treaty between China and that country.[70] The term 'relevant country' includes the country where the foreign enterprise is established by registry or a third country where the enterprise is registered to operate.[71] Representatives of the foreign entities should also submit to the People's Court the documents that prove their identification and the authorization to represent the foreign entities. These documents should be acquired through the same process applied to foreign entities.[72]

Furthermore, China has not established diplomatic relations with 23 countries and, as a result, there is no Chinese embassy or consulate operating in these countries.[73] How can the identity of enterprises registered in these countries be verified for the purpose of Chinese proceedings? The process needs to be facilitated by the assistance of the embassy/consulate of the third country that has diplomatic relations with China. The relevant documents should be notarized by the authorized entities of the relevant country, certified by the embassy/consulate of the third country, and then forwarded to the Chinese embassy or consulate in the third country for a certification.[74] The actual process is complicated and nothing guarantees the cooperation of the third country. It thus imposes barriers for proving identity of foreign entities in these 23 countries and may hamper completely their access to the Chinese courts. **5.49**

VII. REPRESENTATION

Chinese law also provides special requirements for the legal representation of foreign parties conducting actions in China. Only Chinese lawyers can be appointed to represent foreign parties as a lawyer.[75] If the foreign party appoints foreign lawyers as their legal representatives, they are not permitted to be the legal representative in the court.[76] **5.50**

---

70 Ibid., para 2.

71 Ibid., para 4.

72 Ibid., para 3.

73 Budan, Panama, Paraguay, Honduras, Guatemala, Nicaragua, El Salvador, Belize, Dominican Republic, Haiti, Saint Vincent and the Grenadines, Saint Kitts and Nevis, Saint Lucia, Solomon Islands, Nauru, Kiribati, Marshall Islands, Palau, Tuvalu, Burkina Faso, Gambia, Swaziland, São Tomé and Príncipe.

74 2015 Opinion, Art 524.

75 CPL, Art 263.

76 2015 Opinion, Art 528.

5.51 The foreign party could appoint the representative in front of a Chinese judge.[77] If the foreign party signed the letter of authorization in the territory of China, the letter should be authenticated by the Chinese notary or other authorized entity.[78] If the foreign party sends the letter of authorization from abroad to China to appoint a Chinese lawyer or citizen to act as a legal representative, the letter of authorization should be authenticated by the notary in the relevant country, certified by the Chinese embassy or consulate in this country, or follow the treaty procedure if there is a treaty between China and the relevant country.[79] If the foreign party is not within the territory of China, the embassy or consular representing the relevant country in China may authorize its officer to appoint a Chinese lawyer or Chinese citizen to represent the foreign party to conduct the action in China.[80]

VIII. LIMITATION

5.52 The limitation period for filing a defence, submitting an appeal, and delivering judgments in foreign-related litigation is more flexible than in domestic cases. If the defendant is domiciled outside China, he has 30 days to file his defence after the claim forms are effectively served.[81] Chinese courts have discretion to decide whether an extension may be provided upon the defendant's application.[82] If the defendant is domiciled in China, the defendant should file defence within 15 days of service, consistent with the domestic trial.[83]

5.53 If the party wants to appeal, the application should be made within 30 days after the judgment is effectively served, which may also be extended by discretion and upon request.[84] Finally, the CPL does not provide a restriction for the length of trial.[85] It is mainly because foreign-related litigation is more complex in law and in fact and takes time to serve, to translate, to acquire evidence, to summon witnesses, to decide jurisdiction and applicable law, and to prove foreign law. The time that may be spent on trial is unpredictable. However, the complete lack of regulation makes it possible that a foreign-related trial may take much longer than necessary. Since Chinese courts must

77 Ibid., Art 525.
78 Ibid., Art 526.
79 CPL, Art 264.
80 2015 Opinion, Art 529.
81 CPL, Art 268.
82 Ibid.
83 Ibid., Art 125.
84 Ibid., Art 269.
85 Ibid., Art 270.

follow the time requirement in the domestic trial, when workloads increase, priority is given to domestic cases and further delays in foreign-related litigation may be inevitable.[86]

86 For domestic cases, the trial of the first instance should be completed within six months, extended with the approval of the President of the Court by another six months. If further extension is required, it should be reported to the supervisory court for approval: CPL, Art 149.

6

RECOGNITION AND ENFORCEMENT OF FOREIGN JUDGMENTS IN CHINESE COURTS

6.01 Recognition and enforcement of foreign judgments is usually the final stage in international commercial litigation. After the court asserts jurisdiction, decides the applicable law and applies that law to make the decision, the judgment will only have practical value if it can prevent future actions from being brought in the same matter and can be enforced. At the international level the *res judicata* effect and the enforceability of foreign judgments often present difficulties. The effect of any government's acts, including judicial ones, is limited to the territory of the sovereign.[1] Therefore, the judgment of a court normally has no effect outside the territory of its jurisdiction.[2] A judgment has an effect in another country only if the authority of the latter agrees to recognize and enforce it. This chapter focuses on Chinese law and practice on recognition and enforcement of foreign judgments.

1 *Hilton v. Guyot*, 159 U.S. 113,163 (1895).

2 L Collins et al. (eds), *Dicey, Morris and Collins on the Conflict of Laws* (15th ed., London: Sweet & Maxwell 2006) para 14–002.

I. A GENERAL CONSIDERATION

I.1 Recognition v. enforcement

'Recognition' and 'enforcement' are interrelated but different. Briefly speaking, 'recognition' involves a decision not to permit litigation of a specific issue or factual dispute that was previously decided in another court. It grants the foreign judgment the same *res judicata* effect that it has in its country of origin. 'Enforcement' involves the jurisdiction's exercise of its judicial powers to compel compliance with a judgment rendered in another jurisdiction. 'Recognition' is the prerequisite for 'enforcement'. A foreign judgment must be recognized before it can be enforced. However, not all recognized judgments will be enforced,[3] and some judgments need only be recognized but not enforced in the other country, such as an affirmative or negative declaration. **6.02**

I.2 Foreign judgments

The terminology of 'foreign court judgments' can be defined from the following aspects. First, 'foreign' refers to not only foreign countries or nations from the political perspective, but also separate legal regions, such as Hong Kong, Scotland, or California, from the legal perspective, as well as international organizations in the global community, such as the European Court of Justice. **6.03**

Secondly, the so-called 'court' is not limited to a court of justice, but includes administrative organs which exercise particular decision-making power in some special situations, such as the marriage registration office when it issues certificates of marital status. **6.04**

Thirdly, 'judgments' refer to all decisions on the merits of the dispute between the litigants. They are not limited to the adjudicated documents expressly named as 'judgments', but include all rulings, orders, decrees, and decisions which decide the substantive rights and obligations of the litigants. They would exclude rulings on the procedural issues listed in Article 154 of CPL, including: refusal to entertain a case; objection to the jurisdiction of a court; rejection of a complaint; property preservation and advance enforcement; approval or disapproval of the withdrawal of a lawsuit; suspension or termination of legal proceedings; suspension or termination of **6.05**

3 Ibid.

enforcement; cancellation or refusal of enforcing an arbitration award; or refusal to enforce a document of the creditor's rights issued by a notary office.[4]

6.06 In conclusion, 'foreign court judgments' in the recognition and enforcement context may be defined as any decision on the merits by a court or other institutions which are entitled to make a judicial decision from outside mainland China, whatever it is named, including any decree or order, and any determination of costs or expenses, as far as such determination relates to a decision on the merits that may be recognized or enforced under Chinese law. However, since Chapter 13 will specifically address recognition and enforcement of judgments from Hong Kong, Macau and Taiwan, this chapter will only examine enforcement of judgments rendered by the courts in other foreign countries.

II. THE THEORETICAL BASES OF RECOGNITION AND ENFORCEMENT

II.1 Comity

6.07 For centuries, notions of territorial sovereignty focused on the exclusive jurisdiction of a nation over incidents and persons within the boundaries of its territory. In the seventeenth century, Ulrich Huber, a Dutch professor of international law, enunciated three maxims of international law: (1) domestic law of a sovereign state applies within the territory of this state but not beyond; (2) all citizens or institutes within the territory of a state are subjects of the state; and (3) states should give effect to rights created by other states subject to the reservation of states' interest.[5] Huber's concept of comity was originated to establish a theoretical basis for the application of foreign law, but it was widely adopted by national courts as an important foundation in principle for the enforcement of foreign judgments.

6.08 However, the concept of comity is a vague one. In particular, it is uncertain whether it is merely a courteous gesture or is an obligation of a state. Gray J. stated in the U.S. Supreme Court case of *Hilton v. Guyot*:

> 'Comity', in the legal sense, is neither a matter of absolute obligation, on the one hand, nor of mere courtesy and goodwill, upon the other. But it is the recognition which one

4 CPL, Art 154.

5 J.R. Paul, 'Comity in International Law', (1991) 32 *Harvard International Law Journal* 1, 15; E.G. Lorenzen, 'Huber's De Conflictu Legum', in E.G. Lorenzen (ed), *Selected Articles on the Conflict of Laws* (Yale University Press 1947) 136–7.

> nation allows within its territory to the legislative, executive or judicial acts of another nation, having due regard both to international duty and convenience, and to the rights of its own citizens, or of other persons who are under the protection of its laws.[6]

This interpretation leaves the concept of comity undetermined. It is positioned between strict legal obligations on the one hand, and courtesy and good faith on the other. When it should be exercised is a discretionary issue left to the court to decide. More importantly, comity alone would not work appropriately in the international context, where no comity would exist without cooperation and mutual expression of goodwill between countries.[7] This leads directly to the development of the other theory, 'reciprocity', which is adopted more widely by national courts to give effects to foreign judgments. **6.09**

II.2 Reciprocity

As a basis of enforcing foreign judgments, reciprocity means 'the judgment rendered in a foreign country is allowed the same effect only as the courts of that country allow to the judgment of the country in which the judgment in question is sought to be executed'.[8] Reciprocity is deemed an advanced version of comity, i.e., comity only works well if all sovereigns honour the doctrine.[9] It has been stated by Gray J.:[10] **6.10**

> [T]here is a distinct and independent ground upon which we are satisfied that the comity of our nation does not require us to give conclusive effect to the judgments of the courts of France; and that ground is, the want of reciprocity, on the part of France, as to the effect to be given to the judgments of this and other foreign countries.

The doctrine of reciprocity focuses on encouraging other countries to enforce local judgments. By establishing judicial cooperation, both countries establish a reciprocal relationship and will have reciprocal recognition and enforcement of each other's judgments. The rule of reciprocity is rooted in the comity doctrine but it is developed to address the fundamental difficulty that the doctrine of comity may generate in practice. After the doctrine of reciprocity **6.11**

---

6 *Hilton v. Guyot*, *supra* n 1, 163–4.

7 S.L. Stevens, 'Commanding International Judicial Respect', (2002) 26 *Hastings International and Comparative Law Review* 115, 119–20.

8 *Hilton v. Guyot, supra* n 1, 227. For more discussion on reciprocity, see Stevens, *supra* n 7.

9 Stevens, *supra* n 7, 120.

10 *Hilton v. Guyot*, *supra* n 1, 210. For comments, see V. Singal, 'Preserving Power without Sacrificing Justice', (2008) 59 *Hastings Law Journal* 943, 950; Stevens, *supra* n 7, 125–6.

had been established it was quickly adopted by various international conventions and into the domestic law of many countries.[11]

6.12 Support for reciprocity is largely based on pragmatism. Nations have an interest in protecting their citizens and maximizing their interests. Every state has an interest in making its judgments recognizable and enforceable in the territory of other states. Since no country can directly affect the judicial sovereignty of another country, countries would have to find a mutually acceptable method to achieve this aim. The most effective way is to establish cooperation between countries. The doctrine of reciprocity in theory is to 'encourage' states to give effect to each other's judgments.[12] In particular, it may cause foreign judgment creditors to lobby their home country to enforce the judgment of these countries that have adopted this doctrine.[13]

6.13 Reciprocity, however, is also criticized by scholars. It punishes innocent individuals, who are not able to enforce judgments simply because the two relevant states have no reciprocal relationship.[14] It can also cause inefficiency as more disputes arise on whether the reciprocal relationship exists.[15] More onerous duties will be put on the court to determine the foreign attitude towards the local judgment.[16] It may, in fact, not help cooperation but cause retaliation between countries.[17] It is remarkable that the notion of a reciprocity requirement has largely faded. For example, in the US, the Restatement (Second) of Conflict of Laws and the Restatement (Third) of Foreign Relations Law of the United States indicate that the majority of jurisdictions do not require reciprocity to enforce foreign judgments. In Germany, Italy, and the UK, foreign judgments will be recognized pursuant to certain national standards, even if reciprocity is lacking.

---

11 For example, the Brussels Convention on jurisdiction and the enforcement of judgments in civil and commercial matters 1968 states that it aims to secure the simplification of formalities governing the reciprocal recognition and enforcement of judgments of courts or tribunals. See the Brussels Convention 1968, Preamble. See also, CPL, Art 282.

12 For proving the result by using the game theory, see Stevens, *supra* n 7; M. Whincop, 'The Recognition Scene', (1999) 23 *Melbourne University Law Review* 416; R.A. Brand, 'Recognition of Foreign Judgments as a Trade Law Issue', in J.S. Bhandari and A.O. Sykes (eds), *Economic Dimensions in International Law* (Cambridge, CUP 1997) 592.

13 J.F. Coyle, 'Rethinking Judgments Reciprocity', (2014) 92 *North Carolina Law Review* 1109, 1144.

14 R.W. Hulbert, 'Some Thoughts on Judgments, Reciprocity, and the Seeming Paradox of International Commercial Arbitration', (2008) 29 *University of Pennsylvania Journal of International Law* 641, 652; Coyle, ibid., 1124–5.

15 Hulbert, ibid., 651; Coyle, *supra* n 13, 1125–6.

16 Coyle, *supra* n 13, 1120–23.

17 F.K. Juenger, *Selected Essays on the Conflict of Laws* (Transnational Publishers Inc 2001) 312.

Regardless of this trend, reciprocity continues to play a dominant role in China. For example, Article 282 of the CPL explicitly stipulates the principle of reciprocity and reciprocity is strictly applied by Chinese courts. In *Tsuburaya Productions Co Ltd v. Beijing Yansha Youyi Shopping City Co Ltd*,[18] the defendant (Beijing Yansha) sought to rely on a Japanese judgment to support its argument, but the requested Chinese court refused to recognize the Japanese judgment due to the lack of the reciprocal relationship between Japan and China. The majority of Chinese scholars accept the doctrine of reciprocity and believe that no foreign judgments are entitled conclusive effects and they are, at most, the prima facie evidence justifying the merit of the claim.[19] **6.14**

II.3 Vested rights and obligations

This argument extends Dicey and Beale's vested right theory to the enforcement of foreign judgment. According to this theory, a substantive right to the judgment creditor and obligation to the judgment debtor has been created by the appropriate judicial practice under the law of a foreign country.[20] Therefore, the court of the other country will give effect to the judgment not because the foreign power is respected but because the right that is duly created should be enforced. **6.15**

Applying the vested rights theory in foreign judgment recognition suffers two challenges. First, the vested right theory was first established to justify the application of foreign law. The foreign law vests the right on matters subject to its control and the local court recognizes the vested right by giving effects to the foreign law. In the enforcement of judgments, the foreign court renders judgments but the local court enforces the foreign judgment by applying the local law. It is fundamentally different from the vested right in choice of law.[21] Secondly, the judgment rights and obligations are created in the territory of the foreign country, according to its conflict of laws. As a matter of principle, they should be the rights and obligations within the country where the judgment is rendered, instead of rights and obligations of the enforcement country. It is hard to justify why such obligations or rights have extraterritorial effects.[22] This difficulty may be avoided by treating the foreign judgment as a **6.16**

18 No 2 IPC of Beijing Municipality, (2004) Er Zhong Min Chuzi No 12687.

19 WANG Jiwen, 'Lun Woguo Dui Waiguo Caipan Chengren yu Zhixing de Huhui Yuanze—Yi Liyi Hengliang Fangfa wei Gongju [On Reciprocity Principle of Recognition and Enforcement of Foreign Judgments in China: Analysis by Interest-balancing method]', (2012) 6 Faxuejia [*Legal Jurist*] 154, 154–5.

20 J.G. Castel, 'Recognition and Enforcement of Foreign Judgments in Personam and in Rem in the Common Law Provinces of Canada', 17 *McGill Law Journal* 11, 22.

21 Yntema, 'Review: Recognition and Enforcement of Foreign Judgments' (1939) 49 *Yale Law Journal* 1134, 1139.

22 Castel, *supra* n 20, 22.

matter of fact. However, no country would accept that the foreign judgment compels the local court to enforce it. The enforcement and the legal consequence of the foreign judgment depend on the local court, by applying the local law, which creates a local right to enforce.[23]

6.17 Most Chinese jurists reject the vested rights and obligations theory. The vested rights theory shifts the focus on foreign judgment recognition from respecting state sovereignty to the enforcement of individual rights. This is fundamentally different from the underlying policy in China that in general treats foreign judgment recognition as a public matter. Furthermore, the concept of 'vested rights' originated from the protection of private rights and property, a concept largely lacking in the Chinese legal history. The overall concept of 'vested rights' is unpopular in China.

II.4 *Res judicata*

6.18 *Res judicata* grants finality to an effective judgment. It requires a dispute to be put to an end by a legitimate measure and the parties cannot re-litigate the same matter anywhere, either domestically or internationally.[24] Legitimacy depends on the procedural fairness, competence and jurisdiction of the original court and the reasonableness of enforcement. This theory grants the basis to enforce foreign judgments and provides a defence at the same time of safeguarding the interests of the enforcing state.

6.19 However, it is more natural to apply *res judicata* at the domestic than international level. Domestically, the sole policy of stopping re-litigation is enough to justify *res judicata*. At the international level, various policies emerge, these include: the policy of fostering relationships between countries, which is similar to the doctrine of comity; the policy of protecting the interest of litigants; and the policy of protecting the finality of local judgments in foreign states, which shares the root of reciprocity.[25] As a result, *res judicata* may not work alone to justify the enforcement of foreign judgments, because there is always a question as to why foreign judgments should have extra-territorial *res judicata*. This theory should be combined with other policies and doctrines at the international level.

---

23 Ibid., 24.

24 W.L.M. Reese, 'The Status in This Country of Judgments Rendered Abroad', (1950) 50 *Columbia Law Review* 783; Castel, *supra* n 20, 24.

25 C.H. Peterson, 'Res Judicata and Foreign Country Judgments', (1963) 24 *Ohio State Law Journal* 291, 305–206.

II.5 Pragmatism and efficiency

This theory emphasizes the importance of foreign judgment recognition (FJR): efficiency; protection of the party; preventing forum shopping; and fostering international stability.[26] All of these reasons can be placed under the broad concept of efficiency, which includes efficiency for individual litigants, efficiency for individual states, and global efficiency. **6.20**

Cross-border collaboration is crucial for economic development. Refusing to enforce a foreign judgment would cause a series of difficulties that may hamper the economy. The parties may have to re-litigate a matter that has already been adjudicated in another country, which increases public and private costs. The difficulty in enforcing foreign judgments may cause an invisible obstacle for citizens to participate in cross-border transactions, especially with a commercial partner from the country where FJR proves difficult or impossible. For example, if FJR proves more difficult in China than in other countries, it may make it more difficult, or result in higher transaction costs, for Chinese companies to enter into cross-border contracts with foreign companies. It also makes Chinese companies less competitive in the international market. Furthermore, refusing FJR may leave the parties no option but to litigate in an inconvenient forum, which may result in higher litigation and judicial costs. **6.21**

Based on the theory of efficiency, FJR is the need for the development of national economies in globalization. In China, the importance of FJR was recognized only after the 'open door' policy, which led to frequent cross-border connections and transactions. China has made economic development its central task, which has been ranked high in politics and legislation.[27] The efficiency theory is also more comfortably received by Chinese jurists.[28] **6.22**

The efficiency theory, however, has an obvious fallacy. The theory is based on an economic concept. Legal rules and norms are judged in terms of a pragmatic benefit, instead of legal norms such as justice, fairness and equality, or political norms such as sovereignty, power or national interest. However, the legislative and judicial development in FJR in China is heavily influenced by the legal and political norms instead of by economic considerations of efficiency. It is reasonable to argue that the efficiency theory only raises the **6.23**

26 A.T. von Mehren and D.T. Trautman, 'Recognition of Foreign Adjudications', (1968) 81 *Harvard Law Review* 1601, 1601–4.

27 C. Xu, 'The Fundamental Institutions of China's Reforms and Development', (2011) 49 *Journal of Economic Literature* 1076.

28 WANG Jiwen, *supra* n 19, 155–6.

importance and necessity of FJR, but it does not form the theoretical basis for FJR. As a result, the theory of efficiency has never been recognized in Chinese legislation or judicial practice. In China, the only officially recognized doctrine is reciprocity.

III. RECOGNITION AND ENFORCEMENT UNDER INTERNATIONAL TREATIES

6.24 The recognition and enforcement of foreign judgments in China are regulated in Part Four Chapter XXVII of the Civil Procedure Law of the People's Republic of China (2012).[29] Article 282 states that:

> In the case of an application or request for recognition and enforcement of a legally effective judgment or ruling of a foreign court, the people's court shall, after examining it in accordance with the international treaties concluded or acceded to by the People's Republic of China or with the principle of reciprocity and arriving at the conclusion that it does not contradict the basic principles of the law of the People's Republic of China nor violates state sovereignty, security and social public interest of the country, recognize the validity of the judgment by ruling; and if required, issue a writ of execution to enforce it in accordance with the relevant provisions of this Act. Where the judgment contradicts the basic principle of the law of the People's Republic of China or violates state sovereignty, security and social public interest of the country, the people's court shall not recognize and enforce it.

6.25 Therefore, the first step for recognizing and enforcing foreign judgments in Chinese courts is to examine whether there is any multilateral or bilateral treaty of judicial assistance between China and the country from which the judgment originates.[30] In the absence of treaty obligations, the foreign judgment will be recognized pursuant to the principle of reciprocity.

III.1 Judicial cooperation treaties

6.26 China is a member of the Hague Private International Law Conference, and actively participated in the Hague judgment project, which resulted in the 2005 Hague Convention on Choice of Court Agreements. However, China is

---

29 This Act was passed by the National People's Congress on 9 April 1991, first, amended by the NPC Standing Committee in 28 October 2007, and secondly, amended by the NPC Standing Committee in 31 August 2012.

30 But in judicial practice, Chinese courts sometimes applied the international convention incorrectly. Take *HOU Yijun v. HOU Kelis*, Henan Province Zhengzhou IPC, (2013) Zheng Min Er Chu Zi No 001, as an example. The petitioner applied for recognition of a divorce decree (No 873) rendered by a Romanian court on 1 February 2008, Zhengzhou IPC should have made a decision on the ground of the bilateral treaty concluded between China and Romania on 16 January 1991. Unfortunately, it applied CPL, Arts 281 and 282, but ignored the treaty.

not yet a party to the Hague Choice of Court Convention 2005 or any comprehensive multilateral treaty concerning the recognition and enforcement of foreign judgments. A sole exception is the International Convention on Civil Liability for Oil Pollution Damage of 1969, to which the PRC acceded on 5 January 2000. Article 10 of this Convention states any final judgment given within the jurisdiction in accordance with this Convention should be recognized and enforced in another contracting state, except where the judgment was obtained by fraud, or where the defendant was not given reasonable notice and a fair opportunity to present his case. This is the only international convention to which China is a party creating a treaty obligation for the Chinese courts to recognize and enforce foreign judgments.

Since 1987, China has signed bilateral judicial assistance treaties in civil and commercial matters with 36 countries providing rules for the mutual recognition and enforcement of judgments.[31] Table 6.1 below shows all countries that have entered into bilateral civil judicial assistance treaties with China. Judicial assistance is defined broadly to cover: service of process; taking evidence for a foreign proceeding; enforcement of foreign judgments; and enforcement of foreign arbitral awards. Within these 36 countries, except South Korea and Singapore, all other countries have agreed mutual recognition and enforcement of civil judgments with China.[32] **6.27**

The comparative study of the rules on recognition and enforcement of foreign judgments among these treaties shows they are basically similar, except for a few discrepancies caused by the different legal systems, concerns and major demands from different contracting countries. In general, these bilateral treaties adopt the general principle of mutual and reciprocal recognition and enforcement of each other's judgments in civil matters, subject to five refusal grounds discussed in the next section.[33] **6.28**

31 In addition, the Bilateral Treaty on Encouragement and Protection of Investment between China and Australia also provides the rules on recognition and enforcement of court judgments and arbitral awards.

32 Some countries have concluded with China the bilateral judicial assistance treaties in criminal matters, such as Canada (1995), South Korea (2000), the Philippines (2001) and the US (2001). China has also entered into extradition treaties with Russia (1996), Bulgaria (1997), Belarus (1996), Mongolia (1997), Thailand (1994), Ukraine (2000), Uzbekistan (2000), and Cambodia (2000). These treaties do not concern the recognition and enforcement of judgments in civil matters.

33 Art 10.

Table 6.1 List of countries that have concluded civil judicial assistance treaties with China

Signatories	Matters	Signature day	Effective day	Remarks
Bosnia and Herzegovina	Cc1	18 Dec 2012		
Algeria	Cc1	10 Jan 2010	10 Jan 2010	
Brazil	Cc1	19 May 2009	30 Nov 2009	
Peru	Cc1	19 Mar 2008	30 Mar 2009	
Kuwait	Cc1	18 Jun 2007	24 Apr 2008	
United Arab Emirates	Cc1	21 Apr 2004	12 Apr 2005	
North Korea	Cc1	19 Nov 2003	21 Jan 2006	
South Korea	Cc1	7 Jul 2003	27 Apr 2005	No rule on recognition
Argentina	Cc1	9 Apr 2001		
Lithuania	Cc1	20 Mar 2000	19 Feb 2002	
Tunisia	Cc1	4 May 1999	20 Jul 2000	
Laos	Cc1	25 Jan 1999	15 Dec 2001	
Vietnam	Cc1	19 Oct 1998	25 Dec 1999	
Uzbekistan	Cc1	11 Dec 1997	29 Aug 1998	
Singapore	Cc1	28 Apr 1997	27 Jun 1999	No rule on recognition
Tajikistan	Cc1	26 Sep 1996	2 Sep 1998	
Kyrgyzstan	Cc1	4 Jul 1996	26 Sep 1997	
Morocco	Cc1	16 Apr 1996	26 Nov 1999	
Hungary	Cc1	9 Oct 1995	21 Mar 1997	Invalid now
Cyprus	Ccc	25 Apr 1995	11 Jan 1996	
Greece	Cc1	17 Oct 1994	29 Jun 1996	
Egypt	Ccc	21 Apr 1994	31 May 1995	
Thailand	Cc1	16 Mar 1994	6 Jul 1997	
Bulgaria	C	2 Aug 1993	30 Jun 1995	
Kazakhstan	Cc2	14 Jan 1993	11 Jul 1995	
Belarus	Cc2	11 Jan 1993	29 Nov 1994	
Cuba	Cc2	24 Nov 1992	26 Mar 1994	
Ukraine	Cc2	31 Jan 1992	19 Jan 1994	
Turkey	Ccc	28 Sep 1992	26 Oct 1995	
Russia Federation	Cc2	19 Jun 1992	14 Nov 1993	
Spain	Cc1	2 May 1992	1 Jan 1994	
Italy	C	20 May 1991	1 Jan 1995	
Romania	Cc2	16 Jan 1991	22 Jan 1993	

Signatories	Matters	Signature day	Effective day	Remarks
Mongolia	Cc2	31 Aug 1989	29 Oct 1990	
Belgium	C	20 Nov 1987	20 Dec 1987	
Poland	Cc2	6 Jun 1987	13 Feb 1988	
France	Cc1	4 May 1987	8 Feb 1988	

Notes: C=civil matter; Cc1=civil and commercial matters; Cc2=civil and criminal matters; Ccc=civil, commercial and criminal matters.

III.2 Treaty refusal grounds

i. Incompetent foreign court

How to decide whether the original foreign court is competent to hear the dispute? It depends on whether the treaty has provided relevant jurisdiction rules. Some bilateral treaties provide jurisdictional rules to decide the competence of the court, such as the treaties with Italy, Tunisia, Spain, Vietnam, Laos, Egypt and Cyprus. For instance, Article 21 of the China-Spain Treaty states: **6.29**

> For the implementation of this Treaty, a court render [sic] the judgment shall be deemed to be a competent court, where accord with one of the following circumstances:
>
> (a) The defendant's domicile or residence was located in the territory of the contracting country when the proceeding is instituted;
> (b) A representative office was established in the territory of the contracting country, if the defendant was sued owing to a dispute arising from commercial activities;
> (c) The defendant accepted the jurisdiction of the court of the contracting country in writing;
> (d) The defendant had defenced the merit of dispute, but no objection was raised on the issue of jurisdiction;
> (e) In a contract dispute, the places of the contract was concluded, or was performed or should be performed, or the direct subject matter of the action was located in the territory of the rendering contracting-country;
> (f) In a tort case, the place of the occurrence of the infringement act or the place of the occurrence of the result of the infringement was located in the territory of the contracting country;
> (g) In a status or personal relation dispute, the domicile or residence of the relative party was located in the territory of the rendering contracting-country when the action was instituted, the above (a) of this section may not be applied;
> (h) In a dispute concerning maintenance, the domicile or residence of the creditor was located in the territory of the contracting country when the action was instituted, the above (a) of this section may not be applied;
> (i) In succession, the residence of the decedent at the time of his death or the place of main legacy was located in the territory of the rendering contracting-country; and

(j) The subject matter of action was on the right of immovable property located in the territory of the rending contracting country.

6.30 If detailed jurisdiction rules are provided in the bilateral treaty, when the court decides on recognition and enforcement of judgments pursuant to the treaty, it should apply the treaty rules to determine the competence of the original court. However, it is necessary to note that the treaty jurisdiction rules for the purpose of FJR may be inconsistent with the domestic jurisdiction rules to determine jurisdiction of the contracting state. In practice, this may cause a number of problems. First, the treaty jurisdiction rules may be inconsistent with the exclusive jurisdiction in China.[34] Exclusive jurisdiction in Chinese domestic law has a broad scope,[35] which makes it easy to conflict with the treaty jurisdiction rules. Taking the China-Spain Treaty as an example, it does not expressly reserve exclusive jurisdiction rules of either country and the treaty jurisdiction rules are only consistent with the Chinese exclusive jurisdiction in terms of succession and immoveable property. In other disputes, the Spanish court may duly take jurisdiction, which is compatible with the treaty but nevertheless contrary to Chinese exclusive jurisdiction. Some treaties, while listing uniform jurisdiction grounds, expressly make reservations on exclusive jurisdiction.[36] Others, however, do no specifically provide exclusive jurisdiction exception.[37] Internationalists may argue that the purpose of the bilateral treaty is to protect the parties and international commerce from the unforeseeable consequences of unreasonable insistence on juridical sovereignty. Once entering into the treaty without express reservation of domestic jurisdiction rules, the treaty jurisdiction should take priority.[38] Nationalists may, on the other hand, argue that no country would give up its sovereignty demonstrated by the exclusive jurisdiction and the exclusive jurisdiction of each state is reserved unless expressly stated otherwise.[39] Uncertainty, as a result, exists. However, it is possible to claim that even if the internationalist view is adopted by the court and the enforcement is not refused on the competence ground, it may be attacked on the public policy ground if the jurisdiction taken infringes Chinese exclusive jurisdiction.[40] It is likely that domestic exclusive jurisdiction would take priority.

---

34 CPL, Arts 33 and 266. For more discussion on exclusive jurisdiction, see Ch 3, sec II.

35 See Ch 3, sec II.

36 For example, the China-Argentina Treaty lists the jurisdiction grounds for disputes falling outside of either countries' exclusive jurisdiction. The China-Russia Treaty expressly permits the contracting states to refuse recognition and enforcement of each other's judgments based on the exclusive jurisdiction reservation.

37 Such as the treaties with Egypt, Laos, Cyprus, Tunisia, Vietnam, Italy and Spain.

38 XIAO Yongping, *Falixue Shiyexia de Chongfufa [Conflict of Laws from a Jurisprudence Perspective]* (Beijing: Gaodeng Jiaoyu Chubanshe [Higher Education Press] 2008) 365–6.

39 Wenliang Zhang, *Recognition and Enforcement of Foreign Judgments in China* (Kluwer Law International 2014) 215–16.

40 For public policy, see sec v. below.

Secondly, the treaty jurisdiction rules are different from the rules of Chinese law which increases the difficulty in judicial practice. In order to ensure the potential enforceability of judgments, a Chinese court may have to consider first, whether the judgment may require recognition and enforcement in a foreign country; secondly, whether the foreign country and China have entered into any bilateral treaty; and thirdly, whether the treaty has provided a uniform jurisdiction rule. If the Chinese court fails to take these steps and directly applies Chinese domestic jurisdiction rules to assert jurisdiction, there is a risk that the court may be held incompetent pursuant to the treaty rules and the foreign court may refuse to recognize and enforce the judgment. However, in practice, a trial court rarely considers whether its judgment may be enforced in the potential requested court before taking jurisdiction, and would never decline jurisdiction based on this reason. This argument imposes extra burdens to the judge and is incompatible with judicial practice and reality. **6.31**

Thirdly, concluding bilateral treaties may be a relatively easy and realistic way to foster cooperation among countries. However, the vagaries of the negotiation processes and the different requirements of the other treaty state can produce disparate standards. Once treaties proliferate, inconsistencies and complexities are inevitable. This could engender a 'conflict of conventions', which adds further complexity to the conflict between conventions and domestic law.[41] **6.32**

Some treaties do not include detailed jurisdiction rules but provide a general statement that the country of origin is competent pursuant to its domestic law, unless the dispute is subject to the exclusive jurisdiction of the requested court. In other words, the contracting states of the bilateral treaty would mutually recognize each other's domestic jurisdiction rules, subject to the exclusive jurisdiction exception. This approach demonstrates the mutual trust at the higher level between the treaty countries and could effectively facilitate reciprocal enforcement of each other's judgments. The reservation given to the exclusive jurisdiction is also consistent with both states' domestic jurisdiction rules and public policy. Unfortunately, this approach is exceptional and has only been adopted in the China-Russia Treaty.[42] **6.33**

If the treaty does not provide uniform standards to assess the court's competence for the purpose of FJR, the requested court should use its domestic **6.34**

41 Yong Zhou, *International Relations and Legal Cooperation in General Diplomacy and Consular Relations* (Elsevier 2014) 156.

42 China-Russia Bilateral Treaty 1992, Art 20(2).

law to decide whether the court of origin is competent.[43] The domestic jurisdiction rules in the country of origin are no longer relevant. This approach is unfortunate because the diversity of domestic jurisdiction rules would render many judgments given by a court duly taking jurisdiction under its domestic law unenforceable in the other contracting state.

ii. Non-effective judgment

6.35 Only the final and effective judgment can be recognized and enforced under the bilateral treaties. This requirement includes three scenarios. First, the judgment, for the foreign recognition purpose, must be valid under the law of the original country and enforceable by the rendering court. Secondly, the judgment must be final in the original country. Usually, a judgment is final after appeals are exhausted or the time for appeal has lapsed.[44] Thirdly, the judgment must be on the merits to preclude re-litigation. A ruling on dismissals for lack of jurisdiction, improper venue, defective service, and *forum non conveniens* are not judgments on the merits. Sometimes, it is not straightforward whether a judgment is on the merits, such as dismissals for failure to state claims upon which relief can be granted, dismissals under statutes of limitations, or dismissal of claims that were not raised as compulsory counterclaims in previous litigation. The nature of a judgment should be determined by the requested court by applying its own law and standard.

6.36 The applicant must prove the foreign judgment is final and effective. In *Re Application of Schneider Electric Industries SAS for Recognition of the Judgment Delivered by the Tribunal de Grande Instance de Paris*,[45] the application was made by the French party under the China-France Treaty. The petitioner submitted evidence including the original judgment and the certificate issued by the Paris Court of Appeal (Cour D'Appel de Paris) providing the judgment was effective in France and an authorized Chinese translation for both documents. The Wenzhou IPC, however, ruled that the evidence could only prove that neither party had lodged an appeal within the time limit. Pursuant to Articles 540 of the French Civil Procedure Code, there is a possibility of relieving a party from the time bar for lodging an appeal against a judgment rendered by default or deemed to be adversarial where the party, through no fault of his own, was not aware of the judgment in time or if he was unable to

43 The China-Hungary Treaty expressly adopts this approach, providing the requested country uses its own law to decide whether the court of origin is competent.

44 In the US, for example, a judgment may be final even if it may still be subject to appeal. See Y. Zeynalova, 'Law on Recognition and Enforcement of Foreign Judgments', (2013) 31 *Berkeley Journal of International Law* 150, 159 note 56.

45 Zhejiang Wenzhou IPC, (2005) Wen Min San Chu Zi No 155.

act.[46] The Wenzhou IPC refused to recognize the judgment based on the applicant's failure to prove the finality of the judgment.[47]

iii. Inadequate notice

The defendant's right to be heard is a fundamental right, the infringement of which constitutes procedural irregularity. It is therefore a universally accepted principle that a judgment rendered against a party who was not properly notified of the proceedings shall not be recognized and enforced. It serves to protect the interests of the defendant by establishing a purely factual test to ensure that the defendant was properly notified. Non-recognition and non-enforcement are permitted if judicial documents were served on the defendant either not in sufficient time, or not in such a way, to enable the defendant to arrange for his defence. The lack of notice defence can only arise in the case of default judgments. A defendant who actually participated in the foreign action is precluded from relying on the lack of notice defence at the recognition stage. If a defendant is properly served but fails to participate in the foreign proceedings due to his or her own misconduct, the judgment may, certainly, be recognized. **6.37**

How is it decided whether the defendant is properly served? China acceded to the Hague Convention on the Service Abroad of Judicial and Extra-judicial Documents in Civil and Commercial Matters (The Hague Service Convention) on 2 March 1991, which provides international standards for service abroad. If one country is the contracting party of both the Hague Service Convention and a bilateral treaty with China, which also provides service procedure, theoretically the rules in the bilateral treaty prevail. In other words, the procedure of services provided in the bilateral treaty should be considered in recognition and enforcement of judgments, instead of the Hague Service Convention and Chinese domestic law.[48] If the bilateral treaty does not provide service procedure, the service methods in the Hague Service Convention should be applied. If the bilateral treaty does not provide service procedure and the Hague Convention does not apply, Chinese courts should refuse to recognize and enforce foreign judgments under bilateral treaties if documents were served on the defendant in China in a manner incompatible with Chinese domestic law. **6.38**

46 For the information, see 'Procedural time limits – France', http://ec.europa.eu/civiljustice/time_limits/time_limits_fra_en.htm (accessed on 05 April 2015)

47 Another reason for the refusal was that the applicant could not prove that the judgment had been served on the defendant successfully and in a legitimate manner.

48 Point 7 of the Notices of Procedure Regarding Implementing the Hague Service Convention by the SPC, the Foreign Affairs Minister and the Judiciary Minister.

6.39 It is necessary to note that China has made a number of important reservations when acceding to the Hague Service Convention. Two relate to the authorized service methods; first, the first paragraph of Article 8 of the Convention provides a flexible means for serving judicial documents without the application of any compulsion, directly through diplomatic or consular agents. China declares that this means of service may be used within the territory of China only when the document is to be served upon a national of the state in which the documents originate.[49] Secondly, China opposes the service of documents in the territory of China by the methods provided by Article 10 of the Convention, which allows service by post directly to the defendant, service effected by judicial officers, officials or other competent persons of the country of origin directly through judicial officers, officials or other competent persons of the country of destination, and service effected by any person interested in judicial proceedings directly through judicial officers, officials or other competent persons of the state of destination.[50]

6.40 As a result, China has made almost all the reservations allowed in the Hague Service Convention. This may make Chinese law differ from the law of many other countries that have concluded bilateral treaties with China. The difference in the standard of service abroad may add additional uncertainty to the recognition and enforcement of judgments even if bilateral judicial assistance treaties exist. The petitioner should provide evidence proving how the claim forms and other legal documents were served on the dependent in default. In *Re Volga-Dnepr Airline,* the evidence provided by the Russian court only stated that the claim forms were served on the defendant 'by reasonable means', without clarifying the means. The evidence was held insufficient and recognition was refused.[51]

6.41 Finally, adequate service is but a means to an end. The ultimate purpose is to allow the defendant the chance to be heard. Mere service process does not necessarily safeguard the right of defence. However, most bilateral treaties do not expressly protect the defendant's 'opportunity to be heard'. If the defendant is properly served but not properly presented by a qualified legal representative, the defendant has been deprived of his right to be heard and it is uncertain whether this could constitute a legitimate refusal ground.

---

49 Hague Service Convention, Art 8.

50 Ibid., Art 10.

51 *Re the Request to Affirm the Beijing High People's Court's Decision to the Petition of Volga-Dnepr Airline for Enforcement of the Judgment Rendered by the Russian Court,* [2005] Min Si Ta Zi No 33.

iv. *Inconsistent judgments*

As a general proposition, a foreign judgment will not be recognized if it conflicts with an adjudication in the requested country. There is no dispute if the requested court has already delivered the judgment on the same cause of action between the same parties or has recognized the same judgment delivered by a third country. However, recognition and enforcement may be refused if the proceeding in the same cause of action between the same parties is pending in the requested court, and the requested court was seized before the court of origin.[52] This rule aims to prevent concurrent proceedings between contracting states. Although many of the bilateral treaties do not expressly accept *lis pendens*, the negative effect on recognition and enforcement may encourage a court to stay jurisdiction of concurrent proceedings. **6.42**

However, the treaties between China and Mongolia, Greece and Italy adopt a different standard. They provide that recognition may be refused if the same action is pending in the requested country and the requested court was seized before the judgment became final in the country of origin. This provision is unfortunate as it cannot prevent concurrent proceedings or encourage the second seized court to decline jurisdiction. If the foreign court was seized first and judgment was given and one party sues in China before the time limit for appeal in the foreign court lapses, the Chinese court can take jurisdiction and refuse recognizing and enforcing the judgment that eventually becomes final. It may particularly encourage the party that loses in the action and anticipates it may lose again in the appeal to commence the second proceedings in the other country, which would effectively prevent the judgment of the first action to be enforced. **6.43**

v. *Public policy*

A public policy defence is reserved in almost all bilateral treaties.[53] It is the Great Wall, acting as the final defence preventing recognition and enforcement of foreign judgments in all circumstances that may infringe national security, public interest or social order. It is an ambiguous and catch-all concept to safeguard the fundamental interest of a country from the potential negative impact of a treaty.[54] **6.44**

---

52 E.g., the treaties with Argentina, United Arab Emirates, Egypt, Belarus, Bulgaria, Poland, Russia, etc.

53 For example, see the treaty with France (Art 10(5)), Italy (Art 21(6)), Argentina (Art 7), United Arab Emirates (Art 9(1)), Egypt (Art 9), Belarus (Art 11), Bulgaria (Art 8).

54 Almost all international conventions or instruments that facilitate mutual recognition and enforcement of judgments have made the public policy reservation. It is reasonable to argue that countries would not participate in international judicial cooperation without the public policy reservation.

6.45 This defence closely corresponds to the same defence under Chinese national law, although they do not always employ the same terms or expressions. For example, the 2011 China-Algerian Treaty provides that 'if provision of judicial assistance is regarded by the requested country as an infringement of its sovereignty, security or public order, or the requested assistance is beyond the jurisdiction of the judicial organs of the requested country, provision of judicial assistance should be refused'.[55]

6.46 The defence of 'contradiction to the sovereignty, security and public interests' under these bilateral treaties takes different expressions. For most cases, either the term 'public order' or the term 'public interest' is employed; and in some treaties such as in the 1993 China-Spain Treaty, both terms are adopted. However, there is no interpretation of the terms under the treaties. The differences in expressions alone should not justify a different interpretation of the defence, at least to the Chinese side. Nor should the defence be understood in any way differently from the corresponding defence under the Chinese national law.[56]

6.47 Generally speaking, public policy includes procedural policy and substantive policy. Public policy may be offended by procedural irregularities, such as the lack of a fair hearing. It may also be infringed by substantive deficiencies, such as the violation of equality and morality. However, public policy as a defence in international treaties should be construed narrowly in order not to unreasonably prejudice the purpose of the treaties. It has been suggested that public policy should only include 'international public policy', which represents the truly fundamental interest of a country. Even so, the Chinese court will still apply Chinese law in deciding whether the foreign judgment has infringed the 'truly fundamental interest' of China. There is no general guidance on its precise scope. But it is the consensus that the mere fact that a foreign judgment is not accompanied by an opinion or that it is at odds with Chinese substantive, procedural or conflicts law is insufficient to generate the public policy defence.[57] The practice of Chinese courts reveals they would not employ this safety valve in an unduly extensive manner, and Chinese judges can be trusted to determine, on a case-by-case basis, whether a foreign decision is sufficiently offensive to warrant rejection.[58]

---

55 China-Algeria Treaty 2011, Art 8.

56 Wenliang Zhang, *supra* n 39, 223–4.

57 Some treaties explicitly provide restrictions on recourse to this defence, e.g., under the 2008 China-Brazil Treaty, only the infringement of significant public interests can be a well-grounded defence. It implies that the negotiators of the Treaty intended to exclude the infringement of minor public interests from the domain of this defence. See Wenliang Zhang, *supra* n 39, 224.

58 Section IV of this chapter will introduce the practice of Chinese courts in detail.

III.3 Chinese judicial practice

There is limited evidence demonstrating how Chinese courts enforce foreign judgments under bilateral treaties. China has not established a formal case report system. An inclusive, verified study on the situation of application of the treaties is still lacking. The published cases that are available for examination show that where bilateral treaties exist, Chinese courts usually will not be reluctant to enforce foreign judgments, once they are satisfied that no refusal grounds are present.[59] For example, in *Re Petition of B&T Ceramic Group SRL for Recognition and Enforcement of the Judgment on Bankruptcy Rendered by the Italian Court*,[60] Guangdong Province Foshan IPC applied the China-Italy Treaty to recognize the bankruptcy judgment and ordered the transfer of property pursuant to the Italian ruling. This case is unusual in that it concerns the recognition and enforcement of a foreign insolvency judgment. Recognizing and enforcing foreign insolvency judgments is more controversial than other civil and commercial matters. Insolvency of a multinational company may affect the economic and social interests in multiple jurisdictions. Many countries would not recognize the extraterritorial effect of insolvency proceedings and the judgment on insolvency can only affect property located within the territory of the ruling country. The bilateral treaties concluded by China do not usually distinguish insolvency from other civil and commercial proceedings, and the same standards apply to recognize and enforce insolvency judgments of the contracting party. Chinese courts, thus, would give insolvency judgments the same legal effect as domestic judgments on the property located in China. **6.48**

However, one ground that is frequently relied on by the Chinese courts to refuse recognizing foreign judgments, even with bilateral judicial assistance treaties, is the lack of due service because China has made reservation to the Hague Services Convention, and the Chinese law does not recognize service by post. Unless the bilateral treaty expressly allows the service of judgments on the defendant in China by post, recognition of foreign judgments served by post will be refused by the Chinese courts on the ground for the lack of due service.[61] **6.49**

59 E.g., *Schneider Electric Industries SAS supra* n 45; *Re Petition of B&T Ceramic Group SRL for Recognition and Enforcement of the Judgment on Bankruptcy Rendered by the Italian Court*, Guangdong Province Foushan IPC, available in www.pkulaw.cn, CLI.C.829134. In 2014, Shandong Jining Court enforced a judgment under the China-Turkey Treaty upon the request of the Istanbul Sixth Commercial Court of Turkey. China Court Network, 26 February 2014.

60 *Re Petition of B&T Ceramic Group SRL*, ibid.

61 ZHANG Wenliang, 'Recognition and Enforcement of Foreign Judgments in China', (2013) 12 *Chinese Journal of International Law* 143, 156–60. See e.g., *Schneider Electric Industries SAS, supra* n 45 (refusal to recognize French judgments because judgments were served on the defendant by post); *Minsk Automatic*

III.4 Conclusion

6.50 Relying on bilateral treaties for mutual recognition and enforcement of judgments is necessary in the contemporary Chinese legal system. First, it is necessary to recognize that Chinese domestic law is relatively restrictive in enforcing foreign judgments.[62] In the absence of treaties, foreign judgment enforcement would encounter real practical problems that may seriously hamper transnational civil and commercial relationships involving Chinese citizens and companies. It is not easy to conclude a comprehensive and internationally acceptable multilateral treaty to assist with mutual recognition and enforcement. Entering into bilateral treaties is the most feasible and convenient temporary solution. Secondly, there is always a concern that Chinese judges are not competent in dealing with foreign judgments. Bilateral treaties may help Chinese judges to earn adequate experience before more flexible approaches are adopted.[63] Thirdly, practice based on bilateral treaties may provide empirical evidence on the rationale of particular grounds and procedural requirements for recognition and enforcement of foreign judgment, which can be of great value to improve relevant Chinese law in the future reform.

6.51 It is also necessary to note that bilateral treaties are only a temporary solution and should not be the final answer. There are also obvious shortfalls. Bilateral treaties can hardly achieve consistency and uniform results. Multiple bilateral treaties produce disparate recognition standards for judgments from different countries. Although the treaties' conditions are primarily similar, they are not identical. For example, some treaties provide that the applicant should make direct application in the requested court;[64] some require the applicant to apply in the rendering court which will pass the request to the requested court through the central authority;[65] and others permit either the applicant to apply directly in the requested court or for the rendering court to make the application to the requested court through specified channels.[66] As another example, the treaties provide inconsistent rules in determining the competence of the court of origin: some provide that the requested court should apply its

Production Corporation United v. CNMTC, Beijing No 2 IPC, (2001) Er Zhong Min Ren Zi No 1815; Beijing High Court, (2003) Jing Gao Fa No 15; SPC, [2003] Min Si Ta Zi No 4 (refusal to recognize and enforce Belarusian judgments because the judgment was served on the Chinese defendant by post); *Ant A Nicolaides Sanitools v. Beijing Guanghua Times Textile Import and Export Inc* (2007) Min Er Zhong Zi No 12453.

62 Section IV below.

63 Juenger, *supra* n 17, 289.

64 Such as the treaties with France, Tunisia, Spain, Italy, and Argentina.

65 Such as Turkey.

66 Cuba, Argentina, Egypt, Cyprus, Greece, Hungary, Poland, etc.

local law;[67] some presume the rendering court is competent subject to the exclusive jurisdiction of the requested state;[68] and others list the uniform criteria to decide jurisdiction of the rendering court.[69] This inconsistency increases the burden on, and the difficulties before, judges, who should examine different rules in the applications involving different countries. It provides uncertainty for international trade partners. It also increases compliance cost of Chinese companies doing international transactions, which need to understand different treaty rules when dealing with partners from different countries.

IV. RECOGNITION AND ENFORCEMENT OF FOREIGN JUDGMENTS UNDER DOMESTIC LAW OF CHINA

In the absence of international conventions or bilateral treaties to facilitate recognition and enforcement of foreign judgments, Chinese courts apply domestic law to decide the effect of foreign judgments in the territory of China. Given the limited number of existing bilateral judgment treaties concluded by China, the domestic Chinese law is the paramount source in this area.[70] **6.52**

There are three approaches to deciding whether judgments rendered abroad should be given effect locally: (1) the forum may simply disregard foreign decisions; (2) it may recognize only those judgments rendered in countries that honour the local forum's judgments (reciprocity); and (3) it may recognize any foreign judgments that meet certain procedural and substantive standards. Chinese law combines the second and third approaches. In general, except foreign divorce judgments, any other civil and commercial judgments rendered by a foreign court are prima facie unrecognizable and unenforceable in China, subject to exception of reciprocity.[71] Even if the reciprocal relationship exists between China and the foreign country, recognition and enforcement may still be refused on substantive and procedural grounds. The restricted standards provide great difficulties to parties in cross-border disputes; have great influence on the claimant's selection of court; and affect the modernization of Chinese jurisdiction rules.[72] **6.53**

67 Such as Hungary.
68 Such as the China-Russia Treaty.
69 Such as Egypt, Laos, Cyprus, Tunisia, Vietnam, Italy and Spain.
70 ZHANG Wenliang, *supra* n 61, 149.
71 2015 Interpretation, Art 544.
72 See Chs 3 and 4 above.

IV.1 Reciprocity

i. The general principle of reciprocity

6.54 The principle of reciprocity is expressly listed as one of the general and basic principles of the Chinese civil procedure law,[73] and is regarded as having 'the most prominent position' by Chinese scholars.[74] The principle of reciprocity was first provided in the 1982 Civil Procedure Law (For Trial Implementation),[75] followed in the 1991 Civil Procedure Law and its subsequent amendments,[76] and echoed in other legislation and various judicial directions published by the SPC.[77] Both Article 282 of CPL and Article 544 of the 2015 Interpretation make the principle of reciprocity a prerequisite for recognition and enforcement of foreign judgments, except for divorce judgments.[78]

6.55 The CPL and its Opinions do not explain the parameter of 'reciprocity'. In other words, it is unclear how the existence of a reciprocal relationship between China and a foreign country can be proved. Should the Chinese courts adopt the approach of *de facto* or *de jure* reciprocity?[79] *De facto* reciprocity requires actual precedents demonstrating that the foreign country recognized and enforced Chinese judgments in the past. *De jure* reciprocity does not require actual precedents. If, by examining the foreign law, there is a possibility that Chinese judgments may be enforced in the foreign court in principle, the reciprocal relationship exists.[80] It is argued that *de facto* reciprocity may lead to a vicious circle in that if both countries have adopted reciprocity as a precondition to recognizing foreign judgments, neither country will recognize the other's judgment first and for ever.[81] *De jure* reciprocity is a more realistic and flexible approach.[82]

---

73 CPL, Art 5(2) provides that: 'Where the courts of a foreign country impose restrictions on the civil litigation rights of the citizens, legal persons, or other organizations of the People's Republic of China, the people's court shall follow the principle of reciprocity regarding the civil litigation rights of the citizens, enterprises, or organizations of that foreign country.'

74 ZHANG Wenliang, *supra* n 61, 153.

75 Art 204.

76 Arts 267, 268.

77 For example, see PRC Insolvency Law 2006, Art 5; SPC, 'Zuigao Renmin Fayuan Guanyu Zhongguo Gongmin Shenqing Chengren Waiguo Fayuan Lihun Panjue Chengxu Wenti de Guiding de Tongzhi [Provisions on the Procedural Problems in Application of Chinese Citizens to Recognize Foreign Divorce Judgments]', [1991] Fa (Min) No 21.

78 Exception is given to divorce. 2015 Interpretation, Art 544.

79 J.C. Hathaway, *The Rights of Refugees under International Law* (CUP, 2005) 201; E.G. Lorenzen, 'Enforcement of American Judgments Abroad', (1919) 29 *Yale Law Journal* 188, 206.

80 Lorenzen, *supra* n 79, 206.

81 Ibid.

82 The flexible approach to reciprocity has been adopted in Germany. E.g., *German Zublin International Co Ltd v. Wuxi Walker General Engineering Rubber Co. Ltd*, Court of Appeal of Berlin, 18 May 2006, doc no. 20 S ch 13/04.

However, Chinese courts adopt the *de facto* reciprocity approach in practice. If the issue arises for the first time between China and the foreign country and there is no prior practice that may be referred to as a basis for asserting mutual reciprocity between China and a given foreign country, the Chinese court will deny the existence of reciprocity and disregard the effect of the foreign judgment.[83] For example, in *Gomi Akira v. Dalian Fari Seafood Ltd.*,[84] a Japanese citizen Gomi Akira petitioned to the Dalian IPC (the 'Dalian Court') for recognition of the legal effect and enforcement within China of a monetary judgment made by the Japanese court. The court held that China had not concluded or acceded to any international treaty with Japan on mutual recognition and enforcement of judgments or rulings, nor had it established a corresponding relationship of reciprocity with Japan. The enforcement of Japanese judgments was refused for the lack of reciprocity. The decision was later affirmed by the SPC.[85] Since the principle of reciprocity was equally accepted in the Japanese law, recognizing and enforcing judgments between China and Japan would make no progress in the future unless either country revises its law or both enter into a judicial cooperation agreement. Based on the lack of *de facto* reciprocity, Chinese courts refused (either expressly or impliedly) to recognize and enforce judgments rendered in the court of Japan,[86] Germany,[87] England,[88] Australia,[89] the US,[90] and Hong Kong before the China-Hong Kong Arrangement entered into force.[91] 6.56

De facto reciprocity establishes a factual obstacle to recognizing and enforcing foreign judgments. A brief assessment of the published cases shows that in the 6.57

---

83 J.J. Fei, 'Enforcement of Foreign Court Judgments and Foreign Arbitral Awards in China', in M.J. Moser, *Business Disputes in China* (3rd ed., Juris Publishing 2011) 254.

84 *Gomi Akira v. Dalian Fari Seafood Ltd (Application of Gomi Akira (A Japanese Citizen) to Chinese Court for Recognition and Enforcement of Japanese Judicial Decision)*, (1996) 1 SPC Gazette 29.

85 S.C. McCaffrey and T.O. Main, *Transnational Litigation in Comparative Perspective* (OUP 2010) 633; ZHANG Wenliang, *supra* n 61, 155.

86 *Gomi Akira; Application of Awabiya Co for Recognition and Enforcement of Judgment in China,* (2001) Hu Yi Zhong Jing Chuzi No 269.

87 *Re Petition of Deutsche Bank for the Recognition and Enforcement of Judgment 20460/07 of a Frankfurt Court,* [2010] Min Si Ta Zi No 81.

88 *Oliver Otto Dufek v. Siegmund Kahlbacher*, No 2 IPC of Beijing Municipality (2010) Er Zhong Min Tezi No 10324.

89 *Re Arbitration Clause Validity in the Dispute over Transfer Contract for Land-Use Rights in the Case of Hong Kong Ace Medical Packaging Co Ltd v. Dongguan Metal Product Factory Ltd. and Virgin Islands New Guanyu Industrial Co Ltd,* [2007] Min Si Ta Zi No 45.

90 *ZHUO Yue v. Nanjing Diansheng Ltd,* (2004) Ning Min Wu Chu Zi No 7. The case was not about enforcing a foreign judgment but a re-litigation of a dispute that had already been heard and decided in the US. The Jiangsu Nanjing IPC took jurisdiction to hear the dispute based on the SPC judicial interpretation (Art 318 of 1992 Opinion) that in the absence of treaty obligations and reciprocity, the judgment creditor can re-litigate in the competent People's Court.

91 *Petition of Yuanqiao Investment Ltd for the Recognition of the Civil Judgment Rendered by Hong Kong Court,* Fujian Quanzhou IPC, (2001) Quan Min Zi No 1.

absence of bilateral treaty obligations, most applications for recognition and enforcement were declined.[92] China is not the only country that adopts restrictive requirements to recognizing foreign judgments. Recognition of foreign judgments is a traditional difficulty in international civil and commercial litigation. Many countries adopt equally, if not more, restrictive standards.[93] The principle of reciprocity does not work effectively in encouraging recognition of foreign judgments, indeed it acts as a barrier. Secondly, China is not a popular forum or destination for forum shopping. Many parties lack knowledge and confidence in the Chinese judicial system and prefer to bring actions in a more popular forum and enforce the judgment in China. However, given the difficulty in enforcing foreign judgments, such an intention rarely works in practice. Many sophisticated parties would decide to sue in China, where the defendant has assets, to avoid cross-border enforcement difficulty.

6.58 There are three further questions concerning the application of the *de facto* reciprocity approach. The first is whether a more restrictive equal treatment should be imposed. Equal treatment argues that even if the foreign court has recognized Chinese judgments in the past, the Chinese court should still compare the standard to recognizing foreign judgments between two countries. If the foreign standard is more restrictive, the Chinese court can recognize the foreign judgment in principle but should apply the same standard.[94] Secondly, should the characterization of cases be relevant to decide the existence of reciprocity? For example, if the foreign courts enforced Chinese judgments in ordering compensation under contracts, it only means that the reciprocity can be bound in contractual judgments but not others, such as insolvency.[95] Thirdly, in countries with multiple legal districts, such as the US, Germany, and the UK, if one legal district recognizes the Chinese judgment, does the reciprocal relationship exist between China and all other districts of the country?[96] For example, in 2009, California District Court of USA made a ruling to enforce a money judgment in product liability rendered by Hubei High Court of China pursuant to the Uniform Foreign Country

92 The authors have not found any reported case where foreign judgments were enforced in China based on the principle of reciprocity.

93 For example, Saudi Arabia, Mexico, Japan, Spain, etc, have adopted a similar reciprocity principle; Austria, Denmark, Finland, Iceland, Norway and Sweden refuse to recognize foreign judgments in the absence of treaty obligations; Indonesia does not recognize foreign judgments in any circumstances. See J.F. Coyle, 'Rethinking Judgments Reciprocity', (2013) 92 *North Carolina Law Review* 1109, 1154–62; V. Singal, 'Preserving Power without Sacrificing Justice', (2007) 59 *Hastings Law Journal* 943, 955.

94 WANG Jiwen, 'Huhui Yuanze zai Panjue Chengren yu Zhixing Shang de Quexian [The Fallacy of the Principle of Reciprocity in Judgment Recognition and Enforcement]', (2008) 15(3) Yunnan Daxue Xuebao (Faxue Ban) [*Journal of Yunnan University (Law Edition)*] 170, 170–72.

95 Ibid., 172.

96 J. Huang, *Interregional Recognition and Enforcement of Civil and Commercial Judgments* (Bloomsbury Publishing 2014) 63.

Money Judgment Recognition Act.[97] This case suffices to establish the reciprocity between China and California of the USA at least. However, each state of the USA is an independent judicial system and has its own laws to enforce foreign judgments. Substantive differences exist between law and practice of the 50 sister states. Enforcement of foreign judgments in the US is a matter of state law.[98] Although the California Court has recognized and enforced this Chinese court judgment, a Chinese court may refuse to recognize the judgments from other states of the US on ground of non-reciprocity. Since the relationship of *de facto* reciprocity does not exist between China and most foreign countries, these issues are rarely considered by Chinese courts and remain theoretical issues. However, it does not mean that they will never arise. Chinese judgments were recognized and enforced in Germany in 2006[99] and the US in 2009.[100] Chinese courts may need to define reciprocity by taking into account all three questions in the future petition for recognizing German or US judgments.[101]

ii. Comments and suggestions

In Chinese domestic law, reciprocity is a precondition to recognizing and 6.59
enforcing foreign judgments in the absence of treaty obligations. Although the purpose of reciprocity is not to retaliate but to encourage better international cooperation and to improve comity, this purpose is barely achieved in practice. By adopting the same policy in various jurisdictions the direct result is that no country will make the first move to recognize foreign judgments. This doctrine, as a result, causes *de facto* retaliation and hampers comity. Furthermore, even if reciprocity eventually improves foreign judgment recognition, it unfairly punishes individual litigants, who bear all the inconvenience and difficulty and who could not make substantive changes to the situation of the lack of reciprocity. Furthermore, reciprocity cannot achieve efficiency in practice nor ensure the quality of such foreign judgments as may be recognized. Foreign judgment recognition is completely based on the 'pay back' idea, which can lead to arbitrary decisions. Reciprocity, thus, cannot be applied

97 See, *Hubei Gezhouba Sanlian Industrial Co Ltd et al. v. Robinson Helicopter Co Inc*, 06–01798 (CD Cal 2009).

98 The US practice is only partially unified by the Uniform Recognition Act of 1962. L.J. Silberman & A.F. Lowenfeid, 'A Different Challenge for the ALI: Herein of Foreign Country Judgments, an International Treaty, and an American statute', (2000) 75 *Indiana Law Journal* 636.

99 *German Zublin International Co Ltd v. Wuxi Walker, supra* n 82.

100 *Hubei Gezhouba Sanlian Industrial Co Ltd, supra* n 97. XIE Xinsheng, 'Tiaoye yu Huhui Queshi shi Zhongguo Panjue dui Yuwai Zhixing [The Extraterritorial Enforcement of Chinese Court Judgment Without Treaty and Reciprocity]', (2010) 4 Huanqiu Falv Pinglun [*Global Law Review*] 152.

101 Although the Chinese court had the chance to clarify the meaning of reciprocity in *Hukla Matratzen GmbH v. Beijing Hukla Ltd* (2010) Er Zhong Min Tezi No 13890, where the Beijing No 2 IPC was requested to recognize and enforce a German monetary judgment, the court did not consider reciprocity but refused the petition because the judgment was not properly served.

alone and should be accompanied by safeguard measures.[102] Finally, proving foreign practice and law is traditionally difficult and time consuming. *De jure* reciprocity, a more flexible version, requires more than simply ascertaining foreign law and requires an exploration of the foreign legal system and political attitude as a whole. Uncertainty frequently exists,[103] which may prevent this approach from being adopted in China.

6.60 Although the principle of reciprocity is adopted by many other countries as the precondition for foreign judgment recognition and enforcement (JRE), the weakness of the principle is obvious. A number of suggestions are thus proposed. The most advanced approach is to abandon the principle of reciprocity and to adopt a set of criteria that would allow Chinese courts to enforce any foreign judgments that meet the criteria. It adopts a more internationalization approach and may improve recognition of Chinese judgments by other countries adopting the principle of reciprocity. However, if it is difficult to abandon the principle of reciprocity at the current stage, Chinese courts should adopt the *de jure* reciprocity approach, which could not only facilitate more effective recognition of foreign judgments, but also avoid the complexity and uncertainty to determine *de facto* reciprocity.[104] When applying the *de jure* reciprocity, Chinese courts should balance the national interest and private interests when deciding whether the reciprocity exists or not, because the civil judgments mainly influence the litigant's rights and interests clearly.[105] The common approach in proving the foreign law should be adopted.[106]

IV.2 Grounds for non-recognition and non-enforcement

6.61 Where reciprocity exists, the foreign judgment cannot be directly recognized and enforced in China but requires a series of scrutiny first. Article 282 of CPL provides that the Chinese court will only recognize and enforce a foreign judgment if it is not contrary to the 'Chinese general principle of law or sovereignty, national security and public policy'. It does not specify what it is meant by the 'general principle of law' or 'public policy'. In practice, the Chinese courts usually refuse recognition on the grounds of undue procedure. Chinese scholars also claim consideration should be given to the competence of the original court, irreconcilable judgment, and the public policy.

---

102 See IV.2 below.

103 LI Haopei, *Guoji Minshi Chengxufa Gailun [An Introduction to International Civil Procedural Law]* (Beijing: Law Press 1996) 140–41.

104 See sec i. above.

105 WANG Jiwen, *supra* n 19, 154.

106 See Ch 2, VI.

i. Undue procedure

Chinese courts are not reluctant to refuse JRE based on undue procedure. Undue procedure exists if the defendant is not properly served, not duly presented, or deprived of the chance to be heard. Since China has made reservations to the Hague Service Convention, foreign courts may face the relatively restrictive method to serve judicial documents in China. For example, service by post is not allowed. If the foreign process was served on a Chinese defendant in China by post, the defendant is deemed not to have been properly served. If a foreign judgment is posted to a Chinese defendant, this would also lead to the recognition and enforcement application being refused. In *Re Petition of Deutsche Bank for the Recognition and Enforcement of Judgment No 20460/07 by the Frankfurt Court*,[107] for example, a petition was made to recognize a German judgment. There is no bilateral treaty between China and Germany, but the German courts recognized a Chinese judgment in 2006. The Chinese court, however, refused the application based on the fact that the judgment was not properly served on the defendant. The SPC emphasized that China had made reservation to Article 10 of the Hague Service Convention and therefore service, by post, directly to the person located in China was not permitted. Since the German court had posted the judgment to the defendant, this judgment could not be recognized in China. The SPC did not expressly use the term 'undue procedure', but based the decision on the fact that since the judgment was not properly served, it was not effective.[108] **6.62**

ii. Incompetent court

As a universal requirement, all legal systems exercise some form of review of the court of origin's jurisdiction. Jurisdiction grounds vary from country to country. Some grounds, such as *maxim actor sequitur forum rei*, are internationally accepted. Others are more controversial, or obviously excessive, such as the common law's jurisdiction *in personam* based on presence.[109] Each legal system is free to determine which jurisdictional grounds are acceptable for the purpose of recognition and enforcement of foreign judgments.[110] **6.63**

What law should be applied by the requested court to decide whether the foreign court had jurisdiction? Chinese law is silent on this issue. Chinese **6.64**

107 *Re Petition of Deutsche Bank*, *supra* n 87.

108 This ground is equally applied by the Chinese courts to refuse JRE under bilateral treaties. See III.2.iii above. For more discussion, see ZHANG Wenliang, *supra* n 61, 156–60.

109 Such as English common law and the common law in US.

110 Juenger, *supra* n 17, 294.

scholars have reached a common understanding that the concept of jurisdiction differs between trial and enforcement. French law uses two distinguished concepts to describe the two types of jurisdiction: direct jurisdiction (*compétence directe*) and indirect jurisdiction (*compétence indirecte*).[111] Direct jurisdiction allows the court of origin to directly decide its own competence. Indirect jurisdiction permits the requested court to indirectly control the jurisdiction of the court of origin at the enforcement stage.[112] The former is a privilege and right, while the latter is a power.[113] Direct jurisdiction and indirect jurisdiction can only be the same for sister-state judgments or judgments between states with mutual trusts and judicial assistance.[114] In other circumstances, states intend to extend their jurisdictional power, which may include an extended scope for direct jurisdiction and a relatively narrower scope for indirect jurisdiction. In order to protect national interests, it is likely that indirect jurisdiction will be subject to more public policy scrutiny.[115] On the other hand, a country may not adopt some jurisdiction grounds because it has sufficient alternative rules, which, however, may not prevent this country from recognizing the rationale of this jurisdiction ground used by another country. Furthermore, a court may have very restrictive grounds to take jurisdiction and in theory would prefer other countries to hear cases not covered by its own jurisdiction rules. This purpose cannot be achieved if the same jurisdiction grounds are applied to recognize foreign judgments.

6.65 To qualify for recognition, a judgment must comply with both the provisions on direct jurisdiction of the country of origin and on indirect jurisdiction of the requested country. The dual test, however, causes complexity. In practice, the requested court may not review the direct jurisdiction and leave it to the court of origin, but simply apply indirect jurisdiction of the requested country in judgment recognition. As a result, the Chinese law should adopt two different sets of jurisdiction rules, one to decide its own jurisdiction at the trial stage (direct jurisdiction) and another to decide the competence of the court of origin at the enforcement stage (indirect jurisdiction). Chinese domestic law, unfortunately, does not provide any particular rules on indirect jurisdiction.[116]

---

111 E. Bartin, *Principles De Droit International Prive*,§127 (Paris 1930) 317.

112 E. Gottschalk, et al, *Conflict of Laws in a Globalized World*, (Cambridge University Press 2007) 36. See R. Michaels, 'Some Fundamental Jurisdictional Concepts as Applied in Judgment Conventions', (2006) 53 *Duke Law School Faculty Scholarship Series* 1, 8.

113 Michael, ibid., 10.

114 Such as the US, the EU or the Hague Choice of Court Convention. See, Michael, *supra* n 112, 9.

115 A. von Mehren, 'Recognition and Enforcement of Foreign Judgments – General Theory and the Role of Jurisdictional Requirements', (1980) 167 Recueil des Cours 56–8; R Michael, *supra* n 112, 10–11.

116 For example, China-Spain Treaty, Art 21; China-Cyprus Treaty 1995, Art 26; China-Italy Treaty 1999, Art 22; China-Vietnam Treaty 1999, Art 18 of the China-Egypt Treaty 1994, Art 22; and China-Laos Treaty 2001, Art 22.

Chinese courts, therefore, apply the domestic direct jurisdiction provisions to review the foreign rendition court's jurisdiction,[117] even though they may well consult and follow the rules of some bilateral treaties, which provide indirect jurisdiction for enforcement of foreign judgments, as guidance to distinguish between acceptable and exorbitant jurisdictional bases.

iii. Inconsistent judgments

Although the CPL has no provision on this ground, Article 533 of the 2015 Interpretation provides, with the exception of obligations under international treaties, that a foreign judgment will not be recognized and enforced in the PRC if a Chinese court has also reached a judgment on the same matter. **6.66**

First, foreign judgment recognition may be refused if the foreign judgment is irreconcilable with an 'earlier' judgment rendered by a Chinese court. Article 533 of the 2015 Interpretation compares the rendition time of the Chinese court and the time of application for recognition in a Chinese court by the judgment creditor or the request by the foreign court. If the application is made after the Chinese judgment has been rendered, application should be refused. If the foreign judgment is rendered first, Article 533 does not require the Chinese court to refuse recognition. However, this article allows the Chinese court to take jurisdiction over a dispute pending in the foreign court. In practice, these rules may create difficulties. **6.67**

Imagine the hypothetical scenario below. Country A was first seized to hear a dispute, but before the judgment is delivered one of the parties brings the same action in China and the Chinese court takes jurisdiction. Afterwards, the court in Country A delivers its judgment and the applicant applies to the Chinese court to recognize this judgment, while Chinese proceedings are still pending. There is the reciprocal relationship between two countries and there is no other ground to refuse recognition. As a result, by law, the Chinese court may enforce the foreign judgment and terminate Chinese proceedings. In other words, although the Chinese law does not accepts the *lis pendens* rule to prevent concurrent proceedings, concurrent proceedings may be defeated by rushing to a judgment. However, in practice, few Chinese courts would favour the foreign judgement over Chinese proceedings and may nevertheless refuse recognition and continuing Chinese proceedings. **6.68**

Secondly, Chinese law does not define the 'same matter'. Generally speaking, where proceedings involving the same cause of action and the same subject **6.69**

117 As to the direct jurisdictional rules of China, please see Ch. 3.

matter between the same parties are brought in the courts of different countries, they concern 'the same matter'. The proceedings may not be identical and may take different forms. For example, one could be a positive claim for damages while another is a negative declaration for no liability.[118] Chinese law, however, does not provide clarification. Suppose a Chinese seller brings an action in China to enforce a contract and then an Italian buyer commences an action for a negative declaratory judgment in Italy, stating that there had never been a contract between the parties. Obviously, the two claims are not entirely identical, but the same question as to whether the contract is binding lies at the heart of both actions. It is unclear whether the Chinese courts would consider the two actions concerning the 'same matter'. If the Italian judgment seeks recognition in China, would the application be refused pursuant to Article 533 of the 2015 Interpretation? It is suggested that the Chinese court should adopt the broad interpretation and the key test for the existence of the 'same matter' should be whether there will be irreconcilable judgments. In the example given above, the judgment in the positive proceedings to enforce the contract and the negative declaration will be mutually exclusive. While the Chinese court enforces the contract, it is not logically viable to recognize the negative declaration.[119]

6.70 Thirdly, Article 533 states that the foreign judgment will not be recognized after the Chinese judgment is rendered on the same matter between the 'same parties'. In practice, however, it is likely that third parties are involved. When A sues in the foreign court against B, B and C sue in China against A, and the Chinese court delivers the judgment on the dispute between B and C versus A, would the foreign judgment concerning A and B be enforced in China? Article 533 is silent on this issue. It is suggested that even if the parties are not identical, the paramount consideration, again, should be whether the judgments are irreconcilable and mutually exclusive. If the judgment in B and C versus A covers the matter between A and B decided in the foreign court, it could effectively prohibit the enforcement of the foreign judgment in China.

6.71 Fourthly, Article 533 does not consider 'related actions'. It is again suggested that related actions may also lead to irreconcilable judgments. For example, A commences an action against B in Germany for infringement of an IP right,

118 P. Rogerson, *Collier's Conflict of Laws* (4th ed., Cambridge, CUP 2013) 123. Case C-406/92 *Owners of the Cargo Lately Laden on Board the Ship Tatry v. Owners of the Ship Maciej Rataj (The Tatry)* [1994] ECR I-5439.

119 E.g., Professor Martin Gebauer lists four situations: (1) a coercive action in the forum, followed by a negative declaratory action abroad; (2) a coercive action abroad, followed by a negative declaratory action in the forum; (3) a negative declaratory action in the forum, followed by a coercive action abroad; and (4) a negative declaration action abroad, followed by a coercive action in the forum. See E. Gottschalk et al., *Conflict of Laws in a Globalized World* (Cambridge, CUP, 2007) 97–9.

and B seeks a negative declaration of invalidity of the IP right in China. The two actions concern the different causes of action, but they are closely related. If the Chinese court has declared that the IP right is invalid, the German judgment in the tort liability is certainly irreconcilable and cannot be enforced in China.

iv. Public policy

As an internationally accepted principle, a court may refuse to enforce a foreign judgment if it is contrary to the public policy of the forum. The CPL and its judicial interpretations, including all the bilateral treaties, have adopted this ground. But the scope of the public policy ground for refusing recognition of foreign judgments is uncertain because of its intrinsic ambiguity and complexity. Article 282 of CPL, when defining public policy, refers to 'fundamental principles of law in the PRC, or state sovereignty, security, and the public interest'. 'Fundamental principles of law' implies that the mere difference in law and legal provisions would be insufficient to generate the public policy defence.[120] Only when the diversity touches the 'fundamental principle of law', may public policy be used. Unfortunately, what constitutes 'fundamental principles of law of the PRC' is also vague. 'State sovereignty and security' is the core interest of a nation. 'Public interests', however, may have the potential to be interpreted broadly. This gives the Chinese courts the opportunity to apply the public policy defence too readily. **6.72**

Before the 1990s, in the absence of bilateral treaties, Chinese courts employed public policy in an unduly extensive manner. The early version of CPL 1982 referred to public policy as the 'nation and social interests of PRC'.[121] The wording is apparently broader than 'state sovereignty and security and public interest', terminology adopted since 1991. In 1984, The SPC provided instructions not to recognize a legal separation agreement entered into pursuant to Argentinean law because the mere difference in the foreign family law was against public policy.[122] **6.73**

---

120 A.G. Maurer, *Public Policy Exception under the New York Convention* (New York, JurisNet 2013) 64. Including fundamental principles of law in the concept of public policy is not only adopted in the CPL in China, but supported by commentators in other countries, such as Russia, see R. Khodykin, *Arbitration Law of Russia* (New York, Juris 2013) 154; Art 15:101 of the Principles of European Contract Law, see E.H. Hondius, *Towards a European Civil Code* (Nijmegen: Kluwer 2014) 418; Guide to Enactment of UNCITRAL Model Law in International Insolvency; Switzerland, see Swiss Federal Supreme Court, 8 December 2003, at ICCA Yearbook Court Decisions, 838–9 and J.D. Fry, 'Désordre Public International under the New York Convention', (2009) 8 *Chinese Journal of International Law* 81, note 75;

121 CPL 1982, Art 204.

122 Consular Department of Chinese Embassy in Argentina Document, No. 70 (1984), 31 Oct 1984. Answer of SPC to Validity of the Legal Separation Agreement concluded by the Chinese Citizens domiciled in Argentina, Answer No. 14 (1984), dated 5 December 1984.

6.74 The very broad language has changed since 1991. Since Chinese legislators rarely alter the language used in the precedent legislation, unless substantive changes are present, it is assumed that the legislator intends to limit the scope of public policy at the recognition and enforcement stage, an opinion widely shared by Chinese scholars and practitioners.[123] Chinese courts cite public policy to refuse to recognize foreign judgment very prudently, and no refusal was found based on the ground of public policy up to now.

V. CONCLUSION

6.75 Foreign judgment recognition in China could be facilitated through two channels, i.e., the bilateral treaty channel and the domestic rule channel. Since the domestic rule channel relies heavily on the principle of reciprocity and in practice only *de facto* reciprocity is accepted in the courts, FJR through this channel is possible but very difficult. The bilateral treaty channel, on the other hand, brings out some degree of certainty, but problems continue to exist, including the limited number of countries that have entered into bilateral treaties with China, the inconsistency between the treaties and the ambiguity of some rules in the treaties. Where the treaties fail to provide clear rules and guidance, the Chinese courts have to rely on the domestic law while enforcing judgments under one of those treaties. Therefore, the two channels are not mutually exclusive in practice and the implementation of one may rely on the other.

6.76 The difficulty of enforcing foreign judgments is one of the major problems in the current Chinese conflicts system and hampers the development of international cooperation in trade and economy. The difficulty also affects the proper implementation of jurisdiction rules, for example, Chinese courts may refuse to decline jurisdiction in favour of a foreign court chosen by the parties in their exclusive jurisdiction agreement because the foreign judgment cannot be enforced in China; and Chinese jurisdiction rules must include an unusual ground to provide jurisdiction to China in the absence of any other substantive connections if the defendant has assets located in China. This difficulty over enforcing judgments may reduce the confidence of foreign trade partners and affect the competitiveness of Chinese companies.

6.77 The FJR system needs a reform. Four approaches may be adopted. First, China could continue to negotiate bilateral judicial assistance treaties with

---

123 XIAO Yongping, *Falixue Shiyexia de Chongfufa* [*Conflict of Laws from a Jurisprudence Perspective*] (Beijing: Gaodeng Jiaoyu Chubanshe [Higher Education Press] 2008) 218.

foreign countries, especial major trade partners, such as the US, the UK, Japan and Germany. This approach is consistent with Chinese tradition and practice. However, its weakness is obvious. It is piecemeal and takes time to make any progress. Furthermore, it is not easy to enter into such treaties with some countries, which will fail to conclude similar judicial cooperation treaties with China in the future. Some political and economic differences exist and neither country wishes to compromise. It is hard to argue that such a compromise may be reached in the future; and it is predicted that this approach may not make any great progress in the short term.

The second approach is to fundamentally reform the domestic rule channel, abandoning the rigid reciprocity principle and adopting a more flexible criteria for FJR. It could fundamentally change the status quo and largely improve FJR in China. The common criteria that protects defendants, ensures natural justice and due process and protects public interest could form sufficient protection to Chinese sovereignty and national interest. However, legislators seem reluctant to adopt this approach. In the 2012 reform of the CPL and the 2015 interpretation, nothing suggested that the legislators and SPC wish to abandon the basic principle of reciprocity. Adopting a liberal FJR system may prove difficult to implement in China. **6.78**

An alternative approach to reforming the domestic rule channel is to adopt the principle of *de jure* reciprocity instead. Although it could not fundamentally remove the weakness of the principle of reciprocity, it improves the possibility for FJR especially where judgments are given in countries without case precedents of recognizing past Chinese judgments. **6.79**

The fourth approach is to enter into international judicial cooperation treaties facilitating FJR at the international level. The only such treaty covering civil and commercial matters in general is the Hague Choice of Court Convention, which is only enforced among a limited number of countries in the world, and is, further, limited to judgments based on a valid exclusive jurisdiction clause. However, it is still worthwhile ratifying this Convention as it could partially resolve the FJR difficulty and could act as a test for a more general and broad international cooperation treaty in the future. It is suggested that China should and could consider at least approaches three and four above to improve the FJR system. **6.80**

7

RECOGNITION AND ENFORCEMENT OF ARBITRAL AWARDS IN CHINESE COURTS

7.01 Recognition and enforcement of foreign judgments is a traditional difficulty in international society. The difficulty exists not only in China but also in many other countries in the world. Comparatively, arbitration provides an alternative way out. Arbitration can provide a relatively neutral and effective forum for the resolution of transnational commercial disputes. It is based on the parties' consent and cooperation, and many losing parties simply enforce the awards voluntarily. However, when the losing party fails to perform promptly, arbitrators lack the necessary authority to enforce their awards. The prevailing party thus has to turn to the courts for help.

7.02 Which national court may or should be seized to recognize and enforce the arbitral award? This depends on the individual case and the choice of the prevailing party. Normally the place of arbitration is chosen by the parties, it may be a place with which they have no objective connection. The place of enforcement is usually the place where the defaulting party's assets are located.

It would be useless, for instance, to obtain an enforcement order in Chinese courts for seizure and sale of the defaulting party's goods and chattels located outside the PRC. Nor would it be useful to secure an order for the attachment of the defaulting party's bank accounts in China, if these accounts turn out to be overdrawn. This is the reason why an international award needs to be recognized and enforced in a foreign country constantly, not merely in the country in which the arbitral award was made.

Compared to the recognition and enforcement of foreign judgments, foreign arbitral awards circulate more freely in the world, mainly because the recognition and enforcement of foreign arbitral awards is largely facilitated by the United Nations Convention on Recognition and Enforcement of Foreign Arbitral Awards of 1958 (New York Convention) ('NYC' hereafter), which is applicable almost universally.[1] Indeed, as of March 2015, 150 states were parties.[2] This is one of the most successful international treaties in the world. China is a contracting state of the NYC, which means the effect of foreign arbitral awards is much more certain in China than foreign judgments. **7.03**

This chapter integrates the rules on enforcement of foreign arbitral awards in the New York Convention, the CPL of 2012, PRC Arbitration Law of 1994, and some judicial interpretations of China, especially combining the cases of the Chinese courts and to expound Chinese law and practice on enforcement of foreign arbitral awards. For arbitral awards, 'recognition' and 'enforcement' generally run together, because an arbitral award is usually about the payment of money or the performance of some act.[3] **7.04**

I. HISTORY AND STATUTORY FRAMEWORK FOR ENFORCEMENT OF FOREIGN ARBITRAL AWARDS

China has a tradition of avoiding court litigation. For over 2,000 years, Chinese citizens used mediation to resolve civil disputes. This tradition leads to a preference for out of court dispute resolution, including arbitration, in **7.05**

1 UN Treaty Series, Vol. 330, 3.

2 On 23 June 2014, Burundi became the 150th member of the New York Convention. See https://treaties.un.org/pages/UNTSOnline.aspx?id=2, visited 8 March 2015.

3 Of course, this does not preclude the party from only applying recognition of arbitral award in a few cases. Suppose a Chinese company was sued by a foreign supplier for goods sold and delivered, but allegedly not paid for, and an award has been made by a foreign arbitration institution, in which the foreign supplier's claim was dismissed. Under this situation, the Chinese company would request the foreign court to recognize the award as a valid defence to the foreign supplier's claim, but no enforcement would be needed.

modern China. China has one of the most widely used international arbitration entities in the world;[4] but had no legislative ground facilitating enforcement of foreign-related arbitral awards before 1982. These awards, as a result, could not be enforced in court, but the enforcement depends completely on the losing party's voluntary compliance. The situation changed in March 1982 with the Civil Procedure Law of the People's Republic of China (For Trial Implementation) (the 1982 CPL). Article 195 provided a legal basis for the enforcement of arbitral awards made by a 'foreign affairs arbitration organization' of China.[5] If an award was delivered by the foreign organization, it could not be directly enforced by the Chinese court under the 1982 CPL. Such an award had first to be converted into a foreign court judgment. The foreign court then requested the Chinese court to enforce it as a foreign judgment. Due to the difficulty in enforcing foreign judgments, foreign awards rendered by a foreign arbitration entity were never successfully enforced in China before China acceded to the NYC.[6]

7.06 China acceded to the NYC in 1986.[7] The 'Decision on Accession to the NYC' stated that the NYC should be self-executing in China and have priority over domestic laws. Convention arbitral awards were enforceable in China pursuant to the NYC provisions, subject to reciprocity and commercial reservation.[8] The SPC later issued the 'Notice on the Implementation of China's Accession to the Recognition and Enforcement of Foreign Arbitral Awards' ('New York Convention Accession Notice') in 1987, which clarified a number of conceptual and procedural issues concerning the enforcement under the NYC, including the definition of commercial reservation, competent PRC courts, and the time frame.[9] More detailed regulations were provided in the revised

---

4 E. Reinstein, 'Finding a Happy Ending for Foreign Investors', (2005) 16 *Indiana International and Comparative Law Review* 37, 38; M.T. Colatrella, Jr.,'Court-performed Mediation in the People's Republic of China: A Proposed Model to Improve the United States Federal District Courts' Mediation Progress', (2000) 15 *Ohio State Journal on Dispute Resolution* 396–9.

5 CPL 1982, Art 195 provides that when one of the parties concerned fails to comply with a ruling made by a foreign affairs arbitration organization of the PRC, the other party may request that the ruling be enforced in accordance with the provisions of this article by the courts at the place where the arbitration organization is located or where the property is located.

6 R. Peerenboom, 'The Evolving Regulatory Framework for Enforcement of Arbitral Awards in the PRC', (2000) 12 *Asian-Pacific Law and Policy* 1, 15.

7 The NPC Standing Committee adopted the decision on Accession to the Convention on Recognition and Enforcement of Foreign Awards on 2 December 1986.

8 The reciprocity reservation means the NYC should be applied to enforce arbitral awards made in the territory of other contracting states only on the basis of reciprocity. The commercial reservation means the NYC will only be applied in China to enforce foreign arbitral awards in the commercial legal relationship. These two concepts are explained in sec. B below. See Peerenboom, ibid., 15.

9 SPC, Arts 1–5; 'Guanyu Zhixing Woguo Jiaru de "Chengren ji Zhixing Waiguo Zhongcai Caijue Gongyue" de Tongzhi [Notice on the Implementation of China's Accession to the Recognition and Enforcement of Foreign Arbitral Awards]', Fa [Jing] Fa [1987] No 5. Peerenboom, *supra* n 6, 16.

1991 CPL Articles 259, 260 and 269, which are retained by the CPL of 2012 in Articles 273, 274, and 283 respectively. They will be discussed more fully in the next subsections.

On 31 August 1994, the Standing Committee of the NPC passed the Arbitration Law, effective from 1 September 1995. In order to prevent the local protectionism of the local courts and to improve implementation of the NYC, some important regulations were issued by the SPC in various judicial directions and interpretations. The most important judicial interpretations include the 1995 Notice providing a special internal report and review mechanism,[10] the 1998 Fee Regulation providing time limits and fee problems,[11] and the 2006 Interpretation providing instructions for more general issues on the application of the Arbitration.[12] **7.07**

Finally, the 2012 CPL added or revised some provisions for enforcement of arbitral awards, such as property preservation and evidence preservation measures before filing arbitration proceedings, imposing a fine or detention on award debtors who entered malicious arbitration with a third party to evade the obligations of the arbitral award, and the procedural rule that an appeal may not be filed against the ruling of setting aside a arbitral award. The wordings of Articles 273, 274, and 283 for enforcement of foreign arbitral awards are identical with Articles 259, 260, and 269 of the 1991 CPL respectively. **7.08**

II. DEFINING 'FOREIGN ARBITRAL AWARDS' UNDER CHINESE LAW

As a preliminary question, the standard for determining nationality of an arbitral award is, in theory, a very controversial issue. The nationality of an arbitral award is generally decided either by the court entitled to set aside the arbitral award or the court that has been requested to enforce the arbitral award in accordance with their respective domestic laws.[13] Some countries **7.09**

10 SPC, 'Guanyu Renminfayuan Chuli yu Shewai Zhongcai ji Waiguo Zhongcai Shixiang Youguan Wenti de Tongzhi [Notice Regarding Several Issues Relating to the People's Courts' Handling of Foreign-related and Foreign Arbitration Matters]', Fa Fa [1995] 18.

11 SPC, 'Guanyu Chengren he Zhixing Waiguo Zhongcai Caijue Shoufei ji Shencha Qixian Wenti de Guiding [Regulation of the SPC Regarding the Problems of Collecting Fees and Time Limits for Review the Recognition and Enforcement of Foreign Arbitral Awards]', Fa Shi [1998] 28.

12 SPC, 'Zuigao Renmin Fayuan Guanyu Shiyong "Zhonghua Renmin Gongheguo Zhongcaifa" Ruogan Wenti de Jieshi [Interpretation of the SPC concerning Some Issues on Application of the Arbitration Law of the People's Republic of China]' (2006 Arbitration Law Interpretation), Fa Shi [2006] No 7.

13 ZHAO Xiu-wen, *Guoji Shangshi Zhongcai Jiqi Shiyong Falv Yanjiu [A Study of International Commercial Arbitration and Its Application of Law]* (Beijing: Peking University Press 2002) 191; for criticism, see Mauro

determine the nationality of an arbitral award according to the place where the award is rendered.[14] Some determine nationality according to the criterion of the applicable procedure, instead of the geographical criterion.[15] Others combine both criteria and an arbitral award will be foreign only where neither points to the local jurisdiction.[16]

7.10 Chinese law in enforcement of arbitral awards is complicated. In Chinese law, arbitral awards are classified as foreign, foreign-related or domestic.[17] Foreign arbitral awards are all arbitral awards rendered outside China. Foreign-related awards are awards rendered by arbitration institutions of the PRC, which are authorized to handle foreign-related disputes and the dispute in question involves foreign elements. Purely Chinese domestic disputes to be decided by a Chinese local arbitration commission are domestic awards.[18] Only the enforcement of foreign awards is subject to the NYC. Enforcement of foreign-related awards and purely Chinese domestic awards is subject to Chinese domestic law.

7.11 Therefore, the geographic standard is adopted in China, which is consistent with the classification in the NYC, Article 1(1) of which provides: 'This Convention shall apply to the recognition and enforcement of arbitral awards in the territory of a State other than the State where the recognition and enforcement of such awards are sought, and arising out of differences between persons, whether physical or legal.' Clearly the criterion of the NYC for identifying the foreign nature of an award is not the nationality or seat of the arbitration institute, but the place where the award is made.

7.12 Since the key standard is the place where arbitral awards are made, what if a foreign arbitration institution renders the awards in the territory of China? Would these awards be classified as Chinese awards not subject to the NYC? According to the territorial standards, such awards should be classified as non-foreign. However, some courts adopt the standard of both territoriality

---

Rubino Sammartano, *International Arbitration Law and Practice* (3rd ed., Netherlands: Kluwer Law International, 2014) 101–2.

14 Such as Austria, Sweden, Libya, Netherlands, and Egypt. See P. Sarcevic, 'The Setting Aside and Enforcement of Arbitral Awards under the UNCITRAL Model Law', in P. Sarcevic, *Essays on International Commercial Arbitration* (London/Norwell: Martinus Nijhoff 1989) 178.

15 Such as Greece, Germany, and Lebanon. See Sarcevic, ibid., 178–9; Sammartano, *supra* n 13, 103–12

16 Such as Yugoslavia, Hungary, Turkey, etc. Sarcevic, *supra* n 14, 179.

17 J. Fei and R. Hill, 'Enforcement of Arbitral Awards in the PRC', in M.J. Moser, *Dispute Resolution in China* (New York: Juris Publishing 2012) 157, 157. Awards from Hong Kong, Macao, and Taiwan fall into another category, see Ch 13.

18 Fei and Hill, ibid., 158. The foreign affairs arbitration institution of the PRC refers to the China International Economic and Trade Arbitration Commission (CIETAC) and the China Maritime Arbitration Commission (CMAC). There are 209 local arbitration commissions in China.

and nationality of the international institutions and hold that only when both direct to China, the awards are classified as non-foreign.[19] In *Duferco SA v. Ningbo Arts & Crafts Import & Export*,[20] Duferco SA (Duferco), a Swiss company and Ningbo Arts & Crafts Import & Export Co Ltd (Ningbo I&E), a Chinese company, signed a sales contract in 2003, in Ningbo, Zhejiang, China. The contract included an arbitration clause stating that 'all disputes in connection with this contract or the execution thereof shall be submitted to the arbitration commission of the International Chamber of Commerce (ICC) situated in Beijing, China and be arbitrated in accordance with the United Nations Convention on the International Sale of Goods'. When a dispute arose, it was submitted to the ICC according to the arbitration agreement and the ICC rendered the award in favour of Duferco. Ningbo I&E refused to enforce the award, and Duferco initiated an application for recognition and enforcement of the award in the Ningbo IPC ('Ningbo IPC' hereafter).

The Ningbo IPC decided the NYC should be applied to the case,[21] and ruled that the award had been issued by a foreign arbitration institution, i.e., the ICC, rather than a domestic arbitration institution, which made the award an 'arbitral award not considered as domestic'. Since the arbitral award was covered by the NYC, the Chinese arbitration law was irrelevant. The Ningbo IPC, in 2009, ruled that the arbitral award should be recognized and enforced.[22] This approach, unfortunately, is inconsistent with Article 1(1) of the NYC. **7.13**

III. PROCEDURAL ISSUES FOR ENFORCEMENT OF FOREIGN ARBITRAL AWARDS IN CHINA

III.1 Venue and jurisdiction

An application to enforce foreign arbitral awards should be made directly to the Intermediate People's Court (IPC) of the place where the respondent has his domicile or where his property is located.[23] The 1987 NYC Accession Notice further provides that for a natural person, domicile should be his **7.14**

19 *Duferco SA v. Ningbo Import & Export*, Ningbo IPC (2008) Yong Zhong Jian Zi No 4, 22 April 2009. For full description of the case, see Fei and Hill, *supra* n 17, 230–31.

20 *Duferco S,A*, ibid.; Fei and Hill, *supra* n 17, 230–31.

21 NYC, Art 1.

22 It is important to note that in this case the respondent failed to challenge the validity of the arbitration clause in time, and was estoppled from bringing the challenge at the stage of enforcement. As a matter of fact, ICC Arbitration Court has no fixed place of arbitration in China. This was an *ad hoc* arbitration, which is not permitted by Chinese arbitration law.

23 See CPL, Art 273.

registered domicile or where he actually resides;[24] for a legal person or organization, domicile is where its principal place of business is located. If none of the above locations can be determined, the applicant may apply at the IPC where the property is located.[25]

7.15 The literal interpretation of the CPL and the 1987 Notice may be inconsistent. Both accept that more than one IPC may be competent to decide the application. However, a literal interpretation of the 1987 Notice suggests the applicant may only apply in the IPC of the place where the respondent's property is located if the respondent has no registered domicile or place of residence or principal business office. According to Article 273 of the CPL, however, the applicant is free to bring the application to the IPC of either the respondent's domicile or the location of property in any circumstances. There is clearly more freedom to choose the competent court.

7.16 It is suggested that, in practice, Article 273 of the CPL should be followed. First, it is much more recent legislation and should take priority over the older provisions. Secondly, it is in a form of a statute, instead of a 'Notice', which is of the nature of legislative interpretation. Thirdly, Article 273 of CPL is more appropriate, enabling the applicant to choose a more proper venue to apply for enforcement of the arbitral award in any circumstances. Arbitral awards usually are proprietary, and the court that is most convenient to enforce the awards will usually be the court of the place where the property is located. Furthermore, local protectionism may cause practical difficulties and concerns if the applicant applies to the court where the respondent has his domicile, especially where the respondent is a state-owned company. Applying to the court where the property is located may be more effective and appropriate.

III.2 Documentation

7.17 According to Article IV of the NYC, the applicant should supply the duly authenticated original award or a duly certified copy, and the original arbitration agreement or a duly certified copy.[26] If the award or agreement is not made out in the official language of the country in which the award is to be enforced, the applicant should produce a translation, certified by an official or sworn translator or by a diplomatic or consular agent.[27] The documentary requirement is confirmed in Article 20 of the 2006 Interpretation. Besides the

---

24 The registered domicile is called HuKou (户口) in China. See Ch 3, sec IV above.

25 Point 3 of the Notice.

26 NYC, Art IV(1).

27 Ibid., Art IV(2).

documents listed in the NYC, the 2006 Interpretation also requires the applicant to provide an application, an authenticated power of attorney and documentation of the applicant's legal representative, and a notarized and consularized certificate of incorporation or analogous documentation. These documents must be translated into Chinese certified by the Chinese embassy or notarized by the Chinese authority.[28]

In early practice in the 1990s, some Chinese judges had incomplete knowledge of the legal requirements and required the applicant to provide additional documents, such as evidence relied on by the arbitration tribunal in making its award, and its notarization and translation. Such requirements are excessive, can impose extra financial burdens and inconvenience to the application, and may cause delay.[29] The situation is now much improved. In order to facilitate the implementation of foreign arbitral awards in China, some Chinese courts do not even require the applicant to provide the full translation of the arbitral award, but only a translation of the decision part of the award, though this is not clearly stipulated in the law.[30] **7.18**

III.3 Limitation

The 2012 CPL sets forth a unified limitation period for the initiation of enforcement proceedings for domestic judgments, foreign judgments, domestic awards, and foreign awards. Article 239 provides that the limitation period for the submission of an application for enforcement shall be two years, calculated from the last day specified by the award for its performance. If the award does not specify the period of performance, the limitation period should begin on the effective day of the award. An award usually will be effective on the day it was made, unless specified otherwise. However, in practice, it may take time for the foreign arbitral award served on the respondent. Calculating from the date when the award was made may be detrimental to the respondent. In Chinese judicial practice, some courts may calculate the limitation period from the date when the award is served on the respondent.[31] **7.19**

In *Shanghai Jwell Machinery v. Retech Aktiengesellschaft, Switzerland*,[32] the SPC has provided an overly broad interpretation to allow the limitation period to **7.20**

28 SPC, Art 21; 'Guanyi Renmin Fayuan Zhixing Gongzuo Ruogan Wenti de Guiding (Shixing) [Rules on the Several Executive Issues of the People's Court (for the Trial Purpose)'], Fa Shi [1998] No 15.

29 According to a survey of Professor Randall Peerenboom in 1998, see Peerenboom, *supra* n 6, 20.

30 This observation is based on one author's experience practising as a lawyer and arbitrator in China.

31 *Re Application of Louis Dreyfus Commodities Asian Co Ltd for Recognition and Enforcement of Arbitration Award No 3980 of International Federation of Oils, Seeds & Fats Associations*, [2010] Min Si Ta Zi No 48.

32 SPC Guiding Case No 37, published by the SPC on 18 Dec 2014.

start to run when the award creditor knows the debtor has located its property in China, even if the defendant had no bad faith in deliberately hiding its assets. In this case, the CIEFAC delivered the award in favour of the Chinese company on 18 September 2006, ordering the Swiss company to pay money. The application to enforce the judgment in Switzerland was rejected because the translation of the award did not meet the NYC requirement. The Chinese company knew the defendant had located some properties in China for an exhibition and applied for enforcement in China. The SPC confirmed that if both the defendant and its property are located abroad, the two-year limitation period for enforcement would start to run only when the creditor knows the other party or its property is relocated in China. This interpretation aims to protect the award creditor. However, it may prove inappropriate in practice because it artificially extends the limitation period for enforcement even if the failure to enforce in the other country is caused by the claimant's negligence. The claimant may also unreasonably leave the time to lapse in the other country and the concern for enforcement in China may lead the defendant reluctant to do business in China. Some local Chinese courts may be driven by local protectionism and more readily enforce the award against a foreign party. The defendant may successfully defend enforcement in the other country, but be ordered enforcement by the Chinese court.

7.21 The limitation period will be suspended where the creditor cannot exercise his right due to *force majeure* or other obstacles within the last six months of the limitation period. The period will resume from the day when the cause resulting in the suspension is eliminated.[33] *Force majeure* or other obstacles may exist where there is a natural disaster or disease outbreak; it is not always easy to determine when the obstacle is removed. In *Re Scheuer*,[34] the applicant applied after the limitation period had expired. He argued that the delay was caused by the severe acute respiratory syndrome (SARS) outbreak in Beijing, where the competent court was located. There was no official record on when the outbreak was under control and no longer a legal obstacle. The decision was based on the official cancellation of the travel alert to Beijing. However, different institutes made the announcement on different dates. The WHO and Beijing Government made the announcement on 24 June 2003, while the US Government made the same announcement on 11 July 2003. The court did not need to decide which date to choose because it made no difference to the result in this case. However, where differences do occur, determining the date the obstacle was removed would be crucial. Although Beijing had the

33 GPCL, Art 139.

34 *Re Application of Scheuer for Recognition and Enforcement of American Arbitration Association Award*, [2006] Min Si Ta Zi No 35.

authority to determine whether the local SARS outbreak was no longer a barrier for foreign litigants, it was also reasonable for a foreign litigant to determine its travel plan according to the warning of its home state.

Article 140 of the GPCL provides that the limitation period shall discontinue when the creditor files a lawsuit or requests the losing party to perform obligations,[35] or the losing party agrees to fulfil the obligations. The limitation period shall be re-calculated from the discontinued day.[36] However, if the parties simply enter into an agreement to extend or reduce the limitation period, such an agreement is not enforceable in law.[37] The limitation period will not be discontinued if the losing party challenges the award in the supervisory court. In *Re Vysanthi Shipping Co Ltd*,[38] three arbitral awards were rendered in 2001 and 2002. The respondents applied to the English court to set aside the arbitral awards in 2002. The applicant applied for enforcement to the Chinese court in 2004. The SPC held that the challenge in the English court could not discontinue or suspend the limitation period. The application was refused. **7.22**

III.4 The internal report and review mechanism

In 1995, in recognition of the adverse consequences of local protectionism, the SPC issued the 1995 Notice.[39] The 1995 Notice established an internal report/review mechanism with respect to the non-enforcement of foreign-related arbitral awards and arbitral awards made under the NYC or other reciprocal agreements.[40] Under this system, if the IPC finds that an application for the recognition and enforcement of a foreign award should be refused under the NYC or other international treaties to which China has acceded, the court must not render a decision in the matter but must report its **7.23**

35 SPC, 'Guanyi Shenli Minshi Anjian Shiyong Susong Shixiao Zhidu Ruogan Wenti de Guiding [Regulation Concerning Several Issues of Application of Limitation of Action in Civil Case]' ('Limitation Regulation'), Fa Shi [2008] No 11, Arts 10–20 provide detailed regulation on what 'requests' could discontinue the limitation period.

36 SPC, 'Guanyi Shiyong "Zhonghua Renmin Gongheguo Minshi Susongfa" Zhixing Chengxu Ruogan Wenti de Jieshi [Interpretation of the SPC of Several Issues concerning the Enforcement Procedures in the Application of the Civil Procedure Law of the People's Republic of China]', Fa Shi [2008] No 13, Art 28.

37 Limitation Regulation, *supra* n 35, Art 2.

38 *Vysanthi Shipping Co. Ltd v. China Cereals, Oils and Feedingstuff and others*, [2004] Min Si Ta Zi No 32.

39 SPC, 'Zuigao Renmin Fayuan Guanyu Renmin Fayuan Chuli yu Shewai hongcai ji Waiguo Zhongcai Shixiang Youguan Wenti de Tongzhi [Notice on Issues about the Handling of Cross-Border and Foreign Arbitration]', Fa Fa [1995] No 18.

40 The internal report and review mechanism also applies to the court taking jurisdiction based on invalidity of arbitration agreements. See Ch 4, III above.

findings to the HPC for approval.[41] If the latter court concurs with the findings of the lower court, the matter must be reported to the SPC for a reply.[42] Therefore, the approval of the SPC is a prerequisite for a court to refuse enforcement of a foreign-related or foreign award.[43]

7.24 Accordingly, the internal report and review mechanism does not apply to domestic arbitral awards. Furthermore, the internal reporting requirement only applies where the Chinese court determines that enforcement of the foreign-related arbitral award or recognition and/or enforcement of a foreign award should be denied, or where the court determines that a foreign-related arbitral award should be cancelled. There is no requirement to report decisions to enforce a foreign-related arbitral award, or decisions dismissing applications for the cancellation of a foreign-related arbitral award.

7.25 This internal report and review system effectively serves to ensure that different Chinese courts enforce foreign and foreign-related arbitral awards by the same standard. According to a survey, the SPC has denied 80 per cent of the requests to refuse enforcement.[44] However, the internal reporting mechanism may cause delays. Further procedure guidance is provided in the Fee Regulation issued by the SPC in 1998,[45] which provides that if the IPC decides not to recognize foreign arbitral awards falling within the NYC, this decision should be reported to the SPC within two months of admission of the application.[46] This two-month period includes the time to refer the decision to the HPC and the time for the HPC to refer the case to the SPC. However, the law provides no time limit for the SPC to make its decision. Furthermore, after the SPC has made the decision, the SPC will reply to the HPC and the HPC will forward the decision to the IPC, which will make the ruling accordingly. The law again fails to designate a time limit for the HPC to forward the SPC's response and for the IPC to deliver the ruling. Each HPC

41 The report mechanism is also used if the IPC finds an application for the enforcement of a foreign-related award should be refused in the Chinese law. Only enforcement of purely domestic awards will not be subject to this mechanism.

42 Point 2 of the 1995 Notice.

43 In April 1998, the SPC issued a second Notice on the internal report and review system, further extending this system to any decision of the Intermediate or Higher People's Court to cancel a foreign-related arbitral award. SPC, 'Guanyi Renminfayuan Chexie Shewai Zhongcai Caijue Youguan Shixiang de Tongzhi [Notice of the SPC Regarding Matters Concerning Cancellation of Foreign-Related Arbitral Awards]', Fa [1998] 40.

44 See Shengchang Wang, 'Enforcement of Foreign Arbitral Awards in the People's Republic of China', in A.J. van den Berg (ed), *Improving the Efficiency of Arbitration and Awards: 40 Years of Application of the New York Convention* (ICCA Congress Series No 9, 1999) 461–504.

45 SPC, 'Guanyu Chengren he Zhixing Waiguo Zhongcai Caijue Shoufei yi Shencha Qixian Wenti de Guiding [Regulation of the SPC Regarding the Fee and Time Limit for Recognition and Enforcement of Foreign Arbitral Awards]', Fa Shi [1998] No 28.

46 Point 4.

is entitled to issue specific provisions on the time scale of itself and the IPCs in its supervision. For example, the HPC of Jiangsu issued the provisions in 2007, which provides that the HPC should forward the reply of the SPC to the IPC within ten days and the IPC should make a ruling within ten days.[47] However, not every HPC has provided a similar regulation. Furthermore, the HPC has no authority to regulate the time required by the SPC. In practice there are severe delays.

III.5 Consequences of refusal to recognize awards

The court's ruling on enforcement of arbitral awards cannot be appealed.[48] If the court refuses to enforce the foreign arbitral awards, the only remedy for the applicant is the internal report and review mechanism. If the court decides to enforce the arbitral awards, there is no similar review mechanism to protect the respondent. However, if the respondent considers that the award has some errors, he may apply to the original Chinese court or the court at the next higher level for retrial.[49] **7.26**

If enforcement is refused, Article 9 of the Arbitration Law permits the parties to re-arbitrate the same subject matter or to bring the dispute to the court. The refusal, as a result, has the same effect as setting aside the arbitral award and exempting arbitral finality. It is doubtful whether this approach is appropriate in legal theory. When a court refuses to enforce an arbitral award, it only denies the legal effect of the award within the territory of the country where the enforcement is sought. It does not have the effect of invalidating or setting aside the arbitral award, which may still stand and be enforced in another country. Furthermore, the same article also provides that in order for the parties to re-arbitrate, it is necessary for them to conclude a new arbitration agreement. This means that the refusal does not only cancel the award itself, but also the arbitration agreement. However, if the refusal is based on the ground of procedural irregularity or public policy defence, this refusal should not render the original arbitration agreement invalid. From a practical perspective, while the enforcement application is refused, it would be very difficult for the parties to enter into another arbitration agreement. The losing **7.27**

47 Jiangsu HPC, 'Guanyu Xiugai Shenli Minshangshi Zhongcai Sifa Shencha Anjian Ruogan Wenti de Yijian [Opinions of Several Issus concerning Cases of Judicial Review on Commercial Arbitration (Amended)]', Su Gao Fa Shen Wei [2010] No 11.

48 CPL, Art 154.

49 Ibid., Art 178.

party, considering the record in the past arbitration, would refuse to cooperate. The only remedy left for the applicant would be to bring the dispute to the court.[50]

IV. GROUNDS FOR REFUSAL TO ENFORCEMENT OF FOREIGN ARBITRAL AWARDS UNDER THE NEW YORK CONVENTION

7.28 As discussed above, the NYC was designed principally to facilitate the recognition and enforcement of foreign arbitral awards. It imposes a presumptive obligation on contracting countries to enforce awards made in other countries, subject to procedural requirements no more onerous than those for domestic awards. Prior to discussing the specific grounds for refusal, it is necessary to sum up the prerequisites for application of the NYC in PRC. First, the award must be foreign. Secondly, China has declared that the Convention will only apply to awards made in the territory of other Convention signatories. Thirdly, the Convention will only be applied to commercial relationships determined under the China law. Fourthly, there must be a written arbitration agreement available in order to apply the NYC. Fifthly, there are also documentation requirements, under which the party applying must supply: (1) the original of the award or a certified copy; and (2) the original arbitration agreement or a certified copy. Where these are not in an official language of the country where enforcement is sought, i.e., Chinese, they must be accompanied by a certified translation.[51] Subject to the above five relatively straightforward conditions, China may not impose more onerous procedural rules, or a fee or charge that is higher than those applicable to the recognition and enforcement of domestic arbitral awards. In particular, there is absolutely no requirement that the foreign arbitral award should first be confirmed by the courts of the place of arbitration.[52]

IV.1 No valid arbitration agreement

7.29 The existence of arbitration agreements is the fundamental basis for a valid arbitration. As a result, the arbitral award may not be recognized if the arbitration agreement is invalid.[53] However, validity of an arbitration agreement is a question of law, which inevitably gives rise to the choice of law question. Which country's substantive law should be applied to decide the

50 Peerenboom, *supra* n 6, 39.

51 1987 Notice, Arts 1–5.

52 This requirement to first obtain judicial confirmation of the finality of the award is also known as 'double exequatur' and exists under the Geneva Protocol of 1923 and the Geneva Convention of 1961.

53 NYC, Art V(1)(a).

validity of an arbitration agreement? Article V(1)(a) of the NYC provides that non-enforcement may be permitted if:

> The parties to the agreement referred to in Article II were, under the law applicable to them, under some incapacity, or the said agreement is not valid under the law to which the parties have subjected it or, failing any indication thereon, under the law of the country where the award was made.

Article V(1)(a) of the NYC thus categorizes validity into two issues: capacity and other validity issues. If the respondent wants to challenge the capacity of the parties, the law applicable should be the personal law of each party. This, however, does not clarify which law it is. Should it be the law of the party's habitual residence, domicile, or other places? This is left for the national law of the enforcement court to determine. **7.30**

i. Applicable law

As to other validity matters, such as formality or existence of genuine consent, Article V(1)(a) provides that the validity of the arbitration agreement is governed by the law chosen by the parties; if no law is agreed, the law of the country where the award was made would apply to the arbitration agreement. **7.31**

A question that frequently arises is where a choice of law clause is present, whether this is the clause choosing the governing law for the substance of the contract only, or it also applies to the arbitration agreement. In Chinese judicial practice, the Chinese courts do not hesitate to hold that the parties do not agree on the applicable law to the arbitration agreement while there is a general choice of law clause in the contract.[54] Although it is theoretically correct to treat the arbitration clause separately from the main contract, it is rare for the parties to specifically designate a governing law for the arbitration clause. It means the chosen law approach is used in fewer cases than might be expected. **7.32**

ii. Written form requirement

The NYC requires the arbitration agreement to be 'in writing' and 'signed by the parties' or 'contained in an exchange of letters or telegrams'. These provisions on formality are clearly out-dated. Communication by telegram, for example, is extremely unusual in a modern business.[55] Although communication by letters continues to exist, it has, in many circumstances, been **7.33**

54 E.g., *Pany u Chu Kong Steel Pipe v. Shenzhen Fanbang International Freight Forwarder Co Ltd,* [2009] Min Si Ta Zi No 7.

55 L.A. Mistelis, *Concise International Arbitration* (Kluwer Law International 2010) 7.

replaced by the speedier and more convenient means of e-mail. Modern communication technology, unfortunately, is not considered in the NYC. Although the articles of the Convention are not subject to amendment in China, the Chinese law provides a more up-to-date interpretation to Convention formality making it more compatible with the modern communication technology.[56]

7.34 Article 16(1) of the Arbitration Law explicitly requires an arbitration agreement to be in written form, consistent with the NYC. While PRC Contract Law 1999 recognizes oral contracts,[57] any arbitration clause or agreement must be still recorded in writing. This is consistent with the prevailing rule in international arbitration. As for what constitutes a written form, the Arbitration Law does not provide direct answers, but Article 11 of the Contract Law provides that the 'written form' includes any form capable of tangible representation of its content, such as written instruments, letters and electrically or electronically transmitted documents including telegrams, telexes, facsimile, electronic data interchange and e-mail.

7.35 As for the issue of signature, the NYC expressly requires that the 'agreement in writing' should include an arbitral clause signed by the parties. In practice, a 'signature' is not necessary, because it is not a statutory requirement under Chinese law. Furthermore, the exchange of letters or telegrams may also make an arbitration agreement valid, which may or may not include a proper signature. The key for the court is to find consent to the arbitration agreement per se. If the parties do not specifically sign the arbitration agreement, or even the main contract, but there is evidence to prove the parties have notice of the existence of the arbitration agreement and given consent, or they are deemed to give consent, to the arbitration agreement, this agreement will be formally valid.[58] On the contract, even if the parties have signed the main contract containing an arbitration agreement, the court may still hold the arbitration agreement invalid if the parties' consent to this agreement cannot be proved.[59] Although signature is not compulsory, it may be good evidence proving the

---

56 This was also suggested by the UNCITRAL Secretariat in its note of 14 December 2005.

57 Contract Law 1999, Art 10.

58 *Rücker v. Aux Group*, [2008] Min Si Ta Zi No 34, the SPC held that where the assignee of a contract containing an arbitration clause issues a termination notice thereof, it is deemed bound by the contract and arbitration clause; where parties to a contract containing an arbitration clause reach an agreement on matters related to but not included in the contract, such matters may in certain circumstances fall within the scope of the arbitration clause.

59 *Xinfa Alumina v. Transfield Shipping*, [2009] Min Si Ta Zi No 32, the SPC held that where both parties have signed and stamped a confirmation of a contract but have failed to sign and stamp the contract containing the arbitration clause, there is no arbitration agreement between them and the arbitration clause is invalid.

parties' genuine consent. As a result, in *Concordia v. Gangde Oils*,[60] the SPC held that a sales contract and related sales confirmations containing an arbitration clause but signed by only one party are insufficient to conclude that an agreement has been reached. It is thus suggested that a signature is not a formal prerequisite to enforce a foreign arbitral award, but it is recommended as one of the factors to show the arbitration agreement is validly concluded under Chinese law.

iii. Arbitration agreement by incorporation

A common business practice is to conclude a contract which refers to the other contractual documents, such as the general terms and conditions of one of the parties, the master agreement between the contractual partners, and the model terms of a specific trade association, which contain an arbitration agreement.[61] Neither the NYC or Arbitration Law deal directly with incorporation of arbitration clauses by reference. The SPC first confirmed the validity of such an arbitral clause in its 'Judicial Direction issued in 1996'.[62] This was later affirmed in the 2006 Interpretation.[63] However, it does not mean incorporation by reference will make all arbitration agreements valid. Consideration must be given to whether the arbitration agreement is incorporated in a manner that could give the other party adequate notice and make the other party reasonably foresee the consequence of the incorporation. An arbitration clause is not validly incorporated as part of the contract where the reference to it is contained on the reverse side of the contract,[64] and where the reference fails to clearly refer to the relevant party to which the arbitration clause may bind.[65] **7.36**

iv. The parties' true and clear intent to arbitrate

Article 16(2) of Arbitration Law requires that parties to an arbitration agreement expressly mention their intent to arbitrate. Article 17 further provides that such intent must be true, if, by means of duress, one party forces **7.37**

60 SPC, 'Reply of the SPC to Concordia Trading B.V.'s Application for Recognition and Enforcement of a FOSFA Arbitral Award', [2009] Min Si Ta Zi No 22.

61 Mistelis, *supra* n 55, 7.

62 SPC, 'Guanyu Shemeng Jingjihetong Weizhijie Yueding Zhongcai Tiaokuan Ruhe Rending Anjian Guanxiaquan de Fuhan [The Reply of SPC Regarding How to Determine Jurisdiction of a Case when the Mongolia-Related Economic Contract Does not Directly Contain an Arbitration Clause]', Fa Han [1996] No 177. This Judicial Direction was abolished in 2013.

63 Art 11: 'If the contract refers to other contracts or documents which include an arbitration clause to resolve a dispute, when the dispute has arisen, the parties should submit their dispute to arbitration pursuant to the arbitration clause.'

64 *Sinochem v. Haili*, [2009] Min Si Ta Zi No 12.

65 Ibid.

another party to execute an arbitration agreement or an agreement incorporating an arbitration clause, such arbitration agreement will be held invalid.

7.38 The arbitration agreement must record the true, clear and unambiguous intention of the parties to refer specific disputes arising between them to arbitration. If the arbitration provides multiple dispute resolution methods concurrently available to the parties, it would be invalid in China due to a lack of clear and unambiguous intent to arbitrate.[66] For example, the clause could provide that the parties either arbitrate or litigate their dispute or that the parties could choose either arbitration or mediation to resolve their dispute. However, if the clause provides the chronological order for these dispute resolution methods, it may still be valid. For example, the clause may provide that while disputes have arisen, the parties should try to resolve their dispute amicably or by mediation, failing which, the parties should submit their disputes to arbitration.

IV.2 Due process

i. Applicable law

7.39 Article V(1)(b) of the New York Convention permits non-recognition of an award if:

> The party against whom the award is invoked was not given proper notice of the appointment of the arbitrator or of the arbitration proceedings or was otherwise unable to present his case.

7.40 Article 274(2) of the CPL has a similar provision. The due process defence includes two specific requirements: the parties are given proper notice of the arbitration and the opportunity to present their case. However, the NYC does not specify what kind of notice is considered 'proper' nor in what circumstances the parties are deemed to have the opportunity to be heard. The standard of fairness differs from country to country, which, once again, generates the question of the applicable law. Commentators may suggest that the law chosen by the parties to govern the arbitration or the law of the seat should apply to determine the due process of the arbitration.[67] However, nothing could prevent the enforcement court from applying its own procedural standard to assessing the fairness of the arbitration procedure. For

---

66 2006 Interpretation, Art 7. *Lim Teo & Wilkes Design Works Pte Ltd. v. Sanya Mangrove Tourism Resort Co. Ltd*, (2006) Qiong Min Er Zhong Zi No 42.

67 V. den Berg, *The New York Arbitration Convention of 1958: Towards a Uniform Judicial Interpretation* (Kluwer Law and Taxation 1981) 298.

example, one US court explicitly states that Article V(1)(b) 'essentially sanctions the application of the forum state's standards of due process'.[68]

In judicial practice, Chinese courts have taken an internationalization approach to decide procedural irregularities of international arbitration. Recognizing the international and a-national nature of international arbitration, the Chinese courts treat the arbitration procedure differently from judicial procedure and allow the procedure standard to be decided by the parties' agreement or the relevant rules of the arbitration institution. Chinese courts normally would not refuse enforcement of an award based upon the parties' agreed procedure.[69] In the absence of parties' designation, or where the national procedure law is used to fill the gap of the parties' agreement, the Chinese court will consider the applicable arbitration rules of the relevant arbitration institution. For example, in *Haimalu v. Popeyes Foods*,[70] the SPC was requested to consider the due process of service of documents in Korean arbitration proceedings. Instead of applying the specified service methods provided in the Hague Service Convention, the SPC applied the procedure rule of the given arbitration commission. **7.41**

The internationalization approach may be criticized for lacking the minimum standard of protection that Article V(1)(b) may attempt for the respondent. Although most reputable arbitration institutions adopt the advanced arbitration procedural rule in accordance with the legal requirements of the seat, one could not rely on the rule of arbitration institutions alone to provide the minimum due process in arbitration. Furthermore, the parties may designate the procedure that they want to follow although such a designation is always subject to the scrutiny and minimum standard of law. As a result, the role of relevant national law can never be ignored. Finally, no country would be willing to give up the power to protect the basic due process requirement of the domestic law, which may be considered one type of procedure in public policy. As a result, a Chinese court may also refuse to enforce the foreign arbitral award if the arbitration procedure is inconsistent with the fundamental Chinese standard in terms of notification and the right to be heard. **7.42**

---

68 *Parsons & Whittemore Overseas Co v. Société General de L'industrie du Papier*, 508 F.2d 969 (2d Cir. 1974) 975.

69 For one-sided terms, such as where one party may be represented by legal counsel, but the other party may not, one party may present witness testimony, but the other may not, etc, it is unclear whether it is subject to non-recognition under Art V(1)(b) in Chinese courts, because there are no relevant cases.

70 SPC, 'Reply to a Request for Instructions on Denying Recognition and Enforcement of a Korean Commercial Arbitration Board Arbitral Award', [2005] Min Si Ta Zi No 46.

ii. Adequate notice

7.43 Adequate notice requires that the arbitral tribunal informs the respondent of the appointment of arbitrators and of the arbitration procedure. The notice includes the notice of arbitration, which allows the respondent enough time to prepare a presentation for the hearing. Chinese courts have adopted a flexible approach to recognizing the effective means of service. The valid means of service of arbitration documents are determined by the applicable arbitration rule.[71] If the arbitration rule permits the notice to be served by courier, registered mail, ordinary mail or e-mail, the Chinese court will not hold service against the law. Adequate notice also requires sufficient advance notification of the date of hearings.[72]

7.44 As to the burden of proof, Chinese courts adopt inconsistent approaches. In some cases, the courts require the applicant to provide evidence proving that the documents were successfully delivered and received. In the absence of valid proof, adequate notice may be challenged.[73] The requirement for the arbitral tribunal to prove successful delivery applies to both traditional service by mail and to modern communication technology. If the defendant is notified by e-mail, the applicant should provide the evidence proving receipt by the addressee.[74] It is recommended that when sending the e-mail, the arbitration institution should request a message notifying safe delivery of the e-mail. The problem is that then the delivery message will only be sent if the addressee chooses to do so. If the addressee refuses to send a delivery message, then proving that the e-mail was effectively delivered is difficult.

7.45 Enforcement will also be refused if the respondent was not notified because of a mistake or omission by the arbitral tribunal, for example, the tribunal has misspelled the address of the respondent.[75] It is the applicant and the arbitration institution's obligation to find the correct correspondence address of the respondent. It makes no difference if the failure of notice is not due to the mistake of the arbitration tribunal or the applicant. For example, if the respondent's registered address is different from the correspondence address, sending the notice to the registered address is not adequate notice, which would result in enforcement being refused by the Chinese court. In *Mawan*

71 *Cosmos Marine v. Tianjin Kaiqiang*, [2006] Min Si Ta Zi No 34; *Boertong v. Liantaichang Commerce*, [2006] Min Si Ta Zi No 36; *SEMT v. Jianglong Electric Power*, (2006) Sui Zhong Fa Min Si Chu Zi No 2.

72 *SPC, 'Reply to the Application for Annulment of a Foreign-Related Arbitral Award Rendered by the Zhuhai Arbitration Commission'*, [2008] Min Si Ta Zi No 2.

73 SPC, 'Guanyu Jujue Chengren he Zhixing Menggu Zhongcaiyuan Quexi Caijue de Dafu [Reply to the Request for Instructions on Denying Recognition and Enforcement of a Mongolian Arbitration Court Default Award]', [2009] Min Si Ta Zi No 46.

74 *Cosmos Marine v. Tianjin Kaiqiang*, *supra* n 71.

75 *Zhu v. Shanghai Marine*, [2007] Min Si Ta Zi No 7.

Power v. Runhe Development,[76] the applicant and the arbitration institution entrusted a lawyer to find the address of the respondent. The lawyer provided the registered address of the respondent company obtained from the corporate registration authority. The arbitration institution sent the notice of arbitration, arbitration procedure rules, the panel of arbitrators and the applicant's claim to this address, but the documents were returned indicating failure of delivery. The arbitration continued but the Chinese court refused to enforce the arbitral award because the respondent had not been duly notified.

In other cases, the courts have taken a more flexible and pro-enforcement approach. In *Schroeder v. Huada Food*,[77] for example, Zhejiang HPC did not sustain overly formalistic requirements relating to the receipt of notice and filing of application documents. Adequate notice is deemed to exist unless the respondent is able to provide compelling evidence establishing that it had not received any notice of the arbitration proceedings.[78] **7.46**

Neither the pro-respondent nor the pro-enforcement approach is appropriate. As to the former, even if the respondent deliberately hides its address or creates obstacles for service, the Chinese court may still refuse the enforcement of a foreign arbitral award based on the lack of adequate notice. This approach is generally adopted to protect Chinese companies, which are usually the respondents in applications to enforce awards in China. The restrictive requirement for notice creates an imbalance in rights and obligations between the parties. It may also provide incentives for Chinese respondents to refuse to cooperate by giving them the opportunity to escape from arbitration procedure. As to the pro-enforcement approach, it would be difficult for the respondent to prove the negative. It is suggested that the Chinese court should in general require the applicant to prove successful delivery of notice to the respondent, but an exception may be given where the applicant and the arbitration tribunal have taken all the reasonable steps to give notice, or where evidence may be shown that the respondent intentionally changed address or avoided effective service. This more realistic approach has been adopted in a few cases in practice. For example, in *Eastland v. Xinxing Rubber*,[79] the respondent leased a new factory from a third party before the arbitration proceeding, but did not register the change of address with the local authority or notify the other party. The documents concerning appointment of arbitrators and further conduct of the arbitration proceedings were delivered to its **7.47**

76 [2008] Min Si Ta Zi No 1.

77 SPC, 'Application from German Schroeder for Recognition and Enforcement of a Foreign Arbitral Award', [2009] Min San Zhong Zi No 2.

78 *Wai Lana Yoga v. Guangzhou Huanyu*, (2006) Hui Zhong Fa Min Si Chu Zi No 278.

79 (2009) Zhe Tai Zhong Que Zi No 4.

old address. Since the applicant and the arbitration institution had taken all the reasonable steps to notify the respondent, they should not be prejudiced by the failure of delivery caused by the respondent's negligence. The arbitral award was enforced.[80]

7.48 The notice also includes the notice of any procedural matters. For example, if the arbitration rules set up a deadline for rendering the award this may be extended upon notifying the parties. If an arbitral tribunal renders the award after the deadline without proper notice, the enforcement may be refused.[81]

iii. Opportunity to present its case

7.49 A defence of due process will also be available if the respondent is deprived of the opportunity to present his case. Usually, the opportunity to be heard connects closely with the adequate notice. If the respondent receives adequate notice, it is deemed to have had the opportunity to present its case even if it decides not to.[82] On the other hand, if the notice is inadequate, for example, the respondent is not informed well enough in advance to prepare for its presentation or the respondent is not informed of an amendment to the applicant's claim, the procedure has infringed both the requirement of adequate notice and the opportunity for the respondent to present its case.[83] In *Yu v. Hangzhou Youth*,[84] the applicant concealed from the arbitral tribunal the valid mailing address of the other party, relevant arbitration documents were delivered to the last known mailing address and were not received by the respondent. The respondent was deemed neither adequately notified nor having opportunities to present its case.

7.50 The opportunity to present one's case also exists in medi-arbitration, where the arbitrator acts as the mediator to assist the parties to enter into a settlement first, and if unsuccessful, the parties will proceed to arbitration. In *South China Leasing v. Xieya Industrial*,[85] the parties reached settlement during arbitration and the arbitral tribunal provided a conciliation statement based on the parties' settlement. After delivering the conciliation statement, the tribunal found that the evidence submitted by one party was inconsistent with the record registered with the relevant local authority. The tribunal, therefore, held that this party had withheld important evidence and immediately issued a corrected conciliation statement. Conciliation statements have the same legal

80 The same reasoning is provided in *Boertong v. Liantaichang Commerce*, [2006] Min Si Ta Zi No 36.
81 *Shin-Estu Chemical v. Xinmao Science*, [2008] Min Si Ta Zi No 18.
82 Ibid.
83 *Weibei Hongli v. Wah Sang Paper*, [2008] Min Si Ta Zi No 2.
84 *Re Yu Yingru*, [2007] Min Si Ta Zi No 25.
85 *Re South China Leasing Co. Ltd*, [2010] Min Si Ta Zi No 45.

effect as arbitral awards, so, when the arbitral tribunal made corrections to a conciliation statement based on a document that had not been previously submitted to the parties for cross-examination, this unduly deprived the parties of their right to be heard, and also constituted a procedural irregularity.

IV.3 Arbitration in excess of jurisdiction

The Convention arbitral award may also be refused enforcement if the respondent can prove the arbitrator exceeds its jurisdiction to decide the award.[86] If the arbitral award deals with a subject matter not submitted to arbitration, the award will not be enforced. This ground should be interpreted restrictively to protect the implementation of the NYC and is a policy adopted correctly by Chinese courts. **7.51**

In order to apply the jurisdiction defence, the court should first decide the scope of the mandate. The parties should clearly state the subject matter that is to be subject to arbitration. In practice, an *ex ante* arbitration agreement may use clear terms, providing that all 'contractual disputes' arising between the parties should be submitted to arbitration. If the dispute that actually arises is not contractual in nature, arbitration cannot be used unless the parties enter into a new arbitration agreement.[87] Where the parties arbitrate in the absence of a new agreement, the arbitral award may not be enforced in China. However, in many cases the scope of the arbitration agreement is not absolutely clear. As an example, the parties enter into an arbitration agreement in a sales contract (Contract A) providing that 'all disputes in relation to this contract' should be submitted to arbitration. The parties then enter another contract (Contract B) concerning the payment arrangement in relation to Contract A. Where Contract B contains no arbitration agreement, the question is if disputes arise under Contract B whether the parties can arbitrate pursuant to the arbitration agreement in Contract A. In a similar case, the SPC ruled that the arbitration clause in Contract A can be relied on to submit the dispute arising under Contract B to arbitration, because Contract B and Contract A are closely related. Therefore, the dispute arising under Contract B **7.52**

---

86 NYC, Art V(1)(c):

> The award deals with a difference not contemplated by or not falling within the term of the submission to arbitration, or it contains decisions on matters beyond the scope of the submission to arbitration, provides that, if the decisions on matters submitted to arbitration can be separated from those not submitted, that part of the award which contains decisions on matters submitted to arbitration may be recognized and enforced.

87 Article 2 of the SPC's Judicial Interpretations of 8 September 2006, where the parties concerned summarize the matters agreed upon for arbitration as 'contractual disputes', this should include disputes arising on the basis of the formation, validity, change, transfer, performance, liability for breach, interpretation, cancellation, etc., of the contract.

is a dispute in relation to Contract A.[88] The broad interpretation is largely based on the term 'in relation to', which covers all matters that do not directly arise out of a contract, but have connections to the given contract.

7.53 On the other hand, an arbitration clause may be construed narrowly to cover only contractual disputes arising out of its main contract. If the arbitration agreement explicitly covers only one contract, the arbitrator has no jurisdiction to decide disputes arising out of a related contract;[89] if every related contract contains a separate arbitration clause, each clause only covers disputes arising out of the particular contract in which the clause is contained;[90] and if the parties enter into two different contracts and one contains an arbitration clause while the other does not, the arbitration clause cannot be applied to resolve the dispute arising out of the second contract unless the two contracts are closely linked and the arbitration clause is drafted in broad terms.[91]

7.54 After clarifying the scope of the arbitration agreement, the court should then consider whether the award exceeds jurisdiction. If the arbitrator clearly decides issues outside the mandate, the arbitrator has exceeded jurisdiction. However, if the arbitrator only provides an explanation of the consequence of the ruling, this may not be regarded as exceeding jurisdiction. In *Yongxin Auto Components v. SK Central*,[92] for example, the parties requested that the arbitral tribunal determine the termination of a joint venture contract. The award not only considered the termination of the contract, but also addressed the liquidation and dissolution of the joint venture. This award, however, did not exceed jurisdiction because it did not decide a completely new and separate subject matter, but simply explained the consequences of terminating the joint venture contract.

7.55 Finally, arbitral awards are severable; even if the arbitral tribunal exceeds its jurisdiction, it may not render the whole arbitral award unenforceable. If the arbitral award can be split, the court may enforce that part of the award that

---

88 Mistelis, *supra* n 55, 672.

89 *Xi'an Auto v. Jiaqiao Enterprise*, [2010] Min Si Ta Zi No 55, the contracts do not include arbitration clauses, but the parties agree on arbitration by a later exchange of correspondence. This agreement explicitly covers only the question of the validity of one of the contracts. The arbitral tribunal does not have jurisdiction to decide the dispute concerning other contracts.

90 *Re an Application for Annulment of a CIETAC Arbitral Award [2009] CIETAC BJ (0355)*, [2011] Min Si Ta Zi No 13, where parties to a joint venture have entered into two different joint venture contracts, both of which contain an arbitration clause, and where an arbitration is initiated based on the arbitration clause included in the second contract, the arbitral tribunal may not claim jurisdiction over matters falling under the scope of the first contract where there is no express link between the two contracts and the arbitration clause in the first contract appears to be invalid.

91 *Jackin Media v. Honestwin*, (2003) No. 083 by Dalian Arbitration Commission [2004] Min Si Ta Zi No 24.

92 [2009] Min Si Ta Zi No 45.

falls within the scope of mandate and refuse to enforce the part that exceeds jurisdiction.[93]

IV.4 Irregular procedure

Enforcement of Convention arbitration awards may also be refused if the composition of the arbitral authority or the arbitral procedure is incompatible with the parties' agreement, or, in the absence of the agreement, the law of the country where the arbitration took place.[94] **7.56**

Many courts interpret this ground restrictively. The courts will not adopt the 'mirror image' approach to support the procedural irregularity defence wherever there are small discrepancies with the parties' agreement or the law. Instead, the non-compliance should be obvious and serious. As a result, the procedural irregularity ground is rarely relied on successfully.[95] A successful defence will exist if the arbitration procedure clearly infringes the arbitration rule. Procedural irregularity exists if the arbitration institution appoints the arbitrator without following the specific procedural requirements. In *Re Bunge Agribusiness Singapore Pte Ltd*,[96] the parties designated the Federation of Oils, Seeds and Fats Associations (FOSFA) arbitration rules and the English Arbitration Act 1996 to govern the arbitration procedure. The FOSFA arbitration rules provide that if one party fails to designate the arbitrator according to the arbitration agreement, the association will inform that party that the association will appoint an arbitrator on its behalf, unless that party makes the choice within 14 days after the notice. The respondent had appointed one arbitrator according to the agreement, who excused himself before accepting the appointment. The association appointed another arbitrator without notifying the respondent, which was contrary to the arbitration rules. The enforcement was refused. **7.57**

In judicial practice, Chinese courts have refused to enforce arbitral awards based on procedural irregularity where the arbitration institution fails to follow its procedural rules to properly handle the situation; where one of the arbitrators has dissenting opinions and arbitration proceeds with only two **7.58**

93 NYC, Art V(1)(c); *Luoding Power v. Finenco Investment,* [2006] Min Si Ta Zi No 47.

94 NYC, Art V(1)(d).

95 Other jurisdictions also adopt the similar approach. See e.g., Hong Kong Supreme Court, *China Nanhai Oil Joint Service Co v. Gee Tai Holdings Co,* (1995) XX Yearbook of Commercial Arbitration 671; Germany, Oberlandesgericht Dresden, 20 Oct 1998, 11 Sch 4/98; Belgium, Cour d'appel Brussels, 24 Jan 1997, (1997) XXII Yearbook of Commercial Arbitration 643. See also J.D.M Lew and L.A. Mistelis, et al, *Comparative International Commercial Arbitration* (The Hague, Kluwer Law International 2003) 751.

96 [2006] Min Si Ta Zi No 41.

arbitrators;[97] where the parties, in their arbitration agreement, agreed to have amicable negotiations before arbitration but could not prove negotiation had taken place before initiating arbitration;[98] or where the arbitral tribunal failed to verify the qualification of the third-party appraiser or expert and appointed an appraiser which does not possess the qualifications required by law.[99]

7.59 In practice, a dispute may also arise as to which law governs the arbitration procedure. Indeed, the procedure irregularity defence can only be generated if the procedural rule governing arbitration is infringed. In *China Shipping Development v. Anhui Technology*,[100] the arbitration agreement read: 'Arbitration in Hong Kong; English law to apply.' When the respondent failed to respond after a number of notices and requests, the applicant appointed the sole arbitrator to commence arbitration according to the English Arbitration Act 1996. The Chinese court, however, refused to enforce the arbitral award basing the refusal on procedural irregularity. Although the arbitration procedure was in compliance with the English law, the parties' arbitration agreement was interpreted as choosing English law as the governing law to the merit of the dispute. The procedural law to arbitration, as a result, should have been the law of the place of arbitration or the seat of arbitration, which was the law of Hong Kong. According to Article 34C(5) of the Hong Kong Arbitration Ordinance, should parties fail to agree on the number of the arbitrators, they should submit the issue to the Hong Kong International Arbitration Centre (HKIAC). The HKIAC, instead of the applicant, should have made the decision to appoint the sole arbitrator to conduct the proceedings.

i. No binding award

7.60 Enforcement may be refused if the arbitral award is not binding or has been set aside or suspended by the supervisory court.[101] How is it decided whether an arbitral award is 'binding'? The arbitral award can become binding even before all remedies are exhausted.[102] For example, when the final award is decided it becomes binding, although the respondent may challenge the award in the supervisory court, or it has not yet been confirmed by the court according to the law of the seat. Whether an arbitral award is binding, as a result, should be given an autonomous interpretation, instead of being subject

97 *LM Holdings et al v. Jiashijie Group* [2009] Min Si Ta Zi No38.

98 Nadia Darwazeh and Friven Yeoh, 'Recognition and Enforcement of Awards under the New York Convention: China and Hong Kong Perspectives', (2008) 25 *Journal of International Arbitration* 837.

99 *Clinton Engineering v. Dongjun Real Estate* [2004] Min Si Ta Zi No 16.

100 *China Shipping Development v. Anhui Technology* [2008] Min Si Ta Zi No 17.

101 NYC, Art V(1)(e).

102 M. Rubino-Sammartano, *International Arbitration Law and Practice* (3rd ed., New York: Juris 2014) 1444.

to the law governing arbitration.[103] However, the award should be final in the arbitral tribunal. Some arbitration institutions may adopt an appeal procedure. In this case, only the appeal award is binding. In *Continental v. Zhucheng Foreign Trade*,[104] for example, after the Grain and Feed Trade Association (GAFTA) in London tendered an award, the parties appealed the award to a board of appeal of GAFTA. An appeal award was decided. The Chinese court enforced the appeal award, which was the binding award.

ii. Non-arbitrability

Article V(1) of the NYC includes grounds that should be pled by respondents. **7.61**
Article V(2) includes grounds which may be generated by the court by its own motives. Article V(2)(a) concerns arbitrability. Arbitrability generally demonstrates a country's fundamental policy to reserve certain issues to the court. By scoping arbitrability, the legislator expresses the view on what subject matters are not appropriate for private disposal. The criteria usually relate to the country's understanding of public affairs and the national interest. Considering the public policy nature of arbitrability, the enforcing country would not reserve its own law to decide this issue when determining enforcement of a foreign award. A Convention award may not be enforced if 'the subject matter of the difference is not capable of settlement by arbitration' under the law of the enforcing country. Arbitrability, therefore, should be determined by applying the law of the enforcing country.[105]

Chinese law adopts a general pro-arbitration policy and provides a relatively **7.62**
broad scope for arbitration. Some matters subject to exclusive jurisdiction, which excludes the parties' choice of court, may be available for arbitration.[106] In general, three types of matter are non-arbitrable in Chinese law, i.e., disputes concerning personal rights; administrative disputes; and labour and agricultural projects.[107] Even for these matters, arbitration is not completely prohibited but subject to certain restrictions or conditions. For example, although trademark disputes are classified as administrative matters, arbitration can be conducted by the Trademark Review and Adjudication Board.[108] Labour disputes can only be arbitrated by an authorized government body.[109]

---

103 Mistelis, *supra* n 55, 20.

104 *Continental Enterprises Co Ltd v. Shandong Zhucheng Foreign Trade Co Ltd*, (2005) Wei Min Zi No 1.

105 If the non-arbitrability rules of the recognition forum have no connection at all to the parties' dispute or the matters addressed in the award, this approach may not be appropriate.

106 See Ch 3, II.

107 Jingzhou Tao, *Arbitration Law and Practice in China* (The Netherlands: Kluwer Law International 2008) 62–3.

108 Arbitration Law, Art 3(2); see Mistelis, *supra* n 55, 659–60; *Expert Assets et al v. Huayuan Pharmaceutical*, [2006] Min Si Ta Zi No 2.

109 Labour Law, Art 79.

Some matters, as a result, can be arbitrated only in designated specific Chinese institutions. Arbitration by a foreign institution may result in the enforcement being refused.

IV.5 Public policy

i. Introduction

7.63 The catch-all, and last resort, defence is public policy. Public policy is a very vague term and may cover both procedural and substantive matters.[110] Procedural public policy includes any procedural irregularity that is fundamental and may be in breach of natural justice, including corruption, fraud, lack of neutrality, etc. Substantive public policy concerns the content of the award and whether its enforcement may infringe the concept of morality and general principles of law.[111] Public policy should be relied on only in exceptional circumstances. Given the international nature of arbitration and the purpose of the NYC, any contracting state should be cautious relying on public policy defence when refusing to enforce a foreign arbitral award. Furthermore, it is likely that procedural public policy may more easily be supported by the court when it concerns the fundamental rights of the parties. However, some issues in procedural public policy overlap with other refusal grounds, such as due process and procedural irregularity.[112] While the NYC expressly lists due process and procedural irregularity as two refusal grounds, it is probable that other procedural defects may be treated relatively lightly.

7.64 More controversy exists in substantive public policy. It is important to recognize that every country has several mandatory rules concerning public interest of various kinds. In arbitration, the arbitrators usually have the liberty to determine the applicable law, and may apply law that has no connection to the dispute, law that provides the lightest restrictions on the transactions, and even none-state law such as *lex mercatoria*. Permitting a court to refuse enforcement of a foreign award simply because the award was decided according to a law which is contrary to the mandatory rules of the enforcing state would make a refusal too easy. A strict approach has been adopted by many countries and the general approach is that only public policy that could reflect internationally recognized interest and morality can be relied on in Article V(2)(b). Domestic public policy would not be sufficient.

---

110 For more on public policy, see Ch 2, X.

111 See Mistelis, *supra* n 55, 22.

112 See IV.2 and 4 above.

ii. Chinese practice

Since public policy is an ambiguous concept, it is easily abused by the courts, which was true in Chinese local courts, especially before the implementation of the 1995 internal report and review mechanism.[113] Some local courts gave public policy a broader interpretation than the NYC contemplates. Consideration was given, incorrectly, to 'less transparent state interests and unstable short-term policies'.[114] In *Dongfeng Garments Factory of Kaifeng City v. Henan Garments Import and Export*,[115] Zhengzhou IPC held that enforcing the arbitral award against a state-owned company was deemed against public policy. The reason was that the state-owned company was an important local business player and contributed to the local economy. In *Baosheng Environment v. Hefei Environment Bureau*,[116] the local courts used the public policy defence because the local government wasted public funds to purchase equipment which had been left unused. **7.65**

The Chinese courts were thus criticized as being too ready to rely on the public policy defence, which affected their reputation in the international community. The attempt to use public policy was largely driven by the local protectionism.[117] The SPC criticized the tendency of the local courts to extend the use of public policy to refuse enforcement of foreign arbitral awards. In *Dongfeng Garments v. Henan Garments*, for example, the SPC stated that public policy could only be used where the enforcement of arbitral awards may infringe 'fundamental economic interest, general principle of justice, or basic concept of good morals of the forum'. It is obvious that the SPC suggested a narrow and restrictive interpretation of public policy. Bearing in mind the local protectionism and local interest preference of many local courts, the SPC decided to adopt the 1995 internal report/review mechanism. Since then, the situation has largely improved. The local courts may still attempt to use public policy defence but the SPC will have the final word. **7.66**

The SPC has adopted a very tolerant approach to foreign arbitral awards. In *Re Louis Dreyfus Commodities Asian Co Ltd*,[118] the sole arbitrator criticized Chinese law and regulations in the award, stating that the words in Chinese law differed significantly from its implementation in practice and thus could **7.67**

---

113 Yongping Xiao and Zhengxin Huo, 'Order Public in China's Private International Law', (2005) 53 *The American Journal of Comparative Law* 651–2.

114 X.C. Zhang, 'The Agreement between Mainland China and the Hong Kong SAR on Mutual Enforcement of Arbitral Awards' (1999) 29 *Hong Kong Law Journal* 463, 476.

115 Zhengzhou Intermediate People's Ct., 28 Sept 1992.

116 [2005] Min Si Ta Zi No 45.

117 For more discussion, see Z.S Tang, *Jurisdiction and Arbitration Agreements in International Commerce* (London: Routledge, 2014).

118 *Re Application of Louis Dreyfus Commodities supra* n 31.

not be considered significant. Although the Zhanjiang IPC decided that this comment 'seriously challenged the authority of Chinese law and regulations and infringed Chinese public policy', it did not prevent the SPC from enforcing the award. The court should only assess whether enforcing the award will result in infringement of Chinese public policy, but not whether the reasoning or comments in relation to Chinese law may infringe public policy. The SPC has also repeatedly emphasized that awards contradicting mandatory rules or administrative regulations of Chinese law are not equivalent to the infringement of Chinese public policy.[119]

7.68 It is important to note that the improvement in restrictions in applying public policy is largely due to the intervention of the SPC. Nevertheless, some local courts continue to rely rather too easily on the tendency to depend only on public policy. The local courts have, in practice, made a few common mistakes. First, some local courts attempted to examine the substance and merit of the arbitral award. In *GRD Minproc v. Shanghai Flyingwheel*,[120] for example, the dispute was whether the dust pollution in the Shanghai Flyingwheel's factory in China was caused by the quality of the equipment supplied by the supplier. The arbitral tribunal ruled it was not and ordered Shanghai Flyingwheel to cover the arbitration costs of the supplier. The local courts reviewed the fact and the evidence and held that operating the equipment might pollute the working environment and harm the health of employees.[121] The award did not consider the importance of health and safety regulations and breached public policy. This decision clearly exceeds the legitimate scope for review and assesses the quality of decision-making by arbitrators. Secondly, the local courts frequently confuse the direct consequence of enforcing an award with the consequence of a bad business decision. In *Baosheng Environment v. Hefei Environment Bureau*,[122] the local government purchased the recycling equipment that did not work properly due to reasons other than the quality of the equipment. The local courts, however, held that the equipment had cost the government a lot of money and was left unused, which contradicted public policy. This decision was problematic. The waste of public resources was probably against public policy. However, it was not caused by the other party breaching its duty but by a government procurement decision made without the careful selection of more appropriate practices. Refusing enforcement in this case could not be justified. Thirdly, the local courts continue to show their

119 *ED&F v. China National Sugar & Alcohol Group,* [2003] Min Si Ta Zi No 3; *Tianrui Investment v. Yiju Hotel,* [2010] Min Si Ta Zi No 18; *Mitsui v. Hainan Textile,* [2001] Min Si Ta Zi No 12.

120 *GRD Minproc v. Shanghai Flyingwheel,* [2009] Min Si Ta Zi No48.

121 Shanghai HPC judgment in *GRD Minproc v. Shanghai Flyingwheel,* Shanghai High People's Court, (2008) Hu Gao Min Si (Shang) Ta Zi No 2, was reversed by the SPC, ibid.

122 *Baosheng Environment, supra* n 116.

intention of protecting local interests. In both *GRD Minproc* and *Baosheng Environment*, the local courts had taken the financial loss of the Chinese entities into consideration to generate public policy defence. Fourthly, the local courts also have a tendency to construe any breach of Chinese administrative regulation of commercial activities as an infringement of public policy.[123] Although the internal report/review mechanism increases the workload of the SPC and causes delays in enforcement, it still needs to be present as a safeguard so that the Conventional duty is properly performed, until there is an improvement in the overall quality of local courts' decisions and the elimination of local protectionism.

After the implementation of the 1995 internal report/review mechanism, the SPC has only confirmed public policy defence in two reported cases. In the early case *USA Production and Tom and Hulett and Associates v. China Women Travel Service* decided in 1997,[124] the American party and the Chinese event organizer entered into a contract to perform in China. The performer played heavy metal music that was not approved by the Chinese Ministry of Culture. A further performance was banned by the Ministry and the arbitral tribunal ordered the Chinese organizer to pay the American party damages for breach of contract. The SPC approved the local courts' decision to hold enforcement contrary to public policy because the performance was deemed inappropriate for a Chinese audience and caused harm to the Chinese culture. This decision can be criticized for using the public policy defence to protect a purely domestic interest. In *Hemofarm DD et al v. Yongning Pharmaceutical*,[125] the applicant brought a disputed matter that had already been decided by the Chinese court to arbitration. The arbitral tribunal ignored the existence of an effective Chinese judgment and submitted an irreconcilable award. The SPC affirmed the local courts' decision that the award infringed the judicial sovereignty of the Chinese courts and public policy. In this case, the Chinese courts and the arbitral tribunal made different decisions on the scope of the arbitration agreement and the arbitrability of the subject matter. Since the arbitral tribunal was seized after the Chinese courts rendered the judgment on both jurisdiction and substance of the dispute, continuing the proceedings and rendering the award was regarded as manifestly disrespectful to the Chinese courts' authority. Almost every country would also refuse to enforce an award that was irreconcilable with an existing judgment provided by its court, 7.69

123 *ED&F v. China National Sugar & Alcohol Group*; *Tianrui Investment v. Yiju Hotel*; *Mitsui v. Hainan Textile*, all *supra* n 119.

124 (1997) Ta 35.

125 [2008] Min Si Ta Zi No 11.

because this is impractical, causes difficulties and undermines authority of the courts. In this case holding the enforcement to be against public policy was justifiable.

iii. Conclusion

7.70 A careful examination of the Chinese judicial practice reveals that China should no longer be deemed as a country that frequently abuses public policy defences to protect its local interests. The SPC has clearly invoked a policy to treat public policy with caution. This practice is consistent with the purposes of the NYC and the practice in many countries with developed arbitration practice and international judicial cooperation. Local courts, comparatively, are more conservative and have more of an incentive to rely on the public policy defence to protect the local interest. Based on this background, the internal report/review mechanism, regardless of its delays and inefficiencies, should be continuously adopted to allow the SPC to have the final word. The SPC should only be released from this onerous duty when Chinese local courts are equally trained and equipped with relevant legal knowledge and are free from local protectionism.

V. RECOGNITION AND ENFORCEMENT OF NON-CONVENTIONAL FOREIGN AWARDS

7.71 Although most countries are parties to the NYC, it does not mean that domestic rules have few chances to be applied. A few limitations of the NYC should be noted. First, it only applies to commercial matters as described in Chinese law in China. Therefore, any 'non-commercial' foreign arbitral awards are non-Conventional. Secondly, it only applies to arbitral awards rendered in the territory of another signature country, which does not include the arbitral awards rendered by foreign arbitral institutions in the territory of China.[126] These awards are also non-Conventional.[127] A non-Conventional foreign award can be recognized and enforced in China under the Chinese domestic law. Pursuant to Article 283 of the CPL, Chinese courts could enforce non-Conventional foreign awards either under the international reciprocal arrangements or by application of the principle of reciprocity. But because of the weakness of the reciprocal principle, such arbitral awards may hardly be enforceable in China in the absence of treaty arrangements.[128]

---

126 See sec II above.

127 Cf. *Duferco S.A. v. Ningbo Arts & Crafts supra* n 19.

128 See Ch 6, IV.1 above.

VI. CONCLUSION

The legal basis for recognition and enforcement of foreign arbitral awards in China is composed of the NYC, the CPL and Arbitration Law of PRC, and the numerous judicial interpretations of the SPC concerning foreign-related and international arbitration. Unlike many other jurisdictions, China signed up to the NYC on 22 April 1987, prior to the establishment of a national arbitration system in China. As a result the content of the 1995 Arbitration law, the revised CPL, and the plentiful judicial interpretations unambiguously indicate that the SPC has interpreted the Arbitration Law in a purposeful and flexible manner, attempting to ensure that the development of international arbitration in China follows international norms and standards. In this regard the law on recognition and enforcement of foreign arbitral awards in China has had open and international characteristics from the outset. **7.72**

From the judicial interpretations and directions of the SPC, it is apparent that the SPC has been highly supportive of the NYC. Many unmeritorious technical points are discouraged. The grounds for refusal of enforcement as set out in Article V of the Convention have been narrowly construed. The number of foreign awards parties seek to enforce in China is increasing. Although there is still a gap between the practice and the expectation of the international community, Chinese courts pay a lot of attention to ensure that the enforcement process is transparent, foreseeable and in line with international standards. It can be seen that the SPC has always supported the pro-arbitration attitude from the internal report/review mechanism, the extension of the limitation period for application, and enforcement of foreign *ad hoc* arbitral awards, etc. The Chinese accession to the Convention in 1987 has certainly contributed to making arbitration become a more effective means of settling disputes between Chinese and foreign parties. **7.73**

Part III

CHOICE OF LAW

8

CHOICE OF LAW IN CONTRACT

I. INTRODUCTION

Contract is the area where domestic conflict of laws in different countries shares the most similarity and where international harmonization is most likely to be achievable. In the European Union, for example, the harmonization of choice of law rules first started in the field of contract.[1] At the international level, the Hague Conference on Private International Law is in the process of establishing the Hague Principles on choice of law in international contracts.[2] It demonstrates that compared to other areas of law, contractual choice of law rules are well developed in most countries. **8.01**

1 Rome Convention on the Law Applicable to Contractual Obligations of 1980.

2 O. Lando, 'The Draft Hague Principles on the Choice of Law in International Contracts and Rome I', in *A Commitment to Private International Law: Essays in Honour of Hans van Loon* (Cambridge/Antwerp/Portland 2013) 299; A. Dickinson, 'A Principled Approach to Choice of Law in Contracts?', (2013) *Butterworths Journal of International Banking and Financial Law* 151. More information is available at the Hague Conference website, http://www.hcch.net/index_en.php?act=text.display&tid=49 (accessed 14 Oct 2013).

8.02 Chinese conflict of laws in contract is more developed than other fields.[3] As early as 1985, a special choice of law provision was provided for foreign economic contracts.[4] This is the first choice of law provision in PRC history of legislation.[5] The purpose of introducing special conflict of laws for foreign economic contracts is to reduce anxiety of foreign investors and facilitate direct foreign inward investment in China.[6] It adopts the mixed approach, combining the doctrine of party autonomy and the closest connection.[7] The similar approach is later adopted in the General Principles of Civil Law (GPCL) in 1986.[8]

8.03 These choice of law rules are now replaced by the new provisions in the Conflicts Act. The Conflicts Act, by maintaining the traditional approach, has made a few important changes to Chinese choice of law in contracts. Furthermore, extra guidance is provided by the SPC in its judicial interpretation on the application of the Conflicts Act ('Conflicts Act Interpretation I'), which is an important source aiding the interpretation and application of the law in Chinese courts.[9]

II. PARTY AUTONOMY

8.04 The doctrine of party autonomy was adopted in Chinese choice of law in contracts after 1985 as a result of economic reform that started building a market economy.[10] Afterwards the doctrine gradually turned to be the most important conflicts doctrine in contractual choice of law in China.[11] It was confirmed in Article 117(1) of GPCL, Article 99 of the Contract Law, Article

3 Zhengxin Huo, 'An Imperfect Improvement: The New Conflict of Laws Act of the People's Republic of China' (2011) 60 ICLQ 1065, 1085; Guojian Xu, 'Contract in Chinese Private International Law' (1989) 38 ICLQ 648, 649.

4 Zhonghua Renmin gongheguo Waiguo Jingji Hetong Fa [Law of the Foreign Economic Contract of the People's Republic of China] adopted at the Tenth Session of the Standing Committee of the Sixth National People's Congress promulgated by Order No. 22 of the President of the People's Republic of China on 21 March 1985 and effective as of 1 July 1985.

5 Guojian Xu, *supra* n 3, 648.

6 Ibid.; Andrew Armfelt, 'Foreign Economic Contract Law of the People's Republic of China' (1987) 36 ICLQ 151, 151.

7 Foreign Economic Contract Act *supra* n 4, Art 5(1),.

8 GPCL, Art 145.

9 SPC, 'Interpretations of the SPC on Several Issues Concerning Application of the Law of the People's Republic of China on Choice of Law for Foreign-Related Civil Relationships (I)' ('Conflicts Act Interpretation I'), Fa Shi [2012] No 24.

10 Mo Zhang, 'Codified Choice of Law in China: Rules, Processes and Theoretic Underpinnings' (2011) 37 *North Carolina Journal of International Law and Commercial Regulation* 83, 116–17.

11 Not until 1999. Before then Chinese citizens were not permitted to conclude cross-border contracts.

269 of the Maritime Law and two judicial interpretations on the applicable law in cross-border contracts.[12]

Party autonomy in China developed as the consequence of the development of contractual freedom. Parties were not allowed to enter into cross-border contracts in China before the economic reform;[13] and even after economic reform, individuals were still not allowed to conclude cross-border contracts until 1999. The party autonomy doctrine could only apply to contracts signed by companies until the Contract Law 1999 eventually lifted that barrier. Permitting the parties to choose the applicable law for their contractual obligations is consistent with the doctrine of contractual freedom. Where the parties are allowed to use contracts to dispose their rights and obligations, they are similarly allowed to decide which law applies to such rights and obligations. As most transnational activities concern purely private interests between the parties and do not concern public interest, there is no problem applying contractual freedom to such disputes. **8.05**

Party autonomy could provide certainty and predictability and could reduce commercial risk and disputes caused by the uncertainty in the applicable law. Chinese courts have generally applied the doctrine well. It is restated in Article 41 of the Conflicts Act, which reads: 'The parties could, by agreement, choose the applicable law of their contracts.' In practice, if the parties have chosen the applicable law to their contractual relationship, the court usually will enforce this choice.[14] **8.06**

II.1 Implied choice

Although Article 41 does not expressly say so, Article 3 of the Conflicts Act, as a general principle, provides that the choice must be explicit.[15] Explicit choice of law does not mean the choice must be 'in writing'. Oral agreements should be valid in law. However, if there is no express choice and the choice **8.07**

12 One is the SPC, 'Response of the SPC to Certain Questions Concerning the Application of the Foreign Economic Contract Law', Fa [Jing] Fa [1987] 27 (abolished from 2000) and another is SPC, 'Provisions of the SPC on the Relevant Issues concerning the Application of Law in Hearing Foreign-Related Contractual Dispute Cases in Civil and Commercial Matters' ('2007 Provisions on applicable law'), Fa Shi [2007] 14 (abolished from 2013).

13 Mo Zhang, *supra* n 10, 91.

14 *Cinkai Enterprises Ltd v. Asia Pacific Business Link Ltd,* (2012) Hu Gao Min Er (Shang) Zhong Zi No 8 (applying Art 41 of the Conflicts Act to apply Chinese law chosen by the parties); *Tianjng Zhengda Technology v. Chuan Da Distributors (Pty) Ltd,* Tianjing HPC, (2011) Jing Gao Min Si Zhong Zi No 185; *DBS(HK) Ltd v. Bosch and Siemens Home Appliances (Jiangsu),* Jiangsu Province HPC, (2011) Su Shang Wai Zhong Zi No 0072.

15 Conflicts Act, Art 3: 'The parties may explicitly choose the law applicable to their foreign-related civil relation in accordance with the provisions of this law.'

cannot be inferred from the circumstances of the case, the contract should be treated as a contract in the absence of choice.[16]

8.08 The exclusion of implied choice may help reduce uncertainty in litigation and save the parties' time and cost in arguing on the likely tacit choice. However, it is necessary to recognize that sometimes the implied choice does exist in commercial practice, especially between parties with a long-term business relationship. Parties may have concluded a few similar contracts in the past and their new contract will simply provide some new terms without repeating everything that has been discussed before. If the parties have negotiated choice of law in their earlier contracts, it is reasonable to argue that they also have the common intention of applying the same law in the current contract. Refusing to recognize the implied choice is sometimes incompatible with commercial practice.

8.09 Furthermore, implied choice may not always be difficult to prove. In its Conflicts Act Interpretation I, the SPC states that if all the parties have invoked the law of the same country and have not raised any objection to the applicable law, the parties are deemed to have made the choice of the referred law.[17] This is a typical scenario where the implied choice is approved by the parties' conduct. Implied choice in this circumstance will not give rise to many disputes or uncertainty and is accepted by the Chinese courts.

II.2 Choice of an unrelated law

8.10 Chinese law does not require that parties must choose the law with practical connections to the contract. The SPC says in the Conflicts Act Interpretation I that if one party claims that the choice of law invalid because the chosen law has no factual connections with the dispute, this argument will not be supported by the People's Court.[18] As a result, the parties could choose a neutral law to govern their contractual obligations.

8.11 In contrast, more rigid requirements are imposed for choice of court agreements. A valid jurisdiction clause in China must have chosen the forum with 'practical connections' with the dispute.[19] It is unclear why flexibility is provided to choice of law but not choice of court. The possible explanation is

16 Mo Zhang, *supra* n 10, 120.

17 Conflicts Act Interpretation I, Art 8. This practice existed before the publication of the Interpretation, see, e.g., *Tianjing Dongli Yueyang Industry and Trade v. Shiva Chemicals & Pharmaceuticals Services Ltd,* Tianjin HPC, (2011) Jin Gao Min Si Zhong Zi No 15.

18 Conflicts Act Interpretation I, Art 7.

19 Ch 3, sec III.

that choice of court allows the parties to prorogate jurisdiction to a country which concerns a country's judicial sovereignty. Choice of law only grants the parties the free disposal of private substantive rights.

II.3 Change of choice

The parties can change their choice after their original choice is made. The parties' change of choice makes a new choice of law agreement. As a result, all the requirements applying to the choice of law clause should apply to the change of choice. The parties can change their choice only explicitly and any implied change will not be recognized. Parties could change their choice any time before the end of the court debate in the trial at the first instance.[20] If the parties did not choose the applicable law they are competent to choose one during the trial.[21] **8.12**

II.4 *Dépeçage*

Dépeçage means applying different governing laws to different issues in a dispute. Neither the Conflicts Act nor the Conflicts Act Interpretation I explicitly permits *dépeçage*. Its Chinese status needs to be examined on a case-by-case basis. **8.13**

A very broad definition of *dépeçage* means that within one action, the substance and procedure are governed by the law of different countries.[22] No country will apply foreign law to procedural issues. As long as a country adopts modern conflicts rules and permits the application of foreign law to substance, broad *dépeçage* inevitably exists. China is no exception. The 2007 Provisions on Applicable Law provide that the application of foreign law excludes procedure law.[23] Interestingly, after the 2007 Provision was abolished, the SPC failed to provide similar guidance in the Conflicts Act Interpretation I. It, however, could not be interpreted that the Chinese court could now apply a foreign law to govern procedure, which is contrary to Chinese legal tradition and the generally conservative attitude towards the application of foreign procedure law. **8.14**

---

20 Conflicts Act Interpretation I, Art 8.

21 *Alphaint'l Investment Group Ltd v. Nanjing Hongjian Qiti Ltd,* (2012) Su Shang Wai Zhong Zi No 0005.

22 Allan Verman Yap Ong, '*Dépeçage* in Chinese Private International Law' (2009) 8 *Chinese Journal of International Law* 637, 645; Willis L.M. Reese, 'Dépeçage: A Common Phenomenon in Choice of Law' (1973) 73 *Columbia Law Review* 58, 58.

23 2007 Provisions, Art 1; Ong, ibid., 645.

8.15 Secondly, China permits the conflicts clause to be separated from the rest of the contract and subject to a different law. Chinese legislation clearly states the validity of an arbitration agreement to be governed by law different from the *lex causae*. Article 18 of the Conflicts Act provides that: 'The parties could choose the law governing the arbitration agreement. In the absence of choice, the law of the place where the arbitration institute is located or the law of the seat should apply.' The Conflicts Act Interpretation I further provides that while the parties did not specify the arbitration institution or the seat, Chinese law shall be applied to govern arbitration agreements.[24] Neither requires a reference to the *lex causae*. Although no clear guidance exists, in practice, a Chinese court may apply law different to the *lex causae* to determine the validity of a jurisdiction clause in a contract.[25] More uncertainty exists in the choice of law clause. Courts and practitioners rarely consider the applicable law to a choice of law agreement. It is uncertain, when such a question arises, whether the *lex causae* or a different law, may be applied.

8.16 Thirdly, it is unclear whether in China issues concerning the conclusion and formation of a contract, such as existence and validity of a contract, can be governed by different law from the substance and performance of a contract and the parties' rights and obligations therein. In practice, parties usually insert one choice of law agreement into the contract without considering how a contract should be split. Little guidance can, thus, be found in court precedents.

8.17 Fourthly, China does not have a problem applying the general law to one contract but subjecting specific matters to another law. For example, where the contract is governed by the law of a particular country, chosen by the parties, but some rules of the chosen law are contrary to Chinese public policy or mandatory rules, Chinese law may apply to govern these specific issues, while the whole contract is still governed by the chosen law. *De facto dépeçage* exists.

8.18 Finally, China also permits the parties to choose the governing law to some issues but leaves the rest of the contract governed by the law in the absence of choice. If the parties' choice of law is not comprehensive and cannot cover all the issues of a dispute, the law determined by the default choice of law rule should be applied. In *Shanghai Saifeng International Trade Ltd v. Industrial and Commercial Bank of China (ICBC) and Canara Bank*,[26] the parties chose

24 Conflicts Act Interpretation I, Art 14.

25 *Shandong Jufeng v. Korea MGame*, SPC, (2009) Min San Zhong Zi No 4; SPC, 'Zuigao Renmin Fayuan Guanyu Yinfa Zuigao Fayuan Zhishi Chanquan Niandu Baogao (2009) de Tongzhi [Annual Report of Intellectual Property Cases in the SPC (2009)]', [2010] Fa No 173, case 44.

26 Jiangsu Province Changzhou Municipality IPC, 2007.12.26, (2006) Chang Min San Chu Zi No 26.

URC522 to govern the letter of credit. The court further provided that for issues uncovered by URC522 and if the parties did not agree on the applicable law, Indian law should apply based on the principle of the closest connection. Since Indian law could not be proved to the satisfaction of the court, Chinese law thus applied to the rest of the issues under Article 193 of the SPC's judicial interpretation of 1988. Chinese law and URC522 thus applied together as the governing law to the contract.

II.5 Choice of non-state law

Whether non-state law can be applied as the governing law upon the parties' choice is a controversial topic in private international law. In Europe, the Regulation 593/2008 on the law applicable to contractual obligations (Rome I) does not include a provision allowing or prohibiting the choice of non-state law in contracts.[27] Instead, Recital 13 states that non-state law can be 'incorporated' into the contract as a contract term upon the parties' choice.[28] It suggests that the European legislator does not allow the direct choice of non-state law as the governing law to a contract. In some old cases in the US, courts refused to apply non-state law to govern the contract pursuant to the parties' choice.[29] **8.19**

Chinese law is uncertain. The Conflicts Act does not include any guidance. The first draft of the Act included a provision, stating: 'The parties of transnational relationships could expressly choose international custom. If the applicable law is the law of the People's Republic of China and the Chinese law does not provide any regulations on the matter subject to dispute, international customs can be applied.'[30] This provision, however, is deleted in the final Conflicts Act. This is because the legislators believe the complexity and different nature of international conventions and customs makes uniform choice of law provisions inappropriate.[31] **8.20**

27 Regulation (EC) No 593/2008 of the European Parliament and of the Council of 17 June 2008 on the law applicable to contractual obligations (Rome I) [2008] OJ L177/6.

28 Ibid., Recital 13.

29 *Pubali Bank v. City National Bank,* 777 F 2d 1340 (9th Circuit); *Trans Meridian Trading Inc v. Empressa Nacional de Commercializacion de Insumos,* 829 F 2d 949 (9th Circuit). *H Dang*, 'The Applicability of International Law as Governing Law of State Contracts' (2010) 17 *Australian International Law Journal* 133, n 24.

30 PRC Civil Law Code Chapter 9 (Draft), Art 4. See Wei-Di Long, 'The Reach of the CISG in China' in I. Schwenzer and L. Spagnolo (eds), *Towards Uniformity: the 2nd MAA Schlechtriem CISG Conference* (Eleven Publishing 2011), footnote 255 and the accompanying text.

31 http://npc.people.com.cn/GB/13045506.html, accessed on 10 Oct 2012.

8.21 In *Citibank NA v. Shanghai Lansheng Ltd*,[32] URC was chosen by the parties in their contract as the applicable law, the Shanghai High People's Court clearly said that the governing law can be Chinese law, foreign law, international treaties or international customs and called this a 'common understanding in the (Chinese) private international law field'. It is, however, too early to say that consensus is reached in China. The fact is that Chinese private international law research and practice has rarely realized the difference in nature between national law, international treaties and international customs. There is no theoretical justification for the application of international treaties and customs as the governing law of a legal relationship. The occasional application of these types of 'laws' is caused by the lack of understanding instead of sophisticated knowledge and development of legal theories in Chinese law.

i. Choice of conventions not ratified in China

8.22 Interpretation, however, is provided by the Conflicts Act Interpretations I, which provides that if the parties have referred to an international convention not ratified in China, the People's Court can determine the parties' rights and obligations pursuant to the international convention, unless it is contrary to the public interest or mandatory rules of China.[33] It uses the term 'refer to' (yuan yin) instead of choice of the international convention as the governing law.[34] It is not clear whether the SPC treats the international custom as the chosen 'governing law' or as an incorporated contract term deciding the parties' rights and obligations. However, reading the provision as a whole, it seems that the international convention that has no effect in China is treated as the governing law, because its application is not subject to the governing law of the contract but to the public policy and mandatory rules of China. China, as a result, permits the choice of an international treaty, not ratified in China, as the governing law, even though it is non-state in nature.

8.23 This is consistent with past Chinese judicial practice. International conventions not ratified in China have been treated as international customs and some Chinese courts have applied such customs as the governing law to a contract pursuant to the parties' choice. In *China Merchants Godown Wharf & Transportation Co Ltd v. Galaxy Games Centre Ltd*,[35] the parties agreed that all issues relating to the rights and obligations of the carrier should be governed by the Hague Rules of 1924. China is not a signatory of the Hague Rules of 1924, but the SPC gave effect to the parties' choice and applied those Rules to

32 Shanghai HPC, (2000) Hu Gao Jing Zhong Zi No 335.

33 Conflicts Act Interpretations I, Art 9.

34 'Refer to' is 'Yuan Yin' (援引) in the original text.

35 (1997) 1 Zhonghua Renmin Gongheguo Zuigao Renmin Fayuan Gongbao [PRC SPC Gazette] No 14.

the dispute. Although the court provided no justification for this decision, the case shows that the SPC does not mind applying international treaties not ratified in China as an international custom which could be the governing law to a contract.

In *Anhui Clothes Import and Export v. Sudcargos & CGM Tanya SA*,[36] the Wuhan Maritime Court unambiguously used the international convention which was not ratified in China as the governing law of the bill of lading pursuant to the parties' choice. The bill of lading included a choice of court clause choosing '(t)he French law of the 18/06/1966 and relevant edicts, or the International Convention for the Unification of Certain Rules Relating to Bills of Lading of August 25th 1925, as Amended by the Protocol signed in Brussels 23rd February 1926'. The Wuhan Maritime Court held that the parties had expressed the wish for the court to choose either chosen law to apply to the dispute. The court chose the Hague-Visby Rules and applied it as the governing law.[37] **8.24**

ii. Choice of conventions ratified in China

However, the 2012 Interpretations on Conflicts Act does not say the parties could 'refer to' international conventions ratified in China. What the Interpretations say is that if the application of an international convention is involved, the People's Court should make decisions pursuant to Article 142 of the GPCL. Similar provisions also exist in many other domestic statutes or regulations.[38] Article 142 of GPCL provides: **8.25**

> If any international treaty concluded (meaning 'ratified') or acceded to by the People's Republic of China contains provisions differing from those in the civil laws of the People's Republic of China, the provisions of the international treaty shall apply, unless the provisions are ones on which the People s Republic of China has declared reservations. (Explanation added)

Article 142 of GPCL, unfortunately, does not provide clear guidance as to how international treaties ratified in China should be applied. The literal meaning of these provisions suggests that if the applicable law is Chinese law, **8.26**

36 Wuhan Maritime Court, (2001) No 19.

37 See also *Gangying Furniture v. UTI (HK) Ltd*, Wuhan Maritime Court, (2001) Wu Hai Fa Shang Zi No 75; *Shaoxing Yongda v. Mediterranean Shipping Co SA*, Shanghai Maritime Court, (2006) Hu Hai Fa Shang Chu Zi No 276. The similar approach can also be implied from *Zhengda (Tianjin) v. First Steamship SA*, Tianjin Maritime Court, (1998) Jin Hai Fa Shang Chu Pan Zi No 265.

38 The same wording also exists in a number of other special statutes, such as the PRC Environmental Protection Law of 1989, Art 46; PRC Water Law of 2002, Art 78; PRC Negotiable Instruments Law of 1996, Art 96; PRC Seed Law (2004 amendment), Art 77; PRC Civil Aviation Law of 1996, Art 184; RPC Maritime Law of 1992, Art 268.

in the case of conflicts, international treaties ratified by China shall supersede. Therefore, the parties should not choose ratified international conventions directly, but choose the Chinese law instead.[39]

8.27 Judicial practice is not consistent, either. Regardless of the literal meaning of Article 142 of GPCL, some courts allow the parties to directly choose ratified international conventions but this choice is not a choice of non-state law or a choice of the treaty as part of the Chinese legal system, but an intention to choose the Chinese legal system as a whole. If Chinese law is inconsistent with the treaty, the treaty applies; otherwise, Chinese substantive law applies. This interpretation is used in a few cases concerning the application of the Warsaw Convention and other conventions in the Warsaw family in international carriage contracts. In *Wang v. Dragonair*,[40] the carriage of passengers contract provided that the Warsaw Convention of 1929[41] should govern the dispute. The court held the parties' choice of international convention would apply only if its provisions were different from the Chinese substantive law pursuant to Article 142. Since the relevant provisions of the Civil Aviation Law were borrowed from the amended Warsaw Convention and the Guatemala Protocol,[42] they were consistent with international treaties. The court then applied the Chinese Civil Aviation Law, instead of the Warsaw Convention. The court, in fact, treated the choice of convention ratified by China as the parties' intention to choose the Chinese legal system.

8.28 In *Societe Air France v. Geologistics Ltd*,[43] the parties chose the Warsaw Convention to govern the performance of the contract. The court accepted that the parties could choose the convention to govern the contract, but the choice was outdated because China had ratified the Montreal Convention at the time of contracting and the court applied the Montreal Convention instead. Again, the court treated the choice of ratified convention as the choice of the Chinese legal system and applied the updated version as currently applied in China.

---

39 E.g., *Trade Quicker Inc Monrovia Liberia v. Golden Light Overseas Management S.A Panama,* Tianjin Maritime Court, (1993) 3 Gazette of the SPC of the People's Republic of China; *Yantai Dongyao Aquatic Products Ltd v. United Ocean Shipping,* Qingdao Maritime Court, (2008) Qing Hai Fa Yan Que Zi No 22; *Shandong Ocean and Fishery Department v. United Ocean Shipping,* (2007) Qing Hai Fa Yan Que Zi No 1; *H2O Recreation Inc v. Dong Hui Plastic (Shanghai) Ltd,* Shanghai Municipality High Court, (2007) Hu Gao Min Si (Shang) Zhong Zi No 6; *KUB Power Sdn. Bhd v. China Everbright Bank,* Shenyang Municipality Intermediate Court, (2004) Shen Zhong Min Si Wai Chu Zi No 12.

40 Shanghai Municipal Changning District People's Court, (2000) No 233.

41 Unification of Certain Rules Regulating to International Carriage by Air of 1929.

42 Protocol to Amend the Convention for the Unification of Certain Rules Relating to International Carriage by Air, Warsaw 1929, as Amended by the Protocol at The Hague, 1955, Guatemala City, 1971, ICAO Doc 8932.

43 Shanghai No 1 Medium People's Court, (2007) No 27, 12.03.2010.

iii. Choice of other international customs

The Conflicts Act Interpretation I does not address the choice of international customs other than treaties not ratified by China. Reference is again made to Article 142 of the GPCL, the last indent of which provides: 8.29

> International practice may be applied on matters for which neither the law of the People's Republic of China nor any international treaty concluded or acceded to by the People's Republic of China has any provisions.

The provision suggests that if neither the applicable Chinese law nor any international treaties ratified by China include relevant provisions of the matter in dispute, then international custom should be used to fill the gap. In other words, they only allow international customs to fill the gap of Chinese domestic law, instead of applying as independent governing law of a dispute.[44] 8.30

However, in practice, international customs are applied more frequently than 'filling the gap'. Chinese courts usually do not hesitate to apply international customs upon parties' express choice.[45] In *Swiss Newco Commodity AG v. China Construction Bank Jilin Province Hunchun Branch*,[46] China Construction Bank issued a letter of credit for the benefit of Swiss Newco Commodity AG. The letter of credit included an express clause choosing UCP500 as the applicable law. The SPC held that the dispute arising out of the letter of credit should be decided according to the relevant regulation of UCP500. In a number of cases, UCP500 expressly chosen by the parties was applied as the governing law to the parties of a letter of credit.[47] In *Shanghai Saifeng International Trade Ltd v. Industrial and Commercial Bank of China (ICBC) and Canara Bank*,[48] the collection instruction expressly provided for the application of URC522, which was communicated to the other parties according to commercial customs and none of the parties had raised any challenge. The court thus considered the international custom URC522 applied as the applicable law upon the contractual parties' choice.[49] 8.31

44 REN Fanghao, *Guoji Tiaoyue zai Zhongguo Fayuan de Shiyong [Application of International Treaties in Chinese Courts]*, MPhil Thesis submitted to Zhengzhou University in 2007, 12.

45 For example, in *Xiamen Xiangyu Group v. Mechel Trading AG* (2004) Xia Min Ren Zi No 81, the parties agreed that if the CISG did not cover the disputed matter, the law applicable should be ICC Principles of International Commercial Contracts 1994.

46 (1999) 2 *Gazette of the SPC of the People's Republic of China* 71.

47 *Jiaxing Sanzhenzhai Food Co Ltd v. Industrial and Commercial Bank of China*, Zhejiang Province HPC, (2007) Jia Min Er Chu Zi No 96; *Lansheng Ltd v. Citi Bank*, Shanghai Municipality High Court, (2000) Hu Gao Jing Zhong Zi No 335; *Shanxi Cereals, Oil and Foodstuffs Import and Export Co Ltd v. ING*, Beijing Municipality High Court, (2000) Gao Jing Zhong Zi No 295.

48 Jiangsu Province Changzhou Municipality IPC, 2007.12.26, (2006) Chang Min San Chu Zi No 26.

49 The court also relied on Art 126 of the Contract law which permits the parties to choose the applicable law to decide contractual disputes.

8.32 Another interesting case about UCP500 is *Jiangsu Ximen v. Bank of East Asia*,[50] where there was no choice of law clause and the court decided that the law of mainland China should be applied as the governing law according to the closest connection rule. However, the court said UCP500 should also apply because the parties had both referred to UCP500 to support their arguments. It seems that the court applied UCP500 not as part of Chinese domestic law, but as the law tacitly chosen by the parties. Since the common view among Chinese academic writers and practitioners is that the choice of law must be express,[51] this decision is of considerable interest, as it partially based the decision on the fact that all the circumstances demonstrated that the parties had consented to the UCP500 as the applicable law.[52]

8.33 In *Kaide (Qingdao) Ltd v. China Agriculture Bank*,[53] the applicant applied for the China Agriculture Bank to issue a letter of credit using the standard application form provided by the Bank. The form included a choice of law clause choosing UCP400 to govern the letter of credit. The Bank issued the letter of credit based on the application but the letter of credit changed the choice of law into UCP500. The Bank explained that after the UCP500 was issued the Bank had the policy to issue all letters of credit pursuant to UCP500, though the old application forms were provided. The court held that the parties were entitled to change the choice of law clause and applied UCP500.

iv. Conclusion

8.34 It seems that although judicial practice differs from court to court, Chinese judges usually do not intentionally refuse the application of international customs as the governing law pursuant to the parties' choice. The status of international treaties is uncertain, caused because of the uncertainty of the relationship between international treaties and Chinese domestic law. China does not clearly take a monist or dualist approach. There is no clear conclusion as to whether international treaties ratified in China but not converted into Chinese statutes are part of Chinese domestic law and can be applied as such or if they still belong to the independent international law system.

---

50 Nanjing IPC, (2003) Ning Min Wu Shu Zi No 18.

51 The SPC Judicial Interpretation of Law on Economic Contracts Involving Foreign Interests provides that the choice of law must be 'express'. It is important to note that the Law on Economic Contracts Involving Foreign Interests was annulled in 1999 simultaneously with the entry into force of the Contract Law, and the judicial interpretation has also been annulled. However, this interpretation has brought obvious influence to the later judicial practice.

52 Another interpretation probably is that the court applied UCP500 because Chinese law does not contain relevant rules on the issue.

53 [2002] Min Si Ti Zi No 8.

Anyway, the possibility of choosing international customs as the governing law is unusual in the world. It seems that China moves faster than other countries in applying non-state law under party autonomy. However, this is not due to the developed knowledge and understanding of either choice of law or non-state law. The practice and the judicial interpretation, on the contrary, demonstrate the lack of a proper examination of the nature of non-state law and its relationships with conflict of laws. Chinese courts, in most cases, simply fail to distinguish the difference between non-state law and state law and fail to justify whether and why the law designated in private international law refer to not only the municipal law but also international law. Furthermore, neither the cases nor the 2012 Interpretations has considered the potential difficulties in applying non-state law as the governing law to a dispute, such as the quality of law, the clarity and certainty of the content, the interpretation and proof of non-state law, and the comprehensiveness of non-state law. The only public policy or mandatory rules exemptions are not sufficient to address all the weaknesses and difficulties. **8.35**

It is suggested that although more and more commentators propose that non-state law should be allowed to play a role in private international law, legislators are very cautious as to how far party autonomy could go, whether there is the theoretical basis allowing the application of non-state law, and the proper interaction between the doctrines of private international law and public international law. China seems to be too quick to allow the parties to choose international customs as the governing law without adequate justification, and the status of international treaties ratified in China is still uncertain.[54] **8.36**

III. LAW IN THE ABSENCE OF CHOICE

III.1 Development of default choice of law rules in China

Before the Conflicts Act, Chinese law adopted the closest connection doctrine to determine the applicable law in the absence of choice since the 1985 Foreign Economic Contract Law and 1986 GPCL.[55] The SPC issued a Judicial Interpretation on Foreign Economic Contract Law in 1987 providing guidance to decide the closest connection.[56] The 1987 Interpretation provided **8.37**

54 For more discussion, see Z.S. Tang, 'International Treaties in Chinese Private International Law' (2012) 42 *Hong Kong Law Journal* 597.

55 Foreign Economic Contract Law, Art 5; GPCL, Art 145;

56 SPC, 'Response of the SPC to Certain Questions Concerning the Application of the Foreign Economic Contract Law', *supra* n 12.

fixed connecting factors for 11 types of contracts, subject to the escape clause in favour of the country with the 'clearly more significant connection' to the contract.[57]

8.38 The 1987 Interpretation was abolished in 1999 following the promulgation of the Contract Law. Between 1999 and 2007, no judicial directions were available. Although not comprehensive, statistics show that the adoption of the closest connection doctrine in Chinese court practice increased steadily from 31.4 per cent in 2001 to 40 per cent in 2007,[58] there is no clear view, however, as to how the doctrine was applied in each case. It was left to the courts to exercise their discretion to decide which country had the 'closest connection' with the contract.[59] Such flexibility enables Chinese courts to apply Chinese law in most cross-border contracts. Many courts start by considering the link between the dispute and China and if they believe these links are close, they can immediately claim that China is the country with the 'closet connection' in order to apply Chinese law.[60]

8.39 In 2007, the SPC provided judicial guidance to help the People's Court to adopt the right approach in applying the closest connection doctrine.[61] This is the first time that the Chinese authorities adopted the characteristic performance doctrine as a test to determine the closest connection. According to the guidance, the People's Court should consider the special character of each individual contract and the obligation of the party that could demonstrate the most essential and fundamental feature of the contract.[62] This guidance adopts, at least the spirit of, the doctrine of characteristic performance. The judicial interpretation then provided detailed guidance for 17 types of contracts by providing rigid connecting factors that link each contract with a particular country.[63] Most of these connecting factors are decided pursuant to the characteristic performance doctrine. For example, in the contract for the sale of goods, the law of the place where the seller is domiciled should apply, unless the contract was concluded in the buyer's domicile, or the contract expressly states that the goods should be delivered at the buyer's domicile, when the law of that country should apply;[64] in contracts for processing materials supplied by clients, contracts for assembly and other types of

57 Ibid., Art 6.
58 Yu Shuhong et al., 'The Closest Connection Doctrine in the Conflict of Laws in China', (2009) 8 *Chinese Journal of International Law* 423, 432–3.
59 Mo Zhang, *supra* n 10, 125.
60 Ibid., 123; Xu, *supra* n 3, 651; Yu Shuhong et al., *supra* n 58, 439.
61 2007 Provisions on Applicable Law.
62 Ibid, Art 5.
63 Ibid.
64 Ibid., Art 5(1).

contracts for processing, the law of the place where the labour provider/processor is domiciled shall apply;[65] in contracts for leasing moveable property, the law of the place where the lessor is domiciled shall apply;[66] in contracts for the pledge of moveable property, the law of the place where the pledgee is domiciled shall apply;[67] in loan contracts, the law of the place where the lender is domiciled shall apply;[68] in insurance contracts, the law of the place where the insurer is domiciled shall apply;[69] in a guaranty contract, the law of the place where the guarantor is domiciled shall apply;[70] in agency contracts, the law of the agent's domicile shall apply;[71] in commission agency contracts, the law of the agency's domicile shall apply;[72] and in intermediary contracts, the law of the intermediate's domicile shall apply.[73] It finally recommended that if these above described contracts have an obviously closer connection with the other country, the law of that country should apply instead.[74]

Although most of the connecting factors are determined by applying the characteristic performance test, the 2007 Interpretation does not expressly adopt this test as a general rule.[75] Instead, it is a presumption to test whether a country has the closest connections with a contract. Therefore, it is subject to the 'closer connection' escape clause. **8.40**

The 2007 Interpretation arguably has improved Chinese judicial practice.[76] However, the courts rarely use the characteristic performance test and the closest connection principle. Most courts directly apply the hard-and-fast rule **8.41**

65 Ibid., Art 5(2).
66 Ibid., Art 5(5).
67 Ibid., Art 5(6).
68 Ibid., Art 5(7).
69 Ibid., Art 5(8).
70 Ibid., Art 5(12).
71 Ibid., Art 5(13).
72 Ibid., Art 5(16).
73 Ibid., Art 5(17). Some connecting factors are not based on characteristic performance, e.g., contracts for the supply of machinery are governed by the law of the place where the machines are assembled (Art 5(3)); contracts for lease, sale or guaranty of immovable property are governed by the law of the place where the property is situated (Art 5(4)); financial leasing contracts are governed by the law of the lessee's domicile (Art 5(9)); construction contracts are governed by the law of the place of the project (Art 5(10)); storage contracts are governed by the place where the warehouse is located (Art 5(11)); contracts for the issuing, sale or transfer of securities are governed by, respectively, the law of the place of issuing, the place of sale or the place of transfer (Art 5(14)); and contracts for auction are governed by the law of the place of auction (Art 5(15)). For full translation, see ShuhongYu, et al., *supra* n 58, 428–9.
74 2007 Provisions on Applicable Law, Art 5.
75 Cf. Mo Zhang, *supra* n 10, 128.
76 E.g., *Dongguan Qunjun Decoration Light v. Mulinsen Ltd,* Guangdong Dongguan IPC, (2013) Dong Zhong Fa Min Si Zhong Zi No 26; *Qiaoxing Hong Kong Ltd v. Dongguan Yuanda Furniture Ltd,* Guangdong Dongguan IPC, (2012) Dong Zhong Fa Min Si Zhong Zi No 81; *Zhang Jia Cheng v. Dongguan Mao Hong Machinery,* Guangdong Dongguan Intemediate People's Court (2012) Dong Zhong Fa Min Si Zhong Zi No 82.

provided in Article 5 of the 2007 Provision on Applicable Law,[77] because it is much more straightforward and easy to apply. After applying the fixed connecting factors, courts proceeded to apply the law without considering the escape clause at all.[78]

8.42 The 2007 Interpretation was abolished in 2013,[79] following the promulgation and enforcement of the Conflicts Act. The Conflicts Act provides a new provision on deciding law in the absence of choice. It does not depart from previous judicial guidance. Article 41 reads:

> Absent any choice by the parties, the law of the habitual residence of a party whose performance of obligation is most characteristic of the contract or the law that most closely connected with the contract shall be applied.

8.43 The Interpretation on Conflicts Act 2012 does not yet cover any guidance for the application of the closest connection doctrine. Before the publication of the second Judicial Interpretation on the Conflicts Act, it is uncertain how courts should proceed to decide the law in the absence of choice and whether guidance in the 2007 Interpretation would still be considered in judicial practice. This section aims to analyze the new Article 41 and examine how it should be interpreted.

III.2 Characteristic performance doctrine

8.44 The Conflicts Act does not directly use the terminology 'characteristic performance' but the description is compliant with the doctrine of characteristic performance in the EU. This doctrine was introduced first in Switzerland, and developed to its modern form in the Netherlands and Italy.[80] It was later adopted by the EC in the Rome Convention, and followed in the EU Rome I Regulation. Characteristic performance, as a result, has been in use in the EU for over 20 years, but there is still criticism and uncertainty about its

---

77 Yu Shuhong et al., *supra* n 58, 342.

78 E.g., *Dupont Phillip F v. Shaoxing Yuanxing Export and Import Ltd*, Zhejiang HPC, (2010) Zhe Shang Wai Zhong Zi No 92; *Mainstreet Trade Ltd v. Youchang Clothing (Shanghai) Ltd*, Shanghai No 1 IPC (2010) Hu Yi Zhong Min Wu (Shang) Zhong Zi No 15.

79 SPC, 'Zuigao Renmin Fayuan Guanyu Feizhi 1997 Nian 7 Yue 1 Ri Zhi 2011 Nian 12 Yue 31 Ri Qijian Fabu de Bufen Sifa Jieshi he Sifa Jieshi Xingzhi Wenjian (Di Shi Pi) de Jueding [Decision of the SPC on Abolishing Some Judicial Interpretations and Documents of a Judicial Interpretation Nature Which Were Issued from July 1, 1997 to December 31, 2011 (Tenth Group)]', Fa Shi [2013] No 7.

80 H.U.J. D'Oliveira, 'Characteristic Obligation in the Draft-EEC Obligation Convention', (1977) 25(2) *American Journal of Comparative Law* 303, 304.

interpretation and application. It is often described as being one of the most difficult concepts in the Rome I Regulation.[81]

The main purpose of the characteristic performance doctrine is to concentrate the contractual relationship in the one country that is most suitable to determine the obligation owed by both parties, the consequence of the performance and breach, and the effect of the contract as a whole.[82] Which country is entitled to bear this status? It depends on the functioning of law in contracts. Contract terms are usually determined by the parties. The law plays a much less important role with the principle of contractual freedom. The issues which must be determined by law include the supplementary questions where the parties fail to make agreement and the mandatory rules which supersede contractual freedom. The characteristic performer is allowed to consult the law of his home state for supplementing rules. The characteristic performance doctrine concentrates the legal relationship in the home of the performer of the characteristic obligation.[83] **8.45**

The other justification of the characteristic performance doctrine focuses on the 'character' or 'type' of a contract. It locates the contractual relationship in the country where the predominant performance that determines the classification of the contract is located. Such a predominant performance is deemed to be located in the country of the performer. The doctrine is based on the typology of contracts. It presumes that the obligation in the contract differentiates it from other kinds of obligations and thus is the most specific and requires more specific legal guidance than common practice. **8.46**

The characteristic performance doctrine is criticized for failing to pay attention to the importance of the obligation that is not 'characteristic'. If the dispute is on the performance of the non-characteristic obligation, it is questionable whether the law of the characteristic performer should still apply.[84] Furthermore, it locates the contract in the place of a party, instead of the place of performance of the characteristic obligation, while the latter clearly has closer connections with the actual carrying out of the performance and other issues, such as illegality of the performance.[85] Finally, the characteristic **8.47**

81 EU Regulation (EC) No 593/2008 on the law applicable to contractual obligations (Rome I), [2008] OJ L 177/6, Art 4(2); J.J. Fawcett and J. Carruthers, *Cheshire, North and Fawcett: Private International Law* (14th ed., OUP 2008) 712.

82 K. Lipstein, 'Characteristic Performance—A New Concept in the Conflict of Laws in Matters of Contract for the EEC' (1981) 3 *Northwestern Journal of International Law and Business* 402, 410.

83 Lipstein, *ibid,* 410–11; O. Vondracek, 'Art 4 of the Rome Convention on the Law Applicable to Civil and Commercial Obligations' (2007) 8 *Common Law Review* 32, 32.

84 Fawcett and Carruthers, *supra* n 81, 714.

85 Ibid, 716.

performance doctrine is criticized for being one-sided, providing more protection to the supplier than the customer.[86]

8.48 How is the obligation that is 'most characteristic of the contract' decided? There is no consensus. The most widely cited test is the 'payment of money' test.[87] The Giuliano-Lagarde report suggests that if one party's performance is payment of money and the other's is not, the performance that does not involve pecuniary payment is the characteristic performance. This test is summarized from most simple bilateral contracts, such as sale of goods and provision of services contracts. Performance to pay is precise and uncomplicated, and typical in different types of contracts. Performance in kind could categorize a contract and require more supplementary explanations. It also focuses on the functioning of a contract, where performance in kind marks the feature of the contract and distinguishes this contract from another.[88] This test is useful in simple bilateral contract but ineffective in contracts where both or neither parties' performance includes payment of money or in complicated contracts where various complicated performances exist.

8.49 Being aware of the weakness of the money-based test, various alternative tests are provided. For example, the nature of performance test focuses on whether a particular performance could categorize the contract and distinguish this type of contracts from others.[89] This test is more flexible. However, it is important to note that sometimes the nature of a contract depends on the performance of both parties to interact. One party's performance, thus, cannot distinguish this contract from other types.

8.50 Another test focuses on the complexity of the performance. The more complicated an obligation, the more likely it is that it will be characteristic to the contract. Applying this test may provide certainty to the party who endures the higher risk. The weakness of this test is that it is too ambiguous and 'more complexity' of an obligation may be difficult to judge.[90]

8.51 Finally, there is a suggestion that the characteristic performance should be able to demonstrate the social-economic importance of the contracts.[91] This test, again, may not prove practical in practice because great uncertainty exists

86 Vondracek, *supra* n 83, 33.

87 M. Giuliano and P. Lagarde, 'Report on the Convention on the Law Applicable to Contractual Obligations', [1980] OJ C 282/1.

88 D'Oliveira, *supra* n 80, 306.

89 Ibid.

90 Ibid., 307.

91 Ibid., 308.

judging the 'socio-economic' impact of a contract. There are various ways to test characteristic performance, but none of them can claim to work perfectly. In practice, the 'payment of money' test may be able to provide an answer for most straightforward contracts. For other contracts, it is necessary for a court to consider various tests and factors and to exercise discretion. It is also necessary to recognize that for some contracts the characteristic performance doctrine simply cannot work.

The way to identify the characteristic performance is not provided in Article 41 of the Conflicts Act. No guidance can be found either in the current or previous judicial directions. The SPC, in its 2007 Interpretation, avoided giving a general guiding principle but provided fixed connecting factors for 17 contracts. This approach could reduce uncertainty and help Chinese judges to make decisions. It is, however, incomprehensive and, in the long run, unhelpful. However, given the various levels of legal knowledge and judicial skills of Chinese judges, the SPC may not be confident simply providing a general test rule or principle and relying on each judge's judicial discretion. It is expected that detailed guidance depending on the typology of major contracts similar to the 2007 Interpretation may be provided in a future judicial interpretation. In the meantime, while no new interpretation is provided, most Chinese courts are likely to follow the guidance in the 2007 Provisions in their judgments, albeit they have been abandoned. **8.52**

III.3 Closest connection doctrine

The closest connection doctrine is not new in China. It focuses on the centre of gravity of a legal relationship by considering all objective connecting factors, including the place of contracting, the place of performance, the place of breach of a contract, the domicile or place of business of both parties, and the place where the subject matter is located. These connecting factors will be weighed, balanced and accumulated in order to identify the country that has the closest connection with the dispute.[92] **8.53**

The practice in the past few decades demonstrates that Chinese courts could not successfully apply the closest connection doctrine. The flexibility and discretionary nature of the doctrine leads to the 'homeward' trend and makes it possible for a Chinese court to apply Chinese law in most cases without properly conducting the closest connection analysis. In many cases, Chinese courts simply find one fact that relates to China and hence concludes China is **8.54**

92 Fawcett and Carruthers, *supra* n 81, 708–9; Giuliano and Lagarde Report, *supra* n 87, 19–20; Vondracek, *supra* n 83, 33.

the country with the closest connection to the contract.[93] No consideration is given to other factors and no attempt is made to weight compare and balance these factors. Chinese courts, therefore, abuse the very flexible close connection test in order to apply Chinese law.

III.4 Relationship between two doctrines in Article 41

8.55 The most widely criticized point in Article 41 is the confusion over the relationship between the characteristic performance and the closest connection doctrines. Article 41 literally makes the two doctrines alternative. An exact interpretation might suggest that the legislator allows the court to freely choose either doctrine to determine the law in the absence of choice.[94] This approach is uncertain, impractical and not viable. Without judicial guidance from the SPC, some local courts may easily rely on this approach to apply Chinese law in any cross-border contracts. The court may apply either doctrine as long as it leads to the application of China law.[95]

8.56 It is suggested that the relationship between the two doctrines should be clarified by the SPC in the future judicial interpretation. There are a few possibilities for the provision of such an interpretation.

8.57 The first possibility is that the characteristic performance is a test helping determining the closest connection principle. This interpretation was accepted in the 2007 Interpretation, where the SPC suggested that the closest connection doctrine would be determined by the characteristic performance consideration.[96] The importance of this interpretation is that characteristic performance only acts as a test helping determination of the closest connection doctrine. The characteristic performance doctrine, thus, cannot override the closest connection doctrine. If the former leads to a country that clearly has a weaker connection than another, the closet connection doctrine would be used as an escape clause.[97]

---

93 MA Lingxia, 'Lun Zuimixie Lianxi Yuanze de Jiazhi zai Woguo de Shixian [Demonstration of the Value of the Closest Connection Principle in China]' in MA Hai Tao, LI Liang, *Guoji Faxue de Lilun yu Shijian [The Jurisprudence and Practice of International Law]* (China Legal Publishing House 1991), 245; XIAO Yongping, 'Zui Miqie Lianxi Yuanze zai Zhongguo Chongtufa zhong de Yingyong [Application of the Closest Connection Doctrine in Chinese Conflict of Laws]' (1992) 3 Zhongguo Shehui Kexue [*China Social Science*] 146.

94 Huo, *supra* n 3, 1086.

95 For example, see *Vailog (HK) Real Estate Investments Ltd v. Huitong International Trust & Investment Company,* Hainan Province HPC, (2011) Qiong Min San Zhong Zi No 35.

96 2007 Interpretation, Art 5.

97 Ibid.

The second possibility is that the characteristic performance will only be used if the closest connection cannot be determined. Some courts in practice consider all the connecting factors to establish the country with the closest connection to a contract. After this country is determined, they would move on to apply its law without considering the characteristic performance doctrine. In *Vailog (HK) Real Estate Investments Ltd v. Huitong International Trust & Investment Company*,[98] the parties entered into a pledge contract. Pursuant to the characteristic performance doctrine and the 2007 Provisions on Applicable Law the characteristic performer of a pledge contract should be the pledgee. The court, however, did not consider the characteristic performance doctrine but decided that since both the place where the contract was concluded and the place where the subject matter was located were within mainland China, mainland China should be the place with the closest connection to the dispute. After the 2007 Interpretation was abolished, many Chinese courts started to adopt this approach again.[99] How is the country with the closest connection to a dispute designated? Most courts treat the place of performance as a weighty factor. For example, Zhejiang Province Hangzhou Intermediate People's Court says clearly in some cases that the closest connection is determined by the place where the contract is performed.[100] Other courts consider the parties' domicile or habitual residence and the place of performance. In *LIN Binxiong v. XIE Yonghao*,[101] for example, the parties entered into a cross-border loan contract. The court decided to apply Chinese law because the habitual residence of the lender was in China and the loan agreement was performed in China. It seems that the court used the closest connection doctrine by considering two weighty connecting factors, i.e., the lender's habitual residence and the place of performance. Usually, the dispute on applicable law will arise only if the parties have different habitual residence. The place of performance thus acts as a tie breaker.[102] In other words, the country with the closest connection to a contract again will be the place where the contract is performed. **8.58**

98 *Vailog (HK), supra* n 95 .

99 The same approach is used in *GAN Zhengmao v. PENG Rifa*, Yunnan HPC, (2012) Yun Gao Min San Zhong Zi No 55; *Jiangmen X Estate Development Ltd v. JIAN*, Guangdong Jiangmin IPC, (2013) Jiang Zhong Fa Min Yi Zhong Zi No 62; *WU Kunjiao v. ZOU Ying*, Hainan HPC, (2012) Qiong Min San Zhong Zi No 56; *DAI v. JI*, Shanghai No 1 IPC, (2012) Hu Yi Zhong Min Si (Shang) Zhong Zi No S1520.

100 *X Bank Hangzhou Branch v. LI*, Zhejiang Hangzhou IPC, (2012) Zhe Hang Shang Wai Chu Zi No 57; *HONG v. LI*, Zhejiang Hangzhou IPC, (2012) Zhe Hang Shang Wai Chu Zi No 63.

101 Fujian Province Xiamen Municipality Haichang District People's Court, (2012) Hai Min Chu Zi No 2219.

102 *LIN Binxiong v. XIE Yonghao; Jiangmen X Estate Development Ltd v. JIAN; SUN v. LI*, Guangdong Dongguan No 2 IPC, (2013) Dong Er Fa Min Si Chu Zi No 38; *YE Ruilin v. LI Xianyou*, Fujian Xiamen Haichang District People's Court, (2012) Hai Min Chu Zi No 608.

8.59 The third possibility is that the characteristic performance is used in most cases and only if it leads to a country with no substantive connections with the dispute will the closest connection approach will be used. In Chinese judicial practice pursuant to the 2007 Interpretation, most courts apply the characteristic performance, or at least the hard-and-fast rule designated by considering the characteristic performance principle, as the first step. But most courts did not consider the escape clause at all.[103] One interpretation is that these courts did not properly understand the correct procedure proposed by the SPC or the nature of the closest connection escape clause. They were more comfortable applying the hard-and fast rule alone. The other interpretation is that Chinese courts believe the escape clause can only be used in exceptional cases and therefore do not apply it in most cases. After the Conflicts Act entered into force, some Chinese courts continued the practice by directly applying the characteristic performance doctrine without considering the closest connection doctrine.[104]

8.60 Which approach is more appropriate in China? It depends on a few elements. First, is the objective of Chinese legislators to achieve certainty or flexibility? Secondly, which approach is more suitable for Chinese judges to apply considering the legal knowledge and professional skills? It is suggested that due to the average level of Chinese judge's capacity in conducting cross-over disputes and in exercising discretion, the rule that is more certain, with limited and predictable exceptions, should be the best choice. It is thus submitted that the appropriate approach should be: (1) the law of the characteristic performer should apply in most cases; (2) if this place cannot be determined, the law of the country with the closest connection to the contract should apply; and (3) if the law of the characteristic performer leads to a country that does not have real connections with the contract, the law of the closest connection should apply.

IV. SPECIAL CONTRACTS

8.61 One important development in the Conflicts Act is that special choice of law rules are provided for consumer contracts and employment contracts. Before the Conflicts Act, Chinese law did not distinguish contracts with inequality of

103 Yu Shuhong et al., *supra* n 58, 439.

104 *CHOI Won v. XU Chun,* Liaoning Dalian IPC, (2012) Da Min Si Chu Zi No 111; *XIE Yibo v. SHAN Muqing,* Hainan HPC (2013) Qiong Min San Zhong Zi No 3; *WANG Kemin v. ZENG Xiaomin,* Fujian Xiamen Haicang District People's Court, (2012) Hai Min Chu Zi No 1646.

bargaining power from ordinary commercial contracts, which may be unjust to the weaker party.[105]

IV.1 Consumer contracts

The Conflicts Act provides protective choice of law for consumer contracts. Article 42 provides: **8.62**

> A consumer contract is governed by the law of place where the consumer has his habitual residence. If the consumer chooses to use the law of the place where goods or services are provided, or the business has no related commercial activities in the place where the consumer has his habitual residence, the law of the place where goods and services are provided should apply.

Three points should be noted pursuant to this provision. First, the default applicable law for consumer contracts is the law of the place where the consumer has his habitual residence. This is consistent with the tendency to protect consumers as the weaker party in a contract. The weakness exists not only in bargaining power but also in access to information. A consumer has no knowledge of the law in other countries, which hampers consumers' confidence in dealing with foreign traders without knowing the potential law applicable to the contract. Furthermore, many consumers may not be aware of the applicable law problem and presume that they will always be protected by the domestic law of their own country. This approach could protect consumers' reasonable expectations and could ensure that consumers receive protection no lower than in a domestic transaction. **8.63**

Secondly, the default rule can be departed from in two circumstances. The first is that the consumer chooses to use the law of the place where the goods or services are provided. This exemption is unsatisfactory. It is likely that the law of the place where goods or services are provided delivers better protection to the consumer and the consumer would wish to apply the law of that particular country instead of Chinese law. However, there is no clear guidance as to what constitutes the consumer's choice, or how the choice can be expressed. Does it mean a consumer could unilaterally choose to apply the law of the place where goods or services are supplied? Would the choice between businesses and consumers, i.e., a choice of law agreement included in the consumer contract, be a valid choice within the purpose of Article 42? It is common knowledge **8.64**

105 Zhengxin Huo, 'Highlights of China's New Private International Law Act', (2011) 45 *Revue Juridique Themis* 637, 674; Zhang, *supra* n 10, 106.

that most consumer contracts are standard-term contracts, where the consumer is in a take-it-or-leave-it position. Consumers usually do not read the terms and conditions provided by the company and will not negotiate on these terms. Most consumers will not have sufficient professional knowledge to understand the importance and function of the choice of law agreement. If a choice of law agreement included in a standard form contract is regarded as a valid choice, the protection can be denied easily by companies through simply inserting into the standard form contract a choice of law agreement choosing the law of the place where goods or services are supplied.[106]

8.65 A counter argument is that businesses should be allowed to reduce commercial risk by choosing the law of the place where goods or services are supplied. A company cannot cope with multi-national consumer laws in their cross-border practice. It is more commercially effective to allow the business to apply the law of one country. Furthermore, choosing the law of the place where goods or services are supplied is a reasonable choice because this place usually has the closest connection with the contract. Applying this law is more natural and appropriate than the law of the consumer's habitual residence. Moreover, the place where the goods or services are supplied is usually known to the consumers and the application of the law of that country is likely to be expected by consumers.[107]

8.66 It is necessary to mention that the purpose of the protective choice of law is not to apply the law that could substantively provide the most important protection but to provide the consumer with protection no lower than that he could receive in his home state. The most a protective choice of law rule could do is to prevent a business from unilaterally choosing the law of a country that has no connection with the contract and provides the lowest level of protection to consumers. The Chinese protective choice of law does not aim to exclude party autonomy from consumer contracts all together, but to prevent a choice of bad faith.[108]

8.67 Thirdly, the law of the consumer's habitual residence will not apply if the business has not had commercial activities in the consumer's habitual residence. This may occur if mobile consumers travel to the business's domicile to purchase goods or services. Applying the law of the consumer's habitual residence is unpredictable for the business. This condition aims to provide certainty to businesses and reduce commercial risk. The problem is what is

---

106 For justification, see Z.S. Tang, *Electronic Consumer Contracts in the Conflict of Laws* (Hart, 2009) 8–11.

107 Ibid., 208ff.

108 For more discussion, Z. Tang, 'Parties' Choice of Law in E-Consumer Contracts', (2007) 3 *Journal of Private International Law* 113–36.

meant by 'related commercial activities'. Directly supplying goods or services in the consumer's habitual residence, through its own branch, subsidiary, or selling agent, is related activities. What if the business is selling online? Would a website established in the business's home state but accessible in the consumer's habitual residence be regarded as 'related activities'? The answer is that if the goods and services are tangible and require physical delivery, the supply of goods or services to the consumer is the 'related activities' because the business clearly should have knowledge of the place of destination. If goods and services are intangible, businesses should adopt reasonable steps to verify the habitual residence of the consumer. Otherwise, the conclusion of the contract and the performance should be deemed as 'related activities' in the consumer's habitual residence.

In 2013, the NPC amended the Consumer Protection Act.[109] This new law **8.68** increases the standard of consumer protection. It introduces a seven-day cooling-off period for distance selling;[110] provides punitive damages for damage or injury to consumers caused by fraud;[111] allows representative action brought by the consumer association on behalf of multiple consumers;[112] and places the burden of proof on the business.[113] The Conflicts Act could help Chinese consumers to receive at least the same protection when dealing with foreign companies. However, it is also necessary to mention that within the four important improvements on consumer protection, only the cooling-off period and the punitive damages are classified as substance in Chinese conflict of laws and should be determined by applying the governing law. The other two relate to procedure, which, according to choice of law theory, should be preserved by the court.

Finally, it is necessary to note that the Conflicts Act does not define consumer **8.69** contracts. The Consumer Protection Act applies to consumers who 'purchase or use commodities, or receive services for daily consumption'[114] and businesses who 'supply commodities and services to consumers'.[115] The same definitions are likely to be accepted to define the scope of Article 42. However,

109 Zhonghua Renmin Gongheguo Xiaofeizhe Quanyi Baohu Fa [PRC Consumer Protection Act (2013 Amendment)]. Adopted by the 8th NPC Standing Committee 4th Meeting on 31 Oct 1993, first amendment by the 11th NPC Standing Committee 10th Meeting on 27 August 2009, and second amendment by the 12th NPC Standing Committee 5th Meeting on 25 Oct 2013. The 2013 Amendment entered into force on 15 March 2014.

110 Ibid., Art 25.

111 Ibid., Art 55.

112 Ibid., Art 47.

113 Ibid., Art 23.

114 Ibid., Art 2.

115 Ibid., Art 3.

it is still uncertain whether consumer contracts in Article 42 include certain special contracts, such as insurance contracts and financial investment contracts. It largely depends on how broadly 'daily consumption' is defined. If it is defined to cover investment by non-professionals, the buyers of these contracts should qualify as consumers. Since the Conflicts Act does not provide special choice of law for other contracts involving the inequality of bargaining power, it is likely that the legislators want to extend the scope of Article 42 to cover any cases where contracts are concluded between an unprofessional buyer and a professional seller or provider, where the inequality of bargaining power exists.

IV.2 Employment contracts

i. Before the Conflicts Act

8.70 China has adopted a policy in favour of employment of foreign labour working in China. The development of foreign direct investment in China increases the number of foreign employers playing actively in the Chinese market. Foreign-related employment contracts and disputes concerning such contracts are increasing swiftly.

8.71 Chinese conflicts law on foreign-related employment contracts, however, was undeveloped. Before the enforcement of the Conflicts Act, there were no clear legislative provisions on choice of law in foreign-related labour contracts. The 1987 Interpretation on the Application of the Foreign Economic Contract Law first provided guidance that labour disputes should be governed by the law chosen by the parties.[116] In the absence of choice, the law with the closest connection to the dispute should apply, which, in a labour contract, would usually be the place where the labour is provided.[117] This interpretation was abolished in 1999, and no other guidance existed before the Conflicts Act.

8.72 Before the enactment of the Conflicts Act, two opinions existed in Chinese judicial practice and academic writing. The first is that Chinese law should apply as mandatory rules for labour contracts concluded by employers in China. For example, Article 2 of the PRC Labour Contracts Act[118] provides that the establishment, conclusion, performance, variation, termination and ending of labour contracts between employees and enterprises, individual

---

116 SPC, 'Response of the SPC to Certain Questions Concerning the Application of the Foreign Economic Contract Law', *supra* n 12, Art 2(2).

117 Ibid., Art 2(6), (8).

118 Zhonghua Renmin Gongheguo Laodong Hetong Fa [Labour Contracts Law of the People's Republic of China](2007), adopted at the 28th Session of the Standing Committee of the 10th NPC on 29 June 2007, effective from 1 Jan 2008.

economic organizations and private non-enterprise units in China should be governed by the PRC Labour Contracts Act.[119] Furthermore, the Rules for the Administration of Employment of Foreigners in China (2010 Amendment)[120] also provides that if a foreign national entered into a labour contract with employers 'in China' the dispute should be resolved pursuant to the PRC labour law.[121]

The condition applying the PRC Labour Contracts Act as mandatory rules is that the employer is 'in China'. However, it does not apply compulsorily to labour contracts concluded by foreign employers abroad. Pursuant to the Regulation on the Administration of Registration of Permanent Representative Offices of Foreign Enterprises,[122] a permanent representative office of a foreign enterprise can only conduct non-profitable activities relating to the business activities of the foreign enterprise and it does not have legal personality. If an employee entered into a labour contract with such a representative office, he is deemed to enter into a labour relationship with the foreign enterprise and the PRC Labour Contracts Act will not apply as mandatory rules.[123] **8.73**

The other opinion is that the Chinese Labour Contracts Act should not apply as mandatory rules to foreign-related labour contracts where the employers are in China. The provision only states the condition in which the PRC Labour Contracts Act can be used, i.e., the Act can only be used for labour contracts concluded with employers in China, not foreign employers.[124] Furthermore, this provision only grants the Labour Contracts Act the status of domestic mandatory rules.[125] It means the parties shall not by agreement subject their employment relationship to other Chinese statutes, such as the GPCL, Contract Law, etc. to the exclusion of the provisions of the Labour Contracts **8.74**

119 Ibid., Art 2.

120 Waiguoren Zai Zhongguo Jiuye Guanli Guiding (2010 Xiuzheng) [Rules for the Administration of Employment of Foreigners in China (2010 Amendment)], promulgated jointly by the Ministry of Labour, the Ministry of Public Security, Ministry of Foreign Affairs and Ministry of Foreign Trade and Economic Cooperation on 22 Jan 1996, No 29 [1996] of the Ministry of Labour, and Amended by Order No 7 of the Ministry of Human Resources and Social Security on 12 Nov 2010.

121 Ibid., Art 26.

122 Waiguo Qiye Changzhu Daibiao Jigou Dengji Guanli Tiaoli (2010) [Regulation on the Administration of Registration of Permanent Representative Offices of Foreign Enterprises (2010)], adopted by the 132th Executive Meeting of the State Council on 10 Nov 2010, and promulgated and entered into effect on 1 March 2011.

123 *ZHENG Jian Bin v. Taiwan Chun-qiao-tian Ltd,* Fujian Xiamen IPC, (2008) Xia Min Zhong Zi No 3717.

124 *HK Jin Zhi Ma Petroleum Ltd v. YUAN Haiyang,* Fujian Zhangzhou IPC (2004) Zhang Min Zhong Zi No 183.

125 ZHAN Pengpeng, 'Lun Haiwai Yuangong Paiqian zhong de Zhunjufa Weentti [Applicable Law on Overseas Labour Dispatch]', (2010) 13 Zhongguo Guojisifa Niankan [*Chinese Yearbook of Private International Law and Comparative Law*] 122, 135.

Act. Ordinary choice of law rules are still relevant. Some courts have applied the general choice of law rules to employment contracts and determined the applicable law by party autonomy or the closest connection doctrine in the absence of choice. In *ZHENG Baomei v. Fuzhou Yongfeng Deep Sea Fishing Ltd*,[126] the employee died in an accident during work in Sri Lanka. The employment contract included a choice of law agreement choosing Chinese law. The court applied Chinese law to the dispute based on the parties' choice. The court further concluded that, in the absence of choice, China was the country with the closest connection to the dispute because both parties were domiciled in China, the contract was concluded in China, and the ship on which the employee worked was a Chinese flag vessel.

ii. Conflicts Act – party autonomy in employment contracts

8.75 Special choice of law rules are now provided in Article 43 for foreign-related employment contracts. It may be helpful to resolve previous confusion and uncertainty but may not be effective in providing solutions to all disputes. It reads:

> An employment contract shall be governed by the law of the place where the employee works. Where the working place of the employee cannot be ascertained, the law of the principal place of business of the employer shall be applied. Labour dispatch may be governed by the law of the place where the dispatch is arranged.

8.76 This provision does not permit, prevent or restrict party autonomy. It is questionable whether the choice of law rule included in Article 43 is only a default rule applicable in the absence of choice, or it excludes parties' choice. The likely interpretation is that Article 43 excludes party autonomy in employment contracts. Article 6 of the 2012 Interpretation on Conflicts Act provides that if the law does not explicitly allow the parties to choose the applicable law, the parties' choice of law should be invalid. The explicit permission does not exist in Article 43 of the Conflicts Act concerning choice of law in employment contracts. Furthermore, Article 42 also provides the special choice of law for consumer contracts, which should have the same standing in the Conflicts Act as Article 43. Article 42 expressly states that exception to the default rule can be given upon consumers' choice. No similar wording exists in Article 43, which implies that the rule in Article 43 cannot be withdrawn by consent. If this interpretation is adopted, it will be a warning to many foreign businesses where choice of law agreements are frequently used

126 Xiamen Maritime Court, (2003) Xia Hai Fa Shang Chu Zi No 136.

in their employment contracts.[127] Exclusion of choice of law in employment contracts is not ideal in modern employment relationships. Allowing party autonomy in employment contracts but subjecting such a choice to the limitation of mandatory rules is a better approach and is supported by most Chinese commentators.[128]

iii. General rule

The new provision provides clear rules for most cross-border employment contracts, including contracts where the foreign employees are employed by Chinese enterprises, Chinese employees are employed by foreign enterprises, Chinese employees are employed by Chinese enterprises working abroad, and foreign employees are employed by foreign employers working in China. In all of these cases, the law of the place where the employee works should apply.[129] This place has the significant connection with the performance of the contract and the dispute. The place of working is easy to decide if, either according to the employment contract or in practice, the employee is stationed permanently or, in a fixed-term contract, within the fixed term, in one country. If the employee has worked in more than one place, it is suggested that the temporary time away would not affect the place of working. The law of the 'principal' place of working shall apply.[130] However, in certain circumstances, the place where the employee is working cannot be ascertained. For example, the employee is required to work in more than one country all on a temporary basis and change his station frequently; or the employee may not have a 'principal' place of working. In this circumstance, the law of the place that is the principal place of business of the employer shall be applied. **8.77**

iv. Dispatch contracts

The provision specifically provides that 'labour dispatch may be governed by the law of the place where the dispatch is arranged'. It is important to note that the provision has used the word 'may' (*ke yi*) instead of 'shall' (*ying gai*), which is used in other places. In Chinese, 'may' means an alternative option. It probably implies that for labour dispatch, the governing law may be the law of the place of working, the law of the principal place of business of the employer **8.78**

---

127 Choice of law agreements are permitted in many other countries, subject to limitations sometimes. See, e.g., Article 8(1) of the Rome I Regulation.

128 ZHAN Pengpeng, *supra* n 125 140–41.

129 *Zhengzhou City Jinshui District Jishi English Training Centre v. Christopher John Pratt,* Henan Province HPC, (2011) Yu Fa Min San Zhong Zi No 139.

130 The same interpretation is adopted for Article 8 of the Rome I Regulation. See G.J. Morse, 'Consumer Contracts, Employment Contracts and the Rome Convention' (1992) 41 ICLQ 17; Case C-29/10, *Koelzsch v. Luxembourg* [2012] QB 210; Case C-125/92, *Mulox IBC v. Geels,* [1993] ECR I-4075; T. Hartley, 'Article 5(1): employment contract—work in several countries' (1994) 19 *European Law Review* 540; C.M.V. Clarkson and J. Hill, *Conflict of Laws* (4th ed., OUP 2011) 244.

if the place of working cannot be determined, or the law of the place where dispatch is arranged. In other words, the special conflicts rule for labour dispatch is not compulsory but optional. This literal interpretation is undesirable as it causes uncertainty. What criteria should a court follow to decide whether the law of the place of working or the law of the place where dispatch is arranged should be applied? Does it depend on which country has the closer connection to the dispute in particular?

8.79 Cross-border labour dispatch is complicated. It may occur between parent company and subsidiary company, or between an employment agent and its foreign client. The company that arranges the dispatch is called the 'staffing company', the employee who is dispatched to provide labour services is called the 'employee', and the company that uses the employee's services and labour is called the 'receiving company'.[131] The staffing company and the accepting company have a contract for the dispatch arrangement. There may be two possible situations in employment contracts: (1) the employee enters into one contract with the staffing company;[132] or (2) the employee enters into two contracts with both companies.[133] Cross-border labour dispatch could cause complicated choice of law issues.

8.80 If the employee enters into a contract with the staffing company but not the receiving company, the contract is concluded in the place where dispatching is arranged but performed in the place of working. The performance of the employment contract has the closest connection with the place of working.[134] Furthermore, although the receiving company does not enter into the direct employment contract, it still has to perform certain liabilities. The receiving company needs to meet the mandatory requirements of the place of working, for example, by providing a safe working environment and working equipment. Applying the law of the place of working, as a result, will be the most relevant and appropriate law to determine the dispute in question. On the other hand, the employee enters into the employment relationship in the place where the dispatch is arranged and he may receive wages from the staffing company and participate in the pension scheme of that country. The employee and the staffing company usually have the same habitual residence, which is the place of dispatch. Subjecting the relationship to the law of the place where

---

131 Huo, *supra* n 3, 1088.

132 T. Rodgers, 'The Center Cannot Hold: Assessing the Reach of China's Labor Protections to Migrant Workers in Africa' (2012) 35 *Fordham International Law Journal* 1075, 1090.

133 Chinese law requires migrant workers to sign contracts with the direct employers, the receiving companies. See Zhonghua Renmin Gongheguo Jiuye Fa [PRC Employment Promotion Law] (2007), promulgated by the NPC Standing Committee on 30 August 2007, effective 1 Jan 2008, Art 31; Rodgers, ibid., 1090. ZHAN, *supra* n 125, 123.

134 ZHAN, *supra* n 125, 131.

the dispatch is arranged may not be unexpected for both parties. Furthermore, it is important that the applicable law to the legal relationship is determined at the time of contracting. It is possible that where the employee enters into the contract with the staffing company, the staffing company does not immediately know to where the employee should be dispatched, or after several years of performance, the staffing company has dispatched the employee to several places. In such circumstances, applying the law of the place of origin may be more appropriate for the purposes of certainty. Finally, although the place of working has close connections with the performance during dispatch and certain rules concerning health and safety must be followed, these rules are usually classified as mandatory rules and should be applied irrespective of the applicable law.

If the employee enters into contracts with both staffing and receiving companies, both companies should carry certain contractual liabilities. The staffing company, however, has relatively lighter obligations. It may only be responsible for paying social insurance or pension contributions pursuant to the scheme of the country of origin. The receiving company is responsible for paying most of the wages if the employee is providing direct services to the receiving company. However, the employee is still deemed as the employee of the staffing company, which is the parent company in most cases. The contract between the employee and the staffing company is the main contract and the contract entered into with the receiving company is the subsidiary contract.[135] Both contracts are performed in the place of working. The contract with the receiving company will not be governed by the law of the place of dispatch, which does not have substantive connections with this contract. **8.81**

As a result, applying the law of the place where dispatch is arranged is proper to decide contractual obligations arising out of contracts between the employee and the staffing company. It is inappropriate to govern contracts between the employee and the receiving company, though. Given the complexity of overseas labour dispatch, it is recommended that more detailed guidance should be provided by the SPC in interpreting the new conflicts rules in these types of special cross-border employment relationships. **8.82**

IV.3 Conclusion

There has been a recognized improvement of Chinese conflict of laws with the provision of special choice of law rules for special contracts with the inequality of bargaining power. The problem is that the current legislation is not **8.83**

135 ZHAN, *supra* n 125, 137.

sophisticated enough. Several common problems need to be addressed for the conflicts rules for both consumer and employment contracts. The first is the uncertain status of party autonomy. Neither Article 42 nor Article 43 clarifies the effect and validity of choice of law agreements. It is thus uncertain whether the choice of law clause will be invalid in all consumer contracts and employment contracts or if they are valid subject to certain conditions. Secondly, both articles apply the law of a particular country as the default applicable law to protect the weaker party. They do not adopt the concept of domestic mandatory rules. It is possible that the application of the whole set of laws of a particular country may not provide the most appropriate protection to the weaker party, who may need the further protection provided by domestic mandatory rules of a country where the weaker party has his habitual residence. Although all applicable law will be subject to the limitation of overriding mandatory rules and public policy,[136] they are defined narrowly and only apply to exceptional cases. It is doubtful whether overriding mandatory rules and public policy, alone, could provide sufficient protection to consumers and employees in all circumstances. Thirdly, both articles fail to define what consumer contracts and employment contracts mean. In commercial practice, distinguishing special contracts from ordinary contracts is crucial for the proper exercise of protection. It is concluded that the Chinese Conflicts Act has made a pronounced attempt to provide special/protective conflicts rules for consumer contracts and employment contracts, but the detailed rules are still immature.

V. LIMITATION TO THE APPLICABLE LAW: MANDATORY RULES AND PUBLIC POLICY

8.84 Mandatory rules and public policy are the general limitations to the applicable contract law applying to all types of disputes, however, applying these two rules in contract disputes may be more important and necessary. That is because many contractual relationships are governed by the law chosen by the parties. It is almost always commercial parties' intention and nature to reduce transaction costs and to avoid certain rules that they find burdensome and difficult. Contractual parties may intend to choose a law with the lowest threshold for a particular transaction, or they may choose the law of a particular country to validate an otherwise illegal contract. Applying override mandatory rules and public policy to contract disputes has particular importance in combatting the weakness of party autonomy.

136 See section V.A below.

V.1 Mandatory rules

In private international law, mandatory rules are usually of two different types, i.e., domestic mandatory rules and international mandatory rules. The former refer to rules that cannot be contracted out of by the parties' agreements. These rules have mandatory effect within the domestic legal system where they belong. They must be applied if the system of law to which the rules belong is the governing law. International mandatory rules are also called overriding mandatory rules, which could override the effect of conflicts rules. They should be applied regardless of the fact that the choice of law rules may refer to the application of a foreign substantive law.[137] Pursuant to Chinese concepts, if a dispute concerns mandatory rules, Chinese law should be applied automatically without the necessity of considering choice of law issues. **8.85**

Chinese legislation does not clearly distinguish between domestic mandatory rules and international mandatory rules. Where the term 'mandatory rules' (*qiang zhi xing gui ding)* is used in the legislation or judicial interpretation, it refers to international mandatory rules.[138] In the Chinese concept, overriding mandatory rules are unilaterally applicable law, which can be directly applied without the need to refer to conflicts rules.[139] In *ZHU v. Jin Ri*,[140] a Hong Kong company recruited partners and traders to conduct stock exchange transactions through its website. The court of the first instance held that the contract was concluded and performed in China, China had the closest connections to the dispute and Chinese law should apply. Shanghai No 1 IPC, however, on appeal, held that Article 122 of the Chinese Securities Law requires that the establishment of all securities companies be subject to the approval of the securities regulatory unit of the State Council.[141] The Court thus applied Article 122 directly to invalidate the services contract without considering conflicts rules. Article 4 of the Conflicts Act provides mandatory rules shall be directly applied to foreign-related civil relations. The Judicial Interpretation on the Conflicts Act further defines the mandatory rules as rules 'which concern the social and public interest of the People's Republic of China, the applicable of which cannot be excluded from by the parties' agreement, and which are the law and administrative regulations that are **8.86**

137 Fawcett and Carruthers, *supra* n 81, 731ff; J. Hill and A. Chong, *International Commercial Disputes* (4th ed., Hart 2010) 536–8.

138 The original Chinese text for '*Qiang zhi xing gui ding*' is 强制性规定. Conflicts Act 2010, Art 4; Interpretation on Conflicts Act, Art 10. See Ch 2, IX above.

139 Conflicts Act 2010, Art 4.

140 Shanghai No 1 IPC, (2012) Hu Yi Zhong Min Si (Shang) Zhong Zi S1217.

141 Zhonghua Renmin Gongheguo Danbao Fa [PRC Securities Law] (2005 Amendment), revised and adopted at the 18th Meeting of the Standing Committee of the 10th NPC of the PRC on 27 Oct 2005, promulgated and entered into force on 1 Jan 2006.

directly applicable to foreign-related relationship without referring to the conflicts rules'.[142] Examples include rules concerning the protection of employees or labours, food safety or public health, environment protection, foreign currency exchange control, anti-trust and anti-dumping.[143]

8.87 The definition, however, is still very general and vague. For example, one example of mandatory rules is rules that aim to protect employees. However, not all rules protecting employees are overriding mandatory rules. Some of them are simply mandatory in the domestic sense and can be replaced by foreign applicable law. It is important to distinguish overriding mandatory rules from other rules during judicial practice.

8.88 Some Chinese law does use certain terms like 'shall be governed by this'. It raises uncertainty as to whether the law is mandatory in nature. One example is the PRC Labour Contracts Act, which states that it applies to labour contracts with enterprises and other employers in China.[144] The law does not say that it excludes the effect of private international law in a cross-border case. The wording causes confusion among academic writers and practitioners. Three interpretations exist. The first holds that the PRC Labour Contracts Act is mandatory and should be applied to labour contracts concluded by employers in China to the exclusion of private international law. In other words, whenever a cross-border contract is entered into with the employer in China, the PRC Labour Contracts Act shall apply.

8.89 Most law does not state explicitly that it would override an otherwise applicable foreign law. The mandatory nature shall be judged on a case-by-case basis by considering the nature and purpose of the law, the object that it aims to achieve and the intention of the legislator. In *China Bank (HK) v. Guangxi Zhuang Autonomous Region Department of Commerce*,[145] for example, the defendant was the guarantor for the claimant to provide a loan to a company. Upon default of payment, the claimant sued the guarantor for repayment of loan and interests. The guarantee contract chose Hong Kong law as the governing law. However, pursuant to the PRC Guaranty Law,[146] state organs cannot act as guarantors.[147] Such contracts will, as a result, be invalid.[148] The court held that the above requirements and limitations to

142 Art 10.
143 Ibid.
144 Labour Contracts Act, Art 2.
145 Guangxi Zhuang Autonomous Region HPC, (2006) Gui Min Si Chu Zi No 1.
146 PRC Security Law 1995, promulgated and entered into force on 1 October 1995.
147 Art 8.
148 Judicial Interpretation on Security Law, Art 3.

foreign-related guaranty contracts were overriding mandatory rules, which were applicable irrespective of conflict of laws. The guaranty contract was invalid, despite the parties having chosen Hong Kong law. Other overriding rules include rules regulating currency exchange control.[149] In *Bank of China HK v. Hong Ye,* the parties had chosen Hong Kong law to govern their guaranty contract. Since the guarantor did not apply for the approval of administrative authority, this agreement was contrary to the judicial interpretation of the PRC Guaranty Law, which states that a guaranty contract providing guaranty to a foreign entity needs the approval of, and registration with, the competent administrative authority.[150] China is a country that imposes foreign currency exchange control. The requirement for the application to, and approval of, authorities is mandatory to enforce the exchange control, which is important to achieve the purpose of Chinese economic policy. The court thus refused to apply Hong Kong law, but applied relevant Chinese law as mandatory rules to invalidate the guaranty contract.

Because of the vagueness of the concept of mandatory rules and the competence of Chinese judges as a whole, some Chinese courts clearly show confusion and a misunderstanding of the concept of overriding mandatory rules. It is important to note that overriding mandatory rules apply exclusively to substantive domestic law, excluding conflicts rules. In *Shanghai Jumpo-Safety v. Moraglis S.A.,*[151] the Shanghai High People's Court held that for an international sale of goods contracts, the applicable law should be CISG pursuant to Article 4 of the Conflicts Act and Article 142 of the GPCL. The court treated Article 142 as an international mandatory provision. Article 142 GPCL provides if a treaty concluded, or acceded to, by China provides law different to Chinese civil laws, the treaty should be applicable. This provision is not a substantive law provision, but a specialized term dealing with the relationship between Chinese domestic law and international treaties. It does not provide substantive rights and obligations to the parties, and cannot be classified as mandatory under Article 4 of the Conflicts Act. In another case concerning non-contractual obligations, the Guangzhou Maritime Court also treated a conflicts rule as mandatory rules.[152] **8.90**

149 *Bank of China HK v. Hong Ye,* SPC, [2002] Min Si Zhong Zi No 6. See also *Bank of China HK v. Guangdong Zhanjiang No 2 Light Industry United Ltd,* Guangdong HPC, (2004) Yue Gao Fa Min Si Zhong Zi No 26 *Namtuong (Macao) Investment Ltd v. Fuoshan Xinhui,* Guangdong Fuoshan IPC, (2002) Fuo Zhong Fa Min Si Chu Zi No 50; *TAN Liyi v. Bank of Communications HK,* Guangdong HPC, (2004) Yue Gao Fa Min Si Zhong Zi No 46.

150 SPC, Judicial Interpretation of the SPC on Some Issues Regarding the Application of Guaranty Law of the People's Republic of China, adopted by the Judicial Committee of the SPC in its No.1133 Conference on 29 September 2000 and entered into force as of 13 December 2000, Fashi [2000] 44, Art 6(1).

151 Shanghai HPC, (2012) Hu Gao Min Er (Shang) Zhong Zi No 4.

152 *YANG v. ZHONG,* Guangzhou Maritime Court, (2011) Guang Hai Fa Chu Zi 373.

8.91 It is submitted that the application of mandatory rules causes many difficulties in Chinese judicial practice. It is necessary to clarify the concepts of mandatory rules and the nature of different types of mandatory rules. Very often Chinese judges fail to distinguish domestic mandatory rules and international mandatory rules and, thus, grant extended effect to the former. The confusion on the concept of mandatory rules may also lead to the excessive application of Chinese law in many circumstances, which is a traditional problem associated with Chinese judicial practice and needs to be addressed.

V.2 Public policy

8.92 Article 5 of the Conflicts Act provides that Chinese law shall apply if the application of foreign law will infringe Chinese public interests. Usually, public policy acts in a negative manner by attacking a foreign law for its offensiveness and immorality and finally renders the foreign law inapplicable. Chinese conflicts rules clarify that if public policy prevents the application of foreign law, Chinese law shall be the applicable law to fill this gap.

8.93 What is public policy? There is no clear definition. In general, public policy is close to overriding mandatory rules in that both demonstrate the important public interest and fundamental value that a society wants to protect. Traditionally, there may be no clear distinction between overriding mandatory rules and public policy. Courts may use both to justify the application of Chinese law.[153] However, there is a difference between overriding rules and public policy in that public policy usually acts in a negative way by criticizing an otherwise applicable law, while overriding mandatory rules act in a positive way by unilaterally applying to the dispute. In practice, public policy is used in exceptional cases because of the necessity to protect comity.

8.94 Where parties enter into a contract and choose the application of a foreign law, the issue of public policy may arise, if the applicable law will enforce a contract that is illegal either in the place of performance or in China as the forum state. Chinese law does not require Chinese courts to enforce overriding mandatory rules of a third country, but it does not mean China should enforce a contract which may amount to a criminal offence or other illegality in the place of performance, which is a friendly third country. Chinese courts, thus, could rely on public policy to prevent such a contract from being enforced.

8.95 In other cases, public policy may be relied on if the application of a foreign law may infringe an economic policy, affect international relationships and comity,

153 *Bank of China HK v. Hong Ye, supra* n 149.

or breach political strategy. These policies may not be legislated into any legal instruments, and there are no mandatory rules to apply. Chinese courts could rely on public policy to prevent adverse effects from applying a foreign law.

VI. CONCLUSION

The overall structure of design of choice of law in contracts in the Chinese Conflicts Act is consistent with practice in most countries with advanced conflicts systems. It is laudable that party autonomy is fully respected in China, subject to limited restrictions; it is a common practice to adopt the characteristic performance doctrine and the closest connection doctrine to determine the governing law in the absence of a choice; it is also a great improvement to provide special conflicts rules to special contracts where the weaker party needs protection; and the limitation to the governing law by mandatory rules and public policy is also a common practice worldwide. **8.96**

However, looking into details, fallacies are detectable and need to be addressed. From the perspective of legislative techniques, the conflicts rules are too simple in areas which may produce uncertainty in practice. For example, there is no clear guidance as to whether *dépeçage* is allowed in China; whether the parties are free to choose treaties ratified in China and international customs as the applicable law; how to decide which performance is characteristic to the contract; what is the relationship between the characteristic performance and the closest connection doctrines; and what are mandatory rules and public policy. Furthermore, some gaps are not due to undeveloped legislative techniques, but to the poor understanding of some concepts, such as the lack of the distinction between domestic and international mandatory rules in China. **8.97**

Hopefully, the future SPC interpretation to the Conflicts Act could provide satisfactory answers to address the above problems. However, a successful judicial interpretation must take into account not only good legislative techniques and the quality of law, but also the quality of judges. If SPC provides a catchall general principle, its application largely depends on the judges' apprehension and understanding. If the guidance is too flexible, it may be manipulated by the local judges to apply Chinese law. The judicial interpretation, thus, needs to be tailored to properly address the quality of judgments. **8.98**

It is suggested that the following points should be addressed in the future interpretation. As to party autonomy, it is necessary to provide the choice of law rules to decide the existence and validity of party autonomy. More detailed **8.99** guidance is required to determine in what specific circumstances implied choice may be proved. Furthermore, the parties are allowed to choose different laws to govern different issues of a contract, as far as these issues are naturally separable and independent to each other. Finally, the parties could choose not only state law, but also non-state law, including treaties not ratified by China and international customs as a governing law. Treaties ratified by China should be treated as part of Chinese law, the choice of which is valid as the choice of state law.

8.100 Secondly, detailed tests should be provided to determine the characteristic performance of a contract. The SPC could list a number of common contracts and provide them as the fixed place of characteristic performer. For other contracts, the SPC could provide a test combining the 'payment of money', the complexity, the categorization and the socio-economic impact test. In cases where the characteristic performance cannot be identified by any test, and where the place of the characteristic performer has only artificial and no substantive connections to the contract, the closest connection doctrine should apply.

8.101 Thirdly, the SPC should clarify the concept of 'mandatory rules' taking into account the distinction between 'domestic' and 'international' mandatory rules. More guidance is required to determine what domestic rules or regulations are internationally mandatory. This may not be easy and a comprehensive reform of substantive statutes or a judicial interpretation classifying all rules and legislation is clearly impractical.

9

CHOICE OF LAW IN TORT

I. INTRODUCTION

The choice of law process in the field of tort has been said to raise 'one of the most vexed questions in the conflict of laws'.[1] There are various types of torts, such as negligence, defamation, product liability, infringement of intellectual property rights (IPRs), anti-competition, etc, which have different characteristics and generate different policy considerations.[2] Even one type of tort may occur in various scenarios. Furthermore, tort is an unplanned incident, which largely limits the application of party autonomy, a doctrine that may provide certainty and predictability to complicated conflict of laws issues.[3] Choice of law in tort becomes more complicated since the latter half of the twentieth century, as a consequence of the rapid development of science and technology, cross-border transportation and globalization. 9.01

For all these reasons, conflict of laws in tort has been a century-long discussion and debate for private international scholars in the western industrialized countries, and the relevant legislations in those countries have been fairly 9.02

1 *Boys v. Chaplin* [1968] 2 QB 1 (C.A.) 20 per Lord Denning MR.

2 Bryan A. Garner (ed) *Black's Law Dictionary* (9th ed., West 2004) 1626.

3 Alba Mayss, *Principles of Conflict of Laws* (3rd ed., London: Cavendish, 1999) 135.

developed. However, in China cross-border tort did not attract any attention until the country adopted a policy of reform and opening up to the world in the late 1970s, and Chinese legislation in this area remained unsophisticated until 2010 when the Conflicts Act was adopted.[4]

II. HISTORY: FROM GENERAL PRINCIPLES OF CIVIL LAW TO THE CONFLICTS ACT

II.1 Tort choice of law in GPCL

9.03 Before the enactment of the Conflicts Act, the main rules on the law applicable to a tort claim were laid down by Article 146 of the GPCL which provided that:

> With regard to compensation for damages resulting from a tortious act, the *lex loci delicti* shall be applied. If both parties are nationals of the same country or domiciled in the same country, the law of their own country or of their place of domicile may also be applied.An act committed outside the People's Republic of China shall not be treated as a tortious act if under the law of the People's Republic of China it is not a tortious act.

9.04 Given the definition of the *lex loci delicti* is somewhat ambiguous, the SPC set forth in Article 187 of the Opinions on GPCL that:[5]

> The *lex loci delicti* may refer either to the law of the place where the tortious act was committed or to that of the place where the harm of the act occurred and that People's Courts may select either in case where these two laws are different.

9.05 The above articles indicate that Chinese choice of law before the Conflicts Act established a single general rule, a discretionary exception and a compulsory exception. First, the general rule applies the *lex loci delicti,* which includes either the law of the place of occurrence of the tort or that of the place of the occurrence of the results of the tort. The *lex loci delicti* is a classic tort conflict of laws doctrine and applies widely in civil law countries, including Germany and France, and some common law states, including the US and Australia, until the first half of the twentieth century.[6] The theory, dating back at least to

---

4 Zhonghua Renmin Gongheheguo Shewai Minshi Falvguanxi Shiyongfa, [PRC Act on the Laws Applicable to Foreign-related Civil Relationships 2010] ('Conflicts Act').

5 SPC, 'Opinion on GPCL', Art 187.

6 C.G.J. Morse, 'Choice of Law in Tort: A Comparative Study', (1984), 32 *American Journal of Comparative Law* 51; Dan Jerker B. Svantesson, *Private International Law and Internet* (Kluwer Law International 2007) 310.

the fourteenth century, is originally derived from the ancient Latin axiom *locus regit actum*, which means the law of the locality that regulates the thing to be done.[7] In the first half of the twentieth century, it was further endorsed by the vested rights theory.[8] The *lex loci delicti* reflects and protects the legitimate and reasonable expectations of the respective parties. When an individual conducts any activities in a country, this individual should respect the law and tradition of the country where he acts and is liable to adjust his conduct to meet the requirement of this country. Furthermore, this country should have the greatest interest in regulating activities conducted in its territory and implementing the national policy concerning individuals' health and safety.[9]

Chinese legislators believe that the adherence to this theory in general could avoid forum shopping and lead to certain, predictable and uniform results.[10] Where the wrongful act and the harm occur in different countries, the SPC empowers the courts to choose a law of either place at their discretion. Nonetheless, it should be noted that unlike the laws of many other civil law countries,[11] GPCL fails to provide any guideline for judges to follow when they have to choose between the law of the place of wrongful action and that of the place of the damage; arbitrary selections and inconsistent decisions are, therefore, almost inevitable. Indeed, judicial practice in China suggests that Chinese courts might tend to choose the law more favourable to the Chinese parties.[12] The lack of guidelines leads to too much elasticity and flexibility in the application of the *lex loci delicti*, which undermines uniformity, predictability and certainty that private international law purports to safeguard. **9.06**

The *lex loci delicti* is subject to an optional exception where the persons who inflicts the injury and the victim are nationals or domiciliaries of the same state. In such circumstances, the law of the common nationality or domicile may displace the *lex loci delicti*. The rationale for applying common personal law is based on the likelihood that, where such a law exists, it will be more **9.07**

7 Yntema, 'The Historic Bases of Private International Law', (1953) 2 *American Journal of Comparative Law* 304.

8 See generally Perry Dane, 'Vest Righted, "Vestedness" and Choice of Law', (1987) 96 *Yale Law Journal* 1191, 1194–5.

9 See *Spinozzi v. Sherator Corp*, 174 F.3d 842 (7th Cir. 1999).

10 See HUANG Jin (ed), *Guoji Sifa [Private International Law]* (2nd ed., China Law Press 2004) 318–19.

11 For instance, German courts hold that the law most favourable to the victims in this case applies; Swiss private international law provides that if the defendant's act occurs in one state and the harm occurs in another, the latter's law is applicable if the defendant could have foreseen that harm would occur in that state. See Morse, *supra* n 6, 59, 75; see also S.C. Symeonides, 'Rome II and Tort Conflicts: A Missed Opportunity', (2008) 56 *American Journal of Comparative Law* 173, 222, 189.

12 *Tokizaki v. Beijing Hongyun Tianwaitian Restaurant Co Ltd*, Beijing Second IPC, (2001) Er Zhong Min Chu Zi No.3311; *Gansu Highway Department v. Yokohama Rubber Co Ltd*, Xi'an IPC, (2003) Xi Jing Er Chu Zi No.074; Shanxi Province HPC, (2005) Shan Min San Zhong Zi No 19 (appeal withdrawal).

closely connected with the parties or its application better reflects the expectations of the parties.[13] Therefore, the laws of many countries and various international conventions have established that the law of the common personal law of the parties normally prevails over the *lex loci delicti*.[14]

9.08 However, it should be noted that unlike the laws of many countries which provide a systematic and automatic preference of the common personal law over the *lex loci delicti*, the application of the common personal law is discretionary rather than mandatory under the GPCL. The reason for the employment of the alternative reference rule is that although the common personal law is likely to be more closely connected with the tort or better reflects the legitimate expectations of both parties, it is by no means the case that common personal law must in fact be so. In certain cases, the automatic displacement of the *lex loci delicti* in favour of the common personal law is unjustified.[15] What is more, in contrast to the laws of many other countries which provide an exception in favour of the law of another country which has a manifestly closer connection with the tort, the GPCL does not include such an exception. Due to the lack of uniform standards as to when the common personal law should be applied instead of the *lex loci delicti*, the discretionary exception leads to uncertainty and may provide the Chinese courts with another ground to opt for Chinese law.

9.09 Finally, in order for an act committed outside the PRC to be actionable in the PRC, it must necessarily be regarded as a tort in accordance with the domestic Chinese law. This compulsory exception is regarded as a Chinese version of double actionability.[16] Some Chinese scholars argue that the double actionability is based on the consideration that implementing an open-door policy often involves laws of western capitalist countries which may incorporate strict liability principles in dealing with tort and which allows the definition of tort to include a very broad range of acts. The double-actionability rule would limit the adverse impact of the absolute liability doctrine in tort or of the broad coverage of tort being developed in the western legal systems.[17] Although such consideration is not irrational, the reflection of the double-actionability rule in the GPCL has invited a lot of criticism especially since the late 1990s. Many

---

13 Morse, *supra* n 6, 91.

14 See Peter Stone, *EU Private International Law* (Edward Elgar 2006) 340–42.

15 Ibid., 344–5; see also Symeonides, *supra* n 11, 195–7.

16 GPCL, Art 146(2).

17 T.P. Chen, 'Private International Law of the People's Republic of China: An Overview', (1987) 35 *American Journal of Comparative Law* 470; H.R. Zheng, 'Private International Law in the People's Republic of China: Principles and Procedures', (1987) 23 *Texas International Law Journal* 240.

Chinese scholars have questioned the merits and rationality of the incorporation of this common law rule and rejected it as an outmoded remnant of the past.

Furthermore, it is necessary to note that besides the GPCL some other Chinese laws lay down particular rules for certain torts. For example, the Maritime Law of the People's Republic of China, effective as of 1 July 1993, provides conflicts rules for maritime torts in Article 273.[18] Article 189 of the Civil Aviation Law of the People's Republic of China, adopted on 30 October 1995, contains conflicts rules for aerial torts.[19] These special choice of law rules apply together with the choice of law rules in the GPCL. **9.10**

II.2 Conflicts Act

The Chinese choice of law rules in tort before the Conflicts Act is complicated, uncertain, outdated and piecemeal. Major criticisms are the lack of guidance of how judicial discretion should be made to select between the *lex loci delicti commissi* and the *lex loci damni,* and between the *lex loci delicti* and the common personal law where the parties have the same domicile or nationality. The lack of guidance opens the door for Chinese courts to apply Chinese law in most cases, irrespective of other policies, including the protection of the victim, the application of the law that is most appropriate and the application of the law with the closest connection with the disputes. Furthermore, the double actionability approach is parochial, outdated, over-harsh to the victim and contrary to the internationalization policy. These difficulties are addressed in the Conflicts Act 2010. **9.11**

The Conflicts Act contains four articles that deal with torts: Article 44 lays down the main rules on the law applicable to a tort claim; Articles 45 and 46 provide the choice-of-law rules for two particular torts respectively, i.e., product liability and internet defamation; and Article 50 specifies the choice-of-law rules for infringement of intellectual property. Moreover, it is worth emphasizing that Article 51 in Chapter Eight states ambiguously that Article 146 of the GPCL shall be replaced by the relevant articles of the Conflicts Act.[20] **9.12**

18 Zhonghua Renmin Gongheguo Haishang Fa (1992) [PRC Maritime Law (1992)], Art 273.

19 Zhonghua Renmin Gongheguo Minyong Hangkong Fa (1996 [PRC Civil Aviation Law (1996)], Art 189.

20 The GPCL was adopted at the Fourth Session of the Sixth National People's Congress on 12 April 1986, coming into force on 1 January 1987, and is still effective at present, assuming a prominent role in the area of civil law in China. Structurally, the GPCL has devoted an entire chapter to regulating the conflict of laws (i.e., Chapter VIII, Application of Law in Foreign-related Civil Relations), where there is one article (Article 146) dealing with tort. GPCL, Art 146 (1986) (PRC).

9.13 On careful scrutiny of the above articles, one can observe that the Chinese conflicts law in respect of tort is undergoing a fundamental transformation. First, the double-actionability rule in the GPCL is abolished. Secondly, and more strikingly, the Conflicts Act introduces party autonomy to the field of torts. Thirdly, particular rules for product liability, internet defamation, and infringement of intellectual property are laid down by the Conflicts Act. Furthermore, Article 51 of the Conflicts Act indicates that among the tort choice-of-law rules that have existed in various separate laws prior to the date of commencement of the Conflicts Act, only Article 146 of the GPCL is abolished. It therefore follows that the tort choice-of-law rules included in the Maritime Law and the Civil Aviation Law remain unaffected by the new statutory code.[21] As such, this chapter is to examine the statutory reform of tort conflicts that has happened in China, and to critically analyze the problems that have surfaced in this process from the perspectives of both theory and judicial practice. In the end, it attempts to draw a conclusion and to put forward suggestions for improvement.

III. TORT CONFLICTS UNDER THE CONFLICTS ACT

9.14 Abolishing Article 146 of the GPCL, the Conflicts Act prescribes relatively elaborate conflict rules for torts which contain both rules for torts in general and particular rules for certain torts. Generally speaking, the incorporation of various new choice-of-law rules in tort by the Conflicts Act is a response to the fact that increasing numbers of foreign-related tort cases are adjudicated by the Chinese People's Courts, and the existing conflicts rules were unable to provide proper solutions.

III.1 The main rules on torts

9.15 The main choice-of-law rules on torts are provided by Article 44 of the Conflicts Act which applies to most torts. It specifies:

> The laws applicable to tort liability shall be the law of the country in which the tortious act is committed. However, where the parties concerned have their habitual residence in the same country, the tort liability shall be governed by the law of that country. If the parties choose the applicable law by agreement after the tort occurred, their agreement shall prevail.

21 Maritime Law, Art 273; Civil Aviation Law, Art 189.

Under Article 44(1) of the Conflicts Act, tort liability, as a general rule, is governed by the *lex loci delicti*; however, this rule is subject to two exceptions: (i) if both parties are habitually resident in the same country, the tort shall be governed by the law of that country; and (ii) if the parties reach agreement on the applicable law after the tort occurred, the tort is governed by the law chosen by them. Such a triple structure establishes that the Chinese legislators take pains to maintain equilibrium between the orthodox doctrine and modern ones: on the one hand, the general rule of Article 44 is nothing but a restatement of the traditional *lex loci delicti*; on the other hand, the Conflicts Act attempts to substantively reform Article 146 of the GPCL by abolishing the double-actionability rule, introducing party autonomy and choosing habitual residence to replace domicile and nationality as the connecting factor to determine the *lex personalis*. 9.16

i. Lex loci delicti

As the *lex loci delicti* remains the general rule, a question naturally arises: where a tortious act and the ensuing damage occur in different places, which one shall be determinant? Although Article 44 per se fails to provide any guiding principle, one can find the solution by virtue of Article 2(2) of the Conflicts Act. Included in Chapter One 'General Provisions', Article 2(2) provides that a foreign-related civil relationship is governed by the law with the closest connection to it, where neither this Act nor any other law designates the applicable law.[22] Thus, the law that has the closer connection with the tort, between the law of the place of conduct and that of the injury, shall be applied under such a circumstance. Compared with the GPCL which did not provide any guideline for courts to choose between the two laws, the Conflicts Act, obviously, represents an improvement. This approach also, partially, adopts the principle of the closest connection in the field of tort in Chinese law,[23] which has never appeared in previous legislation and judicial practice. Applying the law with the 'closer' connection creates a more appropriate result by locating the dispute at the centre of the state where the legal relationship concentrates. The approach could help achieving appropriateness and justice in individual cases. If this interpretation is adopted by the SPC, it demonstrates an important improvement in Chinese tort conflict of laws. 9.17

However, a related practical problem thus arises. How to decide whether the place of wrongful action or the place of harmful result has the closer 9.18

22 Conflicts Act, Art 2.

23 For the closest connection in tort, see H.C. Morris, 'The Proper Law of a Tort', (1951) 64 *Harvard Law Review* 881; A.A. Ehrenzweig, 'The Not so 'Proper' Law of a Tort', (1968) 17 *International and Comparative Law Quarterly* 1.

connection to a tort? What if, by considering all the objective connecting factors, the court concludes that a third country, in fact, has the most significant connection to the dispute? It is suggested that the general escape clause based on the most significant connection doctrine is not adopted in tort conflict of laws, and the court should not depart from the *lex loci delicti* by applying the law of another country. What the court should do is to compare the connection between the tort action and the two places of tort. But the possibility still exists that neither country has the obvious closer connection with the dispute. If this is the result, how should the court proceed?

9.19 Obviously, leaving the decision completely to the court's discretion is not positive. It has been recognized that a Chinese court has the tendency to apply Chinese law. If any of the places is in China, it may lead to the result that Chinese law will be applied. In *Min Fa Group (HK) Ltd v. Meng Gu (HK) Development Ltd*,[24] regardless of the fact that most of the parties had their domicile/habitual residence in Hong Kong and the wrongful action occurred in Hong Kong, the court applied Chinese law based on the simple fact that the alleged damage occurred in China. In this case, China's position as the more closely connected country compared to Hong Kong is not obvious. It is possible that the decision is simply based on the tendency to apply Chinese law instead of any justifiable private international law doctrines or principles.

9.20 In more complicated cases, the tortious act that gives rise to a harmful result may include several activities occurring in different countries, or one tortious act gives rise to multiple damages in different states. In the circumstances, which country's law should apply? Pursuant to Article 2 and the analysis above, the principle of the closest connection may also be used. However, in these cases, the connections may well spread into multiple countries, which make the closer connected country even more difficult to find.

9.21 Besides, there is another proposal suggesting the applicable law should be the one more favourable to the victim.[25] Instead of relying on the close connection and centre of gravity, Chinese scholars suggest a value-based approach in the Chinese Model Law, i.e., to adopt the value protecting the victim. Which law is more protective may not be hard to decide in tort. If the defendant is liable in one country but not in the other then the former is clearly more protective. The difficulty arises if the defendant is liable under both laws, but the laws provide different rules concerning remedies. For example, one law allows the recovery of psychological injury but not pain and suffering while the other

24 Liaoning High People's Court, (2012) Liao Min San Zhong Zi No 105.

25 Article 112 of the Model Law on Private International Law.

allows the recovery of pain and suffering but not psychological injury. If these issues are classified as substance subject to the applicable law, which law, thus, should govern these issues? Furthermore, this approach may be criticized as too pro-victim, which may create uncertainty for the tortfeasor. One important value of tort conflict of laws is to establish certainty for all the players, and to avoid subjecting them to unexpected risks and liabilities.

A related approach is to leave the choice to the victim. In *Gansu Highway Department v. Yokohama Rubber Co Ltd (YRC)*,[26] for example, a traffic accident occurred caused by the quality of the tyre produced by the defendant, a Japanese company. The tyre was manufactured in Japan but the accident and damage occurred in China. The victim expressly opted to use the Japanese law because of the higher level of liability imposed on the manufacturer and the better protection for the victims. The court held that, because the victims of product liability disputes were usually the weaker party, it should follow the principle of protecting the victim. The law chosen unilaterally by the victim was, thus, applied.[27] It is doubtful whether this approach is appropriate as it is, again, too pro-victim and may result in great uncertainty for the defendant. Furthermore, even if in a product liability dispute, the victim is in a weaker position, this does not necessarily lead to the conclusion that the victim of all tort disputes are in a weaker position versus the defendant. 9.22

ii. Common habitual residence

Article 44(2) of the Conflicts Act ensures that the law of the country where the parties have common habitual residence will prevail over the *lex loci delicti*. What merits particularly strong emphasis is that habitual residence has been elevated to a fundamental status by the Conflicts Act. To be more specific, habitual residence, rather than nationality, has been established as the principal connecting factor to determine *lex personalis*, family law and succession law.[28] There are three reasons for China to deviate from the orthodox position of civil law.[29] First, in a globalized world where human affairs freely cross national boundaries, the connection between a person and his nationality is not as close as it used to be. Secondly, lawsuits are usually brought where parties live, the nexus of habitual residence favours application of the *lex fori*, whereas reliance on the *lex patriae* tends to increase foreign law problems. 9.23

---

26 Shanxi Xi'an Intermediate People's Court, (2002) Xi Jing Er Chu Zi No 74; Shanxi Province HPC, (2005) Shan Min San Zhong Zi No 19 (appeal withdrawal).

27 At the time of dispute, there were no specialized conflicts rules on cross-border product liability. The court made the decision pursuant to GPCL, Art 146.

28 Zhengxin Huo, 'An Imperfect Improvement: The New Conflict of Laws Act of the People's Republic of China', (2011) 60 *International and Comparative Law Quarterly* 1065, 1077.

29 Ibid.

Thirdly, China comprises more than one jurisdiction, under the model of 'One Country, Two Systems'.[30] Within such a setting, nationality cannot determine the internal law to which a Chinese national is subject. As habitual residence enjoys such a fundamental status in the Conflicts Act, it is not surprising that the law of the country where the parties are habitually resident replaces both the *lex partriae* and the *lex domicilii*.

9.24 However, preference for the common habitual residence is not justified in some other situations.[31] For example, the parties may not have known each other before the tort happened and could not anticipate that the other party had the same habitual residence. Applying the law of the common habitual residence instead of the *lex loci delicti* in this case could infringe both parties' expectations. As a matter of fact, this is the reason why Article 146(2) of the GPCL provided that the displacement of the *lex loci delicti* in favour of the common personal law is in any case a matter of discretion, rather than mandatory. Given that Article 44 of the Conflicts Act, like Article 146 of the GPCL, does not include an escape from the common-residence rule, the automatic preference given by Article 44(2) of the Conflicts Act to the common habitual residence is problematic.

iii. Party autonomy

9.25 More strikingly, Article 44(3) of the Conflicts Act gives preference to the law chosen by the parties after the tort has occurred notwithstanding paragraphs (1) and (2).[32] The introduction of party autonomy to tort represents a paradigm shift: in tort, achieving the public interests of justice is traditionally considered to be paramount but adjusting the private interests of the parties is increasingly considered to be also important. The new rule imposes no restriction on the range of legal systems to choose from. Nor does it impose any formal requirements for such a choice to be made. It is thus suggested that the requirements for the choice in contract should be equally applicable here.[33] For example, the parties could choose the applicable law and change this choice at any time before the end of the hearing.[34] Furthermore, the Chinese courts in judicial practice also allow the parties to choose different systems of law to govern different issues in one tort action. For example, in *Seoil Shipping*

---

30 For more discussion, see Ch 13, section I below.

31 See Stone, *supra* n 14, 344–6.

32 Conflicts Act, Art 44(3).

33 See Chapter 7, Section II.

34 *Jiangsu Hong Yu Solar Energy Industry Ltd v. SHEN Zhui and FAN Jinmei*, Jiangsu High People's Court, (2011) Su Shang Wai Zhong Zi No 57.

Co Ltd v. Tangshan Ganglu Steel and Iron Ltd,[35] after disputes had arisen, the parties made agreement that the tort liability of the defendant should be determined according to Chinese law, while whether the carrier had the lien on the property was to be determined by English law. The court allowed such a choice.

Nonetheless, it does not permit a choice before tort takes place, as the parties usually do not contemplate a future tort, and allowing pre-tort agreements may lead to the socially stronger party imposing its unilateral choice on the weaker party.[36] Although this explanation is usually true, it is questionable whether the law should go forward to prevent all pre-tort choices of law, regardless of the quality and authenticity of such a choice. In certain circumstances, the pre-tort choice may exist and demonstrate the genuine intention between the parties. This will usually be the case where tort arises out of contractual relationships between parties where the parties have predicted the potential risk of tort obligations between them. It may also occur if the parties have formed a long-term relationship and wish all their legal relationships, including contractual and non-contractual, to be governed by the law of their choice. If the investigation into the parties' intentions and the circumstances show no irregularity, abuse of power, illegal evading of law or infringement of public policy, there is no reason not to give effect to such a choice. **9.26**

Last, but not least, the practicability of allowing parties to choose the applicable law after the tort has happened may be challenged. The reason is fairly self-evident: after the tort has occurred, the parties are in a position to know their rights and obligations. As reasonable persons, they naturally desire to apply the law that would lead to the result most favourable to themselves, which means that after the occurrence of the tort, each party knows the result of the application of the relevant laws and it is very difficult for the parties to reach an agreement. Such a situation is vividly represented by the following case. **9.27**

On 23 July 2011, two high-speed trains collided in the suburbs of Wenzhou, Zhejiang Province, China when at least 200 were injured and 40 were killed.[37] Among the dead, there were two US citizens (Chinese Americans) and one **9.28**

35 *Seoil Shipping Co Ltd v. Tangshan Ganglu Steel and Iron Ltd*, Tianjin High People's Court, (2012) Jin Gao Min Si Zhong Zi No 4; *ZHANG Xin v. SDT-Holding SA and others*, Tiangjin High People's Court, (2012) Jin Gao Min Si Zhong Zi No 1.

36 See Huo, *supra* n 28, 1089.

37 The investigation blamed faulty signal systems and mismanagement. See http://www.gov.cn/ldhd/2011-12/28/content_2032218.htm; http://en.wikipedia.org/wiki/Wenzhou_train_collision, last visited on 1 January 2012.

Italian citizen (a 22-year-old girl who had come to China for the first time with her boyfriend). After the accident, China's Ministry of Railways announced that the families of each victim would be compensated 915,000 yuan (around $145,000US). As regards the compensation to the foreigners who were killed in the train collision, the Ministry of Railways reiterated on various occasions that the families of the foreign victims would be compensated pursuant to the same standard under the Act on the Application of Laws on Foreign-related Civil Relationships of the PRC and the Tort Liability Act of the PRC.[38] Nevertheless, the families of the foreign victims refused to accept the solution offered by the Ministry of Railways and argued that the law of their home state, rather than Chinese law, should be applied. Up to the end of 2011, no agreement had been reported to be reached between the families of the foreign victims on the one hand, and the Ministry of Railways on the other.[39] This case graphically illuminates that after a tort happens, each party usually tries to apply the law to favour its particular condition, and it is far from easy for an agreement on the applicable law to be reached. In this sense, the feasibility and necessity of introducing party autonomy to tort in this manner is highly arguable.

III.2 Particular torts

9.29 With the increasing complexity of tortious liability, it is widely recognized that there is a need to indicate particular conflicts rules for particular types of torts in addition to providing conflicts rules for tort in general. The Conflicts Act, in response to such needs, incorporates special conflicts rules for product liability, internet defamation and IPR torts.

i. Product liability

9.30 Cross-border product liability generates complicated conflicts issues. The complexities of product manufacturing and distribution mean that potential defendants may involve multiple parties. One product liability dispute may consist of more than one tort action and wrongdoer. The international selling network also means that victims may reside all over the world. Furthermore, the potential risk of a product may cause injury or damage to a third person,

38 HUO, Z., 'Shewaiqinquan Zhizhai de Falvshiyong—yi 7.23 Yongwenxian Tebiezhongda Tielu Jiaotongshiguzhong Waijishangwangchengke de Peichang wei Shijiao' [Applicable Law to Torts – A Commentary on the Dispute Between the Dead and Injured Foreign Passengers and China's Railway Ministry in the Wenzhou Train Collision of July 23] (2011) 28 Fashang Yanjiu [*Studies in Law and Business*] 11.

39 Ibid., 12–13.

who may not be the direct buyer of the product. The victims and their habitual residence may not easily be identified by the defendants.[40]

Establishing product liability conflicts rules, thus, needs to balance a few conflicting interests. On the one hand, the interest of consumers and other individuals need to be protected. On the other hand, the reasonable expectations of the manufacturer, distributor, wholesaler and retailer also require protection. In particular, it is unjustifiable to subject a company to very tough product liability laws imposed in another country that is not its targeted market. Furthermore, domestic product liability laws vary greatly from one country to another. Some law provides excessive damages and penalties, with the purpose not of compensating the victim but punishing the wrongdoers. In some countries, there is a policy of providing a friendlier environment to encourage the growth of companies and industries, which requires the reduction of burdens and commercial risks for companies. In yet other countries, there is a policy preventing the unreasonable enrichment of a victim through tort litigation. These diversities in law and policy determine that establishing a proper conflicts rule for product liability is a huge challenge. **9.31**

In recent years, there have been more cases in China concerning the liability for the harm caused by defective products manufactured in foreign countries,[41] and Chinese courts have not adopted a consistent approach to solving the choice-of-law issues in those cases due to the lack of clear guidance from law. Therefore, it is of considerable significance for the Conflicts Act to provide specific conflict rules for product liability. **9.32**

Article 45 of the Conflicts Act provides: **9.33**

> Products liability is governed by the law of the habitual residence of the victim. Where the victim chooses the law of the place of tortfeasor's principal place of business or the law where the damage occurs, or the tortfeasor does not engage in any business activity in the victim's habitual residence, the law of the tortfeasor's principal place of business or the place where the damage occurs shall be applied.

---

40 See G. Kuhne, 'Choice of Law in Product Liability', (1972) 60 *California Law Review* 1; S.C. Symeonides, 'Choice of Law for Products Liability', (2004) 78 *Tulane Law Review* 1247; H.D. Tebbens, *International Product Liability* (Sijthoff and Noordhoff 1979); W.L.M. Reese, 'Product Liability and Choice of Law', (1972) 25 *Vanderbilt Law Review* 29; R.J. Weintraub, 'Proposed Choice-of-Law Standard for International Products Liability Disputes', (1990) 16 *Brookline Journal of International Law* 225.

41 E.g., *WU Wei-Shan v. Nan'an Min-nan Tire Wholesale Ltd*, Fujian Quanzhou IPC, (2008) Quan Min Chu Zi No 54; *Yun-Nan Hui-Chang Concrete Ltd v. Sanyi Heavy Industry Ltd (Kun-Min)*, Yunnan Kunnin IPC, (2006) Kun Min Liu Chu Zi No 126; *Gansu Highway Department supra* n 26.

9.34 Pursuant to Article 45 of the Conflicts Act, the applicable law should be ascertained in the following order of priority.[42] First, if the claimant chooses to apply the law of the principal place of the defendant or the law of the place in which the damage occurred, the choice of the plaintiff is to be respected. Secondly, if the claimant does not choose a law, or his choice is not valid, the applicable law shall be determined according to whether the defendant has engaged in soliciting activities in the country where the plaintiff is habitually resident or not. If yes, the law of the habitual residence of the plaintiff is to be applied. If not, the law of the defendant's principal place or the law of the place where the damage occurred is to be applied.

9.35 Basically, the primary objective of Article 45 is to protect the interests of the victims as they are usually the weaker party compared with the manufacturers. Therefore, claims for damages relating to product liability are generally governed by the law of the habitual residence of the victims, insomuch as they are usually familiar with this law and will normally expect to be protected under it. However, if they find that the law of the principal place of the defendant or the law of the place where the damage occurred is more favourable to the protection of their interests, they can choose to replace the law of their habitual residence. This is demonstrated in *Gansu Highway Department v. Yokohama Rubber Co Ltd (YRC)*,[43] where the victims chose not to use Chinese law, which was the law of their habitual residence and the *lex loci damni*, but opted for Japanese law, which was the law of the principal place of business of the manufacturer and the *lex loci delicti commissi*. Clearly, approving the choice would enable the victims to choose the law of relevant countries which provided them the higher level of protections. It is reasonable to expect that in almost all cases, victims will not simply apply the default law without making the choice. As a result, the defendant should always be ready to be governed by the law that may grant a higher level of protections to the victim of product liability claims.

9.36 Additionally, certainty and a reasonable balance of interests are also among the concerns of Article 45.[44] Article 45(3) ensures that if the defendant did not engage in any soliciting activities in the country where the claimant is habitually resident, the law of the principal place of the defendant or the law of the place where the damage occurred shall replace the law of the habitual residence of the victims. The reason underlying this exception is that the

42 Conflicts Act, Art 45.

43 *Gansu Highway Department supra* n 26.

44 HUANG Jin (ed), *Zhonghua Renmin Gongheguo Shewai Minshi Falvguanxi Shiyongfa:Shiyi yu Fenxi [Understanding Act on the Application of Laws over Foreign-related Civil Relationships*] (Falv Chubanshe [China Law Press], 2011) 254–6.

reasonable foreseeability of the manufacturer should be protected. If the manufacturer could not, by any means, predict that the products may be distributed in certain countries, victims in those countries should not enjoy the protection of their home states.

It is questionable whether the better law approach may be too strict for the defendant, i.e., manufacturers, distributors, retailers. Given the fact that the defendant should always be familiar with the law of its principal place of business, applying this law should not be contrary to the defendant's reasonable expectation. Furthermore, the defendant will only be subject to the law of the place of the victim's habitual residence if the defendant has targeted that country. Requiring the business to comply with the law of its targeted market should also be reasonably justifiable. Granting the victim the choice aims at preventing the business from manipulating the procedure. Either the country of origin or the country of destination, alone, would encourage the business to rush to the bottom, by either establishing its principal place of business or targeting the market in the place where the law provides lower liability to businesses for manufacturing, distributing or selling defective products. **9.37**

However, there is one question which needs to be answered, i.e., which law, between the law of the principal place of the defendant and the law of the place where the damage occurred, shall be applied, if the defendant did not engage in any soliciting activities in the country where the plaintiff is habitually resident and the plaintiff did not make a valid choice or did not make a choice at all? Regrettably, Article 45 does not contain an answer. The only solution seems to be offered by Article 2(2) of the Conflicts Act, which provides that a foreign-related civil relationship is governed by the law most connected to it in case of a legal vacuum. **9.38**

ii. Internet defamation

A special rule is also considered necessary for defamation via the internet. Defamation raises complicated issues with the use of modern communication technology. First, a defendant may upload the libellous material onto a server, which may be located in a country that has no substantive connections with either party's habitual residence. The place of the wrongful action may be arbitrary and artificial. It can be manipulated and chosen by the offender. Secondly, online material may be accessible in all countries where internet connections are available. If the victim has a reputation in most of the countries where the libel material is accessible, the place of damage may include more than one legal system, which causes difficulties in deciding the applicable law. **9.39**

9.40 The conflicts rules and substantive law on cross-border defamation also have important policy considerations. Defamation law reflects the balance of the conflicting interests: the protection of personality and the protection of the freedom of speech. The conflicts rule should be reasonably predictable to the defendant and should not subject the defendant to a system of law which imposes a greater duty on publishers and the media, the application of which may cause infringement of defendant's freedom of speech as granted by its domestic law. On the other hand, the conflicts law should also protect the victim by granting it the protection of the law within the victim's reasonable expectation. The victim should be confident that the right of his personality and good reputation will not be easily infringed by publishers in another country. Both the freedom of speech and the protection of personality are important human rights. This makes the establishment of proper conflicts rules in cross-border defamation particularly difficult.

9.41 Establishing defamation conflicts rules has encountered much difficulty in the EU, resulting in the exclusion of defamation from the scope of the harmonized choice of law rules on tort obligations.[45] Member States have different domestic interests and policy preferences and no consensus can be reached. Establishing defamation conflicts rules in individual countries may be easier, because the country only needs to consider where the line should be drawn between the protection of personality and the freedom of speech and does not need to consider compromise for other countries.

9.42 The Conflicts Act has established Chinese conflicts rules on cross-border defamation. Article 46 provides: 'Infringements of right of personality, including the right of personal name, portraiture right, privacy, and reputation, via the internet or other means, shall be governed by the law of the victim's habitual residence.'[46] Therefore, a single law will apply even if the victim's personal right is harmed in more than one jurisdiction. Taking the characteristics of internet defamation into consideration, this rule avoids the complexity of applying different laws to a single, and usually indispensible, tortious act. The victim's habitual residence is established as the connecting factor for the following reasons: first, as it is often in the place where the victim is habitually resident that his personal right is harmed most seriously, such a provision is helpful in protecting the interests of the victim; and second, it may also provide the alleged wrongdoer with a certain degree of predictability.[47]

---

45 Regulation (EC) No 864/2007 on the Law Applicable to Non-Contractual Obligations (Rome II), [2007] OJ L 199/40, Art 2(g).

46 Conflicts Act, Art 46.

47 Huang Jin (ed), *supra* n 44, 291.

However, there are a few problems with Article 46 of the Conflicts Act. First, the wording of the article indicates that it governs the infringements of rights of personality via the internet or 'other means'. No guidance is given as to the exact meaning of 'other means'. The vagueness of Article 46 as to its core concepts can lead to uncertainty and unpredictability in judicial practice.[48] Furthermore, this rule demonstrates that personality rights are valued over freedom of speech. It subjects publishers and media to the law of the victim's habitual residence, even though the country of origin may grant greater protection to the freedom of speech to publishers. The law of the victim's habitual residence also applies without the need for the publisher to target or direct the activity to that country. It is questionable whether the rule is proper in all cases. Even if the alleged libel material is not distributed in the victim's habitual residence or the material is not accessible in that country, the law of the victim's habitual residence still applies. If the publisher distributes publications based on subscription, and no one in the victim's habitual residence has subscribed, the victim's habitual residence is not the place of tort. There are no sufficient connections to apply this law to the cross-border defamation in such circumstances. 9.43

iii. Infringement of IPRs

Intellectual property rights have been acknowledged and protected in the PRC since the late 1970s when the country adopted a new policy of reform and opening up to the world. Since joining the World Trade Organization (WTO), China has further strengthened its legal framework and amended its IPR- and IPRs-related laws and regulations to comply with the WTO Agreement on Trade-Related Aspects of Intellectual Property Rights (TRIPs).[49] However, in the existing Chinese law prior to the Conflicts Act, there were no conflicts rules for IPRs which, to a considerable degree, led to the consequence that most Chinese judges and lawyers were not well aware that the disputes involving IPRs posed conflict-of-law issues. 9.44

---

48 So far, there are still various problems when Chinese courts deal with the cases involving foreign elements. The first major problem is that China is short of the rule of law in general and there is a long way to go towards accomplishing the task of building a modern legal system. In particular, judicial corruption has not been effectively checked at the present stage. The removal of Songyou HUANG, Vice President of SPC, in 2008, from office because of corruption may serve as a paradigm. Second, Chinese judges, especially in backward regions, are not well qualified and have not been ready to handle the complicated civil cases involving foreign elements. See Zhengxin Huo, *Private International Law in China* (China Law Press 2010) 107–8.

49 China amended the Patent Law in 1992 and 2000 respectively, the Copyrights Law in 2001, the Trademark Law in 1993 and 2001 respectively. Despite stronger statutory protection, China continues to be a haven for counterfeiters and pirates. According to one copyright industry association, the piracy rate remains one of the highest in the world. http://www.mac.doc.gov/China/Docs/businessguides/IntellectualPropertyRights.htm, last visited on 1 January 2011.

9.45 In order to correct the lack of understanding and to establish a complete conflict of laws regime, the Conflicts Act has devoted an entire chapter, i.e., Chapter Seven, to regulating IPRs. Article 50 provides conflicts rules for infringements of IPRs that are classified as tort. Article 50 states:

> The tort liability arising from an infringement of an intellectual property right shall be governed by the law of the country where protection is claimed; the parties concerned may also choose the *lex fori* as the governing law after the tort has happened by agreement.

9.46 Similar to the law of many other countries,[50] the Conflicts Act establishes that the *lex loci protectionis* is the general rule to govern the infringement of an IPR. This is because the law under which an alleged infringement occurs usually has a greater interest in governing the protection of intellectual property; additionally, in the majority of cases, given the territorial character of intellectual property protection, other laws can rarely govern the issue effectively. Therefore, Chinese scholars believe that Article 50 preserves the universally acknowledged principle in favour of the *lex loci protectionis* and territorial character of an IPR granted or recognized in a given country.[51]

9.47 Moreover, it is important to note that Article 50 permits the parties to an IPR tort case to choose the *lex fori* as the governing law after the tort has happened.[52] Superficially, this is the reflection of a limited party autonomy; essentially, it manifests the legislative intent to expand application of the *lex fori.*

9.48 Nevertheless, if the infringements occur in different countries and the parties do not reach agreement on applying the *lex fori*, should the court apply different laws to what is essentially a single wrong perpetrated by a single infringer? Suppose that a case concerns multiple infringements in different countries, and the claimant has brought proceedings in China, as the country of the infringer's domicile.[53] In principle, each infringement is a separate wrong, each is subject to the law of the country where each infringement

---

50 Josef Drexl (ed), *Intellectual Property Right and Private International Law: Heading for the Future* (Hart 2005) 144.

51 Huang Jin (ed), *supra* n 44, 292. *Compagnie Generaledes Etablissements Michelin v. ZHENG Rong,* Zhejiang Ningbo Intermediate People's Court, (2011) Zhe Yong Zhi Chu Zi No 181; *Schneider Electric SA v. XU Xiao-Xu,* Chongqing No 1 Intermediate People's Court, (2011) Yu Yi Zhong Fa Min Chu Zi No 385; *Honeywell International Inc v. Wenzhou Jiachen Import and Export Ltd,* Zhejiang Ningbo Intermediate People's Court, (2011) Zhe Yong Zhi Chu Zi No 415.

52 *Osram Gesellschaft mit beschrnkter Haftung v. LI Xiao-Hua,* Jiangsu Changzhou Intermediate People's Court, (2012) Chang Zhi Min Chu Zi No 31.

53 Zhonghua Renmin Gongheguo Minshi Susongfa [Civil Procedure Law] Art 22 (1991, revised in 2007).

occurs – a conclusion required by the *lex protectionis* rule. Conceptually this is unproblematic; nonetheless, it has serious practical consequences: it may be both unfair and unrealistic to expect the claimant to sue upon each and every infringement, not least because of the cost and delay involved in seeking to apply the laws of several different countries. The burden involved in applying numerous different laws falls also upon the court.[54]

iv. Unfair competition and antitrust

The Conflicts Act only introduces special conflicts rules for three particular torts, i.e., product liability, defamation, and the infringement of IPRs. There are other complicated torts with special characteristics which may cause difficulties to ordinary tort conflicts rules. However, no special conflicts rules have been introduced for them. **9.49**

One of the special torts is unfair competition. Competition law has special policy considerations, which do not exist in ordinary torts. The law aims to protect competitors, consumers and the healthy functioning of the market.[55] Competition regulation usually reflects the government control of the market and demonstrates the economic policy of a country. Where an infringement occurs, it will usually not only affect the rights and interests of one party, but also the collective interests of all potential competitors and consumers.[56] **9.50**

Applying the ordinary choice of law rules to unfair competition may cause problems.[57] First, the Conflicts Act provides that if the parties have the same habitual residence, the law of common habitual residence shall apply. It is doubtful whether this approach is appropriate for unfair competition, mainly because unfair competition affects not only the interest between the direct parties, but also the commercial ethics, economic or market order, and consumers.[58] Furthermore, party autonomy is not appropriate in competition cases. In the US, for example, if the parties have chosen the law of a particular country, which prevents one party from claiming damages for restraint of competition, the choice of law agreement will be invalid as being contrary to public policy.[59] **9.51**

---

54 Drexl, *supra* n 50, 145. For more discussion on infringement of IPRs, see Ch 12 below.

55 See Recital 21 of the Rome II Regulation.

56 CHENG Weidong, 'Lun Shewai Buzhengdang Jingzheng de Falv Shiyong [Applicable Law on Foreign-Related Unfair Competition]', (1997) 58 Fashang Yanjiu [*Study in Law and Business*] 31.

57 However, China is not the only country where no special choice of law rules are provided for unfair competition. Many other countries, such as France and Italy before the enforcement of the Rome II Regulation, applied the ordinary tort conflicts rules for unfair competition.

58 CHENG, *supra* n 56, 36–7.

59 *George Fischer Foundry v. Adolph H. Hottinger Maschinenbau*, 55 F.3d 1206, 1210 (6th Cir. 1995); *DeGaetano v. Smith Barney*, 983 F.Supp. 459, 467 (S.D.N.Y. 1997).

9.52 The general rule that allows the court to choose between the *lex loci delicti commissi* and the *lex loci damni* is another question. Although it is suggested that a Chinese court should make the choice based on the closest connection principle, most courts might consider that it is permitted to choose the law based purely on its discretion. Given the past tendency of applying Chinese law, most Chinese courts, if seized to hear a dispute, may apply Chinese law without considering policy, governmental interests or closest connections. If the Chinese judge could properly adopt the closest connection test to select between the *lex loci delicti commissi* or the *lex loci damni*, it is expected that in most cases the dispute may have the closest connection with the place where damage occurs, where the market is affected by the competition activities and where the state has the strongest interest to have its law to regulate activities that affects its market order.

9.53 If the ordinary conflicts rule is inappropriate for competition claims, how should the special conflicts rule be designed? Although the Conflicts Act does not distinguish ordinary torts and unfair competition, competition disputes are treated separately in the Model Law[60] and the Draft Chapter Nine of the Civil Code.[61] Both provide that foreign-related unfair competition claims shall be governed by the *lex loci damni*. In unfair competition, the decisive factor is that the unfair competitive behaviour has caused damage to other players in the market and has affected the order and regulation of that particular market. As a result, the market that is affected by the competition activity has the greatest interest in having its law applied.[62] This rule, however, is oversimplified in that it fails to consider certain special cases that may exist in cross-border unfair competition disputes. For example, one activity may cause damage in multiple countries. In this case, if one court takes jurisdiction over all the damages, it may have to apply different laws to damage occurring in different countries.[63] Another example is where the disputed activity only targets and affects one specific competitor; in such a case, there is no sufficient reason not to apply the ordinary tort choice of law rules.[64]

9.54 Another problem that may exist for special choice of law for unfair competition and antitrust disputes is classification. First, the concept of unfair competition differs between countries. In Germany, for example, unfair

60 Art 112.
61 Art 88.
62 CHENG, *supra* n 56, 35–6.
63 Ibid., 37.
64 See, for example, Rome II Regulation, Art 6(2).

competition involves misleading advertising, forced sales, passing off, malicious falsehood, defamation, and disclosure of trade secrets.[65] In Japan, unfair competition mainly includes disclosure and acquisition of trade secrets and activities infringing IP rights.[66] In China, unfair competition includes infringement of trade secrets, passing off and activities infringing IP rights, misleading advertising, commercial corruption, malicious falsehood and defamation.[67] English law has no specific tort on competition.[68] If specific choice of law is provided for unfair competition, it will be classified according to the *lex fori*. Under this rule, activities that are considered ordinary tort in the other country that has the closest connection may be classified as unfair competition, and vice versa. The different classification may lead to the different choice of law rules applying, then different governing law. Secondly, unfair competition, in many cases, may relate to other civil relationships, such as infringement of IP rights, defamation, and breach of contracts. How should the cause of action where unfair competition arises out of IPR infringement be classified? There are a few suggestions. The first one is to treat the IP dispute as the incidental question subject to its choice of law rules. After the incidental question is resolved, the court should consider if the infringement of IP rights also gives rise to damages in competition law.[69] The second argument is that the Chinese Conflicts Act does not provide special conflicts rules for unfair competition, but special conflicts rules for infringement of IP rights. Furthermore, most countries, including China, have well-developed IP law as a separate legal branch, while the development of unfair competition law is more immature. As a result, unfair competition law can only be treated as supplementary to other branches of laws, including IP law, contract law and defamation. Where concurrent liability exists between unfair competition and infringement of IP rights, special conflicts rules for IPR infringement should apply. Special rules for unfair competition will only be applied for activities that do not generate concurrent liabilities.[70]

65 German Act Against Unfair Competition 2010, available at http://www.wipo.int/wipolex/en/text.jsp?file_id=229699, accessed on 19 Dec 2013.

66 Japanese Unfair Competition Prevention Act (Act No 47 of 1993, amended in 1999), available at http://www.wipo.int/wipolex/en/text.jsp?file_id=128371, accessed on 19 Dec 2013.

67 Zhonghua Renmin Gongheguo Fanbuzhengdan Jingzheng Fa [PRC Law Against Unfair Competition], adopted at the third session of the Standing Committee of the Eighth NPC in 1993.

68 J.J. Fawcett and J. Carruthers, *Cheshire, North and Fawcett: Private International Law* (14th ed., OUP 2008), 809.

69 CHENG, *supra* n 56, 37.

70 For example, the 'Principles for Conflict of Laws in Intellectual Property', by the Max Planck Group on Conflict of Laws in Intellectual Property, includes unfair competition that relates to IP infringement into its scope.

v. *Environmental damage*

9.55 Environmental tort is a relatively new topic in modern society. Many countries do not have specialized conflicts rules dealing with the cross-border environment liability.[71] Environmental damage, however, has special characteristics which make special conflicts rules necessary. First, environmental damage, once it occurs, will have significant impact in the country of destination and will cause serious financial cost. The loss may include not only direct financial damage, but also fundamental clean-up costs. Secondly, the environmental policy of the country of destination is closely relevant in cross-border environmental damage, which may generate public policy consideration in private international law. Thirdly, the wrongdoer in environmental damage claims usually acquires economic and financial benefits from its harmful activities.[72]

9.56 Those special concerns in environmental damage disputes suggest that the general rule in allowing the court to choose between the *lex loci delicti commissi* or *lex loci damni*, as adopted in the Chinese Conflicts Act, is an inappropriate approach. There is a strong argument in favour of the victim in environmental damage cases. Given the serious consequences of environmental damage and the international policy of protecting the environment, a requirement that the defendant meets the high standard of environment law is proper and necessary. For example, in the Rome II Regulation, the European legislature adopts the approach of applying the law most favourable to the injured party. Article 7 provides that the injured party is entitled to choose between the *lex loci delicti commissi* and the *lex loci damni*. There is no doubt that the victim will choose the law that grants the highest standard of protection. The race-to-the-top approach is justified because 'there should be a high level of protection based on the precautionary principle and the principle that preventive action should be taken, the principle of priority for corrective action at source and the principle that the polluter pays'.[73] It is laudable to adopt the strict choice of law rule to protect the environment and to impose a high standard on any cross-border activities in terms of environmental protection.

9.57 Could the same approach be adopted in China? There is a potential possibility that Chinese legislators may hesitate to adopt the choice of law in favour of

---

71 For example, before the enforcement of the Rome II Regulation, many EU Member States, such as France, Spain and the UK did not adopt any special choice of law rules for environmental damage. See E. Guinchard and S. Lamont-Black, 'Environmental Law: The Black Sheep in Rome II's Drive for Legal Certainty?', (2009) 11 *Environment Law Review* 161, 166.

72 G. Betlem and C. Bernasconi, 'European Private International Law, the environment and the Obstacles for Public Authorities', (2006) 122 *Law Quarterly Review* 124, 141.

73 Rome II Regulation, Recital 25.

the victim and the race-to-the-top approach to impose the higher standard for environmental protection. In the Model Law of Private International Law and the Draft Chapter Nine of the Chinese Civil Code, the proposed rule is the *lex loci damni*.[74] This approach, however, is criticized for providing a less effective deterrent to polluters and may cause 'mosaic' effects if pollution causes damages in several states.[75]

Would party autonomy be suitable for environmental damage disputes? As a general rule, if both parties agree, after the dispute has arisen, that the law of a particular country should apply, there is no reason to invalidate this choice. However, given the special characteristics of environmental damage, it is suggested that certain issues need to be considered. First, environmental damage, in most cases, has much greater impact than ordinary tort and will injure more than one party. The long-term effect of certain environmental damage may affect the general public. The parties' choice of law, as a result, should not affect the rights of any third parties. Secondly, environmental damage usually generates not only civil liability, but also public law liability, such as administrative regulations and criminal law. The choice of law other than the place of damage should be subject to the mandatory rules and public policy of that country. This may require the court take a special duty to give consideration to overriding rules of the place of damage as a closely related third country.[76] **9.58**

vi. Traffic accidents

The Conflicts Act does not include special choice of law rules for traffic accidents and the general conflicts rules apply to this type of tort. Although many countries do not establish special choice of law rules for cross-border traffic accidents, the Hague Convention on the Law Applicable to Traffic Accidents 1971 has been ratified and accessed by 21 states.[77] The Convention provides special choice of law for traffic accidents. It is necessary to compare the Conflicts Act with the Hague Traffic Accidents Convention to assess whether special conflicts rules are more preferable. **9.59**

Under the Hague Convention, the default applicable law will be the law of the state where the accident occurred.[78] The main rule of applying the law of the place of accident is consistent with the practice of most countries and also to **9.60**

74 Model Law, Art 123; Chapter Nine, Art 89.

75 Betlem and Bernasconi, *supra* n 72, 144.

76 See also ibid., 146–7.

77 For the status of this Convention, see http://www.hcch.net/index_en.php?act=conventions.status&cid=81, accessed on 19 Aug 2015. Portugal signed but did not ratify the Convention.

78 Hague Convention, Art 3.

the ordinary tort choice of law in the Conflicts Act. The place is usually easy to determine and will not cause traditional uncertainty in selecting between the place of wrong and the place of damage.[79]

9.61 This rule will be exempted if only one vehicle is involved in the accident, which is registered in another country, where the law of the state of registration shall apply to the claim made by the driver or owner of the vehicle, the victim passenger whose habitual residence is not in the place of accident, or the victim outside the vehicle who has his habitual residence in the place of registration.[80] Choosing the place of registration as the connecting factor is due to two reasons. First, it is easy to determine.[81] Secondly, it usually coincides with the habitual residence of the owner, the place of business of the insurer, and possibly the law governing the insurance contract.[82] The exception aims to protect the reasonable expectation of the victims in an accident that happened in the territory of another country.

9.62 If more than one vehicle is involved in the accident, the exemption clause applies only if all vehicles have the same state of registration.[83] If one or more persons outside the vehicle or vehicles are involved and may be liable, the exemption clause applies only if all the persons have their habitual residence in the place of registration.[84] These provisions, in principle, allow the common habitual residence of the parties to apply as the exception to the main choice of law. It is consistent with Article 44 of the Conflicts Act.

9.63 Finally, the Hague Convention does not allow party autonomy, which doctrine, nevertheless, is accepted in the Conflicts Act for tort liabilities. It is suggested that most traffic accidents do not have public interest, and do not affect the interest of a third party, except in insurance. As a result, there is no strong argument against the application of party autonomy in traffic accidents, subject to the protection of the interest of insurers. It is also necessary to note

---

79 E.W. Essen, 'Explanatory Report', 3, available at www.hcch.net/upload/expl19e.pdf, accessed on 19 Dec 2013.

80 Hague Convention, Art 4(a).

81 Essen, *supra* n 79, 3.

82 Ibid., 3; European Parliament, Directorate General for Internal Policies, 'Choice of Law for Cross-Border Road Traffic Accidents', 2012, para 2.1.1.

83 Hague Convention, Art 4(b).

84 Ibid., Art 4(c).

that the Chinese Model Law[85] and the Draft Chapter Nine[86] both designated the special traffic accident choice of law rule similar to the Hague Convention.[87]

It is thus suggested that although no special choice of law rule is designed for traffic accidents, applying the ordinary choice of law may lead to very similar results as the Hague Convention on Traffic Accidents. Furthermore, since the Hague Convention was established over 40 years ago, some of the choice of law rules adopted are over-complicated and undeveloped. It was not until the early 2000s that legislators started to expand party autonomy to tort liabilities. Given the background, it is hard to say the Conflicts Act has been left behind by the Hague Convention. On the contrary, the general tort choice of law in the Conflicts Act is more straightforward and easy to apply than the Hague Convention rules. It is suggested that there is no need to introduce special choice of law rules for traffic accidents. **9.64**

IV. CONCURRENT OBLIGATIONS IN TORT AND CONTRACT

One special problem is that in practice sometimes one cause of action may give rise to both tort and contractual liabilities. For example, passengers are injured during the performance of carriage contracts; consumers are injured by products bought under a sale of goods contract; a defendant is claimed to be conducting unfair competition by breaching a restraint of trade clause or a protection of trade secrets clause; or a defendant allegedly has infringed IPRs by breaching the terms of the licensing agreement. In all the above cases, the facts generate both contractual and delictual obligations.While one fact may potentially generate several obligations, the first difficulty faced by the court is classification. Classification is determined pursuant to the *lex fori.* In some countries, contractual and tort liabilities are mutually exclusive. One cause of action can only be classified as delictual if it does not generate contractual obligations.[88] However, most countries allow the claimant to base its claim on **9.65**

85 Art 118.

86 Art 83.

87 For comments on the Draft Chapter Nine, see LI Tao, 'Shewai Gonglu Jiaotong Shigu Sunhai Peichang de Falv Shiyong Wenti Yanjiu [Study of the Law Applicable to the Foreign-Related Road Traffic Accidents]', (2004) 19 Henansheng Zhengfa Guanli Ganbu Xueyuan Xuebao [*Journal of Henan Administrative Institute of Politics and Law*] 20.

88 LIU Xiaohong, 'Lun Guojisifa zhong dui Shewai Hetong Zeren yu Qinquan Zeren Jinghe zhi Chuli [Handling the Coincidence of Contract and Tort Obligations in Private International Law]' (2001) Huadong Zhengfa Xueyuan Xuebao [*Journal of East China University of Political Science and Law*] 24, 25; CHEN Ya-qin, 'Lun Guojisifa zhong Hetong Zeren he Qinquan Zeren Jinghe Wenti de Chuli [On

either obligation of his choice.[89] Chinese practice is consistent with the majority. Since 1989, the SPC provided that if one fact might provide the claimant with two causes of actions, the claimant is free to choose the action that he believes will benefit him most.[90] This approach is confirmed in the PRC Contract Law, which provides that if the breach of contract caused personal injury or damage to property of the other party, the victim is entitled to bring either a contract or tort claim against the defendant.[91] However, it is also necessary to note that in domestic Chinese law, the claimant could not plead both contract and tort on an alternative basis.[92]

9.66 Pursuant to the PRC Contract Law, the claimant has the right to decide whether he chooses to bring a contract or a tort claim. However, there is no consensus on whether classification in private international law depends totally on the claimant's plea.[93] If the claimant demands tort damage, must the court classify the dispute as tort and apply Article 44 of the Conflicts Act or could the court still classify the dispute as contract and apply Article 42 instead? Most Chinese jurists hold the view that the court should respect the claimant's classification.[94]

9.67 The other approach awards the decision to the court and the claimant's claim is not decisive. It is argued that classification is the duty of the court and that although the claimant has the right to base his claim on one liability instead of the other, the court has the power to scrutinize the classification. The claimant's classification may be wrong, unclear or aim to evade the law. The court, in particular, has an obligation to investigate if the defendant is the weaker party. If so, the court may propose to intervene in the claimant's choice. In practice, before the enforcement of the Conflicts Act, some claimants may have wished to plead in tort in order to avoid the choice of law

---

Resolution of the Coincidence of Contractual and Tortious Liabilities in Private International Law]', (2008) 21 Yunnan Daxue Xuebao Faxueban [*Journal of Yunnan University Law Edition*] 129, 131.

89 This is the practice in Germany, the UK and the US. See P. Rogerson and J. Collier, *Collier's Conflict of Laws* (4th ed., CUP 2013) 363; LIU Xiaohong, *supra* n 88, 25; CHEN Ya-qin, *supra* n 88, 131.

90 SPC, 'Zuigao Renmin Fayuan Quanguo Yanhai Diqu Shewai, Shegang'ao Jingji Shenpan Gongzuo Zuotanhui Jiyao [Summary of the National Forum on Trying Cases of Economic Affairs in Coastal Zones Involving Foreign Elements, as well as Hong Kong and Macao]', Fa (Jing) Fa [1989] No 12.

91 Conflicts Act, Art 122. See CHEN, *supra* n 88, 131; LIU, *supra* n 88, 25.

92 *LU Hong v. United Airlines*, Shanghai Jing'an District People's Court, available at www.pkulaw.cn (accessed on 20 Dec 2013).

93 MA Haitao and LI Liang, *The Jurisprudence and Practice of International Law* (China Legal Publishing House 2006) 365.

94 CHEN, *supra* n 88, 132; DU Xinli, *Guoji Sifa Shiwu Zhongde Falv Wenti [Legal Problems in Private International Law Practice]* (CITIC Publishing House 2005) 146.

agreement in their contracts.[95] In *East International Enterpriner Pudong Custom Import and Export Ltd v. Beijing Huaxia Enterprise Transport Ltd Shanghai Branch and Others*,[96] for example, the claimant brought proceedings over fraud. The court found that the dispute was on the liability arising out of delivery of goods without an original bill of lading and decided to classify the action as contractual instead. The SPC also confirmed that classification cannot be totally decided by the claimant. In liabilities arising out of delivery of goods without an original bill of lading, the dispute should be classified as contractual.[97]

What if both parties accept one classification? If such a classification is not wrong in law, could a court change the classification? In general, if both parties agree that the dispute is contractual or tortious, and the classification is not legally wrong, the court should respect the parties' choice.[98] However, the court still has a duty to consider the interest of third parties; the protection of the general public; and public policy. If the parties' classification would help the parties evade mandatory regulations or enable the parties to gain benefits over a third party, the court still has the power to vary the classification. **9.68**

If the claimant makes a wrongful plea, pleads on both obligations, or pleads an alternative, the court will decide the classification without considering the claimant's choice. How could the classification be determined? One of the proposed principles is that of protecting the victim.[99] In *LU Hong v. United Airline*,[100] the claimant sued the defendant for personal injury suffered on board the flight and claimed damages for breach of contract and damages for psychiatric harm. The court held that the claimant had failed to make a valid classification and that the classification should be decided by the court. The court then considered the difference between contractual obligations and tort obligations. As to the former, the liability arose out of the performance of the contract and pursuant to contract terms. As to the latter, the liability depended on the damage caused by the wrongful action. Tort entitles the claimant to recover not only for damage to property but also for personal injury and psychiatric harm. The court relied on the principle to protect the victim and classified the cause of action as tort. **9.69**

95 See CHEN, *supra* n 88, 132. Party autonomy was not allowed in tort before the Conflicts Act.

96 Shanghai Maritime Court, (2003) Hu Hai Fa Shang Chu Zi No 269.

97 SPC, 'Zuigao Renmin Fayuan, "Di Er Ci Quanguo Shewai Shangshi Haishi Shenpan Gongzuo Huiyi Jiyao" [Summary of the Second National Conference on Foreign-Related Commercial and Maritime Trial]', Fa Fa [2005] No 26, Art 101.

98 See *Wanbao Group Guangzhou Feida v. American President Lines Ltd*, [2001] Min Er Zhong Zi No 166.

99 DU, *supra* n 94, 146.

100 *LU Hong*, *supra* n 92.

9.70 Applying this rule, however, is inconsistent with the general choice of law rules in both contract and tort, where the principle of victim protection is not accepted as the common principle. It is uncertain why the victim can receive better protection in concurrent liability disputes than the pure contract or tort dispute. Secondly, this rule creates complexity in that it requires the court to decide both the contractual and the delictual applicable law, and to compare which law would provide the victim with better protection. It will result in prolonged procedures and the 'better' law may not be crystal clear in many cases.

9.71 In summary, the current approach in China is a combination of the claimant's free choice and the court's scrutiny. The claimant, in general, could choose the cause of action on which to base his claim. The court will scrutinize the claimant's choice by considering the legal principle, public interest and the balance of interest between the parties. If the claimant's classification is correct in law, does not contradict public interest or does not show evasion of the law or abuse of power against the defendant, the classification should be allowed. Otherwise, the court could revise the claimant's classification in concurrent obligations. Since party autonomy is now accepted in both contract and tort in determining the applicable law, it is also possible to allow party autonomy in terms of classification in cases of concurrent liabilities. If the parties have agreed on a classification, this will also be allowed, unless the classification is wrong in law, aims to evade law or infringes public policy. When deciding classification, the court usually would take into account the better protection to the victim.

V. REMEDIES AND DAMAGES

9.72 One important difference between different domestic laws in tort is remedy and damages. Damages include issues such as what types of loss are recoverable; how losses and damages are quantified; whether the law imposes the maximum or minimum amount of damages; and whether punitive or excessive damages are allowed. In a simple traffic accident claim, for example, some countries' domestic law allows the recovery of direct pecuniary loss and the medication costs; some countries also allow the recovery of indirect financial losses, such as the loss of wages, loss of working ability, and loss of pension; and other countries even allow the compensation in terms of non-pecuniary loss, such as pain and suffering. Furthermore, the way to calculate and quantify damages also differs between countries. Especially for non-pecuniary loss, the calculation of pain and suffering and psychological loss varies hugely in different systems of law. More importantly, the availability of punitive damages or excessive damages in some countries may cause fundamental differences to the parties when applying different laws. For example, in product liability, some countries grant punitive damages to the victim; others only allow the damage to be compensatory.

The Conflicts Act does not address the applicable law governing remedies in tort obligations. It is questionable whether the law governing the substance of the dispute also governs remedies. It is international common practice that choice of law rules only apply to decide applicable law governing substantive rights and obligations of a dispute. Procedural issues are immune from the conflicts rules analysis and should be determined exclusively according to the *lex fori*. The question is whether remedies are classified as substance or procedure. **9.73**

Classification of remedies and damages is a complicated issue. Some countries treat remedies as substance, because it directly relates to the parties' rights and obligations.[101] In England, the courts traditionally treated items of damage as substance, the quantification of damage as procedure,[102] and the cap or floor of damage as procedure.[103] The Restatement of the Conflict of Laws of the US provides that the *lex causae* should govern the quantification of damage, which shows that all issues of damages are treated as substance.[104] In Australia, quantification of damages is classified as procedural.[105] In the Rome II Regulation, remedies are consistently treated as substance subject to the governing law.[106] **9.74**

No guidance can be found in the Conflicts Act, GPCL, or judicial interpretations. Some commentators argue that substantive issues should have substantial impact on the parties' rights and obligations,[107] while procedure would not largely affect parties' substantive liability. If the criterion to distinguish substance and procedure is the substantive impact on the parties' rights and **9.75**

---

101 LV Guo-Min, DAI Xia, etc., *Guojisifa Chongtufa yu Shitifa [Private International Law: Conflict of Law and Substantive Law]* (Zhongxin Chubanshe [CITIC Press], 2002), 148.

102 *Boys v. Chaplin* [1971] A.C. 356; *Edmunds v. Simmonds* [2001] 1 WLR 1003; *Roerig v. Valiant Trawlers Ltd.* [2002] 1 Lloyd's Law Rep 681; *Hulse v. Chambers* [2001] 1 WLR 2386.

103 *Harding v. Wealands,* [2006] 3 WLR 83; C. Dougherty, 'Private International Law: *Harding v Wealands*', (2007) 56 *International and Comparative Law Quarterly* 443; A. Scotts, 'Substance and Procedure and Choice of Law in Torts', (2007) *Lloyd's Maritime and Commercial Law Quarterly* 44; P. Beaumont and Z. Tang, 'Classification of Delictual Damages', (2008) 12 *Edinburgh Law Review* 131.

104 Art 15(c). See Beaumont and Tang, ibid.; S Symeonides, 'Rome II and Tort Conflicts', (2008) 56 *American Journal of Comparative Law* 1.

105 *Stevens v. Head,* (1992) 176 CLR 433; *McKain v. RW Millar,* (1991) 174 CLR 1.

106 See LV, *supra* 101, 148.

107 DU, *supra* n 94, 120.

obligations, tort damages should be classified as substance. In practice, most cross-border tort cases decided by Chinese courts are subject to Chinese law. The applicable law to remedies thus will not arise. In cases where foreign law applies, the courts rarely consider the classification of remedies, but systematically apply the applicable law to every issues of a dispute. For example, in *Gansu Highway Department v. Yokohama Rubber Co Ltd (YRC)*,[108] the victim chose to apply Japanese law to the product liability claim. The Xi'an Intermediate People's Court held that the claimant who opted to use Japanese law should also provide evidence concerning the quantification of damages under Japanese law. Qualification of damage in tort is thus classified as substance governed by the *lex causae*. However, it is hard to argue that the court, in this case, has seriously considered the classification of remedies. It is more likely that the court simply applied the governing law to any matters arising in the case.

9.76 How should remedies be classified in Chinese conflict of laws? Given the fact that there is no international consensus on the classification of remedies, Chinese law does not have a perfect model to follow. The classification of remedies in China should be determined according to the Chinese conflict of laws theories and the special needs in Chinese judicial practice. Classifying tort damages as substance may cause a few difficulties. First, Chinese courts feel more comfortable applying Chinese law. Requiring Chinese courts to apply the foreign standards in deciding quantification of damages may prove difficult. Secondly, classifying remedies as substance also requires the party to prove the foreign law, which requires extra time, effort and money. Applying Chinese standards systematically may reduce the difficulties. Thirdly, damages in foreign law may provide fundamentally different results to the parties from Chinese law. The damages awarded pursuant to foreign law may be significantly higher than in Chinese law. This could cause serious problems in China, questioning the social impact and justification of such high damages to a victim of product liability. If punitive damages in US law are awarded, it raises a complicated issue as to whether Chinese courts should then invoke a public policy defence because the damage is excessively high. Fourthly, the method of determining the amount of damages differs from country to country. Punitive damages in the US or defamation damages in England, for example, are determined by jury. China has no such jury system to determine civil remedies. Applying US and English law in determining damages may cause substantial difficulties in China. Finally, if the law classifies the head of damages as substance, while quantification of damages is procedure, a difficulty may occur if one head of damages is recognized in the *lex causae* but not

---

108 *Gansu Highway Department, supra* n 26.

in Chinese law. Applying Chinese law to quantifying this type of damages is impractical.

Classification of tort remedies is complicated and important. It is hard to claim that remedies have no substantial effect on the parties' rights and obligations, but there are also practical reasons supporting the simple *lex fori* approach. Given the pragmatism consideration and the competence of Chinese judges in dealing with complicated and innovative issues, it is suggested that classifying damages as procedure governed systematically by the Chinese law as the *lex fori* may meet the purpose. Anyway, no matter how the legislators or SPC eventually decide to classify remedies, it is certainly not appropriate to leave this issue alone. A clear guidance is necessary. **9.77**

VI. CONCLUSION

The enactment of the Conflicts Act has been observed by many Chinese scholars as a benchmark that China has systemized and modernized its conflicts rules.[109] In the field of tort, the improvement is reflected in the following two aspects: first, the Conflicts Act provides a more comprehensive choice-of-law system of tort which includes not only the main rules on torts, but also particular rules for certain specific torts. Second, strongly influenced and much inspired by modern foreign and international legislation, the Conflicts Act abolishes the out-dated rules and incorporates a number of advanced doctrines that have been developed in the western legal system. **9.78**

Nonetheless, Chinese private international law is still in a period of transition, the progress represented by the enactment of the Conflicts Act is but 'an imperfect improvement'.[110] Objectively speaking, China still has a long way to go towards establishing a modern, mature and systematic regime of private international law. Notwithstanding the significant improvement, the rules contained in the Conflicts Act are fraught with various defects. For this reason, the statutory reform of the tort conflicts in China may be considered to taking 'two steps forward, one step back'. **9.79**

109 See Weizuo Chen, 'Chinese Private International Law Statute of 28 October 2010' in Andrea Bonomi, Gian Paolo Romano (eds) 12 *Yearbook of Private International Law* (Sellier 2010) 27.

110 See Huo, *supra* n 28, 1066.

VI.1 The main rules on tort

9.80 First, as the automatic preference to the law of the common habitual residence over that of *lex loci delicti* is not always justified, it is submitted that where the parties have their habitual residence in the same country, the tort liability *may* (instead of shall) be governed by the law of that country. The principle of closest connection has been established as a supplementary rule to determine the applicable law by Article 2(2) of the Conflicts Act, judges are, therefore, entitled to choose a law between the *lex loci delicti* and the law of common habitual residence depending on the judgment of which one is more closely connected with the tort liability.

9.81 Secondly, insofar as the parties can hardly reach an agreement on the applicable law after the tort has happened, the introduction of party autonomy in such a manner is highly debatable. If the Chinese legislators do intend to introduce party autonomy into the field of tort in order to promote predictability and efficiency, they should permit the parties to choose the law governing not only their contract but also the tort liability which would not have occurred but for that contract. Many arguments can be made in support of application of the law chosen by the parties under such a circumstance. First, it is convenient to have all issues arising out of essentially a single relationship governed by one law. Secondly, and more importantly, application of the law chosen by the parties is in conformity with the parties' expectations or intentions. In the practice of international business, it is often the case that the parties agree that the law chosen by them will govern all disputes between them arising in connection with the contract. Indeed, it is unrealistic to assume that non-lawyers understand the distinction between contract and tort.[111] Even if this distinction were appreciated, it is also inconceivable that the parties would expect another law to apply to tort which arises out of the contract, and they may well have relied on the assumption that the same law covers both types of liabilities. Thirdly, application of the law chosen by the parties to the contract to tort liability can increase uniformity of decisions. The parties can choose the law governing their contract is a universally accepted principle; therefore, the same law will be applied regardless of whether an issue which arises out of a contractual relationship is characterized as one of contract or tort.

111 See F. Rose (ed), *Restitution and the Conflict of Laws* (Mansfield 1995) 124.

VI.2 Particular torts

Apart from providing conflicts rules for torts in general, the Conflicts Act lays down special conflicts rules for product liability, internet defamation, and IPR torts. Given those three categories of torts have occurred in China in quantity in recent years, most Chinese scholars argue that the enactment of the rules represents a historic progress.[112] **9.82**

Nevertheless, it should be noted that the progress made by the Conflicts Act in this field is rather limited. As examined above, there are a number of defects or problems, which need to be solved. Moreover, the Conflicts Act neglects some other important types of torts, which call for special treatment, such as unfair competition and environmental pollution, despite the scholars' calls.[113] **9.83**

Indeed, as early as in the late 1990s, when the Chinese Society of Private International Law drew up the 'Model Law of Private International Law of the People's Republic of China' which was expected to serve as a blueprint for the NPC's Standing Committee to enact the Conflicts Act, the scholars reached a consensus on the pressing need to enact particular rules for those specific categories of torts. Therefore, the Model Law contains specific choice-of-law rules not only for product liability, internet defamation and IPR torts but also for unfair competition, environmental pollution, nuclear damage and traffic accidents.[114] The judicial practice during the past decade has shown that there is a greater need to enact particular rules for those special torts; hence, the scholars advocated that the Conflicts Act should include those rules to establish a systematic and elaborate regime of tort conflicts and to meet the demands of judicial practice. Unfortunately, for reasons unknown, this suggestion was rejected by the legislators. **9.84**

VI.3 Ancillary issues

The Conflicts Act also fails to address a few important ancillary issues in tort conflict of laws. First, how should a dispute be classified if it may give rise to both tort and contract? There is no general guidance and court practice is inconsistent. It is suggested that the SPC should provide judicial interpretation permitting the party to select on which course of action it wishes to base its claim, subject to the legitimacy scrutiny of the court. Secondly, there is no **9.85**

---

112 HUANG Jin (ed), *supra* n 44, preface.

113 Chinese Society of Private International Law, 'Model Law of Private International Law of the People's Republic of China' in Petar Sarczvic and Paul Volken (eds) (2001) 3 *Yearbook of Private International Law* 349–90.

114 Model Law, Arts.121, 122, 123, 124.

consideration to the classification of remedy in tort. In past practice, a lot of Chinese courts failed to consider the difference between the substantive obligations and the remedy, and applied the governing law to both questions. This could lead to unreasonable results. For example, in order to prevent the application of the unduly high remedies of another country, the Chinese courts would apply Chinese law completely to the cross-border tort, even if China was not the country with the closest connection to the dispute. It is thus suggested that tort remedy should be classified as procedure subject to the *lex fori*, and Chinese courts should apply the most appropriate law to govern the substance although Chinese law will always apply to assess the remedy.[115]

115 Some materials in this chapter are reproduced with permission from Zhengxin Huo, 'Reshaping Private International Law in China: The Statutory Reform of Tort Conflicts', (2012) 5 *Journal of East Asia and International Law* 93; Zhengxin Huo, *supra* n 28; Zhengxin Huo, 'Choice of Law in Tort', (2009) 4 *Journal of Cambridge Studies* 82.

10

CHOICE OF LAW IN UNJUST ENRICHMENT AND *NEGOTIORUM GESTIO*

I. INTRODUCTION

10.01 The Chinese General Principles of Civil Law provide that obligations between parties include not only contract and tort, but also unjust enrichment[1] and *negotiorum gestio*.[2] A collective terminology for these other obligations is not easily applicable. The common law terminology 'restitution' could perhaps be used, but the definition of restitution is never very clear.[3] More importantly, restitution is a method of remedy, instead of a course of action.[4] This book, thus, does not provide a specific, new terminology for these non-contractual, non-delictual obligations.

10.02 Compared to contract and tort, unjust enrichment and *negotiorum gestio* generate greater difficulties in private international law. First, they both have a relatively shorter history and the legal rules and theories applicable to them

1 GPCL, Art 92.

2 Ibid., Art 93.

3 T.M. Yeo, *Choice of Law for Equitable Doctrines* (OUP 2004) 309–10.

4 A. Chong, 'Choice of Law for Unjust Enrichment/Restitution and the Rome II Regulation' (2008) 57 *International and Comparative Law Quarterly* 863, 868.

are, in many countries, immature. The uncertainty in substantive law inevitably causes difficulties in conflict of laws.[5] Secondly, although these obligations are not contractual or delictual, they usually relate to contracts, formed or unformed, or wrongs. As a result, they may be called quasi-contract, or quasi-delict, obligations, and can be treated in a similar way to contract and tort in the conflict of laws.[6] Inconsistent opinions exist as to whether, for the purpose of choice of law, non-contractual, non-delictual obligations should be classified as *sui generis* obligations, subject to different choice of law rules or if they can bc simply included in the broad classification of contract or tort depending on the characteristic of each specific case.[7] Thirdly, the domestic law of each country varies significantly in non-contractual, non-delictual obligations. The cause of action of some types of non-contractual obligations may not be recognized in some countries. For example, *negotiorum gestio* is unknown in common law.[8] Even where countries recognize both unjust enrichment and *negotiorum gestio*, the domestic rules and concepts vary largely.[9]

10.03 Given the difficulties, Chinese law provided no rules or guidance to decide choice of law in other non-contractual obligations before the Conflicts Act. Although GPCL recognizes unjust enrichment and *negotiorum gestio* as civil obligations separate from contract and tort, GPCL and its judicial interpretation do not provide any separate choice of law rules for them. In judicial practice, courts had to apply either contractual or tort choice of law to decide the applicable law for unjust enrichment and *negotiorum gestio.*[10] The Conflicts Act is the first legislation that provides clear choice of law rules. Interestingly, these two types of obligations are not treated separately, but are subject to the same choice of law rule. This chapter examines the development and the current Chinese choice of law rules for cross-border unjust enrichment and *negotiorum gestio.*

---

5 J.J. Fawcett and J. Carruthers, *Cheshire, North and Fawcett: Private International Law* (14th ed., OUP 2008) 818; Yeo, *supra* n 3, 309.

6 E.g., (EC) No 864/2007 on the law applicable to non-contractual obligations (Rome II), [2007] OJ L 199/40, Art 10; *Cheshire, North and Fawcett,* ibid., 820.

7 P.S. Atiyah, *Essays on Contract* (Clarendon Press, Oxford 1990) 48–56; S. Hedley, *Restitution: Its Division and Ordering* (Sweet & Maxwell, London 2001) 231–2. For criticism, see Chong, *supra* n 4, 571.

8 J. Hill and A. Chong, *International Commercial Disputes* (4th ed., Hart 2010) 617. *Foskett v. Mckeown* [2001] 1 AC 103, 118–9; *Falcke v. Scottish Imperial Insurance,* (1886) 34 Ch D 234; *Re Cleadon Trust,* [1939] Ch 286; *Leigh v. Dickeson,* (1884) 15 QBD 60. Cf. D Sheehan, '*Negotiorum Gestio*: A Civilian Concept in the Common Law?' (2006) 55 *International and Comparative Law Quarterly* 253.

9 *Cheshire, North and Fawcett, supra* n 5, 820; HUO Zhengxin, 'Wuyinguanli de Falvshiyong Guize Tanjiu [Probe into the Application of Law of Negotiorum Gestio]' (2005) 17 Anhui Jinguan Zhiye Xueyuan Xuebao [*Journal of Anhui Vocational College of Police Officers*] 1.

10 For more discussion, see part III below.

II. CONCEPT AND CLASSIFICATION

II.1 Concept

The PRC Economic Contract Law 1982 requires a party to return property obtained under an invalid contract.[11] This rule forms the precedent of unjust enrichment. Unjust enrichment, as an independent obligation, is defined in the GPCL as profits 'acquired improperly and without a lawful basis, resulting in another person's loss'.[12] As the only legislative provision on unjust enrichment, it is very simple but ambiguous. Unjust enrichment is an uncertain concept, not only in China, but also in other countries. In most countries with a relatively long history and mature rules on unjust enrichment, greater diversity exists in domestic concepts. It is thus hard to provide a uniform concept that might be acceptable internationally. It is only possible to summarize the basic features of unjust enrichment, namely there must be enrichment of one party, impoverishment to the other, and that the enrichment either has no lawful basis or is unjustifiable. **10.04**

Negotiorum gestio is defined as 'a person acts as manager or provides services in order to protect another person's interests when he is not legally or contractually obligated to do so'.[13] It is argued by some commentators that *negotiorum gestio* may be viewed as one type of unjust enrichment or be based on unjust enrichment. Unjust enrichment may be acquired in either a positive or negative way. If a person acquires benefits while another provides services without a contract or other liabilities, the service provider suffers loss and may claim restitution based on unjust enrichment or *negotiorum gestio*.[14] However, the common view recognizes *negotiorum gestio* as a restitutionary obligation, which is separate and independent from unjust enrichment.[15] **10.05**

As well as unjust enrichment and *negotiorum gestio,* the European legislators also classify *culpa in contrahendo* as a third type of non-contractual obligation. It covers pre-contractual obligations, such as misrepresentation, non-disclosure and breakdown of contractual negotiations.[16] *Culpa in contrahendo* is different from unjust enrichment and *negotiorum gestio* in that it is not **10.06**

11 Art 16.
12 GPCL, Art 92.
13 GPCL, Art 93.
14 HUO, *supra* n 9, 2.
15 G. Panagopoulos, *Restitution in Private International Law* (Hart 2000) 103–5; *Cheshire, North and Fawcett, supra* n 5, 83–12.
16 Hill and Chong, *supra* n 8, 618.

restitutionary but pre-contractual.[17] Chinese law classifies misrepresentation and non-disclosure as contract matters. Article 42 of the PRC Contract Law provides that the party should be liable for damages if he has not disclosed material facts relating to the contract, has made misrepresentations, or behaved in a manner contrary to the principles of good faith. Thus, *culpa in contrahendo* is classified as contractual obligations in China, not a separate obligation.

II.2 Classification/characterization

10.07 The second difficulty is classification, namely whether unjust enrichment and *negotiorum gestio* should be classified as a *sui generis* category in private international law, or no separate classification is necessary while these obligations shall be classified into the existing categories of contract, tort or property based on the specific characteristics of each case.

10.08 Classification is usually determined by the *lex fori*.[18] However, the *lex fori* in classification does not mean the rigid domestic definition. The court may usually still consider the general principles and international common practice. Especially in cases where the domestic law of the court does not recognize a legal concept, the court has to consider the law of other countries and make classification pursuant to the law that has the closest legal principle as domestic law.[19] The adoption of the liberal *lex fori* increases flexibility of classification and may extend the scope of unjust enrichment and *negotiorum gestio* compared to domestic law.

10.09 The classification of unjust enrichment and *negotiorum gestio* was not clear before the Conflicts Act. The GPCL does not provide clear guidance but it does include unjust enrichment and *negotiorum gestio* in the same section as contracts. It may be interpreted that GPCL classifies unjust enrichment and *negotiorum gestio* as quasi-contract obligations, especially given the fact that most Chinese courts have used the contractual choice of law to determine the governing law for these two non-contractual obligations.[20] A few countries have adopted the same approach by classifying unjust enrichment and *negotiorum gestio* as either quasi-contract[21] or quasi-delict obligations.

17 *Cheshire, North and Fawcett, supra* n 5, 818 and 832.

18 R. Leslie, 'Unjustified Enrichment in the Conflict of Laws' (1998) 2 *Edinburgh Law Review* 233, 235.

19 HUO Zhengxin, *Guoji Sifa zhong de Budang Deli [Unjust Enrichment in Private International Law]*, PhD thesis submitted to the Wuhan University, China, 2005, 149.

20 See Part III below.

21 For *negotiorum gestio,* see JIN Peng-nian, ZHANG Xiao-ke, 'Wuyinguanli Falvshiyong Xintan [New Viewpoints of Application of Negotiorum Gestio in Conflict of Law]', (2001) 31.2 Zhejiangdaxue Xuebao: Renwen Sheke Ban [*Journal of Zhejiang University (Humanities and Social Sciences)*] 104, 105.

The argument supporting no independent classification for unjust enrichment and *negotiorum gestio* has its own advantages. Unjust enrichment, for example, may relate to contract, tort, or property.[22] For example, if one party claims for damages arising out of the breach of a contract and it eventually turns out that the contract is void, would the cause of action be classified as contract or unjust enrichment if the other party acquires benefits from the invalid contract? It is the same for *negotiorum gestio* and some commentators suggest *negotiorum gestio* should be classified into the same category of the pre-existing relationship.[23] Even if unjust enrichment and *negotiorum gestio* are classified as *sui generis* obligations independent from contract, tort or property, their close connections to the pre-existing obligation may make it inevitable for the same governing law to apply to both the pre-existing relationship and the related other obligations. However, this argument fails to recognize the complexity and variety of unjust enrichment and *negotiorum gestio*. Many cases indeed have connections with a pre-existing relationship, but cases also exist where there was no pre-existing relationship between the parties. **10.10**

II.3 Chinese law and practice

Recognizing the above difficulties, the Chinese Conflicts Act classifies unjust enrichment and *negotiorum gestio* as a *sui generis* cause of action. Although they have close connections with contract or tort, they are not treated as quasi-contractual or quasi-delictual obligations. In other words, it is possible for one fact to give rise to concurrent liabilities, i.e., contract or tort liability on the one hand, and unjust enrichment and *negotiorum gestio* on the other. **10.11**

III. CHOICE OF LAW IN UNJUST ENRICHMENT AND *NEGOTIORUM GESTIO* – THEORY

III.1 *Lex fori*

Although applying the *lex fori* to the merit of a claim as a general rule has been abandoned by most countries, this doctrine has remained one of the main conflicts rule for unjust enrichment for a long time.[24] This is mainly because **10.12**

22 Chong, *supra* n 4, 864–8; Hill and Chong, *supra* n 8, 617.
23 Panagopoulos, *supra* n 15, 105.
24 HUO, *supra* n 19, 175.

unjust enrichment was, in history, treated as a form of remedy instead of an independent cause of action.[25] Furthermore, unjust enrichment originates from the concept of 'justice' and, as a result, is regarded as concerning public policy.[26]

10.13 Unlike unjust enrichment, far fewer commentators support applying *lex fori* to *negotiorum gestio.*[27] This is mainly because those common law countries that treat restitution as a form of remedy do not recognize *negotiorum gestio.* Also *negotiorum gestio* has much weaker impact on 'justice' and social order than unjust enrichment.[28]

10.14 The *lex fori* approach, despite having some support in history, has been abolished in most countries in their dealings with cross-border unjust enrichment and *negotiorum gestio.* Nowadays, unjust enrichment and *negotiorum gestio* have developed into independent branches of law and do not represent more public policy consideration than other obligations.[29]

III.2 *Lex personalis*

i. Common lex personalis

10.15 *Lex personalis* suggests that the law applicable to unjust enrichment and *negotiorum gestio* shall be the personal law of the parties. In both unjust enrichment and *negotiorum gestio*, applying the common *lex personalis* of the parties receives much support. Comparatively, more controversy exists if the parties have no common *lex personalis.*

10.16 Regardless of the place where the obligation occurred, if the parties have the same personal law, this law will be the one that is most predictable to the parties, and the parties' expectation will prevail.[30] Furthermore, if the parties have their domicile or habitual residence in the same country and the

25 J. Bird, 'Choice of Law', in F. Rose (ed), *Restitution and the Conflict of Laws* (1995), 103–4; Leslie, *supra* n 18, 235.

26 T.W. Bennett, 'Choice of Law Rules in Claims of Unjust Enrichment' (1990) 39 ICLQ 136, 151; HUO, *supra* n 19, 175–6.

27 ZHANG Jian-liang, HUO Zheng-xin, 'Wuyinguanli de Falvshiyong de Lifasheji yu Lunzheng [Conflict Rules for Negotiorum Gestio: Designing and Demonstrations]', (2005) 58(5) Wuhan Daxue Xuebao (Zhexue Shehuikexue Ban) [*Wuhan University Journal (Philosophy and Social Sciences)*] 607, 610. This approach is used in the Republic of Yemen, see JIN, 'New Viewpoints', *supra* n 21, 105.

28 ZHANG, HUO, ibid., 610.

29 Bennett, *supra* n 26, 151; HUO, *supra* n 19, 176.

30 JIANG Fen, JIN Peng-Nian, 'Lun Shurenfa zai Budangdeli Chongtuguifan zhong de Yingyong [Application of Lex Personalis in Conflict Rules of Unjust Enrichment]', (2011) 29 Hebei Faxue [*Hebei Law Science*] 64, 65; ZHANG, HUO, *supra* n 27, 609. This approach is also adopted in the Rome II Regulation, Arts 10 and 11.

enrichment occurs in another country, the country of the common domicile or habitual residence may have the closer connection to the parties' relationship than the country where enrichment occurs.[31]

ii. Unjust enrichment

If the parties have no common *lex personalis,* it is much more difficult to determine which party's personal law should govern the relationship between them. In terms of unjust enrichment, the most supported approach is applying the *lex personalis* of the debtor. This may be justified because sometimes the debtor does not voluntarily pursue a profit but becomes a debtor of unjust enrichment involuntarily.[32] Applying the *lex personalis* of the debtor could improve the certainty and reduce the risk of cross-border activities. This approach, however, is criticized for being biased and one-sided. Most cases do not show any necessity for protecting the defendant. It is equally important to provide predictability for the claimant. The situation of an involuntary debtor will only occur in exceptional cases and will not be enough to justify the *lex personalis* of the debtor as a general rule.[33] This rule also cannot work if there is more than one debtor residing in different countries.[34] **10.17**

iii. Negotiorum gestio

In terms of *negotiorum gestio,* one interesting view is that *negotiorum gestio* includes the obligation owed by the gestor to the principal and the obligation owed by the principal to the gestor. As a result, the former obligation should be governed by the personal law of the gestor and the latter by the personal law of the principal.[35] The problem is that this approach will lead to *dépaçage* and the splitting of *negotiorum gestio* into obligations owed by either party could lead to incoherence and conflict. Obligations of the principal and gestor co-exist and form the *negotiorum gestio* claim. Applying *dépaçage* in *negotiorum gestio* could not work in practice.[36] **10.18**

Besides, there are also arguments supporting the application of the personal law of the principal. The principal does not intentionally impose on himself any liability. The liability imposed thus should not be more than what is imposed by the principal's law. This approach, however, is criticized for undermining the expectation of the gestor. When the gestor manages another **10.19**

31 Bennett, *supra* n 26, 166.
32 Ibid., 150; JIANG Fen, JIN Peng-Nian, *supra* n 30, 65; HUO, *supra* n 19, 177.
33 Bennett, ibid., 150–51.
34 Ibid., 151; JIANG, JIN, *supra* n 30, 67.
35 ZHANG, HUO, *supra* n 27, 609.
36 Ibid.

person's affair and provides the principal benefits, the gestor should reasonably expect to have its cost recovered pursuant to his personal law. As a result, applying the *lex personalis* of either party cannot achieve the balance of interest, fairness and justice.

III.3 *Lex loci*

i. Unjust enrichment

10.20 *Lex loci* is a traditional conflicts rule adopted to determine the governing law of unjust enrichment and *negotiorum gestio.* It connects the claim with the place where the fact that gives rise to the claim occurs. However, in unjust enrichment, these actions include the action that gives rise to enrichment, loss to the claimant and the enrichment to the defendant. All may occur in different places.[37]

10.21 If one compares unjust enrichment with tort, one may claim that applying the law of the place of action that gives rise to enrichment is similar to the *lex loci delicti commissi.* However, the similarity is rather superficial. The key elements of unjust enrichment do not include a particular activity of the defendant. Instead, they constitute the loss to one party and the benefit to the other. In other words, unjust enrichment is not built on the blameworthiness of an 'action', but on the justice of the 'result'. It means that the focus should be rather on the loss and benefit, instead of action.[38] Furthermore, it is usually hard to ascertain the activity that gives rise to unjust enrichment. For example, in a very typical and simple unjust enrichment case, A paid B money to purchase products, but it later turned out that the contract was void *ab initio.* What activities give rise to unjust enrichment, A's action to pay or the action that makes the contract void? The former is not the fundamental reason why unjust enrichment occurred. Although the place usually has close connections with enrichment, it is wrong to presume that unjust enrichment arises out of pure wrongful payment. The key event that causes unjust enrichment is the underlying transaction.[39] The payment is a consequential event caused by the act that gives rise to unjust enrichment.[40] If the place of action is the latter activity, one needs to further consider the reason why a contract is void; if the

---

37 HUO, *supra* n 19, 179.

38 Ibid., 180.

39 Bennett, *supra* n 26, 148.

40 Ibid.

reason causing invalidity is not a particular 'activity' or 'omission' or the reason constitutes a number of unseverable activities, locating such a reason is not easy.[41]

Applying the law of the place of loss may also be justified by comparing unjust enrichment and tort, where *lex loci damni* applies as the general rule in many countries.[42] However, it is important to recognize the substantial difference between unjust enrichment and tort. Unjust enrichment does not aim to compensate the loss of the claimant, but aims to prevent enrichment or to return benefits obtained without legal justification.[43] **10.22**

Therefore, the third approach, applying the law of the place where enrichment occurs, receives the most support.[44] The spirit of unjust enrichment is to deprive the defendant of the benefit acquired without justification. The place where the enrichment occurs has the closest connection with the essential issue of unjust enrichment. This place will also usually be the place of enforcement where the return or restitution should be ordered.[45] The problem is that the place of enrichment may be hard to determine. In certain circumstances, several places of enrichment may occur: for example, the defendant received the wrongful payment in his account located in country A and invested the money in country B; or country A is the place where the benefit is acquired but country B is the final destination of the enrichment. **10.23**

ii. Negotiorum gestio

In *negotiorum gestio,* a lot of support is given to the law of the place where the gestor acted.[46] This is mainly because liabilities of *negotiorum gestio* are caused by the unauthorized management act and the place where the management activity occurred usually has a close connection with the dispute.[47] Furthermore, this approach could achieve the balance of interest between the principal and the gestor.[48] This approach, however, is criticized because of the possibility it can lead to arbitrary results.[49] *Negotiorum gestio* in modern society shows a variety of different forms caused by the complexity of modern transactions. **10.24**

---

41 Ibid. (an example of the former is incapacity of a party; an example of the latter is a series of negotiations in breach of law); HUO, *supra* n 19, 180.

42 S. Cohen, *Quasi Contract and the Conflict of Laws,* (1956) 31 *Law American Bar Bull* 71.

43 XIAO Yong-Ping, HUO Zheng-Xin, 'Budangdeli de Falvshiyong Guize [Choice of Law Rules in Unjust Enrichment]', (2004) 26 Faxue Yanjiu [*Legal Study*] 128, 130.

44 Bennett, *supra* n 26, 148.

45 HUO, *supra* n 19, 181.

46 Panagopoulos, *supra* n 15, 105.

47 ZHANG, HUO, *supra* n 27, 609.

48 JIN, ZHANG, *supra* n 21, 105.

49 Panagopoulos, *supra* n 15, 105; ZHANG, HUO, *supra* n 27, 609.

In certain cases, there are pre-existing relationships or putative contracts between the parties, which may challenge the place of act as the place with the most significant connections.[50] Furthermore, although the place where the gestor acted is usually easy to determine, difficulties may exist in certain circumstances, for example, the gestor acting in transit or the gestor managing the affirmed at a distance.[51]

III.4 Law of relationship

10.25 A large number of unjust enrichment claims arise out of pre-existing relationships between the parties, for example, payment or property received under an invalid contract; overpayment of a contract; contribution between joint tortfeasors; and constructive trust.[52] Although *negotiorum gestio* usually has no pre-arrangement, an underlying relationship may exist in certain circumstances, for example, the gestor acts exceeding the authority in a contract or the gestor acts after the contract has terminated.[53] In these cases, the pre-existing relationship has very close connections with the other non-contractual obligation claims.[54] Applying the governing law of the relationship to unjust enrichment or *negotiorum gestio* could help to reduce inconsistent results and remove classification difficulties.[55]

10.26 Arguments against this approach suggest that it may complicate the choice of law question by requiring the examination of the law governing the related relationship, such as contract and tort, the applicable law to which is not straightforward.[56] Furthermore, as *dépaçage* is accepted by many countries, if the underlying contract is subject to few governing laws, applying the law of relationship is practically impossible for related unjust enrichment or *negotiorum gestio*.[57] The final criticism is that applying the law of relationship focuses on the importance of the underlying relationship that has connections with unjust enrichment or *negotiorum gestio* instead of such obligations per se.[58]

---

50 ZHANG, HUO, *supra* n 27, 609.
51 Ibid.
52 Bennett, *supra* n 26, 156–7.
53 Ibid.,166.
54 Ibid.
55 HUO, *supra* n 19, 184–187; JIN Peng-Nian, 'Shewai Minshi Guanxi Falv Shiyongfa zhong de Budangdeli Guize [Unjust Enrichment in Applicable Law in Foreign-Related Civil Relationship Act]', (2012) 2 Zhongguo Faxue [*China Legal Science*] 170, 171–4; ZHANG, HUO, *supra* n 27, 609.
56 Leslie, *supra* n 18, 240.
57 Ibid.
58 Ibid.

III.5 Party autonomy

Whether party autonomy could be used in unjust enrichment and *negotiorum gestio* generates debate. Traditionally, the argument against party autonomy in unjust enrichment and *negotiorum gestio* is that these non-contractual obligations are not obligations freely presumed by the parties but obligations imposed by law.[59] This argument, however, has softened with the recent development of private international law in China and worldwide. It is accepted that if the parties have freely made a choice of law to determine their private relationship, and this choice does not infringe interests of third parties or general public or does not contradict public policy of a country, this choice should be recognized by law. Party autonomy has been accepted in non-contractual obligations in both China[60] and EU.[61] **10.27**

Applying party autonomy in unjust enrichment and *negotiorum gestio* may encounter problems of interpretation. If the unjust enrichment arises out of a contractual relationship and there is a choice of law agreement in the contract, could this choice apply to unjust enrichment claims? To answer the question, it is necessary to distinguish party autonomy and the law of relationship.[62] The law of relationship doctrine will apply the chosen law to contract-related unjust enrichment, not because it allows the parties to choose the governing law for unjust enrichment, but because unjust enrichment has the closest connection with the pre-existing relationship, which justifies application of the same law. Party autonomy, instead, allows the parties the freedom of choice of the governing law to unjust enrichment. Applying party autonomy, thus, requires the examination of the scope of the choice of law agreement, i.e., whether the party intended to choose the law to govern the contract only or relationships arising out of, or in relation to, the contract. **10.28**

III.6 Law of the closest connection

A more flexible approach is to apply the law of the closest connection to the claim. The greatest benefit of this approach is the avoidance of rigid choice of law rules by relying on one or few connecting factors. The court will decide the applicable law depending on the specific characteristics of each case.[63] Because various forms of unjust enrichment exist with different natures, applying the **10.29**

59 Chong, *supra* n 4, 874; J. Morris, 'The Choice of Law Clause in Statutes' (1946) 62 LQR 170, 183; JIN, ZHANG, *supra* n 21, 105.

60 Conflicts Act, Art 44 (tort) and 47 (unjust enrichment and *negotiorum gestio*).

61 See Rome I Regulation, Art 14. See also comments in Chong, *supra* n 4, 875–6.

62 See Section III.4. above.

63 Panagopoulos, *supra* n 15, 115–20.

closest connection principle instead of rigid choice of law rules will lead to the application of the most appropriate law in different claims.

10.30 This approach is adopted in the Second Restatement Conflict of Laws of USA.[64] The court needs to consider and weigh all the following factors: the common place of the parties if it has connections with unjust enrichment; the place of enrichment; the place of action giving rise to the unjust enrichment; the parties' domicile, habitual residence, nationality, place of establishment and place of business; and the place where the subject matter of unjust enrichment is located. Similar factors may be considered to decide the law that has the closest connection to *negotiorum gestio*. The disadvantage of this approach is the lack of certainty and predictability.

IV. CHINESE LAW AND PRACTICE

IV.1 Chinese law before the Conflicts Act

10.31 In China's legislation history, choice of law in other non-contractual obligations was established as early as 1918. The Applicable Law Regulations included a very simple choice of law rule, which provided that unjust enrichment and *negotiorum gestio* should be governed by the law of the place where the matter occurred.[65] This law was abolished following the revolution and, after that, there was no choice of law legislation on other non-contractual obligations until the Conflicts Act.

10.32 In 1986, the GPCL recognized unjust enrichment and *negotiorum gestio* as two causes of action for civil obligations.[66] It, however, does not include any choice of law provisions for such non-contractual obligations. In practice, disputes on unjust enrichment and *negotiorum gestio* were rare, mainly due to a lack of sufficient knowledge in this area and the ambiguous substantive law. In cross-border disputes, only a few unjust enrichment cases could be found and no cases on *negotiorum gestio* were reported. When Chinese courts were required to determine foreign-related unjust enrichment claims, they usually decided the applicable law pursuant to choice of law for contractual obligations under the GPCL. Parties were allowed to choose the applicable law to their unjust enrichment disputes.[67] If the parties failed to make a valid choice,

64 Article 221.

65 Applicable Law Regulation 1918, Art 24.

66 GPCL, Arts 92, 93.

67 *Guizhou Wengfu Phosphate Rock Export and Import v. Sino Transpac Corporation*, Guangdong HPC, (2004) Yue Gao Fa Min Si Zhong Zi No 53; *DENG Xinhui v. Suzhou Xiangtong Car-Rental*, Jiangsu Suzhou IPC,

the law applicable would be determined according to the closest connection doctrine.[68] It is necessary to note that Article 145 of GPCL does not expressly apply to unjust enrichment but only to contractual disputes. It is likely that the interpretation of 'contractual disputes' is broad enough to cover all disputes relating to, or arising out of, contracts. If this interpretation is correct, the approach, nevertheless, could not apply if unjust enrichment does not arise out of contract. However, due to the lack of cases, such a particular problem did not appear in judicial practice. This situation provides the false impression that the lack of choice of law rules in other non-contractual obligations does not cause difficulty in practice.

The absence of relevant law is realized by Chinese jurists and legislators. The Model Law on Private International Law includes a provision suggesting that the law of the place where unjust enrichment occurred should apply or where unjust enrichment arises out of a pre-existing relationship the law governing that relationship should apply.[69] It is justified by the impact of unjust enrichment on the public interest of the place where the debt occurred. Furthermore, certainty can be achieved by linking unjust enrichment with the pre-existing relationship,[70] although this is criticized by commentators for being too flexible and uncertain.[71] The Model Law, however, provides a simple rule for *negotiorum gestio*, which suggests that law of the place where the action occurred should govern.[72] In general, the gestor's conduct could benefit the principal and should be encouraged and protected. Applying the law of the place of act could protect the gestor's reasonable expectation and make the legal consequence of the act predictable.[73] **10.33**

In 2002, the Draft Chapter Nine proposed a rather simple choice of law for unjust enrichment. Article 55 of the Draft followed the Model Law in choice of law for *negotiorum gestio*, but provides that unjust enrichment should be governed by the law of the place where the unjust enrichment occurred. This Draft simplified the proposal of the Model Law for unjust enrichment. It accepted the rigid *lex loci* rule, the weakness of which has been widely **10.34**

(2004) Su Zhong Min San Chu Zi No 92; *CHF Enterprise Ltd v. Wujiang Huangshi Art and Costume Ltd*, Jiangsu Suzhou IPC, (2008) Su Zhong Min San Chu Zi No 21; *WANG Huayin v. Dan Yang Hong De Optics Ltd*, Jiangsu Zhenjiang IPC, (2007) Zhen Min San Chu Zi No 50; *Fastwell Industry Co Ltd v. Jiangsu Zhangyu Enterprise Group Ltd*, Jiangsu Suzhou IPC, (2008) Su Zhong Min San Chu Zi No 59.

68 *He x Electric (Shenzhen) Ltd v. Neng x Electric Ltd*, Guangdong Shenzhen IPC, (2010) Shen Zhong Fa Min Si Zhong Zi No 164.

69 Model Law, Art 129.

70 Ibid., explanation to Art 129.

71 HUO, *supra* n 19, 223–4.

72 Model Law, Art 130.

73 Ibid., explanation to Art 130.

recognized by modern jurists. This rule has been abandoned in many other countries. The relevant Draft, as a result, was remarked as being 'disappointing' and was never adopted in the Conflicts Act.[74]

IV.2 Applicable law under the Conflicts Act

10.35 The Conflicts Act, for the first time, provides a special choice of law rule for unjust enrichment and *negotiorum gestrio*. Article 47 provides:

> Unjust enrichment or *negotiorum gestio* shall be governed by the law chosen by the parties via agreement. Absent any such choice by the parties, the law of the common habitual residence of the parties shall apply. Absent any such common habitual residence, the law of the place where the unjust enrichment or *negotiorum gestio* occurs shall apply.

10.36 Compared to the earlier legislative attempt, Article 47 is observed by Chinese commentators as 'showing obvious improvement'.[75] The provision abandons the rigid single connecting factor rule, but combines three doctrines and forms a sophisticated system. The governing law is determined through three steps: (i) if the parties have chosen the applicable law, this law should apply; (2) in the absence of choice, the law of the common habitual residence shall apply; and (3) in the absence of the common habitual residence, the *lex loci conditionis* shall apply. This provision aims to provide both certainty and flexibility. However, three issues deserve some words.

i. Lex loci conditionis

10.37 The Conflicts Act does not define the place where unjust enrichment or *negotiorum gestio* occurs. Unjust enrichment and *negotiorum gestio* may constitute more than one activity, happening in different countries. It has been discussed before that this connecting factor may direct to more than one country. The lack of clarification may certainly be appealing to some Chinese judges who prefer to apply Chinese law, even though a foreign law may be more appropriate and relevant.

10.38 One possible resolution is to adopt the 'closest connection' doctrine to determine the *lex loci conditionis*. This approach, again, grants Chinese judges too much flexibility and the exercise of discretion may well lead to the application of Chinese law instead of the law with the real closest connection. Furthermore, the closest connection may not be easy to determine in some

---

74 HUO, *supra* n 19, 224.

75 JIN Peng-Nian, *supra* n 55.

cases. Determining the country with the closest connection usually requires the accumulation of the factors in one country, or requires one of the factors to have much greater significance than others. The complexity of unjust enrichment and *negotiorum gestio* usually dilutes the importance of traditionally important factors because more than one factor has almost equal importance in one dispute. For example, the parties concluded a contract in country A, which became invalid because of a fact occurring in country B, and the claimant performed the contract in country C, which caused the claimant's impoverishment in country D and the defendant's enrichment in country E. When the claimant claimed for restitution, it is not easy to agree which country has the most significant connection with the dispute. Countries A and B are not the places where the unjust enrichment occurred, but the places where the reasons for unjust enrichment occurred. Countries C, D and E are all relevant places of unjust enrichment. The activity of the claimant, the impoverishment to the claimant and the enrichment to the defendant are all important and unseverable elements for unjust enrichment. It is not easy to say which one should be weighed more heavily than the others.

It is suggested that a hierarchy of factors may need to be provided to determine the closest connection. Otherwise, the *lex loci conditionis* rule may only lead to uncertainty and the application of Chinese law. **10.39**

ii. No escape clause

Another weakness of Article 47 is that there is no escape clause. So the applicable law determined by the three steps is irrebuttable. This leads to rigidity, though the rigidity is softened by the combination of three doctrines designed for different circumstances. It is recognized that this design works appropriately in most cases, but exceptions may exist. For example, if the parties have common habitual residence in country A, but both act in country B, the putative contract existed and was performed in country B, and the impoverishment and enrichment occurred in country B, applying the law of country B may be more appropriate. Furthermore, applying the common *lex personalis* may be appropriate only if both parties expect their personal law to govern their activity. While both parties act in another country, they would expect their activities in the territory of that country to be governed by the *lex loci*. In addition, if the parties have a pre-existing relationship, they may not expect their common personal law to govern later unjust enrichment or *negotiorum gestio* claims. Finally, if unjust enrichment and *negotiorum gestio* include the immovable property, applying party autonomy, the common *lex personalis*, or the *lex loci conditionis* may be less practical than applying the *lex* **10.40** *situs*. Including an escape clause may help to adjust the rigidity that may occur and produce reasonable results in most cases.[76]

10.41 One reason against the inclusion of an escape clause in Article 47 is the concern over the too-flexible approach. As has been explained before, Chinese judges prefer to apply Chinese law and many judges do not have the capacity to apply the escape clause properly. At the current stage, a relatively rigid law may work better in practice than a more flexible approach, although that is sounder in theory.

iii. Inconsistent results

10.42 The Conflicts Act does not accept the doctrine of the law of relationship. The choice of law rule, thus, is criticized as it may lead to irreconcilable judgments if unjust enrichment arises out of a pre-existing relationship, either contract or tort. Some commentators argue that Article 47 is not strictly irreconcilable with the law of relationship doctrine as Article 47 is similar to Article 41 for contract and Article 44 for tort.[77] The similarity between Article 47 and Article 44 is obvious: both follow the party autonomy – common *lex personalis* – *lex loci* process. It is likely that if unjust enrichment relates to an underlying tort applying Article 44 and Article 47 may lead to the application of the same law.[78] However, in theory the parties could choose different laws governing tort and unjust enrichment claims. Furthermore, the *lex loci delicti* and the *lex loci conditionis* may lead to the law of different countries. Although Article 47 appears similar to Article 44, its functioning is never identical.

10.43 The similarity between Article 47 and Article 41 is not obvious. Article 41 allows the parties to choose the governing law for contract. In the absence of choice, the law with the closest connection or the place of characteristic performer applies. It may be arbitrary to argue that the closest connection and characteristic performance doctrines will certainly lead to the application of the law of the common habitual residence of the parties, or the place where the unjust enrichment or *negotiorum gestio* occurs.[79]

---

76 For example, the escaping clause exists in the Rome II Regulation for both unjust enrichment and *negotiorum gestio*.

77 JIN, *supra* n 55, 174; Zhengxin Huo, 'Highlights of China's New Private International Law Act', (2011) 45 RJT 637, 681.

78 JIN, *supra* n 55, 175.

79 Ibid.

V. CONCLUSION

The legislation of conflict of laws in unjust enrichment and *negotiorum gestio* is not well developed in most countries, due to the relatively short history of these subjects; the underdevelopment of the substantive law; the uncertainty of the concepts; and the inherent complexity. Based on the general background, Article 47 of the Conflicts Act is an achievement. It designates a sophisticated choice of law scheme for unjust enrichment and *negotiorum gestio,* which could achieve the balance of certainty, flexibility, justice and practicality in most cases. The rules, in general, are sound in theory and consistent with the common practice in countries with well-developed choice of law rules in other non-contractual obligations. **10.44**

11

CHOICE OF LAW IN PROPERTY

11.01 Chinese choice of law in the transfer of property was undeveloped until very recently. This was largely caused by the under-development of Chinese property law which was once regarded as the weakest area in the Chinese civil law system.[1] The concept of individual property rights was held to be contrary to the public or collective ownership of the socialist legal system until the 1980s. In the early stages of the economic transition, the drawback of the lack of property law was dealt with by strong administrative measures.[2] However, as a consequence of the development of the 'market economy', the legal barrier turned to be a prominent obstacle. Chinese authorities had to confront the legal barrier and various measures were adopted to produce a piecemeal, inconsistent and contradictory framework, including incomprehensive and unsystematic legislation,[3] administrative regulations,[4] and judicial interpretations.[5] The framework was incompatible with the policy of economic transition. After

1 QU Tao, 'Guanyu Zhongguo Wuquanfa Zhidu Sheji de Sikao [Some Thoughts on the System of Chinese Property Law]', Chinese version available at http://www.iolaw.org.cn/showArticle.aspx?id=1466, accessed on 19 June 2015.

2 Wei-chin Lee, 'Yours, Mine, or Everyone's Property? China's Property Law in 2007', (2010) 15 *Journal of Chinese Political Science* 25, 28.

3 GPCL, Arts 71–83; Zhonghua Renmin Gongheguo Tudi Guanli Fa [PRC Land Administration Law] 1999; Zhonghua Renmin Gongheguo Chengshi Fangdichan Guanli Fa [PRC Urban Real Estate Administration Law] 1994; Zhonghua Renmin Gongheguo Nongcun Tudi Chengbao Fa [PRC Contracting of Rural Law] 2002 (amended 2009); Zhonghua Renmin Gongheguo Danbao Fa [PRC Guarantee Law] 1995.

4 Such as State Council, 'Zhonghua Renmin Gongheguo Tudi Guanlifa Shishi Tiaoli [Implementation Regulation for PRC Land Administration Law]', [1991] State Council Degree 73 (abolished in 1999); 'Zhonghua Renmin Gongheguo Chengzhen Guoyoutudi Shiyongquan Churang he Zhuanrang Zanxingtiaoli [Interim Regulations of the PRC concerning the Assignment and Transfer of the Right to the Use of the State-Owned Land in the Urban Areas]', [1990] State Council Decree No 55.

2003, Chinese legislators commenced the legislative process on the PRC Property Law, which was adopted in 2007.[6]

The reform of choice of law in property closely accompanied the development of property law. Before the Conflicts Act was promulgated in 2011, Chinese choice of law in property was incomprehensive and spread through in a variety of statutes. The General Principle of Civil Law (GPCL) provides the *lex situs* rule to decide the ownership of the immovable property,[7] later extended by the SPC to cover all proprietary rights of immovable property.[8] The PRC Maritime Law provides choice of law rules in ship ownership, mortgage, and maritime liens.[9] The PRC Civil Aviation Law also provides conflicts rules to the ownership, mortgage and lien of the civil aircraft.[10] No choice of law rules were provided for other important proprietary rights, such as movable property. **11.02**

The Conflicts Act has made clear improvements. The whole of Chapter 5 of the Act deals with choice of law in property. This Chapter constitutes five articles, providing choice of law rules for the proprietary rights in immovable property, movable property, movable property in transit, securities, and pledge of rights. The choice of law rules in Chapter 5 are rich in content and cover a broad scope. This chapter primarily focuses on proprietary choice of law rules contained in Chapter 5 of the Conflicts Act, but also deals with issues not addressed by the Conflicts Act. **11.03**

I. PRELIMINARY QUESTIONS

I.1 Movable and immovable property

Pursuant to the current Chinese law, rights over immovables are determined by the law of the *situs*; but rights over movables are not necessarily governed by that law. Therefore, the first task of a Chinese court in a foreign-related case when required to decide some questions of a proprietary or possessory nature **11.04**

5 Such as SPC, 'Guanyu Shiyong "Zhonghua Renmin Gongheguo Danbaofa" Ruogan Wenti de Jieshi [Interpretation on Some Issues Regarding the Application of PRC Security Law]', Fa Shi [2000] 44; GPCL Opinion, Arts 84–103.

6 More on the history and political analysis, see in general Lee, *supra* n 2; M. Kielsgard and L. Chen, 'Emergence of Private Property Law in China and its Impact on Human Rights' (2014) 15 *Asian-Pacific Law and Policy* 94.

7 Art 144.

8 Art 186 of the SPC, 'Opinion on GPCL', Fa (Ban) Fa [1988] No 6 (abolished).

9 Conflicts Act, Arts 270–272.

10 Ibid., Arts 185–187.

is to decide whether the item of property that is the subject of the dispute is movable or immovable.

11.05 Classification is a question of law. Under Chinese conflicts law, it is still questionable which law should determine whether the subject matter is movable or immovable. Pursuant to Article 8 of the Conflicts Act of 2010, classification should be governed by the *lex fori*.[11] Therefore, some Chinese authors advocate that the *lex fori* should determine whether a particular thing is movable or immovable in a foreign related dispute.[12]

11.06 Nonetheless, it is universally accepted that if there is a conflict between the *lex situs* and the *lex fori* as to whether a particular thing is movable or immovable, the *situs* at the decisive moment must control.[13] The reason for this rule no doubt is the paramount importance of reaching a decision consistent with what the *lex situs* has decided or would decide, since in the last resort only the *lex situs* has effective control over the thing.[14] Hence, if Chinese courts determine whether the property is movable or immovable under the *lex fori*, instead of the *lex situs*, the harmony in decision-making would be frustrated.

11.07 Suppose A dies intestate, having been habitually resident in Beijing but leaving a house and antiques in London. If dispute arises with regard to the succession to the antiques, Chinese courts would characterize the antiques separated from the house as movable property under the *lex fori*, i.e., Chinese law; therefore, they will be inherited by whoever is entitled to them in Chinese law, since intestate succession to movables is governed by the law of habitual residence of the deceased at the time of his/her death.[15] But, in England, the antiques are classified as 'fixtures', which entail the same legal recognition as in the case of the whole even when the fixtures are separated.[16] Hence, they will descend to whoever is entitled to them by English law, since the *lex situs*

11 Ibid., Art 8.

12 Wenwen Liang, 'The Applicable Law to Rights in Rem Under the Act on the Law Applicable to Foreign Related Civil Relations of the People's Republic of China', in *Yearbook of Private International Law*, Volume 14 (Andrea Bonomi ed., Sellier European Law Publishers 2013) 361.

13 *Dicey, Morris and Collins on the Conflict of Laws* (Lollins of Mapesbury ed., 15th ed., Sweet & Maxwell 2008) 1281.

14 Ibid.; J.J. Fawcett and J.M. Carruthers, *Cheshire, North & Fawcett Private International Law* (14th ed., OUP 2008) 1194.

15 Act on the Application of Laws on Foreign-related Civil Relationships, Art 31(1).

16 Wojciech W. Kowalski, 'Restitution of Works of Art pursuant to Private and Public International Law', *Recueil des cours*, Vol.288 (Martinus Nijhoff 2001) 216.

governs the question of intestate succession to immovable property.[17] Therefore, classifying property into movables and immovables by the *lex fori* is likely to encourage forum shopping; the very thing that conflicts law is dedicated to preventing.

As a result, it is suggested that Chinese courts should not strictly follow Article 8 of the Conflicts Act when required to determine whether a particular thing is movable or immovable; instead, the classification between movables and immovables should be governed by the self-regulated rule of the *lex situs*. **11.08**

I.2 Property, contract and tort

Under Chinese scholarship, property is the right to possess, use, and enjoy a determinate thing, excluding others from interference.[18] Chapter 5 of the Conflicts Act applies to 'proprietary rights'.[19] Proprietary rights are defined in the PRC Property Law as 'the exclusive right of direct control enjoyed by the holder according to law over a specific property, including ownership, usufractuary right and rights for security'.[20] Chapter 5 of the Conflicts Act applies to the same subject matters covered in the Property Law, i.e., civil relationships generated by the ownership and utilization of properties. It does not cover ancillary relations in connection to the ownership and utilization, such as contractual liability in the transfer of property, or tort liability for infringement of proprietary rights. **11.09**

Classification between property and contract is not always easy. In most cases involving a transfer of property there will be a contract to facilitate the sale or assignment. The core element to classify depends on the nature of the cause of action, i.e., whether the action seeks to urge the other party to meet its promise, or to claim title against any third party. For example, in international sales, A concluded a contract to sell the specified goods to B, then sold the same goods to C. When disputes arise as to the true owner of the goods, it should be classified as property. When C sues A for selling the goods over which A had no good title, the dispute concerns whether A has breached the contract term of the sales contract and should be classified as contract.[21] The same confusion also exists in property and tort. Where the defendant infringes the claimant's proprietary rights, the claimant may sue for restitution, removal **11.10**

17 *Duncan v. Lawson* (1889) 41 Ch D 394.

18 *Faxue Cidian* [*Law Dictionary*] (Law Institute of the Chinese Academy of Social Science ed., China Law Press 2004) 702.

19 Proprietary rights is called 'Wu Quan' [物权] in China.

20 Property Act, Art 2.

21 P. Rogerson, *Collier's Conflict of Laws* (4th ed., CUP 2014) 377.

of impairment, elimination of danger, repair, remake, replacement or restoration. The claimant can also claim for damages arising out of the infringement of proprietary rights. Tort liability, however, requires the combination of an act, intention and causation of damage. A property claim does not require examination of the defendant's intention, any damage and the causation. It simply requires the court to restore the proprietor's rights to enjoy, possess, control, use, and dispose of its property.

11.11 Because Chinese legislation did not provide proper choice of law rules for transfer of property, especially movable property, until 2011, and because of the historical ignorance in proprietary rights, in the past Chinese judges frequently confused proprietary and contractual claims. In many cases, where the proprietary dispute related to the contract of sale, the court systematically applied the contractual choice of law to determine all the issues in the case, including property. The *lex situs* was applied not as the proper law to property, but as being designated by the closest connection principle in determining the applicable law in contract.[22] In other cases, although the dispute was about the enforcement of a contract in the transfer of immovable property, the court applied the *lex situs* as provided to immovables to determine the contractual dispute. For example, in *Foshan Municipality Nanhai District Dali Rural Credit Cooperative v. LI Jin and others*,[23] the security was established over the debtor's immovable property. The court held that since the immovable property was located in China, Chinese law should apply to decide the dispute over the contract to create the security. The court applied property choice of law to decide the enforcement of a contract. The Conflicts Act improves the awareness of classification by Chinese courts and in recent cases, Chinese courts have demonstrated their knowledge in classifying the cause of action between contract and property and applying the right choice of law rule.[24]

I.3 *Renvoi*

11.12 *Renvoi* is excluded all together by the Conflicts Act. In transnational property cases, the governing law designated by the Chinese conflict of laws only refers to the domestic law of the foreign country, excluding its choice of law rules.

---

22 Such as *Cosco Japan Co Ltd v. Jincheng Maritime Inc and Others,* Fujian Province HPC, (2011) Min Min Zhong Zi No 410 (applying the contractual choice of law to determine the ownership of the goods); *Qingdao Runshengxiang Trade Ltd v. UK Trans-World (Aluminium) Ltd,* (2000) Jing Zhong Zi No 163 (applying the law governing the sales contract to determine the conflict of titles in multiple sales).

23 (2005) Fo Zhong Fa Min Si Chu Zi No 87.

24 *Foshan X Factory v. LI,* Guangdong Province Dongguan Municipality No 2 People's Court, (2011) Dong Er Fa Min Si Chu Zi No 85.

Excluding *renvoi* may provide certainty and predictability. However, it may not always be appropriate in property cases. The universally accepted *situs* rule shows that the administrative control, sovereign power and enforcement require weight to be given to the law of the country where the property is located. However, if the whole legal system of the *situs* prefers to apply the law of another country, such as the domicile of the proprietor, the judgment based on domestic *situs* law may not fully reflect the interest of the *situs* and may fail to satisfy the above policies. It is also important to reach uniformity by following the approach taken by the court of the *situs* in order to avoid irreconcilable judgments and conflicts in title in land.[25] As a result, although *renvoi* is a dying doctrine, its application still remains in the transfer of property, especially immovable property.[26] It is suggested that the Chinese legislators may need to consider the necessity to adopt *renvoi* in certain proprietary issues when it is necessary and appropriate to do so. **11.13**

II. IMMOVABLE PROPERTY

As a general rule, all questions that arise concerning property rights over immovables are governed by the *lex situs*. The principle is based on the obvious considerations of convenience and expediency.[27] Any other rules would be ineffective because in the last resort only the *lex situs* can control the way in which land, which constitutes part of the *situs* itself, is dealt with. Moreover, the country where immovables are located has a powerful interest in its rule being applied to the rights over them. For many decades, Chinese scholars and judges had followed this principle for similar reasons.[28] **11.14**

The principle has been affirmed by the GPCL, Article 144 provides that 'in disputes involving the ownership of immovables, the law of the place where the property is situated shall apply'.[29] It should be noted that Article 144 confines the application of the *lex situs* to the 'ownership' of 'immovables'. This is a narrow application of the principle compared with general international practice. Moreover, Article 144 speaks only of the 'ownership' of immovables. **11.15**

25 J.W. Singer, 'Property Law Conflicts', (2014) 54 *Washburn Law Journal* 129, 160.

26 The argument for the application of *renvoi* in movable property is much weaker. For example, see English cases, *Iran v. Berend* [2007] EWHC 132.

27 *Dicey, Morris and Collins on the Conflict of Laws*, *supra* n 13, 1331.

28 Before the enactment of the GPCL in 1986, China had no conflicts rules concerning property rights. T.P. Chen, 'Private International Law of the People's Republic of China: An Overview', (1987) 35 *American Journal of Competition Law* 468.

29 GPCL, art 144. This doctrine also applies to real property in intestate succession. According to Art 149, in intestate succession, movable property will be governed by the law of the decedent's last place of domicile and immovable property by the law of the place where the property is located.

If literally interpreted, this would result in the exclusion of its application to property interests other than ownership in immovables.[30]

11.16 Given that the above article as well as others in the GPCL contained a number of problems, the SPC issued 'Opinions on Application of the "General Principle of Civil Law" (For the Trial Purpose)' in 1988 to provide concrete explanations on the abstract or ambivalent articles of the GPCL and to create new provisions to close the legal loopholes left by it. Under Article 186 of this judicial interpretation, the law of the place of immovables governs the civil relations concerning the ownership, sale, lease, mortgage, and use of the immovables. Moreover, 'immovables' refers to land; construction affixed to land; and other fixtures as well as equipment fixed to the construction.[31]

11.17 The SPC makes obvious improvements to Article 144 of the GPCL in two aspects: first, it offers a definition of immovables; second, it extends the *lex situs* to govern, in addition to ownership, sales, lease, mortgage, and use of immovables. Although the improvement is significant, it is far from perfect. First, given that it is widely established that all questions that arise concerning rights over immovables are governed by the *lex situs* as noted above, the extension of the *lex situs* to govern ownership, sales, lease, mortgage, and use of immovables is not extensive enough. Secondly, by offering a definition of immovables herein, the SPC seems to require Chinese courts to classify the property into movable and immovable in conflicts law cases pursuant to the *lex fori*, which is not in conformity with the well-settled principle of the *lex situs*.

11.18 In comparison, the choice of law rule for immovables included in the Conflicts Act is somewhat different although it reaffirms the principle of the *lex situs*. Article 36 of the Act provides that rights over immovables are to be governed by the law of the place where the immovables are located.[32] The wording of Article 36 indicates that the *lex situs* governs all rights over immovables, which is a much broader application of the principle compared with Article 144 of the GPCL. This represents progress.

---

30 Chen, *supra* n 28, 468.

31 Zuigao Renmin Fayuan Guanyu Shiyong Zhonghua Renmin Gongheguo Minfatongze Ruogan Wenti de Yijian [SPC, Opinions on Application of the General Principle of Civil Law of the People's Republic of China], 92 Zuigao Renmin Fayuan Gongbao 22 [Bulletin of SPC] Art 186 (1988) (PRC). M. Zhang, 'International Civil Litigation in China', (2002) 25 *Boston College International and Competition Law Review* 59.

32 Conflicts Act, Art 8(1)

III. MOVABLE PROPERTY

III.1 Introduction

Historically, the Italian statutists of the Middle Ages and their followers in most parts of Europe developed the rule that rights over movables are subject to the law of the domicile of the owner or the possessor: *mobilia personam sequuntur* (movables follow the person) or *mobilia ossibus inhaerent* (movables inhere in the bones).[33] The rationale for this rule is apparent, in a period which did not know mercantilism, articles of personal property were few and cheap, and were usually situated in the owner's domicile. **11.19**

This is not such the case in modern commerce. Today, the modern business system has penetrated almost everywhere with its vast mechanized productive capacity and its efficient means of transportation and communication. Movable property has thus been brought from a secondary to a primary place as an object of wealth. The systems of credit and finance and the growth of corporations have created new kinds of personal property with which different systems of legislation have dealt differently, thus, producing conflicts of enormous importance and difficulty. Under such a historic period, Savigny, in the late nineteenth century, advocated overthrowing the old statutist rule or at least restricting its sphere of application to the case of succession to movables upon death and to the matrimonial property system. Since Savigny's successful avocation of the principle of *lex situs*, most countries switched to the rule that movable property is to be governed by the law of the place where it is situated, subject to certain exceptions.[34] **11.20**

Before 2010, Chinese conflicts law, for a long period, did not provide choice of law rules for movables. Therefore, Chinese courts made decisions according to various rules that were not authorized by law. For example, in *Full Win Developments Ltd v. Chengdu Xinjin Baozhu Alcohol Ltd*,[35] the foreign claimant and the Chinese defendant entered into an international sales contract acquiring title to specified goods stored in the defendant's warehouse in China. Three months after the transaction, the defendant's assets, including the goods transferred to the claimant, were sealed by the local court to enforce debts owned to a third party. The claimant sued to declare the ownership of the goods. At the time of action, there was no legislative choice of law in movable property and the court applied both party autonomy and the place of **11.21**

33 J.H.C. Morris, *The Conflict of Laws* (Sweet & Maxwell 1993) 31.

34 John O'Brien, *Conflict of Laws* (2nd ed., Cavendish 1999) 557.

35 Sichuan Province Chengdu Municipality IPC, (2005) Cheng Min Chu Zi No 548.

performance to determine that Chinese law applies. The court applied contractual choice of law rules to determine the proprietary claim.

11.22 Chinese conflicts scholars eagerly expected that China's first Conflicts Act would establish a systematic private international law regime of movable property.[36] Articles 37 and 38 of the Conflicts Act indeed provide new choice of law rules for movables. However, the choice of law regime is not comprehensive. Although not explicitly stated, 'movables' in the Conflicts Acts only refers to tangible movables.[37]

11.23 Article 37 of the Conflicts Act provides that:

> The parties may choose the law applicable to the rights over movables; where the parties did not make a choice, the applicable law shall be the law of the place where the concerned movable property was located when the relevant legal act occurred.

11.24 The above article indicates that Chinese conflicts law has deviated from the universally accepted principle of the *lex situs*. Under the new rules, party autonomy has been established as the basic principle to determine the law applicable to movables; in comparison, the *lex situs* has been reduced to a rule of secondary importance, which plays a role but in the absence of parties' choice.

III.2 Party autonomy

11.25 Although China is not the first country to incorporate party autonomy into conflicts rules for movables, the Conflicts Act is 'revolutionary' in that it elevates party autonomy to the basic principle to determine the law applicable to movables and that it imposes no limit at all on the parties' choice. Literately interpreted, the parties are entitled to choose a law that has no substantial relation with the movables; they may choose a law applicable not only to the acquisition and the loss of real rights in movables, but also to the content and the exercise of such real rights; moreover, they may even choose a law which is injurious to the interests of a third party.[38]

11.26 So far, the Chinese legislators have not provided a convincing explanation for such a brave innovation. Some Chinese conflicts scholars suggest that the legislative intent of introducing party autonomy to movables is to solve the

36 Zhengxin Huo, 'An Imperfect Improvement: The New Conflict of Laws Act of the People's Republic of China', (2011) 60 *International and Comparative Law Quarterly* 1065, 1083.

37 Intangible movables are covered in Arts 39 and 40.

38 Huo, *supra* n 36, 1084.

complexity of choice of law issues when the transfer of the movable property is made by contract. They go on to specify that the parties usually transfer the property by contract, and that it is often the case that the parties agree in their contract that all disputes in connection with the contract will be governed by the law that they choose. Hence, allowing the parties to choose the law over movables has various merits. First, applying the law chosen by the parties is in conformity with the parties' expectations or intentions, as it is unrealistic to assume that the non-lawyers understand the distinction between contract and property. Even if this distinction were appreciated, it is also inconceivable that the parties would expect another law to apply to the movable property which arises out of the contract, and they may well have relied on the assumption that the same law covers both types of rights. Secondly, applying the law chosen by the parties to the contract to the movable property can increase uniformity of decisions. Since party autonomy is a universally accepted principle in the field of contract, the same law will be applied regardless of whether an issue arising out of a contractual relationship is characterized as one of contract or property. Hence, the introduction of party autonomy to movable property, to some degree, represents the tendency of modern conflicts law.[39]

Although the above arguments sound good, it is submitted that the appli- **11.27**
cation of party autonomy to movables by such a liberal approach, as reflected in Article 37 of the Conflicts Act, may have gone too far.

First, the legislative intent to promote predictability and efficiency by intro- **11.28**
ducing party autonomy into the field of movable property cannot always be accomplished in practice. In the practice of international business, it is by no means rare that the parties fail to choose a law to govern the disputes between them that arise in connection with the contract either because of ignorance or lack of consensus.[40] In such cases, allowing the parties to choose the law governing movable property will not lead to the consequence that the same law applies to both the contract and the movable property transferred by it.

Secondly, as reiterated above, the principle that rights over property, movables **11.29**
or immovables, is governed by the *lex situs* is generally accepted by all legal systems. The country of the *situs* has the effective power over the property and applying this law alone meets the security requirement in international transactions.[41] Nonetheless, the application of party autonomy to property lacks solid ground. Moreover, switching the universally accepted principle to

39 SONG Xiao, 'Yisizizhi yu Wuquan Chongtufa [Party Autonomy and property conflicts]', (2012) Vol 1 Huanqiu Falv Pinglun [*Global Law Review*] 83–4.

40 See Friedrich K. Juenger, *Choice of Law and Multistate Justice* (Special edition, Transnational 2000) 56.

41 *Cheshire, North & Fawcett Private International Law*, *supra* n 14, 1210.

party autonomy which has not been accepted internationally will create the conflict of choice-of-law rules, which, in turn, will undermine decisional harmony.

11.30 Thirdly, property and contract are, after all, two distinct and independent courses of actions. Therefore, it is unjustified to subject them to the same law. A contract creates obligations between the parties only, which will not, usually, influence the interest of a third party; however, property has rights against the entire world and its influence goes far beyond the parties themselves. Hence, allowing the parties to choose the governing law over property may be problematic. Indeed, this is the reason why even the supporters of the introduction of party autonomy to property do not favour an unlimited choice of law.[42]

11.31 It is submitted that if Chinese legislators do intend to introduce party autonomy into the field of movable property in order to promote predictability and efficiency, they should impose certain limits on party autonomy. First, the parties may not choose a law that might prejudice the interest of a third party. Secondly, the chosen law should have a material relationship to the parties or the property, or there is other reasonable basis for the parties' choice. Thirdly, the application of party autonomy should not violate the principle of *numerus clausus* which is a fundamental principle of property law adopted in most civil law countries, including China.[43]

11.32 These limits have been endorsed by some foreign countries which have also introduced party autonomy to movable property. For example, like the Chinese Conflicts Act, the Swiss Code on Private International Law introduces party autonomy to movable property; however, it takes a more restrictive approach that imposes certain limits on the parties' choice. The parties can choose 'the law of the State of shipment, or the State of destination or the law applicable to the underlying legal transaction'.[44] In other words, the parties cannot choose a law that has no substantial relationship with the property or the underlying legal transaction. Secondly, Swiss law limits party autonomy to the issues of the acquisition and the loss of real rights in movables which goes on to specify that the extent and the exercise of interests in movable property shall

---

42 SONG Xiao, *supra* n 39, 85–6.

43 PRC Property Law, Art 5 provides that the types and contents of property rights shall be stipulated by law. Zhonghua Renmin Gongheguo Wuquanfa [Property Law] (2007) art 5. For suggested limitations, see *Nedlloyd Lines B.V. v. Superior Court*, 834 P.2d 1148, 1152 (Cal. 1992).

44 Switzerland's Federal Code on Private International Law, Art 104(1) (1987).

be governed by the *lex situs*.[45] Furthermore, Swiss law states unambiguously that the choice of law shall not be applied against a third party.[46]

The Swiss approach, obviously, is preferable, inasmuch as those necessary limits constitute the reasonable basis for the parties' choice which can prevent party autonomy from being misused. In this light, it is submitted that Article 37 needs amendment and improvement in the future.[47] **11.33**

III.3 *Lex situs*

In the absence of party autonomy, the traditional doctrine *lex situs* applies to the transfer of movables. Applying *lex situs* to movable property may not be as convincing as immovable property. Movable property can be easily relocated to a different country. The alleged sovereign control and practical necessity, as a result, is much weaker. This doctrine, however, may be justified as protecting 'vested rights' and 'security of title of commerce'.[48] Since the proprietary right derived from the property, its acquisition, change, transfer, and elimination exist in the *situs*. The *lex situs* has the closest connection with the change in title. The ownership or other proprietary rights, once acquired under the *lex situs* when the transfer occurs, even if the property is removed to the other country later, the title and the vested right continue to be recognized. Applying the *lex situs* rule is consistent with the universal effect of proprietary rights. Proprietary rights have effect against the world. Attaching importance to the *lex situs* is more realistic than to the place of contracting or domicile of either party, which can only reflect the centre of a contract between the parties. **11.34**

The *situs* of tangible movables is not difficult to determine.[49] The difficulty may arise because movables may be moved from country to country. The application of *lex situs,* thus, depends on the 'moment' when the *situs* is determined. The basic principle is that the *situs* is determined at the moment when the event that allegedly affects the title occurs.[50] For example, when A transferred the title to B, the property was located in England; and when B transferred the property to C, the property was located in China. Where disputes arise as to whether B has acquired the good title, the Chinese court **11.35**

45 Ibid., Arts 100(2), 104(1).

46 Ibid., Art 104(2).

47 The current Chinese law does not impose any specific limitations to party autonomy in property. The only safeguard is the public policy defence. See III.5 below.

48 C.W. Fassberg, 'On Time and Place in Choice of Law for Property', in (2002) 51 *ICLQ* 385, 385.

49 In *Foshan X Factory v. LI,* supra n 23, the court applied the *lex situs* to determine the ownership of equipments in a sale by reservation of title.

50 A. Briggs, *The Conflict of Laws* (3rd ed., OUP 2013) 303.

should apply English law to deciding B's title over the property. Where disputes concern C's title, Chinese law should be applied instead.

III.4 *Res in transitu*

11.36 The transfer of movables while they are in the course of transit raises a difficult question of choice of law.[51] The application of the *lex situs* cannot produce a sound result as the actual *situs* of the *res in transitu* at any given moment is temporary. The *situs* is thus casual, and hardly contemplated by the parties.[52]

11.37 Chinese scholars have advocated several alternatives to the *lex situs*, such as the law of the place of dispatch and the law of the place of ultimate destination. They argue that in international transactions, the law of dispatch is usually favourable to the seller and the law of ultimate destination is favourable to the buyer. Based on this presumption, they submit that Chinese conflicts law should stipulate that the law of the ultimate destination governs the *res in transitu* in order to protect Chinese litigants, as most of the imported goods into China are either expensive high-tech equipment or important mineral resources, while most of exported Chinese goods are cheap products.[53]

11.38 Although the law of the ultimate destination is an appropriate choice in many circumstances,[54] the reasoning of the above argument is problematic. First, the rigid dichotomy between China's imported and exported goods is an over-simplified description of China's foreign trade. As the world's largest trading country and an emerging power,[55] China both imports and exports a huge variety of goods and the simplified classification between China's importations and exportations is apparently groundless. Second, even if the above description of China's foreign trade was true, it cannot follow that the law of ultimate destination would benefit Chinese litigants. Last, but not least, even if it was true and the law of ultimate destination did benefit Chinese litigants, such a parochial ideology is outdated and does not conform to the goal of modern conflicts law, i.e., resolving multistate disputes in a manner that is substantively equitable and fair to the litigants, regardless of their nationalities.

11.39 Before the enactment of the Conflicts Act, Chinese law did not provide choice of law rules for *res in transitu*, nor had Chinese courts had to address the issue

---

51 *Cheshire, North & Fawcett, supra* n 14, 1210.

52 *Dicey, Morris and Collins on the Conflict of Laws, supra* n 13, 1343–4;

53 Du Huanfang, 'Zhongguo Shewai Wuquan Falvshiyongguize zhi Shiyong yu Wanshan' [The Application and Reform of Chinese Property Conflicts] (2013) 5 *Aomen Faxue [Macao Law Review]* 23.

54 *Cheshire, North & Fawcett, supra* n 14, 1221.

55 http://rt.com/business/china-us-largest-trading-country-908/, last visited on 3 September 2014.

of which law should be applied in such a case. This is probably because goods in transit are generally represented by a bill of lading or other documentary symbol of ownership which is capable of an independent dealing.[56] However, this legislative vacuum has been filled by the Conflicts Act, as Article 38 prescribes the following:

> The parties can choose the law applicable to the transfer of a movable property that is being in transit; where the parties did not make a choice, the applicable law shall be the law of the destination of the concerned property in transit.

Under this article, the law applicable to *res in transitu* should be ascertained in the following order of priority. First, when goods in transit are at issue, the parties may choose the applicable law. Secondly, in the absence of parties' choice, the law of the country of destination shall apply. Again, unlimited party autonomy has been established as the general principle to determine the law governing *res in transitu*, and for the similar reasons as analyzed earlier, certain limits on the parties' choice should be imposed.[57] **11.40**

III.5 Public policy defence

Both party autonomy and *lex situs* may lead to the application of a foreign law the application of which may contradict state, national or public interest of China. Since Chapter 5 of the Conflicts Act does not provide specific limitation to the application of foreign property law, the general public policy defence acts as the final safeguard.[58] **11.41**

i. Stolen goods

Public policy defence may be relied on in two typical scenarios. The first is a dispute on the title of stolen goods. Different national practice exists on the conflict of titles. Italy, for example, provides the bona fide buyer for value the good title to the property, even if the seller does not have good title.[59] Under the French and Japanese law, the bona fide purchaser could not receive the good title of the stolen goods, but the title can be acquired after the lapse of time.[60] The UK, on the other hand, adopts '*nemo dat quod non habet*' for stolen goods, which means the purchaser could not receive a better title than the seller.[61] Chinese Property Law adopts '*en fait de meubles, la possession vaut titre*' **11.42**

---

56 Zuigao Renmin Fayuan Gongbao [Bulletin of SPC] (1997) 4 (PRC) 140–41.

57 Huo, *supra* n 36, 1084.

58 Conflicts Act, Art 5.

59 Italian Civil Code, Art 1153.

60 French Civil Code, Art 2279; Japanese Civil Code, Art 193.

61 Sale of Goods Act 1976, s 21(1).

to grant good title to the bona fide purchaser for value.[62] However, it does not provide clear guidance as to whether this rule applies to the transfer of stolen goods. Some courts in practice exclude stolen goods from the bona fide purchaser protection.[63]

11.43 However, it may be too early to conclude that Chinese law applies the *nemo dat* principle to stolen goods. The stolen goods' exemption cannot be implied anywhere in the Property Law or its judicial interpretation. More importantly, the Property Law (draft) included a stolen goods' exemption, which was deleted from the final version. It may imply that legislators had the intention to protect even the bona fide purchaser of stolen goods. Judicial interpretation and directions to other law shows that the authorities recognize the necessity of applying the same bona fide rule to the stolen goods or goods acquired by other illegal means, such as fraud. As early as 1958, the SPC in its Direction to the Guangdong and Hebei HPCs recognized the innocence of both the original owner and the bona fide buyer. The SPC stated that if the bona fide purchaser bought the property in the overt market, the buyer acquired the legal title; if the buyer bought the goods outside the overt market, the property remained with the original owner.[64] The SPC, Supreme People's Procuratorate (SPP), Ministry of Public Security and State Administration for Industry and Commerce jointly published the 'Provisions on Investigate and Deal with Cases concerning Theft and Robbery of Vehicles' in 1998, which explicitly stated that the stolen car should be returned to the bona fide purchaser.[65] In the most recent judicial interpretation to Criminal Cases on Fraud, the SPC and the SPP stated that goods subject to previous fraudulent conversion but bought by the current bona fide buyer will not be recoverable.[66] Although none of these documents attempt to interpret the Property Law, a consistent interpretation is predicted.

62 PRC Property Law, Art 106.

63 E.g., *KANG v. NIU*, Beijing Shunyi District People's Court, (2009) Shun Min Chu Zi 319, the bona fide purchaser was not the legal owner of the stolen car; *WU Mochuan v. ZHAO Huaichao*, Fujian Province Fuzhou Municipality Taijiang District People's Court, (2008) Tai Min Chu Zi No 589, the bona fide purchaser should return the goods to the original owner and claim damages from the seller; *ZHANG v. Ye and Others*, Anhui Province Bangbu Municipality IPC, (2003) Bang Min Er Zai Zhong Zi No 07.

64 SPC, 'Zuigao Renmin Fayuan Guanyu Buzhiqing Maizhu Maide de Zangwu Ying Ruhe Chuli Wenti de Fuhan [Letter in response to the question on how to deal with the stolen goods bought by bona fide buyers]', [1958] Fa Yan Zi 84.

65 SPC, Supreme People's Procuratorate, Ministry of Public Security, State Administration for Industry and Commerce, 'Zuigao Renmin Fayuan, Zuigao Renmin Jianchayuan, Gonganbu, Gongshangju Guanyu Yifa Chachu Daoqie, Qiangjie Jidongche Anjian de Guiding [Provisions on Investigate and Deal with Cases concerning Theft and Robbery of Vehicles]', Gong Tong Zi [1998] No 31, Art 12.

66 SPC and SPP, 'Zuigao Renmin Fayuan, Zuigao Renmin Jianchayuan Guanyu Banli Zhapian Xingshi Anjian Juti Yingyong Falv Ruogan Wenti de Jieshi [Interpretation of the SPC and SPP on Several Issues Concerning the Specific Application of Law in the Trial of Criminal Cases on Fraud]', Fa Shi [2011] No 7, Art 10.

11.44 It is likely that Chinese property law may eventually apply *en fait de meubles la possession vaut titre* to stolen goods. However, since current Chinese legislation does not give a clear answer to the title of stolen goods, public policy defence may not be generated no matter which foreign law applies to this issue. For example, A, a Chinese citizen, is the original owner of a movable property located in China. The property was stolen by B, and relocated to Italy, where the property was sold to C, a bona fide purchaser. C later travelled to China, bringing the property with him and A was made aware of this. A then sued in China for the return of property. Since the property was located in Italy when it was transferred to C, the *lex situs* rule refers to the Italian law, under which C could acquire good title. Even if the goods were not sold in the overt market, China would not generate public policy to prevent the transfer of title. However, if B transferred the property to C in France instead and A sued in China, French law would apply, and A could claim the title of the property within three years of the transfer. A may be successful and recover the ownership of the property. If B transferred the property in England, English law would apply to determine C's title. Under the *nemo dat* doctrine, C could not acquire good title to the stolen goods and A would remain the legal owner.

ii. Cultural property

11.45 The situation is different in the second scenario of cultural property. China is one of the major 'source' countries suffering from the illicit trade in cultural property.[67] In order to prevent illicit trafficking of cultural property, the PRC Cultural Property Protection Law regulates transaction and exportation of cultural property owned collectively or privately,[68] and states that China has ownership of most movable cultural property.[69] Cultural property owned by the country should not be subject to any transaction unless approved by the country; privately owned cultural property may be sold according to the designed procedures and regulations. The protection of cultural property goes beyond civil relationships and enters the field of criminal and administrative regulation. The protection of cultural property reflects the important public and national interest for China to preserve its culture and history. It would override any applicable law that may provide otherwise. Furthermore, this area is also regulated by a number of international conventions, which may also override the application of foreign law.

67 See, in general, J.D. Murphy, 'The People's Republic of China and the Illicit Trade in Cultural Property', (1994) 3 *International Journal of Cultural Property* 227.

68 Cultural Property Protection Law, Art 6.

69 Zhonghua Renmin Gongheguo Wenwu Baohu Fa [PRC Cultural Property Protection Law] 1982 (amended in 1991, 2002, 2007, 2013 and 2015), Art 5.

11.46 The wording of Article 37 of the Conflicts Act suggests that it applies to all movables, including cultural property. As a result, the title of cultural property shall be determined by party autonomy or, in the absence of autonomy, the *lex situs*. The original owner would not participate in the transfer of stolen goods and could not agree on its applicable law. After disputes have arisen, it is more difficult for the parties to agree on the governing law. The governing law is thus determined by the *lex situs* at the time of transfer and is easily manipulated by the illicit trader, who could relocate the property to selected countries to facilitate the transfer of title. The governing law, however, should be subject to two exceptions. The first is the international convention exception. If there is an international convention signed by China and the relevant country, the conventional rule should take priority. The main conventions in this area are the UNIDROIT Convention on Stolen or Illegally Exported Cultural Objects of 1995 and the UNESCO Convention on the Means of Prohibiting and Preventing the Illicit Import, Export and Transfer of Ownership of Cultural Property of 1970. Both Conventions have one important limitation in that they are not retrospective. Furthermore, many countries, especially the destination or market states, have signed but not yet ratified or implemented the Conventions. The second approach is through public policy.[70] Although pursuant to Chinese conflict of laws, the governing law is the *lex situs,* if the application of this law violates Chinese public policy to protect Chinese cultural property, the foreign law should not be applied; Chinese law should be applied instead.[71]

11.47 Although public policy could act as the last defence to prevent illicit transfer of cultural property, the concept of public policy is ambiguous and its application should be subject to reasoning and justification. Although illicit transfer of state-owned cultural property is clearly against public policy, the impact to the social and public interest by the illicit transfer of privately owned cultural property may depend on the level of the breach and the class or type of cultural property subject to the transaction. Some private cultural property may not be classified as of national importance, the trade of which may be treated as stolen goods. Public policy defence may not be appropriately generated. As a result, relying completely on public policy may cause uncertainties and difficulties in practice, and may lead to some courts relying too readily on public policy.

11.48 The alternative approach is to insert a new conflicts rule addressing the illicit trade of cultural property. It is proposed the *lex situs origins* should be the

70 For more on public policy in transfer of cultural property, see T.W. Pecoraro, 'Choice of Law in Litigation to Recover National Cultural Property', (1990) 31 *Virginia Journal of International Law* 1, 1–39.

71 Conflicts Act, Art 5.

proper law to govern the transfer of cultural property.[72] Wherever the cultural property is located at the time of transfer the title should always be determined by the country where the property originated. This rule clearly protects the interest of the source country. Although the *lex situs origins* rule is criticized for not protecting bona fide purchasers and some commentators are concerned that retention by the country of origin may not be the best way to protect cultural property,[73] its necessity in China is undoubted. China has adopted adequate measures to preserve and protect its culture and these attempts lose value if the law of another country eventually applies.[74] Irrespective of some voices for cultural internationalism, China, as well as most other countries in the world, supports cultural nationalism. Furthermore, as *lex situs origins* applies, *renvoi* may be necessary. If the source country prefers applying the other country's law to determine the title of its cultural property, the most appropriate way is to respect this country's policy and to apply the same law to this matter. Uniformity can also be reached wherever the action is brought.

Finally, it is necessary to note that China, or the original private owner of **11.49** cultural property, may only be successful in a restitution claim if the property is located in China. After the court makes the decision, the court could order measures to enforce the judgment easily. If the cultural property is located abroad, while the Chinese claimant may be aware of this matter, suing the Chinese court may not guarantee enforcement and cooperation by the court of the *situs*.

IV. SECURITIES

The Conflicts Act provides conflict rules for securities in Article 39, under **11.50** which securities are to be governed by the law of the place where the rights are to be exercised or the law which is most closely connected with the securities.

Under Chinese scholarship, securities are instruments that evidence the **11.51** holder's proprietary rights or other rights. In the liberal sense, securities cover title documents or documents of claim. Title documents cover bills of lading, warehouse receipts, negotiable instruments, shares and bonds. In the literal

72 See also S.C. Symeonides, 'A Choice-of-Law Rule for Conflicts Involving Stolen Cultural Property', (2005) 38 *Vanderbilt Journal of Transnational Law* 1177, 1185–6; LIU Lin, 'Beidao Wenwu Kuaguo Liuzhuan Suoyouquan Zhengyi Falv Shiyong Guize Tantao [A Study on Conflict Rules Applied to Cross-Border Transactions of Stolen Cultural Properties]', (2011) 9 Shidaifaxue [*Present Day Law Science*] 104, 108.

73 D.L. Crowell, 'Choice of Law in the Protection of Cultural Property', (1992) 27 *Texas International Law Journal* 173, 206.

74 Ibid., 207.

sense, securities cover financial instruments, i.e., equities and bonds.[75] Rights over securities include two distinct categories: (i) the rights to possess and hold securities, i.e., the rights to the securities as such; and (ii) the rights represented by securities, i.e., the holder's rights evidenced by securities.[76] As Article 39 fails to provide any explanation for either the meaning of securities or that of rights over them, the following points, inter alia, are worthy of discussion.

11.52 First, from the wording of this article, it is very difficult to tell whether securities refer to the rights indicated by such securities or the securities as such in the form of pieces of paper or in the digital form.[77] Given that Article 39 is contained in the chapter on rights *in rem*, it can be inferred that the scope includes but the rights *in rem* to securities. Hence, it is submitted that Article 39 is devoted to regulating both the rights to the securities as such and those represented by securities if only they are, in nature, rights *in rem*.

11.53 Secondly, given the diversity of securities, Article 39 enjoys flexibility which, meanwhile, suffers from the uncertainty of judicial discretion since there is little legislative guidance regarding the place where the rights are to be exercised or the place with the closest connection.[78] In comparison, private international law legislation in many foreign states provides more detailed and concrete choice of law rules. For example, English conflicts law follows the *lex situs* rule for securities and provides a detailed definition of the *situs* of securities. For bearer securities, the *situs* of securities is the location of the certificates; for registered securities, the *situs* of securities is the place of incorporation of the issuer or the place of the register for securities transferred by registration.[79] Swiss private international law distinguishes title documents from financial asset securities, which are subject to different choice of law rules.[80] US law has more detailed categories: warehouse receipts, negotiable securities, and shares are governed by different conflict of law regimes respectively.[81] Thus, from the perspective of comparative law, Article 39 of the Conflicts Act looks rather simplistic.

75 Wenwen Liang, *supra* n 12, 361.

76 See HUANG Jin (ed.), *Zhonghua Renmin Gongheguo Shewai Minshi Falvguanxi Shiyongfa Jianyigao Ji Shuangming* [*Proposed Draft Law of the People's Republic of China on Application of Laws to Foreign-Related Civil Relations and Its Explanation*] (Renmin University Press 2011) 81; WANG Limin (ed.), *Minfa [Civil Law]* (China Renmin University Press 2005) 145.

77 Huo, *supra* n 36, 1084.

78 Liang, *supra* n 12, 366.

79 *Dicey, Morris and Collins on the Conflict of Laws*, *supra* n 13, 1294, 1295.

80 Switzerland's Federal Code on Private International Law, arts 105, 106.

81 See American Law Institute, Restatement of the Law—Conflict of Laws (Westlaw 2012), § 216, US Uniform Commercial Code, §8–102(a)15.

Thirdly, Article 39 is intended to apply to securities held directly by investors; therefore, it should not apply in cases where investors hold their securities indirectly through intermediaries and cross-border securities transactions are effected by a mere account transfer.[82] However, as one scholar puts it, 'over the last half century, there has been a marked change in the way that shares, bonds, and other investment securities are held and transferred',[83] and one of the principal changes is the shift from the direct holding system to the indirect holding system. As to the former, a direct relationship exists between the holder and the issuer, and for the latter, interests in securities are held through securities accounts maintained by intermediaries.[84] The lack of choice of law rules for securities held with an intermediary is a disappointment of the Conflict Act. **11.54**

V. PLEDGES OVER RIGHTS

It is interesting to note that the Conflicts Act contains a separate choice of law rules for pledge over rights. Under Article 40, pledges over rights are to be governed by the law of the place where the pledge was established. In order to understand the accurate meaning of this article, it is necessary to examine pledges over rights under Chinese domestic law. **11.55**

First, it should be mentioned that property rights in Chinese legislation literally refer to rights *in rem* over tangibles rather than intangibles, as opposed to the common law of property rights, which extends to both tangibles and intangibles. Property rights over intangibles are governed by other statutes along with the Property Law of the PRC, for example, the Copyright Act of the PRC and the Trademark Act of the PRC.[85] **11.56**

Secondly, pursuant to the Property Law of the PRC, rights *in rem* consist of three categories: ownership, usufruct, and collateral rights.[86] Collateral rights can be further divided into two subcategories: mortgage and pledge. Mortgages may be established over immovables as well as means of transportation, **11.57**

---

82 See Zhengxin Huo, *supra* n 36, 1084.

83 Christophe Bernasconi, 'The Hague Convention of 5 July 2006 on the Law Applicable to Certain Rights in Respect of Securities Held with an Intermediary', *Seminar on Current Developments in Monetary and Financial Law Washington, D.C., Oct. 23–27, 2006*, at http://www.imf.org/external/np/seminars/eng/2006/mfl/cb.pdf (last visited 1 May 2015).

84 Ibid.

85 See Zhonghua Renmin Gongheguo Zhuzuoquanfa [Copyright Act] (1990, revised in 2010); Zhonghua Renmin Gongheguo Shangbiaofa [Trademark Act] (1982, revised in 2013), Art 2(3).

86 Property Law, Art 2(3).

and pledges over tangible movables as well as rights.[87] To be more specific, pledges can be established over any of the following rights which an obligor or a third party has the right to dispose of: (i) bills of exchange, checks, promissory notes; (ii) bonds, deposit receipts; (iii) warehouse receipts, bills of lading; (iv) transferable fund shares or shares of stocks; (v) the rights to exclusive use of trademarks, the property right among patent rights and copyrights which are transferable according to law; and (vi) accounts receivable.[88]

11.58 In this light, it is confusing that pledges over rights are listed separately alongside immovables, movables and securities.[89] Under the current structure of Chapter Five ('rights *in rem*') of the Conflicts Act, immovables are subject to Article 36 of the Act, movables in general are subject to Article 37, and securities to Article 39. These three articles are intended to cover all aspects of rights in *rem* which contain ownership, usufruct and collateral rights (including mortgage and pledge) as well. In contrast, Article 40 is a special rule for pledges over rights only. Hence, a logical conclusion is that mortgages over immovables shall be governed by Article 36 and pledges over movables by Article 37; however, under the principle of *lex specialis derogat generali,* securities generally are to be governed by Article 39 subject to the exception that pledges over rights represented by securities shall be governed by Article 40.

11.59 So far, the rationale behind such an arrangement remains unclear. A possible interpretation is the requirement that publicity of pledges over rights be visible to third parties. The concern for protecting third parties leads to the application of the *lex situs* rule in contrast to the law of the place where the rights are to be exercised or that of the place with the closest connection.

11.60 Under the Property Law, a pledge over rights is established by contract in writing plus formalities. A ledge over bills of exchange, checks, promissory notes, bonds, deposit receipts, warehouse receipts and bills of lading is established on the delivery of title certificates, or upon registration with competent authorities in case there is no title certificate;[90] a pledge over transferable fund shares or shares of stocks and rights in intellectual property rights is established upon registration with competent authorities;[91] and a

87 Ibid., Arts 180, 210.
88 Ibid., Art 223.
89 Liang, *supra* n 12, 367.
90 Zhonghua Renmin Gongheguo Wuquanfa [PRC Property Law] (2007), Art 224.
91 Ibid., Arts. 226, 227.

pledge over accounts receivable is established upon registration with the credit reference agency.[92]

Hence, under Article 40 of the Conflicts Act, pledges over rights incorporated in certificates which are bearer securities shall be governed by the law of the place where the delivery takes place, pledges over rights incorporated in certificates, which are registered securities, shall be governed by the law of the place where the registrar is located; pledges over accounts receivable shall be governed by the law of the place where the credit reference agency is located; and pledges over rights in intellectual property rights shall be governed by the law of the place where the registrar is located.[93] **11.61**

VI. CONCLUSION

The Conflicts Act has established a relatively systematic private international law regime of property, which contains the choice-of-law rules for immovables, movables, securities, and pledges over rights. The Conflicts Act is a milestone in Chinese legislation both in the general area of conflicts law and in the more specified area of property conflicts. **11.62**

In the field of immovables, the Conflicts Act follows the universal rule of the *lex situs*; however, in the field of movables, it has deviated from the universally accepted principle of the *lex situs* and incorporates unlimited party autonomy. Although China is not the first country to introduce party autonomy to the field of movables, the unlimited party autonomy approach to movables may be problematic, as analyzed above. It is suggested that the SPC should interpret Article 37 in a limited manner to impose necessary restrictions on party autonomy, and to provide guidance for the application of law in the sale of stolen goods and culture property. **11.63**

With regard to the choice-of-law rules for securities, Article 39 suffers from overbroad categories. Moreover, judges are left with too much discretion in deciding which is the place where the rights are to be exercised or that with the closest connection. Therefore, when the SPC issues the judicial interpretation in the future, it ought to spell out the meaning of the place where the rights to securities be exercised, and provide a test with the concrete standard to determine the place with the closest connection with the securities. Last, but not least, the Conflicts Act fails to provide rules for securities held with an **11.64**

92 Ibid., Art 228.
93 Liang, *supra* n 12, 368.

intermediary. Given that the Hague Convention on the Law Applicable to Certain Rights in Respect of Securities Held with an Intermediary has provided systematic choice-of-law rules for these types of securities, it is suggested that China should join the Convention in the near future.

12

CHOICE OF LAW IN INTELLECTUAL PROPERTY

I. INTRODUCTION

The Conflicts Act includes one special chapter dealing with choice of law in intellectual property (IP) rights. This is partly due to the complexity of IP and actions arising out of it, and partly due to the special attention paid to the protection of IP rights by Chinese legislators. **12.01**

The first IP legislation in Chinese history, the Regulation for the Award and Promotion of Technology Development, was promulgated in 1889 under the **12.02**

Qing Dynasty. The Chinese intellectual property system was further modernized between 1928 and 1944.[1] However, the process of establishing a modern intellectual property system was delayed by the Communist movement after 1949, when intellectual property rights belonged to the state collectively, not private entities.[2] After the economic reform, Chinese law on IP rights was rehabilitated and China acceded to a number of international IP conventions, such as the Paris Convention,[3] Madrid Trademark Agreement,[4] Berne Convention,[5] TRIPS,[6] WIPO Performances and Phonograms Treaty,[7] and WIPO Copyright Treaty,[8] and entered into bilateral agreements or memorandum with individual countries to strengthen the cooperation in the protection of intellectual property rights.[9]

12.03 At the domestic level, China enacted a series of domestic laws regulating intellectual property and related issues, such as the Trademark Law, Copyright Law and Patent Law, Regulations on Customs Protection of intellectual property rights, GPCL, Law against Unfair Competition, and Advertising Law. The latter three are not specialized intellectual property statutes, but include provisions with the special purpose of protecting IP rights. The PRC government has also adopted a pro-intellectual property rights policy making the protection of intellectual property rights one of the priorities in China's sustainable development plan.[10]

---

1 See C. Devonshire-Ellis, A. Scott and S. Woollard, *Intellectual Property Rights in China* (2nd ed., Springer 2011) 2.

2 Ibid., 2.

3 Paris Convention for the Protection of Industrial Property, acceded to by China in 1984.

4 Madrid Agreement for the International Registration of Trademarks, acceded to by China in 1989.

5 Berne Convention for the Protection of Literary and Artistic Works of 1886, acceded to by China in 1992.

6 Agreement on Trade-Related Aspects of Intellectual Property Rights. In 2007, China approved the Protocol on Revising the TRIPs. See the Standing Committee of NPC (SCNPC), 'Guanyu Pizhun 'Xiugai "Yu Maoyi Youguan de Zhishi Chanquan Xieding" Yidingshu' de Jueding [Decision of the Standing Committee of the National People's Congress on Approving the Protocol on Revising the Agreement on Trade-Related Aspects of Intellectual Property Rights]', 2007.

7 SCNPC, 'Guanyu Jiaru "Shijie Zhishi Chanquan Zuzhi Biaoyan he Luyin Zhipin Tiaoyue" de Jueding [Decision of the Standing Committee of the NPC on Acceding to the WIPO Performance and Phonograms Treaty]', 2006.

8 SCNPC, 'Guanyu Jiaru "Shijie Zhishi Banquan Tiaoyue" de Jueding [Decision of the Standing Committee of the NPC on Acceding to the WIPO Copyright Treaty]', 2006.

9 Such as US (1992, 1995), Switzerland (1992), Sweden (1993), Norway (1995), Russia (1996, 1999), France (1998), Uzbekistan (1999), Ukraine (2002), Italy (2004), Peru (2005), Mongolia (2005), Kyrgyzstan (2006).

10 State Council, 'Guowuyuan Guangyu Yinfa Guojia Zhishi Chanquan Zhanlue Gangyao de Tongzhi [Notice of the State Council about Issuing the Outline of the National IP Strategy]', Guo Fa [2008] 18; General Office of State Council, 'Guanyu Zhuanfa Zhishi Chanquan Ju den Danwei Shenru Shishi Guojia Zhishi Chanquan Zhanlue Xingdong Jihua (2014–2020 Nian) de Tongzhi [Notice on Forwarding the "Action Plan for Implementing the National Intellectual Property Strategy (2014—2020)" of Units Including SIPO]', Guo Ban Fa [2014] No. 64.

The development of the IP rights system in China boosts private enforcement of IP rights. The number of foreign-related or interregional intellectual property rights civil disputes steadily increases, which generates the operation of the conflict of laws. Between 2001 and 2007, the courts of the first instance had only heard 1,634 foreign-related intellectual property cases in six years.[11] In 2009, the courts heard 1,720 foreign-related and interregional intellectual property disputes.[12] Chinese law, however, did not include any IP specialized conflicts rules at that time. The GPCL only covered choice of law rules for contract, tort, immovable property, marriage, divorce, maintenance, and succession. In practice, the courts had to classify IP disputes either as contract or tort, and apply relevant GPCL provisions.[13] If the dispute is about the content, validity and ownership of IP rights, the GPCL is irrelevant and the courts would usually directly apply Chinese IP laws according to the territoriality principle.[14] **12.04**

Due to the importance of IP rights in a future development strategy and the steady increase of cross-border IP right disputes, the Conflicts Act 2010 inserts one chapter, Chapter Seven, to specifically address choice of law rules in IP rights. This is the first time the legislators have clarified the applicable law in cross-border IP disputes. Despite its importance Chapter Seven is drafted in a very simple manner. It only includes three articles, covering the content and ownership, transfer, and infringement of intellectual property rights. Although it covers the most common IP right disputes, it is far from comprehensive. Some IP right issues are not expressly included, such as IP created in the course of an employment relationship. A more detailed judicial interpretation will be necessary to facilitate the smooth implementation of Chapter Seven in practice.[15] **12.05**

---

11 CAO Jianming, 'Zai Di'erci Quanguo Fayuan Zhishi Chanquan Shenpan Gongzuo Huiyi Shang de Jianghua [The Speech of the Vice-President of the SPC, CAO Jianming, in the 2nd Symposium of the Work of intellectual property right Trial of National Courts]', 19 February 2008.

12 'Zhishi Chanquan Sifa Baohu de Baogao [Report on Judicial Protection of intellectual property rights in PRC Courts]' (2008).

13 The GPCL only includes choice of law rules for contract, tort, immovable property, marriage, divorce, maintenance, and succession. It does not provide choice of law rules for other proprietary issues. See Ch 11, section III.1 above.

14 Because GPCL only provides choice of law for immovables. See Ch 11, section II below. Weidong Zhu, 'China's Codification of the Conflict of Laws', (2007) 3 *Journal of Private International Law* 283, 297.

15 Interpretation I does not cover Chapter Seven, which may be covered in the later interpretation.

II. CONFLICTS ACT, DOMESTIC INTELLECTUAL PROPERTY STATUTES AND INTERNATIONAL INTELLECTUAL PROPERTY TREATIES

12.06 The Conflicts Act introduces special choice of law rules for IP rights. It, however, does not immediately simplify judicial practice. The Conflicts Act does not abandon the conflict of laws included in domestic intellectual property statutes or relevant substantive rules in intellectual property treaties. Chinese courts, therefore, can become lost in the statutes and not know which set of conflicts rules or substantive law framework should apply.

II.1 Conflicts Act and domestic intellectual property right statutes

12.07 Article 2 of the Conflicts Act briefly addresses the conflict between the Act and other domestic statutes, providing priority to special statutes. However, the SPC Conflicts Act Interpretation I suggests that the Conflicts Act should take priority over other statutes in determining the applicable law to foreign-related civil relations, except in the areas of bills of exchange, maritime, civil aviation and IP rights.[16] This is mainly because the domestic law of these areas are largely affected by international conventions and many provisions therein directly implement conventional provisions into Chinese domestic law. Granting priority to these special statutes helps China to fulfil its international treaty obligations. It is also consistent with the traditional Chinese principle of giving priority to international treaties and customs. Furthermore, legislators having considered the plurality and complexity of commercial law, decided to leave special choice of law rules in very specialized commercial law areas in the special statutes.[17]

II.2 Conflicts Act and intellectual property right treaties

12.08 International conventions harmonized substantive IP right rules to the extent that the application of conflicts law is irrelevant in such areas. Conflicts law, however, continues to play a role in areas not covered by international conventions and to non-signatory countries to international IP right treaties. The common procedure to deciding the governing law is to consider first, whether the disputes are covered by an international treaty to which both China and the other country concerned are parties. If affirmative, the treaty should apply. If negative, China should apply Chinese conflict of laws

16 Art 3 of the Interpretation I.

17 SPC, 'Zuigao Renmin Faxue Minsiting Buzeren jiu "Guanyu Shiyong Zhonghua Renmin Gongheguo Shewai Minshi Guanxi Falv Shiyongfa Ruogan Wenti" de Jieshi (Yi) Da Jizhewen [Response to Media Inquiries by the Representative of SPC Civil Court No 4 Tribunal about the Application of the Conflicts Act Interpretation I]', published on 6 January 2013.

contained in the Conflicts Act or special IP statutes as described in the previous chapter.

Chinese judicial practice, however, adopts a mixed approach. Some courts follow the above procedure. Others directly apply Chinese conflict of laws to determine the applicable law. If the governing law is Chinese law, the courts then consider whether the Chinese law is consistent or in conflict with relevant international treaties.[18] China follows the principle of giving priority to international treaty and customs over domestic law in civil matters. This principle has been affirmed in a number of statutes.[19] International conventions concluded and acceded to by China have direct effect in the Chinese legal system, which means that the international conventions can be directly applied by the court as a source of law without the necessity of being implemented into domestic law.[20] **12.09**

Intellectual property right treaties, however, are treated differently.[21] Some IP right treaties, such as TRIPS, need to be implemented into domestic Chinese law before they can be applied as a source of law by Chinese courts.[22] Furthermore, many IP conventions only provide the minimum protection standard instead of uniform rules. They can only be enforced after being implemented into domestic law. As a result, Chinese courts can only apply national law concerning IP rights instead of IP right treaties directly. If the parties have chosen TRIPS or other international intellectual property right conventions as the governing law to their disputes, such a choice should be considered invalid. However, if Chinese domestic law provides the standard of protection lower than that provided in the international treaty, the court should rely on Article 142 of the GPCL to apply the international treaty instead. **12.10**

18 *Ferrero SPA v. Zhangjiagang Montresor Food Co Ltd*, [2006] Min San Ti Zi No 3; *Wangreixiang Fashion Co v. Trend Ltd*, Shanghai Municipality No 1 Intermediate Court, (2003) Hu Yi Zhong Min Wu (Shang) Chu Zi No 21.

19 GPCL, Art 142(2); PRC Negotiable Instruments Law 2004, Art 95(1); PRC Maritime Law, Art 268(1); PRC Civil Aviation Law, art 184(1).

20 See Ch 2, II.1.4; in general, Z.S. Tang, 'International Treaties in Chinese Private International Law', (2012) 42 *Hong Kong Law Journal* 597.

21 Conflicts Act Interpretation I, Art 4.

22 N.P. Stoianoff, 'The Influence of the WTO over China's Intellectual Property Regime', (2012) 34 *Sydney Law Review* 65, 74.

II.3 Choice of law in intellectual property rights in the Conflicts Act: an overview

12.11 The Conflicts Act classifies IP right disputes into three categories: property-related, contract-related and tort-related. This classification mimics the traditional classification in the conflict of laws, which classifies most disputes into contract, tort/delict, and property. Intellectual property rights are monopoly rights granted to the proprietor, who has exclusive rights to possess, use, exploit, dispose, licence, and transfer the IP right. The content of the rights is analogical to that of property rights. Therefore, disputes on the creation, ownership, content and termination of intellectual property rights can be classified as property-related rights. Article 48 of the Conflicts Act provides special choice of law rules for deciding this issue.

12.12 Since the proprietor possesses the right to dispose its IP rights, the proprietor is free to transfer the whole or part of the IP rights to the other party, for the other party to exploit and/or use in return for a fee. This is called licensing. Licensing is conducted through a licence agreement between the proprietor, the licensor, and the other party, the licensee. The relationship between the licensor and the licensee is contractual. If the licensee does not use the IP rights in accordance with the manner described in the licence agreement, the proprietor may sue for breach of contract. This type of IP right-related dispute may be comfortably classified as contractual. Article 49 of the Conflicts Act provides a separate and independent choice of law rules for such a claim.

12.13 Furthermore, there may be a party who does not receive permission to use or exploit an IP but nevertheless uses the IP in the absence of agreement, which may cause financial damages to the original proprietor. Since there is no obligation freely assumed between the parties, the proprietor cannot rely on contract to seek remedies. The proprietor, however, could rely on tort claiming infringement of its IP rights. This type of claim is classified as tort, and governed by Article 50 of the Conflicts Act.

12.14 It is necessary to note that these three types of IP right-related disputes may arise on their own, but they may also intertwine with one other. The proprietor may bring the proceedings to seek a declaration of its ownership. The proprietary claim may also arise as a preliminary question of other claims. For example, the proprietor sues for the infringement of his IP right, while the defendant challenges the ownership of the proprietor. The court thus will decide the property-related issue first to clarify the ownership before it can proceed to decide any tort claims. In other cases, the licensee may breach the licence agreement, which may give rise to a claim on either the breach of contract or tort. In these cases, the court uses different choice of law rules to decide different types of the claim in a dispute depending on the claimant's choice.

III. PROPRIETARY PERSPECTIVE OF INTELLECTUAL PROPERTY

III.1 Nature of intellectual property rights

Property aspects of IP rights cover their creation, ownership, content, transferability and termination and are similar to the property rights of ordinary intangible property. Thus, some may directly treat the proprietary prospective of IP rights as a property issue and apply the same conflicts rules as are applicable to intangible property.[23] This approach is problematic both in theory and in practice. The territoriality of IP rights makes it differ from ordinary property rights. Intellectual property rights only exist and have legal effect within the country where they are granted.[24] Some IP rights, such as trademark and patent, are granted upon registration, which includes the operation of state authorities. In the absence of international conventions, a state organ may only grant IP rights legal effect within its own territory and will not affect the administrative power of the other sovereign.[25] Furthermore, applying the property choice of law directly to determine the property perspective of IP rights proves difficult in practice. Article 37 of the Conflicts Act allows the parties to choose the law governing movable property, including intangible movables. However, the creation of some IP rights, such as patent and trademark, depends on the function of relevant government organs. It cannot be changed by parties' agreement. In the absence of choice, the *situs* rule applies to property.[26] How is the *situs* of an IP right decided? The potential option is to rely on Article 40 of the Conflicts Act. This article applies the law of the place where the right is created to the pledge of right. It implies that intangible property situates in the place of creation. Applying a similar principle, IP rights should locate in the place where the rights are granted or acquired. For example, if a patent is registered in China, Chinese law should apply to the ownership and scope of the right. However, determining the *situs* of unregistered rights may still be difficult. For example, **12.15**

23 See L. Collins, et. al. (eds) *Dicey, Morris and Collins: Conflict of Laws* (15th ed., London 2006) para 22–051.

24 T. Kono and P. Jurcys, 'General Report', in T. Kono (ed) *Intellectual Property and Private International Law* (Bloomsbury 2012) 17.

25 Ibid., 18.

26 Conflicts Act, Art 37.

copyrights may have originated in more than one country pursuant to Article 5(4)(a) of the Berne Convention.[27] The copyright, thus, may have more than one *situs.*

12.16 Applying property choice of law to IP rights, as a result, is wrong in theory and difficult in practice.[28] Although the Conflicts Act distinguishes the proprietary aspect of IP rights from other IP right issues, it does not suggest it should be treated as a property right. Instead, the Conflicts Act treats the proprietary issues of IP rights as *sui generis* and provides a different choice of law rules for their proprietary issues.

III.2 The *lex protectionis* principle

12.17 Article 48 of the Conflicts Act provides that: 'Proprietorship and content of intellectual property rights are governed by the law of the place where protection is sought.' It adopts the *lex protectionis* principle to govern the property aspects of IP rights. The *lex protectionis* principle is a widely adopted principle in deciding the applicable law to the proprietary perspective of IP.[29] It closely relates to the territoriality of IP rights. The current international framework and IP rights theory create a country-based system to protect IP rights. The same object may acquire parallel but independent rights in multiple jurisdictions. Intellectual property rights are also policy-oriented, reflecting state policy and demonstrating state sovereignty, which prevents a state from recognizing rights granted and effective in another country. The *lex protectionis* principle allows a country to recognize the IP rights and protect the effect of the right in its own territory pursuant to its own law.[30] Before the enactment of the Conflicts Act, some Chinese courts had used *lex protectionis* as a general international principle to determine the ownership and content of IP rights in the absence of any provisions in Chinese law.[31]

---

27 R. Matulionyte, 'IP and Applicable Law in Recent International Proposals', (2012) 3 *Journal of Intellectual Property, Information Technology and Electronic Commerce Law* 263, 270.

28 The same pragmatic challenge is also recognized in England. See J.J. Fawcett and P. Torremans, *Intellectual Property and Private International Law* (2nd ed., OUP 2011) paras 13.13–13.40.

29 The same rule is adopted in Art 3.201 of the Max Planck on CLIP, 'Principles on Conflict of Laws in Intellectual Property', 2011; Art 5(2) and Art 6bis(3) of the Berne Convention.

30 Fawcett, Torremans, *supra* n 28, para 18.07.

31 For example, in 2009, the Beijing High People's Court in *Ultra Products (US) Co Ltd v. Antec Corporation (US)* (2009) Gao Min Zhong Zi No 5840, concluded that since the GPCL and its Judicial Interpretation did not provide any choice of law rules to determine the property aspect of IP rights, the law applicable should be determined according to the general principle adopted internationally, which is the *lex protectionis*. Since the disputed IP rights were registered and protected in China, Chinese law applied.

What is meant by the *lex protectionis*? The *lex protectionis* is phrased as the law of the country 'for which protection is sought'.[32] For example, if an applicant applies for the registration of its patent or trademark in China, the protection is sought in China and the Chinese law should be applied to determine the creation and content of the IP right. **12.18**

Confusion may exist if the IP right has already been created in country A and the proprietor seeks protection in Chinese courts, either for a declaration relief, or requiring the court to determine its ownership and rights before deciding the substantive claim of infringement. The countries involved include China, where the action seeking to protect the IP right is brought, and country A where protection is granted. Does the *lex protectionis* refer to the law of China or country A? The former focuses on the judicial protection of IP rights, i.e., protection is sought in the court of this country.[33] It leads to the same effect of the *lex fori*. Applying this approach may cause a rigid result. For example, the proprietor sues the defendant in China for infringing his patent registered in the US. The defendant challenges the claimant's ownership as a defence. The strict forum-based approach may lead to the application of Chinese law in all cases, which would not recognize any IP right granted abroad. This result may be abused and encourage infringement of foreign intellectual property rights by Chinese companies. The second approach is based on the vested right, i.e., protection is sought under the system of law that creates the right. This approach leads to uniformity, consistency and stability and helps prevent forum shopping. The majority of commentators and authorities prefer to apply the second approach to interpret the *lex protectionis* as the law of the country where the protection was created and under which the current protection claim is brought.[34] **12.19**

The *lex protectionis* for registered rights is the place where the right is registered. An invention may be registered in multiple countries, but the *lex protectionis* will be the law under which the protection claim is sought. For example, a company registers a patent in country A and country B. The two countries may grant different rights and scopes for the patent. The company wants to sue the defendant for infringement of patent in country A in the Chinese court. The *lex protectionis* is the law of country A. The *lex protectionis* for unregistered rights can be determined in the same way. For example, a **12.20**

32 Fawcett and Torremans, *supra* n 28, para 15.23; Draft CLIP Proposal, Art 3.102.

33 See also Japanese cases, Supreme Court decision of 26 September, 2002, (2002) 56(7) Minshu 1551.

34 See CLIP, s 3:701; ALI Principle, s 301 of the; Transparency Principle, Art 301; Russian Civil Code, Art 1132(1). Matulionyte, *supra* n 27, 264–5. This is an approach accepted by many Chinese commentators. See QI Aimin, HE Peiyu 'Applicable Law to the Foreign-Related Intellectual Property Disputes', (2011) 2 *Intellectual Property* 120, 121; *Ultra Products supra* n 31.

writer's monograph is published in China, Malaysia, and Singapore. He receives copyrights in all three countries. If a dispute arises concerning content of the writer's copyright in Singapore, the Chinese court should apply Singaporean law.

12.21 Although the *lex protectionis* is theoretically different from the *lex fori,* the principles usually refer to the same country in practice.[35] This is because issuance of IP rights sometimes involves the activity of a state organ. Many countries, thus, reserve exclusive jurisdiction to hear disputes in relation to the proprietary perspective of IP rights, especially if the IP right is granted by registration.[36] Other countries, when being seized to hear the dispute, may find they have no jurisdiction,[37] or decline jurisdiction pursuant to *forumn non conveniens*. The court that takes jurisdiction to decide the property aspect of an IP right is usually the place where the IP right is granted. However, this may not be definite. The property aspect of an IP right may arise as an incidental question of other claims. For example, when the proprietor sues the defendant for breach of contract in the defendant's domicile, where it is more convenient to enforce the judgment, the defendant may rely on the scope and limitation of the intellectual property right as a defence. In the absence of judicial cooperation, the court of the defendant's domicile may have to decide the content and scope of the IP right, applying the law under which the protection is sought.

III.3 The scope of Article 48

12.22 Article 48 applies the *lex loci protectionis* to the proprietary issues of IP rights. However, it only expressly covers ownership and content of intellectual property rights. Proprietary issues include creation, ownership, existence, limitation, validity, exception, and transferability of the rights.[38] It is unclear whether Article 48 could be interpreted broadly to cover all proprietary matters of IP rights or it provides an exhaustive list.[39] The latter interpretation clearly leaves many questions unanswered and the gap is probably not what was intended by the legislators. It is thus suggested that irrespective of the narrow wording, Article 48 should be applied to all proprietary matters of intellectual property rights.

35 Matulionyte, *supra* n 27, 265.
36 Brussels I Recast, Art 24(4).
37 Ibid.
38 Kono and Jurcys, *supra* n 24, 135.
39 QI Aimin, HE Peiyu, *supra* n 34, 124.

III.4 Intellectual property rights and employment contracts

In practice, many inventions are created by the employee when performing obligations under an employment contract. When the dispute arises as to the ownership of the intellectual property rights, should Article 48 on the ownership of the intellectual property or Article 43 on employment contracts apply? **12.23**

Article 43 provides special choice of law rules to protect the weaker party, i.e., the employee, in an employment contract to resolve contractual disputes arising out of the employment contract. It, however, may not apply to the property perspective of IP rights. First, the ownership and content of IP rights cannot be classified as a contractual obligation, and thus is not subject to the contractual choice of law. Secondly, Article 48 classifies the property aspect of IP rights a *sui generis* issue. This is a specific choice of law rule designed for IP rights. If the rights are created pursuant to a contract the property aspect will still be determined by Article 48 as the special law takes priority. Thirdly, Article 43 aims to protect the employee and prevent the employer from selecting the law that may deprive the employee-creators of their rights. However, since party autonomy is not applicable to the property aspect of IP rights, the employer is not free to choose the law to govern the ownership of the IP right. Applying Article 48, thus, is not contrary to employee protection policy and should not cause unreasonable results. **12.24**

IV. CONTRACTUAL PERSPECTIVE OF INTELLECTUAL PROPERTY RIGHTS

Contractual perspectives of IP rights may cover a wide range of issues, which can be categorized into three groups. First, assignment or licensing of IP rights, this is the simplest and most straightforward, where the IP right proprietor contracts with the other party to allow the latter to exploit or use the right.[40] Secondly, many IP rights contracts relate closely to other commercial activities. For example, publication contracts include the transfer of copyright from the author to the publisher, and the publisher's activity to copy edit, print, deliver, market and distribute. Franchising agreements requires the franchiser to licence the franchisee to use the franchiser's trademark, design, logo, patent, trade secret, and/or know-how to conduct business and to provide training and support. Distribution contracts usually involve licensing the **12.25**

40 Transfer/assignment differs from licence. The former transfers all substantive rights to the assignee, while the latter transfers only certain rights. See F.B. Schramm, 'Licenses, Contracts and Assignments of Intellectual Property', (1960) 9 *Cleveland-Marshall Law Review* 65, 67.

proprietor's patent to the distributor to market, sell, or use. Sales contracts may also involve transfer of IP rights, such as for the buyer to use patented process, or use the goods sold for particular purposes subject to patent.[41] All these contracts are more complicated than simple transfer of intellectual property rights and include other obligations, such as marketing, distribution, manufacturing, etc, with the transfer of intellectual property rights as one part of the agreement.[42] Thirdly, the joint development agreement is a different type where the parties agree to invent or produce a new intellectual product, such as patent, designs, software, etc, and the agreement provides parties' obligations in the IP right development and ownership and rights over the final product. The subject matter of the agreement is not an existing IP right, but the application of labour, knowledge and skills to produce an intellectual product. Intellectual property right-related disputes usually arise over two aspects: one, the parties' performance of their obligations during the project; and two, the ownership and proprietary rights of the parties over the final product. The first concerns the general contract law and is subject to the contractual choice of law rules. The latter concerns the proprietary aspect of IP rights and should be determined according to the *lex protectionis* rule as described above. This section only focuses on the contractual issues where the IP right is the subject matter and treated as a commodity in the contract. It gives emphasis to examining the first category of the simple transfer of IP rights, before moving on to the more complicated transactions in contracts with mixed purposes.

IV.1 Cross-border transfer of intellectual property rights: the policy

12.26 Cross-border transfer of IP rights involves both private and public interests. The private interest in the transfer of IP rights is primarily analogical to the interest of private parties in an ordinary contract. The parties wish to have certainty and predictability to ascertain the legal consequence of the transaction, to reduce commercial risk and transaction costs, to acquire fair treatments between the parties, and to apply the law that may favour the transaction and/or provide the most favourable result to this particular party.[43]

12.27 The transfer of IP rights, however, involves strong public interest. It is wrong to take market freedom and the right of free disposal of intellectual property rights by proprietors for granted. Countries have policies to balance the protection of innovation on the one hand, and benefit to society and the

---

41 Ibid., 70.

42 Fawcett and Torremans, *supra* n 28, para 14.01.

43 K. Patchel, 'Choice of Law and Software Licenses', (2000) 26 *Brooklyn Journal of International Law* 117, 118–21.

general public on the other. As a result, various policies are imposed to limit the parties' freedom to transfer IP rights. Some countries restrict the length of transfer or licence;[44] some countries limit the types of IP rights that may be transferrable;[45] and others may require compulsory transfer of some IP rights.[46] These public interests inevitably cause a country to make reservations over party autonomy in the transfer of IP rights. A cross-border transfer of such rights may generate the public interest concerns of more than one country. A state has an interest in controlling the transactions and activities occurring within its territory.[47] A state where the IP rights are granted or protected may have the interest to control their disposal. The forum state also has the interest to enforce state policy in relation to the rights.[48] This further complicates conflicts problems. Choice of law rules need to take into account IP right policy, international comity, territoriality of intellectual property rights, and the protection of party autonomy and encouragement of innovation.

Contracts for the transfer of IP rights, therefore, differ from ordinary contracts. First, IP rights are different from ordinary commodities in that they are rights protected by national authorities and usually relate to a country's economic and development strategy. Transfer of the rights, thus, may encounter more restrictions and public policy barriers. This characteristic would be reflected in the conflict of laws by specifically designing connecting factors to determine the country with the most significant connections to the dispute, by considering the overriding mandatory rules of the most closely related country, and by relying on the public policy reservation to the application of forum law. Secondly, the nature and transferability of IP rights are determined by national authorities and have territorial limitations. The transfer of IP rights may inevitably meet the proprietary questions. Consideration should be given as to whether it is more appropriate to apply the same law to govern both the property aspects of IP rights and the transfer of such rights, or to apply different laws to different issues. **12.28**

IV.2 Article 49 of the Conflicts Act

Article 49 of the Conflicts Act provides: **12.29**

---

44 *Horms v. Sterm* 229 F.42, 48 (2d Cir., 1916).

45 For example, the moral rights are not transferable.

46 Compulsory transfer is permitted in China if the proprietor fails to exploit the patent within three years of registering it, the proprietor's activity breaches anti-trust law, the country is in a state of emergency, the country acts for public policy or public health, or a new invention that depends on the exploitation of the patent in question would bring significant development to the economy. Patent Law, Arts 48–51.

47 Patchel, *supra* n 43, 125.

48 Ibid., 126.

> The parties may by agreement choose the law applicable to the transfer and license of intellectual property rights. Absent any choice by the parties, the relevant provisions of this law on contract are applicable.

12.30 Article 49 of the Conflicts Act applies contractual choice of law rules to the contractual perspective of IP rights, i.e., the transfer and licence of IP rights. It clearly states that party autonomy applies as the first principle and, in the absence of choice, the law applicable shall be determined by the conflicts rules in the contract. Finally, the applicable law should be subject to the limitation of mandatory rules and public policy as provided in Articles 4 and 5 in Chapter One 'General Provisions'.

i. Party autonomy

12.31 Intellectual property rights are usually transferred by contract, which usually includes a choice of law agreement. Party autonomy, as a basic choice of law rules for contractual obligations, applies equally in the contract for the transfer of IP rights.[49] However, some special characteristics of transfer of IP rights may challenge the ordinary perspective of party autonomy and require special attention.

12.32 First, party autonomy only applies to the substantive rights and obligations of the parties arising out of the contract to transfer IP rights. It does not regulate the nature and transferability of the subject matter, which are property aspects of IP rights and should be subject to the law designated in Article 48 of the Conflicts Act. It should also exclude the formal requirements utilized by the relevant authority on the transfer of IP rights, such as the requirement of registration. For example, under Chinese law, the right to apply for a patent and the patent itself can be transferred, but the contract for the transfer of the above rights should be in writing, registered in the Patent Office, and announced in a public notice.[50] This requirement cannot be derogated from by party autonomy. If the parties have chosen the law of country A to govern the formation of the contract to transfer a Chinese patent, which does not require the written form, registration and public notice, the transfer is not valid in China.

12.33 Secondly, the method of concluding a contract for the transfer of IP rights may be different from ordinary contracts. Transfer of copyrights of software is usually facilitated by a licensing agreement. This licensing agreement is usually

49 Chosen law has been recognized by Chinese courts in a number of cases. E.g., *Shanghai Jiayang Telecommunication Technology Ltd v. Lingyang Technology Ltd*, (2007) Hu Gao Min San (Zhi) Zhong Zi No 72; *Shandong Jufeng v. MGAME (Korea)*, [2009] Min San Zhong Zi No 4.

50 PRC Patent Law, Art 10.

presented as a shrink-wrap contract. The terms and conditions of the contract are placed inside the package of the software wrapped by plastic and the licensee is bound by the terms and conditions once the seal is broken and the package opened;[51] and licensees are unable to view the full terms and conditions before opening the package.[52] Some licensees may not be aware that the activity of opening the package means they give consent to the terms.[53] Furthermore, most shrink-wrap licensing agreements are used in mass-market consumer sales where inequality of bargaining power exists between the parties.

Shrink-wrap contracts exist in the traditional way to sell software carried in a physical medium. With the development of e-commerce, shrink-wrap contracts are replaced by click-wrap contracts and browse-wrap contracts when selling software online. A click-wrap contract will require the licensee to check the box 'I agree' or 'continue' before he is able to download or install the software. Once the licensee clicks the requested link, he is deemed to have expressed his consent to be bound by the standard terms and conditions of the licensor. A browse-wrap contract does not even require the licensee to actively demonstrate his consent. Simply by continuing browsing the website or continuing transactions, the licensee is deemed to agree on the terms of the licensor. **12.34**

The validity and enforceability of a choice of law agreement contained in the shrink-wrap, click-wrap or browse-wrap contract are in doubt. The effect of this type of licence has been questioned in many countries.[54] Chinese law does not provide clear guidance and no judicial interpretation is provided by the SPC. The Chinese courts, as a result, need to address this issue by exercising their discretion and providing an innovative interpretation of Chinese law. The validity of shrink-wrap licence has been examined in a few cases. In *GUO Li v. Microsoft*,[55] the licensee claimed that 28 terms, including one choice of law clause choosing US law,[56] in the shrink-wrap licence was invalid. The claimant argued that, first, the parties had inequality of bargaining power and the licensor abused its power by 'forcing' the licensee to accept the terms which were not presented in full before purchasing the software. The court, however, refused this argument primarily based on the efficiency consideration. It is **12.35**

51 M.A. Lemley, 'Intellectual Property and Shrink-wrap Licenses', (1995) 68 *South California Law Review* 1239, 1241.

52 Some plastic wraps may show some of the key terms but not all.

53 A warning should usually be provided on the package but many licensees may not pay attention to it.

54 See *Step-Saver Data Systems v. Wyse Technology* 939 F.2d 91 (3d Cir. 1991); *Arizona Retail Systems v. Software Link, Inc.* 831 F.Supp. 759 (D. Ariz. 1993).

55 (2006) Yi Zhong Min Chu Zi No 14468.

56 License Agreement, Art 18.

expensive and inefficient to require a licensor to negotiate every term with licensees in the mass market and the additional cost would be transferred to the licensee eventually through the increased price. Allowing standard contracts would benefit the general public and reduce social costs. Furthermore, when installing the software, the screen displayed all the terms and conditions. The licensee chose to install after seeing all the terms, which demonstrated genuine consent. Finally, it is commercially unviable for a licensor to display the full contract terms on the package of software before the licensee decides to purchase. The licensee secondly, argued that the shrink-wrap contract created unbalanced rights and obligations between the parties. The court, after examining the questioned terms, concluded that the contract was not in breach of Chinese substantive law and did not produce unfairness between the parties. However, the Chinese court invalidated four terms based on the decision that they excluded the licensor's liability compulsory under the Chinese law. In other words, these terms trying to contract out of mandatory rules of Chinese law should be invalid.

12.36 In this case, the Chinese court considered both the contracting process and the substantive validity. It held that shrink-wrap contracts are common commercial practice and justifiable for commercial efficiency. No different treatment, thus, is to be provided for shrink-wrap licences.[57] A term may be invalidated in its substance, but a choice of law clause does not infringe any Chinese mandatory rules and should be substantively valid and enforceable.

12.37 The approach adopted in the Chinese courts may be challenged on three grounds. First, it is too ready to recognize all shrink-wrap types of contracts without imposing any duties of disclosure on the licensor. It would make a great difference if the licensor has taken all necessary steps to provide the licensee with the opportunity to read the terms before entering into the contract on the one hand and if the licensor does nothing or prevents the licensee from fully reviewing the terms on the other. The terms may not be able to bind the licensee if the licensor has abused the shrink-wrap process. Secondly, a difference should be drawn between a business-to-business licence and a consumer licence. In the latter case, consumers are usually weaker and more needs to be done to protect them from the inequality of bargaining power. Simply relying on the mandatory rules is not enough. Furthermore, Article 42 provides special choice of law rules for consumer contracts,[58] while Article 49 provides no different treatment for consumer licences. It increases

57 The same decision was adopted in other cases: see *Eachnet Shanghai v. LIU Songting*, www.chinalawinfo.com, CLI.C.23941; *Intel Corporation v. Beijing Dongxinda Technology Ltd*, (2005) Gao Min Zhong Zi No 1379.

58 For more discussion see Ch 8, section IV.1.

the importance of the correct characterization of purchase of software: if the contract is characterized as a sale of goods or provision of services, the consumer is protected by the protective choice of law;[59] if it is characterized as a licence, no protection is provided. According to PRC Contract law, this transaction should be classified as licence instead of sale.[60] It is, thus, questionable why consumers in ordinary sales are protected while in transfers of IP rights they are not.

ii. Law in the absence of party autonomy

Where the parties do not enter into a choice of law agreement, Article 49 directs 'the choice of law rules applying to contracts'. Article 41 provides the characteristic performance principle or the most significant connection principle as the default choice of law rules for contracts.[61] **12.38**

Who is the characteristic performer of a transfer of an IP right contract? Transfer of IP rights usually involves complicated rights and obligations. In a contract for the transfer of a patent, the original proprietor has an obligation to provide relevant technology, instructions, materials and training. The transferee has an obligation to pay the fees and to utilize the patent according to the contract. In some contracts, the transferee will utilize the patent to produce products, to market and distribute the products and to pay the transferor commissions to an agreed ratio of the profits. It is very difficult to ascertain which party is the characteristic performer. **12.39**

In other contracts, the characteristic performer may be easier to determine. For example, in a publication contract, the writer provides manuscripts to the publisher and transfers copyrights to the publisher. The publisher will copy edit, print, distribute and market the book, and will pay royalties to the writer. The publisher's obligation is more complicated, could demonstrate the characteristic of this type of contract, and makes the publisher carry higher risk. It is reasonable to hold the publisher the characteristic performer of the contract. However, there is no consensus. Some commentators may argue that the writer has the obligation to write and to submit the manuscript, to ensure the manuscript does not infringe others' copyright, and to provide the publisher with an exclusive right to publish and distribute the work in the defined areas **12.40**

59 Conflicts Act, Art 42.

60 PRC Contract Law, Art 137 provides that if the subject matter is computer software or other IP rights, unless the law provides or the parties agree otherwise, the subject matter does not belong to the purchaser. The transaction, thus, does not include the transfer of title and is not a sale.

61 For more discussion, see Ch 8, III.

for an agreed period, and which is equally important, unique to this complicated type of contract.[62]

12.41 It is thus suggested that transfer of IP rights should be considered on a case-to-case basis instead of following a blanket rule. Some may clearly have a characteristic performer, while others may not easily be able to apply the characteristic performance principle. The applicable law to the latter shall be decided according to the most significant connection principle.

12.42 Applying the most significant connection principle to a transfer of IP rights may not be easy, either. Multiple factors may be relevant to the consideration, including the country where the IP right is registered, granted, or protected; the country where the proprietor or the transferee has its habitual residence, domicile or nationality; the country where the transfer is taking place; the country where the obligation is performed; and the country where the contract is concluded. It is impossible to grant a conclusive weight to any of the connecting factors. The court must take a flexible approach to consider all the circumstances of a case. However, in practice, some courts are too ready to hold China the country with the most significant connection to the transfer of IP rights without conducting a comprehensive centre of gravity exercise. For example, in *Beijing Zhimeilida Culture Dissemination Ltd v. WANG Rongfen*,[63] the publication contract was concluded between a Chinese publisher and a German writer. The court held that since the printed books would be disseminated and distributed in China, China was the country with the closest connection with the contract. The conclusion may not have been wrong but the approach in considering only one factor shows the court too ready to apply Chinese law. As far as any substantive factor directs to China, Chinese law applies.

iii. Mandatory rules and public policy

12.43 Chinese courts apply overriding mandatory rules of China to restrict party autonomy and the effect of the applicable foreign law. Due to the authority control of the IP rights, Chinese law imposes restrictions on the transfer of these rights. The restrictions mainly relate to the transferability and formality of the transfer. In general, Chinese courts will only recognize the validity of transfer in the territory of China, if the transfer meets certain formal requirements, including the formality of the contract, the requirement of

---

62 In practice, Chinese courts had applied the most significant connection principle to decide the applicable law for a publication contract: *Beijing Zhimeilida Culture Dissemination Ltd v. WANG Rongfen*, Beijing Municipality HPC, (2008) Gao Min Zhong Zi No 165.

63 Ibid.

registration and public notice. As to the transfer of copyrights, Article 25 of the Copyright Law provides that the transfer of the right of reproduction, distribution, rental, exhibition, presentation, broadcasting, communication through information network, cinematography, adaptation, translation and compilation must be recorded in a written contract. Article 26 further provides that a pledge of copyright requires the parties to register the pledge in the copyright administration department of the state council. The PRC Trademark Law provides that the parties should conclude a contract for the transfer of trademark and apply to the Trademark Office for approval. The transfer is valid only after the application is approved and publicized.[64] Licensing of a trademark should also be recorded in the Trademark Office and publicized.[65] The transfer of a patent also requires a written contract, registration in the Patent Office, and publicity.[66] Furthermore, more procedural requirements are provided to the transfer of a patent from a Chinese proprietor to a foreigner.[67] Some technology is crucial for the national development of economy and technology. Providing exclusive rights for exploiting the patent to foreign companies would bring negative impact to the national interest. The transfer should be jointly approved by the competent department for foreign trade and economic cooperation under the State Council and the administrative department for science and technology under the State Council.[68] If the patent relates to the export of technology that is prohibited, the application will be rejected. If the patent relates to the export of technology that is restricted, the applicants must apply for technology export approval; and after approval, the applicants can use the 'export licensing' to apply for registration of transfer; if the patent can be freely transferred, the applicants should acquire the 'Certificate of the technology export' from the State Council or local commerce administrative department to apply for registration in the intellectual property right Office.[69]

64 PRC Trademark Law, Art 42.

65 Ibid., Art 43.

66 PRC Patent Law, Art 10.

67 Ibid.

68 Art 14 of the Rules for the Implementation of the Patent Law of the People's Republic of China, [2010] Guowuyuan Ling No 569.

69 The PRC intellectual property right Department, 'Announcement on Approval and Registration of the Transfer of Patent Application Rights and Patent to the Foreigners', 26 Dec 2003.

V. INFRINGEMENT OF INTELLECTUAL PROPERTY RIGHTS

V.1 Tort conflict of laws and infringement of intellectual property rights

12.44 Designing a conflicts principle in infringement of intellectual property rights is a conventional difficulty. Legislators face the dilemma between the territoriality of IP rights on the one hand and the international context of infringement on the other. The conflicts rule that is most widely adopted is the *lex protectionis*. Some countries do not have a specific choice of law rules for IP rights, which continue to adopt the traditional *lex loci delicti* or *lex fori* for the infringement of rights. All of these approaches are based on the principle of territoriality.

12.45 International institutions and research groups, however, are working hard to find a new approach that should better suit the internationalization tendency. Proposals have been provided by the American Law Institute, European Max Planck Group on Conflict of Laws in Intellectual Property, the 'Transparency' project in Japan, the Korean Private International Law Association, and the joint project of the Korean Private International Law Association and Waseda University Global COE Project of Japan.[70] Some proposals provide innovative choice of law rules, such as party autonomy and market effect. However, none of the proposals have truly abandoned the *lex protectionis* rule as the basic principle. It is expected that the territoriality approach will continue to play a dominant role in determining choice of law in infringement of IP rights while the internationality approach may only contribute as an exception.

i. Lex loci delicti

12.46 The traditional conflict of laws adopts the *lex loci delicti* rule to determine the law governing the cross-border tort. As the infringement of intellectual property right is also one type of tort, the *lex loci delicti* may be relevant in principle. The *loci delicti* usually includes both the place where the wrongful activity has taken place (*locus delicti commissi*) and the place where the damage or harmful result occurs (*locus damni*). Differences exist as to which law should be applied to a cross-border tort.

12.47 Some countries apply the *lex loci delicti commissi* to tort.[71] Applying the same law to the infringement of IP rights causes two challenges. First, in the infringement of the IP right, the wrongful activity could happen at a distance,

---

70 See Matulionyte, *supra* n 27, 263.

71 Such as Croatia Private International Law Act, Art 28. See I. Kunda, 'Croatia', in T Kono (ed), *Intellectual Property and Private International Law* (Bloomsbury, 2012) 497.

i.e., it may occur in the country where the IP right in question does not exist. Applying this law to decide whether the IP right, which exists and is protected in another country, is infringed causes practical problems and comity concerns. Furthermore, from the governmental interest perspective, the country where the wrongful action occurs has no interest either in determining whether the IP right exists in another country is infringed or in protecting the right. This is fundamentally different from ordinary tort because of the territoriality and sovereign-protection of IP rights. Finally, the claim for the infringement of IP rights usually generates an incidental question of the existence, content and ownership of the rights. The property aspect of IP rights has close connections with state sovereignty and would not be subject to the law of the country where the wrongful action was conducted. *Lex loci delicti commissi,* thus, would cause the application of two substantive laws in the decision. Secondly, the *lex loci delicti commissi* may point to the law of more than one country. For example, the wrongdoer could manufacture pirated products in country A and sell them in country B where the brand is registered. The *locus delicti commissi* includes countries A and B. Which law should apply as the only governing law for the infringement claim?[72] One possible suggestion is that the *locus delicti commissi* should be the country where the 'substantive' infringement activity occurs. Taking into account the territoriality of intellectual property rights, the substantive infringement activity should be the activity to market the product in country B, which generates legal liabilities.

Other countries prefer to apply the *lex loci damni,* which can usually be predicted by the victim, has the closest connection with the victim and would better protect the interest of the victim.[73] In damage to tangible property, the place of damage will be the place where the property is located.[74] In the infringement of IP rights, the location of IP rights is hard to ascertain given its intangible nature. As a result, the infringement of such rights cannot be easily analogized as damage to property. It may be more appropriate to align IP rights with intangible financial interest and agree that the place of damage occurs in the country where the economic interest of the proprietor is hurt. Does the economic interest of the proprietor locate in the place where the proprietor has its habitual residence or domicile, where the market value of the intellectual property right occurs, or where the proprietor's exclusive right to **12.48**

72 D van Engelen, 'Rome II and Intellectual Property Rights', (2008) 4 NiPR 440, 442.

73 See US Restatement of the Conflict of Laws 2nd, Art 37; EU Rome II Regulation, Art 4; Gabon Civil Code, Art 41.

74 Such as Case 21/76 *Bier BV v. Mines de potasse d'Alsaca SA* [1976] ECR 01735, where the wrongdoer produced chemicals in France causing damage to the claimant's plants in the Netherlands. In product liability claims where defective products cause damage to property, the wrongful activity, i.e., manufacturing of products, may occur in another country.

the intellectual property right is deprived? It may be reasonable to argue that the damage occurs in the place where the proprietor has its habitual residence or domicile, because that is the place where the loss of economic interest is felt. This country may be interested in protecting the economic interests of its resident, but it may have no interest in protecting economic interests obtained in another country, nor in protecting an IP right existing in another country. Applying the law of the country where the infringed IP right has its market value is also unreasonable. The right usually has market value in every country irrespective if it is protected there. However, if it is not granted protection in country A, everyone could use or exploit the right in country A and it would not lead to damage in law. Therefore, the most appropriate interpretation is that damage occurs in the place from where the proprietor's exclusive right to use, enjoy and exploit the IP right is deprived, which again is the country where the right is protected.

ii. Lex loci protectionis

12.49 The above analysis shows that the traditional *lex loci delicti* would lead to the application of the *lex loci protectionis*,[75] which is adopted worldwide as the applicable law for infringement of IP rights. Cross-border infringement of IP rights has very close connections with the territoriality of IP rights. Where an IP right is granted in country A, it is protected in the territory of country A under the law of country A, and can only be infringed in country A. For example, if a trademark is registered in Malaysia but not registered or protected in China, the proprietor's claim that the defendant has infringed its trademark in China would not be held successful.

12.50 Intellectual property right holders have an interest in protecting the IP right which is granted and protected by law. As a result, when the right holder alleges that the defendant has infringed its intellectual property right, the right holder will not claim it under the law of another country, but under the law of the country where the protection is granted. The country that has provided protection to the IP right also has governmental interest in protecting the right against any subsequent infringement. Territoriality leads to the worldwide adoption of the *lex protectionis* rule to govern cross-border infringements of IP rights. The *lex protectionis* is closely connected with territoriality of IP rights and enables the application of the same law to both the property aspect and infringement of intellectual property rights.

75 R.A. De Miguel Asensio, 'The Private International Law of Intellectual Property and of Unfair Commercial Practices', in S. Leible and A. Ohly (eds.), *Intellectual Property and Private International Law* (Tubingen, Mohr Siebeck, 2009) 137, 151; T. Petz, in T. Kono (ed.), *Intellectual Property and Private International Law* (Bloomsbury, 2012) 222–5; van Engelen, *supra* n 72, 442

Lex loci protectionis, however, may be criticized in the multi-state infringement. Some IP rights, especially copyrights and famous trademarks, acquire protection in multiple countries. In the digital era, an online infringement may lead to multiple infringements of separate IP rights in every single country, which leads to the application of multiple national laws under the *lex protectionis*. This may cause significant difficulties for the court and also unfairness to the claimant. The claimant may have to prove the law of various countries if wishing to pursue damages in all countries. As a result, many claimants may be prevented from claiming the full damages arising out of one infringement activity and must choose the law of the one or a few countries in which to bring the action.[76] **12.51**

iii. Lex fori

Applying the *lex fori* to cross-border infringement of IP rights is justified for bringing uniformity and certainty and being easy to prove. Uniformity means that it effectively avoids the application of multiple laws in multi-state infringement. Certainty means it avoids the problems of deciding the *situs delicti* in complicated infringement cases. Easy to prove means the court avoids the problem of having to prove foreign law.[77] **12.52**

Applying the *lex fori* may be doubted on three grounds. First, it is questionable how significant an interest the forum may have over the infringement of foreign IP rights, as the right is not protected by the forum and the infringement of it will not affect the forum's policy. One suggestion is that a country could expand its legislative jurisdiction by granting extraterritorial effects to the IP law of the *lex fori*.[78] However, a country's freedom of legislative jurisdiction should be restricted by the public international law principle of comity. This leads to the second ground of refusal that systematically applying the *lex fori* may infringe the sovereignty of the country *protectionis*. Thirdly, since the property aspect of IP rights is exclusively governed by the *lex protectionis*, applying the *lex fori* to the infringement of IP rights may lead to *dépaçage* in some cases. **12.53**

It is necessary to know that except in multi-state infringements of IP rights, in most cases the *lex fori* and the *lex protectionis* would be the same. The claimant usually prefers to bring the tort claim in the country *protectionis*, which is the most convenient forum to determine the ownership, to ascertain the damage, **12.54**

76 R. Fentiman, 'Choice of Law and Intellectual Property', in J. Drexl and A. Kur (eds), *Intellectual Property and Private International Law* (Bloomsbury, 2005) 145.

77 Ibid., 146.

78 Ibid.

and to apply the law. However, this is not definite. In some cases, the claimant may sue in the defendant's domicile for the purpose of enforcement of judgments.

iv. Party autonomy

12.55 Applying party autonomy in tort claims is innovative.[79] It may bring advantages such as certainty and predictability.[80] However, applying party autonomy to IP right infringement may generate more doubts than in other torts. First, IP rights are protected on a country-to-country basis. The protection is restricted within the territory of the country and it is unreasonable and impractical to apply the law of another country to protect the IP right granted and protected in another country. Party autonomy is contrary to the territoriality of IP rights.[81] Secondly, since the protection of IP rights is usually granted and ensured by authorities, applying party autonomy would infringe state sovereignty and public policy. Therefore, applying party autonomy in IP right infringement is controversial and the practice is not widely accepted.[82]

v. Market effect

12.56 The market effect rule is proposed as an alternative or exception to *lex protectionis*.[83] According to this rule, the law of the country where the substantial effect of the infringement occurs may apply. If the infringement conduct does not point to the country *protectionis* and no substantial damage or effects may be felt in this country, the law of this country is not applicable.[84]

12.57 The market effect rule aims to limit the law that may be applicable in multi-state infringement, especially internet infringement. In an online infringement of copyright, for example, the defendant uploads the disputed work, where it is accessible in all countries where the copyright is protected. However, it does not mean that all laws should be applied. The defendant may not target all the countries and only affect the market of a few. The market effect approach would suggest that only the law of the countries that are targeted and/or affected by the defendant may be applicable.

---

79 Conflicts Act, Art 44. See Ch 9 for more discussion. Party autonomy is also adopted in the EU to decide the applicable law in most tort claims. See Rome II Regulation, Art 14. Party autonomy in tort is also accepted in Japan and Switzerland.

80 See Ch 9, III.1 above.

81 Matulionyte, *supra* n 27, 282; A. Kur, 'Applicable Law: an Alternative Proposal for International Regulation', (2005) 30 *Brooklyn Journal of International Law* 952, 975.

82 Although party autonomy in tort is accepted in the Rome II Regulation, Art 8 excludes party autonomy in the infringement of intellectual property rights. However, party autonomy is proposed in CLIP, Art 3:606; Joint Proposal, Art 302(1), (2); Transparency Proposal, Art 305; ALI Principle, s 302.

83 CLIP Proposal, Art 3:602; Joint Proposal, Art 305.

84 Matulionyte, *supra* n 27, 284.

The market effect approach, however, is also subject to criticism. First, it causes design problems. Should the test be based on 'target' or 'factual effects'? The former may be hard to prove, while the latter may cause uncertainty to the defendant, who may not expect that an activity may have a substantial impact in some countries out of its target. Secondly, the application of the market effect rule depends on the court's discretion. The court has to adopt various standards to determine whether substantial effects may be found, which imposes challenges to some courts and causes inconsistency. Thirdly, this approach does not rule out the application of multiple laws where the substantial effects may exist in multi-states. It may only reduce the difficulty caused by the *lex protectionis* approach, but not eliminate it. Fourthly, it artificially prevents the proprietor from full recovery. Although the effects in some countries are unsubstantial, the proprietor's right is indeed damaged in these countries. The proprietor may give up its right to claim damages in the same countries under the *lex protectionis* rule due to the efficiency consideration. However, it is substantively different from the situation where the right to claim is barred. **12.58**

V.2 Article 50 of the Conflicts Act

Article 50 of the Conflicts Act states: **12.59**

> Liability for infringing intellectual property rights is governed by the law of the place where protection is sought. The parties may also choose to apply the law of the forum after the infringement occurs.

According to Article 50 of the Conflicts Act, the applicable law to intellectual property rights should be determined by two steps: (1) the parties could make a choice after the infringement occurred; or (2) in the absence of choice, the *lex loci protectionis* applies. **12.60**

i. Party autonomy

The Conflicts Act adopts party autonomy for the infringement of IP rights. This makes Chinese conflicts rules on infringement of IP rights unique and probably more innovative than that in many other countries. However, the Chinese legislators obviously failed to consider the special characteristics of IP rights. The Conflicts Act provides the same limitations to party autonomy in infringement of IP rights as in ordinary tort claims. The choice can only be made after the infringement occurs.[85] As many IP right infringement cases arise out of breach of contracts, the limitation could avoid the difficulty of **12.61**

85 Conflicts Act, Art 50.

determining whether the contractual choice of law clause should be interpreted to cover the tort claim. The court would ignore any *ex ante* choice of law agreements and, unless the parties entered into a new agreement *ex post,* the court will determine the law according to the *lex protectionis* rule. This requirement may be over-rigid and may not actually simplify the court's work. If the parties have a long-term relationship for the IP right licence and both agree to apply the chosen law to both contractual and tort claims arising out of the licence, there is no reason to refuse to recognize the effect of such a choice.

12.62 It is unclear whether the scope of choice is limited. For example, whether the parties could only choose the law governing the substance of the claim, or also remedies, including limitations of liability; whether the parties can only agree on the applicable law governing rights and obligations between them; or they can also choose the law for the third-party liability.[86] Although the law does not provide any clues, it is very likely that party autonomy in infringement of IP rights will be given a very restrictive interpretation by the SPC. Since most Chinese courts do not clarify remedy as procedure, it is likely that the parties' choice could cover damages.[87] However, the choice may not affect any issues relating to sovereignty of a country, such as the proprietary aspects.[88]

12.63 It is concluded that the Chinese law on party autonomy in the infringement of IP rights has not been well thought through. The provision is vague and unclear on many important issues. The legislators may wish to rely more on mandatory rules and public policy to regulate the negative impact of party autonomy instead of providing clearer instruction at the stage. This may lead to overflexible application of the rule in the choice court.

ii. Lex protectionis

12.64 The Conflicts Act follows the tradition of territoriality and adopts the worldwide accepted *lex protectionis* rule for the infringement of IP rights in the absence of party autonomy. Applying the *lex protectionis,* so far, in practice has not encountered any difficulties. Probably because the Conflicts Act has been in force for only four years, which is not long enough to allow a full empirical survey of its practical impact. Most actions are relatively simple infringement cases, where the claimant sues in China for the infringement of IP rights

86 See Matulionyte, *supra* n 27, 280.

87 See Ch 9, V.

88 Some international proposals even allow party autonomy to determine property issues in relation to infringement claims in order to achieve efficiency. See Matulionyte, *supra* n 27, 281.

protected in China. Chinese courts could comfortably apply Chinese law to these disputes, which is the *lex protectionis, lex declicti commissi* and *lex fori*.[89]

iii. Public policy

The governing law is subject to the public policy defence. Public policy applies not only in the substantive issues, but also in determining remedies. In *Wuhan Jingyuan Environment Project Tech Inc v. Kubota Kasui and Others*,[90] the SPC affirmed the finding that the defendant had infringed the claimant's patent by installing a flue gas desulphurization system subject to the claimant's patent in the factory in Fujian. The court, however, refused to grant the injunction applied for by the claimant but ordered the defendant to pay patent royalties as damages to the claimant. The SPC based this decision on the ground of public policy. Since the system and technology subject to the patent had already been installed in the local factory, an injunction may have caused a significant impact on the social and public interests of Fujian. The PRC Patent Law allows the state to grant compulsory licences in order to protect public interest.[91] In the current case, the SPC's decision was similar to a compulsory licence. The defendant was not barred from continuing using the device and technology in its factory, but had to pay the royalties to the claimant. **12.65**

VI. CONCLUSION

Providing special conflicts rules to intellectual property is an important development. It singles out IP right-related cases from ordinary contracts, tort and property; shows awareness of the special characteristics of IP rights; and fully recognizes the importance of IP rights in China's development strategy. The adopted conflicts rules are largely conventional, following the territoriality principle as a common international practice. However, it also adopts innovative rules, such as party autonomy in determining infringement of IP rights, which is very innovative and unique in comparison with existing conflicts rules in many other countries. **12.66**

There are no enormous errors in Chinese conflicts rules in IP, but the current law is criticized for being oversimplified. As many other conflicts rules in the legislation, they only provide general principles and rules, but fail to provide a **12.67**

89 *Suzuki Motor Corporation v. Changling Group Changchun Motomobile Industry Ltd and Others*, (2010) Zheng Min San Chu Zi No 19 (the disputed logos were designed in Japan but because China is a member of the Berne Convention, Chinese Copyright Law provides protection to the logos in China. The Chinese court, thus, applied Chinese law as the *lex protectionis* to the infringement of copyright claim).

90 *Wuhan Jingyuan Environment Project Tech Inc v. Kubota Kasui and Others*, [2008] Min San Zhong Zi No 8.

91 Patent Law, Arts 48–58.

detailed interpretation. As a result, the application of these rules in practice may cause significant difficulties for judges. It is, in particular, possible that many Chinese judges may not properly understand the meaning of the *lex protectionis*, and may confuse it as being 'the country in which protection is sought', which would lead to the direct application of Chinese law. Furthermore, the provisions fail to consider some special issues in relation to IP rights. What if the infringement of IP rights arises as part of an unfair competition claim? What if an action allegedly infringes IP rights in multiple states? What if the dispute on the ownership of IP rights arises out of an employment contract? What if an infringement arises out of a contract for the transfer of an IP right that chooses a law other than the *lex protectionis*? Should the same conflicts rules apply to ordinary infringement of IP rights, as well as other more special infringements, such as ubiquitous infringement and secondary infringements? All these questions rely on the judicial interpretation and the absence of this causes continuing uncertainty in Chinese practice.

Part IV

INTERREGIONAL CONFLICTS AND COOPERATION

13

INTERREGIONAL CONFLICTS AND COOPERATION BETWEEN MAINLAND, HONG KONG, MACAU AND TAIWAN

13.01 Interregional conflict of laws in China can be regarded as the most complicated topic of conflict of laws in contemporary Chinese law.[1] Interregional conflict occurs as a direct result of the reunification of Hong Kong and Macau with Mainland under the 'one country, two systems' policy and the *de facto* mutual recognition between Mainland and Taiwan of sovereignty over private matters within each other's territory. The specific unification makes Hong Kong, Macau and Taiwan the special regions of China, each with their own high autonomy, special administrative powers, independent judicial systems and separate domestic law. The special circumstances inevitably generate difficult questions on jurisdiction, choice of law, recognition and enforcement of judgments and awards, and other judicial assistance matters.

13.02 Interregional conflicts are a great challenge to Chinese conflict of laws. Before unification, some international treaties on judicial cooperation and assistance applied between Mainland and Hong Kong/Macau. Following unification these treaties were no longer applicable because any conflict is no longer international. Although all the regions have domestic conflicts rules, applying these rules to interregional conflicts may be inappropriate. First, they are conflicts rules in 'foreign'-related proceedings. Applying these rules to interregional conflicts may contradict the 'one country' principle. Secondly, foreign-related conflicts rules may impose a higher threshold for judicial cooperation, the complicated procedural requirements and public policy defence may hamper the cooperation that should otherwise exist between different legal regions in China. Thirdly, all four regions have different domestic conflicts rules. This approach may, in practice, lead to the application of different rules by different legal regions and cause uncertainty, inconsistency and complexity.

13.03 In order to handle the difficulty and uncertainty, the authorities of Mainland, Hong Kong, Macau and Taiwan have entered into a number of arrangements to address interregional conflicts. These arrangements cover interregional service of judicial documents, taking evidence, and recognition and enforcement of court judgments and arbitral awards. The arrangements mainly exist for matters of judicial assistance and there are no arrangements to handle conflicts of jurisdiction and choice of law. Furthermore, these arrangements are generally concluded between the Mainland and the other region on a

1 The expression 'interregional conflict of laws' has many variations. It has also been called 'non-international conflict of laws', 'internal private international law', 'quasi-private international law', 'interprovincial law', 'inter-local law' and 'inter-territorial law'. Other descriptions connected with the specific territorial divisions of particular States are: 'inter-cantonal law' (between the laws of the cantons of Switzerland), 'interstate law' (between the States of the United States), and 'inter-regional law' (in the strict sense between the laws of the States divided into regions, such as Spain).

bilateral basis, resulting in multiple arrangements causing even further complexities and inconsistencies. There is no uniform interregional arrangement covering the whole PRC, nor arrangements between Hong Kong, Macau and Taiwan. Finally, SPC has also published a number of important judicial interpretations to guide People's Courts in Mainland in addressing interregional conflicts with other legal regions.

This chapter focuses on the interregional conflict of laws between Mainland on one hand and Hong Kong, Macau and Taiwan on the other,[2] primarily from Mainland's perspective. The interregional conflict of laws cannot be properly understood without fully understanding the historic and political background of the four legal regions in China. The first section starts by providing a comprehensive introduction to the 'one country, two systems' policy and the emergence of interregional conflicts. **13.04**

I. 'ONE COUNTRY, TWO SYSTEMS' AND EMERGENCE OF INTERREGIONAL CONFLICT OF LAWS IN CHINA

I.1 'One country, two systems'

The Chinese government and scholars consider the period from 1842 to 1949 a 'century of humiliation', during which China was demoted to a semi-colony.[3] In 1842, the island of Hong Kong was ceded in perpetuity to Britain based on the Treaty of Nanking with the Qing government following the first Opium War. Pursuant to the First Convention of Peking in 1860, Kowloon and Stonecutters Island were also ceded in perpetuity to Britain. In 1898, Britain received a 99-year lease over the New Territories on Mainland China immediately across from Hong Kong Island. Pursuant to the terms of the 1898 treaty, the lease expired on 30 June 1997, and the New Territories reverted to China on 1 July 1997. **13.05**

After the Opium War ended in 1842, the Portuguese captured Taipa and Coloane Islands from the Qing government. Three decades later, in 1887, the Qing government concluded that Portugal had jurisdiction over Macau in perpetuity and signed the Sino-Portuguese Treaty of Peking, also known as the Protocol of Lisbon. This treaty permitted the Portuguese to reside in and **13.06**

2 This chapter does not involve the application of rules on these questions between Hong Kong and Macau, between Hong Kong and Taiwan, or between Macao and Taiwan.

3 See J.A. Cohen and H. Chiu, *People's China and International Law: A Documentary Study* (Princeton University Press, 1974) 3–22.

govern Macau as a colony, but limited Portugal from transferring Macau's sovereignty to another country. Following the signing of this agreement, China and Portugal signed the Treaty of Commerce and Friendship in 1888. This treaty finally authorized the transfer of Macau's sovereignty to the Portuguese government.

13.07 After the PRC was established in 1949, the defeated Kuomintang (KMT), while retaining control only over Taiwan and nearby smaller islands,[4] continued to assert the existence of the Republic of China (ROC). At the same time, China was isolated from the rest of the world for almost three decades because of ideological and political differences. China's economy remained fragile during its isolation, but began to improve in the 1980s, when the government began to implement economic reform policies. China, for economic, political, and historic reasons, has always considered sovereignty as a matter of fundamental principle, which cannot be compromised and which has always been the highest political objective of the PRC government. Reuniting Taiwan, Hong Kong and Macao was unsurprisingly seen as one of the main tasks of the PRC government.[5]

13.08 After the Cultural Revolution,[6] the Chinese government adopted a pragmatic attitude towards reuniting Hong Kong, Macao and Taiwan with Mainland. The idea of granting high autonomy to a special region within one sovereign China was first proposed by DENG Xiaoping as an innovative approach for the peaceful unification of Taiwan.[7] In 1981, the Chairman of the NPC, the late Mr YE Jian-Ying, made a statement on the eve of National Day that:

> after peaceful reunification, Taiwan may become a special administrative region with a high degree of autonomy which means that the existing social system, economic system and life-style of Taiwan will remain unchanged, and so will Taiwan's economic and cultural relationship with foreign countries.[8]

13.09 Mr YE's statement was preceded by the Report on the Amendment of the Constitution of the PRC by the late Mr PENG Zhen, Chairman of the NPC.

---

4 The full area of 'Taiwan' under control of the KMT included only the islands Taiwan and the Pescadores and the offshore islands Quemoy and Matsu.

5 The Preamble of the Constitution of the PRC of 1982 stated: 'Taiwan is part of the sacred territory of the People's Republic of China. It is the lofty duty of all Chinese people, including our compatriots in Taiwan, to accomplish the great task of reunifying the motherland.'

6 The Cultural Revolution started in 1966 and ended in 1976 during which veteran revolutionaries and scholars suffered tremendously and the entire country was in disorder.

7 This idea was mentioned on a few different occasions and talks in Nov 1978, Jan 1979 and March 1979.

8 See the Special Group on the Relationship between the Central Government and the SAR, 'Final Report on the Relationship Between the Basic Law and the Constitution', 2 (10 February 1987).

The report emphasized the importance of the unification and recommended that the government establish special administrative regions (SARs), if necessary, in order to achieve the goal. It was understood that the SARs' social, economic, and legal systems might be different from those of the rest of China. In other words, within the same country, different systems could co-exist. In September 1982, in his meeting with then British Prime Minister Margaret Thatcher, DENG Xiaoping proposed that reintegrating Hong Kong into China could be resolved through a policy of 'one country, two systems'.[9]

When the policy of 'one country, two systems' was first announced, not even the Chinese government was certain of its content. The negotiation and signing of the Joint Declaration on the Question of Hong Kong between China and Britain (the 'Joint Declaration') provided an opportunity to define the policy. In the view of the Chinese government, despite their 'high degree of autonomy', SARs should not be considered states of a federal nation.[10] These SARs are local governments and their powers and autonomy must be delegated by the Central Government. 'Two systems' is necessary as a means of reuniting China, but it is not the objective. For the Chinese government, sovereignty and unification of the country is the final aim.[11] 13.10

I.2 'One country, two systems': Mainland, Hong Kong and Macau

Eventually, the 'one country, two systems' was incorporated by the PRC in two Joint Declarations, between the PRC and Britain for the handover of Hong Kong in 1997, and between the PRC and Portugal for the handover of Macau in 1999. The two Joint Declarations set out basic principles that Hong Kong and Macau would enjoy a high degree of autonomy and have executive, legislative, and independent judicial power; the laws currently in force would remain 'basically unchanged'; their courts would exercise judicial power independently and be free from interference; and the current social system, lifestyle, and economic system in Hong Kong would remain unchanged. These Joint Declarations were later implemented and acquired legal effect through two Basic Laws: Hong Kong Basic Law[12] and Macau Basic Law,[13] both 13.11

9 When this phrase was first used, there were eight Chinese characters: 'Yi Ge Guo Jia, Liang Zhong Zhi Du' (一个国家，两种制度). Later, they were simplified to four characters 'Yi Guo Liang Zhi' (一国两制).

10 See XIAO Weiyun (ed.), *Yiguo Liangzhi yu Xianggang Jibenfa [One Country, Two Systems and the Basic Legal System of Hong Kong]* (Beijing Daxue Chubanshe [Peking University Press] 1990) 124–33.

11 XIAO Weiyun, 'Xianggang Bibenfa: Chuangzaoxing Lifa de Jiezuo [The Hong Kong Basic Law: A Masterpiece of Creative Legislation]', (1995) 3 Zhongguo Faxue [*China Legal Science*] 87.

12 Zhonghua Renmin Gongheguo Xianggang Tebie Xingzhengqu Jiben Fa [Basic Law of Hong Kong Special Administrative Region, PRC], adopted in the 3rd meeting of the 7th NPC in 1990 and entered into effect since 1 July 1997.

ensure that the domestic law of Hong Kong and Macau, with the exception of foreign affairs and defence, remain in effect for 50 years after the handover.

I.3 'One country, two systems': Mainland and Taiwan

13.12 The situation with Taiwan is different. After the end of the civil war in 1949, the defeated Kuomintang government took control of Taiwan[14] and claimed to be the only legitimate government over the territory of China, including Mainland. The PRC government insisted on having sovereignty over the whole of China, including Taiwan. The tensions completely broke civil and commercial connections between the two sides. After 1983, Mainland started to officially propose a peaceful reunification under the 'one country, two systems' policy, offering Taiwan adequate autonomy, including having its own government, separate law and independent legal system; this, however, was rejected by Taiwan, which proposed equal governments in Taipei and Beijing.[15] The political negotiation made no obvious progress, but the 'one country, two systems' policy remains recorded as the basic Taiwan policy by the Mainland.[16]

13.13 Regardless of the difficulties in politics, both governments relaxed the restriction for private contacts between the two sides. The civil and commercial relations between citizens on either side grew quickly. Both governments recognize the importance of protecting citizens in these relationships and are willing to recognize the authority of the other over private matters.[17] The common interest and understanding established the basis to *de facto* 'one country, two systems' between Mainland and Taiwan and eased the feasibility of applying interregional conflicts rules to facilitate private relationships between the two sides.

---

13 Zhonghua Renmin Gongheguo Aomen Tebie Xingzhengqu Jiben Fa [Basic Law of the Macau Special Administrative Region, PRC], adopted in the 1st meeting of the 8th NPC in 1993 and entered into effect since 20 Dec 1999.

14 The full area of 'Taiwan' under control of the KMT includes only the islands Taiwan and the Pescadores and the offshore islands Quemoy and Matsu.

15 For Taiwan's official position on the 'one country, two governments' idea and for the PRC's firm negative response, see *New Changes in the Relations Between the Two Sides of the Strait as Seen from the Proposal on 'One Country Two Governments'*, Foreign Broadcast Information Service-Daily Report, China 31 May 1989.

16 The State Council's White Paper on 'the Taiwan Question and the Reunification of China' ('White Paper'), Part III. The policy was reaffirmed by President Jiang Zemin in his 1997 new year's greeting. Chinese President's New Year Greeting, Xinhua News Agency, 1 Jan. 1997. The policies were subsequently reaffirmed by the Chairman of the NPC in an interview with a US journalist. NPC Chairman Accepts Interview by US Journalist, *Xinhua News Agency*, 16 Jan. 1997, available in LEXIS, Asiapc Library, XINHUA File.

17 See Tung-pi Chen, 'Bridge across the Formosa Strait: Private Law Relations between Taiwan and Mainland', (1990) 4 *Journal of Chinese Law* 101, 112; S. Cooney, 'Why Taiwan is not Hong Kong', (1997) 6 *Pacific Rim Law and Policy Journal* 497, fn 27–34.

II. THE FEATURES OF INTERREGIONAL CONFLICT OF LAWS IN CHINA

The whole landscape of legal systems of Mainland, Hong Kong Special Administrative Region (HKSAR), Macau Special Administrative Region (MASAR) and Taiwan could be characterized by '1–2-3–4', that is one country (China), two systems (the capitalist and socialist systems), three legal families (common law, civil law and Chinese socialist law) and four legal territories or districts. The interregional conflict of laws problems in China are complicated and unique in several perspectives. **13.14**

II.1 Different legal and socio-economic systems

China's interregional conflict of laws is unusually complicated because it involves not only conflicts between different legal regions of the same socio-economic systems, but also conflicts between legal regions of different socio-economic systems, i.e., socialism and capitalism. Furthermore, even within the similar socio-economic systems of capitalism in Hong Kong, Macau and Taiwan, the legal system in each region has been shaped by different legal doctrines and heritages, commonly called the 'law families'. For example, the legal systems in Macao and Taiwan have been profoundly influenced by the continental European civil system, whereas the legal system in Hong Kong was derived from the English common law system.[18] By contrast, the interregional conflict of laws in most other countries arises in the context of a unified socio-economic system.[19] **13.15**

II.2 Unique central/local relations in a unified country

Interregional conflicts problems in China are different from the conflicts issues that arise within a federal state. The degree of autonomy enjoyed by Hong Kong and Macau is unique. First, although Hong Kong and Macau enjoy a high degree of autonomy, they are local administrative entities within a unitary political system. These SARs are directly under the supervision of the central government of Mainland, whose sovereignty is laid down in the Basic Laws. **13.16**

Secondly, compared with federal states, the autonomy enjoyed by the SARs is as large as, or even larger, than that commonly enjoyed by the territorial units **13.17**

18 Jin Huang and Andrew Xuefeng Qian, 'One Country, Two Systems, Three Law Families, and Four Legal Regions: the Emerging Interregional Conflicts of Law in China', (1994) 5 *Duke Journal of Comparative and International Law* 304, 304–5.

19 In North America, there are two such areas (Louisiana and Quebec), where the French legal tradition is still alive. Both are members of federal states dominated by the common law.

of a federation. For example, the Hong Kong Basic Law established a new Court of Final Appeal, which replaced the UK's Privy Council as the ultimate judicial authority. The previously named Supreme Court was renamed the High Court and the former High Court was renamed the Court of First Instance. The Court of Final Appeal in Hong Kong has the right of final adjudication, which shows that the Hong Kong enjoys more autonomy in the exercise of judicial power than a federal state.[20]

13.18 Thirdly, unlike other autonomous areas in the PRC,[21] the autonomy of Hong Kong and Macau is not merely a domestic arrangement but also China's commitment under the Joint Declarations respectively with the British and Portuguese governments. To implement the policy of 'one country, two systems', the SARs need more authority, both quantitatively and qualitatively. The relations between the central government and the SARs are based on the division of power, not on the division of functions. Hence, the SARs are not merely an administrative body primarily responsible for implementing the central government's policies under local conditions, they possess a wide scope of autonomy that defies interference from the central government at will. This special autonomy is guaranteed not only by the Chinese Constitution but also by the Basic Laws.

13.19 Fourthly, from a political perspective, the laws of the SARs are local laws and as such are inferior to the national laws of PRC. This is illustrated by the following reasons: (a) partial national laws of Mainland cited in the Annex of the Basic Law must be applied in the SARs, but no law of the SARs may be applied directly in Mainland;[22] (b) laws enacted by the SARs must be reported to the Standing Committee of the NPC (SCNPC) for the record. If the SCNPC considers a law to be incompatible with provisions of the Basic Law regulating relations between the central authorities and the SARs, it may reject the law in question. Any law rejected by the Standing Committee is immediately invalid; and (c) the power to amend the Basic Law belongs to the NPC. The power to interpret the Basic Law is vested in the SCNPC, which is bound

20 See section II.4 below.

21 China has five autonomous regions for areas with high populations of minority ethic groups, Inner Mongolia, Xinjiang, Guangxi, Ningxia and Tibet.

22 Annex III of the HKSAR Basic Law 'National Laws to be applied in the Hong Kong SAR': (1) Resolution on the Capital, Calendar, National Anthem and National Flag of the PRC; (2) Resolution on the National Day of the PRC; (3) Order on the National Emblem of the PRC proclaimed by the Central People's Government, Attached: Design of the National Emblem, Notes of Explanation and Instruction for Use; (4) Declaration of the Government of the PRC on the territorial Sea; (5) Nationality Law of the PRC; (6) Regulation of the PRC Concerning Diplomatic Privileges and Immunities. On November 4, 1998, the Standing Committee of the NPC voted to add the Regulation on the Exclusive Economic Zone and Continental Shelf of the PRC to Annex III.

by the Chinese Constitution when making its decisions. The SCNPC authorizes the courts of the SARs to interpret any provisions of the Basic Law falling within the scope of the autonomy of the SARs. However, if the courts of Hong Kong or Macau need to interpret provisions of the Basic Law concerning affairs under the jurisdiction of the central government or the relations between the central authorities and the SAR, they must first request the NPC Standing Committee to interpret the relevant provision. The query must be made before giving a final judgment without a possibility of appeal if such interpretation could affect the outcome. The interpretation of the SCNPC is binding on the courts of the SARs whenever the relevant provision is applicable.[23]

From a legal perspective, however, the SARs are legal regions whose laws enjoy the same legal status as those enacted by the NPC and its Standing Committee (except the Basic Law). The ordinary hierarchy of legislation, which gives priority to national law over local law generally, does not apply to Hong Kong and Macau. In the majority of cases, the courts of Hong Kong and Macau can apply their own law without having to consider giving priority to national law. Furthermore, the judgments rendered by the judicial bodies of these legal regions are authentic and qualifies for mutual recognition between each other. **13.20**

II.3 International treaties

The power to enter into international treaties is usually reserved by the central government in all states, including federal states, and once a treaty is concluded or acceded to, it has the effect in all territories of the country. However, the central government consults Hong Kong and Macau before deciding whether an international treaty signed by Mainland would apply to these special administrative regions.[24] **13.21**

Secondly, local government usually has no right to enter into international treaties. But some international economic treaties permit local or regional governments to become signatory parties. Before the 1997 handover, Hong Kong entered into some multilateral international treaties, such as the Agreement Establishing the Asian Development Bank. The right to continue to enter into international economic treaties in the name of 'Hong Kong, China' and 'Macau, China' is granted by the Basic Laws. According to the Basic Laws, the HKSAR and MASAR governments are authorized to enter into **13.22**

---

23 Xiao Yongping, 'The Conflict of Laws between Mainland and the HKSAR: the Choice of Coordination Models', (2002) 4 *Yearbook of Private International Law* 171–3.

24 MASAR Basic Law, Art 138.

non-political treaties with foreign states and regions and international organizations, in the area of economic affairs, trade, finance, shipping, communications, tourism, culture and sports.[25] It follows that the international treaties signed in the name of Hong Kong or Macau before the reunification continue to apply to the SARs.

13.23 Furthermore, from the principle of state sovereignty it follows that the international treaties signed by the British or Portuguese governments should have ceased to be effective in Hong Kong or Macau after the handover. However, one major objective for reunification is to maintain the prosperity of the SARs. In particular, Hong Kong has established itself as an international financial, trading and shipping centre, playing an important role in the international market. Reunification should not affect its external commercial environment, which requires that the previous international treaties that applied in Hong Kong and worked well to facilitate international trade and finance should continue to apply. If these treaties stopped being effective in Hong Kong, it would cause concerns about Hong Kong's commercial stability and prosperity after reunification. A more realistic solution is to continue implementing these treaties in Hong Kong, except those in relation to national sovereignty and defence or contradictions with the Basic Law. This solution was reached in the Sino-British Joint Declaration (Appendix I) and adopted by the Sino-Portuguese Joint Declaration.[26] However, the question whether a specific treaty would continue to apply, fully or in part, or not apply at all, is very complicated in practice. It is necessary to take a different approach to different treaties, having regard for the Basic Law, state sovereignty and the local interest. Taking Hong Kong as an example, when the Sino-British Joint Declaration was signed in 1984, both sides agreed to set up a Sino-British Joint Liaison Group. One of the group's tasks was to examine and determine the action to be taken by both sides: (a) to ensure Hong Kong's participation in the GATT, the Multi-fibre Arrangement (International Textile Product Trade Agreement) and other international arrangements; (b) to ensure the continued application of international rights and obligations affecting Hong Kong; and (c) to assist Hong Kong in maintaining and developing economic and cultural relations and conclude agreements on these matters with states, regions and relevant international organizations. After negotiation, both sides later agreed that Hong Kong should continue to participate in the intergovernmental activities of 34 international organizations. Hong Kong was permitted to join 19 intergovernmental international organizations, including the International

25 HKSAR Basic Law, Art 151; MASAR Basic Law, Art 13.

26 See, in general, XU Chongli, 'Jiuqi Zhihou Guoji Jingji Tiaoyue Ruhe Jixu Shiyong yu Xianggang [Application of International Economic Treaties in Hong Kong After 1997]', (1998) 1 Zhongwai Faxue [*Peking University Law Journal]* 104.

Civil Aviation Organization and the International Monetary Fund, and to attend their meetings in the capacity of a 'member of the delegation of the Chinese Government'. As a member or associate member and in the name of 'Hong Kong, China', Hong Kong continues its membership of 15 intergovernmental international organizations, including the Asia Development Bank and the International Maritime Organization. Of the 300-plus international treaties once applicable in Hong Kong, 214 continued to apply after 1 July 1997. These included ones to which China was a party, as well as treaties that China has not yet joined. Therefore, most international agreements and treaties in effect in Hong Kong and Macau when the PRC took control continue to be effective.

Finally, applying treaties of which both Mainland and the SARs are parties **13.24**
also encounters challenges. Without any controversy, these treaties would continue to apply to Hong Kong or Macau in handling the relationship with other party states or regions. However, the application of these treaties between Mainland and Hong Kong or Macau becomes complicated. Before the handover, these treaties, such as the Hague Service Convention and New York Convention (NYC), applied between Mainland and Hong Kong/Macau, each belonging to a separate sovereignty. After the reunification, Hong Kong and Macau become part of China and belong to one sovereign state as Mainland. These treaties, while aiming to deal with international relationships and judicial cooperation between different sovereign states, would cease to be effective interregionally. Therefore, the interregional conflicts between Mainland, Hong Kong and Macau may become more complicated from the perspective that some conflicts and judicial cooperation treaties that applied in the past cannot continue to be relevant after the reunification.[27]

II.4 No common supreme judicial organ

Unlike other legal systems with more than one territorial unit, China has no **13.25**
common supreme judicial organ to coordinate and resolve conflicts among the independent courts of the SARs. Each region has a court of final adjudication, independent of all other regional and PRC courts. Prior to 1997, the Supreme Court of Hong Kong had no power of final adjudication. Parties wishing to appeal a judgment of the Supreme Court could do so before the Privy Council in London. The Basic Law has vested the power of final adjudication of the HKSAR in the Supreme Court of the HKSAR, now called the Court of Final Appeal. Similarly, the Court of Last Instance of Macao was established in 1999 and enjoys the power of final adjudication in the MASAR. It is a rare

27 See sections III, IV and V below for more discussions.

situation anywhere in the world for a court of an administrative region to enjoy the power of final appeal.

13.26 Moreover, the courts in the SARs have jurisdiction over all cases in their region, with the exception of matters concerning acts of state such as defence and foreign affairs. It is ambiguous as to which acts qualify as an 'act of state'. The decision whether a matter actually relates to defence or foreign affairs is to be made solely by the Chief Executive of each region and cannot be challenged in the courts.

13.27 The lack of a supreme judicial organ in China, in practice, causes difficulty. If there is difference in interpreting the law between different regions, which leads to conflict in the jurisdiction, applicable law or judicial assistance, there is no final authority to impose a solution on all regional final courts. The only resolution method is communication and negotiation between different regions, which inevitably causes uncertainty and difficulty.[28]

II.5 Mutual trust and diversity

13.28 The law, economy and judicial system between sister states in most federal states usually share similar standards and develop at a similar level, which makes interregional cooperation and mutual trust easy to establish.[29] This similarity, however, does not exist in China. In terms of economic and political power, population, and international importance, Mainland is much stronger than the other regions, but this does not assist interregional mutual trust, but rather causes concern to the other regions. In terms of legislative, judicial and enforcement quality, Hong Kong and Macau are nevertheless superior. The diversity causes difficulties in establishing mutual trust and cooperation.[30] For example, it proves very difficult for Mainland to enter into judicial assistance/cooperation arrangements with Hong Kong. The Mainland-HK Judgment Arrangement entered into in 2006 is an example of very restrictive rules, which excludes many civil and commercial judgments from its scope.[31] It demonstrates Hong Kong's lack of trust in Mainland judgment and judicial practice, which hampers a more efficient interregional judicial cooperation.

---

28 GUO Yujun, XU Jingtang, 'Zhonguo Quji Falv Chongtu Jiejue Lujing Tanxi (Shang) [A New Perspective of Chinese Interregional Law Conflicts (I)]', (2008) 6(1) Shidai Faxue [*Contemporary Law Science*] 13, 22.

29 The similarity is present not only in federal states, such as the US, Germany, and India, but also regions with similar history, legal culture and judicial system, for example, the high level of mutual trust and cooperation also exists between the Member States of the European Union.

30 GUO Yujun, XU Jingtang, *supra* n 28, 20.

31 See below section V.1.

III. APPROACHES IN RESOLVING INTERREGIONAL CONFLICTS

There are various approaches for resolving interregional conflicts.[32] The first allows all regions to apply domestic conflicts rules for international disputes to interregional cases. Most common law countries have adopted the first approach by applying the same conflicts rules to both international and interregional conflicts. This approach conceptually treats other regions as separate 'countries' no different from foreign countries in private international law. This approach avoids adopting a dual system applying to international and interregional cases and provides consistency and convenience in practice. However, although the same choice of law or jurisdiction rules may apply to international and interregional cases based on the grounds of separate legal systems, other rules more closely relevant to judicial assistance and judicial authority may not. Even in jurisdiction and choice of law issues, different standards may apply to several issues demonstrating national interest, public order, cooperation and mutual trust and respect, such as parallel proceedings and public policy. Therefore, this approach cannot systematically resolve all interregional conflicts. Finally, since different regions have different domestic conflict of laws, this approach may only produce consistency in terms of one region, but not in the whole country.[33] **13.29**

The second approach permits all regions to adopt their own interregional conflicts rules. This approach leaves the solution completely to each region and cannot contribute to consistency and uniformity. **13.30**

The third approach suggests that the central/supreme legislative organ of the nation should enact the uniform interregional conflicts statutes applying to all regions. It is the most ideal solution, providing uniformity, equality and certainty in practice. However, adopting this approach to resolve interregional conflicts in China is, at the current stage, unrealistic. First, since the SARs have great autonomy and reserve legislative power, most Mainland law does not apply to the regions, except those relating to international affairs and defence. It is hard to argue that there is a national supreme organ to enact national uniform conflicts rules. This approach is inconsistent with the 'two systems' principle. Secondly, unlike Hong Kong and Macau, Taiwan is not **13.31**

32 YU Fei, 'Yelun Jiejue Haixia Liang'an Minshangshi Falv Chongtu de Moshi [The Mode of Solving the Conflict of Civil and Commercial Laws in Cross-Strait]', (2006) 91(1) Taiwan Yanjiu Jikan [*Taiwan Research Quarterly*] 8, 8–9.

33 This is the case in China. Mainland applies its jurisdiction and choice of law rules to international cases and to HK, Macau or Taiwan-related cases; Hong Kong applies Hong Kong domestic conflict rules to Mainland, Macau, or Taiwan-related cases; Macau applies Macau conflict rules to Mainland, Hong Kong or Taiwan-related cases. There is no unified approach in China.

formally reunified with Mainland. The Taiwan government does not officially accept the 'one country, two systems' principle or the existence of any 'supreme' or 'central' legislative organ. Thirdly, given the different legal traditions, culture and development of rule of law, uniform conflict of laws is unlikely to be accepted by all regions at this stage.[34]

13.32 The final approach suggests regions enter into judicial cooperation and conflicts arrangements. It encourages dialogue and communication between regions, which is believed to produce mutual trust and mutual respect and result in interregional conflicts arrangements. This approach is helpful in providing uniformity and encouraging judicial cooperation. It is consistent with the 'one country, two systems' principle, by fully respecting each region's autonomy. It is also realistic and pragmatic. However, one weakness of this approach is it may progress slowly and can lead to piecemeal arrangements. It is hard for the authorities of all regions to enter into a 'one-stop' arrangement for all conflicts issues between all regions. This approach may only improve interregional cooperation gradually. But it would be a necessary and practical method to assisting mutual understanding and much wider cooperation in the future.

13.33 The current approach adopted in China is the mixture of approach one, two and four. Mainland enters into a few arrangements with each region respectively, which provides piecemeal harmonization of rules in service, taking evidence, and recognition and enforcement of judgments. Nothing prevents Hong Kong, Macau and Taiwan from entering conflicts arrangements between each other. Each region is free to apply its international conflicts rules or enact its domestic interregional conflicts rules to resolve interregional cases for issues falling outside the existing arrangements. For example, both Mainland and Hong Kong apply the foreign-related conflicts rules to interregional conflicts;[35] and Macau enacted the Macau Civil Code in 1999, which expressly provides the same conflicts rules to international and interregional conflicts. The Macau Civil Code adopts habitual residence to replace nationality as a connecting factor, showing a clear intention to apply to interregional conflicts cases.[36] Taiwan enacted the Regulations Governing the Relations

34 GUO Yujun, XU Jingtang, 'Zhongguo Quji Falv Chongtu Jiejue Lujing Tanxi (Xia) [A New Perspective of Chinese Interregional Law Conflicts (II)]', (2008) 6(2) Shida Faxue [*Contemporary Law Science*] 8, 11.

35 27 December 2010, the SPC of the PRC promulgated a judicial interpretation entitled 'Guanyu Shenli Shetai Minshangshi Anjian Falv Shiyong Wenti de Guiding [Provisions on Application of Law in the Trial of Taiwan-Related Civil and Commercial Cases]', Fa Shi [2010] No 19, according to which the Conflicts Act is extended to apply to the Civil and Commercial Cases that involve Taiwan Element.

36 Arts 30(1) and 83(1).

between Peoples of the Taiwan Region and the Mainland Area in 1992[37] and Act Governing Relations with Hong Kong and Macau in 1997.[38]

IV. SERVICE BETWEEN MAINLAND, HONG KONG, MACAU AND TAIWAN

IV.1 Service between Mainland and Hong Kong

i. China-HK service arrangement

Before the Hong Kong handover, although Article 247 of the Civil Procedure Law of 1991 provided the method for serving judicial documents on foreign parties, Chinese courts did not consider service to Hong Kong as falling into the scope of this article. The SPC provides judicial guidance on service to Hong Kong in a few documents, which, however, provide inconsistent rules and do not much help practice.[39] In 1988, the Guangdong HPC (with the approval of the SPC) and the Supreme Court of Hong Kong reached an agreement on assistance on service. This agreement is the first official mutual assistance agreement entered between China and Hong Kong and has historical significance:[40] it is not, however, widely used in practice. From 1988 to 1991, only 126 judicial documents had been served from Guangdong to Hong Kong with 11 documents going in the reverse direction.[41] This is partly because of the narrow focus of the Agreement and the complicated procedure provided by it. After China joining the Hague Service Convention in 1991, that Convention applied to judicial assistance and service between Hong Kong and China.[42] **13.34**

37 It has been amended numerous times. The latest amendment to this Act was in 2010.

38 Amended in 1998, 1999, 2004 and 2006. For more, see GUO Yujun, XU Jintang, *supra* n 34, 12–13.

39 See SPC, 'Guanyu Shenli Shegang'ao Jingji Jiufen Anjian Ruogan Wenti de Jieda [Answer on Several Issues Regarding the Trial of Hong Kong and Macau-related Economic Disputes Cases]', Fa (Jing) Fa [1987] No 28 (abolished); SPC, 'Quanguo Yanhai Diqu Shewai Shegang'ao Jingji Shenpan Gongzuo Zuotan Huiyi Jiyao [Summary of the Panel Discussion on the Adjudication of Foreign-related and Hong Kong and Macau-related Economic Cases in Coastal Regions]', Fa (Jin) Fa [1989] No 12.

40 TANG Dehua, the then vice-president of the SPC, said this:

> is a legal document of historical significance. It will play an important role in providing for the quick and efficient protection for an immediate and fair mutual solution of civil and economic disputes. It also reflects our high concern about safeguarding the legitimate rights and interests of the parties concerned from both sides including Hong Kong compatriots.

People's Daily (overseas edition), 31 March 1999.

41 FENG Xia, *Zhongguo Quji Sifa Lun [On Interregional Private Law in China]* (China, Renmin Fayuan Chubanshi [*People's Court Press*], 2006) 250.

42 General Office of the SPC, 'Zuigao Renmin Fayuan Guanyu Zuigao Renmin Fayuan Guanyu Jiang "Haiya Gongyue" Shiyongyu Xianggang de Tongzhi [Concerning the Application of the Hague Convention to Hong Kong]', Faban (1992) No 86.

13.35 The July 1997 handover has rendered the Hague Convention inapplicable to service assistance between Mainland and Hong Kong because there has been a fundamental change in the nature of their relationship: from a situation where they were governed under different sovereignties, to the situation of 'one country, two systems'. In such cases, China notified the Netherlands government, the depository state of the Hague Service Convention, that after the handover the Convention would continue to be applicable to Hong Kong by virtue of China's ratification. At the same time, the administrative office of the Chief Secretary's Office was named as the regional authority to undertake service requests from, or to, Hong Kong. As a consequence, legally speaking, Britain's ratification of the Hague Convention no longer applies to Hong Kong; and technically, China's ratification does not cover some of Hong Kong's practice under the common law tradition either, such as postal service to a foreign defendant, due to China's declared reservation. This unique situation poses a challenge to both sides to find an acceptable solution so that single state sovereignty, the principle of 'one country, two systems', and judicial efficiency can be maintained.

13.36 In 1999, pursuant to Article 95 of the Basic Law of the HKSAR and after the consultation between the two sides,[43] the SPC and the High Court of HKSAR reached an arrangement for mutual service of judicial documents.[44] The courts of both sides may entrust each other to serve judicial documents in civil and commercial proceedings.[45] Request for service of judicial documents shall be made through the Higher People's Courts in the Mainland and the High Court of the HKSAR. The SPC may also make direct requests to the High Court of the HKSAR for service of judicial documents.[46] When requesting service of judicial documents, the entrusting party shall produce a letter of entrustment in the Chinese language, or accompanied by a Chinese translation, duly sealed with its official seal, setting out the name of the entrusting party, the full name and description of the person to be served, his or its detailed address and the nature of the proceedings involved.[47] Upon receipt of the letter of entrustment, the entrusted party shall effect service promptly and, in any event, no later than two months from the day when the letter of entrustment is received.[48] After effecting service, the relevant Mainland court shall issue a

---

43 Art 95.

44 SPC, 'Zuigao Renmin Fayuan Guanyu Neidi yu Xianggang Tebie Xingzhengqu Fayuan Xianghu Weituo Songda Minshangshi Sifa Wenshu de Anpai [Arrangement for Mutual Service of Judicial Documents in Civil and Commercial Proceedings between the Mainland and Hong Kong Courts]', Fa Shi [1999] No 9. Meanwhile, HKSAR issued it in (1999) Law Announce No 39.

45 Art 1.

46 Art 2.

47 Art 3.

48 Art 4.

return form on the service, and the HKSAR court shall issue a certificate of service. In the event service cannot be effected, the entrusted party shall state on the return form or the certificate of non-service the reason for non-service, or, where acceptance of service is refused, the reason and the date of refusal.[49] Service of judicial documents shall be effected free of charge. If the entrusting party in the letter of entrustment requires a special method of service, it shall be responsible for the charge and expenses arising from the request.[50]

Some special characteristics deserve explanation. First, even if the date for appearance in court or the time limit specified in the document has expired, the entrusted party is still responsible for serving the judicial documents.[51] If the entrusting party makes the request too late, it may deprive the defendant of the opportunity to be heard. The arrangement, therefore, requires the entrusting party to make the request in 'reasonable' time.[52] But what is a 'reasonable' time? Should the entrusting or entrusted party determine whether the time is reasonable? What is the consequence of unreasonable delay? Would it entitle the entrusted party not to serve the document? None of these questions are given a clear answer. Secondly, this arrangement implies that neither side will refuse to serve the judicial documents based on the violation of public policy. This reflects the principle of 'one country', and increases the rate of service. Service may only be refused if the address is wrong, making service practically impossible.[53] 13.37

As the first interregional judicial cooperation agreement, this arrangement not only establishes a formal channel for mutual service of judicial documents between Mainland and HKSAR, but also provides a model for judicial assistance in other fields between the two sides and between Mainland and other regions. More importantly, it establishes the principle of equality and expands the scope of judicial assistance to the relations between HKSAR and other provinces, autonomous regions and municipalities within Mainland.[54] The arrangement improves successful service between Mainland and HKSAR. However, the success rate is relatively higher in the Mainland than in HKSAR. Take Guangdong Province as an example. In 2000, Guangdong HPC entrusted the High Court of HKSAR in 97 cases and the success rate 13.38

49 Art 5.

50 Art 8.

51 Art 4.

52 Ibid.

53 Art 5.

54 FENG Xia, 'Woguo Neidi Quji Minshangshi Songda Zhidu de Sifa Tansuo [Judicial Approach in Interregional Service for Civil and Commercial Matters]', (2006) 8 Renmin Sifa [*Peoples Judicature*] 79, 80.

was only 35 per cent; the High Court of HKSAR entrusted Guangdong HPC in 33 cases and the success rate was 87 per cent.[55] Between 2002 and 2004, Guangdong HPC entrusted the High Court of HKSAR in 554 cases with a success rate of 31.2 per cent; the High Court of HKSAR entrusted Guangdong HPC in 89 cases with a success rate of 60.7 per rate.[56] The success rate for the whole Mainland is relatively lower than Guangdong, but still higher than HKSAR. In 2003, for example, the Mainland HPC entrusted the High Court of HK to serve in 849 cases and the success rate was 45 per cent; the High Court of HK entrusted Mainland HPC to serve documents in over 72 cases and the success rate was 51 per cent.[57] The low success rate in HKSAR is primarily due to two reasons: difficulty in identifying the correct address and no one being present to receive the documents.[58] Furthermore, under the traditional practice, Hong Kong courts usually did not take responsibility for service and the responsibility for serving judicial documents was assigned to the claimant and its representatives. The Mainland courts, on the other hand, have a tradition of serving judicial documents as part of the exercise of state power. Therefore, Mainland courts are willing to work hard to look for recipients while Hong Kong courts usually have no motive to do the same.

13.39 Service through judicial cooperation may cause delay. The arrangement only permits the HPC or SPC to send the letter of entrustment directly to the High Court of HKSAR. When the lower courts wish to serve in HKSAR, they should transfer the relevant documents to the HPC. The low success rate and delays generate criticism of the arrangement. The recognized service method is too limited, relying on the cooperation of both courts and excluding more effective and efficient modern channels.

ii. China-HK/Macau service provisions

13.40 On 16 February 2009, the Judicial Committee of the SPC passed the SPC's Provisions Regarding the Service of Judicial Documents in Hong Kong and

---

55 The Guangdong HPC, *Zhongguo Shewai Shangshi Shenpan Redian Wenti Tanxi [Exploration on hot issues in China's Foreign Commercial Trial]* (Law Press, 2004) 265.

56 SONG Xixiang, 'Neidi yu Gang'ao Quji Minshangshi Sifawenshu Songda Xianzhuan Jiqi Wanshan Sikao [Status quo and Improvement of Interregional Service of Judicial Documents in Civil and Commercial Cases between Mainland and Hong Kong and Macau]', (2013) 15 Yiguoliangzhi Yanjiu [*One Country Two System Study*] 121, 124.

57 Feng, *supra* n 54, 80.

58 Ibid. In 2003, for example, 464 services were unsuccessful, within which 156 were due to the lack of correct address.

Macau-related Civil and Commercial Cases ('China-HK/Macau Service Provisions').[59] These provisions provide multiple and flexible methods for Mainland courts to serve judicial documents in Hong Kong and Macau, partly imitating the CPL provision on service abroad.[60] Judicial documents may be directly served on the Hong Kong recipient, who is present in the Mainland,[61] through the recipient's representatives,[62] or upon an authorized agency.[63] All legal representatives or representative agents of the recipients are presumed to be competent to accept legal documents on behalf of the recipients, unless the agency/representative agreement provides otherwise. This is in order to prevent some representatives from refusing to receive the documents based on the excuse that they are not authorized to do so expressly by the agency agreements.[64] However, arguably express authorization is required if the courts wish to directly serve judicial documents on the branch or business agency.[65] This is primarily because the authorization and power of the branch or business agency differs from the representative or representative agent. The former usually are empowered to conduct business-related activities only on behalf of the recipient, while the latter have much broader competence and authorization.

For recipients with no representatives or agents in Mainland, the provisions confirm service by judicial cooperation provided in the arrangement. If the evidence of successful service is not received within three months after the documents are delivered to the High Court of HKSAR, the service is deemed unsuccessful and the Chinese courts are entitled to rely on Articles 7, 8, 9 and 12 to adopt alternative methods to serve in HKSAR. Alternative methods include service by post, by electronic means, by public announcement, or through leaving judicial documents with the recipient. If service is made by **13.41**

59 SPC, 'Zuigao Renmin Fayuan Guanyu She Gangao Minshangshi Anjian Sifa Wenshu Songda Wenti Ruogan Guiding [Provisions Regarding the Service of Judicial Documents in Hong Kong and Macau-related Civil and Commercial Cases]', Fa Shi (2009) No 2.

60 CPL 2007, Art 245 (now Art 267). See Ch 5, s.II above.

61 HK-Macau Service Provisions, Art 3 of the provides that judicial documents may be served upon natural persons, legal representatives of the legal person or other organizations, or principal leading personnel of any other organizations directly, if they are in Mainland.

62 Ibid., Art 4 provides judicial documents may be served through the litigation representative, with an exception that the litigation representative is not empowered explicitly by the recipient of the service to receive the judicial documents.

63 Ibid., Art 6 provides judicial documents may be served upon the representative agency, branch, or business agent of the recipient of the service whom are authorized to receive the judicial documents within the territory of Mainland.

64 REN Xuefeng, 'Guanyu Shegang'ao Minshangshi Anjian Sifa Wenshu Songda Wenti Ruogan Guiding de Lijie yu Shiyong [Apprehension and Application of the "Provisions Regarding the Service of Judicial Documents in Hong Kong and Macau-related Civil and Commercial Cases"]', (2009) 7 Renmin Sifa [*People's Judicature*] 20, 21. See Ch 5, s.II.1.iv above.

65 Ibid., 21.

post, a return form on the service should be attached. If the recipient of the service refuses to sign the return form, but signs on receipt of the mail, the service shall be considered completed, and the date of receipt as signed by the recipient of the service will be regarded as the date the document is served. In the event that no receipt is returned within three months of the date on which the document was posted, but the recipient of the service mentioned the judicial document, or performed pursuant to the judicial document before the court, the service shall be deemed completed upon the expiration of the time limit.[66] Service made through electronic means include telefax, e-mail, or other means that receipt can be confirmed.[67] The modern service methods should improve efficiency, reduce costs and improve the success rate.[68] A public announcement can be used if none of the above-mentioned methods can be employed. The contents of the announcement should be published in newspapers on the Mainland and the domicile of the recipient of the service, and the service will be considered complete three months after the date when the public announcement was issued.[69] Finally, judicial documents can be left at the place where the recipient of the service stays, if he is present in Mainland and refuses to accept the judicial document.[70]

IV.2 Service of process between Mainland and Macau

13.42 Before 1999, service between Mainland and Macau was based on the Hague Service Convention.[71] In practice, service requests between Mainland and Macau were very rare because of the weak civil and commercial relations between the two regions. Before 1999, Mainland made service requests in only three cases, and Macau did not make any such requests in accordance with the Convention.[72] The Hague Service Convention stopped applying between Mainland and Macau after the reunification in 1999.

13.43 In 2001, in accordance with the provisions of Article 93 of the Basic Law of MASAR, China and Macau entered into an Arrangement Concerning

66 HK-Macau Service Provisions, Arts 7 and 12.

67 Ibid., Art 8.

68 For more discussion on service by electronic means, see Ch 5 above.

69 HK-Macau Service Provisions, Art 9.

70 Ibid., Art 11. But the person serving the document shall ask the representatives of the relevant basic organization or unit to which the recipient of the service belongs to appear on the scene, explain the situation to them, and record the reasons of the refusal and the date on the receipt. After the person serving the document and the witnesses have affixed their signatures or seals on the receipt, the document may be left at the place where the recipient of the service stays, and the service shall be considered completed. The person serving the document may also use photographs, video and other means to record the delivery process. See CPL, Art 86.

71 Portugal government ratified to access the Hague Service Convention in 1973, which extended to Macau.

72 FENG Xia, supra n 41, 260.

Mutual Service of Judicial Documents and Taking of Evidence in Civil and Commercial Matters between the Mainland and Macao Special Administrative Region ('Macau Service and Evidence Arrangement').[73] This is the first arrangement on mutual legal assistance between Mainland and MASAR. Compared with the arrangement with HKSAR, the Macau Service and Evidence Arrangement provides more flexible methods for service. It permits direct service on recipients present in Mainland,[74] and service by post, electronic means, public notice and leaving at the place where the recipient stays.[75] The entrusted court cannot refuse cooperation based on the ground that it has exclusive jurisdiction, or that the requested matters are not recognized in its law.[76] However, the entrusted court could refuse execution if it believes service will infringe its public policy.[77] The public policy defence may be questioned on its consistency with the 'one country' policy. However, it is recognized that even within one county, different regions still have different cultures and local interests. Reserving public policy is more reasonable and realistic. Furthermore, sister states in the federal countries all reserve public policy in judicial cooperation between each other. Reserving public policy does not infringe the principle of 'one country'.

Therefore, the effect of implementation of the Macau Service and Evidence Arrangement was significantly better than the HK Service Arrangement. It is also necessary to note that the 2009 HK-Macau Provisions also applies to reciprocal service of judicial documents between Mainland and Macau. Since the service methods provided in the provisions are close to those in the Macau Service and Evidence Arrangement, the enforcement of the provisions does not change the methods and efficiency of service much. Comparatively, many fewer requests are sent between these two sides than those between Mainland and HKSAR, but the success rates are much higher. The data for service between Mainland and Macau can be found in Tables 13.1 and 13.2 below. **13.44**

73 SPC, 'Zuigao Renmin Fayuan Guanyu Neidi he Aomen Tebie Xingzhengque Fayuan jiu Minshangshi Anjian Huxiang Weituo Songda Sifawenshu he Diaoqu Zhengju de Anpai [Arrangement Concerning Mutual Service of Judicial Documents and Taking of Evidence in Civil and Commercial Matters between the Mainland and Macao Special Administrative Region]', [2001] Fa Shi No 26.

74 See Macau Service and Evidence Arrangement, Arts 3, 4 and 5.

75 See ibid., Arts 7, 8, 9 and 11.

76 Ibid., Art 8.

77 Ibid.

Table 13.1 Record of Mainland court's request to Macau court to service and/or take evidence (2001–2011)

Year	Request	Settled	Unsettled	Success rate (%)
2001–2002	33	27	6	81.8
2002–2003	53	44	9	83
2003–2004	67	49	18	73.1
2004–2005	78	60	18	76.9
2005 2006	50	44	6	88
2006–2007	41	32	9	78.1
2007–2008	33	28	5	84.8
2008–2009	37	32	5	86.5
2009–2010	32	30	2	93.8
2010–2011	39	29	10	74.4

Source: SONG Xixiang, Guo (Qu) Ji Minshangshi Sifa Huodong de Chongtu yu Xietiao, Conflict and Coordination of Civil and Commercial Judicial Activities between Countries or Regions (China Law Press, 2014) 121.

Table 13.2 Record of Macau court's request to Mainland court to service and/or take evidence (2001–2011)

Year	Request	Settled	Unsettled	Success rate (%)
2001–2002	3	2	1	66.7
2002–2003	8	6	2	75
2003–2004	8	7	1	87.5
2004–2005	8	7	1	87.5
2005–2006	14	14	0	100
2006–2007	14	14	0	100
2007–2008	27	21	6	77.8
2008–2009	17	15	2	88.2
2009–2010	31	24	7	77.4
2010–2011	34	28	6	82.4

Source: SONG Xixiang, Guo (Qu) Ji Minshangshi Sifa Huodong de Chongtu yu Xietiao, Conflict and Coordination of Civil and Commercial Judicial Activities between Countries or Regions (China Law Press, 2014) 122.

IV.3 Service of process between Mainland and Taiwan

13.45 For a long time, there was no coordination mechanism on service of judicial documents between Mainland and Taiwan. The courts of the two sides did not entrust each other to serve judicial documents. In practice, the usual service methods between the two sides included service through public announcement, by attorney, or by post. None proved effective or satisfactory. The effectiveness of a public announcement was hampered by the lack of communication between the two sides. Newspapers and other media in Mainland could not usually be circulated in Taiwan and vice versa.[78] Service through attorney is almost always expensive. Service by post was largely hampered by the lack of direct postal services between the two sides until 2008. All mail between Mainland and Taiwan had to be redirected to Hong Kong or Macau before reaching its final destination, which induced delay and uncertainty.[79]

In order to improve judicial cooperation, the SPC issued the 'Several Provisions Regarding the Service of Civil Judicial Documents in Taiwan-related Civil Matters' ('2008 Taiwan Service Provisions') in 2008.[80] These are the first provisions on service of judicial documents between Mainland and Taiwan. In terms of serving documents in Taiwan, the provisions adopt all the service methods provided in the HK-Macau Provisions: judicial documents may be served directly on the recipient in Mainland; through representative, representative agent, branch or business agent; or by post, electronic means and public announcement.[81] In 2009, the Straits Exchange Foundation (Taiwan) and the Association for Relations Across the Taiwan Straits (Mainland) entered into the 'Agreement on Common Fight Against Crime and Mutual Judicial Assistance' ('2009 Taiwan Agreement on Mutual Judicial Assistance'),[82] which facilitates judicial assistance in civil and criminal matters, including service of judicial documents, collection of evidence, and enforcement of civil judgments. The two sides agreed to make best efforts to provide judicial assistance in accordance with their own regulations.[83] The agreement explicitly provides that the requested party shall try to serve within three months from the date of receipt of the request, shall inform the result to the requesting party, and promptly return the supporting document to the requesting party, whether or not the service is successful.[84] **13.46**

The provisions and the agreement contributed greatly to the service of cross-strait judicial documents. According to the SPC's statistics, as of May 2011, Taiwan courts requested Mainland courts to assist in service of judicial **13.47**

78 HE Qisheng, *Yuwai Songda Zhidu Yanjiu [Study of Extraterritorial Service]* (Peking: Peking University Press, 2006) 287.

79 Ibid., 291.

80 SPC, 'Zuigao Renmin Fayuan Guanyu She Tai Minshi Susong Wenshu Songda de Ruogan Guiding [Several Provisions Regarding the Service of Civil Judicial Documents in Taiwan-related Civil Matters]', Fa Shi [2008] No 4.

81 Taiwan Service Provisions, Arts 3–4.

82 Published on 26 April 2009 and entered into force on 25 June 2009.

83 Taiwan Agreement on Mutual Judicial Assistance, Art 7.

84 Ibid.

documents in 10,216 cases, 8,300 of them served. Meanwhile, Mainland courts requested Taiwan courts to assist service of judicial documents in 201 cases, 161 served. The success rate of service reached 80 per cent.[85] However, this agreement is not a SPC judicial interpretation or an arrangement between two governments. It is an agreement between two non-governmental associations and its formal legal effects may be of concern. In order to more effectively implement the 2009 Agreement, the SPC issued the 'Provisions on the People's Courts' Handling of Cases of Mutual Judicial Assistance in Terms of Serving Legal Documents, Investigation and Evidence Collection between Both Sides of the Taiwan Strait' ('2010 Taiwan Judicial Assistance Provisions') in 2010.[86] These provisions confirm the service methods provided in the 2008 Taiwan Service Provisions, but provide more detailed regulation on other procedural matters, including the power and responsibility of courts at different levels, the timelines, costs and fees. The SPC is the primary organ for the connection with the competent departments in Taiwan, responsible for consulting, coordinating and communicating with the competent departments of Taiwan on the matters involving the People's Courts' work; guiding, supervising, organizing and coordinating the local courts of all levels; and timely notifying the higher people's courts of the liaison information designated by this court and the competent departments of Taiwan.[87] The HPCs authorized by the SPC could directly connect with the competent departments of Taiwan on serving legal documents between both sides. The HPCs shall be responsible for guiding, supervising, organizing and coordinating the people's courts under their respective jurisdictions; directly contacting the competent departments of the business in terms of serving legal documents; registering and summing up the cases handled by the People's Courts under their respective jurisdictions; regularly reporting the information regarding serving legal documents handled by the People's Courts under their respective jurisdictions to the SPC; timely reporting the liaison information of the reporting court to the SPC; and simultaneously notifying the liaisons in Taiwan and the People's Courts at lower levels.[88] The IPCs and the BPCs shall be responsible for handling the specific cases of mutual judicial assistance; regularly reporting on the information regarding the mutual judicial assistance in serving legal documents between both sides handled by the reporting court to the higher

85 SONG Xixiang, Guo (Qu) Ji Minshangshi Sifa Huodong de Chongtu yu Xietiao [Conflict and Coordination of Civil and Commercial Judicial Activities between Countries or Regions] (China Law Press, 2014), 142.

86 SPC, 'Zuigao Renmin Fayuan Guanyu Renmin Fayuan Banli Haixia Liang'an Songda Wenshu he Diaocha Quzheng Sifa Huzhu Anjian de Guiding [Provisions on the People's Courts' Handling of Cases of Mutual Judicial Assistance in Terms of Serving Legal Documents, Investigation and Evidence Collection between Both Sides of the Taiwan Strait]', Fa Shi [2011] No 15.

87 Taiwan Judicial Assistance Provisions, Art 4.

88 Ibid., Art 5.

People's Courts level by level; and timely reporting of the names, contact information and change of the personnel of the reporting court responsible for the mutual judicial assistance between both sides to the higher People's Courts level by level.[89]

The provisions also provide detailed timelines for prompt service. After the lower court submits the judicial documents and mutual assistance request to the HPC, the HPC should complete investigation within seven working days and, when satisfied, transfers the documents to Taiwan immediately.[90] After receiving the response from Taiwan, the HPC should inform the lower court within seven working days.[91] If there is no response within four months, service is deemed to have failed.[92] After receiving the service request from Taiwan, the HPC should complete investigation within seven working days and transfer the documents to the relevant People's Court for service. The relevant court should register the case within five working days. Service should be processed within 15 days, and in no means longer than two months.[93] The timeline assists speedy service and increases the predictability of the parties and the other side. However, it does not provide the process time for the Taiwan part, which may cause delays for serving documents in Taiwan. **13.48**

Implementation of the 2010 Taiwan Mutual Assistance Provisions hs proved successful. People's Courts have successfully served documents from Taiwan in difficult and complicated cases, including cases where the recipient was located in an isolated area,[94] where the recipient changed address and had no other contact information,[95] and where a large number of recipients located in multiple cities were served.[96] In 2014, Fujian HPC received the request to serve 1,200 judicial documents on 602 recipients located in 64 cities in the Fujian province. In this complicated service case, the success rate was 73 per cent and service on average only took 15 days.[97] **13.49**

---

89 Ibid., Art 6.

90 Ibid., Art 11.

91 Ibid., Art 12.

92 Ibid.

93 Ibid., Art 13.

94 Zhejiang Zhoushang IPC Assists Taiwan Pingdong Court to Serve Judicial Documents in SPC, 'Renmin Fayuan Shetai Sifa Huzhu Dianxing Anli [Sample Cases on Taiwan-Related Mutual Judicial Assistance by the People's Court]', published on 20 June 2014.

95 Zhejiang Zhoushang IPC Assists Taiwan Pingdong Court to Serve Judicial Documents and Jiangsu Wuxi IPC Assists Taiwan Taipei Court to Serve Judicial Documents, in 'Sample Cases on Taiwan-Related Mutual Judicial Assistance', *ibid*; Guangdong Dongguan IPC assists Taiwan Xinbei Court to service documents, in SPC, '2014 Nian Renmin Fayuan Shetai Sifa Huzhu Dianxing Anli [2014 Sample Cases in Taiwan-Related Judicial Assistance]', published on 30 June 2015.

96 Fujian 64 courts assists Taiwan courts to serve judicial documents, in '2014 Sample Cases', ibid.

97 Ibid.

V. TAKING OF EVIDENCE BETWEEN MAINLAND, HONG KONG, MACAU, AND TAIWAN

V.1 Taking of evidence between Mainland and HKSAR

13.50 The Hague Evidence Convention applied to taking evidence between Mainland, Hong Kong and Macau, before the reunification. After Hong Kong and Macau returned to the PRC this Convention was no longer applicable as the basis of taking evidence between the regions. No agreement has been reached between Mainland and HKSAR on mutual assistance in taking evidence. Thus, the courts on both sides obtain evidence located in the other area in accordance with the local rules. Because of the fundamental differences in the judicial systems there are enormous difficulties in taking evidence between HKSAR and Mainland.

13.51 Hong Kong requires each party to obtain and present its evidence.[98] A party or its attorney can take whatever steps it sees fit in another jurisdiction to obtain evidence, as long as the steps are lawful in that other jurisdiction and neither invades a right of the other party before the Hong Kong court nor amounts to unconscionable conduct. The Hong Kong court cannot object if the party applies to a foreign court for discovery against a third party, or if a party interviews a witness abroad with a view to calling him at trial or serving a statement taken from him.[99] In the absence of formal judicial assistance, a party should take the responsibility to take evidence in Mainland to present in Hong Kong courts. The individual may suffer difficulties and costs in obtaining evidence. If the party needs evidence by deposition, the party may apply for a letter of request to be sent from the Hong Kong High Court to the requested court for assistance. The Hong Kong High Court may also appoint a special examiner to take evidence on oath.[100] However, since there is no judicial assistance arrangement between the two regions or judicial interpretation guiding the practice of Mainland courts, whether Mainland courts would wish to cooperate is unknown. In practice, due to the complexity and uncertainty of this method, most evidence in Mainland is collected by the party or its attorney.[101]

---

98 Renshan Liu, 'Recent Judicial Cooperation in Civil and Commercial Matters between Mainland China and Taiwan, the Hong Kong S.A.R. and the Macau S.A.R.', (2009) 11 *Yearbook of Private International Law* 235, 243.

99 S. Cromie, *International Commercial Litigation*, (Butterworths 1997), 407–8.

100 The Rules of the High Court (HKSAR), Ch 4A, Order 39, point 2.

101 SONG Xixiang, WANG Hongyan, 'Zhongguo Neidi yu Gang'ao Quji Quzheng Zhidu de Chengxiao, Wenti Jiqi Gaijin Jianyi [Effectiveness, Problems and Reform of Interregional Evidence Collection between Mainland and Hong Kong and Macau]', (2012) 11(1) Yiguo Liangzhi Yanjiu ['*One Country, Two Systems' Study*] 123, 124.

Hong Kong courts, in principle, could accept the letter rogatory from the Mainland court requesting assistance in taking evidence. According to Articles 75–77 of the Evidence Act of Hong Kong, the letter of request should be sent to the Hong Kong High Court. On obtaining the request, application is made to the Hong Kong court without notice to the other party. This is made by filing an affidavit, which will usually ask for a particular person to be appointed as examiner and ask for orders as to the time and place of the examination, the examiner's powers to administer oaths, whether foreign lawyers may participate, whether videotaping is to be permitted, and so on. The witness or the other party may apply to the court for the order to be set aside based on the ground that it falls outside the functions of the court in that state or that the request would prejudice the state's sovereignty or security. **13.52**

Although the formal assistance may be possible,[102] in the absence of legislative authorization of procedure for formal judicial assistance, more informal approaches are frequently adopted in practice. Because HKSAR has adopted a liberal stance with regard to the voluntary giving of evidence in Hong Kong, the courts in Mainland utilize the following routes to take evidence in HKSAR: (a) the parties to the litigation present the evidence themselves; (b) the attorney practising in HKSAR or Mainland entrusted by the parties to the litigation takes evidence; (c) Mainland organizations in Hong Kong and private detectives appointed by the court that requires the evidence could gather evidence; (d) the Hong Kong notary public authorized by the Justice Department of PRC can handle matters related to notarization; and (e) judicial officers in the name of business, tourism, or visiting relatives can enter HKSAR to take evidence in the case of particularly serious or urgent cases.[103] Within these methods, the first four are private actions and do not infringe the law of HKSAR or Mainland. However, the authenticity and reliability of the evidence taken by the parties completely out of jurisdiction may be questioned. Furthermore, it is inconsistent with the basic principle of evidence collection in Mainland, where the parties have an obligation to produce evidence and the court may also of its own motion take evidence when necessary.[104] Method (e) is particularly controversial as it allows evidence to be taken by a Mainland judicial officer. Such conduct can amount to the exercise of judicial power in another jurisdiction. Judicial officers entering Hong Kong to conduct judicial **13.53**

102 The SPC recognized that although there is no formal arrangement, the courts in Mainland and HKSAR have provided judicial assistance in individual cases in practice. See SPC, 'Guanyu Jinyibu Guifan Renmin Fayuan Shegang'aotai Diaocha Quzheng Gongzuo de Tongzhi [Notice on Further Regulating Investigation and Evidence Collection Involving Hong Kong, Macau or Taiwan by People's Court]' ('2011 Evidence Notice'), Fa [2011] No 243.

103 FENG Xia, *supra* n 41, 292–3; SONG Xixiang, WANG Hongyan, *supra* n 101, 124.

104 CPL 2012, Art 64.

activities without notifying Hong Kong authorities and without authorization and permission infringe the 'two system' policy and judicial autonomy of HKSAR in the absence of the authorization of the relevant authority of HKSAR, which directly affects the legitimacy and admissibility of the evidence.[105] Being aware of the inappropriateness of such actions, the SPC stated in 2011 that Mainland courts should not permit officers to enter into HKSAR, MASAR and Taiwan to take evidence unless it is necessary in special circumstances, reported to the SPC and authorized by relevant central authorities.[106] Although the SPC aims to regulate the behaviour of the local courts, it still permits such evidence collection methods in exceptional cases, although it is still inappropriate and controversial in the 'one country, two systems' principle.

V.2 Taking of evidence between Mainland and MASAR

13.54 Taking evidence between Mainland and MASAR is utilized by the 2001 Macau Service and Evidence Arrangement.[107] This arrangement does not adopt the 'central authority' channel provided by the Hague Evidence Convention, but establishes the directly entrusted courts channel, normally through the HPC of PRC and the Final Appeal Court of MASAR. The SPC of PRC and the Final Appeal Court of MASAR may also mutually request the taking of evidence.

13.55 The requesting court should send the letter of request to the requested court. The letter of request should be in Chinese or accompanied by a Chinese translation. It should specify: (a) the name of the requesting court; (b) the names and addresses of the parties to the proceedings and their representatives, if any; (c) the reason why the evidence is required, and the specific issues of the evidence; (d) the names and addresses of the persons to be examined, and the questions to be put them; (e) any special method or procedure to be followed; and (f) any other information beneficial to the execution of the request. The 'evidence' covers oral evidence from parties to proceeding, witnesses, and experts; testimonial; judicial inquest; and other documents related to the proceeding.

13.56 The requested court shall complete the evidence collection task within three months. If the requested court holds that the letter of request does not comply with the provisions of the arrangement, it shall promptly notify the requesting

105 SONG Xixiang, WANG Hongyan, *supra* n 101, 126.
106 SPC, '2011 Evidence Notice', *supra* n 102, point 1.
107 See section IV.2 above.

court and require that court to issue supplementary materials if necessary. The methods and procedure for taking the evidence should be governed by the law of the requested court. However, if the requesting court requires special procedures to be followed, this may be respected unless it contradicts the forum law or is impossible due to different local procedure and practice. The execution of the request may be refused only on two grounds: (a) the execution of the request does not fall within the functions of the court; or (b) the execution of the request may infringe the public policy of the requested court.

Upon the request of the requesting court, the requested court shall notify the date and address of evidence collection, so that the persons concerned may be legally present. In executing the request, the requested court may allow the judicial officers of the requesting court to attend. The judicial officers of the requesting court may examine and cross-examine the witnesses and experts with the permission of the requested court, if necessary. This approach should improve the efficiency of judicial assistance. Allowing the requesting judicial officers to take evidence could improve the quality and admissibility of the evidence taken. **13.57**

The requested court may assist in arranging local witnesses and experts to testify in the requesting court upon the request of the requesting court and the assent of the witnesses. During their stay in the requesting court, the witnesses and experts shall not be liable to criminal prosecution, detention, deprivation of property, withholding of identity documents, or any other way of restriction of personal freedom. The requesting court shall reimburse the fees and cost thereof.[108] **13.58**

A written document establishing the execution of the request shall be sent by the requested court to the requesting court. In every instance where the request is not executed in whole or in part, the requested court shall so inform the requesting court, explain the reasons in writing, and immediately return the letter of request and all accompanying documents. If the parties to the proceeding and witnesses refuse to give evidence under the law of the requested court, the requested court shall inform the requesting court, explain the reasons in writing, and immediately return the letter of request and all accompanying documents. **13.59**

The arrangement is implemented well in practice. Between 2001 and 2008, MASAR courts received nine requests from Mainland, eight of which were executed successfully with the success rate 89 per cent; Mainland received 28 **13.60**

108 SONG Xixiang, *supra* n 85, 175–8.

requests from MASAR and successfully executed 16, the success rate 57.14 per cent.[109] Although the success rate is higher in MASAR, it is proportionate with the smaller number of requests. However, although the implementation is in general satisfactory, the arrangement mainly facilitates evidence-taking through formal judicial assistance, which requires cooperation between the two courts and results in high costs and complicated procedures. The success largely depends on whether the requested court expends its best efforts to execute the request. The requesting court will have to wait until the request is executed. The arrangement requires evidence to be taken no later than three months after receiving the letter of request.[110]

V.3 Obtaining evidence between Mainland and Taiwan

13.61 The 2009 Taiwan Agreement on Mutual Judicial Assistance also includes terms utilizing mutual assistance in taking evidence. Article 8 provides that the two sides agree to make their best efforts to provide assistance in obtaining evidence in accordance with their own regulations, which includes gathering testimony and statements, providing documentary evidence, physical evidence and audiovisual material, confirming the relationship between the parties and its identification; inquests, identifications, inspections, visits, and surveys; and searches and seizures, etc.

13.62 With the implementation of this agreement, the result of the cross-strait mutual legal assistance in taking evidence is remarkable. From 2009 to September 2013, the courts in Mainland received the evidence-taking request from Taiwan in a total of 497 cases, respectively six cases in 2009, 116 in 2010, 137 in 2011, 122 in 2012, and 123 in 2013. The successful rate reaches 82 per cent. Correspondingly, the courts in Taiwan received the evidence-taking request from Mainland in 234 cases, respectively one case in 2009, eight cases in 2010, 12 in 2011, 69 in 2012, and 144 in 2013. 199 cases were successfully executed, which attain the success rate of 85 per cent.[111]

13.63 In order to more effectively implement the Agreement of 2009, the SPC issued the 'Provisions Regarding the Service and Gathering of Evidence between the Both Sides of Taiwan Straits' in 2010.[112] This provision defines a wide scope of evidence-taking between the two sides. Evidence should include taking testimony and statements; providing documentary evidence, physical evidence and

---

109 SONG Xixiang, WANG Hongyan, *supra* n 101, 126.

110 Macau Service and Evidence Arrangement, Art 5.

111 SONG Xixiang, *supra* n 85, 188.

112 SPC, Provisions, *supra* n 86.

audiovisual material; confirming the relationship between the parties and its identification and criminal record; and inquests, identifications, inspections, visits, surveys, searches, seizures, and other means of taking evidence.[113] The methods and procedure of taking evidence by the courts in Mainland shall comply with the civil procedural law, criminal procedural law, administrative procedural law and the relevant judicial interpretations of PRC.[114] The Provisions also reserve a public interest defence in that the People's Courts should assist in taking evidence according to the request of Taiwan courts, but taking evidence cannot infringe Chinese law or relevant regulations, prejudice the social public interests, or hinder the ongoing proceedings.[115]

The provisions provides detailed timelines for assisting in taking evidence. The SPC and the High People's Courts shall finish the review on the request within seven days.[116] The specific competent court shall file a case by the cause of action of 'assistance Taiwan in investigation and evidence collection' within five working days from the date of receipt of the materials transferred by the High People's Court, shall finish the investigation and taking evidence within one month, not exceeding three months from the date of the filing. **13.64**

The evidence and judicial documents obtained in Taiwan in accordance with the agreement and the provisions do not need notarization, authentication, or any other forms of proof.[117] This largely reduces judicial cost and improves judicial efficiency. **13.65**

V.4 Conclusion

Judicial assistance in interregional evidence-taking respectively exists between Mainland and MASAR and between Mainland and Taiwan. Although there is room for further development, the current practice is in general satisfactory. Comparatively, the most difficulty exists between Mainland and HKSAR. Apart from absence of a mutual arrangement, Mainland does not have unilateral rules providing any guidance on collecting evidence in HKSAR. This is primarily due to the difference in judicial systems and evidence rules. Mainland, MASAR and Taiwan follow the civil law tradition and the court takes an active role in collecting or assisting in collecting evidence. HKSAR follows the common law tradition where judges do not usually take part in evidence-gathering on behalf of the parties. Formal judicial cooperation **13.66**

113 Ibid., Art 15.
114 Ibid., Art 16.
115 Ibid., Art 2.
116 Ibid., Art 10.
117 Ibid., Art 24.

usually requires the requested court to take evidence on behalf of the requesting court, which may be much easier to implement in other regions than HKSAR.[118] Furthermore, HKSAR provides very detailed and complicated rules on evidence, many of which are unknown in Mainland. Conducting mutual assistance or following an unknown procedure to collecting evidence may prove difficult in practice. For example, HKSAR courts may summon witnesses to give evidence, while Mainland courts would not use any compulsory measures for this purpose.[119] Given the differences, both mutual arrangements and unilateral provisions in relation to evidence-taking between Mainland and Hong Kong prove difficult.

VI. ENFORCEMENT OF JUDGMENTS BETWEEN MAINLAND, HONG KONG, MACAU AND TAIWAN

13.67 In order to facilitate integration between Mainland, Hong Kong, Macau and Taiwan, save judicial resources and protect the private rights of civil parties effectively, the four regions respectively enacted some regulations on the interregional enforcement of judgments. After Hong Kong and Macau reunited with the PRC, the three regions signed two bilateral arrangements on mutual recognition and enforcement of judgments, namely the Mainland-Macau Judgment Arrangement 2006,[120] and the Mainland-HK Judgment Arrangement 2006.[121] Furthermore, Mainland and Taiwan entered into the Agreement on Mutual Judicial Assistance in 2009.[122]

VI.1 Enforcement of judgments between Mainland and HKSAR

i. Mainland-HK Judgment Arrangement 2006

13.68 The Mainland-HK Judgment Arrangement was concluded in 2006 and entered into effect following the SPC judicial interpretation[123] and HKSAR

118 SONG Xixiang, WANG Hongyan, *supra* n 101, 127.

119 Ibid.

120 SPC, 'Guanyu Neidi yu Aomen Tebie Xingzhengque Xianghu Renke he Zhixing Minshangshi Panjue de Anpai [Arrangement between the Mainland and the MASAR on the Mutual Recognition and Enforcement of Civil and Commercial Judgments]', [2006] Fa Shi 2.

121 'Neidi yu Xianggang Tebie Xingzhengqu Fayuan Xianghu Renke he Zhixing Dangshiren Xieyi Guanxia de Minshangshi Anjian Panjue de Anpai [Arrangement between the Mainland and the HKSAR on Mutual Recognition and Enforcement of Civil and Commercial Judgments Pursuant to Choice of Court Agreements]', signed on 14 July 2006, came into force as of 1 August 2008 by the SPC judicial interpretation, Fa Shi [2008] No 9.

122 Haixia Liang'an Gongtong Daji Fanzui ji Sifa Huzhu Xieyi [Agreement on Common Fight against Crime and Mutual Judicial Assistance between Both Sides of the Taiwan Straits] 24 June 2009.

123 Interpretation No 9 [2008] of the Supreme People's Court on 3 July 2008.

implementation legislation,[124] both done in 2008. Prior to this arrangement, enforcing judgments between two regions caused real difficulties and uncertainties.[125] This arrangement produced certainty in enforcing monetary judgments in civil and commercial matters and further assisted Hong Kong to become a major dispute resolution centre, with particular privileges for helping enforce judgments in China. Most foreigners feel more comfortable taking proceedings in Hong Kong rather than Mainland and, because enforcing foreign judgments in Mainland is still not easy, suing in Hong Kong provides a practical solution.[126]

The arrangement largely mirrors the Hague Choice of Court Convention, which is reflected in its rules and its scope. The arrangement only applies to monetary judgments in civil and commercial matters pursuant to an exclusive choice of court agreement in writing. This limitation is caused by the difficulty of reaching consensus between two regions with differences in their legal systems, litigation culture and procedures. Enforcing monetary judgments in civil and commercial matters raises the least controversy and the existence of an exclusive choice of court agreement is the common jurisdiction ground for both regions causing the lightest challenge to jurisdiction. **13.69**

Judgments that fall within the narrow scope should be mutually enforced between Mainland and HKSAR, unless one of six grounds refusal are found, i.e.: the choice of court agreement is invalid; judgments are wholly satisfied; the enforcement court has exclusive jurisdiction over the subject matter; the court proceedings are unfair and irregular; the judgment is obtained by fraud; or the judgment is irreconcilable with an earlier judgment rendered by the requested region and enforcement may infringe the public policy of the requested region. **13.70**

An application under the arrangement should be submitted to the IPC either in the domicile or residence of the respondent or in the place where the respondent's assets are located. The alternative jurisdiction provides the applicant with freedom of choice. Usually, the applicant may wish to choose the locality of the assets in order to smooth enforcement. The application should be made pursuant to the procedural law of the requested court.[127] The applicant submits an application form, a duplicate of the judgment affixed with the seal of the court, a certificate issued by the judgment court proving **13.71**

---

124 Mainland Judgments (Reciprocal Enforcement) Ordinance and its (Commencement) Notice, Ord. No. 9 of 2008, L.S. No.2 to Gazette No. 27/2008.

125 See discussion in Ch 6.

126 James Illman, 'HK Courts Accord to Open China Market', *Legal Week* (11 May 2006).

127 Mainland-HK Judgment Arrangement, Art 8.

that the judgment is final and can be executed at the jurisdiction of origin, and an identity certificate. Any document submitted to the Chinese court should be in Chinese. If the original documents are in another language, the applicant submits a certified translation. Application for Chinese judgments enforced in Hong Kong should be made within two years from the last day of the time limit for voluntary execution as stated in the judgment, and if the judgment is to be executed by stages, from the last day of the time limit set for each stage, or, if there is no time limit in the judgment, from the day when the judgment becomes effective. For a judgment made in HKSAR to be executed in Mainland, the time limit shall be calculated from the day when the judgment becomes enforceable.[128]

13.72 The arrangement significantly contributes to the civil and commercial connections between Mainland and HKSAR and largely improves judicial certainty. However, the arrangement cannot provide a one-stop solution for mutual enforcement of judgments between Mainland and HKSAR. The arrangement has a narrow scope. In the absence of a jurisdiction clause meeting the requirement of the arrangement, in non-monetary judgments such as injunctions, in areas outside civil and commercial disputes, and in explicitly excluded areas, such as employment contracts, consumer contracts and family matters, the arrangement is not applicable. This narrow area is inspired by the Hague Choice of Court Convention, which is criticized by commentators for being too narrow and restrictive for interregional cooperation, although it may be realistic for an international framework.[129]

ii. Judgments out of the scope of the Mainland-HK Judgment Arrangement 2006

13.73 Although mutual enforcement of judgments between Mainland and HKSAR is facilitated by the 2006 Arrangement, judicial cooperation does not exist in judgments falling outside its scope. In order to ensure enforcement of such judgments the two regions have to rely on their unilateral domestic law. Since Chinese legislation does not clearly address this issue there is uncertainty and three approaches can be made. The first is to treat HKSAR as on an equal footing with other regions and apply any existing provisions for other regions to Hong Kong judgments. Since the SPC has issued the 'Provisions on Recognition of Civil Judgments of Taiwan Courts',[130] and because both Hong Kong and Taiwan are treated as separate legal regions by the Mainland, Hong Kong could be analogized as Taiwan and the rules in the Taiwan Judgment

---

128 Ibid.

129 HKSAR LC Paper No. CB (2) 722/01–02 (04), para 18.

130 SPC, 'Zuigao Renmin Fayuan Guanyu Renmin Fayuan Renke Taiwan Diqu Youguan Fayuan Minshi Panjue de Guiding [Provisions on the People's Court's Recognition of Civil Judgments made by Relevant Courts in the Taiwan Region]', Fa Shi [1998] No 11.

Provisions apply.[131] The second approach analogizes Hong Kong as a foreign country and applies Article 282 of the CPL for recognition of foreign judgments to enforcing Hong Kong judgments.[132] This approach may lead to a refusal to recognize most Hong Kong judgments falling out of the Arrangement due to the narrow grounds for enforcing foreign judgments in China.[133] Further, it is doubtful whether this approach is appropriate for interregional enforcement of judgments under the 'one country' policy. The third approach would systematically refuse enforcement of these Hong Kong judgments because excluding them from the Arrangement might imply an intention not to enforce them.[134] This approach is criticized for being too rigid. It may also misinterpret the legislative purpose. These judgments are excluded from the Mainland-Hong Kong Judgment Arrangement because they cause more controversy between two sides that may prevent them from being automatically enforced. It does not mean that legislators do not intend to enforce them at all.[135]

There is no definite answer as to how to handle applications to recognize and enforce court judgments from HKSAR. However, the relatively restrictive interpretation of approaches two and three (above) is, in practice, that normally adopted by Mainland courts. Regardless of the reunification, which makes judgments recognition and enforcement an interregional problem, Mainland courts have tended to apply the traditional approach, unless different rules are expressly provided by law. Furthermore, judges have little discretion and are trained to apply the given law. In the absence of legislative provisions, judges are likely to follow the principle not to give extraterritorial effect to judgments in another jurisdiction. Given the narrow scope of the Mainland-HK Judgment Arrangement, the current situation for mutual enforcement of judgments remains one of its major shortfalls. **13.74**

---

131 Xianchu Zhang and Philip Smart, 'Development of Regional Conflict of Laws: On the Arrangement of Mutual Recognition and Enforcement of Judgments in Civil and Commercial Matters Between Mainland and Hong Kong ASR', (2006) 36 *Hong Kong Law Journal* 553, 555; Huang Jie, 'Interregional Recognition and Enforcement of Civil and Commercial Judgments: Lessons for China from US and EU Laws', Duke Law Theses and Dissertations 90 (2010).

132 *Application of Quanqiao Investment Co to Recognize a Hong Kong Civil Judgment,* Fujian Quanzhou Intermediate People's Court, (2001) Quan Yin Zi No 1; *Jiangmen Xinhua Paper Mill v. Tak Lee Metal &Paper Co,* Guangdong Province HPC, (1999) Yue Fa Jing Er Zhong Zi No 322.

133 See Ch 6 above.

134 *Re Application of NORSTAR to Recognition of the Order of the Court of HKSAR*, [2011] Min Si Ta Zi No 19. The applicant applied for the recognition of an HKSAR liquidation order. This issue is out of the Mainland-HK Judgment Arrangement. The SPC refused to apply Art 265 of the CPL on recognition of foreign judgments to a HKSAR court order. The SPC finally stated that the liquidation order was not recognizable for the lack of legal basis. Huang Jie, *supra* n 131, 91–2.

135 For more discussion of the three approaches, see Huang Jie, ibid.

VI.2 Enforcement of judgments between Mainland and MASAR

13.75 Mutual enforcement of judgments between Mainland and Macau is facilitated by the Mainland-Macau Judgments Arrangement 2006.[136] Before the arrangement entered into force, Macau unilaterally recognized and enforced most Mainland's judgments according to its unilateral domestic rules. Macau judgments could not often be treated reciprocally in the same way because of the rigid Mainland law in this aspect.[137] The arrangement brings about mutual benefits for both sides, especially for Macau.

13.76 Compared to the Mainland-HK Judgment Arrangement, the Macau Arrangement is much broader in scope. It covers all civil and commercial judgments, monetary or non-monetary, including some controversial areas, such as employment disputes. It also extends to civil compensation in criminal proceedings.[138] A judgment eligible for enforcement under the arrangement must be 'effective' pursuant to the law of the judgment-rendering jurisdiction.[139] Such judgments should be enforceable by the other side in principle, unless common exceptions apply, such as: infringement of exclusive jurisdiction of the requested jurisdiction; the existence of an irreconcilable judgment in the requested court has recognized or enforced earlier judgments or awards in a third country; procedural irregularity; an ineffective judgment; or public policy.[140]

VI.3 Enforcement of judgments between Mainland and Taiwan

13.77 Mainland has always held a positive attitude to the civil judicial assistance between Mainland and Taiwan. As early as April 1991, President REN Jianxin of the SPC of the PRC stated, in the Work Report, that:

> Taiwan residents' civil acts in Taiwan Region and the civil rights under the laws of Taiwan may be recognized by Mainland courts, as long as it dose not violate the fundamental principles of law of PRC, or social public interests. The civil judgments

136 SPC, 'Zuigao Renmin Fayuan Guanyu Neidi yu Aomen Tebie Xingzhengque Xianghu Renke he Zhixing Minshangshi Panjue de Anpai [Arrangement between the Mainland and the Macau Special Administrative Region on the Mutual Recognition and Enforcement of Civil and Commercial Judgments]', [2006] Fa Shi 2.

137 For discussion of Macau's domestic law in recognition and enforcement of foreign judgments, see Guangjian Tu, 'Recognition of Enforcement of Non-Local Judgments in Macau: A Critical Review', (2012) 42 *Hong Kong Law Journal* 640. Since this book mainly focuses on the conflict of laws in Mainland, Macau law is not discussed in detail.

138 Macau Arrangement, Art 1.

139 Ibid., Art 3.

140 Ibid., Art 11.

of Taiwan courts will also be recognized in accordance with this principle and the different circumstance of the individual case.[141]

Before 1 July 2015, enforcement of Taiwan judgments in Mainland was utilized by four SPC judicial interpretations: the 'Provisions on Enforcement of Taiwan Judgments' (1998),[142] 'Reply on Recognition of Civil Mediation Agreements'(1999),[143] 'Reply on Recognition of Payment Order' (2001),[144] and 'Supplementary Provisions on Enforcement of Taiwan Judgments' (2009).[145] These four documents largely provided certainty that Taiwan judgments in civil and commercial matters would be effective; however, the application of four different documents increased complexity. In 2009, the two sides entered into the 2009 Agreement on Mutual Judicial Assistance, Article 10 of which provides a very general principle for the mutual enforcement of civil judgments and arbitral awards based on reciprocity and protection of public policy. This provision only sets out a very basic principle without providing any practice procedure for its implementation. In 2015, the SPC published the more comprehensive 'Provisions on the Recognition and Enforcement of Civil Judgments by the Courts of the Taiwan Region' ('Taiwan Judgment Provisions 2015'),[146] which entered into force from 1 July 2015 and abolished all four judicial interpretations. **13.78**

These provisions requires Mainland courts to recognize and enforce Taiwan civil judgments as a matter of principle, provides detailed procedures, and clarifies certain exemptions. Civil judgments are broadly defined to include all effective judgments, rulings, settlement agreements, mediation agreements, payment orders, and civil remedies provided in criminal proceedings.[147] Application should be made in the IPC of the place where the domicile, or **13.79**

---

141 The Gazette of Supreme People's Court of PRC, 1991.

142 Fa Shi [1998] No 11, *supra* n 130.

143 SPC, 'Guanyu Dangshiren Chi Taiwan Diqu Youguan Fayuan Minshi Tiaojieshu Huo Youguan Jigou Chujude Huo Querende Tiaojie Xieyishu Xiang Renmin Fayuan Shenqing Renke Renmin Fayuan Yingfou Shouli de Pifu [Reply regarding whether People's Court shall Accept the Application for Recognition of the Civil Mediation Agreement by relevant Court in Taiwan Region, or Issued or Confirmed by relevant Institutions in Taiwan Region]', Fa Shi [1999] No 10.

144 SPC, 'Guanyu Dangshiren Chi Taiwandiqu Youguan Fayuan Zhifu Minlin xiang Renminfayuan Shenqing Renke Renminfayuan Yingfou Shouli de Pifu [Reply regarding whether People's Court shall Accept the Application for Recognition of the Payment Order by relevant Court in Taiwan Region]', Fa Shi [2001] No 13.

145 SPC, 'Guanyu Renminfayuan Renke Taiwandiqu Youguan Fayuan Minshi Panjue de Buchong Guiding [Supplementary Provisions of the SPC on the People's Courts' Recognition of Civil Judgments of the Relevant Courts of the Taiwan Region]', Fa Shi [2009] No 4.

146 SPC, 'Guanyu Renke he Zhixing Taiwandiqu Fayuan Minshipanjue de Guiding [Provisions on the Recognition and Enforcement of Civil Judgments by the Courts of the Taiwan Region]', Fa Shi [2015] No 13.

147 Taiwan Judgment Provisions 2015, Art 2.

habitual residence, of the applicant or respondent is located, or where the respondent's assets are located.[148] The applicant should provide the application form, final judgment and its certificate,[149] and evidence proving the judgment is authentic and in effect.[150] The application should also provide the certificate proving that the Taiwan court has followed the legal procedure to serve the defendant if judgment is made in default.[151] The court should register the case in the record within seven days of receiving the application and make a decision within six months of registration.[152] In procedural issues, difficulties usually exist over what certificate is needed to prove the authenticity and effect of the judgment. Before the 2015 Provisions, the parties could provide notarized documents, courts' certificates or apply for the requested court to conduct an investigation. The absence of uniform standards led to uncertainty and some courts simply refused to enforce the Taiwan judgment straightaway. The 2015 Provisions provides clear guidance. Article 9 provides that the requested court investigate under the existing rules in taking evidence in Taiwan,[153] either upon application or by its own motive. It simplifies the procedure for the applicant and provides the uniform procedural standards. The problem is that it takes all responsibility from the application and imposes it on courts. Although it is more reliable, it increases the court's workload, and the mutual assistance procedure in taking evidence is usually complicated and time consuming. This inevitably causes delay and raises costs. Although the court is required to make a decision within six months, the time spent in taking evidence is excluded. The procedure, as a result, is inefficient and too complicated. It is necessary to trust the applicant to provide evidence certified by authorized organs.

13.80 Recognition and enforcement will usually be granted, unless one of the exception grounds exists: the defendant is deprived of the opportunity to be heard; the case falls within the exclusive jurisdiction of Mainland; Taiwan courts take jurisdiction in breach of a valid arbitration agreement; the case has already been heard and decided by the Mainland court or tribunal; the same dispute has already been heard and decided by the HKSAR, MASAR or foreign court which is recognized by the Mainland court; the arbitral tribunal of Taiwan, HKSAR, MASAR, or a foreign country has given an award on the same matter which is recognized by the Mainland court; and the infringement

---

148 Ibid., Art 4.
149 Ibid., Art 7.
150 Ibid., Art 9.
151 Ibid., Art 7.
152 Ibid., Arts 8, 14.
153 See s V.3 above.

of public policy.[154] Most exceptions are common exceptions for enforcement of foreign judgments. As to the public policy defence, it has been reserved in most documents concerning interregional conflicts, but the Taiwan Judgment Provisions specifically name the 'one country' principle as an example.[155] It is understood as being especially designed for Taiwan-related matters, reflecting the political difference between the two sides. Therefore, Mainland courts may exercise discretion as to whether an interest or order is public policy, but certainty is provided for the 'one country' policy. Except for the 'one country' policy, Mainland courts need to apply public policy defence restrictively and only in exceptional cases. What judgments may infringe the 'one country' policy? It is likely that the 'one country' policy in the public policy defence must include the full meaning of the policy. Any diverse interpretation may cause the judgment not to be recognized. If the judgment expressly or impliedly states Taiwan as a country, recognizes one country, but treats the central government as on an equal footing as the Taiwan government, records the Taiwan 'one country, two areas' policy instead of 'one country, two systems', it infringes this policy. However, this may only have symbolic and academic value. Such contents may not normally exist in most civil and commercial judgments.

VII. ENFORCEMENT OF ARBITRAL AWARDS BETWEEN MAINLAND, HONG KONG, MACAU AND TAIWAN

Arbitral awards were enforced pursuant to the NYC between Mainland and Hong Kong/Macau before reunification. Afterwards, the NYC was no longer applicable and the enforcement of foreign awards was complex because awards, rendered in the different regions, were subject to contrasting special rules. Taiwan is not a signatory of the NYC and the mutual enforcement of arbitral awards between Mainland and Taiwan had, from the beginning, been governed by the domestic instead of the conventional rules. This section explores the respective legal bases for recognition and enforcement of arbitral awards among the four regions. **13.81**

VII.1 Enforcement of arbitral awards between Mainland and HKSAR

Current enforcement of arbitral awards between Mainland and HKSAR is unitized by the 'Arrangement on the Mutual Enforcement of Arbitral Awards between the Mainland and the HKSAR 1999' ('Mainland-HK Awards **13.82**

154 Taiwan Judgment Provisions 2015, Art 15.

155 Ibid.

Arrangement'), in effect since 2000.[156] This arrangement had retrospective effect, applying to any awards after the Hong Kong handover on 1 July 1997.[157]

13.83 The arrangement does not define the scope of awards that may be enforced. China has made a reservation to only enforce 'commercial' awards under the NYC,[158] while no such reservation was made by Hong Kong. Therefore, it is uncertain whether the Mainland-HK Awards Arrangement only covers awards that are classified as 'commercial'. Two interpretations exist: (a) since the arrangement largely follows the NYC, both jurisdictions should retain the same scope of subject matter under the arrangement. Therefore, HKSAR may enforce awards in any area, while Mainland may only enforce Hong Kong awards in commercial matters according to Mainland law. This interpretation undermines the principle of reciprocity and places Hong Kong and Mainland in unequal footing; and (b) the NYC reservation cannot be naturally transplanted in the interregional arrangement, which is different from international convention. In the absence of express definition, the arrangement should have a broader scope to cover wider matters. This interpretation is more realistic. In practice, some Mainland courts indeed enforce HK awards outside commercial matters.[159]

13.84 The applicant could apply to the court for enforcement in the place where the other party resides or the property concerned is located.[160] In the Mainland, the relevant court is the IPC, and in the HKSAR it is the High Court.[161] If the respondent's residence and location of assets are in Mainland and HKSAR respectively, the applicant may only file his application in the court in one place at a time. He may not file his second application unless he is unable to fully recover the award from the first proceeding. In any event, the sum enforced by the courts of the two jurisdictions shall not exceed the amount awarded.[162] The applicant should submit the enforcement application, the

156 SPC, 'Zuigao Renmin Fayuan Guanyu Neidi yu Xianggang Tebie Xingzhengqu Xianghu Zhixing Zhongcai Caijue de Anpai [Arrangement on the Mutual Enforcement of Arbitral Awards between the Mainland and the HKSAR 1999]', Fa Shi [2000] No 3.

157 For more discussion, see M.J. Claver-Carone, 'Post-handover Recognition and Enforcement of Arbitral Awards between Mainland and Hong Kong SAR', (2002) 33 *Law and Policy in International Business* 369, fn 101–135

158 New York Convention, Art I(3).

159 WU Lijing, TIAN Xiaoyun, 'Lun Neidi yu Xianggang Xiuanghu Zhixing Zhongcai Caijue de Falv Wenti [Legal Issues on Mutual Enforcement of Arbitral Awards between Mainland and Hong Kong]', (2011) 3 Tequ Jingji [*Special Zone Economy*] 15, 16.

160 Mainland-HK Awards Arrangement, Art 1.

161 Ibid., Art 2.

162 Ibid.

arbitral award and the arbitration agreement.[163] As compared with Article IV of the NYC, which mentions only the arbitral award and the arbitration agreement, a party seeking to enforce an arbitral award under the arrangement may have to produce more supporting documents. For example, the applicant should also produce a copy of its business registration, the particulars and grounds of the enforcement application, and the conditions of the property concerned. If the applicant is a foreign legal person or organization, the documents need to be notarized and attested.[164] None of these requirements are present in the NYC.

The limitation issue is governed by the law of the place where the enforcement is sought.[165] This, however, causes different levels of rights and obligations between Hong Kong and Mainland applicants, due to different domestic law of limitation. In the Mainland, application to enforce arbitral awards is two years from the last day of the performance period specified in the arbitral award.[166] In HKSAR, the limitation period can be as long as six years.[167] As such, a party seeking to enforce a Hong Kong arbitral award in his favour in the Mainland has far less time than his counterpart seeking to enforce a Mainland award in Hong Kong. **13.85**

The law governing the enforcement procedure is determined by the *lex fori*.[168] This is a common conflicts rule dealing with procedure. In HKSAR, the applicant has the right to appeal after the ruling of rejection; while in Mainland, the ruling of IPC on enforcement application is final, subject to the internal report and review scheme.[169] **13.86**

The refusal grounds translate Article V of the NYC virtually word for word. Finally, the SPC applies the arrangement to ad hoc arbitral awards and awards made by foreign arbitral tribunals in Hong Kong.[170] **13.87**

163 Ibid., Arts 3, 4.
164 Ibid., Art 4(3), (4).
165 Ibid., Art 5.
166 Art 239 of the CPL 2012.
167 Hong Kong Limitation Ordinance (Cap 347), s 4(1)(c).
168 Mainland-HK Awards Arrangement, Art 6.
169 See Ch 6, section III.5.
170 SPC, 'Zuigao Renmin Fayuan Guanyu Xianggang Zhongcai Caijue Zai Neidi Zhixing de Youguan Wenti de Tongzhi [Notice on Issues concerning the Execution of Hong Kong Arbitral Awards in the Mainland]', Fa [2009] 415.

VII.2 Enforcement of arbitral awards between Mainland and MASAR

13.88 On 30 October 2007 Macau and Mainland China signed the 'Arrangement Concerning the Mutual Enforcement of Arbitral Awards between the mainland and the MASAR' ('Mainland-Macau Arbitral Award Arrangement').[171] It is very similar to the NYC. It is applicable to all arbitral awards made after the handover on 20 December 1999, on the condition that the application for recognition and enforcement was made after the effective date of the arrangement, i.e., after 1 January 2008. For arbitral awards made after 20 December 1999 and before the effective date of the arrangement, the time limit applicable to application for recognition and enforcement shall commence from the effective date of the arrangement. Mutual enforcement of arbitral awards is guaranteed, subject to seven refusal grounds. The first six grounds for refusal of enforcement correspond with the first six grounds set out in Article V of the NYC. In respect of the seventh ground, the arrangement provides for refusal if enforcement would be contrary to 'the basic principle of law or the public interests of Mainland China' or if enforcement would be contrary to 'the basic principles of law the public order of the MASAR'. The Mainland-Macau Arbitral Award Arrangement is generally similar to the Mainland-Hong Kong Arbitral Award Arrangement with some improvements.[172]

VII.3 Enforcement of arbitral awards between Mainland and Taiwan

13.89 Although political tensions between Mainland China and Taiwan remain, their trade ties have become stronger. Taiwan and Mainland China have not entered into any particular bilateral arrangement on mutual recognition and enforcement of arbitral awards, except that the 'Agreement on Common Fight against Crime and Mutual Judicial Assistance between Both Sides of the Taiwan Straits' provides a very general and ambiguous principle on reciprocal recognition of arbitral awards.[173] Therefore, given the current relationship with China, the enforcement of arbitral awards within Taiwan is regulated by separate frameworks depending on which side of the Taiwan Strait is involved.

---

171 In Mainland the Arrangement was adopted on 31 October 2007 by the 1437th session of the Judicial Committee of the SPC, 'Zuigao Renmin Fayuan Guanyu Neidi yu Xianggang Tebie Xingzhengqu Xianghu Zhixing Zhongcai Caijue de Anpai [Arrangement Concerning the Mutual Enforcement of Arbitral Awards between the mainland and the MASAR]' ('Mainland-Macau Arbitral Award Arrangement'), Fa Shi [2007] 17, promulgated on 12 December 2008. In Macau it was published by order of the Chief Execution on 12 December 2007. The Arrangement entered into force on 1 January 2008.

172 Robert Pe and Michael Polkinghome, 'Two Steps Forward, One Step Sideways', (2008) 25 *Journal of International Arbitration* 410–412.

173 Art 10.

On the Mainland side, the 2015 'Provisions on Recognition and Enforcement of Arbitral Awards in the Taiwan Area' ('Taiwan Awards Provisions') entered into force from 1 July 2015.[174] All civil and commercial arbitral awards, including ad hoc awards, may be enforced in Mainland under the procedure and standard of the Provisions. The Taiwan Awards Provisions provides the same procedure rules as the Taiwan Judgments Provisions,[175] and similar refusal rounds as Article V of the NYC.[176] **13.90**

VIII. CONFLICT OF JURISDICTION AND PARALLEL PROCEEDINGS

There is no arrangement between the regions on dealing with concurrent proceedings and conflicts of jurisdiction. This issue is thus left completely to the domestic rule of each region. As far as Mainland is concerned, it does not enact any special jurisdiction rules addressing interregional conflicts and parallel proceedings. In principle, the same international jurisdiction rules should be applicable, which do not include the *lis pendens* rule and the legislators hold the view they should not tackle concurrent proceedings between different judgments but recognize and respect judicial sovereignty.[177] **13.91**

Would the same view apply to interregional conflicts? The then Vice President of the Supreme People's Court, WAN E'Xiang, suggested that where both Mainland and Hong Kong/Macau have jurisdiction, and one party has sued and been heard in Hong Kong/Macau, the People's Court 'should' take jurisdiction if one of the parties subsequently brought the same action to Mainland. It does not matter if the Hong Kong or Macau courts have delivered final judgments or not.[178] *Lis pendens*, again, is irrelevant in conflict of jurisdiction between different regions of China. Mr WAN E'Xiang, on the other hand, discouraged concurrent proceedings between two People's Courts in Mainland. He stated that if a dispute was heard in Hong Kong or Macau, and another People's Court had accepted the application to consider the recognition and enforcement of the judgment delivered in Hong Kong or Macau, or another People's Court has already recognized and enforced the judgment given by the courts in Hong Kong or Macau over the same issue, the **13.92**

174 Fa Shi [2015] No 14.

175 See VI.3 above.

176 Art 14.

177 See discussion in Ch 4, section VI.2.

178 WAN E'Xiang, 'Quanguo Shegang'ao Shangshi Shenpan Gongzuo Zuotanhuishang de Jianghua [The Talk of the Vice President of the Supreme People's Court WAN E'Xiang in the National Seminar of the Trial Concerning Hong Kong and Macao Related Commercial Matters]', published on 22 November 2007.

People's Court should decline jurisdiction.[179] This opinion was later adopted in the Taiwan Judgment Provisions 2015,[180] which officially approves handling concurrent jurisdiction between Mainland and Taiwan.

IX. CONCLUSION

13.93 The current interregional private interregional law system in China constitutes three parts. First, to deal with the jurisdiction and choice of law issues in interregional cases, the courts of the regions apply their respective rules of private international law, however there is no conformity among these regional rules. Secondly, the bilateral regimes in the form of interregional arrangements were reached between Mainland and HKSAR, between Mainland and MASAR, and between Mainland and Taiwan. But these arrangements only touch upon the issues of service, the taking of evidence, recognition and enforcement of judgments, and recognition and enforcement of arbitral awards. These arrangements established the basic framework of interregional laws in China. Thirdly, the unilateral regimes in the form of regional laws were used to implement the arrangements, or were applied to the issues outside the scope of the arrangements. For example, the judgments excluded by the arrangements are recognized and enforced according to regional laws, such as the Mainland CPL and its judicial interpretations, the Macau Civil Procedure Code, and Hong Kong common law.

13.94 The bilateral arrangement approach among the Chinese regions generates a divergence of the arrangements. The best method of resolving the conflict of laws problems in China may be to enact uniform conflict of laws rules at a national level. Such an approach would have several benefits. First, uniform rules would eliminate forum shopping since the courts of different regions would apply the same conflicts principles, thus ensuring that the issues of the case would be handled in the same way. Secondly, enacting uniform conflicts rules could be achieved more easily than unifying substantive rules. Thirdly, this approach would prevent clashes between interregional conflicts rules, thus avoiding the problem of *renvoi*. Furthermore, enacting uniform national conflicts rules would lay the foundation for a possible unification of the substantive law. Certainly, this would be a gradual process. Until its completion, each region would use its own existing conflicts rules to address problems relating to the conflict of laws.

---

179 Ibid.

180 Articles 11 and 12. See section VII.3 above.

Part V

FINAL REMARKS

14

CHINESE CONFLICT OF LAWS: PAST, PRESENT AND FUTURE

I. DEVELOPMENT OF CHINESE CONFLICT OF LAWS

Chinese conflict of laws has been gradually developed and updated over the past three decades, as a direct consequence of the economic and political reform. The development of Chinese conflicts rules has gone through three stages: foundation, progression/transition, and modernization. The formation stage started from the 1978 economic reform until the mid-1990s, with the adoption of conflicts rules in foreign-related matters in a number of legislative works, including the GPCL (1986), CPL (1991), Maritime Law (1992), Arbitration Law (1994), Civil Aviation Act (1995) and Bill of Exchange Act (1995). The early system covered many areas and provided common conflicts issues, responding to the urgent needs to improve international civil and commercial relations following the 'open door' policy.[1] **14.01**

The early system was piecemeal, oversimplified and impractical. The implementation of the system encountered many uncertainties and, in practice, proved difficult. Fortunately, the SPC published a series of important judicial interpretations and provided numerous directions to the lower courts, **14.02**

1 For more discussion on the history, see Ch 1, IV.1.

filling in the gaps in the legislation.[2] The SPC interpretations and directions played an invaluable role in the implementation and improvement of the Chinese conflicts system; continuously enriching and improving it by various judicial interpretations and reform and enactment activities. Two major events further contributed to the need for improvement. One was the reunification of Hong Kong and Macau and the improved civil and commercial relationship with Taiwan, which resulted in the establishment of interregional conflicts system.[3] Another was China's entry into the WTO, after which the deepened economic reform and strengthened cross-border connections again called for a more modernized and internationalized system and resulted in the reform of the CPL in 2007 and 2012,[4] the adoption of the first codified choice of law statutes the Conflicts Act in 2010,[5] and the contribution by judicial interpretation on CPL in 2015 and on the Conflicts Act in 2012, which marked a staged achievement in the development of the Chinese conflicts system.

14.03 It is appropriate to argue that the new CPL and Conflicts Act and their judicial interpretations demonstrate that China has already formed an up-to-date and comprehensive, though not perfect, conflicts system and marked the end of the progression/transition stage. The Chinese conflicts system is now entering the stage of modernization.

II. CHARACTERISTICS OF THE CURRENT CONFLICTS SYSTEM

II.1 Partial internationalization

14.04 Internationalization means that the Chinese conflicts system borrows common rules, practice and usages from international conflicts conventions or advanced foreign legislation and transplants them into Chinese soil. For example, it adopts conflicts doctrines and principles widely accepted internationally and representing common practice of most countries in the world into Chinese law, such as the characteristic performance and the closest connection principle in contract,[6] *lex loci delicti* in tort,[7] *lex situs* in property,[8]

2 SPC, 'Opinion on Several Questions in the Implementation of the PRC Civil Procedure Act' ('1992 Opinion') (Abolished), Fa Fa [1992] 22; SPC, 'Opinion of the SPC about Several Issues on the Implementation of the "General Principle of Civil Law" (For the Trial Purpose)' ('Opinion on GPCL'), Fa (Ban) Fa [1988] No 6 (abolished).

3 Ch 13.

4 Ch 1, IV.1.

5 Law of the People's Republic of China on the Laws Applicable to Foreign-Related Civil Relations ('Conflicts Act') (2010); Ch 1, IV.

6 Conflicts Act, Art 41; Ch 8, III.

7 Ibid., Art 44; Ch 9, III.

and *lex protectionis* in intellectual property rights.[9] It also adopts the common law *forum non conveniens* doctrine into foreign-related procedure.[10] Some interregional arrangements directly borrow from international conventions, for example, the Mainland-HK Judgments Arrangement mirrors the Hague Choice of Court Convention 2005,[11] and both the Mainland-HK Awards Arrangements and the Mainland-Macau Awards Arrangements learn from the New York Convention.[12] Internationalization is also demonstrated by China's commitment to participating in international treaties or agreements. China has entered into a number of multilateral international conventions, such as the New York Convention, the Hague Service Convention, the Hague Evidence Convention, and numerous bilateral agreements.[13]

However, compared to other countries active in the international market, the number of international treaties signed by China is limited. China, for example, has not yet signed the Hague Choice of Court Convention. In those treaties signed or acceded to by China, China has made many reservations and only partial commitment.[14] Furthermore, China does not adopt some of the common approaches accepted by most countries advanced in international trade and private international law practice, such as a more flexible approach to choice of court agreement,[15] and a more liberal approach to enforcing foreign judgments.[16] The Chinese conflicts system is thus characterized by partial-internationalization and partial-nationalization. **14.05**

It does not, however, follow that full-internationalization must be the final aim of modernization. It is necessary to recognize that conflict of laws is a domestic law representing domestic interests. Internationalization and international commitments are only 'approaches' not 'goals'. They are approaches adopted to further the interest of a country. China has an interest in developing its economy, improving international trade and transactions, **14.06**

8 Ibid., Art 36; Ch 11, II and III.

9 Ibid., Art 48, 50; Ch 12, III and V.

10 Article 532 of the SPC, 'Interpretation of the SPC on the Application of the PRC Civil Procedure Law' ('2015 Opinion'), Fa Shi [2015] No 5; Ch 4, V.

11 SPC, 'Arrangement between the Mainland and the HKSAR on Mutual Recognition and Enforcement of Civil and Commercial Judgments Pursuant to Choice of Court Agreements', Fa Shi [2008] No 9; Ch 13, s.VI.1.

12 SPC, 'Arrangement on the Mutual Enforcement of Arbitral Awards between the Mainland and the HKSAR 1999', Fa Shi [2000] No 3; SPC, 'Arrangement Concerning the Mutual Enforcement of Arbitral Awards between the mainland and the MASAR' ('Mainland-Macau Arbitral Award Arrangement'), Fa Shi [2007] 17; Ch 13, s. VII.1 and 2.

13 For details of bilateral judicial assistance agreements entered by China, see III.1.

14 For example, reservations are made in the Hague Service Convention, see Ch 6, s.III.2.iii and IV.2.i above, and the New York Convention, Art 1, see Ch 7, s.I above.

15 See Ch 3, III.

16 See Ch 5 III and IV in general.

strengthening cross-border communications and connections and protecting Chinese individuals and companies in international relations. China has adopted the common conflicts rules and practice used worldwide not because China wants to be the same as other countries, but because these rules prove effective and useful, and consistency at some levels could improve parties' experience and reduce difficulties, risk and costs. As a result, modernization does not mean China must abandon any nationalized approaches. Instead, China should carefully balance internationalization and nationalization.

14.07 An example of an area where nationalization may be more appropriate than internationalization is interregional conflict of laws. The special characteristics of the interregional conflicts between Mainland, Hong Kong, Macau and Taiwan are unique. Practices in other countries with multiple legal regions, such as the UK, the US, Germany, Russia, etc, may be examined, considered, and even learnt from, but they cannot be copied to resolve the interregional conflicts in China. In the absence of comparable samples or precedents, internationalization is inappropriate and China should only adopt the nationalized approach to attend this issue.[17]

II.2 Partial pragmatization

14.08 Pragmatization means that the legislators and judges adopt an efficiency-oriented policy to establish a Chinese conflicts system. Efficiency includes two requirements, i.e., easy application of the law and an improvement to the effectiveness and impact of the law. Compared to the previous Chapter Eight of GPCL, the Conflicts Act is much more systematic and comprehensive, covering all major issues of cross-border applicable law.[18] The Conflicts Act is easier to use in practice. In terms of practical impact, procedural efficiency is one of the main concerns in cross-border jurisdiction, demonstrated by the Chinese style, efficiency-oriented *forum non conveniens* introduced by the CPL Interpretation 2015;[19] party autonomy is recognized and adopted as an efficient tool to resolve most choice of law issues;[20] and a modern way for serving judicial documents out of jurisdiction are accepted improvements to efficiency.[21]

17 For the unique nature of interregional conflicts in China, see Ch 13, II above.

18 For more introduction and comments, see Ch I, IV.

19 2015 Opinion, Art 532.

20 It is important to note that party autonomy is adopted not only in contract, but also in tort, unjust enrichment, transfer of movable property, and transfer of intellectual property rights. Conflicts Act, Arts 44, 47, 37, 49.

21 See CPL, Art 267(7) and Ch 6, s.I; Mainland-HK-Macau Service Arrangement and Ch 13, s.IV.1 above.

However, it is also necessary to note that although pragmatism and efficiency are accepted objectives of the Chinese conflicts system, they cannot override another major purpose, that of protecting national judicial sovereignty. Where legislators believe national interest is involved and decide to reserve state control, they would restrict the application of more effective conflicts rules, as shown in the area of judicial cooperation. For example, there is no rule to deal with concurrent proceedings,[22] even at the interregional context;[23] recognition and enforcement of foreign judgments largely rely on the principle of reciprocity and remain difficult;[24] and there is unnecessary restriction to party autonomy in jurisdiction.[25] The Chinese conflicts system, therefore, only achieves half pragmatization. 14.09

II.3 Partial standardization

Standardization means applying uniform and consistent standards to all cases, which greatly improves certainty, predictability and consistent decisions by judges. Standardization requires the law to be detailed and comprehensive and requires the similar interpretation and implementation of law by legal professionals. Standardization includes two perspectives, i.e., by legislation and by implementation. Standardization by legislation requires the law to be full, comprehensive, detailed and consistent throughout. Since Chinese conflicts rules are scattered through various judicial documents, including legislation, legislative interpretations, multiple judicial interpretations and judicial directives, administrative documents, etc, there are frequent inconsistencies.[26] This can only be resolved by more comprehensive codification and updated judicial interpretations. Although important progress was made in the new Conflicts Act, the CPL reform and the publication of new judicial interpretations, full standardization in legislation has not been achieved, because of the lack of a comprehensive conflicts code. Furthermore, legislative provisions are usually simple and have inevitably to be supplemented by various judicial interpretations and directions, again causing possibility for inconsistency.[27] The only resolution would be to improve the quality of judicial interpretation by paying more attention to the consistency of different interpretative documents. 14.10

In terms of standardization by practice, Chinese judicial practice demonstrates great inconsistencies between courts at the different levels and in different 14.11

22 See Ch 4, II above.
23 Ch 13, VIII above.
24 Ch 6, IV above.
25 Ch 3, III above.
26 See Ch 2, III.
27 See Ch 3, II.1.

regions. In general, judicial practice in the SPC appreciates the importance of the conflicts of laws and demonstrates good knowledge of applying conflict of laws to meet the economic and practical needs. Besides judicial interpretation, the SPC has also issued judicial directions to local courts in terms of a specific question in a particular case; and the SPC also decides conflicts disputes directly either in appeal or in judicial review.[28] The lower courts, however, may tend to misinterpret the conflicts rules.[29] In terms of different regions, it is generally recognized that courts in the regions with a more advanced economy and more frequent cross-border connections, such as East-South Coastal cities, such as Jiangsu, Zhejiang, Fujian and Guangdong, or major inner cities, such as Beijing, Nanjing, Wuhan, and Chengdu, apply the conflicts rules more appropriately and effectively. Local courts in less developed regions demonstrate higher incidence of local protectionism and a tendency to misapply the law.

II.4 Partial modernization

14.12 Modernization is demonstrated by the quality of the conflicts provisions. China is one of the few countries that permits party autonomy in non-contractual obligations, such as tort, infringement of IPRs and the transfer of movables;[30] China is also one of the few civil law countries adopting a tailored common law concept *forum non conveniens* in cross-border jurisdiction;[31] China law provides specialized provisions to unjust enrichment and *negotiorum gestio*;[32] China provides specialized intellectual property choice of law;[33] and China also provides special conflicts rules and interpretations in relation to special challenges imposed by the internet.[34] All demonstrate the advance of a Chinese conflicts system. However, this does not mean Chinese conflicts rules are fully modernized: some issues involving judicial cooperation and state sovereignty lag behind.[35] The current Chinese conflicts system can only be recorded as 'partially-modernized'.

---

28 Such as the internal-report/review mechanism. See Ch 4, III.2 and Ch 7, II above.

29 For example, the lower courts may have the tendency to abuse 'public policy' defence. See Ch 7, IV.5.

30 Conflicts Act, Arts 44, 49, 37.

31 2015 Opinion, Art 532.

32 Conflicts Act, Art 47.

33 Ibid., Arts 48–50.

34 Conflicts Act, Art 46; 2015 Opinion, Arts 20 and 25.

35 These are specifically shown in the area of service of process (Ch 5), recognition and enforcement of judgments (Ch 6), enforcement of foreign choice of court agreements (Ch 3, III.4 and Ch 4, IV) and dealing with concurrent proceedings (Ch 13, VIII).

II.5 Difference between 'private' and 'public' matters

The four characteristics discussed above also show the different levels of development between 'private' and 'public' matters. 'Public' matters do not mean the dispute concerns public issues, but the conflicts issues relating to national power and judicial sovereignty, and classified as 'sovereign-sensitive'. 'Private' means the conflicts issues not concerning government power or national interest but individual rights and obligations between the parties that may be freely disposed of. For example, most choice of law issues are characterized as 'private' conflict of laws matters, concerning private parties' substantive rights and obligations. As long as the disputed matter does not enter into the zone of public law or mandatory rules, the general liberal conflicts rules are adopted. Therefore, Chinese conflicts rules in choice of law are generally more internationalized, modernized and efficiency-driven. However, judicial cooperation matters concern a country's judicial sovereignty, where a much more conservative approach is adopted. Jurisdiction sits somewhere between 'private' and 'public' matters. The conflicts rules on jurisdiction, as a result, stand between the liberal approach and the conservative approach. **14.13**

This observation reveals the direction for future development. While some issues in 'private' matters, such as choice of law, may need to be further improved, the current level of modernization is laudable and the need for improvement is not urgent. What seriously restrains the pace of modernization is the area that is classified 'public' or 'half-public'. It is understandable that reform in these fields is more difficult, concerning not only pragmatic rules and efficiency, but also some interests that a country may feel reluctant to lose or traditionally fears to be intervened or infringed. These matters are more policy-driven, politics-oriented, and sovereign-sensitive. **14.14**

III. MODERNIZATION POLICY

III.1 From sovereignty to efficiency

The transition of Chinese conflict of laws has shown the trend to gradually move from the sovereignty-oriented to efficiency-oriented approach. The tradition of the Chinese conflicts system was based on the concept of allocation of sovereign power,[36] pursuant to which China acted ambitiously to protect its sovereign interest, which led to the lack of procedural efficiency, **14.15**

36 This concept is not only the basis for the traditional Chinese conflicts system, but was accepted by most other countries at the early stage. See J. Trachtman, 'The International Economic Law Revolution', (1996) 17

weak international cooperation, absence of protection for private interests and local protectionism. This system was not compatible with the Chinese policy for economic reform.

14.16 Realizing the barrier to the international trade and Chinese economy, the Chinese conflicts system has been reformed by weakening state control and improving private interest and certainty. This path should be continuously followed at the modernization stage. It is necessary to recognize the practical importance of the conflicts system and its objective to serve the needs for economic development, and the liberalization-trend in the civil and commercial field. This does not mean that the final result of the modernization would exclude the sovereign interest and state control completely. Instead, sovereign interest is an inevitable consideration in cross-border affairs but it should be carefully framed within the public matters. One of the major weaknesses of the current Chinese conflicts system is the lack of a clear distinction between private and public matters, which results in the over-broad scope of matters where private interest is largely ignored. The first issue that modernization needs to resolve is to determine which areas are truly 'public' and sovereign-focused, where private interest may be superseded, and which areas include both public and private interests where consideration should be given to properly balancing these interests. If the balancing exercise shows that more private interests are involved, a partial liberal approach should be adopted subject to the restriction of state interest; if, on the contrary, public interests override private interests, the sovereign-oriented approach should be maintained but supplemented by exceptions to private interest and efficiency.

III.2 From local protectionism to comity

14.17 The second primary modernization policy is to abandon local protectionism. In the past few decades, the SPC has provided numerous judicial interpretations, judicial directions and guidance to supervise the practice of the local courts. It is fair to comment that the SPC has played an important role in controlling local protectionism. Significant improvements are shown in some areas, such as international commercial arbitration.[37] However, local protectionism continues to exist in some local courts. Typical examples include the trend to apply Chinese law, and the readiness to generate mandatory rules or public policy defence when applying foreign laws.[38]

University of Pa Journal of International Economic Law 33, 40; H.L. Buxbaum, 'Conflict of Economic Laws', (2002) 42 *Virginia Journal of International Law* 931, 936.

37 For example, the internal report and review concerning international arbitration was provided in SPC, 'Notice on Issues about the Handling of Cross-Border and Foreign Arbitration', Fa Fa (1995) No 18.

38 For the modernization of judicial practice, see IV.2 below.

Local protectionism does not only exist in judicial practice. It also exists in conflicts legislation. Although the system has been largely updated and improved, some fields continue to show the sign of local protectionism. For example, the weight given to a choice of court clause is balanced in favour of choosing Chinese courts over foreign courts;[39] more over-restrictive rules are provided for foreign claimants serving judicial documents in China than for Chinese claimants serving process abroad;[40] and most foreign judgments in civil and commercial matters can only be recognized based on reciprocity.[41] Although the Chinese conflicts system is adopting a more and more international approach, traces of local protectionism have not been completely removed during the transition. Modernization thus requires the full abandonment of local protectionism not only in legislation but also in judicial practice. **14.18**

III.3 Balancing internationalization and nationalization

The third policy is to find an appropriate 'biting point' between internationalization and nationalization. Although common practice adopted internationally may provide China with an advanced sample to follow, it is wrong to argue that the Chinese conflicts system should be fully internationalized.[42] Not all common practice is feasible for China and, given the complexity of the conflicts rules, some widely-adopted rules suffer equally from criticism and controversy.[43] Furthermore, some conflicts issues are Chinese-specific, such as the interregional conflicts between four regions, which means internationalization may not be an answer.[44] **14.19**

Therefore, the proper policy should not be the full-internationalization of Chinese conflict of laws, but an appropriate balance between internationalization and nationalization. It is necessary to learn from the international practice and commonly adopted rules, but very careful analysis and selection is required before they can be implanted into the Chinese soil. The analysis should include the technical pros and cons of these rules, theoretical justification, evidence and empirical data of their enforcement in other countries, and the specific culture, tradition, and economic policy of China. **14.20**

39 For more details, see Ch 4, IV and V.2.

40 See Ch 5, II and Ch 6, III.2.iii and IV.2.i.

41 See Ch 6, IV.1.

42 See more discussion in II.1 above.

43 Such as the common law liberal approach for taking evidence abroad; the approach to permitting private parties to serve judicial documents; the common law anti-suit injunction.

44 See Ch 13 above; II.1 above.

III.4 Policy and rules

14.21 Finally, given the legal history and tradition of China, there will usually not be any debate on whether the Chinese conflicts system should follow the policy-oriented or rules-based path. The policy-oriented path suggests conflict of laws should reflect a nation's substantive policy and therefore a flexible 'approach' should be adopted to replace rules.[45] This approach, however, is not appropriate for China. Although Chinese conflicts legislation has adopted some general 'principles' instead of 'rules', these principles cannot be properly enforced in practice without detailed interpretation being provided by the SPC. It is fair to argue that the Chinese conflicts system is rule-based and it cannot be functional without rules.[46]

14.22 The modernization of the Chinese conflicts system should focus on improvement of the quality of the 'rules', instead of replacing the rules by more general and flexible policies. It is true that 'rules' may be rigid and inflexible, but this weakness may be reduced by improving legislative skills. Furthermore, Chinese conflicts legislation is largely general and simple, while most rules are provided by the SPC interpretation, which is easier to update than legislation. This model worked well in the past and could be reserved in the modernization of the Chinese conflicts system.

IV. MODERNIZATION PROCESS

IV.1 Democratization

14.23 Democratization means that the formation and development of the Chinese conflicts system has been contributed to by various participants and reflects the interests of different stakeholders. The progression of the Chinese conflicts system is also driven by a mixture of legislators, judges, scholars, legal practitioners and other stakeholders. Legislators directly make and reform the law. SPC judges publish judicial interpretations and judicial directions, which are treated as the *de facto* source of law in China. Judges in local courts contribute by applying the law and seeking directions from the SPC.

14.24 Scholarship also contributes to the modernization. First, when Chinese judges were poorly trained to handle cross-border disputes or to apply the conflicts provisions properly at the early stage after the Chinese conflicts system was

45 B. Currie, 'The Constitution and the Choice of Law' (1958) 26 *University of Chicago Law Review* 9.

46 See Ch 1 for history and tradition of Chinese conflicts rules.

established, Chinese scholars undertook the obligation to educate, introduce and train legal professionals on conflict of law theories and principles by publications, lectures and providing public training. Secondly, the scholars' opinions were frequently consulted by SPC judges when judicial interpretations were produced. Scholars proposed the appropriate interpretation of the current law, the possible ways for law reform, and introduced foreign approaches into Chinese law. Some scholarly proposals were later approved and adopted in judicial interpretation.[47] Thirdly, some Chinese scholars are directly involved in legislative work, by responding to consultations of the legislative body. Other stakeholders, including legal practitioners, international commercial participants and individuals also contribute by expressing opinions to the proposals of legislation.

However, compared with the legislators and SPC, the contribution of scholars and stakeholders is indirect and rather limited.[48] Most scholars and stakeholders can only contribute by responding to a public consultation paper. There is no effective regulation on how the consultation works. Responses are not revealed, analyzed, or publicized in any way and no one knows the detailed data of the responses or the result of the consultation. This lack of transparency affects most stakeholders' confidence and their incentive to participate. Future modernization needs a more standardized procedure to consult the public and to truly take public opinions into consideration. **14.25**

IV.2 Improving judicial practice

Modernization does not only include modernization of law, but also modernization of judicial practice. In practice, poor implementation of the law hampers the purpose of conflicts legislation. As a result, one important perspective of modernization is to improve the knowledge and skills of judges. **14.26**

Current judicial practice in the field of private international law shows the unbalanced development between conflicts legislation/judicial interpretation and court practice, between courts at different hierarchies, and between courts in different areas. In general, the overall court practice in the country falls below the level of the development in legislation and judicial interpretation. The judgments of lower courts sometimes show a total ignorance of relevant conflicts questions in a cross-border case; a fundamental misunderstanding of **14.27**

47 For example, the 2015 CPL Interpretation adopts *forum non conveniens* in China, which is partially based on the comments and suggestions of Chinese conflicts scholars.

48 It is primarily drawn from the judicial practice and partially from academic writing and scholarship.

conflicts concepts; and a misinterpretation of the relevant rules.[49] Comparatively, the superior courts usually have a better comprehension of private international law.[50] Judges in economically advanced areas implement conflict of laws more appropriately and professionally than judges in undeveloped areas. Modernization in Chinese conflict of laws requires a systematic improvement in the professional competence and standard of all Chinese judges, which will involve the provision of more effective training and assessments for specialist judges in foreign-related disputes.

V. CONCLUSION

14.28 Remarkable achievements have been made to update the Chinese conflicts system, but more has to be done to facilitate its modernization. Modernization needs to focus on enforcement of foreign judgments, international judicial cooperation and procedure, and international jurisdiction. In particular, the difficulty in recognizing and enforcing foreign judgments forms an inevitable barrier not only concerning foreign judgments *per se* but also preventing the full modernization of jurisdiction rules. As to the choice of law rules, it is recognized that the Conflicts Act has generally proved to be up-to-date and successful. The gaps and oversimplified rules may be compensated for by the detailed rules provided in the SPC judicial interpretation. The choice of law system is not in urgent need of reform, but the final modernization may require a more systematic and comprehensive code, synthesizing choice of law rules in other specialized statutes, and a more mature legislative technique to improve the quality and reduce uncertainty of some legislative provisions. Modernization also needs the contribution of all stakeholders in a more organized, systematic and transparent manner, and requires the improvement of not only legislative quality but also the competence of judges in implementing the law in judicial practice.

---

49 For example, the following judgments show a misunderstanding of conflicts concepts or the homeward trend of local courts: *Chancery plc (United Kingdom) v. Sukissed Marine Co. Ltd (Greece)*, Guangzhou Maritime Court, 29 Feb. 1996; *Compania Sud Ameicana De Vapore S.A v. Hin-proInternational Logistics Ltd,* Zhejiang HPC, (2013) Zhe Xia Zhong Zi No 145; *Dongfeng Garments Factory of Kaifeng City v. Henan Garments Import and Export,* Zhengzhou Intermediate People's Ct., 28 Sept. 1992; *Baosheng Environment v. Hefei Environment Bureau,* [2005] Min Si Ta Zi No 45 (SPC overruled the local court's judgment); *GRD Minproc v. Shanghai Flyingwheel,* [2009] Min Si Ta Zi No48 (SPC overruled the local court's judgment).

50 See Ch 14, II.3 above.

BIBLIOGRAPHY

ENGLISH MATERIALS

American Law Institute, Restatement of the Law—Conflict of Laws (Westlaw, 2012)

Armfelt, Andrew, 'Foreign economic contract law of the People's Republic of China' (1987) 36 International and Comparative Law Quarterly 151

Asensio, R.A. De Miguel, 'The Private International Law of Intellectual Property and of Unfair Commercial Practices', in S. Leible and A. Ohly (eds.), *Intellectual Property and Private International Law* (Tubingen, Mohr Siebeck, 2009)

Atiyah, P.S., *Essays on Contract* (Clarendon Press, Oxford, 1990)

Bartin, E., *Principles De Droit International Prive* (Paris, 1930)

Beaumont, P. and Z. Tang, 'Classification of Delictual Damages' (2008) 12 Edinburgh Law Review 131

Bennett, T.W., 'Choice of Law Rules in Claims of Unjust Enrichment' (1990) 39 International and Comparative Law Quarterly 136

Bernasconi, C., 'The Hague Convention of 5 July 2006 on the Law Applicable to Certain Rights in Respect of Securities Held with an Intermediary', Seminar on Current Developments in Monetary and Financial Law Washington, D.C., Oct. 23–27, 2006, at http://www.imf.org/external/np/seminars/eng/2006/mfl/cb.pdf (last visited 1 May 2015)

Betlem, G. and C. Bernasconi, 'European Private International Law, the Environment and the Obstacles for Public Authorities' (2006) 122 Law Quarterly Review 124

Bird, J. 'Choice of Law', in F. Rose (ed), *Restitution and the Conflict of Laws* (Mansfield, 1995)

Brand, R.A. 'Recognition of Foreign Judgments as a Trade Law Issue', in J.S. Bhandari and A.O. Sykes (eds), *Economic Dimensions in International Law* (Cambridge, CUP, 1997)

Briggs, A., *The Conflict of Laws* (3rd ed., OUP, 2013)

Brilmayer, L., 'Governmental Interest Analysis' (1985) 46 Ohio State Law Journal 459

Carter, P. B. 'Domicil: The Case for Radical Reform in the United Kingdom' (1987) 36 International and Comparative Law Quarterly 713

Castel, J.G., 'Recognition and Enforcement of Foreign Judgments in Personam and in Rem in the Common Law Provinces of Canada' 17 McGill Law Journal 11

Chen, Albert Hung-yee, *An Introduction to the Legal System of the People's Republic of China* (LexisNexis, 2004)
Chen, T.P., 'Private International Law of the People's Republic of China: An Overview' (1987) 35 American Journal of Comparative Law 445
Chen, Weizuo, 'Chinese Private International Law Statute of 28 October 2010', in A. Bonomi and G.P. Romano (eds) 12 *Yearbook of Private International Law* (Sellier, 2010)
Chen, Weizuo, 'The Necessity of Codification of China's Private International Law and Arguments for a Statute on the Application of Laws as the Legislative Model' <http://www.tsinghua.edu.cn/docsn/fxy/tclr/issue/.../CHEN%20Weizuo.pdf>
Chen, Xingliang, 'China's Guiding Case System: A Study on the Mechanisms of Rule Formation' (2014) 1 Peking University Law Journal 215
Chong, A., 'Choice of Law for Unjust Enrichment/Restitution and the Rome II Regulation' (2008) 57 International and Comparative Law Quarterly 863
Clarkson, C.M.V. J. and J. Hill, *Conflict of Laws* (4th ed., OUP, 2011)
Claver-Carone, M.J., 'Post-handover Recognition and Enforcement of Arbitral Awards Between Mainland and Hong Kong SAR' (2002) 33 Law and Policy in International Business 369
Cloherty, Daniel J., 'Exclusive jurisdiction and the eleventh Amendment: Recognizing the Assumption of the State Court Availability in the Clear Statement Compromise' (1994) 82 California Law Review 1287
Cohen, J. A. and H. Chiu, *People's China and International Law: A Documentary Study* (Princeton University Press, 1974)
Colatrella, M.T. Jr.,'Court-performed Mediation in the People's Republic of China: A Proposed Model to Improve the United States Federal District Courts' Mediation Progress' (2000) 15 Ohio State Journal on Dispute Resolution 396
Collier, J.G., *Conflict of Laws* (3rd ed., CUP 2001)
Collins, L. (et. al) eds, *Dicey, Morris and Collins on the Conflict of Laws* (15th ed., Lawrence Collins ed., Sweet & Maxwell, 2012)
Cohen, S., 'Quasi Contract and the Conflict of Laws' (1956) 31 LA Bar Bulletin 71
Cooney, S., 'Why Taiwan is not Hong Kong' (1997) 6 Pacific Rim Law and Policy Journal 497
Coyle, F., 'Rethinking Judgments Reciprocity' (2014) 92 North Carolina Law Review 1109
Cromie, S., *International Commercial Litigation* (Butterworths, 1997)
Crowell, D.L., 'Choice of Law in the Protection of Cultural Property' (1992) 27 Texas International Law Journal 173
Currie, B., 'The Constitution and the Choice of Law' (1958) 26 University of Chicago Law Review 9

D'Oliveira, H.U.J., 'Characteristic Obligation in the Draft-EEC Obligation Convention' (1977) 25(2) American Journal of Comparative Law 303

Dane, Perry, 'Vest Righted, "Vestedness" and Choice of Law' (1987) 96 Yale Law Journal 1191

Dang, H., 'The Applicability of International Law as Governing Law of State Contracts' (2010) 17 Australian International Law Journal 133, n 24.

Darwazeh, Nadia and Yeoh, Friven, 'Recognition and Enforcement of Awards under the New York Convention: China and Hong Kong Perspectives' (2008) 25 Journal of International Arbitration 837

den Berg, V., *The New York Arbitration Convention of 1958: Towards a Uniform Judicial Interpretation* (Kluwer Law and Taxation, 1981)

Derr, E.J., 'Striking a Better Public-Private Balance in *Forum Non Conveniens*' (2008) 93 Cornell Law Review 819

Devonshire-Ellis, C., A. Scott and S. Woollard, *Intellectual Property Rights in China* (2nd ed., Springer, 2011)

Dickinson, A., 'A principled approach to choice of law in contracts?' (2013) Butterworths Journal of International Banking and Financial Law 151

Dika, M., 'Boundaries of Arbitrability—Reflections on Draft Croatian Law on Arbitration: Arbitrability and Exclusive Jurisdiction of Courts of Law' (1999) 6 Croatian Arbitration Yearbook 27

Dougherty, C., 'Private International Law: *Harding v Wealands*' (2007) 56 International and Comparative Law Quarterly 443

Drexl, Josef (ed), *Intellectual Property Right and Private International Law: Heading for the Future* (Hart, 2005)

Ehrenzweig, Albert A., 'The Not so "Proper" Law of a Tort' (1968) 17 International and Comparative Law Quarterly 1

European Parliament, Directorate General for Internal Policies, 'Choice of Law for Cross-Border Road Traffic Accidents' 2012

Fassberg, C.W., 'On Time and Place in Choice of Law for Property' (2002) 51 International and Comparative Law Quarterly 385

Faxue Cidian [*Law Dictionary*] (Law Institute of the Chinese Academy of Social Science ed., China Law Press 2004)

Fawcett, J.J. and J. Carruthers, *Cheshire and North's Private International Law* (14th ed., Oxford University Press, 2008)

Fawcett J.J. and P. Torremans, *Intellectual Property and Private International Law* (2nd ed., OUP, 2011)

Fei, J. and R. Hill, 'Enforcement of Arbitral Awards in the PRC', in M.J. Moser, *Dispute Resolution in China* (New York: Juris Publishing, 2012)

Fei, J.J. 'Enforcement of Foreign Court Judgments and Foreign Arbitral Awards in China', in M.J. Moser, *Business Disputes in China* (3rd ed., Juris Publishing, 2011)

Fentiman, R., 'Choice of Law and Intellectual Property', in J. Drexl and A. Kur (eds), *Intellectual Property and Private International Law* (Bloomsbury, 2005)

Fry, J.D. 'Desordre Public International under the New York Convention' (2009) 8 Chinese Journal of International Law 81

Garner, B.A. (ed) *Black's Law Dictionary* (9th ed., West, 2004)

Giuliano, M. and P. Lagarde, 'Report on the Convention on the Law Applicable to Contractual Obligations', [1980] OJ C 282/1

Gottschalk, E., et al, *Conflict of Laws in a Globalized World* (Cambridge University Press, 2007)

Guinchard, E. and S. Lamont-Black, 'Environmental Law: The Black Sheep in Rome II's Drive for Legal Certainty?' (2009) 11 Environment Law Review 161

Haitao, M. and L. Liang, *The Jurisprudence and Practice of International Law* (China Legal Publishing House, 2006)

Hartley, T., 'Article 5(1): Employment Contract—Work in Several Countries' (1994) 19 European Law Review 540

Hathaway, J.C., *The Rights of Refugees under International Law* (CUP, 2005) 201

Hedley, S., *Restitution: Its Division and Ordering* (Sweet & Maxwell, London, 2001)

Hill, J. and A. Chong, *International Commercial Disputes* (4th ed., Hart, 2010)

Hondius, E.H., *Towards a European Civil Code* (Nijmegen: Kluwer, 2014)

Huang, J., *Interregional Recognition and Enforcement of Civil and Commercial Judgments* (Bloomsbury Publishing, 2014)

Huang, Jin and Huo, Zhengxin, 'A Commentary on Private International Law in East Asia', in Wang (ed), Wen-Yeu, *Codification in East Asia: Selected Papers from the 2nd IACL Thematic Conference* (Springer, 2014)

Huang, Jin and Andrew Xuefeng Qian, 'One Country, Two Systems, Three Law Families, and Four Legal Regions: the Emerging Interregional Conflicts of Law in China' (1994) 5 Duke Journal of Comparative and International Law 304

Hulbert, R.W., 'Some Thoughts on Judgments, Reciprocity, and the Seeming Paradox of International Commercial Arbitration' (2008) 29 University of Pennsylvania Journal of International Law 641

Huo, Zhengxin, 'A Tiger without Teeth: The Antitrust Law of the People's Republic of China' (2008) 10 Asian Pac Law Pol J 36

Huo, Zhengxin, 'An Imperfect Improvement: The New Conflict of Laws Act of the People's Republic of China' (2011) 60 International and Comparative Law Quarterly 1065

Huo, Zhengxin, 'China's Codification of Conflicts Law: Latest Efforts' (2010) 51 Seoul Law Journal 279

Huo, Zhengxin, 'Choice of Law in Tort' (2009) 4 Journal of Cambridge Studies 82

Huo, Zhengxin, 'Highlights of China's New Private International Law Act' (2011) 45 Revue Juridique Themis 637

Huo, Zhengxin, *Private International Law in China* (China Law Press, 2010)

Huo, Zhengxin, 'Reshaping Private International Law in China: The Statutory Reform of Tort Conflicts' (2012) 5 Journal of East Asia and International Law 93

Huo, Zhengxin, 'Two Steps Forward, One Step Back: A Commentary on the Judicial Interpretation on the Private International Law Act of China' (2013) 43 Hong Kong Law Journal 710

Jinxian, Zhang, *China's Maritime Courts and Justice*, I.C.C. International Maritime Bureau (Witherby Publishers, London, 1997)

Juenger, Friedrich K., *Choice of Law and Multistate Justice* (Transnational Publishers, 2000)

Jie, Huang, 'Interregional Recognition and Enforcement of Civil and Commercial Judgments: Lessons for China from US and EU Laws' (2010) Duke Law Theses and Dissertations 90

Karayanni, M.M., 'The Public Policy Exception to the Enforcement of Forum Selection Clause' (1996) 34 Duquesne Law Review 1009

Kay, H.H., 'Currie's Interest Analysis in the 21st Century' (2001) 37 Willamette Law Review 123

Khodykin, R., *Arbitration Law of Russia* (New York, Juris, 2013)

Kielsgard, M. and L. Chen, 'Emergence of Private Property Law in China and its Impact on Human Rights' (2014) 15 Asian-Pacific Law and Policy 94

Kong, Qingjiang and Hu, Mingfei, 'The Chinese Practice of Private International Law' (2002) 3 Melbourne Journal of International Law 202

Kono, T. and P. Jurcys, 'General Report', in T. Kono (ed) *Intellectual Property and Private International Law* (Bloomsbury, 2012)

Kowalski, W.W., 'Restitution of Works of Art Pursuant to Private and Public International Law' Recueil des cours, Vol 288 (Martinus Nijhoff 2001)

Kuhne, G., 'Choice of Law in Product Liability' (1972) 60 California Law Review 1

Kunda, I., 'Croatia', in T. Kono (ed), *Intellectual Property and Private International Law* (Bloomsbury, 2012)

Kur, A., 'Applicable Law: an Alternative Proposal for International Regulation' (2005) 30 Brooklyn Journal of International Law 952

Lando, O., 'The Draft Hague Principles on the Choice of Law in International Contracts and Rome I', in *A Commitment to Private International Law: Essays in Honour of Hans van Loon* (Cambridge/Antwerp/Portland, 2013) 299

Lazic, V., 'Arbitration Law Reform in the Netherlands' (2007) 11 Electronic Journal of Comparative Law 17

Lee, 'Wei-chin, Yours, Mine, or Everyone's Property? China's Property Law in 2007' (2010) 15 Journal of Chinese Political Science 25

Lemley, M.A., 'Intellectual Property and Shrink-wrap Licenses' (1995) 68 South California Law Review 1239

Leslie, R., 'Unjustified Enrichment in the Conflict of Laws' (1998) 2 Edinburgh Law Review 233

Lew, J.D.M and L.A. Mistelis, et al, *Comparative International Commercial Arbitration* (The Hague, Kluwer Law International, 2003)

Li, Yuwen, *The Judicial System and Reform in Post-Mao China* (Ashgate Publishing, 2014)

Lin, Feng, *Constitutional Law in China* (Sweet & Maxwell, 2000)

Lipstein, K., 'Characteristic Performance—A New Concept in the Conflict of Laws in Matters of Contract for the EEC' (1981) 3 Northwestern Journal of International Law and Business 402

Liu, Renshan, 'Recent Judicial Cooperation in Civil and Commercial Matters between Mainland China and Taiwan, the Hong Kong S.A.R. and the Macau S.A.R.' (2009) 11 Yearbook of Private International Law 235

Lo, Vai Io and Tian, Xiaowen, *Law and Investment in China: The Legal and Business Environment after China's WTO Accession* (Routledge, 2005)

Long, Wei-Di, 'The Reach of the CISG in China' in I. Schwenzer and L. Spagnolo (eds), *Towards Uniformity: the 2nd MAA Schlechtriem CISG Conference* (Eleven Publishing, 2011)

Lorenzen, E.G., 'Huber's De Conflictu Legum', in E.G. Lorenzen (ed), *Selected Articles on the Conflict of Laws* (Yale University Press, 1947)

Lorenzen, E.G., 'Enforcement of American Judgments Abroad' (1919) 29 Yale Law Journal 188

McCaffrey, S.C. and Thomas O. Main, *Transnational Litigation in Comparative Perspective* (OUP, 2010)

Mann, Michael, 'The Seventh Report of the Private International Law Committee on Domicile' (1963) 12 International and Comparative Law Quarterly 1326

MAO Tse-Tung, *Selected Work of Mao Tse-Tung*, Vol. IV (1st ed., People's Publishing House, Peking, 1961) (in English)

Matulionyte, R., 'IP and Applicable Law in Recent International Proposals' (2012) 3 Journal of Intellectual Property, Information Technology and Electronic Commerce Law 263

Maurer, A.G., *Public Policy Exception under the New York Convention* (New York, JurisNet, 2013)

Max Planck on CLIP, 'Principles on Conflict of Laws in Intellectual Property' 2011

Mayss, Alba, *Principles of Conflict of Laws* (3rd ed., London: Cavendish, 1999)
Michaels, R., 'Some Fundamental Jurisdictional Concepts as Applied in Judgment Conventions' (2006) 53 Duke Law School Faculty Scholarship Series 1
Mistelis, L.A., *Concise International Arbitration* (Kluwer Law International, 2010)
Mistelis, L.A. and S.L. Brekoulakis, *Arbitrability: International and Comparative Perspectives* (Kluwer Law International, 2009)
Morris, J.H.C., 'The Proper Law of a Tort' (1951) 64 Harvard Law Review 881
Morris, J.H.C., 'The Choice of Law Clause in Statutes' (1946) 62 Law Quarterly Review 170
Morris, J.H.C., *The Conflict of Laws* (Sweet & Maxwell, 1993)
Morse, C.G.J., 'Consumer Contracts, Employment Contracts and the Rome Convention' (1992) 41 International and Comparative Law Quarterly 17
Morse, C.G.J. 'Choice of Law in Tort: A Comparative Study' (1984) 32 American Journal of Competition Law 51
Murphy, J.D., 'The People's Republic of China and the Illicit Trade in Cultural Property' (1994) 3 International Journal of Cultural Property 227
O'Brien, J., *Conflict of Laws* (2nd ed., Cavendish, 1999)
Ong, Allan Verman Yap, 'Dépeçage in Chinese Private International Law' (2009) 8 Chinese Journal of International Law 637
Palmer, M. and C. Xi, 'The People's Republic of China', in C. Hodges, S. Vogenauer, M. Tulibacka (eds), *The Costs and Funding of Civil Litigation* (Bloomsbury, 2010)
Panagopoulos, G., *Restitution in Private International Law* (Hart, 2000)
Patchel, K., 'Choice of Law and Software Licenses' (2000) 26 Brooklyn Journal of International Law 117
Paul, J.R., 'Comity in International Law' (1991) 32 Harvard International Law Journal 1
Pe, R. and M. Polkinghome, 'Two Steps Forward, One Step Sideways' (2008) 25 Journal of International Arbitration 410
Pecoraro, T.W., 'Choice of Law in Litigation to Recover National Cultural Property' (1990) 31 Virginia Journal of International Law 1
Peerenboom, R., 'The Evolving Regulatory Framework for Enforcement of Arbitral Awards in the PRC' (2000) 12 Asian-Pacific Law and Policy 1
Peterson, C.H., 'Res Judicata and Foreign Country Judgments' (1963) 24 Ohio State Law Journal 291
Pogue, R.W., 'Exclusive Jurisdiction' (1973) 43 Antitrust 313
Rabel, E., *The Conflict of Laws, A Comparative Study* (University of Michigan, 1968)

Reese, W.L.M., 'The Status in This Country of Judgments Rendered Abroad' (1950) 50 Columbia Law Review 783

Reese, W.L.M., 'Product Liability and Choice of Law' (1972) 25 Vanderbilt Law Review 29

Reese, W.L.M. 'Dépeçage: A Common Phenomenon in Choice of Law' (1973) 73 Columbia Law Review 58

Reinstein, E., 'Finding a Happy Ending for Foreign Investors' (2005) 16 Indiana International and Comparative Law Review 37

Richman, William M. and Milliam L. Reynolds, *Understanding Conflict of Laws* (LexisNexis, 2003)

Rodgers, T., 'The Center Cannot Hold: Assessing the Reach of China's Labor Protections to Migrant Workers in Africa' (2012) 35 Fordham International Law Journal 107

Rogerson, P., *Collier's Conflict of Laws* (4th ed., CUP, 2013)

Rose, Francis, (ed), *Restitution and the Conflict of Laws* (Mansfield, 1995)

Sammartano, Mauro Rubino, *International Arbitration Law and Practice* (3rd ed., Netherlands: Kluwer Law International, 2014)

Sanders, P., *Het Nederlandse arbitragerecht—nationaal en internationaal* (4th ed., Deventer: Kluwer, 2001)

Sarcevic, P., 'The Setting Aside and Enforcement of Arbitral Awards under the UNCITRAL Model Law', in P. Sarcevic, *Essays on International Commercial Arbitration* (London/Norwell: Martinus Nijhoff, 1989)

Schramm, F.B., 'Licenses, Contracts and Assignments of Intellectual Property' (1960) 9 Cleveland-Marshall Law Review 65

Scotts, A., 'Substance and Procedure and Choice of Law in Torts' (2007) Lloyd's Maritime and Commercial Law Quarterly 44

Sheehan, D., '*Negotiorum Gestio*: A Civilian Concept in the Common Law?' (2006) 55 International and Comparative Law Quarterly 253

Shuhong, Yu, et al., 'The Closest Connection Doctrine in the Conflict of Laws in China' (2009) 8 Chinese Journal of International Law 423

Silberman, L.J. and A.F. Lowenfeid, 'A Different Challenge for the ALI: Herein of Foreign Country Judgments, an International Treaty, and an American Statute' (2000) 75 Indiana Law Journal 636

Singal, V., 'Preserving Power without Sacrificing Justice', (2008) 59 Hastings Law Journal 943

Singer, J.W., 'Property Law Conflicts' (2014) 54 Washburn Law Journal 129

Stavrianos, L.S., *A Global History: From Prehistory to the 21st Century* (Prentice Hall, 1999)

Stevens, S.L., 'Commanding International Judicial Respect' (2002) 26 Hastings International and Comparative Law Review 115

Stoianoff, N.P., 'The Influence of the WTO over China's Intellectual Property Regime' (2012) 34 Sydney Law Review 65

Stone, Peter, *EU Private International Law* (Edward Elgar Publishers, 2006)
Suk, Kwang Hyun, 'The New Conflict of Laws Act of the Republic of Korea', in *Yearbook of Private International Law* (P. Sarczvic and P. Volken eds. Kluwer Law International, 2003) 1
Svantesson, Dan Jerker B., *Private International Law and Internet* (Kluwer Law International, 2007)
Symeonides, S.C., 'A Choice-of-Law Rule for Conflicts Involving Stolen Cultural Property' (2005) 38 Vanderbilt Journal of Transnational Law 1177
Symeonides, S.C., 'Choice of Law for Products Liability' (2004) 78 Tulane Law Review 1247
Symeonides, S.C., 'Rome II and Tort Conflicts: A Missed Opportunity' (2008) 56 American Journal of Comparative Law 173
Tang, Z.S., 'Declining Jurisdiction by *Forum Non Conveniens* in Chinese Courts' (2015) 45 Hong Kong Law Journal 351
Tang, Z.S., 'Effectiveness of Exclusive Jurisdiction Clauses in the Chinese Courts—A Pragmatic Study' (2012) 61 International and Comparative Law Quarterly 459
Tang, Z.S., *Electronic Consumer Contracts in the Conflict of Laws* (Hart, 2009)
Tang, Z.S., 'International Treaties in Chinese Private International Law' (2012) 42 Hong Kong Law Journal 597
Tang, Z.S., *Jurisdiction and Arbitration Agreements in International Commerce* (Routledge, London, 2014)
Tang, Z.S., 'Parties' Choice of Law in E-Consumer Contracts' (2007) 3 Journal of Private International Law 113
Tao, Jingzhou, *Arbitration Law and Practice in China* (The Netherlands: Kluwer Law International, 2008)
Tebbens, H.D., *International Product Liability* (Sijthoff and Noordhoff, 1979)
Tu, 'Guangjian, Recognition of Enforcement of Non-Local Judgments in Macau: A Critical Review' (2012) 42 Hong Kong Law Journal 640
Tung-Pi Chen, 'Bridge across the Formosa Strait: Private Law Relations between Taiwan and Mainland', (1990) 4 Journal of Chinese Law 101
Uzelac, A., 'Arbitrability and Exclusive Jurisdiction' in S. Kroll, L.A. Mistelis, P. Perales Viscasillas and V. Rogers (eds), *International Arbitration and International Commercial Law: Synergy, Convergence and Evolution* (Kluwer Law International, 2011)
van Engelen, D., 'Rome II and Intellectual Property Rights', (2008) 4 NiPR 440
Vondracek, O., 'Art 4 of the Rome Convention on the Law Applicable to Civil and Commercial Obligations' (2007) 8 Common Law Review 32
von Mehren, A., 'Recognition and Enforcement of Foreign Judgments—General Theory and the Role of Jurisdictional Requirements' (1980) 167 Recueil des Cours 56

von Mehren, A.T. and D.T. Trautman, 'Recognition of Foreign Adjudications' (1968) 81 Harvard Law Review 1601

Wagner, W.J., 'The Original and Exclusive Jurisdiction of the United States SPC' (1952) 2 Louisiana University Law Journal 111

Wang, Shengchang, 'Enforcement of Foreign Arbitral Awards in the People's Republic of China' in A.J. van den Berg (ed), *Improving the Efficiency of Arbitration and Awards: 40 Years of Application of the New York Convention* (ICCA Congress Series No 9, 1999)

Wei, Li, 'Judicial Interpretation in China' (1997) 5 Willamette Journal of International Law and Dispute Resolution 87

Weintraub, R.J., 'An Inquiry into the Utility of "Domicile" as a Concept in Conflicts Analysis' (1965) 63 Michigan Law Review 961

Weintraub, R.J., 'Proposed Choice-of-Law Standard for International Products Liability Disputes' (1990) 16 Brookline Journal of International Law 225

Whincop, M., 'The Recognition Scene' (1999) 23 Melbourne University Law Review 416

Wojewoda, Michal, 'Mandatory Rules in Private International Law' (2000) 7 Maastricht Journal of European and Comparative Law 183

Wolff, Martin, *Private International Law* (2nd ed., Clarendon Press, 1950)

Yongping, Xiao, 'The Conflict of Laws between Mainland and the HKSAR: the Choice of Coordination Models' (2002) 4 Yearbook of Private International Law 171

Xiao, Yongping and Huo, Zhengxin, 'Ordre Public in China's Private International Law' (2005) 53 American Journal of Competition Law 653

Xiao, Yongping and Weidi Long, 'Mandatory Rules in China's Private International Law' (2012) 10 Social Sciences in China 107

Xu, C., 'The Fundamental Institutions of China's Reforms and Development' (2011) 49 Journal of Economic Literature 1076

Xu, Guojian, 'Contract in Chinese Private International Law' (1989) 38 International and Comparative Law Quarterly 648

Yeo, T.M., *Choice of Law for Equitable Doctrines* (OUP, 2004)

Yntema, H., 'Review: Recognition and Enforcement of Foreign Judgments' (1939) 49 Yale Law Journal 1134

Yntema, H., 'The Historic Bases of Private International Law' (1953) 2 American Journal of Comparative Law 304

Zeynalova, Y., 'Law on Recognition and Enforcement of Foreign Judgments' (2013) 31 Berkeley Journal of International Law 150

Zhang, Mo, 'Codified Choice of Law in China: Rules, Processes and Theoretic Underpinnings' (2011) 37 North Carolina Journal of International Law and Commercial Regulation 83

Zhang, Mo, 'Choice of Law in Contracts: A Chinese Approach' (2006) 26 Northwestern Journal of International Law and Business 299

Zhang, Mo, 'International Civil Litigation in China' (2002) 25 Boston College International and Competition Law Review 59

Zhang, Wenliang, *Recognition and Enforcement of Foreign Judgments in China* (Kluwer Law International, 2014)

Zhang Wenliang, 'Recognition and Enforcement of Foreign Judgments in China' (2013) 12 Chinese Journal of International Law 143

Zhang, X.C., 'The Agreement between Mainland China and the Hong Kong SAR on Mutual Enforcement of Arbitral Awards' (1999) 29 Hong Kong Law Journal 463

Zhang, X.C. and P. Smart, 'Development of Regional Conflict of Laws: On the Arrangement of Mutual Recognition and Enforcement of Judgments in Civil and Commercial Matters Between Mainland and Hong Kong ASR' (2006) 36 Hong Kong Law Journal 553

Zheng, H.R., 'Private International Law in the People's Republic of China: Principles and Procedures' (1987) 23 Texas International Law Journal 240

Zhou, Yong, *International Relations and Legal Cooperation in General Diplomacy and Consular Relations* (Elsevier, 2014)

Zhu, Lijiang and Chengyuan Ma, 'Chinese Practice in Public International Law' (2013) 12 Chinese Journal of International Law 363

Zhu, Weidong, 'China's Codification of the Conflict of Laws' (2008) 3 Journal of Private International Law 283

Zweigert, K. and H. Kötz, *Introduction to Comparative Law* (3rd ed., Clarendon Press, 1998)

CHINESE MATERIALS

CAO Fagui, 'Xiamenshi Zhongji Renminfayuan Shewai Minshangshi Anjian de Shenli he Yanjiu [Adjudication of Foreign-Related Civil and Commercial Cases by the Xiamen Intermediate People's Court]', (2007) 3 Renmin Sifa [People Judicature] 46

曹发贵, "厦门市中级人民法院涉外民商事案件的审理和研究", (2007) 3 《人民司法》 46

CHEN Chenglong, 'Zhongguo Sifajieshi de Diwei yu Gongneng [The Status and Function of Judicial Interpretation in China]' (2003) 1 Zhongguo Faxue [China Legal Science)] 24

陈春龙, "中国司法解释的地位与功能", (2003) 1《中国法学》24

CHEN Xuebin, 'Jurisdiction of the People's Republic of China on Pollution Discharged by Vessels in Its Exclusive Economic Zone', (2006) 2 Hebei Faxue [Hebei Law Science] 118

陈学斌, “刍议中国对专属经济区船舶污染的司法管辖权”, (2006) 2 《河北法学》 118
CHEN Ya-qin, 'Lun Guojisifa zhong Hetong Zeren he Qinquan Zeren Jinghe Wenti de Chuli [On resolution of the coincidence of contractual and tortious liabilities in private international law]', (2008) 21 Yunnan Daxue Xuebao Faxueban [Journal of Yunnan University Law Edition] 129
陈亚芹, “论国际私法中合同责任和侵权责任竞合问题的处理”, (2008) 21 《云南大学学报法学版》 129
CHEN Yong-can, 'Jiedu Minshi Susongfa Xin Xiuding [Interpretation of the Amendment of the Civil Procedure Law]'
陈永灿, “解读民事诉讼法新修订” http://www.wjnco.com/cn/articles_show.asp?Articles_id=248 (accessed on 4 June 2013)
Cheng Dejun, Wang Shengchang and Kang Ming, *Guoji Guanli he Shewai Zhongcai Shiwu [International Practice and Arbitration Involving Foreign Elements]* 258–9 (Zhongguo Qingnian Chubanshe [China Youth Press] 1993).
程德钧, 王生长, 康明: 《国际惯例和涉外实务》(中国青年出版社, 1993)
CHENG Weidong, 'Lun Shewai Buzhengdang Jingzheng de Falv Shiyong [Applicable Law on Foreign-Related Unfair Competition]', (1997) 58 Fashang Yanjiu [Study in Law and Business] 31
程卫东, “论涉外不正当竞争的法律适用”, (1997) 58(2)《法商研究》31
DING Wei, 'Woguo Shewai Minshangshi Susong Guangxia Zhidu de Wanshan [On the Perfection in the Legal System of China's Jurisdiction over Foreign Civil and Commercial Disputes]' (2006) 24 Zhengfa Luntan [Journal of China University of Political Science and Law] 152
丁伟, “我国涉外民商事诉讼管辖权制度的完善”, (2006) 24 《政法论坛》 152
Dong Likun, *Guoji Sifa [Private International Law]* (Revised ed, Falv Chubanshe [China Law Press] 2000)
董立坤: 《国际私法》(修订版)(法律出版社, 2000 年版)
DONG Qin, 'Application of labour law in Foreign-Related Labour Disputes' (2005) Jianghua Luntan [Jiang Huai Forum] 72
董勤, “涉外劳动争议中劳动法适用问题”, (2005) 11《江淮论坛》 72
DU Huanfang, 'Ruhe Queding yu Xingshi Shewai Minshangshi Guanxiaquan [How to determine jurisdiction in cross-border civil and commercial matters]'
杜焕芳, “如何确定与行使涉外民商事管辖权”, available at http://www.zwmscp.com/a/susongchengxu/susongchengxu/2010/0709/6826.html (accessed on 10 Oct 2012)
DU Huanfang, 'Zhongguo Fayuan Shewai Guanxiaquan Shizheng Yanjiu [Empirical Study of Extra-territorial Jurisdiction of Chinese Courts]' (2007) 2 Faxuejia [Jurist] 152
杜焕芳, “中国法院涉外管辖权实证研究”, (2007) 26《法学家》 152

DU Huanfang, 'Zhongguo Shewai Wuquan Falvshiyongguize zhi Shiyong yu Wanshan' [The Application and Reform of Chinese Property Conflicts] (2013) 5 Aomen Faxue [Macao Law Review] 23

杜焕芳, "中国涉外物权法律适用规则之适用与完善", (2013) 5《澳门法学》 23

DU Wanhua, 'Strengthen Supervision and Guide, Promote Judicial Harmony, Improve the Development of Civil Trial – The Talk in the Symposium on Civil Trial in Chengdu and Shantou', 2007

杜万华, "加强监督指导促进司法和谐努力推动民事审判工作新发展——在成都, 汕头召开的民事审判专题座谈会上的讲话", 2007, a Chinese version is available in chinalawinfo, reference code: CLT.3.110448

DU Xinli, *Guoji Sifa Shiwu Zhongde Falv Wenti [Legal Problems in Private International Law Practice]* (CITIC Publishing House, 2005)

杜新丽,《国际私法实务中的法律问题》(中信出版社, 2005)

FEI Zongwei and TANG Chengyuan, *Zhongguo Sifa Xiezhu de Lilun yu Shijian [The Theory and Practice of Judicial Assistance in China]* (Renmin Fayuan Chubanshe [People's Court Press] 1992)

费宗祎, 唐承元: 《中国司法协助的理论与实践》, (人民法院出版社 1992 年版)

FENG Xia, 'Woguo Neidi Quji Minshangshi Songda Zhidu de Sifa Tansuo [Judicial Approach in Interregional Service for Civil and Commercial Matters]', (2006) 8 Renmin Sifa [Peoples Judicature] 79

冯霞, "我国内地区际民商事送达制度的司法探索", (2006) 8《人民司法》 79

FENG Xia, *Zhongguo Quji Sifa Lun [On Interregional Private Law in China]* (China, Renmin Fayuan Chubanshi [People's Court Press] 2006)

冯霞,《中国区际私法论》(人民法院出版社, 2006)

GUO SuLi, 'Guoji Minshangshi Guanxiaquan Chongtu Jiqi Jiuji—dui Zhongguo Shijian de Kaocha [Conflict of Civil and Commercial Jurisdiction and Remedies—A Study of Chinese Practice]' (2000) 7 Faxue [Legal Science] 12

郭树理, "国际民商事管辖权冲突及其救济——对中国实践的考察", (2000) 7 《法学》 12

GUO Tinyi, *Jianmin Zhongguo Xiandaishi [A Brief of Modern Chinese History]* (Shanghai People's Press, 2009)

郭廷义,《简明中国现代史》(上海人民出版社, 2009)

GUO Yujun and XU Jingtang, 'Zhongguo Quji Falv Chongtu Jiejue Lujing Tanxi (Xia) [A New Perspective of Chinese Interregional Law Conflicts (II)]', (2008) 6(2) Shida Faxue [Contemporary Law Science] 8.

郭玉军, 徐锦堂, "中国区际法律冲突解决路径探析(下)" (2008) 6 (2) 《时代法学》 8

GUO Yujun and XU Jingtang, 'Zhonguo Quji Falv Chongtu Jiejue Lujing Tanxi (Shang) [A New Perspective of Chinese Interregional Law Conflicts (I)]', (2008) 6(1) Shidai Faxue [Contemporary Law Science] 13
郭玉军, 徐锦堂, "中国区际法律冲突解决路径探析（上）"（2008）6（1）《时代法学》13
HAN Depei and XIAO Yongping, *Guoji Sifa* [*Private International Law*] (Renmin Fayuan Chubanshe [China People's Court Press] 2000)
韩德培, 肖永平,《国际私法》, 人民法院出版社 2000 年版
HAN Depei, *Guoji Sifa* [*Private International Law*] (Gaodeng Jiayu Chubanshe [China Higher Education Press] 2001)
韩德培主编,《国际私法》, 高等教育出版社 2001 年版
HE Qisheng, 'Woguo Yuwai Songda Jizhi de Kunjing yu Xuanze [Difficulties and Reform for Service out of China]', (2005) 27 Faxue Yanjiu [Cass Journal of Law] 126
何其生, "我国域外送达机制的困境与选择",（2005）27（2）《法学研究》126–137
HE Qisheng, *Yuwai Songda Zhidu Yanjiu [Study of Extraterritorial Service]* (Peking: Peking University Press, 2006)
何其生,《域外送达制度研究》（北京大学出版社, 2006）
HU Angang, 'Gaige Quanguo Renda Changweihui Youhua Zucheng Renyuan Jiegou [Reforming the Standing Committee of the NPC, Optimizing the Composition of its Members]' 21 Jan. (2003) Ershiyi Shiji Huanqiu Baodao [Global News of the 21st Century] 15. Available at http://news.sina.com.cn/c/2003–01–21/1509882585.shtml (visited 20 April 2013)
胡鞍钢, "改革人大常委会,优化组成人员结构", 载《新浪网》http://news.sina.com.cn/c/2003–01–21/1509882585.shtml
HU Tugui, 'Quanguo Renda Ying Chongfen Xingshihao Lifaquan [The NPC Should Fully Exercise Its Legislative Power]' (1995) 2 Faxue [Legal Science] 8
胡土贵, "全国人大应充分行使好立法权", 1995 年第2期《法学》8
HUANG Jin (ed), *Zhonghua Renmin Gongheguo Shewai Minshi Falvguanxi Shiyongfa: Shiyi yu Fenxi* [*Understanding Act on the Application of Laws on Foreign-related Civil Relationships*] (China Law Press, 2011)
黄进主编:《‹中华人民共和国涉外民事关系法律适用法›释义与分析》（法律出版社 2011 年版）
HUANG Jin (ed.), *Zhonghua Renmin Gongheguo Shewai Minshi Falvguanxi Shiyongfa Jianyigao Ji Shuoming* [*Proposed Draft Law of the People's Republic of China on Application of Laws to Foreign-Related Civil Relations and Its Explanation*] (Renmin University Press 2011)
黄进（主编),《中华人民共和国涉外民事法律关系适用法建议稿及说明》（人民大学出版社, 2011）

HUANG Jin, *Guoji Sifa [Private International Law]* (2nd ed., China Law Press 2005)
黄进,《国际私法》（第二版,中国法律出版社，2005）
HUANG Liangyou, WEN Tingting, 'Wangshang Gonggao Songda Zhidu Yanjiu [Study of Service by Online Public Notice]', (2013) 34 Jishou Daxue Xuebao Shehui Kexueban [Journal of Jishou University (Social Science Edition)] 114
黄良友,文庭婷, "网上公告送达制度研究",（2013）34（1）《吉首大学学报：社会科学版》114
HUANG, Qiu-feng, 'Zhonngguo Ying Queli Bufangbian Fayuan Zhidu [Set up the Doctrine of *Forum Non Conveniens* in China]', (2010) 28 Hebei Faxue [Hebei Law Science] 70
黄秋丰, "中国应确立不方便法院制度", (2010) 28 《河北法学》 70
HUO Zhengxin, 'Wuyinguanli de Falvshiyong Guize Tanjiu [Probe into the Application of Law of *Negotiorum Gestio*]' (2005) 17 Anhui Jinguan Zhiye Xueyuan Xuebao [Journal of Anhui Vocational College of Police Officers] 1
霍政欣, "无因管理的法律适用规则探究",（2005）17《安徽警官职业学院学报》1
HUO Zhengxin, *Guoji Sifa zhong de Budang Deli [Unjust Enrichment in Private International Law*], PhD thesis Wuhan University, 2005
霍政欣,《国际私法中的不当得利》武汉大学博士论文, 2005
JIA Chenhao, LIU Yantao, 'Sifa Wenshu Dianzi Songda [Electronic Service of Legal Documents]', (2014) 240 Lilun Xuekan [Theory Journal] 107
贾宸浩, 柳砚涛, "司法文书电子送达",（2014）2 《理论学刊》107
JIANG Fen, JIN Peng-Nian, 'Lun Shurenfa zai Budangdeli Chongtuguifan zhong de Yingyong [Application of Lex Personalis in Conflict Rules of Unjust Enrichment]', (2011) 29 Hebei Faxue [Hebei Law Science] 64
蒋奋, 金彭年, "论属人法在不当得利冲突规范中的应用", (2011) 8 《河北法学》 64
JIN Peng-Nian, 'Shewai Minshi Guanxi Falv Shiyongfa zhong de Budangdeli Guize [Unjust Enrichment in Applicable Law in Foreign-Related Civil Relationship Act]', (2012) 2 Zhongguo Faxue [China Legal Science] 170
金彭年, "涉外民事关系法律适用法中的不当得利规则", (2012) 2《中国法学》 170
JIN Peng-nian, ZHANG Xiao-ke, 'Wuyinguanli Falvshiyong Xintan [New Viewpoints of Application of Negotiorum Gestio in Conflict of Law]', (2001) 31.2 Zhejiangdaxue Xuebao: Renwen Sheke Ban [Journal of Zhejiang University (Humanities and Social Sciences)] 104
金彭年, 章晓科, "无因管理法律适用新探", (2001) 31《浙江大学学报：人文社科版》 104
Jin Zhengjia, Guo Shengping, 'Shewai Haishi Shenpan zhong de Falv Shi-yong' [The Application of Law in Foreign Maritime Judicature] (1989) 6 Faxue Pinglun [L. Rev.] 73

金正佳,郭生平, “涉外海事审判中的法律适用”, 1989 年第 6 期《法学评论》 73
JU Haiting, 'Dianzi Fangshi Songda Falv Wenshu Wenti Yanjiu [Study of Problems in Electronic Service of Legal Documents]', (2006) 6 Renmin Sifa [People's Judicature] 67
鞠海亭, “电子方式送达法律文书问题研究”, (2006) 6《人民司法》 67
LU Jun, *Guojisifa zhi Lilun yu Shiji [Theory and Practice of Private International Law]* (China University of Political Science and Law Press 1998)
卢峻,《国际私法之理论与实践》, 法律出版社 2000 年版
LI Guilian, *Shen Jiaben Zhuan* [*Biography of Shen Jiaben*] (China Law Press 2000)
李贵连, 《沈家本传》, 法律出版社 2000
LI Hao, 'Minshi Susong Zhuanshu Guanxia Zhidu Yanjiu [Study of Exclusive Jurisdiction in Civil Procedure]' (2009) 26 Fashang Yanjiu [Study in Law and Business] 94
李浩, “民事诉讼专属管辖制度研究”, (2009) 26 《法商研究》 94
LI Haopei, *Guoji Minshi Chengxufa Gailun [An Introduction to International Civil Procedural Law]* (Beijing: Law Press 1996)
李浩培,《国际民事程序法概论》(法律出版社, 1996)
LI Li-Min, 'Brief Study of the Quantitative Assessment of Judges'
李立民, “浅谈法官的量化考核”, published on http://www.hicourt.gov.cn/theory/artilce_list.asp?id=1943&l_class=6 (accessed on 10 Oct 2013)
Li Shuangyuan and Xie Shisong, *Guojiminshisusong Gailun* [*An Introduction to International Civil Procedure*] (Wuhan University Press 2001)
李双元,谢石松: 《国际民事诉讼导论》, 武汉大学出版 2001 年版
LI Shuangyuan, *Guojisifa [Private International Law]* (2nd ed., Peking University Publishing 2007)
李双元,《国际私法》(第二版, 北京大学出版社, 2007)
LI Tao, 'Shewai Gonglu Jiaotong Shigu Sunhai Peichang de Falv Shiyong Wenti Yanjiu [Study of the Law Applicable to the Foreign-Related Road Traffic Accidents]', (2004) 19 Henansheng Zhengfa Guanli Ganbu Xueyuan Xuebao [Journal of Henan Administrative Institute of Politics and Law] 20
李涛, “涉外公路交通事故损害赔偿的法律适用问题研究”, (2004) 19《河南省政法管理干部学院学报》 20
LI Wang, 'Guojisifa Zhongguoji he Zhusuo de Queding [Determining the Chinese Nationality and Domicile in Private International Law]', (2010) 31 Faxue Zaizhi [Law Science Magazine] 62
李旺, “国际私法中国籍和住所的确定”, (2010) 3 《法学杂志》 62
LIAO Zhonghong, 'Xieyi Guanxia: Wenti, Yuanyin Jiqi Gaige Shexiang [Agreement Jurisdiction: the Problems, Reasons and Reformation Plan]' (2008) 10 Xinan Zhengfa Daxue Xuebao [Journal of Southwest University of Political Science and Law] 110

廖中洪, "协议管辖: 问题, 原因及其改革设想", (2008) 10 《西南政法大学 学报》 110

LIU En-yuan, 'Zhongguo Chengren yu Zhixing Waiguo Panjue de Jichu Tiaojian [Basic Conditions for China to Recognize and Enforce Foreign Judgments]', (2008) 23 Fazhi [Journal of Shanghai University of Political Science and Law] 63

刘恩媛, "中国承认与执行外国判决的基础条件", (2008) 23 《法治》 63

LIU Li, 'Shewai Jicheng Anjian Zhuanshu Guanxia Kao [Study on Exclusive Jurisdiction in Cross-Border Succession]' (2009) 2 Xiandai Faxue [Modern Law Science] 138

刘力, "涉外继承案件专属管辖考", (2009) 2《现代法学》 138

LIU Lin, 'Beidao Wenwu Kuaguo Liuzhuan Suoyouquan Zhengyi Falv Shiyong Guize Tantao [A Study on Conflict Rules Applied to Cross-Border Transactions of Stolen Cultural Properties]', (2011) 9 Shidaifaxue [Present Day Law Science] 104

刘琳, "被盗文物跨国流转所有权争议法律适用规则探讨", (2011) 9 (1) 《时代法学》 104

LIU Xiaohong, 'Lun Guojisifa zhong dui Shewai Hetong Zeren yu Qinquan Zeren Jinghe zhi Chuli [Handling the Coincidence of Contract and Tort Obligations in Private International Law]' (2001) Huadong Zhengfa Xueyuan Xuebao [Journal of East China University of Political Science and Law] 24

刘晓红, "论国际私法中对涉外合同责任与侵权责任竞合之处理", (2001) 《华东政法学院学报》 24

LIU Xingli, 'Lun Woguo Haishi Qinquan ji Chuanbo Pengzhuang de Falv Shiyong [Applicable Law to Maritime Tort and Collision between Ships]', (2002) 12 Xueshu Yanjiu [Academic Research] 87

刘兴莉, "论我国海事侵权及船舶碰撞的法律适用", (2002) 12 《学术研究》 87

LIU, Jia-Liang, 'Shixian Minshi Susongfa Quanmian Xiugai de Lingyizhong Shijiao—"Zhongcaifa Jieshi" Pingjia [Complete Revision of Civil Procedure Law—Assessment of the Interpretation of Arbitration Law]', (2008) Journal of Shandong Police College 29

刘加良, "实现民事诉讼法全面修改的另一种视角—《仲裁法解释》 评介", (2008) 20 《山东警察学院学报》 29

LV Guo-Min, DAI Xia, etc., *Guojisifa Chongtufa yu Shitifa [Private International Law: Conflict of Law and Substantive Law]* (Zhongxin Chubanshe [CITIC Press], 2002)

吕国民, 戴霞, 郑远民《国际私法冲突法与实体法》(中信出版社, 2002)

MA Lingxia, 'Lun Zuimixie Lianxi Yuanze de Jiazhi zai Woguo de Shixian [Demonstration of the Value of the Closest Connection Principle in China]' in MA Hai Tao, LI Liang, *Guoji Faxue de Lilun yu Shijian [The*

Jurisprudence and Practice of International Law] (China Legal Publishing House, 1991)

马灵霞，"论最密切联系原则的价值在我国的实现"，马海涛，李亮（编），《国际法学的理论与实践》（中国法制出版社, 1991）

MA Zhang-Kai, 'Comments on Network Copyright Disputes and the "Judicial Interpretation"'

马章凯， "网络著作权案件《司法解释》评解"， http://www.china-review.com/laf.asp?id=13321, accessed on 20 November 2011

QI Aimin, HE Peiyu, 'Shewai Zhishi Chanquan Jiufen de Falv Shiyong [Applicable Law to the Foreign-Related Intellectual Property Disputes]', (2011) 2 Zhishi Chanquan [Intellectual Property] 120

齐爱民, 何培育, "涉外知识产权纠纷的法律适用", (2011) 2《知识产权》 120

QU Tao, 'Guanyu Zhongguo Wuquanfa Zhidu Sheji de Sikao [Some Thoughts on the System of Chinese Property Law]',

渠　涛, "关于中国物权法制度设计的思考", http://www.iolaw.org.cn/show Article.aspx?id=1466, accessed on 19 June 2015

REN Fanghao, *Guoji Tiaoyue zai Zhongguo Fayuan de Shiyong [Application of International Treaties in Chinese Courts]*, MPhil Thesis submitted to Zhengzhou University in 2007

任晧, 国际条约在中国法院的适用, MS thesis, 郑州大学, 2007

REN Xuefeng, 'Guanyu Shegang'ao Minshangshi Anjian Sifa Wenshu Songda Wenti Ruogan Guiding de Lijie yu Shiyong [Apprehension and Application of the "Provisions Regarding the Service of Judicial Documents in Hong Kong and Macau-related Civil and Commercial Cases"]', (2009) 7 Renmin Sifa [People's Judicature] 20

任雪峰, "《关于涉港澳民商事案件司法文书送达问题若干规定》的理解与适用", (2009) 7 《人民司法》 20

SHEN Juan (ed.), *Guoji Sifa [Private International Law]* (China Social Sciences Press 2006)

沈涓主编: 《国际私法》（中国社会科学文献出版社 2006 年版）

SONG Xiao, 'Yisizizhi yu Wuquan Chongtufa [Party Autonomy and Property Conflicts]', (2012) Vol 1 Huanqiu Falv Pinglun [Global Law Review] 77

宋晓, "意思自治与物权冲突法", (2012) 1环球法律评论 77

SONG Xixiang, 'Neidi yu Gang'ao Quji Minshangshi Sifawenshu Songda Xianzhuan Jiqi Wanshan Sikao [Status quo and Improvement of Interregional Service of Judicial Documents in Civil and Commercial Cases between Mainland and Hong Kong and Macau]', (2013) 15 Yiguoliangzhi Yanjiu [One Country Two Systems Study] 121

宋锡祥， "内地与港澳区际民商事司法文书送达现状及其完善思考", (2013) 15 《'一国两制' 研究》 121

SONG Xixiang, *Guo (Qu) Ji Minshangshi Sifa Huodong de Chongtu yu Xietiao [Conflict and Coordination of Civil and Commercial Judicial Activities between Countries or Regions]* (Law Press, 2014)

宋锡祥, 国（区）际民商事司法活动的冲突与协调, (法律出版社, 2014)

SONG Xixiang, WANG Hongyan, 'Zhongguo Neidi yu Gang'ao Quji Quzheng Zhidu de Chengxiao, Wenti Jiqi Gaijin Jianyi [Effectiveness, Problems and Reform of Interregional Evidence Collection between Mainland and Hong Kong and Macau]', (2012) 11(1) Yiguo Liangzhi Yanjiu ['One Country, Two Systems' Study] 123

宋锡祥, 王红燕, "中国内地与港澳区际取证制度的成效, 问题及其改进建议", （2012） 11 （1）《'一国两制' 研究》 123

TAN Yue-qi, 'A Milestone in the Development of Chinese Maritime Litigation', (2000) 5 Faxue Pinglun [Law Review] 73

谭岳奇, "中国海事诉讼发展的里程碑", 2000《法学评论》 73

The Guangdong HPC, *Zhongguo Shewai Shangshi Shenpan Redian Wenti Tanxi [Exploration on Hot Issues in China's Foreign Commercial Trial] (*Law Press 2004)

广东省高级人民法院,《中国涉外商事审判热点问题探析》（法律出版社, 2004）

WAN E'Xiang, 'Zai Quanguo Shewai Shangshihaishi Shenpan Gongzuo Huiyishang de Jianghua [Speech in the Conference of National Foreign-Related Civil and Commercial Trial Work]', in *Zhongguo Shewai Shangshi Haishi Shenpan Zhidao yu Yanjiu [Guidance and Study of China Foreign-Related Civil and Commercial Trial]* (2002, Vol 1) 54

万鄂湘, '在全国涉外商事海事审判工作会议上的讲话', 2002 年第一卷《中国涉外商事海事审判指导与研究》 54

WANG Fuhua, 'Xieyi Guanxia Zhidu de Jinbu yu Juxian [Development and Limits on Prorogation Jurisdiction]' (2012) 30 Falv Kexue: Xibei Zhengfa Xueyuan Xuebao [Law Science: Northwest University of Political Science and Law Journal] 163

王福华, "协议管辖制度的进步与局限", (2012) 30《法律科学: 西北政法学院学报》 163

WANG Guozheng, 'On the Perfection of China's System of Regional Jurisdiction of Joint Defendants' (2002) 1 Zhongguo Haiyang Daxue Xuebao (Shehui Kexue Ban) [Journal of Ocean University of Qingdao (Social Science)]

王国征, "浅议完善我国共同被告地域管辖制度–兼析我国《 民事诉讼法》 第 22 条第 3 款", (2002)《中国海洋大学学报: 社会科学版》

WANG HanBin, 'Guanyu "Zhonghua Renmin Gongheguo Minshi Susongfa (Shixing)" (Xiugai Cao'an) de Shuoming' [Explanation on the Civil Procedure Law of the People's Republic of China (for Trial Implementation) (Amendment Draft)]', the 4th Meeting of the Seventh NPC, 2 April 1991

王汉斌, "关于《中华人民共和国民事诉讼法(试行)》(修改草案)的说明", http://cpc.people.com.cn/GB/64184/64186/66684/4494177.html (accessed on 10 Oct 2013)

WANG Jiwen, 'Huhui Yuanze zai Panjue Chengren yu Zhixing Shang de Quexian [The Fallacy of the Principle of Reciprocity in Judgment Recognition and Enforcement]', (2008) 15(3) Yunnan Daxue Xuebao (Faxue Ban) [Journal of Yunnan University (Law Edition)] 170

王吉文, "互惠原则在判决承认与执行上的缺陷", (2008) 15(1) 《云南大学学报(法学版)》 170

WANG Jiwen, 'Lun Woguo Dui Waiguo Caipan Chengren yu Zhixing de Huhui Yuanze—Yi Liyi Hengliang Fangfa wei Gongju [On Reciprocity Principle of Recognition and Enforcement of Foreign Judgments in China: Analysis by Interest-balancing method]', (2012) 6 Faxuejia [Legal Jurist] 154

王吉文, "论我国对外国判决承认与执行的互惠原则——以利益衡量方法为工具", (2012) 6 《法学家》 154

WANG Limin (ed.), *Minfa [Civil Law*] (China Renmin University Press 2005)

王利民(主编),《民法》(人民大学出版社, 2005)

WANG Qi, LU Jianhua, 'Woguo Guonei Xieyi Guanxia Zhidu de Wanshan [Improving Chinese Domestic Prorogation Jurisdiction]' (2009) Hainan Daxue Xuebao (Renwen Shehui Kexueban) [Hai Nan University Journal (Art and Social Science)] 167

王琦, 陆建华, "我国国内协议管辖制度的完善", (2009) 2 《海南大学学报: 人文社会科学版》 167

WANG XiaoYan, *Study on Domicile of Natural Person in Private International Law,* PhD Dissertation, Southwest University of Political Science and Law (2009)

王晓燕, 《国际私法中的自然人住所制度研究》, 西南政法大学, 博士论文 2009

WU Lijing, TIAN Xiaoyun, 'Lun Neidi yu Xianggang Xiuanghu Zhixing Zhongcai Caijue de Falv Wenti [Legal Issues on Mutual Enforcement of Arbitral Awards between Mainland and Hong Kong]', (2011) 3 Tequ Jingji [Special Zone Economy] 15

吴莉婧, 田晓云, "论内地与香港相互执行仲裁裁决的法律问题", (2011) 3 《特区经济》 15

WU Yi-Min, 'Liangda Faxi zhong de Bufangbian Fayuan Yuanze ji zai Zhongguo de Heli Jiejian [*Forum non conveniens* in Two Legal Systems and its Adoption in China]', (2008) 1 Xinan Zhengfa Daxue Xuebao [Journal of SWUPL] 2

吴一鸣, "两大法系中的不方便法院原则及在中国的合理借鉴", (2008) 1《西南政法大学学报》 2

XI Xiao-Ming, 'Bufangbian Fayuan Zhidu de Jidian Sikao [Several Thoughts on *Forum Non Conveniens*]' (2002) 24 Faxue Yanjiu [Legal study] 81
奚晓明，"不方便法院制度的几点思考", (2002) 24《法学研究》 81
XIAO Weiyun (ed.), *Yiguo Liangzhi yu Xianggang Jibenfa [One Country, Two Systems and the Basic Legal System of Hong Kong]* (Peking University Press, 1990)
肖蔚云（主编),《一国两制与香港基本法律制度》（北京大学出版社，1990）
XIAO Weiyun, 'Xianggang Bibenfa: Chuangzaoxing Lifa de Jiezuo [The Hong Kong Basic Law: A Masterpiece of Creative Legislation]', (1995) 3 Zhongguo Faxue [China Legal Science] 87
肖蔚云，"香港基本法：创造性立法的杰作"，（1995）3《中国法学》 87
XIAO Yongping, 'Zui Miqie Lianxi Yuanze zai Zhongguo Chongtufa zhong de Yingyong [Application of the Closest Connection Doctrine in Chinese Conflict of Laws]' (1992) 3 Zhongguo Shehui Kexue [China Social Science] 146
肖永平，"最密切联系原则在中国冲突法中的应用"，（1992） 3《中国社会科学》 146
XIAO Yongping, *Falixue Shiyexia de Chongfufa [Conflict of Laws from a Jurisprudence Perspective]* (Beijing: Gaodeng Jiaoyu Chubanshe [Higher Education Press] 2008)
肖永平,《法理学视野下的冲突法》（北京,高等教育出版社，2008）
XIAO Yongping, *Guoji Sifa Yuanli [The Principle of Private International Law]* (Law Press, Beijing 2003)
肖永平,《国际私法原理》（法律出版社，2003）
XIAO Yong-Ping, HUO Zheng-Xin, 'Budangdeli de Falvshiyong Guize [Choice of Law Rules in Unjust Enrichment]', (2004) 26 Faxue Yanjiu [Legal Study] 128
肖永平, 霍政欣，"不当得利的法律适用规则", (2004) 26《法学研究》 128
Xiao Yongping, *Zhongguo Chongtufa Lifa Wenti Yanjiu* [*A Study on the Legislative Issues of China's Conflicts Law*] (Wuhan University Press 1996)
肖永平，《中国冲突法立法问题研究》（武汉大学出版社 1996 年版）
XIE Xinsheng, 'Tiaoye yu Huhui Queshi shi Zhongguo Panjue dui Yuwai Zhixing [The Extraterritorial Enforcement of Chinese Court Judgment Without Treaty and Reciprocity]', (2010) 4 Huanqiu Falv Pinglun [Global Law Review] 152
谢新胜，"条约与互惠缺失时中国判决对域外执行——以美国法院执行中国民商事判决第一案为视角",（2010）4《环球法律评论》 152
XU Chongli, 'Jiuqi Zhihou Guoji Jingji Tiaoyue Ruhe Jixu Shiyong yu Xianggang [Application of International Economic Treaties in Hong Kong After 1997]', (1998) 1 Zhongwai Faxue [Peking University Law Journal] 104

徐崇利, "'九七'之后国际经济条约如何继续适用于香港", (1997) 《中外法学》 104–110

XU Gong-wei, 'Bufangbian Fayuan Yuanze zai Zhongguo de Yunyong [The Application of the Principle of *Forum Non Convenience* in China]', (2003) 21 Zhengfa Luntan [Tribune of Political Science and Law] 161

徐伟功, "不方便法院原则在中国的运用", (2003) 21 《政法论坛》 161

XU Gong-Wei, 'Woguo Buyi Caiyong Bufangbian Fayuan Yuanze [*Forum Non Conveniens* is Inappropriate for China]' (2006) 24 Faxue Pinglun [Legal Forum] 146

徐伟功, "我国不宜采用不方便法院原则——以不方便法院原则的运作环境与功能为视角", (2006) 24 《法学评论》 146

XU Qian-fei, 'Zailun Zhongguo Faguan de Suzhi [Re-Evaluation of Quality of Chinese Judges]', (2002) Renmin Sifa [People's Judicature] 33

许前飞, "再论中国法官的素质", (2002) 1《人民司法》 33

XU Qian-fei, 'Zhongguo Faguan Suzhi Pingxi [Evaluation of the Quality of Chinese Judges]', (2001) 9 Renmin Sifa [People's Judicature] 8

许前飞, "中国法官素质评析", (2011) 9《人民司法》 8

XU Yan, 'Interpretation of the 2012 New Civil Procedure Law Part II'

徐艳, "2012新民事诉讼法解读（二）", published on the website of the Yun Xi District Court on 25 February 2013, available at http://yxqfy.chinacourt.org/public/detail.php?id=290 (accessed on 2 June 2013)

XUE Hui, *Zhongmei Pingxing Susong Wenti zhi Bijiao Yanjiu [Comparative Study of Parallel Proceedings between China and USA]*, MS Dissertation, Dalian Haishi University, submitted in 2007

薛辉, 《中美平行诉讼问题之比较研究》, 大连海事大学, 硕士论文, 2007

YAN Lin, 'Guojisifa shang Ziranren Zhusuo Zhidu jiqi Jiejian Yiyi [Domicile of a Natural Person in Private International Law]' ((2007) 16 Huaiyin Gongxueyuan Xuebao [Journal of Huai Yin Gong Xue Yuan] 31

颜林, "国际私法上自然人住所制度及其借鉴意义" (2007) 16 《淮阴工学院学报》 31–36

Yao Zhuang and Ren Jishen, 'Lun Guojisifa de Duixiang yu Fanwei [On the Object and Scope of Private International Law]' (1980) 3 Faxueyanjiu [Journal of Chinese Law]

姚壮, 任继圣, "论国际私法的对象与范围", (1980) 3《法学研究》

YU Fei, 'Yelun Jiejue Haixia Liang'an Minshangshi Falv Chongtu de Moshi [The Mode of Solving the Conflict of Civil and Commercial Laws in Cross-Strait]', (2006) 91(1) Taiwan Yanjiu Jikan [Taiwan Research Quarterly] 8

于飞, "也论解决海峡两岸民商事法律冲突的模式", (2006) 91(1) 《台湾研究集刊》 8–13

YU Fei, *Zhongguo Guoji Sifa Lilun yu Lifa [Theory and Legislation of Chinese Private International Law]* (China Law Press 2004)

于飞,《中国国际私法理论与立法》（中国法制出版社, 2004）

YU Xianyu (ed.), *Chongtufa* [*Conflict of Laws*] (China Law Press 1989)

余先予主编,《冲突法》（法律出版社 1989 年版）

YUAN Mingsheng, 'Sifa Jieshi Lifahua Xianxiang Tanwei [A Commentary on the Legitimacy of Judicial Interpretation of the SPC]' (2003) 2 Fashang Yanjiu [Studies in Law & Business] 3

袁明圣, "司法解释立法化现象探微", (2003）2《法商研究》 3

Z Huo, 'Shewaiqinquan Zhizhai de Falvshiyong—yi 7.23 Yongwenxian Tebiezhongda Tielu Jiaotongshiguzhong Waijishangwangchengke de Peichang wei Shijiao'[Applicable Law to Torts–A Commentary on the Dispute Between the Dead and Injured Foreign Passengers and China's Railway Ministry in the Wenzhou Train Collision of July 23] (2011) 28 Fashang Yanjiu [Studies in Law and Business] 11

霍政欣, "涉外侵权之债的法律适用——以"7.23　甬温线特别重大铁路交通事故"外籍伤亡乘客的赔偿为视角", (2011）28《法商研究》 11

ZENG Er-xiu, 'Lun Zhongguo Haishi Qinquan de Falv Shiyong [On the Law Applicable to Maritime Tort in China]', (2012) 23 Zhongguo Haishangfa Yanjiu [Chinese Journal of Maritime Law] 27

曾二秀, "论中国海事侵权的法律适用", (2012） 23 中国海商法研究 27

ZENG Jianpin, 'Budongchan Jiufen Zhuanshu Guanxia Tanxi [Study of exclusive jurisdiction on immovable property]' (2008) 2 Xinan Nongye Daxue Xuebao (Shehui Kexue Ban) [South West Agriculture University Journal (Social Science)] 22

曾建平, "不动产纠纷专属管辖探析", (2008) 2 《西南农业大学学报 (社会科学版)》 22

ZHAN Pengpeng, 'Lun Haiwai Yuangong Paiqian zhong de Zhunjufa Wenti [Applicable Law on Overseas Labour Dispatch]', (2010) 13 Zhongguo Guojisifa Niankan [Chinese Yearbook of Private International Law and Comparative Law] 122

詹朋朋, "论海外员工派遣中的准据法问题", (2010）13 《中国国际法年刊》 122

ZHANG Jian-liang, HUO Zheng-xin, 'Wuyinguanli de Falvshiyong de Lifasheji yu Lunzheng [Conflict Rules for *Negotiorum Gestio:* Designing and Demonstrations]', (2005) 58(5) Wuhan Daxue Xuebao (Zhexue Shehuikexue Ban) [Wuhan University Journal (Philosophy and Social Sciences)] 607

张建良,霍政欣, "无因管理的法律适用的立法设计与论证", (2005) 58 (5) 《武汉大学学报(哲学社会科学版)》 607

ZHANG Shu-Dian, 'Lun Woguo Bufangbian Fayuan Yuanze Shiyong de Ruogan Zhenyi Wenti [Study on Problems on *forum non convenience* in court]', (2009) 30 Xingzheng yu Fa [Public Administration and Law] 96
张淑钿, "论我国不方便法院原则适用的若干争议问题", (2009) 30 《行政与法》 96
ZHANG, Xianming, 'Zhengque Shenli Shewai Minshi Anjian Qieshi Weihu Shehui Gonggong Liyi [Trying the Foreign-related Civil Cases in an Appropriate Way to Safeguard the Social Public Interests, Answer of the Fourth Civil Division of the SPC to the Press]', *Renmin Fayuanbao* [People's Court Daily], 7 Jan. 2013)
张先明, "正确审理涉外民事案件,切实维护社会公共利益",《人民法院报》2013 年 1月 7 日第 6 版
ZHANG Yan, *Lun Woguo Fayuan Shewai Anjian zhong Jujue Guanxiaquan de Jichu [The Bases for the Chinese Court to Decline Jurisdiction]*, MPhil thesis submitted to Shanghai Jiao Tong University in 2008
张妍, 《论我国法院涉外案件中拒绝管辖的基础》, 硕士论文,上海交通大学, 2008
ZHAO Cheng-Tao, 'A Dispute on the Jurisdiction Clause in the Bill of Lading', (1999) Yearbook of Chinese Maritime Law 402
赵程涛, "一起提单管辖权条款纠纷案之我见", (1999) 《中国海商法年刊》 402–411
ZHAO Xianglin (ed),*Guoji Sifa* [*Private International Law*] (Press of China University of Political Science and Law 2011)
赵相林主编, 《国际私法》 (第三版, 中国政法大学出版社 2011 年版)
ZHAO XiangLin, Guoji Sifa Jiaoxue Anli Pingxi [Private International Law Case Study] (China CITIC Press 2006)
赵相林,《国际私法教学案例评析》 (中信出版社, 2006)
Zhao Xiu-wen, *Guoji Shangshi Zhongcai Jiqi Shiyong Falv Yanjiu [A Study of International Commercial Arbitration and Its Application of Law]* (Beijing: Peking University Press 2002)
赵秀文, 《国际商事仲裁及其适用法律研究》 (北京大学出版社, 2002 年)
ZHENG Zhi-Hua, 'Tidan Beimian Guanxia Tiaokuan Xingzhi Ruogan Wenti Tanxi [Analysis of Several Issues concerning Jurisdiction Clauses in the Back of the Bill of Lading]' (2004) 32 Haishi Sifa Luntan [Maritime Judicial Forum] 59
郑志华, "提单背面管辖条款性质若干问题探析", (2004) 32《海事司法论坛》 59
Zhenjia Jin, *Zhongguo Dianxing Haishi Anli Pingxi* [*An Analysis of Typical Chinese Maritime Cases*](China Law Press 1998)
金正佳,《中国典型海事案例评析》 (法律出版社 1998 年版)

INDEX